John J. Pershing and the
American Expeditionary Forces
in World War I, 1917–1919

American Warriors

Throughout the nation's history, numerous men and women of all ranks and branches of the U.S. military have served their country with honor and distinction. During times of war and peace, there are individuals whose exemplary achievements embody the highest standards of the U.S. armed forces. The aim of the American Warriors series is to examine the unique historical contributions of these individuals, whose legacies serve as enduring examples for soldiers and citizens alike. The series will promote a deeper and more comprehensive understanding of the U.S. armed forces.

Series editor: Joseph Craig

An AUSA Book

John J. Pershing and the American Expeditionary Forces in World War I, 1917–1919

VOLUME 4
MARCH 21–MAY 19, 1918

Edited by John T. Greenwood

This volume was funded in part by the Pritzker Military Museum & Library.

Copyright © 2024 by The University Press of Kentucky

Scholarly publisher for the Commonwealth, serving Bellarmine University, Berea College, Centre College of Kentucky, Eastern Kentucky University, The Filson Historical Society, Georgetown College, Kentucky Historical Society, Kentucky State University, Morehead State University, Murray State University, Northern Kentucky University, Spalding University, Transylvania University, University of Kentucky, University of Louisville, University of Pikeville, and Western Kentucky University.
All rights reserved.

Editorial and Sales Offices: The University Press of Kentucky
663 South Limestone Street, Lexington, Kentucky 40508-4008
www.kentuckypress.com

Cataloging-in-Publication data available from the Library of Congress

ISBN 978-1-9859-0076-9 (hardcover)
ISBN 978-1-9859-0078-3 (pdf)
ISBN 978-1-9859-0077-6 (epub)

This book is printed on acid-free paper meeting the requirements of the American National Standard for Permanence in Paper for Printed Library Materials.

Manufactured in the United States of America.

 Member of the Association of University Presses

Contents

Introduction to Pershing's Wartime Correspondence   vi

Introduction to Volume 4   xxi

1. March 21–March 31, 1918   1

2. April 1918   114

3. May 1–May 19, 1918   386

Bibliography   553

Index   561

Introduction to Pershing's Wartime Correspondence

A Multivolume Series

When I was researching and editing *My Life before the World War, 1860–1918: A Memoir*, by General of the Armies John J. Pershing, for publication by the University Press of Kentucky (2013), I spent many hours working in the Pershing Papers in the Manuscript Division of the Library of Congress. In the process, I became very familiar with the entire collection and realized that the treatment of Pershing's enormous role in World War I deserved to be expanded beyond the existing biographies to include a collection of his extensive correspondence. Pershing's role in the war, both at home in the United States and overseas in Europe, was exceedingly prominent, more so than any other American military leader and also more than most of the civilian political leaders.

Accordingly, I proposed a project on Pershing's wartime correspondence to Dr. Roger Cirillo, lieutenant colonel of the U.S. Army (retired), then the director of the Book Program of the Association of the U.S. Army, and he readily agreed to support the undertaking. As a result, I embarked on a long journey that took in virtually all of Pershing's papers in the Library of Congress as well as available collections of those military and civilian American leaders with whom he mostly corresponded. However, without the resources for extensive travel to explore all of the possible research holdings where copies of his correspondence might be held, I decided to rely primarily on Pershing's collection and the official records in the National Archives and Records Administration (NARA). I found that except in some relatively rare cases, I was able to secure the majority of Pershing's correspondence that was relevant to my project.

Sources. In the following paragraphs, I will review the primary sources upon which I have relied to build this series of volumes.

Papers of John J. Pershing, Library of Congress. In this project, my focus was on Pershing's official correspondence as commander-in-chief, American Expeditionary Forces (CINC, AEF), and not on his private, personal correspondence with his son Francis Warren (known by his middle name, Warren), his brother and sisters, his in-laws—other than his father-in-law, Senator Francis E. Warren (Wyoming)— other close relatives, civilian friends, or Micheline Resco, his paramour and companion after the summer of 1917. In addition, I have not included most congratulatory, commemorative, introductory, and seasonal (Christmas and New Year's) cables and messages unless Pershing himself made a special note of them.

However, I ran into several obstacles in taking this approach. One major problem arose from the many years during which Pershing's collection was shuffled around among various offices in Washington, DC, that Pershing occupied after his return to the United States in September 1919 and during his years as chief of staff (1921–1924), as the chairman of the American Battle Monuments Commission from its establishment in March 1923 until his death, and as general of the Armies. In addition, he and his personal staff worked through his papers extensively and reorganized them while compiling his memoir of World War I, published in 1931 in two volumes as *My Experiences in the World War,* and then the subsequent drafts of his prewar memoir, which I mentioned above. I believe that during this time some correspondence might well have been lost. Moreover, the Manuscript Division has organized and reorganized and boxed and reboxed the papers in the years after they were first acquired in 1951. A myriad of researchers have now used them for many decades. Naturally, despite the precautions of the staff of the Manuscript Division, documents do stray between folders on occasion.

I also believe that Pershing himself may have removed some documents from his papers that he felt were inappropriate for retention or later viewing by others. Above all, Pershing was a very proper and honorable nineteenth-century gentleman who would not reveal unseemly and negative information about others. I know from his extensive correspondence with his father-in-law, Senator Warren, a powerful figure in the Senate for many years, that they agreed to destroy certain letters beginning in late February 1918. On March 27, Warren replied to letters of February 25 and 27 from Pershing that were marked "Personal and Confidential" and apparently carried a note from Pershing to destroy them after he read them. Other letters, which I could not locate but found specific reference to include Warren to Pershing on March 18, 1918, Pershing to Warren on April 15, 1918, and Pershing to Warren on July 29, 1918. How many other letters there were that were destroyed or what those letters discussed, I have no way of determining.

In a February 2 letter Pershing had already written to Warren stating that "as to letters, if you wish to send me a confidential letter and you know of no one to send it by, I would suggest, that you might have it put, in the Embassy bag at the State Department and send it in care of our Ambassador, who would then have it delivered to me in person. I have little confidence in the mails, and shall not risk sending anything to you in the open mail which might possibly fall into unfriendly hands." Pershing usually used an official Army courier or officer whom he trusted, and who was going to Washington, to carry his letters to Warren and sometimes to Secretary of War Newton D. Baker, and suggested that Warren do likewise. In an effort to track down these letters, I contacted the American Heritage Center at the University of Wyoming, which holds Warren's papers, and they were unable to locate these letters mentioned above in the senator's papers.

An important problem cropped up right in the Manuscript Division of the Library of Congress. The personal papers of Baker, one of Pershing's most important and frequent correspondents, are held there. After collecting all of the Baker-Pershing correspondence from the Pershing papers, I turned to the Baker papers to cross-check and to make sure I had all of the relevant documents. After an extensive review of the available microfilms of Baker's collection and discussions with the staff of the Manuscript Division, I determined that the microfilms contained no copies of any Baker-Pershing correspondence from 1917 through 1919. Where those documents are now no one at the Manuscript Division could determine.

The problem of missing correspondence was not limited to either the Pershing-Warren or Pershing-Baker letters. Often, I could not locate correspondence that was clearly referred to. In these instances, I have annotated the correspondence accordingly to inform the reader that the document could not be located.

National Archives and Records Administration. From my many years of research in its collections, I knew from the outset that NARA held significant amounts of the relevant Pershing correspondence. The large amount of official AEF documentation is held both in NARA's Record Group (RG) 120, Records of the American Expeditionary Forces, and specific Pershing materials in PRSHG (formerly RG 200), a large collection of the office files from his years as general of the Armies. RG 120 itself contains thousands of boxes of documents and PRSHG, another thirty-five boxes. These particular boxes duplicated some of the files in Pershing's papers at the Manuscript Division but more often date from after September 1919 and dealt heavily with his postwar activities. At first I chose not to research these collections due to constraints of time and resources. Rather I decided to rely on the enormous collection of edited AEF records contained in the seventeen volumes of the *United States Army in the World War* (*USAWW*) because those editors not only had direct and complete access to all the AEF documents then in the possession of the Army War College's Historical Division but also had plenty of time to review and select such an exhaustive compilation. However, experience proved me wrong. I finally had to turn to RG 120 and RG 165, Records of the War Department General and Special Staffs, to fill in some important omissions in the *USAWW* and locate critical communications from the U.S. Military Attaché in London and the U.S. Military Mission in Paris during the war's opening months. I believed that these communications would provide important background on just exactly what information Pershing had available to him and his key staff before he sailed for Europe on May 28, 1917. Hence, I have added a number of these reports and cables to show that Pershing had an enormous amount of detailed information at his disposal to study during the weeks he spent in Washington, DC, before his departure.

The documents in RG 120, especially the records of the assistant chief of staff, Operations (ACS, G-3), were of great importance. All operational planning in General Headquarters (GHQ), AEF, centered in this staff, first under John McAuley Palmer, and then his successor, Fox Conner. While there are many important files in the G-3 records, file 1003: Employment of Troops (folder 681, box 3112) held a large number of critical planning studies that Pershing had personally requested. One of the most significant of these was "A Strategical Study on the Employment of the A. E. F. against the Imperial German Government," which Fox Conner, LeRoy R. Eltinge, and Hugh A. Drum submitted on September 25, 1917. This exhaustive study basically laid down the AEF's strategic path in Europe for the remainder of the war, and Pershing followed it closely thereafter.

Equally important was the large cache of original and duplicate correspondence between Pershing and GHQ, AEF, and Ferdinand Foch, Henri-Philippe Pétain, Douglas Haig, and their headquarters, which are located in file 1003, folders 649–672, boxes 3110–3111. Among them were copies of original, signed correspondence that were not located in any of Pershing's files in the Library of Congress. This correspondence was predominantly from the year 1918 and, hence, very critical to this collection.

United States Army in the World War. While comprehensive, the volumes of the *USAWW* are not easy to use and often contain significant omissions. The editors scattered documents among the various volumes, so it is often difficult to piece together the flow of correspondence and events. They often did not refer the users to the related preceding or succeeding key documents, leaving the user to search among volumes for the document, if they were published at all, which they often were not. They also edited out large parts of documents, again leaving the user to wonder what was said and if it were of any importance. I have tried to repair these faults where I was in possession of the entire document from Pershing's papers or another source, especially the official French Army history of the World War.

The French Army History. The tendency of the *USAWW*'s editors to delete parts of documents was especially marked where French documents were concerned. Fortunately, the *USAWW* editors frequently cited documents reprinted in the narrative and documentary volumes of the French official history, *Les armées françaises dans la Grande guerre* (*The French Army in the Great War*), prepared by the Service Historique, État-major de l'armée (Historical Service, French Army General Staff) and published by the Ministry of War in Paris from 1922 to 1938. Thanks to the former French Ministry of Defense, now called the Ministry of the Armed Forces, and today's Service historique de la Défense (Defense Historical Service) at Château de Vincennes (successor to the former French Army Historical Service), these invaluable sources are now available on the internet.

Of the eleven narrative volumes in the French Army history, I was only concerned with the volumes directly dealing with the time of the American involvement in the war and the armistice period from April 1917 through August of 1919. My focus thus encompassed narrative volumes 5 through 7 (a total of six separate volumes) and their annexes (appendices). The second part of volume 7 of the French Army history dealing with the period from September 26, 1918, to June 28, 1919, sadly contained only nineteen documents relating to the important immediate post-armistice and occupation period (November 11, 1918) up through the signing of the peace Treaty of Versailles. The annexes of those narrative volumes accounted for nine volumes of documents, all well organized and numbered for easy use. Ready access to these documentary volumes (the annexes) allowed me to check the original French documents cited in *USAWW* and insure that the documents were complete according to the French version. This was important because I soon discovered that the *USAWW* editors also omitted a number of French and American documents that passed between Pershing and Foch, Pétain, and other French leaders, which provided a clearer picture of the entirety of Franco-American cooperation and often conflict during and after the war. Moreover, there were often disparities between the French and American versions of published documents, which I have attempted to resolve.

I have focused heavily on the French documents that dealt with American involvement in the war and with Pershing and the AEF. Beginning even before American entry into the conflict on April 6, 1917, the French political and military leaders were developing plans and estimates of what they required from the United States to reinforce their war effort against Germany. The visit to Washington, DC, of the French Mission under René Viviani during April and May 1917 became a defining moment for laying down the details of exactly what the French desired in the way of American assistance in the war. It also introduced Marshal Joseph Joffre to the War Department's leaders, including Pershing, and it was Joffre who did so much to advise and assist not only Pershing during his early months in France but also his own government and military leaders on how to deal with the American presence and character.

These French background documents often clearly lay out the prevailing French views and policies as well as their heavy demands for substantial manpower and material support from the United States. Without them, critical aspects of the Franco-American relationship and Pershing's decision-making during the war would not be easily understandable to the reader. A number of these documents passed back and forth between Foch, Pétain, French Premier Georges Clemenceau, and the Ministry of War and the French Military Mission with the AEF at Chaumont. I have assumed that most of these documents were meant for Pershing and the GHQ, AEF as background or points of departure for more extensive discussions on an issue. Although I assume that there were many also specifically limited to "French Eyes Only," I have not yet seen one so marked.

The Papers of Woodrow Wilson. The collection of Woodrow Wilson's wartime papers, edited by Arthur S. Link, et al., and published by Princeton University Press in volumes 42 through 62 from 1983 to 1990, proved to be an invaluable source. These volumes allowed me to review Wilson's correspondence with and about Pershing without the time of searching Wilson's personal papers in the Library of Congress. From these volumes, I was able to obtain the details about how and when various Pershing cables and letters reached Wilson, usually forwarded from Secretary of War Newton D. Baker or others in the War Department in his absence, and the president's responses to them. This was the important and often missing link interconnecting presidential and War Department orders and directives to the actions of Pershing and the AEF in France.

Microfilm Collections. Also, I soon realized that NARA had already microfilmed a number of relevant collections that I could more easily access. Thus, I also consulted NARA Microform Publications M923: *Records of the American Section of the Supreme War Council, 1917–1919* (containing many of General Tasker H. Bliss's papers and correspondence with Pershing from January 1918 to August 1919); M930: *Cablegrams Exchanged between General Headquarters American Expeditionary Forces and the War Department, 1917–1919*; and M990: *Gorrell's History of the American Expeditionary Forces Air Service, 1917–1919*, which contains extensive collections of primary documents and cablegrams; and MF1024, *Records of the War*

Department General Staff: Correspondence of War College Division and Related General Staff Offices, 1903–1919. Of these microfilms, the more than seventeen thousand cables exchanged between the AEF and War Department were by far the most valuable in filling out the story of Pershing's interaction with the War Department and especially the secretary of war and chief of staff. Fortunately for my progress, I was able eventually to access those collections which Fold 3 has graciously now placed online for researchers at www.fold3.com. While certainly much easier and more convenient to use than the microfilms, these files also require a high degree of familiarity with the documents and their organization before one can really use them productively. I have noted much more about these cablegram files in the *Editor's Note* following Pershing's cable No. 1 to the War Department on June 8, 1917.

Cablegrams. The AEF-War Department cablegrams came to form a critical part of my collection. Scholars have seldom deeply explored these important sources due to their enormous number and the difficulty in using them. These coded cables were the only swift method that Pershing had for communicating with Washington and the War Department. Letters and documents had to be carried by an Army courier or reliable officer on a one-way trans-Atlantic voyage that took upward of a week at sea. Thus, cables were the only means for any quick and convenient communication of the AEF's major concerns to the decision-makers in Washington, and vice versa. The cables carried virtually all of the administrative, personnel, financial, contracting, materiel and equipment, procurement, etc., business that the AEF conducted with the War Department until July 19, 1918. Then the less critical or more bulky items went by couriers as "Courier Cables" until August 29, 1919. In my collection, I have not used any of the AEF's various official weekly, semiweekly, or daily "Summaries" of operations that were issued from October 30, 1917, to May 14, 1918, when the first of 227 daily "American Official Communiques" were sent in a series that lasted through December 13, 1918.

A reading of even a fraction of these cables will reveal the enormity of the task that Pershing and the AEF confronted in France after their arrival. They were dependent on the French for all their bases, training areas, billeting, supplies, transportation, and very heavily so for military equipment, armaments, and ammunition. Before an operational American army could even be imagined, an entire line of communications had to be created from virtually nothing because Pershing soon realized that the French could not effectively provide everything he required—wharves and dock facilities at ports of debarkation to receive shipments of officers, men, and supplies from the United States; barracks to house the men and warehouses to store the supplies; railway equipment and a transportation network to move the men and supplies to whatever base area was given to the AEF; a functioning storage and distribution system to assure continuing support to the troops; weapons and ammunition from infantry small arms to heavy artillery; military aircraft and engines of all varieties; and the training needed for officers and men to use the weapons and to learn the techniques of modern war as it was then being waged in the trenches. Pershing's cablegrams fully tell the story of his ceaseless drive for the men, equipment, and support required from the War Department and the United States from millions of feet of lumber to thousands of machine guns, aircraft and engines, trucks and cars, and artillery pieces, and millions of rounds of ammunition for infantry and artillery weapons. I have selectively included a number of these critical cablegrams so that the reader can more completely understand the demands of modern warfare that underpinned Pershing's planning and requisitions and relations with the Allies as well as the War Department.

Library of Congress Collections. In addition to Pershing's Papers in the Manuscript Division, a number of other collections there are of particular importance. The extensive papers of Gen. Tasker H. Bliss are of special note. Bliss was not only acting chief of staff subbing for Maj. Gen. Hugh L. Scott when Pershing left for France, he was later chief of staff (September 1917 until May 1918), although from January through May 1918 he was chief, American Section, and American permanent military representative, Supreme War Council (SWC) at Versailles and only the titular chief staff. His role on the SWC was critical for the AEF and Pershing, and he remained in that post well past Pershing's departure from France in September 1919. It is important to note that NARA's M923, the Records of the American Section, SWC, is missing at least seventy-nine of the most important files (out of a total of 377). These were transferred to Bliss and now rest in Bliss's papers in the Manuscript Division. Among these files are his correspondence with President Woodrow Wilson, Secretary Baker, Chief of Staff Gen. Peyton C. March, Pershing, and many other American and foreign military and political leaders. Though some his correspondence with Baker and March can be found scattered in various files in M923, by far the majority of it is in Bliss's own papers. These files are to be found in Part II: Personal File, 1917–1920, boxes, 244–317, and Part II: Office File—Supreme War Council, 1917–1930, boxes 317–87.

Also most important in the Manuscript Division are the papers of Gen. Peyton C. March, acting chief of staff and chief of staff (February 1918–September 1919), and Maj. Gen. James G. Harbord, who was probably Pershing's most trusted military subordinate, both as his chief of staff (May 1917–May 1918; May–August 1919), commanding general, 4th Marine Brigade (May–July 1918), and 2nd Division (July 1918), and as commanding general, Services of Supply, AEF (July 1918–May 1919). Other collections of value are Maj. Gen. Hugh L. Scott; Maj. Gen. George Goethals; Maj. Gen. Benjamin D. Foulois, Chief, AEF's Air Service (November 1917–May 1918) and then with Air Service in the Zone of Advance, First U.S. Army; Lloyd C. Griscom, Pershing's representative with the secretary of state for War and British War Office (chief of the Imperial General Staff) in London (see the following paragraph for an additional comment); Maj. Gen. Robert Bullard; Maj. Gen. Henry T. Allen; and Col. Paul M. Clark, Pershing's liaison officer with Marshal Henri-Philippe Pétain, General Headquarters, French Army, and commander-in-chief, Armies of the North and Northeast; Adm. William S. Sims, Force Commander, U.S. Naval Forces in European Waters; and Bishop Charles H. Brent, Pershing's chief chaplain for the AEF.

Lloyd C. Griscom played a pivotal role in maintaining Pershing's relations with Lord Milner, the secretary of state for War, and the British General Staff in London from June 1918 through the AEF's departure from France in September 1919. Griscom was also an acquaintance of Col. Edward M. House, President Wilson's most trusted confidential advisor, and frequently corresponded with him, often through Pershing. It is important to note that Griscom's personal papers at the Library of Congress contained very little of his extensive correspondence with Pershing, and none with House that I could locate. Where those papers are today, I could not determine. However, I was able to gather the Griscom-House correspondence as well as the House-Pershing correspondence from the Edward M. House papers at Manuscripts and Archives at Yale University Library.

Yale University Library. The Edward Mandell House papers at Manuscripts and Archives, Yale University Library, were an important source to me. I obtained copies of House's correspondence with Pershing, which often filled in important gaps, and also his correspondence with Lloyd C. Griscom, as mentioned above. In addition, series II of House's papers include his extensive diaries, which provided his personal conversations with and about Pershing that often furnished important details. These diaries are now available online at Yale University Library Digital Collections at web.library.yale.edu/digital-collections.

My Experiences in the World War. Pershing's two-volume memoirs of World War I were published by Frederick A. Stokes of New York in 1931. Pershing and his personal staff crafted these volumes very carefully over a number of years before publication, but they were severely edited and reduced in length for commercial publication. In addition to the many weaknesses of these volumes, which Fr. Donald Smythe has pointed out in his *Pershing: General of the Armies,* pp. 288-95, I would add the rather abrupt termination of Pershing's story in November 1918 in volume 2, chapter 51. I have relied heavily on Pershing's own accounts of personages, meetings, and events to provide important additional details that he so often leaves out of his personal diary entries. I believe it is important that these details be included so that the reader can more fully understand the background of the events and persons mentioned as well as Pershing's perspectives on them in his own words.

Organization of the Volumes. I have had to change my original concept for the organization of the collection into eight chronological volumes, with four quarterly volumes devoted to 1918 and two additional volumes for 1919. Because of the large amount of critical documentation pertaining to the events of 1918, which I amassed during continuing research, I have concluded that a restructuring of the remaining volumes is required to assure a thorough treatment of Pershing and the AEF. Because 1918 was the decisive year of the war, it demands such coverage. Thus, I have developed a revised organization for Volumes 3 to 8:

Volume 1	April 7–September 30, 1917
Volume 2	October 1–December 31, 1917
Volume 3	January 1–March 20, 1918
Volume 4	March 21–May 19, 1918
Volume 5	May 20–July 14, 1918
Volume 6	July 15–September 25, 1918
Volume 7	September 26–December 31, 1918
Volume 8	January 1–September 3, 1919

A Daily Structure Adopted. Each volume is organized by day, with all correspondence and cable traffic included under the date of origin, completion, or dispatch—not the date of receipt. The first item each day is an entry from Pershing's personal diary that he and his aides kept from May 1917 until he returned to the United States on

September 1, 1919. Every day in each volume does not have an entry from Pershing's diary because some entries were too mundane and unimportant to merit inclusion, or simply did not exist. The Manuscript Division of the Library of Congress has now digitalized all of these wartime diaries, which are now available online beginning with May 1917 at hdl.loc.gov/loc.mss/ms013112.mss35949.003 (the original pages are in Set 1, which continues through .007 for the period until Pershing leaves France on September 1, 1919). The diary entries used in this collection are not from the War Diary, General Headquarters, American Expeditionary Forces, which was kept by the Operations Section of the General Staff for most of the war. They are also not the diary entries that Pershing and his colleagues concocted for his *My Experiences in the World War,* which Fr. Donald Smythe in his *Pershing: General of the Armies,* called "fictitious. Instead of the one kept during the war, it was a composite formed by combining the wartime diary with other headquarters records" (p. 290).

I have opted to begin each day with an entry from Pershing's personal diary when appropriate because it is the best indication of his exhausting daily routine and schedule as the CINC, AEF, from mid-June 1917 through September 1, 1919. While much of what was recorded in these entries might be seem routine, I have included many such entries because they clearly indicate the rigorous schedule that Pershing kept, including his frequent travels, visits, and meetings with Allied military and political leaders, inspections of troops and installations, meetings with correspondents and visiting congressmen, and on and on and on.

On many key occasions, such as meetings with or visits to his fellow Allied commanders, Foch, Haig, and Pétain, or his numerous visits to AEF or Allied units, Pershing usually recorded extensive comments, which form an important source of information. Pershing was an astute observer and excellent writer who clearly laid down his views and reasoning in these discussions and the decisions reached.

Pershing usually met with his chief of staff and key staff officers daily, and often saw his subordinate commanders and staffs for important discussions of policy and strategy, to issue directives or orders, or to correct deficiencies he had noted in behavior or performance. He was in many ways a micromanager who kept his fingers on everything that was going on in the GHQ and AEF. If anyone questions that assertion, a review of Harbord's wartime papers as the AEF's chief of staff in the Manuscript Division will quickly end such a fantasy. During August 1917, Harbord wrote of this trait of Pershing in a letter to his wife, later published as part of his *Leaves from a War Diary:*

> General Pershing is a very strong character. He has a good many peculiarities, such I suppose as every strong man accustomed to command is apt to develop. He is very patient and philosophical under trying delays from the War Department. He is playing for high stakes and does not intend to jeopardize his winning by wasting his standing with the War Department over small things—relatively unimportant, though very annoying as they occur. He is extremely cautious, very cautious, and does nothing hastily or carelessly. He spends much time rewriting his cables and other papers I prepare for him, putting his own individuality into them. He is the first officer for

whom I have prepared papers who did not generally accept what I wrote for him. It is very seldom I get anything past him without some alteration, though I am obliged to say I do not always consider that he improves them, though often he does. He edits everything he signs, even the most trivial things. It is a good precaution, but one which can easily be carried to a point where it will waste time that might better be employed on bigger things, but it is probably justified in the preliminary stages in which we are. (James G. Harbord, *Leaves from a War Diary* [New York: Dodd, Mead, 1931], 124.)

A good example of Pershing's control over the GHQ AEF's activities is the following memorandum that he sent to Harbord on October 17, 1917:

Headquarters American Expeditionary Forces.

October 17, 1917.

Confidential.

Memorandum for the Chief of Staff.

    1. Please have Colonel Conner [Acting Chief, Operations Section] prepare weekly report of our forces for the British General Headquarters and have a copy sent to the British War Office, the latter to be sent to General Robertson [Chief, Imperial General Staff].

    These reports should be, of course, very confidential and should be the same as we are sending General Petain weekly. Let me add here that a copy of the one sent to General Petain should also go to General Foch in Paris. Let this be the rule hereafter.

    2. Please have study made with as little delay as practicable as to the rapidity with which Germany could bring divisions from the eastern to the western front. I think the French have made a study of this and possibly we may be able to obtain that through our mission. In any event, I desire a separate study made by our own General Staff.

    3. For Captain de la Farranay [French ADC]: Please obtain as early as practicable from the French War Officer or other source, information as to the amount of wheat available in France for the use of both the army and the people.

    4. As to paragraph three, please direct Colonel Nolan [Assistant Chief of Staff, Intelligence] also to get what information he can on this subject. This is important for two reasons. The first is the question of making up the deficiency and the second affects our own transportation problems.

    5. Please submit to me a report on all unanswered questions that are now before the General Staff. Referring to my remark the other day, I do not desire the General Staff to get into the habit of holding these questions for an indefinite time. They must, as well as other people, understand that work should be turned out promptly. Let us not fall into the habit which

seems to prevail in the War Department of allowing things to become buried in the General Staff.

6. I desire the Operations Section take up the study of some of the principal battles of the war and present them in such shape that they can be used not only by division and brigade commanders but by all staff officers as well. It is desired that they become a part of division instruction as well as instruction of the staff schools.

7. I am rather under the impression that from now on, communications addressed to the British and French General Headquarters relating to troops and other matters, except routine, turned over to the staff should be generally submitted to me for comment and possible signature before being sent.

8. The question of the location of the headquarters for the line of communications has never been given serious consideration by the General Staff. Please have this taken up at once by the proper section and invite their attention to the fact that the Commander of the Line of Communications, himself, is of the opinion that the headquarters should remain in Paris or possibly placed at Tours or some other city along the line. I, myself, am inclined to think that the Line of Communications Commander should be here. and such assistants as may be necessary to keep him advised of conditions and to carry out his instructions should be located at various ports and depots further back. I think also that a staff officer of ability should represent him in Paris.

9. This question of personnel is one that must be solved at once. I do not see any other way than to turn it over to one of the General Staff sections whose business it should be to do this and nothing else. This is a large question and one that might mean success or failure for us. I have thought of placing it under the Adjutant General and have also thought of placing it under one of my personal staff officers—possibly the Military Secretary, who would work out the various questions involved and be ready to present to me at any time records of officers and recommendations for their assignment. It seems to me that this must be of a confidential nature and possible the latter plan would be the better.

10. Please let me know the organization of the General Staff as it exists now, with recommendations as to the detail of other officers for duty here. Either our officers are overworked or else they are not the class of officers we would wish. Of course I know the latter, to a large extent, is unavoidably true. My recollection of the British General Staff is that they have not such a great number of officers at general headquarters, but of course they have not now the many details to work out that our General Staff has. Let me have this in the next day or two if possible.

J. J. P.

(Library of Congress [LC], Papers of Maj. Gen. James G. Harbord, folder: Correspondence with John J. Pershing, box 11.)

Pershing was on top of all major and most minor issues that came into the GHQ. He would cite War Department or AEF cables by number and paragraph and ask what action had been taken or was to be taken and who was working the issue. He sent many daily "J.J.P.s," memos to the chief of staff or whatever staff officer was lucky enough that day to receive the initialed memo, which meant that it came directly from Pershing through his aides and personal staff. Frederick Palmer, who was his chief press censor in France, had known Pershing well since they first met in Manchuria in 1905 when Pershing was a military observer with the Imperial Japanese Army and Palmer a well-respected war correspondent. In his *John J. Pershing, General of the Armies: A Biography*, which was written well before Pershing's death but not published until after it, Palmer includes chapter 12, "Initialed 'J.J.P.,'" in which he writes about the ubiquitous "J.J.P.s": "There was no doubt on the part of the pioneer staff or ever to be who was running the AEF. It was the man who wrote the bold J. J. P. under instructions or comment on a pad in letters as clear as though they were block—. . . . Rarely was he referred to by those close to him as the Chief, or the General, practically never as the Old Man, but almost invariably as 'J.J.P.'" (Frederick Palmer, *John J. Pershing, General of the Armies: A Biography* [Harrisburg, PA: Military Service Publishing, 1948], 101). Any researcher who has worked in Pershing's papers is very familiar with "J.J.P.s" and those strong, distinct, and unquestionable initials.

It is well-known that Pershing had an extremely strong personality and held his views with a high degree of intensity. He was not a person to be intimidated by any foreign civilian or military leader. He came to France with specific instructions from the president, the secretary of war, and the chief of staff (see May 27, 1917), and he held to those instructions with a fervor that appalled and often infuriated both British and French leaders. This was especially so with his adamant refusal to consent to the amalgamation of American soldiers or small units (company or battalion) into British or French line units and his equally adamant insistence upon the autonomy of the American forces and the eventual creation of an autonomous American army occupying its own sector of the front. His often rigid stance on these main issues truly incensed both British prime minister David Lloyd George and French premier Georges Clemenceau. Indeed, Clemenceau became so infuriated with Pershing that he even tried to force Marshal Ferdinand Foch, the Allied commander-in-chief, to undermine or remove him from command in October 1918 (see December 23, 1917, *Editor's Note* following Pétain, CINC, Armies of the North and Northeast, and Pershing, CINC, AEF; January 2, 1918, *Editor's Note* following TAG, War Department, to Pershing, Cable A-588-R; and January 5, 1918, Pershing to Clemenceau, President of the Council, Ministry of War, Paris; and especially October 22, 1918, *Editor's Note* following *Pershing's Personal Diary*). Lloyd George went behind Pershing's back on several occasions in an effort to undermine him with President Wilson and Secretary Baker (see April 7, 1918, *Editor's Note* following Baker-Pershing conference with Generals Whigham and Hutchinson, and April 27, *Editor's Note* following *Pershing's Personal Diary*). In his memoirs, Lloyd George makes unmistakably clear his personal dislike for Pershing and his positions (see David Lloyd George, *War Memoirs of David Lloyd George* [London: Odhams Press, 1938], vol. 2, 2nd ed., 1800–1825).

The trials and tribulations of Pershing's often stormy and sometimes difficult relations with the Allies are very clearly played out in his exchanges with them. Moreover, he also had more than his share of fiery tangles with American civilian and military leaders at home, especially in the War Department, when he could not obtain what he wanted in France for the AEF. One thing Pershing was not was shy. He defended his positions, himself, his key staff officers, and his officers and men against all comers. While he was not always on the side of the angels in all of his disputes, he held his ground and argued his points aggressively and frankly.

Pershing's most enduring official wartime relationship in Washington was with the Secretary of War Newton D. Baker, whom he greatly respected. In his numerous letters and cables to Baker, he laid out his positions clearly and firmly. His relations with Chief of Staff Peyton C. March were not nearly so gracious or smooth, for the two did not see eye to eye on many critical issues once March became acting chief of staff early in March 1918. Again, Pershing was not reticent to put his case before March, nor was March to put his before Pershing. The latent hostilities built up during the war were to be played out much more fully with the appearance of their respective postwar memoirs as well as in those of their confidants, such as Harbord. (See Donald Smythe, *Pershing: General of the Armies* [Bloomington: Indiana University Press, 2007], 292–95.)

Linked Correspondence. In each entry in the daily catalog of correspondence, whether letter, memorandum, or cable, I have added reference to the date of any reply received, if I have located any, so that the reader can more easily and quickly access the response and follow the continuation of the discussion already begun. Fortunately, this was very easy to do with the AEF-War Department cable traffic because the AEF copies (those used by NARA) were all annotated with the cable number and paragraph of the reply. I simply adopted the AEF's annotation procedure for referring to replies or additional cables. For example, on December 20, 1917, Pershing cabled the War Department about the shipment of supplies to the Red Cross in P-399-S, paragraph 3B (annotated P-399-S-3B) and at the end of that paragraph will be found [Reply—December 24, A-561-R-7], meaning the answer will be found on December 24 in cable A-561-R, paragraph 7. By using this procedure, I was able to link all applicable correspondence so that a chain of continuity would be formed, allowing the user to locate all relevant documents pertaining to the subject being discussed.

Organization of Daily Documents. The documents for each daily entry are organized in a specific manner to provide continuity of coverage. Following the entry from Pershing's personal diary, I have placed documents in the following order, if there were any for that particularly day:

1. Documents from French civil and military leaders and organizations.
2. Documents from British civil and military leaders and organizations.
3. Documents originating in the staff of the GHQ, AEF.
4. Documents originating in AEF commands and units.
5. Documents from American civilian and military leaders in Europe but not assigned to the AEF, such as Gen. Tasker H. Bliss, Arthur H. Frazier, Edward M. House, etc.

6. Pershing's correspondence with the American civil and military leaders or personal friends in the United States, including President Wilson, Secretary Baker, General March, Senator Warren, etc.
7. Pershing's cables to the War Department (P-series, Main and Confidential).
8. War Department cables to Pershing and the AEF (A-series, Main and Confidential).

Each document contains a source citation at the end so that the user will know where the information came from and where the document can be located. I believed that some such structure was needed so that I could organize the documents in an orderly and repetitive manner that the reader could readily understand and follow. I hope my scheme adequately meets that goal.

Editor's Notes. I have used two varieties of Editor's Notes in these volumes: (1) parenthetical notes are indicated by *Ed.* and refer specifically to the subject matter where it is located to fully explain information that may not be clearly understood, or to add pertinent information for clarification; (2) *Editor's Note* indicates substantive additional information pertaining to the correspondence or subject matter cited to provide sufficient details for the reader to more fully understand the context of the document. I have been very liberal in my use of an Editor's Note to add important details to some of Pershing's often very succinct and not particularly informative entries in his personal diary or to add an event or meeting that Pershing simply left out. His two-volume *My Experiences in the World War* often provided the detailed accounts and personal perspective that Pershing had skipped. On a number of occasions, I also chose to include material from published sources, such as the two volumes of Charles G. Dawes's *A Journal of the Great War* (Boston: Houghton Mifflin, 1921), which gave the details I believed were necessary to understand Pershing's decisions and activities.

Identification of Persons. I have made no effort except coincidentally to identify the many civilian and military leaders and personages with whom Pershing interacted or corresponded during his time as CINC, AEF. A large number of biographical dictionaries exist online and in print that provide the reader with sufficient biographical details.

Illustrations. I have tried to illustrate the volumes with pertinent maps and photographs that will enhance the reader's understanding. The maps used are drawn from Pershing's two-volume *My Experiences in the World War* or from various volumes of *The United States Army in the World War*. I have specifically chosen the less complicated maps to increase the ease of use. Photographs are from the U.S. Army Signal Corps collection (RG 111) in the NARA's Still Picture Branch, Special Archives Division; the collections of the Prints and Photographs Division of the Library of Congress; or from sources identified in the photograph's caption. The Signal Corps photographs are particularly difficult to use because they are arranged in no logical, organizational, or chronological order. They were apparently added to the photograph collection as they were received from the AEF, resulting in significant mixing of images into a jumbled mass. In addition, the dating of the images is often inaccurate as is the identification of locations, personages, and events shown in them. Because of this, numerous images were found unusable for illustrative purposes. From the Library of Congress, I have focused primarily on the collections from Pershing's personal papers. Whether from the National Archives or the Library of Congress, many of the images lacked captions that contained basic, accurate information such as date, location, people, and detailed descriptions of the subject matter in the image. As with the Signal Corps images, in many cases this problem made it impossible to use numerous images that could not be identified or placed accurately in the volumes. I have tried to place the images used on the exact date they were taken or when the event occurred and link them to the text for a graphic enhancement of the narrative.

As editor, I alone am responsible for the organization and accuracy of all documents contained in these volumes.

Introduction to Volume 4

The long-anticipated great German offensive (Operation Michael) struck the British front on the Somme in the early morning hours of March 21, 1918. Quickly dislodging much of the Third and Fifth Armies, the German surge continued; by April 6 the Germans had pushed the British back thirty-seven miles, to just east of Amiens. Three days later, on April 9, a second German offensive (Operation Georgette) on the Lys River to the north struck in the Armentières area and continued until April 27. These two massive blows radically transformed the Allied situation on the British sector and required the French to send divisions north to take over part of the front, changing the entire strategic situation in the West within weeks. The rupture of the British front also completely altered Pershing's long-range plans for the building of the American Expeditionary Forces (AEF). The growing crisis soon embroiled him in more controversies with the British and French political and military leaders, who desperately sought American manpower to replace their mounting losses and to compensate for their increasingly critical shortages of manpower.

By pure coincidence, Pershing and Secretary of War Newton D. Baker visited General Henri Philippe Pétain, French Commander-in-Chief, and his General Headquarters (GHQ) at Compiègne on March 21 and received a briefing on the initial French estimate of the German offensive. Baker was then involved in much of the frenetic activity among the Allies that followed the German breakthrough, assisting Pershing and General Tasker H. Bliss, American Permanent Military Representative, in establishing American positions on critical issues requiring quick Presidential action. A number of these issues in which Baker was involved, especially the British leaders' resurrection of the idea of amalgamating American troops into their divisions and Lloyd George's efforts to undermine Pershing, would cause the American commander-in-chief (CINC) many uneasy and difficult moments in the months to come.

The initial German grand offensive of March 21 dramatically changed Pershing's world. The crisis about which the British and French leaders had so worried since Russia left the war some months earlier was now a dangerous reality. Pershing swiftly acted to meet with French military leaders. On March 25 he journeyed to Compiègne to meet with Gen. Pétain, French Army CINC. On March 28, he traveled to Clermont to confer with Georges Clemenceau, French Prime Minister and Minister of War, and Gen. Ferdinand Foch, French Chief of Staff and newly ordained coordinator of Allied military operations at the Anglo-French conference at Doullens on March 26. During his meeting with the French leaders, Pershing offered the full support of the AEF to Foch in these famous words: "There is at this moment no other question than that of fighting. Infantry, Artillery, Aviation—all that we have—are yours to dispose of as you will." The gravity of the crisis forced Pershing to discard temporarily his hard-won plans for the creation of an American Army and the phased preparation of the AEF for combat—he offered his as yet not fully trained combat divisions to the French for service on the front lines. Within days of the German attack, he would see the January agreement and the Six-Division Plan with Britain buried under an avalanche of British and French demands for the immediate shipment of only infantry and machine-gun units to the exclusion of other divisional, corps, army, and Services of Supply supporting units. Once again, the fractious issue of amalgamation of American troops into depleted British and French combat divisions became a major subject of debate among the Allies as the British and French struggled to survive rapidly mounting combat losses.

Three major Supreme War Council meetings, those at Beauvais (April 3), Abbeville (May 1–2), and Versailles (June 1–3) (see Vol. 5), dominated the ensuing inter-Allied relations and strategic planning to regain control of the situation on the Western front. Pershing was intimately involved in all these meetings, as the Allied leaders fought to change the priorities in the flow of American troops to emphasize mainly infantry and machine-gun units. Such changes would overturn the AEF's existing scheme of balanced priority shipments designed to build the supporting line of communications in the rear as well as the AEF's combat forces at the front. These conflicting priorities pushed Pershing into a sustained struggle for the AEF's future and its American identity with Lloyd George and Georges Clemenceau, who often actively worked against Pershing to pursue the resources they desperately needed to salvage their own war efforts.

British and French leaders met at Doullens on March 26 in an attempt to forge some unity of command to save the deteriorating situation on the northern Allied front. Foch, Chief of the French Army General Staff, was appointed the nominal Allied Commander-in-Chief with limited powers to coordinate Allied operations. Two days later, on March 28, Pershing offered Clemenceau and General Foch all the forces at his disposal, whether completely ready for combat or not. Pershing fully realized that this decision compromised his plans for an independent American Army under American command on its own sector of the front, but the survival of the Allied coalition was his paramount concern. He was fortunate that Secretary of War Newton D. Baker had arrived in France early in March for his first visit to the AEF and Allied leaders, so he was present for personal consultations and discussions with Pershing and Bliss throughout this critical period.

The situation for the Allies had now grown so critical that Clemenceau called a meeting of the Supreme War Council at Beauvais on April 3 to discuss two major issues: the unity of command on the Western Front and American cooperation. The first issue was dealt with relatively easily, as the Allied leaders and their governments granted Foch the powers of *generalissimo* to coordinate, plan, and execute operations, although with some significant limitations. The second issue, however, soon became very contentious.

Lloyd George, ever the manipulator, had gone behind Pershing's back to President Woodrow Wilson in late March and early April in an attempt to undermine Pershing's authority as CINC, AEF, and reverse his policies. At Beauvais in the discussions on American cooperation, he even went so far as to blindside Pershing with a theatrical display and reading of a cable from Lord Reading, British Ambassador in Washington. Lloyd George contended that President Wilson promised the shipment of 120,000 American troops per month through July. Pershing had received no such cabled information and quickly stated that he would seek confirmation from Washington. The confirmation, of course, did not support Lloyd George's statements (see April 5, cable 79-S, and April 6, cable 45-R). Indeed, Tasker Bliss, who was an active participant in the Beauvais discussions, would write to Secretary Baker, who was in Italy at the time of the Beauvais meeting, after the Abbeville Conference on May 4, "When General Pershing and I told you of this statement, at General Pershing's house in Paris, you telegraphed to the President to ascertain what engagements he had made. He replied, as I remember it, to the general effect that he had made no such specific engagement, as to numbers and time. Mr. Lloyd George's statement was based on a telegram from Lord Reading in Washington which he read to the Conference at Beauvais [see March 30, cable no. 1360, in Editor's Note following Storr to Bliss]. As long as the statement made by Mr. Lloyd George at Beauvais remains uncorrected and, on the contrary, is given official circulation, it will be the cause of misunderstanding." That it certainly was.

As American divisions entered the front lines during April, Pershing struggled to come to an agreement with the British and French on the shipment of American troops to France. Poor communication and coordination with Washington once again undermined his position in these discussions, as they had in December 1917 (see Vol. 2). On April 19, Secretary Baker, back in Washington, sent a memorandum to the British Ambassador, known as the "Baker Memorandum," with a draft cable to Pershing on the matter of American troop shipments. The British Ambassador quickly made this available to the British and French governments, but Pershing never received a copy until his return to Chaumont on April 26 from his visit to London (see April 26, cable A-1184-R, and Editor's Note following). This serious lack of coordination by Washington leaders seriously compromised Pershing's position, as he noted in his memoirs:

> This concession went further than it was necessary to go and much further than I had expected. Realizing the complications that might arise from commitments so far in the future and the delay in forming an American army that would follow, I did not agree in later discussions at the Supreme War Council with all that the Allies now felt justified in demanding. I was opposed to the action of the Council in assuming the power to dispose American troops under any circumstances. Moreover, it was not in any sense a prerogative of this body. (Pershing, *My Experiences in the World War*, vol. 2, pp. 7–8.)

Secretary Baker was so concerned about the disarray shown in this entire matter that he wrote lengthy letters to Pershing and Bliss on April 29 explaining what had happened (see April 29, Baker to Pershing, and Editor's Note following; and Baker to Bliss). Another lengthy letter from Baker to Pershing on June 6 (Vol. 5), responding to Pershing's cable reporting on the Versailles Conference, further explained the difficulty of negotiations with the British and French on this matter and Baker's lack of clarity regarding Pershing's discussions with the Allies in Europe. Baker told Pershing that "as soon as I discovered how much confusion was being created I recommended to the President strongly that further agreements on this subject be made only by you." Basically, he correctly left the final decisions on any future agreements on troop shipments up to Pershing, the American commander in the field.

Efforts to reach an understanding on troop flows dominated much of April following the Beauvais Conference. In an attempt to resolve the main issues with the British, Pershing traveled to London, where negotiations with Lord Milner, Secretary of State for War, resulted in the London Agreement of April 24 on the transportation of American troops to France. In order to reassure the French concerning the arrangements made with Lord Milner, on April 25, as he was returning from London, Pershing met with Foch at his GHQ at Sarcus to inform him of the provisions of the London Agreement. Unfortunately, Foch was not pleased, and the French leadership reacted extremely negatively to this agreement, believing that it favored troops going to support the British Armies and shorted the French. This resulted in a British-French meeting at Abbeville on April 27, without any American presence, to thrash out their differences and produced a call for another Supreme War Council session at Abbeville to resolve this lingering issue (See Editor's Note, April 27).

The Supreme War Council gathered at Abbeville on May 1–2 to review the entire issue of the employment of American troops, which continued to fester with the British and French, as well as some other strategic questions. The first day was largely devoted to dealing with the movement and employment of American troops, a discussion in which Pershing held his own on most points and had the Allied leaders accept his request for the formation of an American Army. Ultimately, he arrived at an agreement, known as the Abbeville Agreement, which provided for certain levels of troop movements in May (130,000) and June (150,000) and placed a priority on infantry and machine-gun units in addition to the six divisions already committed for shipment to train with the British. In the Council's Resolution No. 6 (May 2), these force levels were recognized, as was the formation of an American Army "as soon as possible." However, the priorities for infantry and machine-gun units also resulted in a serious limitation on the number of line of communications (Services of Supply), corps, and army support units reaching France, including artillery, which eventually would have profound consequences for Pershing and the AEF once large-scale offensive operations began in September.

Anticipating another German offensive in the near future, Pershing had continued to build the AEF as best he could and resolve the many problems facing it. Because American divisions were now scattered all along the front and in training areas in the rear of the British and French sectors, Pershing maintained a busy schedule of visits to his troops and meetings with Allied leaders to resolve outstanding issues and to address future operational plans. In meetings with Foch at Versailles on May 18 and Pétain at Chantilly on May 19, Pershing thoroughly discussed the AEF's current status in supporting the French front and his plans for an American sector.

Both Foch and Pétain agreed to the formation of an American sector on the front once the present emergency had passed. Both also asked for American troops to reinforce their weakened divisions, but Pershing tactfully demurred on their requests. In his memoirs, he briefly explained his answer to Pétain: "While his needs were appreciated, this was another request that could not be granted without yielding in my determination to bring about the formation of an American army" (*My Experiences in the World War*, vol. 2, p. 54).

1

March 21–March 31, 1918

March 21

Pershing's Personal Diary

Arrived at Compiègne about 11 a.m. We were met at the train by a few French officers and Major [Paul H.] Clark and Major Freeborn of the American Mission at French headquarters. We went to General Pétain's headquarters, and the Secretary, General Pershing and General Pétain had a talk, General Pétain explaining to the Secretary the possibilities as to the German attack. The Secretary, General Pershing, General Black and Colonel Boyd had luncheon at General Pétain's mess. The other members of the party lunched at General Barescut's mess. We could hear very distinctly the steady rumble of bombardment to the north. General Pétain said it was possibly the beginning of the long-heralded German offensive. After lunch the party divided; the Secretary's party, Colonel Collins and Major Palmer went by motor to Montreuil; Colonel Boyd and myself went to Paris, arriving there at about 3 p.m. I saw Mr. Pomeroy Burton [General Manager of Britain's Associated Newspapers] and worked in quarters for the remainder of the day.

LC, Pershing Papers, Diary, May 7, 1917–September 1, 1918, box 4.

Editor's Note—Although the British and French had been anticipating a major German spring offensive for many months, they were not prepared when this offensive, the first of five from March 21 through mid-July (see Map 1), struck the British lines. In his wartime memoirs, Pershing commented extensively on the German offensive and the British and French lack of preparedness in meeting it (see Map 2). He focused heavily on two issues that he constantly strove to instill in the AEF: training in open (mobile) warfare and attention to maintaining adequate reserves.

On March 21st the great German offensive began against the British armies between the Oise and the junction of the French and British lines, on a front of fifty miles in length, extending from near La Fère to Arras. Near the center of the attack was General Gough's Fifth Army, with the Third Army under General Byng on its left. The artillery bombardment preceding the infantry advance was of short duration but of great intensity, with an unusually high proportion of gas shells. Following a heavy barrage, the German infantry, using the same tactical methods that had been so successful at Riga and Caporetto, delivered its blow. The weather favored the enemy, as a heavy fog continued intermittently for three days, much to the disadvantage of the defense. The overwhelming force of sixty-four specially trained German divisions out of their 192 then on the Western Front compelled the British lines to yield. Although at the end of the first day the Fifth Army had not entirely given away, its losses had reached several thousands and there was no question that the Germans were making a serious attempt to separate the British and French armies.

While there seemed to be every confidence before the attack that the lines could hold, full consideration had not been given to the certain use of open warfare tactics by the Germans, in which neither the British nor the French had been sufficiently trained. Adherence by the Allies on the Western Front to trench warfare methods proved advantageous to the Germans. Except for the Verdun affair of 1916, Germany had been on the defensive in the West while completing the conquest of Russia and the Near East. As expected, the collapse of Russia and the total defeat of Roumania released a large number of German divisions for the 1918 offensive in the West, where the Germans gained numerical superiority for the first time since 1914. With this advantage, they promptly began training for open warfare with the object of forcing their adversaries out of the trenches and beating them in the open. In this sort of warfare the British were seriously handicapped on account of their long adherence to stabilized warfare. Their officers said that when the men had to leave the trenches they acted as though something were radically wrong in that there was not another trench somewhere for them to get into.

On the second day of the battle the last of Gough's reserves were put in, yet he received no support to stop the widening gap in the British front until the following day, when one French infantry division and one French dismounted cavalry division arrived. On the 24th four other French divisions got into position. These divisions and others that came in the next two or three days were put into battle by General Fayolle without regard to the integrity of units or the order of their entry, some of them being very short of ammunition.

The British Fifth Army was evidently sorely pressed from the start, yet no British reenforcements were sent to Gough until the 24th, and then only one division, no others arriving during the first week. By the end of the fifth day the German forces had driven a salient into the British front some thirty-seven miles deep and were threatening the important railway center of Amiens, the capture of which would probably have made a complete breach between the French and British armies....

In view of the agreement for mutual support, it is not clear why the British and French should not have had a greater number of reserve divisions within easy reach of the point of juncture. Certainly it seemed logical that the enemy would endeavor to separate the two armies by attacking at that point. In fact, our information for some time previous indicated that he intended to do so. In the extension of the British front, the French had gained several divisions for their reserves, but when the blow came few of them were near enough to be of immediate service. The French staff seemed to fear that their front might be the German objective, and this might account for the lack of French reserves near the junction of the two armies. Whether the general reserve would have been adequate or not, there is no doubt that the substitute agreement for mutual support did not fully meet the situation. (*Ed.*—For additional background on the disagreement between Haig and Pétain concerning reserves and mutual support arrangements, see Vol. 3.) (Pershing, *My Experiences in the World War*, Vol. 1, pp. 353–56.)

Col. H. W. Thornton, British Army, Deputy Director General of Movements and Railways, War Office, Paris Representative, to Pershing.

Personal.

In regard to the shortage of wagons which you are experiencing at your ports and which you mentioned to me recently, the Inter-Allied Transportation Council has now been formally brought into being, and General Nash, the British Delegate, who is largely responsible for its creation, is now in Paris. I have mentioned our conversation to him and you may rest assured that he fully appreciates the pressing need of early assistance. The first undertaking of the Council will be the consideration of your position with respect to transport, and I believe a way will be found to afford relief.

There is, however, another aspect which has a direct bearing on the shortage of wagons which confronts the American Expeditionary Force and which I want to touch upon—not so much as a British Officer, but as a friend and one who is intensely interested in the successful participation of the United States in the war.

The increased size of the British Army, the necessity of maintaining an army in Italy, as well as French Military and Civil needs, have placed a very heavy burden on the French Railways, notwithstanding the importation of 916 locomotives and 51,000 wagons "ten-ton units" from England, most of which were taken out of service at a time when the Railway traffic of the United Kingdom was at a maximum and increasing rapidly. In fact today, owing to the reduction in coastal trade and the general increase in internal traffic, the British Railways are handling by far the greatest tonnage in their history. To still further aggravate the position, it is imperative to move 9,000 tons of coal a day by all rail routes to Italy, and 6,000 tons a day by rail to Marseille, and thence by sea. While the Italians are providing most of the rolling stock for this service, a substantial amount must come from the French supply. In short, as it stands today, the capacity of the French and British transportation machines is now strained to the limit, without additional burdens.

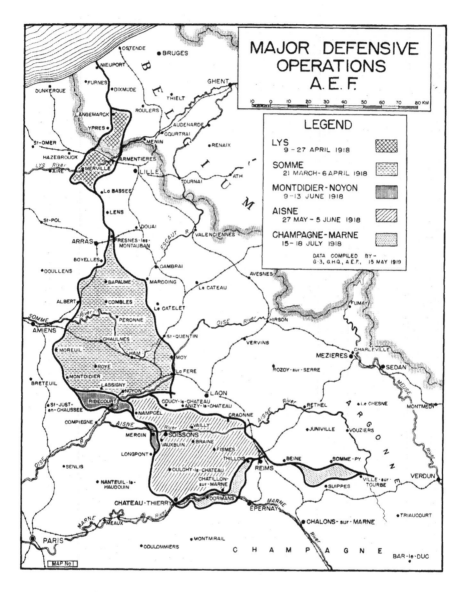

Map 1. Major Defensive Operations, AEF. A series of five major German offensives struck the Allied lines from March 21 through mid-July 1918. The first two attempted to break the British armies, split them from the French, and push them back to the Channel. The next three were aimed at the French, but only that on the Aisne River in late May presented a major threat. While the AEF had only minor engagement in the first two offensives against the British, it played a large part in defeating the last three German drives. Source: *The United States Army in the World War*, vol. 1, p. 15.

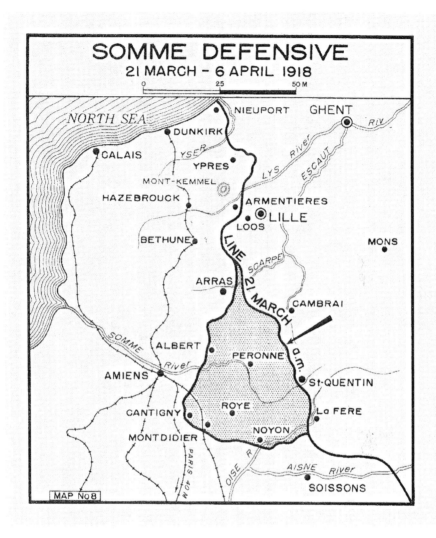

Map 2. The Somme Defensive, March 21–April 6, 1918. The first great German offensive of 1918, Operation Michael, very nearly succeeded in breaking though the British front. Through a desperate effort and with French cooperation, the British were able to stabilize their front as the German offensive ran out of steam early in April. Source: *The United States Army in the World War,* vol. 4, p. 26.

This brings me to the particular point I wish to urge upon you. The American Expeditionary Force is here in advance of its railway transport, which, for the time being, must be largely provided from sources in France, until you are able to catch up. In the face of what I have said above, this additional and considerable burden jeopardizes the safety of the whole proposition, and I think you ought to reduce the number of men despatched to France and increase your export of transportation equipment, *unless you have at your disposal sufficient shipping to do both in proper proportion*. I fully recognise the necessity of sending a considerable Army to France for sentimental and other reasons, but I feel that that point has now been reached. At all hazards from now onwards you must keep your equipment ahead of the arrival of your men; any other course is not only folly, but is courting failure for you and disaster for all. These are strong words, but I want to put it clearly and emphatically. I am prepared to stand by what I have said and I may add that I am not alone in this opinion. If you agree with me, I venture to suggest that Secretary Baker should be fully informed of the position before he returns to America, and I have no objection to your using this letter in any way you may desire.

Finally, I want to make it perfectly clear that this letter is not written in a spirit of criticism or in any desire to dodge an issue or shift a responsibility. The necessity which rested upon the American Government to bring a considerable force to France immediately, is fully recognised, but I now feel the time has come when the situation should be carefully reviewed in connection with the transportation difficulties which exist here.

Irrespective of what may happen, you may be certain of whole-hearted and enthusiastic British support, and I have no doubt the French Government will view the matter in the same spirit. [Reply—March 24, Pershing to Thornton]

LC, Pershing Papers, folder: Col. H. W. Thornton, box 196.

Brig. Gen. Benjamin D. Foulois, Chief, Air Service, SOS, AEF, to CINC, AEF, in reply to request from Lt. Col. James A. Logan, Jr., ACS, G-1, GHQ, AEF, March 19 (not located), in addition to Foulois to Logan, March 20.

(*Ed.*—A handwritten note on the copy of this memorandum states: *"Reply to General P memo for Col Logan dated March 19/18."*)

Subject: Air Service Program.

1. Present Air Service program, as approved by General Staff, contemplates 120 Service Squadrons for front line service by December 31, 1918.

2. Present plans contemplate having 60 Service Squadrons ready by June 30, 1918, for front line service, provided aeroplanes, aeroplane engines and truck transportation can be provided.

The English, French and Italian sources of supply are being utilized to the fullest extent to obtain aeroplanes, aeroplane engines and truck transportation, but due to their own needs and the shortage of raw materials, the Allies are having great difficulty in supplying the needs of the American Air Service.

This condition of affairs renders the American Air Service program very uncertain until the American production begins to come through to France in sufficient quantity to make us independent of the French, English and Italian sources of supply.

3. Present policy contemplates that all training of pilots, observers, gunners and mechanics shall be trained to fullest extent at training stations in the United States,

and that the training stations in France will give a finishing course of about one month before personnel is sent to the front.

Due to lack of sufficient aeroplanes in the United States, at the present time, suitable for "advanced" training, the American Air Service training stations in France are giving all pilots, observers, and gunners the necessary "advanced" training and will so continue until the work can be taken over by the stations in the United States.

4. Under the present American Air Service organization, all enlisted personnel coming from the United States, is held in England, where they are given a complete training in English factories, aerodromes and schools.

This arrangement has enabled the British to send approximately 15,000 additional mechanics to the front. This arrangement has also saved the United States great expense in the construction of buildings and establishment of mechanics' schools in France, and affords us a better method of training by utilizing the entire training personnel and material of England.

5. There are at the present time the following training schools in operation is France and Italy:

(a) Clermont-Ferrand (Bombardment).
(b) Issoudun (Pursuit-Fighting).
(c) Tours (Preliminary Flying–Artillery Observation).
(d) Foggia, Italy. (Preliminary Flying and Bombardment).
(e) Army Corps Schools (Training Artillery Observers).
(f) Vadanay (Balloon School).
(g) St. John (School of Aerial Fire).

6. All Pilots, Observers, Gunners and Mechanics, (except such necessary number to maintain schools), as soon as they complete their individual training are grouped into squadrons and sent to the Zone of the Advance for Organizational training.

There are three Organizational Training Centers, as follows:

(a) Romilly—(Bombardment).
(b) Villeneuve—(Pursuit).
(c) Amanty—(Observation).

The squadrons at the Organizational Training Centers are grouped with French squadrons and gradually work over the front lines, until they are reported upon by a board of expert and experienced officers as ready to go, as finished squadrons, for front line service.

Balloon companies and balloon squadrons, as soon as they finish at balloon schools, are sent direct to the front line, and are attached to French balloon units for service work.

7. Under the present policy, all aero squadrons and balloon squadrons, as soon as reported upon as fit for front line service, are attached to French and British air units and remain with these units until needed for service with our own troops.

8. It is the proposed policy that all American Air Units not actually needed for tactical work with the ground armies, shall be formed into independent groups for strategic purposes, and for combined offensive operations with the British and French Air Services.

9. The present Americas Air Service organization consists of the following sections:

(a) Training)   Air Service Headquarters
(b) Personnel)   at
(c) Supply)   Tours
(d) Advanced Section, Air Service—Zone of Advance.

The Advance Section, Air Service, Zone of Advance, is principally employed in the construction of aerodromes and the establishment of advance depots for supplies.

10. Attached herewith is a summary of personnel and location of same.
[Enclosure]

Report on United States Air Service in Europe.	
1. Squadrons	
Total number of aero squadrons	133
Total number of balloon squadrons	2
In England, aero squadrons	66
In France, aero squadrons	67
In France, balloon squadrons	2
2. Cadets	
Total number of cadets	1,676
3. Complete Personnel	
Total Commissioned Officers	1,763
Total Enlisted Personnel	26,288
In England:	
Officers	353
Enlisted	10,512
In France:	
Officers	1,373
Enlisted	15,382
In Italy:	
Officers	37
Enlisted	394
4. Aeroplanes:	
Total Aeroplanes all types in service	1,224
Total Aeroplanes all types on order in Europe	2,706

LC, Foulois Papers, folder 10: AEF—Organization, Program, 1917–1918, box 10; enclosure is from LC, Pershing Papers, folder: Air Service, AEF, box 8. See also Vol. 3, March 16, Editor's Note following Foulois to Secretary of War.

Editor's Note—In his report of January 29, 1919, Foulois explained why this day, March 21, became so fateful for the Air Service's future development:

> On March 21, 1918, the long-expected Spring offensive of the Germans commenced and from that time on, until well into the Summer, all questions of priority of Air Service personal was [sic], necessarily, subordinated to the transporting of a maximum number of ground combatant troops. This fact however did not relieve me from my responsibility in connection with the organization, training, supply, maintenance, repair and operation of the Air Service, A.E.F., nor, in my opinion did it relieve the General Staff, A.E.F., from the responsibility of arriving more promptly at some definite decision as to priority of Air Service troops in coordination with the general priority for other services, especially during the months of December 1917 and January, February and March 1918. [See April 1, Foulois to Chief of Staff] (NARA, RG 120, M990, Gorrell's History of the American Expeditionary Forces, Air Service, 1917–1919, Series A, vol. 1: Foulois, Air Service Lessons Learned during the Present War, January 29, 1919, roll 1; see also online "Gorrell's History—AEF Air Service," at https://www.fold3.com.)

Arthur H. Frazier, U.S. Embassy, Paris, for Pershing, to Secretary of State, for House, Counsellor to the President, Washington, reply to Polk for House to Frazier for Pershing, cable, March 11.

Cable 33, March 21, 4 p.m.
For Colonel House. With reference to your suggestion, believe party personally qualified but think his being an officer in the army and his having been an Ambassador would be something of a handicap. However, if you have full confidence in him, suggest that you have a talk with him and leave final decisions until after his arrival here.

Edward Mandell House Papers, Manuscripts and Archives, Yale University Library, Series 1: Correspondence, folder 3072: John J. Pershing, box 89.

Pershing to TAG, War Department, in addition to Pershing to TAG, War Department, cable P-577-S, February 6.

Cable P-759-S.
1. For Chief of Staff. Lessons drawn from Tuscania disaster show necessity for further attention to ships drill, particularly in practical use of davits and ships gear. Actual practice in lowering all boats into water and unhooking falls should be had before leaving harbor. Losses which actually occurred due largely to lack of drill in

lowering boats. Crew busy elsewhere. Suggest that Commanding Officers be directed to detail from their troops mature non-commissioned officers for each trip to assist ship's crew in lowering boats. All on board should know where to find water, food, matches and compass in lifeboats and use of flares and how to light same. Much unnecessary suffering in open boats due to lack of this instruction. Destroyers averted larger loss of life on Tuscania by removing 1350 who were still on board owing to many lifeboats being smashed by improper handling. Has Navy given attention to above since the disaster? [Reply—March 28, A-1001-R-3]

NARA, RG 120, M930, Main Series, AEF to War Department, roll 2. (These cables are available online at www.fold3.com, a subscription service, under "WW I Cablegrams—AEF and War Dept.")

Pershing to TAG, War Department, in part in reply to TAG, War Department, to Pershing, cable A-918-R, March 14; in addition to Pershing to TAG, War Department, cables P-454-S, January 5, P-521-S, January 20, P-591-S, February 11, and P-705-S, March 10.

Cable P-760-S. Confidential.
For the Chief of Staff.

1. Reference our recommendations regarding material and supplies in accordance with Phase Program of Priority Schedule [October 7, 1917], am making further detailed investigation with view to considerable reduction in shipments from America of all classes of building material and other supplies, either by postponement or cancellation in order especially to assist you in tiding over next 3 or 4 months. Shall have revision made in automatic and exceptional requisitions of material and supply and will send them to you as soon as possible. Meanwhile it will be possible to regulate immediate shipments by present method. But think it necessary that these revised requisitions should be in your hands as general guide. Fully realized here that shortage in tonnage makes stringent revision necessary at this time.

1A. Reference your confidential cable 918, see subparagraph L, paragraph 1, our confidential cable 705. No reduction whatsoever or temporary omission in Service of Rear troops called for by 1st, 2nd and 3rd Phases our Priority Schedule must be made. Port situation due to failure to send labor troops and material becoming serious. The dispatch of combat troops out of 3d Phase in advance of remaining service of rear troops of 1st Phase not yet supplied, and in advance of Service of Rear troops of 2nd and 3rd Phases will not hasten creation of formidable Army to put against enemy. Expediting movement combat troops by advancing their order of priority will surely result in confusion and delay. Leading elements 3rd and 5th Division, combat units of third phase, now commencing to arrive. Strongly urge completion of first phase service of rear, corps troops and army troops. Existing shortage first phase: service of rear, 28,000, Corps troops, 9,000, army troops, 12,000. Also strongly urge that completion of second phase, service of rear, corps troops and army troops before commencing third phase. Second phase Priority Schedule calls for 73,000 service of rear and 16,000 army troops which should be moved by our tonnage simultaneously with movement of six divisions of Second Corps by British for training with British Army. So far as third phase is concerned, note A Page 16 Priority Schedule states "At least 50% of the Service of Rear troops should precede combatant troops. The other 50% may be shipped simultaneously with the first half of combatant troops". The total number of Service of Rear troops called for this phase 52,000. We are making every endeavor to procure European labor. Impossible to estimate at this time results our endeavors this particular [procurement of European labor]. As this labor becomes available we will recommend corresponding reductions in unskilled military labor units shown our Priority Schedule in third phase. Important that no reductions be made in Service of Rear troops of first or second phases on this account, that the third phase be fully organized, and that reduction in third and succeeding phases be made only after recommendation from here.

1B. Attention is invited to paragraph A, our cablegram 591, stating four Negro regiments not available for labor as previously proposed in paragraph 1H, our cablegram 454. For this reason they must not be confused with any pioneer regiments of corps, army or Service of Rear.

1C. On account military importance aviation do not now desire any reduction in existing Aviation Program. This question being studied and if any reduction found advisable will cable.

1D. Renew previous recommendation that all skilled labor troops bring their tools with them on same boat, so as to prevent delay in getting to work.

1E. Attention again invited to necessity expediting every possible way movement car and locomotive repair men called for in paragraph 1B, C, D, E and F, our cablegram 521. Is foregoing thoroughly understood and will recommendation be followed? [*Ed.*—No response has been located.]

NARA, RG 120, M930, Confidential Series, Pershing to War Department, roll 7; see also *USAWW*, vol. 2, pp. 246–47.

TAG, War Department, to Pershing, in part in reply to Pershing to TAG, War Department, cable P-753-S, March 19; in addition to TAG, War Department, to Pershing, cable A-915-R, March 15.

Cable A-956-R.

6. Reference my 915, your 753. The effect on your General Staff if all the Officers desired at this time were taken exclusively from it was considered and appreciated and that was the reason why in the despatch to you you were directed to select "From the American Expeditionary Forces including the Officers at your own and other headquarters 30 Officers who are qualified for General Staff work." These Officers need not be Officers who are now performing General Staff duty necessarily, although such Officers are preferred. It was neither supposed nor intended that the 30 Officers would be taken exclusively from the General Staff Officers both detailed and attached at your Headquarters. The scheme of dividing up these 30 Officers among all arms

including the Staff Corps was designed to put the smallest possible burden upon you consistent with getting the machinery of the Department here working harmoniously with the American Expeditionary Forces. The requirements of the fighting forces in France are my first consideration in all recommendations affecting personnel and it is believed that the value to you of having Officers on the ground here familiar with conditions in France will far outweigh any value these individuals may have in France taken as they would be from the whole body of Officers there. Unless you desire to present further facts for information of the Acting Secretary of War and with this new presentation of the case for your information it is desired that you carry out the program indicated in our 915. March. [Reply – March 27, P-793-S]

NARA, RG 120, M930, Main Series, War Department to AEF, roll 11.

TAG, War Department, to Pershing, reply to Pershing to TAG, War Department, cable P-705-S, March 10.

Cable A-957-R. Confidential.

1. With reference to paragraph 1, your 705 confidential. Conference here with British authorities yesterday relative to transportation of six divisions for training with British, developed two vital differences of opinion relative to this movement. First, instructions from British Ministry to their representatives here, contemplates that the movement of the six divisions will be made by using all commercial tonnage under British flag except the *Aquitania, Mauretania, Olympic, Czar, Czaritza, Dwinsk* and *Kursk* and that the British obligations to transport American troops other than those pertaining to the six divisions is limited to 12,000 per month. Second, that the movement of these divisions by British tonnage does not contemplate the transportation of motor vehicles and trains referred to in your recent instructions. As a matter of fact their instructions restrict shipment to personal troop equipment without transport and heavy equipment.

1A. Our understanding here has been from the start that the movement of the six divisions for training with the British was to be made without interfering with the transportation of troops to France necessary to meet our obligation to the Allies of two divisions per month. This obligation was based upon the assumption that commercial tonnage used, which has averaged approximately 15,000 troops per month exclusive of *Olympic, Aquitania* and *Mauretania*, would continue to be used in carrying into effect the regular program. The *Olympic* and *Aquitania* and the *Mauretania* were loaned specifically under separate agreement to the United States for the transportation of troops. It now appears that these vessels are to be used in carrying out the obligations of the British to transport 12,000 troops per month in addition to the six divisions for training on British front.

1B. In effect, the agreement as understood by the British representatives here, will result under best possible conditions of turn around, in a monthly reduction of troop capacity from 30,000 to 18,000 in British tonnage, and if their contention that no cargo excepting light troops equipment is to be transported by them, this will require additional cargo vessels to move motor transportation and heavy equipment referred to in paragraph 1E, your 705.

1C. Should we receive confirmation that your agreement of January 30 is that our share of British tonnage is only 12,000 men per month and that agreement is effective from March 1 then all troops transported by British tonnage during March on account your regular schedule will be charged against a total of 36,000 men which British here believe to be our quota for the three months March, April and May.

1D. Unless British are prepared to assign additional troop vessels for the movement of the six divisions it is manifest that this movement will materially interfere with our regular program of despatching two divisions per month. This could be overcome if British authorities will consent to permitting additional vessels used in the transportation of six divisions to England to continue in service after this movement is completed and assist in making up shortage of 10,000 per month which will occur during this movement. In view of new developments, your recommendation desired. March.

1E. Cablegram transmitted by British representative here to British Ministry follows:

"Kindly transmit to Shipping Controller, London—Your 817. We have as instructed seen Foreign Office telegram number 1494 from Derby to Reading [*Ed.*— Cable 1494 from Lord Derby, Secretary of State for War, to Lord Reading, Ambassador, Washington, concerned the existing confusion concerning the responsibilities for transporting American troops of the Six-Division program to Europe for training with the British. Not reproduced.] and after fully discussing matter with Ambassador have had conferences yesterday and today with representatives of the United States Chief of Staff and Chief of Embarkation. As it was evident to us that there were considerable differences between General Pershing's instructions to United States authorities here and your instructions to us we considered it was absolutely necessary that the following messages should be shown to the United States authorities and this was done—namely F. O. telegram 1494 and your telegram numbers 688, 893, 155, 187 and in return we were handed copies of General Pershing's telegram number 705.

You will note the following difference between the above message and instructions you have already given us—firstly—according to Foreign Office Telegram 1494 Robertson writing to General Pershing on February 13 [*sic*, January 30] stated that we would transport 6 divisions without transport and heavy equipment. This does not agree with instructions contained in General Pershing's telegram which if carried out would mean following space for each division would have to be allotted—312 tons or 584,188 cubic feet. Secondly—Our understanding is the six divisions will disembark in English ports but from General Pershing's telegram it is not clear whether troops will arrive at Cherbourg direct or via England. Thirdly—United States authorities here have been working on the following trooping program for General Pershing's troops, viz: about 12,000 per month in British liners as heretofore, plus *Olympic, Aquitania* and *Mauretania*. These three ships were given to Americans on condition that they paid all expenses. Fourthly—It is not clear who will maintain the six divisions.

Meanwhile with a view to meeting difficulty number 3 above we have made following proposals to United States authorities, subject your approval, viz: that seven transports *Aquitania, Mauretania, Olympic, Czar, Czaritza, Dwinsk* and *Kursk* for which United States authorities are liable for all expenses should be available exclusively for (a) troops without regard to monthly average carried but any shortages below 12,000 per month to be made up by British liners. We estimate 3 vessels making regular voyages should carry 18,000 troops per month based on: big vessels doing round trip in 30 days and four Russian vessels in 50 days. We believe this proposal will be accepted provided guarantees can be given that on completion of the transport of the six divisions any shortage against their anticipated program will be made up by British tonnage. United States authorities here state they have no knowledge of arrangements whereby four Russian vessels are available for them nor do they know the terms. They are uncertain whether speed of these four vessels will permit of their sailing in United States troops convoys.

British Military Attaché states that of six divisions one should be moved in March, two in April, three in May but with tonnage so far nominated this movement would be seriously affected by trooping arrangements for General Pershing as understood by United States authorities here. We have made every endeavor to comply with your instructions but until the differences outlined above are arranged on your side in order to avoid delay to vessels we have had to continue shipping troops under (a) but if agreement mentioned in F. O. Number 1494 is to be carried out it will mean that our obligations under (a) will result in only 36,000 men being transported in divisions, April and May, of which at least 23,000 will have been transported in March.

This telegram has been laid before the meeting of the United States authorities and agreed to by them. Their cable to General Pershing has also been concurred in by meeting.

We have arranged with the United States authorities to commence movement of personnel of first of six divisions, which is seventy-seventh division on *Carmania*, but pending settlement of the differences referred to above, conference agreed that it was undesirable to make further assignments of B troops.

As a result of conference, Chief of Staff has sent the following cable to General Pershing and General Pershing has been sent copies of this telegram." [See below, March 23, 1918, War Office to Brig. Gen. C. M. Wagstaff, Chief, British Military Mission to GHQ AEF.] [Reply—March 24, P-778-S]

NARA, RG 120, M930, Confidential Series, War Department to AEF, roll 18.

March 22

Pershing's Personal Diary

At Paris. Worked in quarters in the morning. Gave short sitting to an artist named Wolfe who insisted on painting my picture. In the afternoon went to Versailles and had talk with General Bliss. Returned to quarters and received there Mr. Sidney Veit, who brought an artist, Mr. Henri Boudet, who presented me with a collection of his pictures entitled "Les Fils de Washington en France." Saw also Mrs. Ella Wheeler Wilcox. Saw General Atterbury and Colonel Andrews at about 11 p.m.

LC, Pershing Papers, Diary, May 7, 1917–September 1, 1918, box 4.

Brig. Gen. Camille Ragueneau, Chief, French Military Mission with the American Army, to CS, AEF, Chaumont, reply to Maj. Gen. James G. Harbord, CS, GHQ, AEF, to Chief, French Military Mission, March 13.

No. 7999/TR
Subject: Machines, Cars on the Railroads.
    1. Upon receiving your letter of the date of March 13, on the same subject, I investigated with the French Authorities in regard to the questions you were so good as to submit to me.
    2. I have received assurances from our Minister of Public Works and Transportation as well as from the 4th Bureau of the Staff of the Army that particular attention has for a long time been given to the important question of the freight cars which remain a long time in the same place. A permanent information department gives notice of long delays and makes it possible to remedy the situation in the least time, even placing responsibility for it. Furthermore the figures show that while the cars available in service on the French Railroads are almost the same as to number, the kilometric tonnage has increased by 41% since the war; certain experts call this result remarkable, and assert that the best possible use of the available cars has been made.
    Nevertheless, it is always possible that there are abuses or cases of negligence, and the French Authorities are fully determined to punish them; but in view of the general results attained it is not enough to call attention in general to the fact that freight cars remain unused, and it would be very desirable if the facts noted and called to the attention of General Pershing were specified exactly as to number, place, and if possible, length of time. It is quite difficult in such a matter to keep clearly in mind facts which rest on statements without exact data.
    Finally we are particularly grateful for the efforts you are so kind as to promise on your own part with the idea of reducing the delays in the case of the American Army, and of increasing the speed of movement in our rolling stock.
    3. The French Authorities are especially concerned with the number of cars. It is indeed true that the English have furnished the General Park of the French Railroads with slightly more than 35,000 cars: but the total is employed in the service of the British Army. Furthermore, France has to assume, with her own resources, the burden of the transport for Italy, which requires the constant service of 26,000 cars. She has assumed similarly the transportation by train of the American Army in Europe, and up to the present the assistance you have been able to render us, is, according to the latest information, 160 cars in service.
    Now, these military transports were only assured by reducing to the extreme passenger traffic in France; this has decreased since the war, by 65%; freight traffic must also be reduced, but not too much, because of the absolute necessity of supplying our

war industries with raw materials—these are almost the only remaining industries in France. It is further necessary to move the manufactured articles, and any new decrease seems well-nigh impossible. The situation is no less serious in the matter of engines. It is to be noted among the causes of the decrease in the efficiency of our rolling stock, that the intensive service which has been required during more than three and a half years of war, and the lack of raw materials and scarcity of labor render it difficult to maintain and repair the stock proportionally to the wear and tear. This is not exclusively true of France, as in the case of the Central Powers our information leads us to believe that this wear and tear and the difficulties of repair are even more serious there.

However, the measures now necessary, and which it is time to follow with all the energy and speed possible are as follows:

1. The importation of cars for the transport of the American Army.
2. The continued importation of engines.
3. The rapid repair of rolling stock; the assistance which you have so kindly promised in this matter will be very precious.
4. We beg you to accept our assurance that this situation is one which occupies us seriously and is the object of the particular attention and constant effort of M. Claveille, our Minister of Public Works and Transportation. It is a matter of equal concern to our English Allies who recently ordered their General Director of Transportation in France to make a minute investigation. As a result of this investigation, General Sir Philippe Nash, whose great technical skill is known to you, submitted a report of which I have a French translation that I send you with pleasure. I shall be grateful if you will return it to me after you have had a copy or a translation made if you so desire.

NARA, RG 120, Office of the Commander-in-Chief, Office of the Secretary of the General Staff, Entry 22, Reports of the Commander-in-Chief, folder 34: GHQ War Diary, January 24–April 28, 1918, diary entry March 25, 1918, 289 a, pp. 243–45, box 4.

Pershing to TAG, War Department, in addition to Pershing to TAG, War Department, cables P-637-S, February 23, and P-745-S, March 18 (not reproduced).

Cable P-764-S.

1. For the Chief of Staff. 1C. With further reference to paragraph 3, our cablegram 637, and paragraph 9, our cablegram 745 [not reproduced]. On account tonnage situation and scarcity forage in France recommend discontinuance all shipment animals after April 1st to France. Study now being made looking to very material reduction in authorized allowances animals to units. Believe we can get through French and British all animals we require during next 4 or 5 months. British will turn over to us animals for all division units training with them. This reduces number to be supplied from French to completion First Phase allowances, Artillery Corps

troops and army troops Second Phase and entire Third Phase with replacements. Under circumstances do not feel justified in allowing shipment heretofore recommended of 2,000 heavy draft animals per month after April 1st. If any indication of breakdown develops on part French will cable in ample time to resume supply from American. Acknowledge. [*Ed.*—The War Department immediately complied with Pershing's request and informed the AEF on March 29 in cable A-1005-R-2 that the "Quartermaster Corps directed to ship no animals after April 1st."] [Reply—Vol. 5, June 26, A-1609-R-3; in addition—Vol. 5, June 29, P-1390-S-1B]

NARA, RG 120, M930, Main Series, AEF to War Department, roll 2.

TAG, War Department, to Pershing, in part in reply to Pershing to TAG, War Department, cable P-741-S, March 16.

Cable A-961-R.
    5. Stevens in message to Shipping Board states British Ministry of Shipping desires settle financial arrangements relative to *Olympic, Mauretania,* and *Aquitania.* Preliminary negotiations relative to use of these vessels made here as well as financial arrangements relative to *Olympic.* Desirable that negotiation relative to terms and final settlement of these matters be handled in War Department. British representative requested Jan. 7th to inform War Department definitely relative to terms of operation of 3 vessels named.
    5A. Chartering of vessels for War Department can best be handled here and it is requested that all be advised that final arrangements will be handled by War Department.

NARA, RG 120, M930, Main Series, War Department to AEF, roll 11.

TAG, War Department, to Pershing, in part in reply to Pershing to TAG, War Department, cable P-669-S, March 2.

Cable A-962-R.
    1. Attention Air Service. With reference to paragraph 5F, your 669. DH 4 floated March 15th prepared in 2 cases fuselage in 1 piece. Subsequent shipments will carry 4 planes in 9 boxes with fuselage in 2 pieces. Blueprints showing latest packing scheme and detailed instructions for unpacking and assembling being prepared and will be forwarded as soon as completed. Special messenger First Lieutenant Carl F. Clark will leave with shipment with instructions to report to you by wire immediately on arrival. If machine is to be flown recommend Walter Morris, John Munford, Frank Murray or Perry Graves Liberty engine experts now in Europe be called in to inspect start and tune up for flight. [*Ed.*—In its P-967-S-6E on April 20, the AEF informed the War Department that the DH 4 had never arrived and requested a trace on the shipment. On April 27 in A-1196-R-2B, the War Department replied that it had received a telegram from Lt. Clark on April 16 informing them that the

transport was delayed indefinitely at Fort Monroe, Virginia, and would proceed as soon as necessary repairs were completed.]

NARA, RG 120, M930, Main Series, War Department to AEF, roll 11.

TAG, War Department, to Pershing, in reply to Pershing to TAG, War Department, cables P-637-S, February 23, P-710-S, March 12, and P-729-S, March 14 (not reproduced).

Cable A-963-R. Confidential.
   1. With reference to your 637, paragraph 3, and your 710 and 729, regarding purchase of animals in France. Following divisions go overseas without animals and will require animals after completion training. With British about following dates: 77th, May 15th, 83rd, June 1st, 28th, June 15th, 78th, June 30th, 80th, July 15th, 30th, July 31st. Requested you purchase in France and Spain as many as possible each class horses and mules required there 6 divisions per tables of organization, January 14, 1918, reporting by cable number each class you desire shipped from this country to complete allowance each of these divisions.
   2. Also requested you purchase in Europe necessary animals for Army and Corps headquarters units. [Reply—April 19, P-950-S-2D]

NARA, RG 120, M930, Confidential Series, War Department, to AEF, roll 18.

TAG, War Department, to Pershing, in part in reply to Pershing to TAG, War Department, cable P-714-S, March 11; in addition to TAG, War Department, to Pershing, cable A-872-R, March 6.

Cable A-967-R.
   4. With reference to paragraph 1, your 714, and paragraph 10, our 872. Disregard tabulations mailed you showing tentative organization of tank service. Your project of February 18th for Tank Corps is approved except as follows [a series of enlisted personnel changes]. . . . Preparation of Tables of Organization in prescribed form replacement, await your reply. Reference appointment: Welborn, an extra Colonel was added to your project in order to provide a regular officer of sufficient service and experience to select, organize and supervise the preliminary training of tank companies in United States. Impossible to secure officer of the rank suggested by you with sufficient experience and ability to do this work. Necessary to have at least 2 Majors in United States to command camps. Have you 2 that you can return for this purpose? March. [Reply—Vol. 5, May 27, A-1406-R-2; in addition—Vol. 5, June 6, P-1258-S-2B; and Vol. 6, July 25, P-1513-S-1A] [*Ed.*—In his reply to the Chief of Staff in cable P-806-S, paragraph 1G, March 28, Pershing accepted these changes, said he did not have 2 majors to return to assist training, and would send Lt. Col. Clopton in mid-April once he had finished his course of instruction with the British and French.]

NARA, RG 120, M930, Main Series, War Department to AEF, roll 11.

March 23

Pershing's Personal Diary

Left Paris at about 8:30. We did not realize till the next morning that for half an hour or so before we left Paris the town was being bombarded by a long-range German gun. Stopped en route to Chaumont for lunch at the Hotel Audre at Vendeuvre.

LC, Pershing Papers, Diary, May 7, 1917–September 1, 1918, box 4.

Summary of Decisions taken at the 22nd Meeting of the Military Representatives, held in the Council Chamber, Versailles, on Saturday, March 23, 1918, at 10 a.m.

S.W.C. 136
S.W.C. (M.R.) 22
Present
France	General Weygand
Great Britain	General Rawlinson
Italy	General Giardino
America	General Bliss

* * * * * *

Chairman—General Bliss

* * * * * *

General Bliss invited attention to the fact that the third subject was not on the Agenda, but consideration had just been requested by General Rawlinson.

* * * * * *

Reinforcement of British Army by American Troops
General Rawlinson submitted a paper on the question of the reinforcement of the British Army in France by drafts or battalions of American troops which was read and translated into French [no copy located]. General Rawlinson was called out of the room.
General Montgomery stated that this matter was considered most important and most urgent and suggested it might be discussed informally and then noted on tomorrow at a meeting to be held at 10.30 a.m. He further said that tomorrow there would be submitted forecasts of the probable British losses at the end of April, May and June, which would show that whatever plans may have been made for the American Army, and however good these plans for the use of the American Army may be, they would not be of help if the British Army has ceased to exist. He thought that the circumstances had changed since the matter was discussed by the Supreme War Council.
General Weygand found that what makes the solution of this problem hardest is that it affects the ultimate effectiveness of the American Army. It was evident to him

that the English Army cannot hold as large a line if reduced by losses. In view of this fact, General Pétain has already arranged to relieve the British Army of the line as far as Peronne. He can only do this because he finds that American Divisions are taking over a part of the Front. [*Ed.*—See Map 3.] If General Rawlinson's proposal were carried out, the American Army would be broken up unnecessarily. In the speaker's opinion, the British requirements would be satisfied if the American Government were asked to give the British a number of battalions equivalent to three of the six Divisions which they are bringing over.

General Rawlinson, who had returned, said he did not intend to break up any existing Divisions now ready to take their place in the line, but to use, to reinforce the British Army, troops now in training. General Bliss stated that at least they would have the six divisions to be transported in British bottoms. This question was then postponed to the next Meeting.

Summary of Decisions Taken.
3. Incorporating of American Troops. It was decided to postpone the discussion on the question of incorporating American troops as drafts or battalions in the British Army till the next sitting. [See March 24.]

NARA, RG 120, M923, Records of the American Section, SWC, file 299: Minutes (with Annexes and Joint Notes) of Meetings of the Permanent Military Representatives, Dec. 4, 1917–Nov. 4, 1919, document 299-22, roll 17; see also online "WW I Supreme War Council, American records," at https://www.fold3.com.

Maj. Gen. Maurice de Barescut, Chief of Staff to Pétain, CINC, Armies of the North and Northeast, to CINC, GAE, Miracourt, and Chief, French Military Mission with the American Army, Chaumont.

No. 4863 and 4864/M.
Encrypted Telegram.
 1. The battle engaged in forces us to create withdrawal availabilities on the front. It is necessary that the available American troops enter the passive fronts to relieve French units.
 2. 1st Infantry Division U.S. can expand its front by putting three infantry regiments on line. The 26th and 42nd Infantry Divisions U.S. can take the fronts of French divisions of G.A.E. after a short rest.
 3. The 26th Infantry Division U.S. would be available in the movement area where it is scheduled to arrive on March 27 or 28.
 The movements of the U.S. 42nd Infantry Division, which are expected to commence on the 25th current, will be countermanded and the division will be placed in the area of Baccarat.
 The 26th and 42nd Infantry Divisions U.S. would be made available to G.A.E. for relief on the front under conditions to be determined by agreement with the U.S. command.

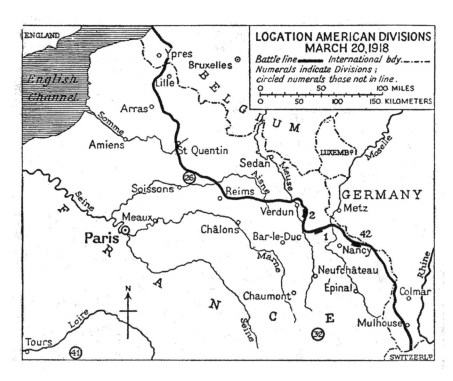

Map 3. Location American Divisions, March 20, 1918. On the day the great German offensive began, the AEF had six divisions in France: three were in the trenches, the 1st and 2nd holding parts of the St. Mihiel salient, and the 42nd in the Vosges; one, the 26th, was completing its trench combat familiarization training with the French and preparing for its frontline assignment; the 32nd Division was at the 10th (Prauthoy) training area in the Haute-Marne, temporarily acting as the Replacement Division for the I Corps; and the former 41st, now redesignated the 1st Depot Division for I Corps, was in the St. Aignan-Noyers region east of Tours. Source: Pershing, *My Experiences in the World War*, vol. 1, p. 369.

The 2nd Infantry Division U. S. will be used in the Heights of the Meuse sector.

4. Please submit these proposals to General Pershing and make known reply as soon as possible to the General in Chief and the General Commander G.A.E.
Les armées françaises dans la Grande Guerre, Tome 6, vol. 1, Annexes, vol. 2: Annexe No. 550, pp. 93–94.

Ragueneau, Chief, French Military Mission with the American Army, Chaumont, to CINC, AEF.

1. Following my verbal communication this afternoon, I have the honor of specifying the request I am charged to make to you from the C-in-C of the Armies of the North and Northeast

2. Gen. Pétain believes that the battle engaged demands the briefest delay in the formation of all reserves made available by the withdrawal of large French units from parts of the western front which are not likely to become the field of active operation.

3. Consequently he asks that the 1st Division, A.E.F., extend its front by putting three regts. inf. into the line. It does not appear that there can be any difficulty in doing this in view of the fact that the 1st Brigade has already had a fairly long rest since last relieved, sufficient for the entry into the sector of at least one of its regiments to be considered. He asks that the 26th and 42d Divisions go to the front after a short rest, in the French Groupe d'Armées de l'Est (Eastern Group). I am asking urgently the general in command of the Eastern Group how he proposes to carry out this relief, and I will hasten to inform you as soon as I am informed. Thus, as I have informed you, Gen. Pétain asked that the order directing movements of the 42d Division which should have started the 25th of this month be countermanded, and I thank you for having ordered it. This division will be left at rest in the region of Baccarat awaiting a further decision in regard to it. As for the 26th Division, it would be advisable that it make the travel anticipated to reach the zone of Lafauche where it should arrive March 27 or 28.

4. No changes under consideration for the 2d Division. There is every advantage that it remain in the Hauts-de-Meuse sector as long as possible.

5. I would be very grateful to be informed of your reply because General Pétain is anxious to receive it as soon as possible.

USAWW, vol. 3, pp. 482–83.

Field Marshal Sir Douglas Haig, CINC, BAF, to Pershing.
I should be much obliged if you would inform me if it would be possible for you temporarily to make available for urgent work in the zone of the British Army, one or two of your Regiments of Engineers. These would be of especial use to me at this juncture in connection with the construction of a rear line of defence which I am constructing behind the defences prepared by the several Armies.

If you should also be able to place temporarily at my disposal any heavy artillery for which you may not have immediate use, I should be most grateful if you would let me know.
[Reply—April 1, Pershing to Haig]

NARA, RG 120, Office of the Commander-in-Chief, Office of the Secretary of the General Staff, Entry 22, Reports of the Commander-in-Chief, folder 34: GHQ War Diary, January 24–April 28, 1918, diary entry April 2, 1918, 297-g, p. 270, box 4; copy LC, Harbord Papers, folder: Military Activity: I, Official War Activity, p. 160, box 8.

War Office, London, to Brig. Gen. C. M. Wagstaff, GS, Chief, British Military Mission to GHQ AEF, Chaumont, for Pershing.
54886 cipher.

The following telegram to Lord Reading [British Ambassador on Special Mission in Washington] has been sent today:

> Your 1194 of March 20. You should explain to President that we are engaged in what may well prove to be decisive battle of the war. The Germans are concentrating the greater part of their available forces against the British front and are pushing their attacks with the greatest determination. We have every hope of checking him, but our losses have been very heavy and will be heavier. This is only the beginning of the campaign of 1918 and we have to look to the future. In the present state of our manpower resources we cannot keep our divisions supplied with drafts for more than a short time at the present rate of loss, and we shall be helpless to assist our Allies if, as is very probable, the enemy turns against them later. We have the divisional cadres ready with all necessary services and what we require is men to help us to keep them filled. You should appeal to the President to drop all questions of interpretation of past agreements and send over infantry as fast as possible without transport or other encumbrances. The situation is undoubtedly critical and if America delays now, she may be too late.

You should make what use of this with General Pershing as you may think fit.

LC, Pershing Papers, folder: Data for Book *My Experiences in the World War*, folder 11: Extracts from official records of British War Office, *The Progress of the American Army in France*, vol. 2, document no. 102, box 354; *USAWW*, vol. 3, pp. 71–72.

Harbord, CS, GHQ AEF, to Army Artillery Commander.

3d Section, General Staff
General Headquarters, A.E.F.
[Extract]

    1. The Commander-in-Chief directs that you be charged with and take up at once the whole problem of antiaircraft organization and defense for the A.E.F. Your responsibility for the study, and upon approval of the plan proposed for the installation of proper defense measures extends over all the area now occupied by our forces, except the sectors of the front line where antiaircraft defense is provided by the French armies with which our units are serving.

    2. It is considered that antiaircraft defense must be handled as a sector or area problem, the least area within which along the front there can be no division of command, being that occupied by an army. There must be coordination of defense between the front and rear areas. With no present responsibility for defense in the sectors of the front line, your work of actual defense installations for the present should be directed toward the rear areas, but your study of the problem of the proper administrative and command organization apart from the study of the ground organization for any particular locality, must have in view the extension of the defense

scheme toward the front. Immediate attention should be given to the installation of a defense for Is-sur-Tille, and for Chaumont and Jonchery.

3. Considerable study has already been given to the whole antiaircraft problem, and some definite conclusions have been reached in regard thereto. It is considered that you will be best informed of these, and as well of the present status of the personnel and materiel for this service, by having one of your staff officers confer direct with G-3, these headquarters. . . . [Reply, March 27, Conner to Harbord]

USAWW, vol. 2, p. 250.

Col. Charles G. Dawes, GPA, AEF, SOS, Paris, to CINC, GHQ, AEF.

Telegram.

1. Have just received telegram from Cutcheon as follows "Think something will be accomplished. No idea yet how much. Have had no answer telegrams to you probably leave Saturday night." Yesterday afternoon I wired Cutcheon as follows "Your letter received. General Pershing and I are making strong representation by cable to the State and Treasury Departments in this connection and suggest that Crosby hold matters in status quo until they are heard from." In view of Cutcheon's telegram do you not think it would be well to defer sending our cablegrams to Washington and for you to wire Cutcheon as follows "On account of your telegram to Dawes which indicates probability of granting our request by Italian Govt have deferred sending cable to Washington recommending ultimatum. Keep Dawes informed of the situation and he will advise me." The above telegram is simply to indicate how my mind is running on the situation and you will no doubt improve on these suggestions.

LC, Pershing Papers, folder: Gen. Charles G. Dawes, 1918, box 59.

TAG, War Department, to Bliss, Chief, American Section, and Permanent Military Representative, SWC, Versailles. Copy to Pershing.

Cable 38-R.

2. Full information as to shipping schedule for transportation of 6 American divisions cabled General Pershing. Get it from him and arrange for prompt interchanging of such important cablegrams. That cable took 2 clerks 15 hours to code. [See March 21, TAG, War Department, to Pershing, A-957-R.]

NARA, RG 120, M923, American Section, SWC, file 316: Cablegrams Received from the War Department, Jan. 23, 1918–Nov. 19, 1919, roll 18; see also online "WW I Supreme War Council, American records," at https://www.fold3.com.

TAG, War Department, to Pershing, in part in reply to Pershing to TAG, War Department, cable P-683-S, March 5.

Cable A-970-R.

7. With reference to paragraph 4D, your 683. Joint resolution has been requested authorizing acceptance by our officers and men of decorations awarded by Allied service. [*Ed.*—After several cables from Pershing questioning when this action would be taken, March informed Pershing in cable A-1577-R-3, on June 21, that "provisions incorporated in present Army Appropriations bill, and should become a law before August 29th."]

7A. Provisions of General Orders Number 6, 1918, authorizes award of Distinguished Service Crosses and Distinguished Service Medals to any person serving in any capacity with the Army. This is held to include officers and enlisted me of Allied service so serving.

7B. The award of Medals of Honor is limited by law to officers and enlisted men of our Army. It is not desired to request additional legislation on this matter now unless circumstances demand it. Is this satisfactory? [*Ed.*—In cable P-786-S-6, on March 26, Pershing notified March that "no additional legislation desired at this time."]

March.

NARA, RG 120, M930, Main Series, War Department to AEF, roll 11.
TAG, War Department, to Pershing.

Cable A-972-R.
11. Desire daily summary of activities along British front as far as you can furnish it during progress of present drive. March.

NARA, RG 120, M930, Main Series, War Department to AEF, roll 11.

Editor's Note—On September 30, 1917, Pershing initiated his general information reporting to the War Department and Chief of Staff with four "weekly summaries" as confidential cables with the expressed "purpose to send each week an estimate and information of the enemy's strength, intentions, political and economic conditions from all sources." His first summary was in confidential cable (P-195-S), which was followed by three others on October 8 (P-207-S), 15 (P-223-S), and 21 (P-238-S). Following this, from October 30, 1917, to January 5, 1918, these "summaries of information" were sent as cablegrams on a weekly basis and included information on Allied operations. From January 6 until March 24, these became semiweekly before changing to a daily issuance until April 26 in response to the War Department's request in A-972-R above for daily updates on operations after the German offensive of March 21. These summaries were included in Pershing's numbered P-cables in both the Main and Confidential Series. While the original summaries were still being sent, the AEF began another series of fifty-eight "Summary of Activities" running from March 11 to May 14, which were also in Pershing's numbered Confidential Series of P-cables. For information on the continuation of these daily summaries, see Editor's Note following May 6, A-1255-R.

March 24

Minutes of the Meeting of the Military Representatives, held in the Council Chamber, Versailles, on Sunday, March 24, 1918, at 10:30 A.M.

S.W.C. 141/1
S.W.C. (M.R.) 23.
Present
France   General Weygand
Great Britain   General Sir H. S. Rawlinson
Italy   General Giardino
America   General Bliss

Chairman—General Sir H. S. Rawlinson
    1. *General Rawlinson* places before the Military Representatives a draft note on the subject of the incorporation of the American army with the British army [no copy located].
    General Bliss accepts this note in principle, but draws attention to the fact that it involves a complete change in the American military programme. The question would, therefore, have to be placed before Congress.
    General Weygand urges that in principle the proposals contained in General Rawlinson's draft note should be made applicable to all the Allies and not only to Great Britain, whilst recognizing that priority should be given to the reinforcements for the British troops which are now being attacked.
    The Military Representatives invited General Rawlinson to prepare a new draft resolution for the next meeting giving effect to the suggestions made by General Weygand.

Summary of Decisions
Despatch American Troops
    The Military Representatives, after considering the text of a resolution to be embodied in a Joint Note, in connection with the despatch of American troops to France, decided to give the final form to their resolution at their next meeting. [See March 27.]

USAWW, vol. 3, pp. 72–73; NARA, RG 120, M923, American Section, SWC, file 299: Minutes (with Annexes and Joint Notes) of Meetings of the Permanent Military Representatives, Dec. 4, 1917–Nov. 4, 1919, document 299-23, roll 17; see also online "WW I Supreme War Council, American records," at https://www.fold3.com.

Maj. F.L. Dengler, Member, American Military Mission at French GHQ, to ACS, G-2, GHQ, AEF, Chaumont.
    ... reports ... regarding the general situation at French G.H.Q., of which the substance is as follows:

1. The total number of German Divisions admitted by the French as being on the Western front is 192, of which 44 are known to be in reserve. The total includes 4 divisions from Russia, and two others from (?), not before known.

2. The total number of German divisions admitted by the French to be in the attack zone is between 56 and 57, which agrees very closely with the British estimate of 60, reported by me in my letter of March 23rd.

3. It has been officially announced that all of the bureaus would move on March 27th. The place was not stated, but I have been reliably informed that it is Chantilly.

4. I learn that an official announcement of the firing on Paris of the German 240 mm. gun from near Laon has been made. It is reported that the gun is located at or near Crepy, to the West of Laon. It is also rumored that the Germans have been bombarding London recently with another gun of the same type.

5. I have been unable as yet to learn any details of the damage received last night from the raid here. It is understood that the railroad station was again the objective, and that some damage was done to the tracks. A bomb also struck the barracks here – I hear there were a few casualties.

Additional report from Major Dengler, at 11.30 P. M., this date:

1. Orders were transmitted orally and received later (8.00 P.M.) officially today to prepare for a possible change of base tonight. Everything is packed and it is probable that the move will take place during the night. This step is believed to be due to developments of the last day or two, the constant bombing of this place from the air and the probability of its being shelled by long range artillery.

2. So far as I can see the French morale is decidedly good. They appear to regard the general situation as quite serious but show absolutely no signs of being stampeded.

3. Since my report of about 10.30 A.M., today, I have been able to gather very little definite information from the 2nd Bureau. They naturally are busy and I did not believe it to be wise to press them at all.

4. About 2.00 P.M., I was told that the line was holding north of Saint Quentin and that yesterday seven heavy enemy attacks had been broken up. At 11.15 P.M. tonight I called again and was told that "the line is now on the Somme and the Germans have entered Chauni (?) (spelling is phonetic and from memory); it is west of La Fere. They are beginning to bother us now by attacks toward Oise-Reims".

5. From another source I learned that the French took over the sector south of Peronne to La Fere and had augmented the 4 divisions originally sent to that region on March 22nd by two armies.

6. Lieut. Freeborn of the Mission returned today from Paris and stated that the long-range gun was shelling very regularly every 15 minutes. He states that the noise of arrival is scarcely noticeable and that the explosive effect is slight considering the calibre 240 mm. (10.6"). That is logical, since the tremendous range attained would require an enormous velocity which in turn would require strong shell structure with diminished bursting charge capacity.

7. The bombing of last night and early this morning damaged a number of houses, caused two fires and damaged the tracks and railway station—nothing

serious accomplished from a military standpoint. Tonight there were two alarms, much firing but no bombing.

8. A French officer just came in and told me that we would not go to Chantilly but to Senlis—where sealed orders would be received indicating destination.

NARA, RG 120, Office of the Commander-in-Chief, Office of the Secretary of the General Staff, Entry 22, Reports of the Commander-in-Chief, folder 34: GHQ War Diary, January 24–April 28, 1918, diary entry March 24, 1918, 288-e, pp. 242–43, box 4.

Pershing to Col. H. W. Thornton, British Army, Deputy Director General of Movements and Railways, War Office, Paris Representative, reply to Thornton to Pershing, March 21.

Personal.

I have your note of March 21st and fully realize the gravity of the transportation situation. As you know, already every possible effort is being made to remedy it. I am urging the shipment of cars and locomotives from the States, but much more can be done here than is being done. A complete reorganization is necessary, and all railways must be under one control.

LC, Pershing Papers, folder: Col. H. W. Thornton, box 196.

Pershing to the Secretary of War, then in London.

With reference to a branch of the Judge Advocate General's Office in France to review certain court martial proceedings after they have been acted upon by the Judge Advocate here, the reason for this is not clear.

It submits to review cases within the jurisdiction of department commanders in time of peace and is in direct conflict with the broad and liberal character of the President's instructions at inauguration of command. Any authority outside of control of the Commander-in-Chief will cause delay in handling cases. Beyond doubt, punishment for desertion or misconduct in front of the enemy must be almost summary if it is to have deterrent effect.

This is practiced in both the British and French armies. Any method that causes delay and possible miscarriage of justice would be unfortunate for us and injurious to the morale of our allies.

The circumstances under which we are serving are in no sense comparable to our Civil War conditions as here we are fighting a strong and virile foreign nation and every possible means must be placed in the hands of the supreme commander to enable him to maintain the morale and integrity of the army. Any thought in the minds of men that they can possibly escape punishment for such misconduct, would be disastrous. I am very strongly of the opinion that final authority in these cases should rest with the supreme commander here.

LC, Pershing Papers, folder: vol. 2: Memoranda, A.E.F., 1918, box 133.

Secretary of War Newton D. Baker, London, to Bliss, Versailles.

(Confidential)
I fancy this letter will find you at Versailles although it may have to wait a day or two for your return from Italy. I am writing it because my plans are apparently changed by uncontrollable events from day to day and I am therefore not certain that I shall have a chance to see you before I leave. I regretted that it was not possible for me to come to London at the time suggested in your first telegram. One difficulty was that about the same time I was urged to go to Paris for a conference and also received a somewhat conflicting later invitation for another conference in London all of which led me to feel that unless I pursued the course mapped out I would probably not be able to make a thorough and consistent study of the line of communication. I further had the feeling that if I were to leave France even for a few days before I had seen our own soldiers in their training camps and at the Front some disappointment would be created and some anxiety, perhaps, as to the gravity of events which would cause me to change my known plans and hasten to London. The car question, of course, is of vital importance and yet it didn't seem to me that any permanent and unalterable project would be determined upon, and so I have adhered to the plan made by General Pershing with immensely satisfactory and informing results to me and I hope with no serious disappointment to you.

I arrived in London last night and will be here until Tuesday morning. I am to see several members of the Government, including the Prime Minister, and will doubtless learn from them the state of the projects which were discussed at your last meeting here. Meantime I think it would probably be wise if you could find the time to send me a letter—in care of the Embassy at Paris—giving me just a summary view of the determinations arrived at with regard to the Reserve Army and the present state of the car question, and any other matters which you think I ought to know, so that if I should be so unfortunate as not to see you again I can have the last word from you on the subject. Of course the strong likelihood is that I shall see you at Versailles if you have returned there from Italy by the time that I shall return from Italy, which ought to be about the 30th or 31st of the present month, the plan being for me to be in Paris about the 30th for a day or such a matter, before starting for the boat.

The car question as stated in your telegram perplexes me deeply. Obviously we cannot have a large Army in France if its supplies of cars and engines is to be subject to any sort of prolonged interruption. Of course it is entirely possible for us to send over cars and engines, and we are doing it, but they become a part of the common stock and are distributed by the French railroad management so that there is no assurance that even our own cars will be available for our own transportation of supplies and subsistence; yet without such an assurance an entirely new element of hazard is brought into the proposed large numerical increase in our Expeditionary Force. Perhaps after all this question gets back to the question of ocean tonnage, and its solution may lie in our giving immediate preference to the shipment of cars and engines thus delaying for a bit troop and supply transportation but not making any permanent modification in the military programme.

I am writing this from Mr. Page's house in London and will enquire on my return to Paris on Tuesday whether you have returned from Italy. Of course I cannot expect you to have received this letter by that time in the present uncertain state of the mails, but if I find that you are back from Italy I will send you word to Versailles the exact date of my return to Paris from Padua. [Reply—March 28, Bliss to Baker]

LC, Bliss Papers, folder: General Correspondence—Newton Diehl Baker to Bliss, March 1918–March 1920, box 250.

Col. James L. Collins, ADC to Pershing, then in London with Secretary of War Newton D. Baker, to CINC, AEF.

Telegram L. R. No. 1128.
    March 24th. Personal. The Secretary of War believes inadvisable because of serious military situation in France for you to accompany him to Italy. Might be misunderstood by public opinion in United States. However leaves the matter to your judgement. Requests that you ascertain if railroad situation is such that his visit to Italy would in any way embarrass French railroads authorities in which case regrets would be made to Italy and he return to United States at an earlier date than now contemplated. Cable me care of Embassy London. Collins.

LC, Pershing Papers, folder: Colonel James L. Collins, box 49.

Editor's Note—Pershing responded by telegram the next day that he had "already reached same conclusion" but wished "to confer with him upon his arrival in Paris." He also informed Collins that he did "not think the Secretary's visit would embarrass French railroads." Pershing conferred daily with Secretary Baker in Paris and Chaumont from March 26 to 29 before the Secretary and his party left Chaumont for Italy in Pershing's private railway car on the evening of March 30.

Pershing to Bliss, Chief, American Section, and Permanent Military Representative, SWC, Versailles.
    Will you kindly let me have copies of the proceedings of the Military Representatives of the Supreme War Council since the last general meeting held in Paris? None have been sent me since that time.
    Thanking you in advance.
[Reply—March 26, Bliss to Pershing]

LC, Pershing Papers, folder: Supreme War Council, February–April 1918, box 193.

Bliss, American Section, SWC, Versailles, to Pershing.

Telegram No. 31.
    The Executive War Board and the Committee of Military Representatives have asked me to say that they urgently request you to have an interview with them at 3

o'clock tomorrow, Monday afternoon [March 25]. Matter is of great importance and cannot wait. I told them that you would leave in a day or 2 with Mr. Baker. Can you let me know by tomorrow morning? [*Ed.*—Pershing was unable to meet on March 25 because of his scheduled conference with Pétain at French GHQ at Compiègne that day. He did meet with them on Tuesday, March 26.]

NARA, RG 120, M923, American Section, SWC, file 317: Telegrams sent by the American Section, Jan. 21, 1918–Dec. 5, 1919, roll 19; see also online "WWI Supreme War Council, American records," at https://www.fold3.com.

Pershing to Maj. Gen. John Biddle, CG, Base Section No. 3, SOS, AEF, London, for Vice Admiral William S. Sims, Commander, U.S. Naval Forces Operating in European Waters, in reply to Sims to Pershing, March 11, and 1488 (not located).

Telegram.
Subject: Transportation of Troops
    March 24th. Confidential for Admiral Sims, London.
    With reference to your cablegram 1488 and your cablegram to OpNav replying to their No. 3615. As understood the statement that British shipping is in hand to transport troops from the United States at the rate of 60,000 per month means that the British are not counting upon supplying British ships except for the movement as previously agreed upon of 12,000 per month for A.E.F. and the six divisions for training with the British. It is my understanding that the agreement as to the transportation of these troops in British ships from the United States was to be made exclusively in the *Aquitania*, *Mauretania* and *Olympic*. These ships had been lent to us specifically and they have been counted upon by me to meet the situation stated in the cablegram 3615 to you requiring us to dispatch two divisions per month in addition to those which the British agreed to transport in British Ships. Trust my understanding as herein stated will be confirmed by the British. Early reply requested. [Reply—March 26, Sims to Pershing, telegram 1721]

NARA, RG 45, ONRL, 1803–1859, T829, Miscellaneous Records of the Navy Department, Miscellaneous Materials, 1–6/1918, 7–12/1918, Miscellaneous Material Printed Files, World War, roll 408; see also Naval History and Heritage Command, website: Wars, Conflicts, and Operations, World War I, Documentary Histories, March 1918, Pershing to Biddle for Sims, March 24, 1918; original document at NARA, RG 45, ONRL, Entry 517B.

Pershing to TAG, War Department.

Cable P-777-S.

For General March.
    Have you received copy of letter dated March 1st subject "Report on port facilities and necessary measures which must be taken to obtain maximum capacity

32   John J. Pershing and the American Expeditionary Forces

therefrom"? This report was sent as enclosure in letter to you to be delivered by General J. Franklin Bell. [*Ed.*—On March 25 in A-982-R-3, March replied, "Letters and inclosures handed to me by Major General J. Franklin Bell this morning."]

NARA, RG 120, M930, Confidential Series, AEF to War Department, roll 2, and War Department to AEF, roll 11.

Pershing to TAG, War Department, in reply to TAG, War Department, to Pershing, cable A-957-R, March 23, in addition to Pershing to TAG, War Department, cables P-555-S, January 30, and P-705-S, March 10, and Pershing to Biddle for Sims, March 24, telegram.

Cable P-778-S. Confidential.
For Chief of Staff.
    1. With reference to paragraph 1, your cablegram 957 confidential.
    1A. Our understanding of the British undertaking in the transportation of our troops in British ships agrees with yours as stated in paragraph 1A, your cablegram 957. Attention invited to my confidential cablegram 555 embracing original agreement. In other words there was to be no change in the arrangements existing at that time for bringing over American troops. This with the object of bringing over 2 divisions per month. That is, the tonnage we were using was to continue in our service and not be diverted to bring over the 6 divisions.
    1B. This is understood to include the use of the *Olympic, Aquitania* and *Mauritania*. The motor transport mentioned in our 705 for these 6 divisions it would be preferable to send it with the troops, but in view of the urgent necessity for expediting our troop movement in British ships and via England, it is recommended that if the tonnage arrangements required for this motor transport involved any serious difficulties in being transported with troops, it may be shipped later. It was the agreement that the British should transport only the personnel of the 6 divisions with personal equipment. We fully understand originally that we should transport all equipment except this light equipment. However, paragraph 1, our cablegram 705, was submitted in the hope that the British would make the concession, if possible. Urgency of this should be strongly impressed upon British.
    1C. It is the understanding that the 6 divisions for training with the British will move via England. However, there should be no objection if the British should land these troops directly at their French debarkation ports.
    1D. We cabled Sims, London, today as follows: "With reference to your cablegram 1488 and your cablegram to OpNav replying to their number 3615. As understood the statement that British shipping is in hand to transport troops from the US at the rate of 60,000 per months means that the British are not counting upon supplying the British ships except for the movement as previously agreed upon of 12,000 per month for AEF and the 6 divisions for training with the British. It is our understanding that the agreement as to the transportation of these troops in British ships

from the US was to be made exclusive of the *Aquitania, Mauretania* and *Olympic*. These ships have been loaned to us specifically and they have been counted upon by us to meet the situation stated in the cablegram 3615 to you requiring us to dispatch 2 divisions per month in addition to those which the British agreed to transport in British ships. Trust our understanding as herein stated will be confirmed by British. Early reply requested." On receipt of reply from Sims, we shall advise you fully. In view of new developments, the urgency of the situation requires that every effort be made to expedite arrival here of our combat forces. [*Ed.*—Sims's reply received on March 26, Sims to Pershing, cable no. 1721, but no promised cable from Pershing to the War Department has been located.]

NARA, RG 120, M930, Confidential Series, AEF to War Department, roll 7.

Pershing to TAG, War Department, in part in reply to Maj. Gen. Enoch H. Crowder, Judge Advocate General, War Department, to Pershing, February 25, in addition to Pershing to TAG, War Department, cable P-680-S, March 4.

Cable P-779-S.
    1. For Chief of Staff. It is understood that many National Army Divisions have been called upon to furnish so many men for special work that they are filled up with new men with little training. If this is so, suggest the advisability of combining divisions so that the average training in each resulting Division will be approximately same for all officers and men. Present prospects indicate that there will be little opportunity to train here after arrival except in specialties. [In addition—April 2, P-836-S-2C.]
    3. For the Judge Advocate General. With reference to your letter February 25th. Johnson's promotion along with many others in the various Staff Departments seems quite out of proportion, and the Line and Staff Officers here feel that such promotions made at home are unfair to men who are serving in France. I have tried to impress this upon the War Department but the Staff Departments at Washington evidently continue to press for promotion and men promoted at home are now relatively very far ahead of men serving over here. I hope that the plan proposed in paragraph 1, my cablegram 680, and approved by the Secretary of War will receive earnest consideration and that it will be adopted. This plan will relieve us all of probable error in commitment to individuals, so many of whom fail to achieve after promotion what was expected of them. I cannot too strongly urge the adoption of the plan proposed and think it should apply to all the staff at home as well as to our forces abroad. In the meantime no further promotions ought to be made at home until the proposed system is adopted or rejected. May I ask that this matter be discussed with General March.
    3A. With reference to a branch of the Judge Advocate General's Office in France to review certain court martial proceedings after they had been acted upon by the Judge Advocate here, the reason for this is not clear. It submits to review

cases with the jurisdiction of Department Commanders in time of peace and is in direct conflict with broad and liberal character of President's instructions at inauguration of command. Any authority outside of control of the Commander-in-Chief will cause delay in handling cases. Beyond doubt punishment for desertion or misconduct in front of the enemy must be almost summary if it is to have deterrent effect. This is practiced in both the British and French armies. Any method that causes delay and possible miscarriage of justice would be unfortunate for us and injurious to morale of our Allies. The circumstances under which we are serving are in no sense comparable to our Civil War conditions as here we are fighting a strong and virile foreign nation and every possible means must be placed in the hands of the supreme commander to enable him to maintain the morale and integrity of the Army. Any thought in the minds of men that they can possibly escape punishment for such misconduct would be disastrous. I am very strongly of the opinion that final authority in these cases should rest with the supreme commander here.

NARA, RG 120, M930, Main Series, AEF to War Department, roll 2.

Pershing to TAG, War Department.

Cable P-781-S. Confidential.
For Chief of Staff and Acting Secretary of War.
　In view of the great need for labor and the shortage of tonnage, every endeavor is being made to secure labor from Italian government. Therefore, request you present following letter from Colonel Dawes to Secretary McAdoo:
　"Because of the great necessity existing for building line of communications we are employing about 20,000 combatant troops for labor purposes. For every civilian laborer we can secure at present, we can release a soldier for combatant activity at the front. The emergency is evident. The Italian government has already furnished 100,000 militarized laborers to the French. Have sent Captain Cutcheon to Italy with Crosby to urge our necessities to the Italian government concurrent with Crosby's consideration of the Italian request for a loan of $30 million from the United States. Crosby's concern in this situation is of course not direct but very sympathetic. Captain Cutcheon reports his belief that if Mr. Crosby persists strongly he can get, without creating any serious strain, considerable number of men immediately and probably more later and says that if Mr. Crosby concedes what the Italian want in the nature of exchange provisions before leaving and without getting a definite promise in our matter, his task will become practically hopeless. And that the American Ambassador agrees with his view. Having procurement of labor in charge, strongly feel that the State and Treasury Departments in consultation should instruct Crosby and the American Ambassador to urge the matter of supplying at once at least 15,000 militarized laborers to the A.E.F. and that unless some concessions are made further negotiations in connection with the loan must be suspended. Dawes."

Have requested Crosby to hold loan in abeyance until this matter could be taken up. I believe it only necessary to suggest this situation to the virile departments of the United States Government which have so far supported the A.E.F. to have them create the proper atmosphere around their representatives at Rome which will result in an arrangement through which all our combatant troops can be released for the front. In my judgment this result can best be obtained by the attitude suggested in Colonel Dawes' telegram.

NARA, RG 120, M930, Confidential Series, AEF to War Department, roll 7.

March 25

Pershing's Personal Diary

Worked in the office in the morning. In afternoon left by motor with Colonel Boyd for Compiègne. Arrived there about 10 p. m. General Pétain had changed houses since we were last there. At headquarters they left a guide who took us to his new abode. We found him, General Anthoine, his Chief of staff, General Ragueneau and Commandant Cochet waiting for us. General Pétain had ready the map of the right of the French line where the American divisions had been serving. No time was wasted; everyone talked fast; Cochet and Boyd both interpreted as rapidly as they could. I agreed to General Pétain's urgent request that American divisions take their place as soon as possible in quiet sectors of the line so that French divisions might be relieved and sent to the battle. I had insisted that it be the policy to work toward the formation of an American Corps, and General Pétain agreed to this principle. Each of us agreed that it is not now the time to form this corps. General Pétain and I were in perfect agreement on all points. He told me that by doing this the Americans are rendering the maximum aid with the troops which they have at their disposition. Left about 11 p. m. for Paris.

LC, Pershing Papers, Diary, May 7, 1917–September 1, 1918, box 4.

Pershing-Pétain Conference at French General Headquarters on the Formation of an American Corps.

Notes on Conversation between General Pershing and General Pétain, March 25th, 10:15 p.m.
    General Pershing stated that he had come to discuss the matter of putting American divisions into the line.
    General Pétain stated that he would like to see these divisions placed in line as soon as possible in order to take the place of French divisions which were needed on the present battle front.

General Pershing stated that he was willing to put these divisions in line, and brought up the question of having them united on the front as an American corps.

General Pétain replied that it would be well to have the American troops united if they had had sufficient experience to justify this, but that he did not consider that they had yet sufficient experience to justify entrusting a part of the front to a corps which had not yet functioned. He remarked that only one of the divisions had as yet functioned as a division; that all of the reserves are to be taken away from the rear of the troops holding the French line; that if the Germans should by chance break through there would be no reserves to fall back on; that it would be necessary to do this in order to withstand the shock which the Germans are apparently going to make in the north; that eventually every division on the right of the line shall pass through the fight in the north and that if the American troops could take place in the line so as to relieve French troops which might go to the battle, they would render a very great aid.

General Pétain again remarked that the American division and corps staffs had not yet had sufficient experience to justify at present placing on them the responsibility of holding a sector on the front.

General Pershing stated that he was willing and anxious to do what is best to meet the present emergency; he, however, wished it understood that it shall be the policy to work toward the organization of an American corps on the front and that as soon as practicable he wishes to see the American troops united on the front under the command of their corps commander. He pointed out that though his troops had been for some time on the front, only one of his division commanders had had an opportunity to exercise command of his division and that his corps commander had had no experience at all.

General Pétain stated that he agreed with this policy and thought that we should work toward it; that, however it would be impossible at present to fix any date for the organization of an American corps. He stated that it is to the interest of us all to see an American army as such on the front, but that we are at present going through a crisis; that it may become necessary to manoeuvre even on the right of the French line. He stated for example that the Verdun salient might be straightened out by withdrawal of the French in order to release three or four divisions; that similarly a straightening of the front might occur in the vicinity of Nancy and Toul; that in this event we would have during this period of straightening out a war of movement and that it would be a delicate manoeuvre, which should be entrusted only to staffs that have had experience.

General Pétain suggested that the most certain aid which the Americans could give at present would be of letting the 1st and 2d Divisions remain where they are; placing the 26th Division in line in the vicinity of the 1st Division, perhaps with its two brigades separated by some French troops and some French troops between the 1st and 26th Divisions, and by having the 42d Division go into line in the vicinity of Baccarat, a sector with which it is more or less familiar.

General Pershing stated that he would agree to this proposition in principle, but asked why the 42d Division should not be brought up nearer to the other American divisions.

General Pétain remarked that it was a question of convenience, and that as the division is in the vicinity of Baccarat it is more or less familiar with the sector.

General Pershing stated that this was satisfactory to him. He also stated that he is hoping to see arrive from now on two American divisions per month, and that there are also the troops which were to have been trained with the British; that he did not see how there would be means for giving these troops instruction with the British and that if these troops could be of any assistance he would be glad to use them. He added that these divisions having received more instruction in the United States, arrive with their training further advanced than the divisions which came ahead of them.

General Pétain replied that these divisions could render the very greatest service by placing them in quiet sectors on the front, by battalion or larger unit, with French troops. He stated that he will from now on be withdrawing divisions from the fight where they will have lost from two to three thousand men; that these divisions cannot go to rest, but will necessarily have to take a place in line in a quiet sector in order to release other French troops who will be sent to the battle; that these American troops could be placed for service with the depleted French divisions and would render a very great service in this way.

General Pétain went on further to state that as the French divisions now have three regiments of infantry, it might be arranged to have eventually two French regiments and one American regiment per division, and possibly later on two American and one French regiment per division. Finally all the infantry of the division might be American and only the artillery French the division being then called an American division. He stated that naturally the French would furnish the artillery and artillery personnel up to this point, and that later on, if desirable, the French artillery personnel might be gradually replaced by American artillery personnel, when the division will become entirely American. He recommended further that as American divisions arrive, those of them which would be able to begin at once on this scheme be sent to the front; that those that are in need of further training before beginning on this scheme be held near the coast for this instruction so as to avoid encumbering the roads and billets near the front with troops which are not actually taking part in the battle. He remarked that there will from now on be a great deal of movement along the front.

General Pershing assured General Pétain that he wished to aid in every possible way during the present crisis and that he could be counted on to do his utmost; that the American divisions stood ready to go into the battle and they were glad to do so.

General Pétain stated that he knew this to be General Pershing's motive, and that he did count on General Pershing to the very limit of American resources in France; that he would not like to see American divisions sent to battle now, but that a little later on it may be advisable to withdraw the best instructed of them, giving them a little training in open warfare and let them go through the battle.

LC, Pershing Papers, Conferences and Agreements, folder 1, box 50; see also *USAWW*, vol. 3, pp. 273–75.

Resumé of Conversation of General Pershing and General Pétain at French General Headquarters, March 25, 1918. Prepared by General Ragueneau, Chief, French Military Mission with the American Army.

General Pershing acknowledges receipt of General Pétain's request to employ available American troops for the relief of French divisions on quiet parts of the front and to free these divisions for battle.

General Pershing, anxious to lend every possible assistance to General Pétain, approves in general the immediate entry into sector of the American 26th and 42d Divisions. In carrying this out he would, however, like to have his brigade and division commanders exercise actual command of a sector. He would also like to have the American I Army Corps organized as soon as possible to hold an American front. He considers the present situation offers an opportunity for it.

General Pétain objects as follows:

The training of the divisions does not appear at this juncture to have reached a point that would enable them to hold a division sector of their own.

It is premature to want to form an American sector to be turned over to the I Corps, because:

The staff of this corps is not yet ready for the duty.

If several American divisions—even two divisions—were assembled side by side, they would occupy a rather considerable front and it is to be feared they would be unable to resist a violent attack, a thing which is always possible.

In such case, it would be prudent, to say the least, to support them with French divisions in reserve, which it is impossible to do at this time.

Just at this time it might be necessary to maneuver, conduct a retreat on the front held by the American I Corps, etc. The American I Corps is not yet prepared to carry out operations of this description.

In short, it is impossible, or at least unwise, to form the American sector during the crisis.

General Pershing yields to these reasons, insisting, however, that the question be kept in mind and that this sector for the I Corps be created as soon as possible.

General Pétain agrees to this, with the sole reservation as to the time when this operation will be possible.

General Pershing reverts to the matter of putting the divisions on the line in separate sectors. He again lays stress on the necessity of training his brigades and division commanders in their duties. General Pétain agrees that the 42d Division can go into sector, not by separate regiments inserted on the line in regiments of a French division (3 regiments in line, 1 in reserve), as General de Castelnau suggested, but on a brigade front. If the two brigades were placed in line, instead of one behind the other, it would be possible to have all the generals in the division exercise actual command.

General Pétain makes no objection generally to this last proposition.

Summing up, as to the first question, it is agreed:

1. That the 1st Division go into sector complete, by extension to the left (3 regiments in line).

2. That the 2d Division remain until further orders where it is—in the heights of the Meuse (by regiment in the infantry divisions of the XVII A. C.).

3. That the 26th Division go into sector, beginning its movement about April 4 or 5, as may be directed by the Group of Armies of the East (brigade sector south of the St-Mihiel salient).

4. That the 42d Division go into sector on a brigade front, beginning its movement about March 31 or April 1, on the present front of the right division of the VII A. C., the General-in-Chief not objecting to having the brigades go in line side by side, each with one regiment in front line.

General Pétain thoroughly appreciates General Pershing's desire to form the I A. C. as soon as possible, and to give it responsibility for its own front. He repeats that it is not possible during the present crisis, but that he will do his utmost to satisfy this desire as soon as he can.

* * * * * *

Divisions of the American II and III A. C.

General Pershing, affirming his very keen desire to help the French Commander-in-Chief in every possible manner during the battle, to this end offers the use of the divisions of the II and III A. C., which are beginning to arrive.

He expresses doubt that the divisions of the II Corps could at this time go to the British area for training. He is of the opinion that all these divisions, having had their initial training in America, could, on arrival, be employed on the front by regiment or separate battalions inserted between French units. General Pétain accepts this offer.

However, if certain divisions have not had enough training, they will be assembled after debarkation, to complete that training in billeting areas in the interior (areas situated on the lines of communication, for example), General Pétain asking that the zone of the armies be as free as possible, on account of the considerable movements of troops to be anticipated.

He discloses that the drain on our divisions is going to be considerable and that some units will have to be inactivated on account of reduced strength.

This being the case, he suggests that in the French divisions, thus reduced, first one, then two American regiments be placed, in proportion to the inactivation of French units. The artillery of the American divisions would carry on its training in the camps, while the infantry would go on the front line in this manner in French divisions; the artillery personnel would later replace French personnel and take over the materiel of the French divisions.

General Pershing takes up the proposition again. It is understood that American troops, thus placed in French divisions which are at reduced strength, could be sent to some part of the front or other, into quiet sectors.

As to the dispatch to the French front of the divisions transported in British bottoms, *General Pétain* states that it devolves upon General Pershing, who took the initiative in the matter, to come to an understanding with Marshal Douglas Haig, whose consent is indispensable.

The conversation ends with *General Pershing's* affirmation that he will do his utmost to cooperate in the battle. He believes he can only do what lies within the compass of the agreements just made, but that he is ready to accept any suggestions on the subject. *General Pétain* contemplates the possibility, if General Pershing so desires, of getting American divisions into the fight. Once a division has served some time in a sector, it could be withdrawn, placed in the rear for a while to train in the warfare of movement, and then be used like a French division in a French army. A start could be made with the 1st Division, whose training is rather more advanced than the others.

General Pershing accepts this suggestion.

USAWW, vol. 3, pp. 275–77; *Les armées françaises dans la Grande Guerre, Tome 6,* vol. 1, *Annexes*, vol. 2: *Annexe* No. 668, pp. 197–99.

Pershing to Sims, Commander, U.S. Naval Forces in European Waters, London, in reply to Sims to Pershing, March 18.

Personal.

Please accept my sincere thanks for your letter of March 18th enclosing copy of a chart showing the submarine sinkings during the month of February, 1918.

I am very glad to have the remarks contained in your letter with reference to the shipping situation, and wish to express my appreciation of the close cooperation between the Naval authorities and Military authorities on all questions relating to this expedition.

LC, Pershing Papers, folder: Sim (Adm. Sims document misfiled), box 184.

Secretary Newton D. Baker, then in London, to CINC, GHQ, AEF.

Cable 1137—L. R. Very urgent.

I have just had a long talk with the Prime Minister. He urges 3 proposals for your consideration. First, that our divisions in France be placed immediately in line to relieve French divisions for service elsewhere; quiet sectors being chosen for troops with least training. Second, that all available Engineer troops be taken from lines of communication work and sent to aid of British engineers preparing positions back of present lines. It is urged that the suspension of our work would be but temporary and that the work suggested is imperative. Third, that infantry be sent first of the entire 6 divisions to be transported by British in view of present acute needs of that arm. No answer to the foregoing is necessary until I see you tomorrow when we can discuss the suggestions fully. If railroads in France are too fully occupied to make Italian trip possible, I would abandon it. At any rate we should not permit diversion of engines and cars if they can be used in present emergency. We leave here tomorrow Tuesday at 7:30 for Paris.

LC, Pershing Papers, Conferences and Agreements, folder 1, box 50; *USAWW*, vol. 2, p. 252.

Editor's Note—It is important to understand that Prime Minister David Lloyd George strongly opposed Pershing in the ongoing debate about incorporating American units into the British and French Armies, which were then sorely pressed for able-bodied, trained men to replace their heavy losses, especially those then occurring due to the ongoing German offensive. Baker met with Lloyd George and Foreign Secretary Arthur Balfour in London on March 25, after which Balfour sent a cable to Edward M. House, Wilson's close confidential advisor, reporting on the meeting with Baker and the discussions therein, requesting that he take action to obtain "from the proper authorities assent to" the proposals of Lloyd George and Balfour. In his *War Memoirs*, Lloyd George commented:

> Prime Minister and I saw Mr. Baker this morning and earnestly pressed upon him the urgency of obtaining from the proper authorities assent to the three following suggestions:
> First. That the four American divisions should be used at once to hold the line and relieve further French divisions.
> Second. We understand that transport is available for bringing six complete American divisions to this country. We strongly urge that, in the present crisis, this tonnage would be more usefully employed if it were not used to carry complete divisions with their complement of artillery, etc., but if it were used in the main for the transport of infantry, of which, at this moment, we stand in most pressing need.
> Third. That, as a temporary expedient, American engineer units in France now engaged in preparing the bases and lines of communication of the future American Army and said to include many skilled engineers, should be diverted from present occupations and utilised as extemporised engineer units for construction of defenses, etc., in the rear of our armies.
> Fourth. That one of the American displacement divisions, which is reported to be complete with transport, should also be employed in the line, either as a separate division, or to increase the infantry of the combatant divisions.
> Mr. Baker seemed personally favourable to these suggestions.
> ... Colonel House replied on the 26th to Mr. Balfour's cable, saying that he had passed it to the President with his recommendation that orders should be issued on the lines suggested. ... On the 27th we had a further telegram from him saying:
> "The President agrees with practically every suggestion that you make regarding disposition of our Army. I am glad to inform you that Secretary Baker, after consulting with General Bliss and Pershing, has given orders making effective the recommendations set forth in your telegram." (David Lloyd George, *War Memoirs of David Lloyd George*, vol. 2, pp. 1811–13.)

Lloyd George then noted that the Permanent Military Representatives that day in Versailles had approved Joint Note No. 18 (see March 27, Minutes of the Meeting of the Military Representatives, held in the Council Chamber, Versailles, on Wednesday, March 27, 1918, at 3 p.m.) Pershing was present during the extensive discussions and clearly laid out the definite limits that he thought appropriate to place on the use of American forces during the present crisis. Lloyd George did not address Pershing's point, but then commented:

> All who have not experienced the vainglorious inflexibility of the professional mind where questions of status and authority are concerned would think that an order from the head of the Government countersigned by the Secretary of War would have settled this unfortunate dispute.
>
> When General Pershing learned of this resolution he was thoroughly upset, for it seemed to him that here was another attempt to rob him of his American Army. He got hold of Secretary Baker, and laid his misgivings before him. To meet them, Baker sent a covering note to President Wilson with the recommendations of the military representatives, in which he suggested that their proposals "ought to be conceded only in view of the present critical situation and continued only so long as that situation necessarily demands it." [See March 28, cable 67-S, Bliss, Chief, American Section, and Permanent Military Representative, SWC, for the Secretary of War Newton D. Baker to TAG, War Department, for President Wilson, especially Baker's personal comments to Wilson in paragraph 3, and his personal cable to Wilson that follows.] (David Lloyd George, *War Memoirs of David Lloyd George*, vol. 2, p. 1813.)

Lloyd George lamented that Wilson had approved the limitations that Baker and Pershing requested on the implementation of the Military Representatives' Joint Note No. 18, because "it practically left action entirely to the discretion of General Pershing." Lloyd George continued in the following weeks to work through Lord Reading to influence President Wilson to reverse the recommendations of Baker and Pershing in these matters (see March 28, cable 67-S). Lloyd George's policy would continue to bedevil Pershing and the GHQ, AEF, for weeks and months to come. (David Lloyd George, *War Memoirs of David Lloyd George*, vol. 2, p. 1814.)

Balfour's cable to House following the meeting with Baker on March 25 was just the beginning of an onslaught of cables between Lloyd George and Balfour and Lord Reading, British Ambassador in Washington, over the next several months. The British leaders repeatedly went behind Pershing's back to Wilson and House in attempts to convince the administration to overrule Pershing's opposition to their plans. These cable exchanges can be found in Link (ed.), *The Papers of Woodrow Wilson*, vol. 47: *March 13–May 12, 1918*, pp. 181–83 (March 28), 183 (March 28), 203–5 (March 29), 213–14 (March 30), 221–22 (April 1), 229–30 (April 2), 256 (April 4), 280–81 (April 7), 369–72 (April 18), 386–88 (April 20), and 393–94 (April 21); LC, Pershing Papers, folder: Data for Book *My Experiences in the World War*, folder 11: Extracts from official records of British War Office, *The Progress of the American*

Army in France, vols. 2 and 3, box 354; Lonergan, *It Might Have Been Lost!* passim; and Lloyd George, *War Memoirs*, vol. 2, passim.

Pershing to the Secretary of War, then in London.

<u>Confidential</u>.
Memorandum for the Secretary of War:

1. Americans recently visiting our training areas and coming in contact with officers in high command have received a note of deep pessimism, including apprehension of undue hardships to be undergone, of the disadvantages of billeting as compared to field conditions that have prevailed in our own country, of the great numbers of our enemy, and a belief in the impregnability of his lines, mingled with some comment on the peculiarities of our Allies, and generally have come away with an impression that the war is already well along toward defeat for our arms. It is especially to be regretted that such an impression has been derived mainly from general officers who, if prompted by considerations of soldierly duty, of leadership, of patriotism, fortitude and ambition, should maintain quite an opposite attitude.

2. While realizing that optimism cannot be created by order, it should be unnecessary to point out that such a state of mind on the part of officers in responsible positions is at once reflected among their troops, and it is not an over statement to say no officer worthy of command would give expression to thoughts of depression, much less communicate to untutored civilians false ideas of the morale of our troops. A conservative firmness and faith in our cause is not inconsistent with a serious estimate of an enemy's forces or even of a grave strategic or tactical situation, but I hardly need add that a temperament which gives way to weak complaining; which views with apprehension the contact with the enemy; which carps at the individuality of our allies, and querulously protests at hardships such as all soldiers must expect to endure, marks an unfitness for command of such an officer, and indicates his practical defeat before he goes to battle.

3. The officer who cannot read hope in the conditions that confront us; who is not inspired and uplifted by the knowledge that under the leadership of our chief executive, the heart of our nation is in this war; who shrinks from hardship; who does not exert his own personal influence to encourage his men; and who fails in the lofty attitude which should characterize the general that expects to succeed, should yield his position to others with more of our national courage. The consciousness of such an attitude should in honor dictate an application for relief. Whenever the visible effects of it on the command of such an officer reach me in future, it will constitute grounds for his removal without application.
[Handwritten note: *"Copy of a letter written to a Division Commander in Dec. 1917."*]
[*Ed.*—See Vol. 2, December 13, 1917, Pershing to Sibert, for background and the original letter.]

LC, Pershing Papers, folder: Newton D. Baker, January–June 1918, box 20.

Col. Fox Conner, ACS, G-3 (Operations), GHQ, AEF, to CS.
[Extract]

1. The following points were brought out in the conference with the Commander-in-Chief this morning which he wished noted in brief form:

1. The operations view is that in the present emergency the 2d Division should be left with the French; that the 42d Division should go in on the right of the 1st Division, that the 26th Division should go in on the left of the 1st Division, the left of our line to extend as far as the Meuse and the right to extend to the present right of the French 69th Division; the whole to be under the corps commander.

2. Due to difficulties of supply of troops to the west of the Meuse it would be preferable not to extend beyond the river.

3. As to the availability of the 26th and 42d Divisions, it is to be noted that the march of the 26th Division will not be completed before March 29. The division should have 7 days' rest, after which it will require 3 days' march to reach the front proposed for it. The earliest date at which the division could properly go into the line would therefore be April 8 (about). For the 42d Division the march from its present rest billets around Baccarat to the sector on the right of the 1st Division would require about 5 days. The earliest date at which it would be put into the line would therefore be about April 6 (allowing 7 days' rest).

4. Should we take over portions of the front as proposed above it would be necessary to supply the Corps Sector with some heavy batteries for counter-battery work. Our Corps Artillery is not yet available. There are, however, 32 8-inch howitzers at Mailly which are suitable for counter-battery work. We have in our depots nearly 27,000 rounds of 8-inch howitzer ammunition. This would supply sufficient ammunition at the usual rate of expenditure for 6 batteries for one month.

For personnel it is believed that we can draw on the Coast Artillery Brigade at Mailly for sufficient officers and men to form several batteries of 8-inch howitzers. No transportation would be essential as we could utilize trucks to draw the guns to the sector in question. Three of the battalions of the Coast Artillery Brigade are now absent from Mailly; one of these battalions is in the vicinity of Charmes where they are preparing railroad emplacements under the direction of the French; another battalion is at Brienne where it is constructing an ammunition depot; another is near Royaumeix constructing railroad emplacements.

In accordance with the directions of the Commander-in-Chief, orders will be sent this afternoon to the Commanding General, Coast Artillery Brigade, to begin the organization of provisional batteries to serve the 8-inch howitzers. In the absence of further directions no orders will, however, be given which would disturb the battalions which are now working for the French as above noted.

NARA, RG 120, Office of the Commander-in-Chief, Office of the Secretary of the General Staff, Entry 22, Reports of the Commander-in-Chief, folder 34: GHQ War Diary, January 24–April 28, 1918, diary entry March 28, 1918, 292-d, pp. 254–55, box 4; a partial extract containing only paragraphs 1–3 is at *USAWW*, vol. 3, p. 277.

Pershing to TAG, War Department, in addition to Pershing to Secretary of War, March 1 letter.

Cable P-782-S.
  2. For the Chief of Staff. 2A. Understand a centralized bureau of statistical information under Stettinius has been created to secure and maintain accurate information as to the state of the military program in ships, men in training, special troops, munitions, supplies, and all other information relating to the military program. Understand that in this bureau master charts will be available on which such information will be graphically displayed. Suggest plans be made to send over sufficient personnel entirely familiar with the work of the bureau in order that identical charts may be maintained here subject to constant change and development based on advises from Washington. If such a plan is feasible it would greatly aid communications between Headquarters here and Washington as to development of entire program. Headquarters here and Washington would then be communicating upon identical bases of fact as to the conditions of the program which would be reproduced here in identical manner. This plan would greatly aid in the development of our purchasing program with French and English. Desire full information as to what steps can be immediately taken to put such a plan of statistical information into practical operation. [Reply—March 31, A-1018-R-3] [*Ed.*—On April 8, in cable A-1066-R-2, the War Department informed Pershing that 6 National Army officers and 9 enlisted men or field clerks who were fully trained by the Statistical Branch, War Department General Staff, would be sent to France with the necessary supplies and equipment and complete plans for setting up the statistical system. It was only on May 30, in cable A-1422-R-15, that the War Department informed the GHQ AEF that Lt. Col. L. P. Ayers, later the AEF's Chief Statistician, was being sent to France with 7 officers and 9 Army field clerks to establish the statistical branch.]
  2I. Reference my confidential letter March 1st to the Secretary of War on port facilities, most urgently necessary that rolling stock be forwarded with all possible expedition. Present situation by congestion of cars practically places embargo on movement from ports.

NARA, RG 120, M930, Main Series, AEF to War Department, roll 2.

Pershing to TAG, War Department, in reply to TAG, War Department, to Pershing, cable A-921-R, March 18.

Cable P-783-S. Confidential.
For the Chief of Staff. 1A. With reference to paragraph 4, your cablegram 921. It must be remembered that in cases such as this request for food and forage we are dealing with French bureaus individually. If we are kept informed by you of United States tonnage assigned to French, and purposes for which assigned, we can arrange to satisfy demands of various French bureaus, adjusting such on a basis of the tonnage and replacement relations they bear each other, and leaving matters involving broader

policy to be treated through other channels. Answering specifically above referred to cable French High Commission in United States should handle the matter, but as far as possible these supplies should be shipped in tonnage that we have already allotted French, and vessels carrying these supplies should not be destined for any of our berths in French ports. [Reply—April 6, A-1050-R-6]

NARA, RG 120, M930, Confidential Series, AEF to War Department, roll 7.

TAG, War Department, to Pershing, in part in reply to Pershing to TAG, War Department, cables P-669-S, March 2, and P-716-S, March 13, in addition to TAG, War Department, to Pershing, and A-913-R, March 14.

Cable A-984-R.

1A. With reference to your 669, paragraphs 2B, C, D. Monthly deliveries of 9.2-inch howitzer ammunition of mark 1 at dock as follows. as June 5,000; July 10,000; August 25,000; September 30,000; October 30,000; November 35,000, and December 35,000. [Reply—April 4, P-856-S-3]

1I. With reference to your 716, paragraph 2 [*Ed.*—P-716-S-2 requested monthly deliveries at seaboard for the next 6 months of 155-mm gun batteries complete, 155-mm gun ammunition, and 4.7-inch gun ammunition.] Delivery 155-m.m. guns given our 913, paragraph 1G. Approximate estimate deliveries seaboard 4.7-inch shells: August 75,000, September 100,000. 4.7-inch shrapnel: April 5000, May 20,000, June 25,000, July 30,000, August 35,000, September 55,000. 155-m.m gun shells September 100,000. 155-m.m. shrapnel September 5000. Wheeler [Acting Chief of Ordnance]. [Reply—April 22, P-977-S-5D]

1L. . . . General Staff has decided that Vickers [machine guns] be shipped unaltered for either ground or air service. If you will notify us what quantities are to be used in France for Air Service alterations can be made in United States. Wheeler [Acting Chief of Ordnance]. [Reply—April 13, P-912-S-1A]

NARA, RG 120, M930, Main Series, War Department to AEF, roll 11.

March 26

Pershing's Personal Diary

At Paris. Worked in quarters in morning. In the afternoon went to Versailles and had talk with General Rawlinson who brought up again the question of drawing on America for reserves to fill up British ranks [see below, Rawlinson to Bliss, copy to Pershing]. Had also a conversation with the Italian Military representative at Versailles, General Giardino, who gave several of his own reasons why Italy would be glad to see Americans fighting on the Italian front. In the evening went to the Gare de Nord to meet the Secretary of War who was returning from London. Saw a large number of refugees at station who said that they were being evacuated from Compiègne. They stated they were put on the trains and transported free of charge, and were told after they got on board where they were going. They made a very pitiful sight.

LC, Pershing Papers, Diary, May 7, 1917–September 1, 1918, box 4.

Editor's Note—Pershing later wrote of the long-term consequences to the AEF of placing American troops on the Italian front, as Giardino requested:

> He argued that their presence would be tangible proof of the intense feeling of cooperation that inspired the American nation, that it would encourage those Italian working people who had been in America, that it would increase their confidence in the successful outcome of the war, and that, above all, they needed help. No doubt much of this was true, but it would have opened the way for similar concessions to the other Allies and in the end our forces would have been frittered away probably to little or no purpose. These appeals by the Allies, presented anew from time to time, only served to fix in our minds the idea that each was thinking in terms of its own army rather than of benefit to the Allies as a whole. (Pershing, *My Experiences in the World War*, vol. 1, pp. 358–59.)

Gen. Rawlinson reported the results of this meeting with Pershing to Gen. Wilson, CIGS, War Office, who dutifully reported that information to the War Cabinet when it met on the morning of March 27:

War Cabinet 374. Extract from Minutes . . .
8. Assistance by United States troops in France. With reference to War Cabinet 373, Minute 6. The Chief of the Imperial General Staff reported that General Rawlinson has seen General Pershing at Versailles yesterday, and that General Pershing would not agree to put the American battalions in the British divisions, as he was very anxious to keep his organization of divisions intact. He had, however, agreed to send American engineers to the front, and to put American divisions into the line to relieve French divisions. General Wilson said that there was to be another meeting at Versailles today.
The War Council decided that—
A strongly worded telegram drafted by the Prime Minister, with a view to ultimate publication, should be sent to President Wilson from the War Cabinet, explaining the whole situation [see below, March 30, Storr to Bliss, Editor's Note following]. (LC, Pershing Papers, folder: Data for Book *My Experiences in the World War*, folder 11: Extracts from official records of British War Office, *The Progress of the American Army in France*, vol. 2, document no. 105, box 354.)

Gen. Sir Henry Rawlinson, British Permanent Military Representative, SWC, Versailles, to Bliss, Chief, American Section, and Permanent Military Representative, SWC, Versailles. A copy sent to Pershing.

[Handwritten] *"This is the Memorandum a copy of which I forwarded to Genl Pershing."*

Telephone Message from Secretary, War Cabinet, to Lord Milner.

Prime Minister wishes you to discuss following possibilities with General Pershing: He has already had a preliminary discussion of them with Mr. Baker, Mr. Balfour being present:

1. Cannot American Divisions take over more of the Allied Line in order to enable French Divisions to be withdrawn for support of British? Such American Divisions might be placed more thickly in the line than the French whom they relieve, viz: 3 American Divisions where there were two French.

2. For the present, American Infantry only should be shipped to France.

3. Engineer and other American troops, etc. now employed in making or improving communications for the American Army in France should suspend their present work and be drafted behind the Allied front in order to construct fresh defensive lines.

Subsidiary Points:

(a) It is believed that there are in France some American batteries, with trained crews, in excess of their Divisional establishments. Could not these be sent to the British Front, or be sent to the French Front, to enable French batteries to be withdrawn for British support?

(b) It is not known whether the British recent Artillery losses comprised gun-crews as well as guns. If gun crews have been lost as well, could not American Artillerymen be sent to British batteries to replace losses of our Artillery personnel?

In my previous message I omitted to include a suggestion that one of the American Divisions which is reported to be complete with transport should also be employed in the line either as a separate Division or to increase the Infantry in the Combatant Divisions.

LC, Pershing Papers, folder: Conferences and Agreements, Folder No. 1, box 50.

Doullens Conference and Agreement.

[*Ed.*—The conference of British and French political and military leaders at Doullens, France, was a critical step in the eventual creation of the unified command of the Allied Armies on the Western Front under Ferdinand Foch, and for that reason is included here. The decisions reached at the Doullens Conference will also come up at the Beauvais Conference of April 3.]

O.A.D. 795
Record of Third Conference held at Doullens at 12 noon, March 26, 1918
Present
M. Poincaré
M. Clemenceau
M. Fouchel
General Foch
General Pétain
General Weygand
Field-Marshal Sir Douglas Haig, Commanding-in-Chief [sic]
General Sir H. A. Lawrence
General Sir H. Wilson
Lord Milner
General Montgomery
[Extract]

The *Field Marshal Commanding-in-Chief* pointed out the absolute necessity of the French hurrying forward as large reinforcements as possible from the south to support General Gough's army which had been in the battle since the 21st without a pause.

General Pétain said that the Fifth Army was no longer a fighting force. He explained the French situation, and what action he had taken. The French were detraining at Moreuil and Montdidier. He explained the dangers involved by pushing these troops in in driblets. Nine divisions were already engaged; fifteen more divisions were being brought up to the battle.

After some discussion it was unanimously agreed that "Amiens must be covered at all costs." The point was how to do it and who was to replace General Gough's tired troops in front of Amiens. This was the difficulty. All the French troops are being hurried up as fast as possible.

It was agreed that it was essential that all British troops must hold on from Arras to the Somme at all costs or another break might take place which would be very much more dangerous to the safety of Amiens. General Pétain said that the leading division from the north had had to be moved up to Moreuil instead of detraining at Abbeville.

Lord Milner impressed on the meeting the importance of putting in fresh troops at once, as although our men were tired, so were the Germans.

General Pétain said he was moving everything as fast as possible.

General Foch emphasized the necessity of instant action and of impressing on all troops that they must give up no ground.

General Wilson said he entirely agreed with General Foch.

Sir Douglas Haig thought that he could guarantee to do this without French help provided the French did not uncover his flank south of the Somme. General Gough had been ordered to hold on to Bray with his left.

It was also agreed that the French were to hurry on all movements of troops to the utmost. All troops south of the Somme, British and French, were to be ordered to hold on whether tired or not. The French would be responsible for the front south of the Somme.

M. *Clemenceau* pointed out that in his opinion the burning question was, at present, not how many divisions can be spared from the French front but how quickly reinforcements can arrive on the battle front. Time was of vital importance.

Everyone at the meeting was in agreement with this.

General Pétain explained how long it would take his troops to arrive.

M. *Clemenceau* then said he thought that all were agreed on the principles involved and what it was essential for the French and British to do. The only difficulty was the realization of the measures involved in these principles.

After private discussion between ministers and generals concerned, a resolution by M. Clemenceau was drawn up proposing that General Foch be appointed to coordinate the operations of the Allied armies about Amiens to cover that place.

The *Field Marshal* pointed out the difficulty of such a task unless General Foch had full authority over all the operations on the western front. M. Clemenceau agreed, and this proposal was unanimously adopted by the representatives of the French and British Governments. G.H.Q., March 26, 1918.

Doullens, March 26, 1918.

Doullens Agreement

General Foch is charged by the British and French Governments with the coordination of the military operations of the Allied armies on the western front. To this end, he will make arrangements with the Generals-in-Chief, who are requested to furnish him all necessary information.

Clemenceau.
Milner.

USAWW, vol. 2, pp. 253–54.

Pershing to Maj. Gen. Francis J. Kernan, CG, SOS, AEF, Tours, in reply to Kernan to Pershing, telegram, March 20.

[Extracts]

1. Receipt is acknowledged of your letter of the 20th inst., wherein you state your understanding of the relationship that now exists between the S.O.S. [Services of Supply] and the D.G.T. [Director General of Transportation]. Your understanding in this case is correct.

2. The letter of January 28th, 1918, of these headquarters, referred to in General Atterbury's telegram dated February 26th, 1918, was, of course, modified by G.O. 31, C.S., G.H.Q., which put into effect our reorganization of the L. of C. and directed the

chiefs of all the Administrative and Technical Staff Services to exercise their functions in the matter of procurement, supply and transportation under the direction of the C.G., S.O.S. [Commanding General, Services of Supply]

3. General Atterbury is in charge of a large subdivision of your office, but he possesses no powers which you do not possess over and above him and this includes all matters of administration, sanitation and discipline.

4. In effecting the reorganization of the L. of C. and the assembling of the services at Tours, under you, it was desired to give you all the power necessary to enable you to perform the great task with which you are now charged. Under the old arrangement the C. G. L. of C. [Commanding General, Line of Communications] was charged with certain duties, but the means which he had to employ in the performance of these duties were not entirely under his control. This has been corrected in the new organization. You have now the full power to administer all these agencies as the demands of your duties require.

7. The C. in C. desires you to know that you will be given the fullest support in the administration of your office and that the staff at these headquarters will give you every possible assistance.

NARA, RG 120, Office of the Commander-in-Chief, Office of the Secretary of the General Staff, Entry 22, Reports of the Commander-in-Chief, folder 34: GHQ War Diary, January 24–April 28, 1918, diary entry April 7, 1918, 302-c, p. 281, box 4.

Harbord, CS, GHQ, AEF, Chaumont, to Pershing, Paris, with reference to Pershing to TAG, War Department, cable P-779-S, March 24.

Telegram.

With reference to your telegram to General Crowder (March 24, P-779-S-3A). General Kreger states that he does not feel that he can with propriety officially comment against an order but states that the requirement that he shall pass on the bare legality of sentence will result in the least delay practicable. That he and Bethel [AEF's Judge Advocate General] will work together but he does agree with me that any arrangement in times like these which depends on the personality and ability of two officers to get together is a weak arrangement. He does not know whether the order emanates from Crowder or the Secretary. The execution of negro soldiers was coincident with a number of dismissals of officers from here and different parts of the United States about which when asked by politicians the War Department replied that it was not familiar with details. Someone then hunted up this statute of 1863 and the order is the result. Certainly believe that in times of stress like these no administrative machinery should depend on personality of officers to make it work.

LC, Harbord Papers, folder: correspondence with John J. Pershing, box 11.

Conner, ACS, G-3, GHQ AEF, to CS.

There were present at this conversation Colonel de Chambrun and Colonel Fox Conner, Asst. C. of S., G-3.

1. The chief of the French Military Mission proposed a plan for the employment of our troops in the existing emergency which was somewhat different and more detailed than the plan proposed by the Chief of Staff of the French Military Mission this morning.

2. For the 42d Division the Chief, French Military Mission, proposed that the division be put into a sector as a division with three regiments in line, the sector to be on the right of the VII Army Corps. As an alternative the Chief, French Military Mission, proposed that the 42d Division be put in by regiments, the division being brought together later. The Chief of Staff accepted the proposition to put the 42d Division in as a division.

3. For the 1st Division, General Ragueneau proposed that the front be extended as far as the Meuse by bringing up at least one of the regiments of the brigade in reserve. Coupled with this it was proposed to put the 26th Division in with its right resting on the Moselle, the 69th Division thus being between the 26th Division and the 1st Division.

It was proposed to put the 26th Division in either by regiments or as a division. Considerable discussion arose over this. The Chief of Staff stated that this was entirely different from the agreement made between General Pétain and General Pershing as he (General Harbord) understood that agreement from a telephone conversation with General Pershing today. The Chief of Staff stated that his objection to this plan was that it would delay the functioning of the corps as such.

As an alternative to the proposition made by the Chief, French Military Mission, the Chief of Staff suggested that instead of extending the front of the 1st Division to the Meuse by putting in the remaining elements of that division, it might be possible to put the 26th Division, less one brigade, in on the left of the 1st Division, the corps commander, I Army Corps, assuming command of the two divisions which would thus be in line side by side.

The Chief, French Military Mission, stated that he was not authorized to accept this solution and that he would have to communicate with French G. H. Q. The Chief of Staff pointed out that a solution today was not essential as the 26th Division is still marching and would not be available before April 1.

The matter was finally left to be decided after the return of General Pershing, or if practicable by telephone, during the next 24 hours.

4. With reference to the sector to be occupied by the 26th Division, it was pointed out that the solution proposed by the Chief of Staff would be no more dangerous than the solution proposed by the French. In effect, placing the 26th Division in on the left of the 1st Division would extend the line to the Meuse as was desired by the French, but such extension would be accomplished in greater strength than would be the case by extending through bringing troops of the 1st Division now in reserve on the line to the left of the present front.

It was also pointed out that in all probability this sector was less likely to be attacked than the sector on the heights of the Moselle in which the French proposed to put the 26th Division. [*Ed.*—Probably meant "Meuse," as mentioned in paragraph 4.]

USAWW, vol. 3, pp. 278–79.

Harbord, CS, GHQ, AEF, to Chief, French Military Mission with the American Army, Chaumont.

1. In accordance with the understanding between the Chief of Staff, French Mission, and myself, I submit a resume of the conversation between us and the action taken by me thereon.

2. Orders have been given the Commanding General, 42d Division, to place his division at the disposition of the Commanding General, French VII Army Corps.

This order contained no limitations. If practicable, however, it is desired that the 42d Division have two or three additional days of rest. It is requested that so far as practicable the artillery of the division be used to support its own infantry.

It is understood that if opportunity offers the division will soon be brought together as a division under the tactical command of its commanding general.

3. Orders have been given to expedite the return of the 26th Division to its area. The manner of employing this division was not settled between us, but will be taken up with the American Commander-in-Chief.

The 26th Division will, it was agreed, be ready to start for the front on or about April 1

4. Orders have been given to form 6 howitzer batteries (8-inch) from available American personnel and materiel now at Mailly. It is hoped that these batteries may be available after a period of 10 to 15 days. We desire to employ these batteries, if needed, in sectors held by our troops.

5. In addition to the batteries noted above, we are prepared to furnish, with a brief delay, 3 other batteries provided the French Command can return to Mailly the 2d Battalion, 53d C. A. C. [Coast Artillery Corps], now at Brienne-le-Château. (This battalion is now constructing an ammunition depot.)

It is requested that you take this matter up with the proper authority.

6. You will, of course, understand that the desires which I have expressed as to the method of employing our troops are not to be construed as hampering the French command in utilizing the units placed at their disposition in the present emergency.

Allow me to express our satisfaction at being able to contribute something toward meeting the present emergency and to regret that we have not 20, instead of 2, divisions to place alongside our French comrades.

USAWW, vol. 3, pp. 279–80.

Harbord, CS, GHQ, AEF, Chaumont, to Maj. Gen. Clarence R. Edwards, CG, 26th Division, AEF.

Subject: Criticism.

1. The Commander-in-Chief directs me to say that there has been brought to his attention much that is creditable regarding the good appearance, discipline and smartness in saluting in your division, as well as the good conduct of its regiments during its recent tour in the line. He regrets, however, that there has been at the same time brought to his attention the fact that you frequently indulge in criticisms of other officers, in some cases your superiors.

2. Temperate criticism of officers of your command, if made to the officer and with disciplinary intent, is of course, with your sphere when properly given.

3. I am to say that this habit of loose comment on other officers goes far to outweigh the commendable conditions mentioned in par. 1. It is especially harmful from a General Officer of the Regular Army commanding a National Guard unit. Criticism of officers outside your command, especially in the presence of junior officers, is inexcusable and must cease.

[Reply—March 31, Edwards to Harbord]

Clarence R. Edwards Papers, folder 18: 1917–1919, Commendatory and Personal Letters to Edwards, box 22, Massachusetts Historical Society, Boston.

Bliss, Chief, American Section, and Permanent Military Representative, SWC, Versailles, to Pershing, reply to Pershing to Bliss, March 24.

Until I received the War Department telegram No. 38, herewith, I supposed, without having given any special thought to it, that an interchange of important Communications had been going on between my office in Versailles and your headquarters [see March 23, 38-R-2]. I found that it had been overlooked and I at once gave orders to have copies made of all correspondence except the purely routine kind, and it was ready for transmission to you before I received your note of the 24th instant about the proceedings of the Military Representatives of the Supreme War Council. Expecting that you would be in Paris yesterday or today, I have held them to hand them to you when you come. I have given instructions that hereafter all such documents be promptly communicated to you.

Several times my colleagues here have asked me about the progress made in the program for the transportation by the British of the six divisions which they agreed to bring over after your conference here with Mr. Lloyd George and others on this subject on January 29th. I told the British that I understood that the program was entirely in their own hands; that we had designated the divisions that were to come and that I supposed it as entirely a matter of their providing the shipping to bring them over in accordance with their agreement. Finally, in order to satisfy them, I telegraphed to Washington to find out what the program there was. That resulted in paragraph 2 of despatch number 38 from Washington, signed by March and McCain [see March 23, 38-R].

Hoping that I may see you today...

Inclosures [copies of documents received and sent by Bliss from arrival in Paris to the present].

LC, Pershing Papers, folder: Supreme War Council, February–April 1918, box 193; see also LC, Bliss Papers, folder: American Expeditionary Forces and American Forces in France, January–December 1918, box 248.

Sims, Commander, U.S. Naval Forces Operating in European Waters, London, to Pershing, in reply to Pershing to Sims, March 24.

Telegram. Very Secret.
1721. For General Pershing. Referring to your cable March 24, the whole subject of ships to transport U.S. troops is being handled by the War Department in Washington and is under discussion there at the present moment with British Representatives. No decision has as yet been reached as to the British ships that will be allocated for carrying U.S. troops to France. I shall advise you if I am informed of the decisions reached in Washington.

NARA, RG 45, ONRL, 1803–1859, T829, Miscellaneous Records of the Navy Department, Miscellaneous Materials, 1–8/1918, Miscellaneous Material Printed Files, World War, roll 411; see also Naval History and Heritage Command, website: Wars, , World War I, Documentary Histories, March 1918, Sims to Pershing, March 26, Conflicts, and Operations 1918; original document at NARA, RG 45, ONRL, Entry 517B.

March 27

Pershing's Personal Diary

At Paris. The Secretary of War and party stopping at the house, 73 Rue de Varenne. In the morning talked with the Secretary and also with Messrs. Crosby and Cravath. In the afternoon went to Versailles and talked with General Bliss.

LC, Pershing Papers, Diary, May 7, 1917–September 1, 1918, box 4.

Minutes of the Meeting of the Military Representatives, held in the Council Chamber, Versailles, on Wednesday, March 27, 1918, at 3 p.m.

S.W.C./153
S.W.C. (M.R.) 24
Present
France	Major Pagezy
Great Britain	General Rawlinson
Italy	General Giardino
America	General Bliss
	accompanied by General Pershing

* * * * * *

Chairman—General Giardino

General Giardino: In accordance with the desire expressed by Military Representatives in their meeting of March 24, General Rawlinson had proposed a resolution for discussion with regard to the incorporation of American forces. He favored this project, except in certain particulars. He wished that the question be solved not with regard to England alone, but that the principle be established for all the Allies.

Major Pagezy made a remark with regard to the phrase "Since the English Army is bearing all the weight of the struggle," and the modification "having borne at the beginning . . ." was adopted. He also requested an explanation regarding the 150,000 men asked for by General Rawlinson.

General Rawlinson explained it by the present losses of about 80,000 men and 45,000 prisoners.

General Bliss being consulted asked General Pershing to speak.

General Pershing made, in substance, the following statement:

"You may remember General Rawlinson that when this matter was first discussed here with General Robertson and Mr. Lloyd George, it was decided that 6 divisions rather than 150,000 infantry would be transported in British ships. I desire to help in every way possible, but I am not ready to commit myself, or my government, to furnish this number of infantry first to England and then to France. This would require nearly all available shipping until late in the autumn, without our being able to bring over a proportionate number of artillery and auxiliaries in time to complete their training. It would amount to the United States giving up any expectation of participating in the war with a force adequate to accomplish anything; would be practically agreeing to maintain the British and French divisions at full strength. This would in my opinion not be best either for the United States or for the Allies. A better procedure would be for the Allies to amalgamate their weakened divisions into a lesser number and let the American divisions take their proper places in the line wherever that may be. I think this the safest and most rational plan. The question may arise as to whether the American divisions are competent to take their places as suggested, to which I answer decisively and without hesitation in the affirmative. I am prepared to put the American divisions on the line as fast as they arrive. They have had much training at home and the short experience on the front would enable them to make a creditable showing.

However, in order to show my desire to cooperate and help, I am ready, in view of the heavy losses of the British to agree that infantry be sent according to the existing agreement with the British under the condition that their artillery may be brought over when we ask for it, and that the infantry units be withdrawn and united in their own divisions when required by the American Commander-in-Chief. I therefore suggest that the resolution take about the following form:

> 'It is believed that in view of and during the present emergency on the western front, the infantry of the American divisions that are to be trained with the British should be given precedence in sea transportation and that the

agreement made between the British and Americans regarding training of divisions with the British should be modified to that extent, with the understanding that this is a temporary measure and that these units of infantry are to be reunited with their artillery and auxiliary units when so desired by the Americans, in order, as planned, that an American army may be built up which shall take its place beside the other Allied armies.'"

General Giardino then called attention to the fact that apparently this proposal referred only to the 6 American divisions to be transported by the English, and inquired whether if the German attack should exhaust the Italian effectives, the American army would be able to furnish them infantry.

General Pershing stated that he understood only the present emergency was being considered, and that the step proposed applied only to the 6 divisions to be transported in the English shipping. That the question of sending American troops to Italy could be settled only by his Government.

General Giardino said that he wished to know whether it was intended that the text offered by General Pershing should acknowledge the general principles of the resolution as first proposed by General Rawlinson.

General Pershing thought he could clear the matter up. He said it had been agreed that the British should transport 6 divisions and that the infantry of these divisions should be trained with the British; that the artillery of these divisions was to be trained under him. To meet the emergency, he now proposed that all of the infantry of these 6 divisions should be brought over first; and the artillery subsequently. As to France, this same procedure had been followed all along. He had had one division, and he just added 2 divisions, the infantry of which was training with the French divisions, and the division commanders of which were training with the corps commander. If they had to participate in the fight, they would fight. This plan had been agreed upon by General Pétain who is perfectly satisfied with it. The completion of the French and British divisions by drafts of the American troops had not been contemplated.

General Giardino thought that they were not looking at the matter from the same point of view. He desired to know whether it was deemed necessary to meet the German attack, and our infantry were disrupted, would the American army furnish more infantry to replace it.

General Pershing stated that the United States would be undertaking a very large contract if they agreed to this, and he was not sure that they were prepared to do so.

General Giardino said he did not doubt the American divisions would be most helpful; but the critical question now was one of time, and they would not be on time if the Allies had already suffered defeat. While the Americans were bringing over two complete divisions a month, they could be bringing the infantry of at least four, and the needed help would therefore be more likely to arrive in time; this seemed especially important to the French and English.

General Rawlinson pointed out that the decisive battle is at this moment being fought; it is all a question of time; and requested that infantry and machine guns be brought, if transports are not full of artillery and other services, they will be able to bring us a greater number of infantry. He said the English and the French require the infantry of six divisions.

General Pershing declared himself ready to recommend the bringing over first of the infantry of the six divisions intended to be trained with the British; he thought that this would provide for British needs arising out of the present emergency; after considerable study and discussion, he and General Pétain had arrived at the arrangement now in force with the French army, and they were both entirely satisfied with this arrangement. He did not think it necessary to make a radical change to meet a future emergency until the latter should have arisen.

General Pershing then left.

General Bliss remarked that General Pershing expressed only his personal opinion, and that it is the Military Representatives who must make a decision.

General Bliss then proposed a version to which all the military representatives agreed. This, with a part of General Rawlinson's scheme, formed the subject of Collective Note No. 18.

Joint Note No. 18
Joint Note to the Supreme War Council by its Military Representatives. American Reinforcements—Western Front

To: The Supreme War Council

(1) In paragraph 4 of Joint Note No. 12, dated January 12, 1918, the Military Representatives agreed as follows:

After the most careful and searching inquiry they were agreed on the point that the security of France could also be assured. But in view of the strength of the attack which the enemy is able to develop on this front, an attack which, in the opinion of the military representatives could reach a strength of 96 divisions (excluding reinforcements by "*roulement*" [rotation]); they feel compelled to add that France will be safe during 1918 only under certain conditions, namely:

(a) That the strength of the British and French troops in France are continuously kept up to their present total strength, and that they receive the expected reinforcement of not less than two American divisions per month.

(2) The battle which is developing at the present moment in France and which can extend to the other theaters of operations may very quickly place the Allied armies in a serious situation from the point of view of effectives, and the Military Representatives are from this moment of the opinion that the above detailed condition (a) can no longer be maintained and they consider as a general proposition that the new situation requires new decisions.

The Military Representatives are of the opinion that it is highly desirable that the American Government should assist the Allied armies as soon as possible by permitting, in principle, the temporary service of American units in Allied army corps and divisions, such reinforcements must however be obtained from other units than those American divisions which are now operating with the French, and the units so temporarily employed must eventually be returned to the American Army.

(3) The Military Representatives are of the opinion that, from the present time, in execution of the foregoing, and until otherwise directed by the Supreme War Council, only American infantry and machine-gun units, organized as that Government may decide, be brought to France, and that all agreements or conventions hitherto made in conflict with this decision be modified accordingly.

Weygand [French Military Representative]
Rawlinson [British Military Representative}
Giardino [Italian Military Representative]
Tasker H. Bliss [American Military Representative]
Versailles 27th March, 1918.

LC, Pershing Papers, folder: Supreme War Council, February–April 1918, box 193; NARA, RG 120, M923, Records of the American Section, SWC, file 299: Minutes (with Annexes and Joint Notes) of Meetings of the Permanent Military Representatives, Dec. 4, 1917–Nov. 4, 1919, document 299-24, roll 17; see also online "WW I Supreme War Council, American records," at https://www.fold3.com.

Editor's Note—Pershing was not an official member of this body, so he left prior to the vote. His view on the outcome of the day's discussions was noted in his wartime memoirs, as were the actions he then took:

> The situation was considered so serious that the Military Representatives seemed to think it necessary to recommend that all previous plans for the shipment of American troops be disregarded and that nothing but infantry and machine gun units be shipped until otherwise directed by the Supreme War Council. This they did in the form of a joint (or unanimous) note, which was, of course, approved by the Supreme War Council. I was very much surprised at the attitude of General Bliss, our military representative with the Council, as without his consent the joint note could not have been submitted to the Council.
>
> The presence of the Secretary of War fortunately afforded me the opportunity to discuss with him not only the demands of the particular situation existing at the time but the general attitude of our Allies regarding the manner in which Americans should be employed. When the joint note [Joint Note No. 18] was presented to Secretary Baker, I pointed out to him and to General Bliss [during the March 28 meeting] that the proposal, if approved by the President, would place the disposition of American units entirely in the hands of the Supreme War Council and take them quite out of our control, even for training, and would without doubt destroy all possibility of our forming an American army. The Secretary was as strongly opposed to any such outcome as I was and after some discussion he dictated his views in a cable to the President, explicitly recommending that the control of our forces should be retained by our Commander-in-Chief and that the joint

note be approved only in that sense.... [See March 28, cable 67-S, especially paragraph 3, and also March 28, Baker to Wilson, cable.]

This action by the Military Representatives just at this crisis was intended to put the weight of the Supreme War Council behind the idea of maintaining the strength of Allied units by American replacements as a policy. The text of the joint note made it entirely plain that this was their purpose. (Pershing, *My Experiences in the World War*, vol. 1, pp. 360, 362.)

Pershing was certainly most unhappy with Bliss's actions in crafting his revisions to Joint Note No. 18 after Pershing left the session of the Permanent Military Representatives. He had persistently fought vigorously against any concessions that would allow amalgamation of American troops into the deleted British and French military units. And yet this is exactly what Bliss had effectively done, although he also added some conditional phrases in paragraph 2 of the Note. Don Smythe explained the problem and its resolution:

After Pershing left, Bliss remarked: "General Pershing expressed only his personal opinion... it is [we] who must make a decision."

Bliss then proposed a resolution which was substantially that of Rawlinson's and which was unanimously adopted and sent to the SWC as Joint Note #18: "It is highly desirable that the American Government should assist the Allied armies as soon as possible by permitting, in principle, the temporary service of American units in Allied army corps and divisions.... In execution of the foregoing, and until otherwise directed by the Supreme War Council, only American infantry and machine-gun units [should] be brought to France...."

Bliss did add certain saving phrases that he thought Pershing would want. The proposed reinforcements were to come from America and not from American divisions already in France, which should be preserved intact. Also, amalgamated units "must eventually be returned to the American army." Nonetheless, Pershing was shocked at Bliss's resolution and considered himself somewhat undercut. It would stop practically all shipments of artillery, technical units, service of the rear, corps, and army troops—in other words, stop the formation of a separate American Army.

Since Secretary Baker was still in Europe, Bliss presented Joint Note #18 directly to him in Paris. Baker was aware that Allied proposals for amalgamation, at least during the emergency, had considerable merit. Many patriotic Americans supported them, for example, Bliss, Wood, Sims, and House....

Baker must also have been aware of considerable Allied bitterness over America's meager manpower contribution after one year of war....

Accordingly, Baker overruled Pershing and on March 28 recommended that President Wilson approve Joint Note #18 "in view of the present critical situation" [see March 28, cable 67-S]. Shipments of infantry and machine-gun

General Tasker H. Bliss. After his appointment as the American Military Representative to the Supreme War Council at Versailles in January 1918, General Tasker H. Bliss played a pivotal role in the Allied deliberations on the conduct of the war. He also became an important and trusted advisor to Pershing, although the two often had divergent views on major issues. However much he may have disagreed with Pershing in private, Bliss consistently supported him in public. In 1918, the War Department commissioned American artist Joseph Cummings Chase and sent him to the American Expeditionary Forces in France to "obtain the likenesses of our more distinguished solders" for the permanent pictorial record. With Pershing's complete support and cooperation, Chase traveled throughout the AEF to sketch subjects from the highest commanders to ordinary soldiers. These sketches were published in his collection *Soldiers All* in 1920. Source: Joseph Cummings Chase, *Soldiers All: Portraits and Sketches of the Men of the A.E.F.* (New York: George H. Dorn Co., 1920), p. 77.

units would be given preference, even though this necessarily postponed organization and training of complete American divisions and thus delayed the formation of an independent American army. No specific numbers of troops were mentioned, nor the length of time that they would be given preferential shipment. On arriving in Europe, they would be directly under Pershing for training and use, and ultimately be gathered by him into a separate American Army. (Smythe, *Pershing*, pp. 100–101.)

Pershing, Paris, to Prime Minister Georges Clemenceau, etc.

Will you permit me to express, thus informally, my extreme gratification that a solution to the question of a generalissimo for the Allied armies has at last been reached and that you have been selected? I wish to assure you of my loyal support and to express the hope that American divisions may have an early opportunity to demonstrate in action our unqualified devotion to the cause. With unity of command there can be none to doubt a victorious outcome of the war.

LC, Pershing Papers, folder: Georges Clemenceau, box 47.

Ragueneau, Chief, French Military Mission with the American Army, Chaumont, to CINC, AEF, in reply to Harbord, CS, GHQ AEF, to Chief, French Military Mission, March 26.

In reply to your letter of March 26 and following the conversations which I had yesterday and this morning with your Chief of Staff, I have the honor to confirm the following dispositions which were drawn up after agreement with the French Command.

(1) The 42d Division, which was placed yesterday, March 26, at the disposition of the French VII Corps, will occupy the division sector under the orders of its general in the eastern part of the present sector of the French 128th Division (Baccarat-Badonviller). It will have three regiments in line and one regiment in reserve.

(2) The 1st Infantry Division receives today the order to take its second Brigade to the front. That division will extend its sector towards the west in such a manner as to relieve one regiment of colonial infantry of the French army. The division will thus have three regiments in line and one regiment in reserve.

(3) The American 26th Division, available from and after March 29, will enter by brigades the sector actually held by the French 69th and 42d Divisions, in such a way as to make free one of these divisions, the 42d. The 26th Division will be placed under the orders of the French 69th Division.

General Liggett, commanding the American I Corps, will take his place alongside of the General commanding the XXXII Corps for the purposes of information, but General Liggett will not exercise tactical command until further orders.

(4) The American 2d Division, remaining in its present place, will receive the orders of the French command for the execution of such dispositions as may be necessary to permit the relief of one French infantry division.

I shall hasten to communicate to you all the supplementary information which I may receive concerning the details of execution, as well as the reply of the General Commander-in-Chief on the subject of your proposal as to the employment of heavy batteries of 8-inch mortars.

The French command deeply appreciates the valuable assistance which you have been kind enough to bring it through enabling the French command to render available from the present time four infantry divisions, and it does not doubt but that similar assistance will be available in the future to the full extent that events may require.

[GHQ AEF Action forwarding Ragueneau's letter.]
March 27, 1918
CS, GHQ AEF, to CG, I Corps, AEF.

1. Herewith, for your information, is a translation of a letter received from the Chief of the French Mission.

2. You have already been informed as to the details of the agreement as set for in the translation herewith. It is therefore hardly necessary to add that the translation represents the agreement made with the French.
[Unsigned]

USAWW, vol. 3, pp. 280–81.

Harbord, CS, GHQ AEF, to Pershing, then in Paris.

Sir Douglas Haig telegraphs thanking you for engineer regiments [see March 23, 1918, Haig to Pershing]. Another subsequent telegram suspends movement engineers until further notice. Am having them held in readiness.

LC, Pershing Papers, folder: Gen. James G. Harbord, 1910–1918, box 87.

Conner, ACS, G-3, GHQ, AEF, to CS, in reply to Harbord, CS, to Army Artillery Commander, March 23.

1. Conforming to the idea of the Commander-in-Chief, that antiaircraft defense should be a separate organization, there are herewith, a general order [omitted] providing for the establishment of an antiaircraft service at these headquarters, and a special order [omitted] for the detail of such officer as the Commander-in-Chief may decide upon as chief of this service.

2. This order has in view a separate organization in charge of a chief who works through the Chief of Staff, A. E. F. His duties are prescribed in the order only in general terms because working under the chief of staff, his activities can always be regulated by the proper sections of the general staff.

3. It is considered desirable that a selection be made at once of an officer to act as chief of this service. While the materiel immediately available for antiaircraft defense

Lt. General Hunter Liggett. When Hunter Liggett first arrived in France as commanding general of the 41st Division in October 1917 for his orientation tour, Pershing viewed him unfavorably due to his weight and was inclined to reject him for assignment to the AEF. However, he retained Liggett at the last moment. He became so impressed with Liggett's energy, leadership qualities, tact, clear thinking, and intelligence that he appointed him to command the AEF's newly organized I Corps in January 1918. Pictured here as a Lt. General on November 5 at his command post while commanding the U.S. First Army, Liggett organized and trained the divisions of the I Corps and proved to be an outstanding combat leader throughout his time in command. He replaced Pershing as commander of First Army on October 16, 1918, and remained in high command positions in the AEF until he returned to the United States in the summer of 1919. Source: NARA, Still Picture Branch, RG 111, 111-SC-30944.

is very small, the matters of proper organization and administration can be settled upon at once. Schemes for organization, for employment, and detailed defense plans for a number of specified points are in possession of this section and can be turned over to the chief of the antiaircraft service as soon as he is appointed.

USAWW, vol. 2, p. 260.

Logan to Chief, French Military Mission with the American Army, Chaumont. Copy to CG, SOS, on March 27.

Subject: Areas for troops near ports.

1. Your attention is invited to the advisability of having reconnaissance made immediately for the purpose of determining whether or not it will be possible to obtain billeting areas for six divisions in the immediate vicinity of our ports of debarkation.

2. As the use of these areas would be only temporary, it would not be advisable to undertake any new construction. It would, however, simplify our supply situation, due to the temporary shortage of railroad cars, if these areas could be found in the immediate vicinity of the ports of Brest, St. Nazaire and Bordeaux.

3. You have already been kind enough to have had reconnaissances made of certain areas in the zone of our Services of Supply but unfortunately these, due to the present railroad car shortage, are a little too far away from the ports to accomplish the desired results.

4. The request in this particular does not conflict with our previous request for reconnaissances of certain areas in the neighborhood of Le Mans and to the west of Tours, referred to in our, letter dated March 15, 1918, for permanent areas for Depot Divisions. These latter of course will be needed.

5. A prompt reply will be very much appreciated.
By direction.

[GHQ AEF Background]
Harbord, CS, GHQ, AEF, to the ACS, G-1.

The Commander-in-Chief is convinced that the scarcity of railroad transportation and the fact that the troops are to be crowded on to us very soon will necessitate the selection of a number of areas for divisions near the ports.

What have you already listed and reconnoitered in that line?

Attached is a proposed location of Divisions, Corps and Army troops, 3rd Phase, under certain eventualities, furnished by the Assistant Chief of Staff, G-1, to the Chief of Staff, A.E.F.

On March 26th the above list of proposed locations was returned by the Chief of Staff to the Asst. Chief of Staff, G-1, with the following memorandum:

"This list of areas does not fill the requirements. What is wanted is a number of areas very near the ports obviating the use of railroad transportation. Some of these places will answer.

Please prepare a letter to the French Mission stating that the scarcity of railroad cars and a threatened congestion necessitate the selection of at least six areas for divisions very near our ports of debarkation.

Ask them to have their reconnaissances made at once and let us know at the earliest practicable moment.

J.G. Harbord
Chief of Staff"

NARA, RG 120, Office of the Commander-in-Chief, Office of the Secretary of the General Staff, Entry 22, Reports of the Commander-in-Chief, folder 34: GHQ War Diary, January 24–April 28, 1918, diary entry March 28, 1918, 292-i, pp. 255–56, box 4.

Secretary of War Baker, then in Paris, to President Woodrow Wilson.

For the President.

I have returned to Paris and leave tonight for visit to Italian headquarters. Will sail for home April 1st. The situation here is very grave but seems better this morning than at any time since the offensive began. The French have taken over a substantial part of the British line and reserves of both armies are now concentrated near chief point of attack which seems to be Amiens which is rail head for supplies of British front. Its capture would be serious. A part of the German plan is to drive in between the French and British forces and for a while they were out of touch with one another. Contact was reestablished last light [night] and the line of defense is now unbroken. General Pershing is in full accord with General Pétain and General Haig and is placing all our men and resources here at their disposal. Our engineer troops are being brought up from the line of communications to aid Haig in the construction of new defensive positions and Pétain in [is] placing four of our divisions [1st, 2nd, 26th, and 42nd Divisions] in the line thus freeing French divisions for use as battle reserves. This is the best use to be made of them all agree. They will be in action but not as a corps as they have not had corps experience except in association with French divisions and under French Corps Commanders. Both British and French people calm but serious. British have control of air but enemy is still able to use air service effectively. Baker.

LC, Baker Papers, folder: Personal Correspondence, Woodrow Wilson, January–February 1918, microfilm reel 5; see also Link (ed.), *The Papers of Woodrow Wilson*, vol. 47: *March 13–May 12, 1918*, p. 166.

Secretary of War Baker, then in Paris, to President Wilson.

For the President.

Had decided to postpone visit to Italian front. Next few days are critical with regard to the German offensive. I will go to General Pershing's headquarters at Chaumont as my being at either Paris or Versailles might suggest my having political rather than purely military object here. Will report military developments to you from Chaumont. General Foch has been chosen Supreme Commander [March 26 at Doullens Conference], acting under Mr. Clemenceau. General Pershing will visit him tomorrow and arrange to cooperate fully. This arrangement is everywhere regarded as most happy and will probably mean a Supreme Commander for the rest of the war. Baker.

LC, Baker Papers, folder: Personal Correspondence, Woodrow Wilson, January–February 1918, microfilm reel 5; see also Link (ed.), *The Papers of Woodrow Wilson*, vol. 47: *March 13–May 12, 1918*, pp. 160–61.

Sims, Commander, U.S. Naval Forces Operating in European Waters, London, to Operations, Navy Department (OpNav), in reply to Operations, Navy Department (OpNav), to Sims, March 12, cable 3775.

Cable 5635.
Very Secret
5635 Your 3775. The Ministry of Shipping have been anxious to utilize Brest for *Olympic, Aquitania,* and *Mauretania*. Admiralty officials opposed use of harbor owing exposed anchorage and lack of port facilities. Ministry sent two representatives in February to inspect harbor. These men interviewed pilots and shipping men and reported against use of the port for large ships for following reasons:

"(a) Bad holding ground.
(b) Lack of port facilities.
(c) Liability of much delay in disembarking and coaling owing to bad weather and exposed condition.
(d) No repair facilities.
(e) Fresh water supply insufficient.

Additional equipment required 30 coal barges, six winch barges, two tugs and necessary coaling gear, derricks, chutes, etc. Also necessary skilled coolies and collier service from England and tank steamer."

Admiral Wilson reports as follows: "It will be necessary to supply nine mooring anchors 18,000 lbs., and 495 fathoms 3½- to 4-inch chain in fifteen fathom shots.

There is no shore storage equipment or labor available at Brest for coaling this vessel. Coal must be carried afloat and there will be required a minimum of twenty lighters each 200 tons with ground tackle, a collier service and 600 laborers. Troops can be landed in 7 days. Present railroad facilities from Brest will handle only transports already assigned this port. Date at which U.S.S. *Leviathan* could be received depends on delivery foregoing equipment. She could be turned around in 10–14 days. I believe this scheme to be doubtful practicability and with difficulties which may or may not be balanced by accruing advantages."

It is very desirable to have *Leviathan* make monthly trip. Under present conditions there is no way of accomplishing this in Liverpool until Landing stage is dredged, the date of which is indefinite. Furthermore the additional British liners soon to be placed in trade to carry U.S. troops will further congest the port of Liverpool and delay dredging operations as well as coaling. I have sent Captain [Henry F.] Bryan to Brest to familiarize himself with harbor and select suitable position for planting mooring buoy. With present facilities however Brest will be unable to furnish the *Leviathan* more than a small amount of coal.

I suggest Department investigate possibility of utilizing present ballast and freshwater tanks for carrying 3000 tons oil and converting a few boilers to burn oil. By this means it may be possible to make round trip and take only limited amount of coal at Brest. Increased draft of ship would be no disadvantage. Brest Harbor could then be used and ship make round trip a month. Further report will be forwarded by mail and additional report submitted on return of Captain Bryan. [Reply—April 2, Benson to Sims, cable 4475.]

NARA, RG 45, ONRL, T829, Miscellaneous Records of the Navy Department, Miscellaneous Materials, 1–8/1918, Miscellaneous Material Print Files, World War, roll 411; see also Naval History and Heritage Command, website: Wars, Conflicts, and Operations, World War I, Documentary Histories, March 1918, Sims to OpNav, March 27, 1918; original document at NARA, RG 45, DNA, Entry 517B.

Editor's Note—Despite the problems he clearly states in this cable, Sims recommended that the U.S.S. *Leviathan* use Brest rather than Liverpool as its debarkation port. The shipment of American troops and their equipment through England and then across the Channel to France was originally intended to relieve congestion at the French Atlantic ports, but the policy presented problems for both the AEF and the British. For the AEF, it meant a delay for the troops reaching France to begin training. For the British, it placed additional burdens on the British ports, railroads, and shipping across the Channel. The British response to the German offensive of March 21 placed enormous new demands on these systems, which required a change in the American approach to transporting troops to France. The use of fast, large liners like the *Leviathan, Great Northern, Northern Pacific*, and others as troopships to Southampton, Brest, or Cherbourg rather than Liverpool would not only relieve some pressure on the British transportation system, but would also hasten the arrival of American troops in France. Except for those divisions specifically intended for training with the British, most of which were carried in British ships docking in Liverpool, Pershing and the AEF preferred American troops to debark at Brest, Cherbourg, or French Atlantic ports to facilitate their movement inland to training and billeting areas. The incessant demands of the Allies for large increases in the shipment of American infantry and machine-gun units in response to the German spring offenses were accommodated more easily with the large liners carrying much of the increased flow of troops to Brest while most cargo continued to go to the French Atlantic ports. A critical factor in adopting this approach was the growing success of Allied anti-submarine efforts against the German U-boats. (Pershing, *My Experiences in the World War*, vol. 1, p. 389; Sims, *The Victory at Sea*, pp. 355–58; Still, *Crisis at Sea*, p. 363.)

Senator Francis E. Warren, U.S. Senate, Washington, to Pershing.

Somehow, from somewhere, comes a letter addressed to me; and after breaking through a couple of seals, there develops your "Personal and Confidential" letters of February 25th and 27th. [*Ed.*—Neither letter was located in Pershing Papers or Warren Papers. See Editor's Note below.]

Before going further, I want to say that we are pretty blue and down-hearted here at the Capitol and elsewhere owing to the movements of the great battle of the last four or five days.

The newspapers seem to be trying to make it seem more of a victory or less of a defeat than what the facts, as they detail them, seem to warrant; but we are hoping for the best, and yet believe that there will be a turn in affairs soon.

You probably noticed in the service papers and in the daily mail that there were notices that General Wood would be called before the Senate Committee on Military Affairs on his return here. Well, on Monday morning the cards were out for a 10:30 meeting of the Committee—or, rather, the cards were sent out the night before. Promptly at 10:30, General Wood came in with his aide. I was already there, as were two or three other members of the Committee, and hand-shakings followed. The Chairman asked when it would be convenient for him to talk to the Committee. He replied, "Any time," so I asked, "Why not now?"

He then spoke up and said, "I have not yet paid my respects to the War Department; haven't called there, and think I had better go there first." The Chairman then asked him to name a time when he would be able to come, and he fixed 3:30 Monday afternoon.

He came before us at that hour and talked to the Committee and answered questions until about 5:30. No stenographer was present; no newspaper men; not anyone, in fact, except members of the Senate. Nearly all of the committeemen were present and ten or fifteen other Senators.

The General was invited to tell us what he saw, etc., over on the other side. He commenced by describing the trip, how the slowness of the convoys exposed the ships to the attacks of the U-boats, and said it added 30% to the risk by reason of the ships being so much longer open as targets for the U-boats, and besides this, with our faster boats, transports if properly armed and with fast-sailing convoys could to a far greater extent avoid or overpower submarine warfare.

He then spoke of the British soldiers and was quite elaborate in his praise of the British Army, the Generals and all, and spoke incidentally and modestly about seeing this, that, and the other celebrity. I think he said he stayed with French, former commander-in-chief. He spoke of interviews with Robinson [Robertson] and, I think, Haig.

A great many questions were asked him, of course, which he answered freely, as is his wont; and while protecting the English all right, as he did later the French, he scored the Administration and its handling of war matters here on this side, taking up what we have become painfully cognizant of, of late—the shortage of our shipping facilities, the greater shortage of air service, of our big guns, etc. He was very vicious in his attack against the Ordnance Department, and declared that the British

Enfield rifle, as they had used it, was far better for the kind of fighting over there than the Springfield rifle or the new modernized Enfield; that we might have had millions of the first-named and all our troops armed with them as well as all the Lewis machine guns we needed, had not our War Department and especially the Ordnance branch so completely fallen down; that the British had found the Lewis gun to be absolutely satisfactory, etc.

He spoke of the French soldiers, I thought, in rather warmer terms than of the English, but all of them he praised as to their good condition, discipline, and ability. He did not mention the American troops at all until pretty late, say within the last fifteen minutes of his talk, when he was asked whether he had visited our American forces and what he had to say about them. He said yes, he had seen them; not many of them; that he had visited one division; that they were splendid soldiers, of course not as hardened as were the old soldiers of the allies; as that our Army was constituted, of course, of State guards, National Army, and Regular Army—with most of the regiments of Regulars split into three parts and recruited up to full capacity which made the division still more acute; and that of course, practically speaking, our Army was mostly new recruits who should have the best of drill here and over there; and that everything had been wrong on this side, as they hadn't had their rifles and machine guns, etc.

Naturally, the questions fired at him took in the whole gamut of equipment, time, etc. He mentioned your name only once, and that was in relation to something which the Secretary of War had said here—that General Pershing and General Wood had both agreed to something in relation to equipment which, as a matter of fact, neither he nor Pershing had agreed to. Nobody asked him anything concerning Pershing or anything very pointed about the troops. I assume perhaps my presence may have had something to do with that. But to give the General credit, he really did not say a word in belittlement of anything connected with our forces over on the other side. He told how they were located, how many there were, etc.

There was another Senate Military Committee meeting called for 10:30 Tuesday morning, and when I appeared there I was told it was for the consideration of routine matters, and I therefore went to a subcommittee meeting on a big appropriation bill. A little before 12 o'clock I moved up again to the Military Affairs room, and found they had adjourned. General Wood was in the room with his aide. I asked him if he had been testifying further and he said no; that when he came the Committee had already adjourned, and that he wanted to see Senator Thomas of Colorado, who at the time was making a speech on the Floor. Now, referring to your letter of 27th ult.: I do not feel any too well acquainted with either Martin Egan or Griscom, though I have seen much more of Griscom and really have a good deal more confidence in him and as to his being just the right man, than I have in Egan. I have not heard from the party at the State Department who sent the cables regarding the proper man for you, except that, three or four days after the cables were sent, the party sending them said he had not heard from you although he had suggested a reply. He assumed it was because you were away from your headquarters with the Secretary of War and others, probably. I suggested yesterday to the Chairman of the Committee,

Chamberlain, that as General Bell had also returned with Wood and had made a somewhat similar trip, and as both had been at times Chief of Staff, both had gone from captain to brigadier (Wood stopping for a few days as colonel of volunteers), and as Bell was a West Pointer, had been in fights and had commanded troops, while Wood had had education as a medical man and had been up through that ladder, I thought it might be well to hear from Bell. Chamberlain said, "All right; we'll get him." I am not at all certain that he will. I have understood that Bell is here in the city, the same as Wood. The papers have mentioned that both would be subjected to the examination as to physical fitness, etc.

With much love to you, and the hope that you are well.

Editor's Note—Senator Warren's opening comment about a "Personal and Confidential" package contained Pershing's letters of February 25 and 27, 1918, is not the first indication of special correspondence between the two men, which commenced with these letters. In a February 4 letter Pershing wrote to Warren, "As to letters, if you wish to send me a confidential letter and you know of no one to send it by, I would suggest, that you might have it put, in the Embassy bag at the State Department and send it in care of our Ambassador, who would then have it delivered to me in person. I have little confidence in the mails, and shall not risk sending anything to you in the open mail which might possibly fall into unfriendly hands." Pershing hereafter usually used an Army courier or officer whom he trusted who was going to Washington to carry his letters to Warren and suggested that Warren do likewise. A number of such letters would have followed thereafter, none of which have yet been located in Pershing's papers and are considered to have been destroyed at the time. I contacted the Western Historical Collection at the University of Wyoming, which holds Warren's papers, and they were unable to locate such letters in the Senator's papers.

LC, Pershing Papers, folder: Senator F. E. Warren (1918), box 394.

Pershing to TAG, War Department, in part in reply to TAG, War Department, to Pershing, cables A-896-R, March 10, A-912-R, March 13; in addition to Pershing to TAG, War Department, cable P-673-S, March 3.

Cable P-789-S.

2. For Felton. Cable DGT 70. With reference to paragraph 1. Your cablegram 896 understood.

2A. With reference to paragraph 2, same cable [A-896-R]. Your mileage figures are safe. We expect largely to increase them. French are furnishing us much less than our car requirements and consequently situation is grave. Remedy lies in sending our new cars at rate of 1,500 per month and in hurrying locomotive and car repair men with tools and equipment covered by paragraph E, cablegram 673. [*Ed.*—In its reply on April 2, cable A-1022-R-1, the War Department told Atterbury it understood and "will continue to use mileage figures referred to in making future estimates."]

2R. With reference to paragraph 2, your cablegram 912. Owing to lack of tools our car erecting output is limited to approximately 500 monthly. We can arrange with Middletown Car Company for erection of approximately 500 to 750 cars monthly. This would make our present capacity 1,000 to 1,250 cars monthly. If you can hasten to us within next month all tools required for 35th Engineers, the combined output of our erecting shop and Middletown Car Company should be gradually increased to from 2,000 to 2,400 cars monthly by July 1st. We are now doing the best we can with no tools or equipment and are turning out cars bolted up instead of riveted, thus requiring their later return to shop. With this knowledge before you cable when we may expect tools for 35th Engineers also rate of shipment of cars and proportion of various types so we may prepare in advance for distribution of work between our shop and Middletown Car Company. [In addition—April 13, P-907-S-2A.]

NARA, RG 120, M930, Main Series, AEF to War Department, roll 2.

Pershing to TAG, War Department, in part in reply to TAG, War Department, to Pershing, cable A-914-R, March 14.

Cable P-790-S.
   1. For Chief of Staff. 1A. [*Ed.*—This paragraph replied to cable A-914-R-3 and listed a number of officers recommended for promotion.]
   2. For Chief Signal Officer. What are your plans if any for providing Liberty motors to England, France and Italy? Italians want to know how many of their original 3,000 they can expect to get and when. In view of revised schedule of production appreciate statement showing what you are planning to set aside for each ally by months. [Reply—April 4, A-1039-R-1, 1A]

NARA, RG 120, M930, Main Series, AEF to War Department, roll 2.

Pershing to TAG, War Department, in reply to TAG, War Department to Pershing, cable A-956-R, March 21.

Cable P-793-S.
For Chief of Staff.
   Reference paragraph 6, cablegram 956. Agree with your views as to your necessity for officers to build up General Staff. But further emphasis fact that there are few such officers here that are not on important General Staff duty from which they cannot possibly be spared as already reported. There are of course a number of young officers under instruction but they are too inexperienced for our work. My requests on War Department in the past for personnel for General Staff work have been only partially complied with as you know and do not equal number of officers you have

asked for. Your attention is invited to seriousness of developments that are now taking place on battle front and the increasing demands for trained staff officers here and demands for staff officers for corps, for First Army and for Army artillery. Secretary of War is of opinion that selected staff officers should first be sent over here for a period of training so that we should not be left shorthanded. In view of above, if you still think it wise at this time to carry out plan you propose shall do the best possible to start plan and after selecting officers shall have them at headquarters for a few days instruction and if time permits will send to the front for short time all those who have not had that experience, as I consider this of prime importance. But must urge that you start over at once an equal number of capable officers at least to replace the field officers as these officers will be of little value until they have served here 3 or 4 months.

NARA, RG 120, M930, Main Series, AEF to War Department, roll 2.

Editor's Note—During Secretary Baker's visit to Chaumont on March 17–21, Pershing took the opportunity to speak with him on a number of pressing issues, one of which was the proposed exchange of General Staff Officers with the War Department. He explained in his memoirs:

> I brought to the attention of the Secretary our serious handicap due to an insufficient number of general staff officers and urged that more should be sent over in view of the approaching German offensive. We discussed the exchange between general staff officers at home and abroad, which had been suggested by the Chief of Staff in order that he might have more officers at home familiar with our difficulties in France. The idea would have been carried out later, but events of such importance followed one after another that our officers could not be spared and the principle never found regular application. (Pershing, *My Experiences in the World War*, vol. 1, p. 350.)

TAG, War Department, to Pershing, in part in reply to Pershing to TAG, War Department, cable P-699-S.

Cable A-993-R.
    1. Attention Air Service. 1A. With reference to your 699, paragraph 6. Aircraft Board requests full information by letter as to present status and activity of Paris Committee and your views as to desirability of continuing same as committee of army personnel exclusively.

NARA, RG 120, M930, War Department to AEF, roll 11.

Editor's Note—The future of the Joint Army and Navy Aircraft Committee became a matter of discussion in April when on April 7 Cone informed Adm. Sims that the committee should be continued in some form. However, on April 11 Foulois sent a lengthy and detailed memo to the Chief of Staff, AEF, recommending that the committee be transitioned into an Army-only organization. Despite Foulois's lengthy and detailed memo, the GHQ, AEF, had taken no action on it by the time that Brig. Gen. Mason M. Patrick replaced Foulois as Chief, Air Service, AEF, on May 24, 1918. Indeed, no further action on this memo or the committee was apparently ever taken at all during the remainder of the war. As Maj. Foster Crampton, the Secretary of the Committee, wrote in the introduction to the "History of the Joint Army and Navy Aircraft Committee":

> So far as I have been able to ascertain, the formal status of the Joint Army and Navy Aircraft Committee is today what it was on the date of its first and last formal meeting, February 9th, 1918. It has virtually been supplanted or has transformed itself into the American Section of the Interallied Aviation Committee.

Crampton's history and the key documents on the Joint Army and Navy Aircraft Committee are at NARA, RG 120, M990, Gorrell History of the U.S. Army Air Service, American Expeditionary Forces, "History of Joint Army and Navy Aircraft Committee," in Series A, vol. 2: Histories of the Bolling Mechanics, the Joint Army and Navy Aircraft Committee, the Interallied Aviation Committee, and Reports on the Establishment of Air Service Headquarters Overseas, roll 1.

TAG, War Department, to Pershing, in part in reply to Pershing to TAG, War Department, cable P-693-S, March 7.

Cable A-995-R.
    4. With reference to paragraph 2C, your 693. Action on recommendations is suspended pending the receipt of all your recommendations for promotion to grades of general officers. Please expedite, as appointments are being held awaiting your recommendations. There are 10 vacancies for Major General and 17 for Brigadier General. March. [Reply—April 1, P-834-S-1D]

NARA, RG 120, M930, Main Series, War Department to AEF, roll 11.

March 28

Pershing's Personal Diary

    At Paris. Had conference with Secretary of War and General Bliss. The Secretary of War, his party, Colonel Collins and Major Palmer left by motor for Chaumont. I took Colonel Boyd and Captain de Marenches and left after luncheon for Clermont. We were somewhat delayed en route by numerous motor truck columns on the road. Incidentally they were not well closed up.

On arriving at Clermont we went to Headquarters of the 3d French Army where I talked to the General commanding the artillery of the army and he assured de Marenches that he was absolutely ignorant as to whether or not General Foch was in town. An old friend of de Marenches there on the Staff of the 3d Army also claimed absolute ignorance as to where General Foch was or had been, or whether he was expected in the town. The Chief of Staff, however, put beside our driver a man who guided us to the edge of the town and through a gate which let us into a lane made of double rows of trees on each side which led up to a house setting well back up on the hill among the trees.

While waiting to see General Foch, I went out and walked in the garden with Boyd. We admired a cherry tree which was in full bloom. There was no sound or sight that would make one realize that not more than 30 kilometers to the northeast the French were at that moment counterattacking furiously against Montdidier and to the east. This latter is the counterattack which I had said to the Secretary of War a few hours before should in all probability take place.

I soon went in to see M. Clemenceau, General Foch, General Pétain and M. Loucheur. They explained the situation to me. M. Clemenceau and General Pétain went out in the yard and I said to General Foch what I had come to say, namely that we are ready and anxious for a chance to do our part in the fight and that I stood ready for any suggestion as to how we might help.

General Foch was manifestly touched and insisted that we go at once to M. Clemenceau. We went into the garden and saw him and General Pétain standing in the gravel walk by a cedar tree. General Foch in his enthusiasm rushed across the lawn, holding me by the arm as he went. He told them quickly what I had to say. M. Clemenceau showed a buoyancy and gleam of fire in his face that made me realize why they call him "*Le tigre.*" General Pétain, who has a very unchangeable face and manner for a Frenchman, reflected the appreciation of his comrades. They were all manifestly touched. Under the inspiration of the moment, Boyd says, I out-Frenched the French; that my subconscious mind came into play and that I spoke to them in their own language with words which I could not have commanded ten minutes before or ten minutes afterward. What I said appears in the press account given below.

General Pershing Offers American Army for Great Battle
In the course of a meeting held yesterday at the front and attended by General Pétain, M. Clemenceau and M. Loucheur, General Pershing went up to General Foch and said to him:

"I have come to tell you that the American people would consider it a great honor for our troops to be engaged in the present battle; I ask you for this in their name and my own.

Infantry, artillery, aviation, all that we have, is yours; use it as you wish. More will come, in numbers equal to requirements.

I have come especially to tell you that the American people will be proud to take part in the greatest and finest battle of history."—Havas. N. Y. Herald (Paris), March 30, 1918.

General Foch stated that the details for carrying out this offer of mine could be arranged by myself and General Pétain who was charged with the "manoeuvre" of the troops. General Pétain spoke up and said that he and I were already in agreement as to the way the American troops should be employed. I suggested that the American people would feel proud to have our soldiers do their part in the battle and that my divisions would be eager to go. I suggested that the 1st Division might be ready now. General Pétain said we would see; that all the French divisions would take their turn on the battle front and that perhaps the 1st American Division might also go; that we would see.

I left a few minutes later with a distinct feeling of admiration and sympathy for the French generally and in particular for these men.

I left without learning definitely who is really in command. General Bliss had reported March 27th to the Secretary of War and to me in a note that at a meeting at Doullens on March 26th, at which were present Lord Milner, General Haig, M. Clemenceau, General Foch and General Pétain, it had been decided that Clemenceau should be Generalissimo, with Foch as C. of S. Some of the British Mission at French G.H.Q., however, stated that Foch was only playing a liaison role.

LC, Pershing Papers, Diary, May 7, 1917–September 1, 1918, box 4.

Pershing to General Ferdinand Foch, Chief of Staff, French General Staff, Ministry of War.

[later written down by Pershing]
"I have come to say to you that the American people would hold it a great honor for our troops were they engaged in the present battles. I ask it of you in my name and in that of the American people.

There is at this moment no other question than that of fighting. Infantry, Artillery, Aviation—all that we have—are yours to dispose of as you will. Others are coming who will be as numerous as may be necessary. I have come to say to you that the American people would be proud to be engaged in the greatest battle of history."

[Note] General Pershing's statement to Marshal Foch "in which, on March 28, 1918, he offered all available troops of the American Expeditionary Forces to the Marshal in the emergency arising from the successful German offensive of March 21, 1918."

Autograph signed copy.

LC, Pershing Papers, folder: Marshal Foch, 1917–1918, box 75.

March 21–March 31, 1918   77

Editor's Note—In his memoirs, Pershing wrote of his trip to Foch's headquarters at Clermont-sur-Oise on the afternoon of the 28th:

> As soon as I learned of the action of the Doullens Conference I decided that General Foch himself should know of our desire to do whatever we could to strengthen the Allies. Although I had offered our troops to Pétain on the 25th, it seemed to me that it might be better to make it emphatic by letting Foch know that I was prepared to put into the battle every man that we could muster. I had often thought of the possibility of a crisis that would require such a step and I wished Foch to know our attitude. . . .
>
> The place was quaintly picturesque and quiet, entirely undisturbed by the sound or sight of anything suggestive of war. Yet only a few miles to the northeast the French were at that moment making a furious counterattack against the enemy at Montdidier in one of the critical battles of the war. As were entered the house, Clemenceau, Foch, Pétain, and Loucheur were intently studying a map spread on the table. The situation was pointed out to me, showing that already the British had thirty divisions and the French seventeen against the German's seventy-eight. It seemed to be the opinion that the British Fifth Army was getting back on its feet and that the lines would hold for the time being.
>
> Intimating that I had come to see General Foch, the others withdrew into the yard, leaving us alone. I told him that the Americans were ready and anxious to do their part in this crisis, and that I was willing to send him any troops we had. I asked him for suggestions as to how we might help. He was evidently very much touched and in his enthusiasm took me by the arm and without hesitation rushed me out across the lawn to where the others stood and asked me to repeat what I had said to him. They, of course, showed keen interest, especially M. Clemenceau, as I told them what I had said to General Foch. Colonel Boyd, my aide, was kind enough to say that, under the inspiration of the moment, my French was spoken with a fluency that I could not have mustered ten minutes before or after. It appeared in the French papers the next morning, although I feel certain that it was written up in much better French than I actually used. . . .
>
> At the conclusion of my visit, the details of making use of our troops were left to be arranged with Pétain, who remarked that he and I had already discussed their employment. If the responsibility had been mine, I should not have hesitated at moment to put into battle any or all of our five divisions then in France. . . . As our divisions were more than twice as large as theirs, it amounted to almost immediate reinforcement of ten divisions. (Pershing, *My Experiences in the World War*, vol. 1, pp. 364–65.)

Marshal Foch, in his own *Memoirs*, commented thusly on Pershing's visit and offer:

A few hours before this meeting [with Clemenceau, Foch, Pétain, and Loucheur], General Pershing had come to see me and, with magnificent spirit, spontaneously offered to throw immediately into battle all the trained American divisions. General Bliss, the American representative on the Versailles Committee, animated by a similar sentiment, exclaimed to me: "We have come over here to get ourselves killed; if you want to use us, what are you waiting for?" (Foch, *Memoirs*, p. 270.)

Col. George S. Simonds, CS, II Corps, AEF, with the BEF, to G-3, GHQ, AEF. Forwarded to Pershing.

1. The following sources and methods of obtaining information are being used.

I have at Château Bryas a British Liaison Officer and through him and personally am keeping in close touch with the headquarters of the First Army and the headquarters of the First Corps which are close by. At British G.H.Q., Major Quekemeyer and I are in close touch with the Operations and Intelligence people. Today or tomorrow I shall send an officer or go myself to the headquarters of the Third Army. Am also able to pick up a good deal of information from British aviators who are in this vicinity and from officers of the First Army who are in communication with the Third Army on their right. Colonel Bacon is rendering assistance at G.H.Q. in keeping us in touch with the bulletins that come into his office and the views of the various officers of the British Staff.

General Considerations

2. Since the beginning of the fight a week ago today weather conditions have favored the Bosche [Boche]. For the first three days of the fight a heavy fog came in from the sea which extended as far south as Amiens. This prevented efficient work by the British Air Service, which throughout has maintained its superiority over the German. But the fog and mist from time to time lifted sufficiently to permit the necessary registration by the German artillery. There has been no rain, the ground is very dry and everything favors movement. The nights have been generally clear with moonlight enough to permit troop movements and great activity of the Bosche planes.

Aviation

3. The air fight has from the beginning taken a peculiar course. For several days prior to the beginning of the fight and all during the fight the British have maintained constant superiority in the daytime, but just at the time most favorable to the Bosche the weather conditions were unfavorable for observation. For three or four days prior to the beginning of the fight a great number of German planes were brought down, but since that time the reports have not been so convincing. However, the British have undoubtedly accomplished great things with their planes. Day before yesterday it is reported that the air was full of them and that all day they took an active part in the fight, using machine guns and bombs on the advancing

Germans in mass formations and on their trains and supply columns. The aviators with whom I have talked are full of fight and maintain that they have it on the Bosche. One man, however, gave it as his opinion that although he believed they did considerable damage to the enemy, he did not believe they really slowed up their advance very much. At night it has been quite different. The air has been full of German planes and they have bombarded trains, railroads, airdromes, ammunition dumps and trains of lorries moving troops on the road. It cannot be said with what effect, but it has at least caused much consternation, inconvenience, and considerably delayed movement.

Artillery

4. There seems to have been in this battle far less artillery preparation in the different phases than has characterized the other big battles of this trench warfare. The first day the preparation was most violent and effective but short. Since that time it has been much less. The remark is frequently heard that it is a machine gun and infantry fight, although upon looking into it this is seen to be an exaggeration, for it now appears that the Germans have succeeded all along the line in getting forward and getting into the fight considerable numbers of their 77's and 5.9's. Although the British have suffered heavy losses in artillery, reports from the Third Army indicate that some of it well paid for itself in the rear-guard actions before being captured. It is reported that they have succeeded in getting out considerable numbers of their larger calibres.

Machine Guns

5. All are agreed as to the effective use of machine guns on both sides. The Germans have gotten them forward in large numbers with their infantry and are using them with their infantry. The British have exacted their greatest losses by the use of machine gun fire. It has been the real feature of their really great work. They have attached to each of their batteries one or two Lewis guns and by the efficient use of these few guns with small infantry supports they have time and again held up German infantry until the guns could be pulled out and gotten away. An American surgeon in charge of one of our hospitals up here, who has had considerable experience on this front, tells me that a larger proportion than ever before of wounds has been caused by machine gun fire.

Infantry

6. The Infantry on both sides is doing wonderful work. There is a note of admiration prevalent in all I have heard from British officers of the way the German infantry comes on regardless of loss. On the other hand, the British infantry with machine guns is time and again holding out until they are killed or captured.

Cavalry

7. There is as yet no definite evidence of the use of any large bodies of German cavalry. There have been instances of cavalry fights, but always of small bodies. A rumor was prevalent yesterday that a British cavalry division had been defeated, in the angle between the Ancre and the Somme by a larger German cavalry force

driving toward Amiens. Upon further investigation I believe this to be nothing but the rear-guard action of some dismounted British cavalry which had been sent in here and was simply swept back by the ordinary German infantry advance. I am still looking for German cavalry and believe that if they ever clearly break through that some will appear.

Tanks

8. There is no evidence of the use of German tanks. The Germans claim to have captured numbers of British tanks, but this is not understood as it was not expected that these would be used on the defensive, and I do not know that considerable numbers of machine guns from the tanks have been sent up into the line with the infantry.

Wire Cutting

9. There is as yet no satisfactory explanation of how the Germans have cut the wire. The first day it is believed that it was done in the usual way. Since then there are reports to the effect that special squads prepared for this work have whenever necessary pushed out ahead of the advancing troops, gone in and cut the wire, and taken the extermination that is coming to them. There have been rumors that advancing troops have thrown themselves upon it and others marched over them. It is believed that a possible partial explanation of it is that after the first day the Germans passed through areas which have not been properly wired for defense. Of course, no admission has been received from anyone that this is the case, but my observations are that the defensive measures have not been as complete as they might.

Gas

10. In the first bombardment there was a large amount of gas and a great many gas casualties. Since then we have heard almost nothing of it.

Casualties

11. There are meager reports as to casualties on either side. My impressions are that the British have lost heavily in killed, wounded and prisoners. Last Tuesday the Germans claimed 45,000, but since then have heard of no claims. It must be many more. The German losses have undoubtedly been enormous. The British have lost probably in excess of 1,000 guns.

Situation

12. In spite of their heavy losses and rapid retreat, it is evident that the British have maintained their lines unbroken. Their rear-guard actions have been well carried out and all gaps have been speedily plugged up. It appeared for a time that a bad situation existed in the Fifth Army, and although our reports from there are meagre, the French must have gotten in there in time to prevent a complete break through. It is very evident that the Bosche's main idea is to separate the French from the British, although out here in the First Army there is much concern for fear that he will make a sudden smash further to the north. It is understood that the French are concentrating a large force to the West of Amiens and when the proper time comes they will hit the Bosche a telling blow. The speedy assistance given by the French to the Fifth

Army and the determined resistance and well-conducted rear-guard actions of the Third Army have prevented any disastrous break and things in general look much better this morning than yesterday.

Morale

13. The morale of the British officer and man is just what would be expected of the British soldier. They do not have the attitude of a year ago, but they do show that they are full of fight. One gains the impression that they are out to stay with it to the last regardless of cost and that they expect to be able to hold the German until the French arrive, and that ultimately he will be stopped as have all of the offensives on the Western Front heretofore. There is no air of gloom and in watching the soldiers moving to the front they seem to be taking it as all in a day's work. Those coming back tell how many Bosche they killed and say that he can keep it up. Their spirit is admirable.

As to the Bosche, if there has been any deterioration of his morale, it is not evident. They have apparently gone into this thing in high spirit and determination to put it through.

1. Following items of interest have been received from the Intelligence Officer, First Army:

(a) A verification of previous report on the valuable service rendered by machine guns with batteries of artillery in the retreat.
(b) He gave an account of two batteries of the 34th Division which covering the retreat of their divisions served their guns till the last and with the assistance of some small parties of infantry and four Lewis guns held up the German advance for a sufficient period to get away a large number of other guns and considerable materiel. The men finally got away with their breech blocks and with the infantry rear guard made their getaway.
(c) No tanks have been in use by either. The tanks reported to have been captured by the Germans were probably in an area from which the British did not have time to get them out.
(d) Criticisms from numerous British infantry officers as to the effect this trench warfare has had on their men:

"They get out into the open and act as though they were suddenly thrust naked into the public view and didn't know what to do with themselves, as if something were radically wrong and that there ought to be another trench somewhere for them to get into."

My impression was not that there was any doubt about their willingness and ability to fight but that too much trench warfare had had its effect.

2. There was a German demonstration this morning and later a more determined attack against the First Army front near Oppy, but the Germans were thrown back—probably a reconnaissance in force on their part to find out in what strength the British are holding their lines up there.

3. I don't know how general this is in France but in the towns around here all the 15, 16 and 17 year old boys are being mobilized—I understand to be sent for work at munition factories.

4. It is reported here that General Foch has been placed in command of all armies in France.

5. Enclosed herewith is a map giving the present line.

Quekemeyer is sending his usual Order of Battle and Changes to Intelligence.

Montreuil, 5:30 p.m.

Latest reports indicate a bad situation around Montdidier belying somewhat the optimism in the previous paragraph on the "Situation." However reports all day indicate that in the past 36 hours the British have given but little ground, have given up none north of the Somme, and in some cases have gained back some lost.

The hopeful feature about the British end of it is that they are so full of fight after such a retreat.

As to the situation near Montdidier, everything is obscure.

The line on the enclosed map [*Ed.*—not included] shows it as near as can be determined.

Following has been obtained on good authority:

"That the Chief of Operations here telephoned to General Montgomery (Gen. Montgomery has been the Chief of Staff to Gen. Rawlinson but is now apparently with General Foch) at Gen. Foch's Headquarters that the Fifth Army (British) was hard pressed and that Gen. Gough, commanding Fifth Army had reported that he probably would not be able to keep the enemy from reaching Amiens unless he was reinforced by some French divisions. General Montgomery wired back that he did not anticipate that any French Divisions could be sent to the east of Amiens for four days."

(signed) G. S. Simonds

I prefer that it not be known that I have this.

G.S.S.

March 30, 1918.

Chief of Staff:

I desire that such extracts be made from this memorandum as will be applicable to our divisions preparing to undertake serious business. It should be gone over very carefully with that end in view.

J.J.P.

NARA, RG 120, Office of the Commander-in-Chief, Office of the Secretary of the General Staff, Entry 22, Reports of the Commander-in-Chief, folder 34: GHQ War Diary, January 24–April 28, 1918, diary entry March 30, 1918, 294-g, pp. 262–66, box 4; *USAWW*, vol. 3, pp. 119–22; for more on the American divisions with the British, see Mitchell A. Yockelson, *Borrowed Soldiers: Americans under British Command, 1918* (Norman: University of Oklahoma Press, 2008).

Conner, ACS, G-3 (Operations), GHQ, AEF, to CS.

1. It would appear that the question underlying the substance of this telegram [See March 23, A-957-R] relates to the responsibility for disembarking and caring for our troops.

2. A letter from Colonel Simonds dated March 1, 1918 [see Vol. 3, March 1], to the Chief of Staff, reads in part as follows:

I have maintained that the entire question of the transportation of these divisions from the United States until arrival in their areas is assumed to be handled by the British. . . .There is a clear understanding between us that for any troops landed at ports under British control, they retain all responsibility for getting them through the ports, and there is consequently no question to be settled in the use of Le Havre and Cherbourg.

3. These headquarters have always maintained that under the agreement made with the British, the British authorities are responsible for all questions connected with the physical transportation and disembarkation of these six divisions.

4. With reference to the control of these troops the following is quoted from a memorandum signed by the Chief of Staff, British General Headquarters, dated March 12, 1918 [not reproduced]:

The American corps headquarters . . . and will be responsible for the general control and supervision of all the American divisions, and will be authorized to visit and inspect these divisions irrespective of the army to which they are attached.

5. The above quotations and the statement made above as to the attitude of these headquarters indicates that the understanding of these headquarters has always been that the British were responsible for all the physical features connected with the transportation of these six divisions, that with the exception of the artillery to be trained separately, the British were to train the troops in accordance with a program to be prepared at these headquarters, and were to exercise tactical command over these troops when in the British lines. It is further evident that these headquarters retained general control and supervision over the divisions in question.

6. Assistant Chief of Staff, G-5, agrees with the above as representing the attitude of these headquarters and the agreement with the British.

7. It is believed that G-1 has arranged certain details concerning transportation, etc., and it is suggested that G-1 be consulted before final action.

USAWW, vol. 3, pp. 74–75.

Bliss, Versailles, to Secretary of War Newton D. Baker, then in France, in reply to Baker to Bliss, March 24.

I have just received your letter of March 24th written at Mr. Page's house in London and which came by the Ambassadorial pouch from London to our embassy here and was delivered to me from there this afternoon.

I knew perfectly well that you would find it most difficult to go to London at the time that I suggested your visit in my first telegram to you from there. I sent that telegram with great reluctance and told Lord Derby and Lord Milner so, they being the ones who first urgently requested me to communicate with you. I knew that you had an itinerary marked out in order that you might get an orderly view of the general situation in your mind; and as I knew that you hoped to visit London some time before your departure for America, my own opinion was that it would be better for you to meet those Gentlemen and discuss the difficulties of the transportation question after you had seen for yourself what the situation was.

Immediately on my return to Paris on March 17th, I sent a telegram to General Pershing at Chaumont [see Vol. 3, March 17, telegram No. 21], having been informed that you would arrive there with him about 1 P.M. of that day. In that telegram I stated more fully the reason why Lord Derby and others were so anxious to see you in London. You will probably remember the telegram and that I stated that the view of officials of the War Cabinet in London, based on a report recently made by their railway transportation expert (General Nash) to the effect that we would probably have to suspend bringing over our troops and supplies until we had equipped ourselves with rolling stock and completed certain railway construction; that I referred to M. Clemenceau's declaration at the Session of the Supreme War Council to the effect that he would guarantee the movement of all American troops and supplies from the ports of debarkation to the American Front; that, in view of this, I had protested to General Wilson against any hasty judgment in the matter, and that he had told me that the British Government was sending over General Nash at the same time with myself in order that he and General Atterbury and M. Claveille could personally inspect our transportation facilities and decide, yes or no, whether we would have to give precedence for a time to transportation of railway material; and that I suggested that your visit to London might well be deferred for a week, at the end of which time General Nash and the others would make their final report and you could be fully advised of their view as to the situation.

Today, an hour after I said good-by to you at General Pershing's house, General Nash came to Versailles and asked me whether M. Claveille had made a personal report to you of the situation. I told him that he had not done so while I was with you, nor had I heard you mention it. General Nash expressed some anxiety, saying that M. Claveille had promised him that immediately on your return to Paris from London he would advise you as to the situation. He told me that he and Gen. Atterbury and M. Claveille had personally inspected the situation and had arrived at a conclusion which they had communicated to General Pershing; and, he added, that he was authorised to say that General Pershing was in accord with their view. This view, as he briefly stated it to me, was to the effect that if we did not promptly get over sufficient rolling stock it might be found very difficult to properly supply the American troops now here. But, he said, he had learned from Gen. Atterbury that our cargo transport service as now of a capacity that, beginning with the month of April, the Americans could bring over railway cars at a certain rate per day (I think he said 65) and locomotives at a certain rate per month. If we could do that, he said, he did not think there should be any difficulty in continuing our present program of transporting troops to the capacity of our troop transports.

I told him that I was sorry that he had not informed me of this earlier in order that I could have communicated it to you; but, as his committee was not appointed by the Supreme War Council nor was it directed to report to us, I had no right to expect it.

In case you return to Paris even for a few hours in the near future, I hope very much you will arrange to have a talk with General Nash, provided he has not at that time returned to London. I am telegraphing him at this moment asking him to give me a brief statement of his view as to the situation which I can transmit to you at Chaumont, in case you should have no opportunity to meet him.

[*Ed.*—In the following paragraphs, Bliss answered Baker's questions about the General Reserve and actions of the SWC's Executive War Board.]
[Reply—April 29, Baker to Bliss]

LC, Bliss papers, folder: General Correspondence—Bliss to Newton Diehl Baker, December 1917–May 1918, box 250.

Bliss, Chief, American Section, and Permanent Military Representative, SWC, for the Secretary of War Newton D. Baker, to TAG, War Department, for President Wilson. Copy to General Pershing by Col. Fox Conner, G-3, GHQ, AEF.

Cable 67-S.

1. The Secretary of War this morning [Baker then in France] directed this telegram be sent direct to the President with copy for Secretary of State and Secretary of War and Acting Chief of Staff. Following Joint Note 18 of the Permanent Military Representatives with the Supreme War Council is transmitted for the action of the President. Following the text of the Joint Note are the recommendations of the Secretary of War dictated by him this morning.

2. The following Joint Note 18 was adopted by the Permanent Military Representatives March 27, 1918

"(1) In paragraph 4 of Joint Note 12 dated 12th [21] January, 1918, the Military Representatives agreed as follows:

After the most careful and searching enquiry they were agreed on the point that the security of France could also be assured. But in view of the strength of the attack which the enemy is able to develop on this front, an attack which, in the opinion of the Military Representatives could reach a strength of 96 Divisions (excluding reinforcements . . .); they feel compelled to add that France will be safe during 1918 only under certain conditions, namely:

(a) That the strength of the British and French troops in France are continuously kept up to their present total strength, and that they receive the expected reinforcements of not less than two American Divisions per month."

(2) The battle which is developing at the present moment in France and which can extend to the other theatres of operations may very quickly place the Allied Armies in a serious situation from the point of view of effectives, and the Military Representatives are from this moment of opinion that the above detailed conditions (a) can no longer be maintained and they consider as a general proposition that the new situation requires new decisions.

The Military Representatives are of opinion that it is highly desirable that the American Government should assist the Allied Armies as soon as possible by permitting, in principle, the temporary service of American units in Allied Army Corps and Divisions, such reinforcements must however be obtained from other units than those American Divisions which are now operating with the French, and the units so temporarily employed must eventually be returned to the American Army.

(3) The Military Representatives are of opinion that, from the present time, in execution of the foregoing and until otherwise directed by the Supreme War Council, only American infantry and machine gun units, organized as that Government may decide, be brought to France, and that all agreements and conventions hitherto made in conflict with this decision be modified accordingly."

3. The following is the action recommended by the Secretary of War.

"To the President:

The foregoing resolutions were considered by General Bliss, General Pershing and me. Paragraph 3 proposes a change in the order of shipment of American troops to France and necessarily postpones the organization and training of complete American divisions as parts of an independent American army. This ought to be conceded only in view of the present critical situation and continued only as long as that situation necessarily demands it. The question of replacements will continue to embarrass the British and French governments, and efforts to satisfy that need by retaining American units assigned to them must be anticipated, but we must keep in mind the formation of an American army, while, at the same time, we must not seem to sacrifice joint efficiency at a critical moment to that object. Therefore I recommend that you express your approval of the joint note in the following sense:

"The purpose of the American Government is to render the fullest cooperation and aid and therefore the recommendation of the military representatives with regard to the preferential transportation of American infantry and machine gun units in the present emergency is approved. Such units when transported will be under the direction of the Commander-in-Chief of the American Expeditionary Forces and will be assigned for training and use by him in his discretion. He will use these and all other military forces of the United States under his command in such manner as to render the greatest military assistance, keeping in mind always the determination of this government to have its various forces collected, as speedily as their training and the military situation will permit, into an independent American army, acting in concert with the Armies of Great Britain and France and all arrangements made by him for their temporary training and service will be made with that end in view. Baker"

[Reply—March 29, cable 39-R, and March 30, cable 40-R]

LC, Pershing Papers, folder: Supreme War Council, February-April 1918, box 193; NARA, RG 120, M923, American Section, SWC, file 315: Cablegrams Sent to War Department, Jan. 22, 1918–Dec 10, 1919, roll 18; see also online "WW I Supreme War Council, American records," at https://www.fold3.com; Link (ed.), *The Papers of Woodrow Wilson*, vol. 47: *March 13–May 12, 1918*, pp. 175–76.

Secretary of War Newton D. Baker, then in Paris, via Department of State, to President Wilson.

Cable.

A joint resolution of the advisors of the Supreme War Council will reach you today with my recommendation appended [see above, Bliss for Baker to TAG, War Department, for Wilson]. It seems important for us not to insist upon carrying out an ideal program in a moment when all agree that the greatest need here is infantry and the use of shipping for other personnel decreases the number of infantry possible to be transported. Nevertheless I agree with General Pershing that we should keep constantly before the British and French that all our plans are ultimately in that direction. This for two reasons: (1) we do not want either nation to rely upon us for replacements, and (2) we want the Germans to know that we are augmenting the present Allied forces and not merely making good [their] losses. Moreover, (American!) sentiment must be satisfied. After full consideration I believe you should approve the joint resolution in the manner suggested in my note attached to the copy sent you by General Bliss. General Pershing will then be free to make necessary stipulations with French and British commanders for the use and ultimate return of these units and General Pershing's judgment of the military situation will determine when they can safely be reincorporated in American forces. Baker.

U.S. Department of State, *Papers Relating to the Foreign Relations of the United States, 1918. Supplement 1: The World War*, Vol. 1, pp. 177–78; see also Link (ed.), *The Papers of Woodrow Wilson*, vol. 47: *March 13–May 12, 1918*, p. 174.

Pershing to TAG, War Department.

Cable P-801-S. Confidential.
For the Chief of Staff.

1. Have just returned from French Field Headquarters and conferred with Foch and Pétain. Find situation improved but Germans still have many fresh divisions. British line north of Albert holding well and British Fifth Army appears to be getting a foothold across the Somme east of Corbie for protection of Amiens. French have launched a counterattack against Montdidier today. French Third Army is counterattacking northward between that point and Lassigny and have made considerable

progress this afternoon. Success of the counteroffensive very important. French are in fine spirits and both armies seem confident.

2. Have made all our resources available and our divisions will be used if and when needed. 26th and 42d are to relieve French divisions in Lorraine. 1st Division is considered fit for any service and will probably be taken at early date if battle continues.

NARA, RG 120, M930. Confidential Series, AEF to War Department, roll 7.

*татом

TAG, War Department, to Pershing.

Cable A-998-R. Confidential.
Please cable at once actual number of combat planes, advance training planes and training planes now in the hands of American Expeditionary Forces. March. [Reply—March 29, P-818-S-3B]

NARA, RG 120, M930, Confidential Series, roll 18.

TAG, War Department, to Pershing, in part in reply to Pershing to TAG, War Department, cable P-759-S, March 21.

Cable A-1001-R.
3. With reference to paragraph 1, your 759. Steps will be taken to carry into effect your recommendations relative to Tuscania.
4. Chief of Naval Operations has suggested the use of slower vessels in coal and channel service. Shipping Control Committee of opinion that lake and other steamers suitable for this service upon their arrival abroad should release larger vessels now in that service which are capable of transatlantic trade. Navy suggests that slow vessels like Winnebago and Hattie Luckenbach be used for service abroad. Shipping Control Committee however do not recommend this as they consider these vessels too large to be used economically in such service. Your definite recommendations desired relative to vessels now in coal trade which in your opinion can be released upon assignment of lake tonnage or other suitable tonnage for that service. [Reply—April 20, P-970-S-1]
March.

NARA, RG 120, M930, Main Series, War Department to AEF, roll 12.

March 29

Pershing's Personal Diary

Left Paris at 7:15 a. m. for Chaumont. Took Mrs. Boyd and Ann; dropping them at Fontainebleau. Colonel Boyd and I made a record trip by the way of Sens; actual running time between my quarters in Paris and my quarters in Chaumont 4 hours 12 minutes. Worked in office in the afternoon. General Ragueneau brought a proposition from General Pétain to let the 1st Division go into the battle. I accepted this proposition and gave orders for the Division to be withdrawn from the front so as to prepare it for the fight. I afterward told the Secretary of War of this decision, and he heartily approved, stating that this move is one that would be enthusiastically approved by the people at home. Mr. Paul Cravath dined at the house and did much talking about the unity of command. It seems that he has done some talking in England on this subject and that he favors the war being directed on the Western front by a committee composed of Generals Pétain, Haig and myself.

LC, Pershing Papers, Diary, May 7, 1917–September 1, 1918, box 4.

De Barescut, Chief of Staff, Armies of the East, to French Military Mission with the American Army, Chaumont, for CINC, AEF.

No. 5483/M

By mutual agreement of the Commanders-in-Chief, it has been decided that the American 1st Division shall participate in battle.
Therefore:
(1) Prepare for the earliest possible relief of the 1st Division by the American 26th Division.
(2) Provide for the movement by rail of the 1st Division.

USAWW, vol. 3, p. 485.

TAG, War Department, to American Section, SWC, Versailles, for Secretary of War Baker, reply to Bliss to TAG, War Department, cable 67-S, March 28.

Cable 39-R.
Reference Cablegram 67 signed Bliss. The action of the President is as follows:
"The President concurs in the Joint Note(s) of the Permanent Military Representatives of the Supreme War Council in the sense formulated in your Number 67 March 28th and wishes you to regard yourself authorized to decide questions of immediate cooperation or replacement."
March.

[Note at the bottom of the page: *"Forwarded to Secretary of War by Lt. Col. Poillon leaving Paris 8 p.m. train for Chaumont Mar 30, '18."*]

NARA, RG 120, M923, American Section, SWC, file 316: Cablegrams Received from the War Department, Jan. 23, 1918–Nov. 19, 1919, roll 18; see also online "WW I Supreme War Council, American records," at https://www.fold3.com.

Bliss, Chief, American Section, and Permanent Military Representative, SWC, Versailles, to Pershing.

Telegram No. 39.
For the Secretary of War. The following has been handed me by the Military Representative of Great Britain and is transmitted for the information of the Secretary of War and General Pershing:
"Secret. From the Prime Minister.
Subparagraph A. Please communicate to General Bliss that I have cabled to President Wilson asking him to approve of Foch exercising the same coordinating authority over the American Army as he is now exercising over the British and French. To send men over to France with the utmost possible speed to make good losses and to agree to arrangements made by General Pershing to their being brigaded as they become available with French and British Divisions for the duration of the crisis.
Subparagraph B. The Prime Minister thinks that before this fighting is over, every man may count, and he can see no other way of making splendid American material available in this crisis of the war."

NARA, RG 120, M923, American Section, SWC, file 317: Telegrams sent by the American Section, Jan. 21, 1918–Dec. 5, 1919, roll 19; see also online "WW I Supreme War Council, American records," at https://www.fold3.com.

Brig. Gen. Alfred E. Bradley, Chief Surgeon, HQ, SOS, AEF, Tours, to Pershing.

Memorandum on the proposition of the General Staff to suspend work on portion of the authorized hospital construction.
1. There are at this time only 23,411 available beds; 19,409 in Base and Red Cross Military Hospitals and 9,002 in Camp Hospitals. There are included in the latter figure 1,592 beds in field and evacuation hospitals which should not be counted in bed capacity. The bed capacity of the Base Hospitals is only .063 of the strength of' command.

2. The Engineers estimate completion for June 30, 1918, on projects now under way is 68,237 beds or 8,763 beds less than the original estimate and is only 357 beds more than the reduced percentage is now proposed to adopt.

3. Under the proposed revision, i.e. 20% of beds for 40% of the strength of command as combatant and 6% of beds for of the command as line of' line of communications troops 67,880 beds will be required by June 30, and 98,253 beds by September 30th. So far not a single Base Hospital under construction by the Engineers has been completed and it seems improbable owing to the difficulties of labor and with their best effort that they will complete 41 hospitals in 3 months by June 30th and 71 hospitals in 5 months October l, 1918.

4. Of the 91,479 beds authorized, 79,870 are authorized under contract, of which 60,870 are under way and 17,000 not yet started. Only 11,609 beds are under construction by army labor, 1,000 of this number by mixed labor and contract.

These hospitals are in the Zone of the Advance where they are very much needed and where the work has progressed to a stage where it would be unwise to stop construction. The number of men employed is comparatively small.

5. With the prospect of more active work at the front we will need more beds than are now in sight for margin of available beds is being reduced, and it would be difficult to select any project which could be discontinued.

Our allies need all the bed capacity they can obtain and we should not call on them for aid.

6. In reference to the offer of the Service de Santé of 10,238 beds for American hospitalization, it must be remembered that these hospitals are in units from 250 to 1200 beds in inconvenient places and that these figures include the beds necessary for our personnel which materially reduces the number.

7. I would therefore urge that all of the projects under way, the most of which are contract work, be carried on as it seems probable that the beds will be urgently needed before they can be completed. [In addition—March 30, Bradley to Pershing]

LC, Pershing Papers, folder: Hospital Units—Hospitalization, box 97.

Pershing to TAG, War Department, in part in reply to TAG, War Department, to Pershing, cable A-947-R, March 19.

Cable P-808-S.

1. For Chief Signal Officer. 1C. Our agreement of December 5 to put 15,000 men in England must be kept. After that squadrons may come to France direct or via England depending on tonnage available. Some should go to England because we can withdraw squadrons only in excess of 15,000 to be maintained there. The first to arrive in England should be fairly trained now. Very desirable to draw trained men from there. [Reply—April 5, A-1045-R]

NARA, RG 120, M930, Main Series, AEF to War Department, roll 2.

Pershing to TAG, War Department, in part in reply to TAG, War Department, to Pershing, cable A-892-R, March 9.

Cable P-812-S.
    2. For Chief of Ordnance. With reference to paragraphs 1A, B, C, and D, your cablegram 892. Bomb requirements as stated in paragraph 6, our cablegram 661 [not reproduced], were based on the following squadrons: Day bombing squadrons April 1, May 4, June 9, July 10 extra 1, August 12 extra 3, September 14 extra 5, October 16 extra 7, November 18 extra 9, December 20 extra 11; night bombing squadrons September 3, October 6, November 9, December 12. It is not at all certain that this program will be met, but it is the only basis at present available for bomb estimates. [Reply—April 15, A-1106-R-2A]

NARA, RG 120, M930, Main Series, AEF to War Department, roll 2.

Pershing for Baker to TAG, War Department.

Cable P-813-S. Confidential.
For the President
    Reports from all sources indicate generally better and improving situation. Both French and British lines are holding and French reserves are arriving in battle area in numbers which seem to assure arrest of German forward movement. Fighting continues heavy but German communique of last night much less confident in tone. Amiens less in danger than it was 2 days ago. General Pershing is with General Foch today. On his return here I will send you real situation with regard to Supreme Commander [see March 30, P-820-S]. No announcement has been permitted on the subject and some confusion exists as to just what has been done. Both French and British armies are fighting splendidly and together have suffered less loss than the Germans. British losses much heavier so far than French on account of greater number engaged. 30 British divisions and 17 French have been engaged against 78 German divisions. As French have many fresh divisions now moving in better situation is expected constantly. Baker [Chaumont].

NARA, RG 120, M930, Confidential Series, AEF to War Department, roll 7.

Pershing to TAG, War Department, in part in reply to TAG, War Department, to Pershing, cables A-468-R, December 2, A-522-R, December 16, A-797-R, February 17, and A-913-R, March 14, and A-998-R, March 28.

Cable P-818-S.
    1. For Chief of Ordnance. 1B. With reference to paragraph 1G, your cablegram 913. According to present information the French cannot arm our troops with

155-m.m. G.P.F. materiel as fast as required. Exact figures cannot be given now. Possibility of shortage of materiel for at least 4 regiments during the next 3 months.

1C. With reference to paragraph 1G, your cablegram 913, shows later deliveries of 4.7-inch guns than specified in paragraph 1E, your cablegram 797 and later deliveries of 6-inch guns than specified in paragraph 3, your cablegram 522, and paragraph 1, your cablegram 468. [Reply—April 15, A-1105-R-5E]

1D. Request that you give your personal attention to the earlier delivery of these guns and ammunition to France to supply deficiency which may be expected, and that manufacture of 4.7-inch and especially 155-m.m. G.P.F. guns be pushed at utmost speed to supply guns for replacements as well as for armament. [Reply—April 27, A-1189-R-1A]

3. For Chief of Staff. With reference to recent Press dispatches showing that sentences of 4 men for sleeping on post which were sent to the War Department for action of the President under the law have been made the subject of petitions for clemency by large number of persons, recommend that in future similar cases be given no publicity. Whole effect here is subversive of discipline and demoralizing.

3A. Secretary of War [then in France] has today prescribed rule for handling publicity of matters pertaining to troops and operations. He rules that all matters pertaining to events, persons, policies or operations here will only be officially given out from these headquarters. Similar matters effecting forces at home will be given out from the War Department.

3B. With reference to your 998. Actual number of planes as follows: combat planes 78, advance training planes 996, training planes 236.

NARA, RG 120, M930, Main Series, AEF to War Department, roll 2.

TAG, War Department, to Pershing.

Cable A-1004-R.

Transmit following message to General Foch: "May I not convey to you my sincere congratulations on your new authority? Such unity of command is a most hopeful augury of ultimate success. We are following with profound interest the bold and brilliant action of your forces. Woodrow Wilson".
March.
[Handwritten note: *"Transmitted by CinC thru French Mission."*]
[*Ed.*—The copy in Pershing's papers has the following note written in longhand:
Dear Mr. Secretary:
This message rather indicates the President's view of the new arrangement. I have just received it. J.J.P.]

NARA, RG 120, M930, Main Series, War Department to AEF, roll 12; LC, Pershing Papers, folder: Newton D. Baker, January–June 1918, box 20.

March 30

Pershing's Personal Diary

Worked in office all day. Saw General [Roy] Hoffman, commanding the 93d Division; also Colonel Moore of the Inspector General's Department, Mrs. Lars Anderson and Mr. Paul Cravath. Saw Messrs. B. L. James, New York Times, and Don Martin of the New York Herald; also General Hines. The Secretary and party and Lieutenant Colonel Mott left at 8 p. m. in my private car for Italy.

LC, Pershing Papers, Diary, May 7, 1917–September 1, 1918, box 4.

Lt. Col. L. Storr, Secretary, British Section, SWC, to Gen. Tasker H. Bliss, American Military Representative, SWC, Versailles.

Very Secret (Typewritten by a General Staff Officer).

I have received instructions through the Secretary British War Cabinet to communicate the following to you and to ask that it may also be communicated to Secretary Baker and General Pershing.

"Mr. Lloyd George is dispatching a cable based on the following considerations to the President of the United States [*Ed.*—No. 1828, March 30 (not reproduced)]. Apart from exigencies of the present great battle he regards manpower as the essential problem confronting the Allies. He is of the opinion that upon the ability of the Allies to refit and maintain armies in time to counter a second blow, which the enemy will certainly deliver, in view of their pronounced intention to break our line, the whole military future will depend. Up to the present, that is after one week's fighting, the British losses amount to 120,000 men. We can barely make this good by sending out all our trained and partially trained reserves in England, and this will involve the complete exhaustion of those reserves. Immediate steps are being taken by the British Government to raise from 400,000 and 500,000 men by taking boys of 18, by raising the military age to 50, by drastic combing out and similar measures. But it will be at least another 4 months before these men will be sufficiently trained for employment in France. Consequently in May, June and July—the very months when we may expect the Germans to make their next big effort—there will be a dangerous gap. During these months, therefore, the deficiency must be made good by American troops, if we are to make certain of holding the enemy then, and of frustrating his intention of dealing the decisive blow of the war on the western front. In no other way can the Allies hope to make their position secure.

According to our calculations British shipping can embark in the United States in April 60,000 men. The carrying capacity of the American fleet is estimated by Admiral Sims to be 52,000 troops a month. By using certain other ships which are also available the total of troops which can be transported from the United States is 120,000 in April next, and it is possible that this total could be increased to some extent in the ensuing months.

Mr. Lloyd George is therefore asking President Wilson to authorize the despatch from the United States, from now until the end of July, of 120,000 American infantry. He is urging that, as the American regiments arrive in France, their battalions should be brigaded with British or French divisions on the same basis as that planned for the infantry of the six divisions, in regard to which the Military Representatives resolved on March 27th that the American troops to be sent over should consist of infantry and machine gun units only. In the case of the above 120,000 troops, just as was agreed in that of the 6 divisions, battalions as soon as trained can be reformed in regiments and sent to General Pershing as he may require them.

Mr. Lloyd George is aware that President Wilson will place great reliance upon the advice tendered by Mr. Baker, General Pershing and General Bliss, and he is anxious therefore that they should be informed of the proposal he is making and Mr. Lloyd George hopes that his proposal will meet with their support. Mr. Lloyd can see no other way in which, in this vital crisis of the war, hundreds of thousands of trained or partially trained men now in the United States can be made available to meet that crisis. Every single trained man may count before the struggle is ended. The Germans can replenish and refit her armies from her existing reserves. Moreover, German newspapers report that already some 250,000 Austrian troops are on the Western front, Germany will have a chance of delivering the knock-out blow whereby her leaders hope to win the war, unless the Allies can refit their armies as quickly as the enemy can. Now, when everything hangs in the balance, our necessary reinforcements can only come from America, and it seems possible to make these reinforcements available, only in the manner suggested above. The responsibility therefore of making the Allied cause secure rests upon the United States of America."

[Handwritten: *"To General John J. Pershing, Comd'g Am. Ex. Force in France. Copy goes at same time to the Secretary of War. Tasker H. Bliss, Am. Per. Mil. Rep. S.W.C."*]

LC, Pershing Papers, folder: Supreme War Council, February–April 1918, box 193.

Editor's Note—Lord Reading's reply (cable No. 1360 below) to Lloyd George's initial cable No. 1828 (March 30) would soon become a major problem for Pershing and led to significant misunderstandings between Great Britain and the United States. For that reason, it is reproduced here:

No. 1360. Very Secret.
Following for Prime Minister:

I had an interview with the President today. He began by referring to the two requests in your cablegram No. 1793. On the 28th of March I cabled a report to you of my interview with him and stated that he would give an answer after he had received the full message from Secretary Baker. The President informed me that he had now received it and he had yesterday instructed Secretary Baker to cooperate with you in respect to (1) sending American troops to France at the utmost speed and (2) the method of making American forces now in France available. The President said that Secretary Baker had proposed the same. The President had cabled to Secretary Baker to act in accordance with the proposals submitted by him to the President.

I delivered a paraphrase of your cablegram No. 1828 to the President with the exception of the part marked confidential. He requested me to inform you that he would issue instructions to the proper authorities to act in accordance with your request and desired me to assure you that, in every respect in which it is possible for him, he would cooperate with the Allies in meeting the necessities of the situation. Accordingly he will direct that 120,000 infantry be embarked for transport to Europe in each of the months of April, May, June and July, making a total of 480,000 always provided the ships and necessary equipment would be available and of which he had not the details. In principle he approves the employment of the troops in the manner desired but leaves details to his military chiefs.

This decision is in accordance with the willingness of the President repeatedly expressed to me to send more men to Europe provided proper and sufficient transportation and terminal facilities could be given. He said that the difficulty hitherto had been that although the United States Government had been ready to fulfil the programme arranged at the Paris conference [*Ed.*—He probably is referring to the SWC meeting January 30–February 2] it could not be carried out owing to insufficient accommodation facilities at the French ports. With regard to the use of the American forces the President, as I informed you early in February, had given the fullest powers to General Pershing to dispose of the American troops in an emergency or otherwise as he thought best. The President is ready to send even a larger number of troops than requested if only sufficient transport and other facilities can be found. He desires me to inform you that it is only the limitations in shipping and port and railway capacity in Europe which prevents him sending a larger number of troops than requested by you. (Link (ed.), *The Papers of Woodrow Wilson*, vol. 47: March 13–May 12, 1918, pp. 213–14.)

Lloyd George expressed great pleasure in learning of President Wilson's apparent agreement with the requests in his previous cables of March 28 (No. 1793) and March 29 (No. 1828), especially of the British demand for 120,000 men in infantry and machine gun units monthly from April through July. Confusion would soon reign as to exactly what Wilson had actually agreed to. That caused a serious problem for Pershing, who knew nothing of the President's decisions until at the Beauvais Conference on April 3, when Lloyd George confronted him with Lord Reading's cables reporting his meetings with Wilson (see April 3). The most important of these cables was Reading's No. 1360 (above), which Lloyd George so brazenly used to upstage Pershing at Beauvais. For Bliss's comments on this unfortunate incident, see April 3, Editor's Note following Lloyd George, Memorandum, April 3, 1918. (See Beauvais Conference minutes, "Cooperation of the United States of America.")

In his *War Memoirs*, Lloyd George wrote:

A very satisfactory reply was received from President Wilson to this request. Lord Reading cabled me on March 31st [received in London] to inform me that the President had substantially agreed to my proposals; that he would issue directions for 120,000 infantry a month to be embarked during April, May, June and July, if the necessary shipping and equipment were available; and that only the limitations of shipping and port facilities hindered him from sending them faster. He also approved in principle the method of employment of troops suggested by me, but left the details of their disposal and use to be settled by General Pershing. (David Lloyd George, *War Memoirs*, vol. 2, p. 1818.)

For Pershing this was merely a continuation of his ongoing differences and skirmishes with Lloyd George and the British. However, it also marked the beginning of another major dispute, this one between Pershing and Peyton March, which extended far beyond the war itself and well into the 1930s in a "battle of the books." When Pershing's memoirs appeared in 1931, March was livid with the account and determined to correct the story. Among other things, he believed that Pershing gravely misrepresented his actions and those of the War Department in their dealings with Lord Reading and the British and French over the question of shipping 120,000 American infantry and machine gun units per month and that correction was required. In his *The Nation at War* (1932), he vigorously defended his own actions and attacked Pershing. Naturally, Pershing counterattacked. Rather than directly rebutting March, which he deemed would only bring more attention to March and his book, he did so through Harbord. His former Chief of Staff and close colleague did the heavy lifting, but in a less personal and low-key manner in his *The American Army in France* (1936). For more on this continuing drama, see March, *The Nation at War*, pp. 79–94; Harbord, *The American Army in France*, pp. 256–62 and fn 2, pp. 110–11; Smythe, *Pershing*, pp. 293–95; Coffman, *The Hilt of the Sword*, pp. 236–40.

Bradley, Chief Surgeon, Hq. SOS, AEF, Tours, to Pershing, in addition to Bradley to Pershing, March 29, 1918.

Since writing to you yesterday the study of the hospitalization situation has been completed and I herewith transmit for your information the result of our study. I believe that this is correct as far as it can be made so at this time. In view of the present situation and probability that long before the hospitals which are authorized are available our needs will be more urgent, and probably much greater than at present. I strongly urge that all the projects now under way be permitted to go on to completion.

Dates of Completion Phase of Troop Arrivals	1st—April 1st	2nd—June 30th	3rd—Sept. 30th
Number of Troops	304,000	282,000	261,000
Beds Provided Present Base and Camp Hospitals	26,864		
Beds Necessary 20% or 40% and 6% of 60%		67,860	98,253
Construction Engineers Estimates of Completion		68,237	119, 237
Base Hospitals Arriving	18 here now	30	29
Evacuation Hospitals Arriving	3	9	12
Original Estimate Ordinary Accumulative Regardless of Evac. Hosps.	30,400	76,000	119,900

[Handwritten:] AEB [Alfred E. Bradley] 3/30/18.
[Ed.—Table reoriented to facilitate use.]

LC, Pershing Papers, folder: Hospital Units—Hospitalization, box 97.

Col. T. Bentley Mott, GHQ, AEF Representative with Italian GHQ, then at Chaumont, to CINC, GHQ, AEF.

Under this date, Colonel T. Bentley Mott, U.S. Army, submits the following report to the Chief of Staff, A. E. F., regarding the Italian situation.

Italian forces: 49 organized divisions, also 80 battalions armed and instructed, in the depots.

French forces: 6 divisions; 2 en route now for France, leaving 4 in Italy. British, 5 divisions, 2 en route for France, leaving 3 in Italy. Franco-British, 7 divisions.

Total Ally—56.

Enemy forces: 46½ divisions, all Austrian.

The instruction of the Italian army has been progressing since January, due to Franco-British example and influence, rather than to the independent action of the Commando Supreme. The latter have shown themselves jealous of any attempts of French and British to improve the instruction of the Italian army and it was only by arranging for an exchange, on terms of entire equality, that it was obtained to have Italian officers sent to the schools of the French and British armies in Italy.

The weak point of the Italian army is its ignorance of the most modern methods of fighting, especially artillery work and liaison. There are plenty of men of capacity in all grades in the army but they have not been taught the newest methods. What prevents this is alleged Italian pride and susceptibilities.

The private soldier is brave, self-sacrificing, most patient under privation. He is badly led, especially at the top. The morale of the army is constantly improving and is now good. The disaster in October was more due—at least in its extent—to faulty military dispositions than to any treason or propaganda. The latter causes, freely alleged at first, are now seen to be small as compared with the military vices existing and faults committed. This is the view of the British, French and American observers and of most Italian officers. Just after the disaster, socialists, clericals, civilians in the rear, generals at the front—each found in the other the causes of the defeat. The matter is now better understood.

The Commander-in-Chief at the time was Gen. Cadorna. He was relieved and at first sent to represent Italy at Versailles. He is now replaced there by Gen. Giardino. Gen. Diaz took the place of Commander-in-Chief with Gen. Badoglio as assistant. The British and French have no great confidence in Gen. Diaz as a general, and his pride and distance do not make for good cooperation.

The Italians do not like the French; they want their divisions in Italy, indeed claim it as a right, but show no gratitude. They have none of this resentment toward the British but even to them show little appreciation of the aid they sent.

The Italians have persistently exaggerated the number both of German and Austrian divisions on their front and have constantly asserted that a great offensive was preparing there. Yesterday, March 29, the Chief of Staff of the French army in Italy asserted that he saw no reason to expect an Austrian offensive in the near future—there were no signs of it. The Austrians are only too glad to be let alone.

The British and French Generals-in-Chief and their officers work in perfect harmony in Italy. Both have striven earnestly and tactfully to help the Italians, especially in the matter of instruction and in correcting vital defects in locating lines and occupying them. The lower Italian officers willingly accept and sought this cooperation but Gen. Diaz has refused it as far as he could.

The morale of the interior is better now than it was before the disaster of October and the army and the interior act and react on each other in a healthy way.

NARA, RG 120, Office of the Commander-in-Chief, Office of the Secretary of the General Staff, Entry 22, Reports of the Commander-in-Chief, folder 34: GHQ War Diary, January 24–April 28, 1918, diary entry March 30, 1918, 294-b, pp. 259–60, box 4; copy *USAWW*, vol. 2, pp. 265–66.

Secretary of War Baker, Chaumont, to Pershing.

As I am about to leave your headquarters, and may not return here on this visit abroad, I want to thank you for the hospitality of my reception and the helpfulness with which you have made it easy for me to see the American Expeditionary Forces and its undertakings, speedily and comprehensively & particularly want to renew and emphasize my expressions of approval and confidence in the broad planning and rigorous execution which has characterized the worn back of the troops, upon which their supply must rest, and the very remarkable schools and system of instruction which are rapidly giving our men and officers the finishing touches necessary to qualify them to bear their part in the great struggle worthily. My whole visit has been surrounded by considerable attentions from the members of your splendid staff, and take back to the United States a sense of inspiration and satisfaction which, if I can adequately convey it, will bring to you and your co-laborers the grateful approval of the whole country.

I venture to enclose a word of encouragement which, if opportunity arises and you approve, might be published to our army here four or five days after I have sailed for home.

[Enclosure]
The Secretary of War
Washington

After a thorough inspection of the American Expeditionary Force I am returning to the United States, with fresh enthusiasm, to speed the transportation of the remainder of the great Army of which you are the vanguard. What I have seen here gives the comfortable assurance that plans for the effectiveness of our fighting forces and for the comfort and welfare of the men have been broadly made and vigorously executed. Our schools and systems of instruction are adding to the general soldier training the specialized knowledge which has developed among our French and British associates during the four years of heroic action which they have displayed from the beginning of the war.

Fortunately the relations between our soldiers and those of the British and French are uniformly cordial and happy and the welcome of the civil population of France has been met by our soldiers with chivalrous appreciation and return.

We are building a great army to vindicate a great cause and the spirit which you are showing, the courage, the resourcefulness and the zeal for the performance of duty both as soldiers and as men is not only promising of military success, but is worthy of the traditions of America and of the Allied Armies with which we are associated. Press on!

Editor's Note—This enclosure to Baker's letter to Pershing was subsequently published to the AEF as General Orders No. 57, April 7, 1918, with the following addendum from Brig. Gen. James G. Harbord, the AEF's Chief of Staff, and republished in Volume 1 of Pershing's *My Experiences in the World War*:

"In adding his own high appreciation of the splendid spirit of our army, the Commander-in-Chief wishes to impress upon officers and men of all ranks a keen sense of the serious obligations which rest upon them, while at the same time giving forth fresh assurance of his complete confidence in their loyalty, their courage, and their sincere devotion to duty.

2. This order will be read to each company and separate detachment at first assembly after the receipt of the order."

LC, Pershing Papers, folder: Newton D. Baker, January–June 1918, box 20; see also Pershing, *My Experiences in the World War*, vol. 1, pp. 385–86.

Pershing to The Adjutant General, War Department, Washington, in addition to Pershing to TAG, War Department, cable P-714-S, March 11.

[No cable number given]
1. The American Expeditionary Forces now have available 21,340 beds. Upon arrival in France of personnel to operate same, the 28,000 beds will be available as stated in par. 1, subparagraph G, Cable AGWAR, March 11, 1918 [P-714-S-1G].
2. According to present program, based on all projects underway, we shall have available within the next months 118,930 beds. An appreciable number of these will be available in the very near future.
3. It is impossible at present to express a trustworthy opinion as to the probable date upon which battle casualties in appreciable numbers may be expected to begin arriving in the United States. It will probably be a matter of several months.
4. It is not the intention that any sick or wounded shall be sent to the United States except such as give no indication of ever being able to return to the firing line.

NARA, RG 120, Office of the Commander-in-Chief, Office of the Secretary of the General Staff, Entry 22, Reports of the Commander-in-Chief, folder 34: GHQ War Diary, January 24–April 28, 1918, diary entry March 30, 1918, 294-d, p. 261, box 4.

Senator Francis E. Warren, U.S. Senate, Washington, to Pershing, in addition to Warren to Pershing, March 27.

Additional to my personal letter of March 27th:
We had General Bell before the Committee yesterday (Friday) morning. We did not have a full attendance of the Committee. In fact, we seldom do. But there was a bevy of newspaper men, anywhere from eight to a dozen at different times, at the opposite end of the table, and an official committee reporter as well as some shorthand-writing newspaper men. And so the General dictated his statement, very slowly and ceremoniously, something like one would do with a $60.00-a-month stenographer in the presence of the mighty, interjecting as he went along, "paragraph," "period," "comma," etc., and often asking to have the questions re-stated, etc. What he said was good. To begin with, he gave some description of what he saw over there. He was asked what about the older officers retained in the service by our allies—those beyond the age for retirement. He handled the subject very well; said that the

trenches must be visited frequently and continuously by commanders of brigades; occasionally—and oftener if necessary—by commanders of divisions; seldom if ever by corps commanders (lieutenant generals), as they were more territorial commanders; not necessarily by commander-in-chief, as he had everything to provide and everybody and everything to provide for. He said it was always better to have younger men or not-too-old men for commanders-in-chief, if they could get men of sufficient ability, experience, and excellence, such as, for instance, General Pershing; that he thought there was a possibility of retiring or at least keeping in this country general officers who might well act as division commanders in France because they would not be required to endure the hardships of the brigade commanders and those below that rank; and that often or always the experience and judgment of such officers were valuable.

He said that he himself had been examined the day before to see whether he was fitted for active service, and he very much hoped that he might pass as he was anxious to be at the front and would like to return immediately to France, taking his command (what was left of it) with him, etc.

He was asked about the present situation, the battle now going on, etc., and some other pretty close questions, which he parried, saying he would rather talk to us in executive session about those things.

Generally speaking, the Committee listened to his slow dictation very patiently, and asked but few questions. Thomas of Colorado rebelled at one point, saying that what he supposed they would hear was something about matters of to-day and the late battles; that he was rather busy elsewhere, etc.

Later, after a little recess, Bell returned to the Committee—or the part of it which came back to hear him—and a stenographer and the committee clerk were the only others present. He then talked more rapidly and openly, and finally, when something was very close, he asked the stenographer to lift his pen, and, presto change! he struck out at a gait faster than General Wood had talked at the earlier time (General Wood's remarks were all in executive session, with no shorthand reporter or newspaper men present). He then went over the situation as he viewed it now, from the point of what the newspapers were saying, and added here and there quite a good deal of information as to what the British and French were thinking about; responded promptly as to the outfitting you had; said the troops were all in fine condition; that this falling back from the front to lines in the rear did not necessarily mean defeat; in fact, so far it augured toward final victory or at least one of those times where we fight and run in order to live and fight again. He was warm in his protestations that we are bound to win in the long run; said we must hurry men and supplies and equipment abroad; expressed himself as eager for the fray; and, in fact, acquitted himself very well, and splendidly well in all the latter part of his remarks. Senators present expressed themselves afterwards as noting the wonderful change in the free-handed talk that he gave us which was not to be reported.

When he had finished, I invited him and his aide, Captain Crutcher (or something like that), to go to luncheon. He agreed, but said he wanted to do some telephoning. In the meantime I was called away on an important matter (a roll-call to vote upon universal military training as an amendment to a draft bill, the amendment being finally defeated); and when I returned to the Committee room ten minutes later, he had left, and they pointed to a distant door and I caught sight of him flying out at high speed into the open.

Previously, before I left the Committee Room, he had remarked to me Pershing wanted him to return to France and that he was tremendously anxious to do so; that he expected soon to hear his fate.

When I overtook him, he begged to be excused from luncheon, but upon my insistence he stayed. He immediately informed me that he had just had a telephone message from the War Department to the effect that he had passed, and he now hoped to be ordered to France; that he was perfectly willing to admit that Pershing should have been made the commander-in-chief on account of advantage in age; that he hoped to be in the thick of things and to distinguish himself; and then, in low-down confidence, he said he wanted finally to get retirement as a lieutenant general or more because he felt that he had more claim to a position like that than had many others who had gone before, like Bates, Chaffee, Young, et al. In other words, he uncovered himself as being full to the brim of ambition. He said he was well and weighed 40 lbs. less than formerly.

I am enclosing some clippings—first, one from a Star of a few days ago, which states the great interest felt in the coming examination of General Wood. About the middle of the week, some of the Senators had 'phone messages from New York, from George Perkins and others, expressing the fear that Wood was to be retired; what a shame it would be; that it must not happen; rebellion must be made against it, etc. Wood himself said nothing, when before the Committee, about his own examination; simply referred to older men as I indicated in my former letter.

Then last night's Star said he had been examined by the doctors named in the article. To-day we hear that he has passed all right; that the only Regular Army doctor on the board was Brigadier General William H. Arthur; that Wood objected to him and that some Medical Reserve Corps officer was put on in his place, leaving no Regular Army officer on the examining board.

It occurred to me yesterday that Mayo, one of the Mayo Brothers, had been a great builder of notoriety for their concern and was liable to be a participant in or believer in the notoriety emphatically worked up for General Wood; that the regular Roosevelt-Perkins-Boston Transcript-Senator Lodge-Ex-Senator Root (I think)-combinations have kicked up such a dusty; an ex-editor of the Transcript having been engaged in writing occasional articles for a Washington paper, that it was likely Wood would be passed and Bell had been passed as a sort of prelude. They would rather pass two men, or perhaps any number who might be in bad condition, provided they could work in the well-advertised General Wood, who always has about him a publicity bureau and to whom the papers generally seem to be always open.

This evening's Star, just out, has an editorial and also an article, which I enclose.

Of course, as matters turned and we were rushed into war, the President before that making a strong argument in his first message against any additional army or preparation, added to Wood's constant cry for the last few years against unpreparedness, Wood is put a great ways to the good in the press, etc. He was at times extravagant and even impudent in some of his excessive demands for preparation, as it seemed <u>then</u>. But all of that has since become under rather than over what we should have done, in the light of what has happened.

I think the President knows (I am told that he does) how disloyal and abusive Wood has been concerning Wilson and the Administration. I feel quite sure that Baker knows, because he has spoken to me of Wood's insubordination. Auchincloss knew, and I & others have told him a little about it; and of course that means that Colonel House knew it, and I should think it would mean that the President must know of his recent back-hand work over on the other side.

But we shall see what we shall see. The President has the name of being careful to return tit for tat and to be really vindictive against his accusers. Of course we know what he did to Roosevelt, and I suppose we shall find out in due season what he proposes to do with Wood.

By the way, Bell in confidence to me expressed himself rather bitterly toward Wood. Of course I had almost nothing to say in reply.

Perhaps the President may ease himself by "passing the buck" up to you.

LC, Pershing Papers, folder: Senator F. E. Warren (1918), box 394.

TAG, War Department, to American Section, SWC, Versailles, reply to Bliss to TAG, War Department, cable 67-S, March 28, in addition to TAG, War Department, to American Section, SWC, cable 39-R, March 29.

Cable 40-R. Confidential.

With reference to your 67, the recommendations of Secretary of War to President in your paragraph 3 that preferential transportation be given to American infantry and machine gun units in present emergency understood and will be followed. The following general statement is submitted for your information:

Division Headquarters, Headquarters Troop, 4 Camp Infirmaries, Infantry and Machine Gun Units, including personnel of their Field Trains, of 3 divisions, will at once be given preferential transportation over other units of divisions. Motors and animal drawn vehicles of trains will not accompany troops but will follow when possible. This arrangement includes the 77th Division now embarking on British transportation, the 3rd and 5th Divisions on our own transportation; total 50,000 men. Equipment will be complete with exception of machine guns, automatic rifles and other articles of ordnance not available in this country but issued to troops upon arrival in France. After above are embarked, certain field artillery, services of the rear, army and corps troops, which are already at ports, must be interpolated until infantry of other divisions can arrive at ports of embarkation. The infantry and machine gun units of 3 of these divisions will be ready to embark about the middle of April and the infantry and machine gun units of at least 3 more about May 1st.

In following this plan every effort will be made to carry out the shipping schedule of October 7th, 1917, as regards the completion of each division and phase as shipping space becomes available and as far as consistent with vested authority new instructions to give preferential transportation to infantry and machine gun units. Report promptly to General Pershing. [Reply—April 3, P-844-S]
March.
[Handwritten note: *"Repeated immediately after receipt to Gen. Pershing."*]

[*Ed.*—Bliss sent a copy of War Department Cable 40-R to Pershing in his Telegram No. 44, April 1.]

LC, Pershing Papers, folder: Supreme War Council, February–April 1918, box 193; NARA, RG 120, M923, American Section, SWC, file 316: Cablegrams Received from the War Department, Jan. 23, 1918–Nov. 19, 1919, roll 18; file 317: Telegrams sent by the American Section, Jan. 21, 1918–Dec. 5, 1919, roll 19; see also online "WW I Supreme War Council, American records," at https://www.fold3.com.

Pershing for Baker to TAG, War Department, in addition to Bliss, Chief, American Section, and Permanent Military Representative, SWC, for the Secretary of War Newton D. Baker to TAG, War Department, for President Wilson, March 28, cable 67-S.

Cable P-820-S. Confidential.
For the President.

I have just been shown a copy of a message from Lloyd George to you with regard to General Foch and American troops [see March 28, cable No. 1793]. The situation seems to be that Lloyd George is personally in favor of a Supreme Commander but fears British opinion will be the other way because such a Commander could sacrifice the Channel ports to the defense of Paris. The arrangement, therefore, is that General Foch is to be supreme enough to coordinate but without being called Supreme Commander. General Pershing will, of course, act under General Foch as Pétain and Haig have already agreed to do. I venture to suggest that in replying to that part of Lloyd George's message you might go further than he asks and say that we are willing to accept a general supreme command whenever the French and British are. Perhaps the relative smallness of our present force and our having no immediate defensive object in France would make it unwise for us to urge the point though the present events would seem to have demonstrated the need. The second part of Lloyd George's message is covered by joint note of Versailles conference about which I wired you 2 days ago [see March 28, Bliss for Baker to TAG, War Department, for

President Wilson]. General Pershing's prompt and fine action with regard to the use of our troops and facilities here in the emergency has won enthusiastic commendation from French and British. Our First Division will shortly be withdrawn from trenches and used in battle.
Baker. [Chaumont]

NARA, RG 120, M930, Confidential Series, AEF to War Department, roll 7.

Pershing to TAG, War Department, in addition to Pershing to TAG, War Department, cable P-508-S, January 17.

Cable P-823-S.
    3. For Director of Gas Service. 3A. Before beginning of present battle the enemy fired 150 to 200,000 shells of 475 [unidentified poison gas] on 4 successive nights. Practically all cases were lung and eye cases. Extremely low percentage of body burns, this percentage being only about 1 and 1/2. Reports are that some shells filled with 475 were exploded just above ground in same manner as shrapnel. No high explosives accompanied the gas. Either due to bursting gas shell above ground or the mixture with some other gas, or possibly to a better solvent, the enemy have gotten better vaporization of 475 which possibly accounts for the lack of body burns. Nearly every case showed more or less burning of the face under the mask. Men wore the masks to the point of physical exhaustion. The face under the mask then became moist and soft from trapped moisture and when the mask was removed the face was affected in the same way as any other moist tissue. Probably the majority of casualties was caused by too early removal of the mask. Hundreds of casualties might have been avoided if men had worn masks for 3 hours beginning at sun-up. The nights being cold, the gas remained on the ground in the liquid form, quickly volatilized with warm sun of morning. Woods, valleys, unprotected dugouts or dugouts contaminated from gassed men entering therein, were the greatest sources of casualties. Men on knolls high ground suffered less. Beginning of battle Germans used quantities of lethal gasses, coupled with lachrymators, along whole front forcing the troops to wear masks and reduce bodily vigor and fighting efficiency. The gassing was probably timed so that enemy could cross same area after the gas became too thin to affect troops but while defending troops were still suffering from wearing mask. These experiences indicate the tremendous value of comfort in a mask. It is believed that the coming mask must omit the mouthpiece and nose clip.
    4. For the Chief of Staff. 4A. Reference our cablegram 508, believe work of chaplains would be facilitated if they were not given military rank. I have personally held this view for a long time. Many of our principal ministers believe that their relations would be closer if they did not have military title and did not wear insignia. They should be given assimilated rank and pay. The above view is held by Bishop Brent, Bishop McCormick and many others whom I have consulted. Recommend that the

matter be given consideration in connection with bill now pending before Congress. [Reply—April 17, A-1120-R-3, see note for additional information.]

NARA, RG 120, M930, Main Series, AEF to War Department, roll 2.

TAG, War Department, to Pershing, in part in reply to Pershing to TAG, War Department, cable P-655-S, February 27.

Cable A-1009-R.
    2. Air Service. 2D. With reference to your 655, paragraph 2, urging production of Caproni parts for your assembly in France. Refer Aircraft Board via Department of State, number 3159, subject: Standardization on One Type Night Bomber Airplane [not located]. Had good manufacturer ready to take hold of Caproni as soon as sample and drawings were approved. Italy, however, has now withdrawn order for 1,000 sets of parts. Question: Do you want us to manufacture both Caproni and Handley Page parts? If so, give us your reasons and cable quantities wanted, output per day and whether we should supply equipment, material and personnel for assembly at Air Production Center Number 2 [Romorantin]. [Reply—April 19, P-964-S-4]

NARA, RG 120, M930, War Department to AEF, roll 12.

March 31

Pershing's Personal Diary

    Worked in quarters all day. Saw Bishop Brent; also had talk with Colonel Ardery [Edward D., Assistant to the Chief, Gas Service, AEF] on the subject of "Lifire". Sent him to Paris to see Mr. Garland.

LC, Pershing Papers, Diary, May 7, 1917–September 1, 1918, box 4.

Foch, Chief of Staff, General Staff, Ministry of War, to the Minister of War (Clemenceau).

General Headquarters,
General Staff
    Prompted solely by the demands of the present situation, I am submitting the attached memorandum to you.
    Would you be good enough to inform me as to your reaction to my recommendation.

Memorandum
Personal and Secret.

In order to gain the best results from the strategic combination on the various fronts as well as power in the present battle it seems necessary to supplement the decision adopted March 26 in the following respects:

1. It would be expedient to request the Italian Government to give its assent to this arrangement with a view to having the operations on the Italian front incorporated in the overall scheme of the contemplated strategic combinations and hence the movements of the troops between this front and the French-British front as well.

2. To complete, under this arrangement, the terms defining the function of General Foch: "To coordinate the action of the Allied armies on the western front. For the purpose of accomplishing this an arrangement will be reached by him with the Commanders-in- Chief who are invited to furnish him all necessary information."

By the following terms:

"He is instructed at the same time to direct the total operations in conformity with the views of the governments to apportion the offensive and defensive missions among the various fronts and make appropriate allotment of the necessary supplies to those fronts. He has the authority to inform the commanders in chief of the directives which shall result from these duties and to see to their execution. The commanders-in-chiefs will continue to direct the conduct of the operations on their various fronts."

3. It is of course understood that if the point of view set forth in paragraph 2 is accepted, it is the final draft of the British and French Governments that should be submitted to the Italian Government.

USAWW, vol. 2, p. 267; see also *Les armées françaises dans la Grande guerre, Tome 6, vol. 1, Annexes, vol. 2: Annexe No. 1225*, pp. 705–6.

Editor's Note—Within days of the Doullens Agreement, Foch realized that the strategic situation had changed and that his coordination of British and French forces to stem the German offensive would soon have to give way to full strategic planning for future operations. Hence, he sent the above memorandum to Clemenceau, the Minister of War, which was the first of his three pivotal notes of March 31 and April 1. In them, he advocated for a revised charter from the Allied leaders that would give him directive authority to issue orders on military planning and operations along the entire Western Front from the North Sea to the Adriatic. If this took place, it would add the Italian theater as well as the Belgian front to his oversight responsibilities. However, in Belgium and Italy the respective kings commanded their fighting forces. This raised difficult constitutional issues in both countries, which took many months to resolve. Nonetheless, the Supreme War Council held a lengthy discussion of this matter during the Abbeville meeting early in May. (See Foch, *Memoirs*, pp. 275–76; Maxime Weygand, *Mémoires: Idéal vécu* (Memoirs: Ideal Lived) (Paris: Flammarion, 1953), pp. 486–87; Greenhalgh, *Victory through Coalition*, pp. 198–99, and *Foch in Command*, pp. 308–9; and Lord Hankey, *The Supreme Command, 1914-1918*, vol. 2, p. 797.)

Maj. George S. Patton, Jr., CO, 1st Light Tank Center, Bourg, to Pershing.

I have just received a letter from Col. Stanton [*Ed.*—Probably Charles E. Stanton, a longtime friend of Pershing's and then the AEF's Chief Disbursing Officer, who had given the July 4, 1917, speech at Picpus Cemetery ending with "Lafayette, we are here!"] inclosing these two clippings which he says are for your scrapbook. He adds that if you have not such a book you should start it. I respectfully concur in his recommendation.

I have ten tanks here now and eight of them work every day from eight fifteen A.M. to five P.M. I would consider it an honor if you could inspect them some day. If you would let me know in advance I could arrange a small maneuver for you. I regret that they did not arrive in time for Mr. Baker's inspection.

I have had very good accounts of my family especially of Anne [Nita]. I have as yet no details as to the death of Mr. Ayer [Patton's father-in-law].

LC, Pershing Papers, folder: Col. and Mrs. Geo. S. Patton, box 155.

Edwards, CG, 26th Division, AEF, to Harbord, CS, GHQ, AEF, Chaumont, in reply to Harbord to Edwards, March 26.

Subject: Criticism.
  1. I have your letter of March 26th on this subject, and must say that I am entirely unconscious of having offended in any way indicated.
  As I have already explained to you in person, the instances you gave me during our recent conversation convince me that I have been either misquoted or misunderstood, and that a false and unjust impression has been thus gained.
  2. I know that my heart is pure. Nevertheless, I wish you would assure the Commander-in-Chief that in the future he can count upon me to play with particularity the role of Caesar's wife.

Massachusetts Historical Society (Boston), Edwards Papers, folder 18: 1917–1919, Commendatory and Personal Letters to Edwards, box 22; Vandiver, *Black Jack*, vol. 2, p. 962, fn 66.

Editor's Note—Pierpont Stackpole, Liggett's aide, provided an insight into the background of Edwards's reply to Harbord from a visit Liggett made to Robert Bullard's 1st Division headquarters on March 28. Edwards was also a guest at dinner that evening and in a conversation with Liggett "afterwards said he had been summoned to GHQ to answer some atrocious lies, and he had smoothed it over all right with Harbord." Stackpole, *In the Company of Generals*, p. 45; for more on the background of this particular incident, see Shay, *Revered Commander*, p. 148.

Bliss, Versailles, to Secretary of War Newton D. Baker [later handed to him in Paris].

I have had a most interesting and instructive day, of which I will give you a hasty account.

Yesterday, General Foch sent me word from Beauvais asking me to come up and pass the day at his headquarters. I went up in the morning and found him waiting for me. He took me into his little private office and, after the usual pleasant preliminary banalities, he said that he wanted to explain the whole situation to me. He showed me on his maps (which were practically identical with those which we have kept at Versailles, based on the same information) what the exact situation was on the opening day of the battle and how it had progressed up to that moment. He showed me his orders for the bringing up of all of the British and French reserves. He showed me the then exact position of each division on the map, the route that it was following, and the calculated date and hour of its arrival at its initial place. He pointed out where the indications were that a fresh German attack was being prepared and the possibilities of relieving their pressure at that point by an offensive of the Allies elsewhere.

He seemed fairly well content with the situation as it stood for the moment, but at the same time, he spoke quite freely of its gravity. He said, "The Germans have taken the initiative just as we expected, but they have succeeded to a greater extent than we thought would be the case, and it is they who are now making our plans."

At first, I thought that he was telling me all this as a matter of courtesy and because of our relations together on the Executive War Board. But, once or twice, when I got up with the idea of taking my departure, saying to him that I could not take up any more of the time of a man who was still engaged in the conduct of a great battle, he pressed me back into my seat (the second time placing his hands on both shoulders), and said, "I want to talk to you. I can do nothing more now here. All the orders have been given and it is the people out yonder who must do the rest." It then began to dawn on me that he was merely relieving his mind to a man who, as he well knew, had the greatest sympathy for him. I had already discovered this feeling on his part in our meetings of the Executive War Board, of which he is the executive head. After a long discussion in which I had taken no part because it related to some situation in which the Americans by no possibility could play any part, he would turn to me (my seat was on his right) and say, "I want to know what General Bliss thinks." If I replied that I thought it was a question to be settled by the British and French he would say, "It is just because you are out of it that I want your opinion." As a matter of fact, my opinion was generally acceptable to him. The only question on which there was a radical difference of opinion between himself and me was the organization of the General Reserve; but it produced no feeling and I know he thought none the less of me for it.

And so he talked and talked until well on in the afternoon, making no complaints about the situation or the causes which had led to it, criticizing no one, praising the British in the highest terms, and expressing the greatest confidence in the American troops. General Pershing had already made his offer to use the American troops at any place or in any way where they could do the most good, and this had pleased General Foch very much. He had also just received, almost at the moment of my arrival, the telegram sent to him by President Wilson, and this had touched him very deeply. He asked me to tell you this, which I did in a telegram to General Pershing, and to say that he was about to make an appropriate reply.

Altogether he impressed me as being the right man in the right place; cool, imperturbable, in no way depressed by what had happened but realizing the gravity of the situation, and very quick to see the requirements of that situation and to make his decisions.

Finally, he said to me that he had arranged a meeting for me with General Humbert, commanding the 3rd French Army in front of Montdidier and operating down as far as Lassignies and Noyon. I motored over to Clermont, the headquarters of General Humbert, passing on the way great numbers of British troops who were just off the firing line, having been relieved by new French divisions that had come up. I had met General Humbert at his headquarters in Noyon last December. He had then taken me out to his most advanced line at Coucy-le-Château where we looked across to the Chemin des Dames which had recently been taken after a bloody fight, and which the Germans were then trying to get back. Although General Humbert's army was then engaged in the last fierce struggle of the first eight days of the battle, he received me very cordially and with a black crayon he showed me on his map the dispositions which he was then making; how the Germans had that morning captured an important point of his line and he was then endeavoring to retake it by two counter-attacks. It was not until after I left [for] Paris that I learned of the success of his operation. Of course I did not take the time of a man who was at that moment engaged in the conduct of a fight and after a few minutes with him I left for Versailles.

While at Beauvais I learned that General Maistre, who has been commanding the French divisions in Italy, had been ordered back to take command of a group of French armies. If General Foch has many such men as Humbert and Maistre (The latter I met in Turin at our conference with General Diaz), I feel sure that the French will do everything that is humanly possible to do.

LC, Bliss papers, folder: General Correspondence—Bliss to Newton Diehl Baker, December 1917–May 1918, box 250.

Bliss, in Beauvais visiting Foch, to Pershing.

Telegram No. 27.

Arrived here this morning. Please tell Secretary of War that General Foch has received a telegram of congratulation from President Wilson which has touched him very deeply. He wishes Mr. Baker to know that he is very well satisfied with the present situation.

LC, Pershing Papers, folder: General Tasker H. Bliss, 1917–1918, box 26.

Pershing to TAG, War Department, in part in reply to TAG, War Department, to Pershing, cable A-810-R, February 19.

Cable P-826-S.
   7. For Chief of Staff and Chief Ordnance Officer. With reference to paragraph 7, your cablegram 810. Now clear your program for 14-inch guns for American Expeditionary Forces is 120 tubes and 60 carriages and for 16-inch howitzers provides 50% spares for mortars. This program approved. Shipment upon completion of materiel dependent upon actual tonnage situation at that time as per paragraph 1, my cablegram 607 [as corrected].

NARA, RG 120, M930, Main Series, AEF to War Department, roll 2.

TAG, War Department, to Pershing, in part in reply to Pershing to TAG, War Department, cables P-537-S, January 27, P-693-S, March 7, and P-790-S, March 27, and letter, Pershing to Secretary of War Baker, March 1.

Cable A-1014-R.
   4. [*Ed.*—This paragraph referenced specific paragraphs of the above-cited cables, which had requested promotions of certain officers in the AEF and informed Pershing that the officers "have already been promoted, or are about to be promoted, to the grades recommended by you."] March.
   6. Reference your letter of March 1st to Secretary of War on the subject of port facilities and measures necessary to obtain maximum capacity thereof, report what storage facilities you now have at each port, giving capacity thereof. Will you be able to unload steamers at maximum capacity before the additional storage recommended by you is actually provided? At least 2500 car repair men will have sailed by March 31st, the balance will follow soon thereafter. Locomotives and cars will go forward at rate you recommended. Goethals. [Reply—April 1, P-834-S-1A; April 17, P-941-S-1]

NARA, RG 120, M930, Main Series, War Department to AEF, roll 12.

TAG, War Department, to Pershing, in reply to Pershing to TAG, War Department, cables P-739-S, March 16, and P-782-S, March 25.

Cable A-1018-R.
   3. With reference to paragraph 2A, your 782. Standardized statistical plans being rapidly developed by statistical branch, General Staff. Will advise as soon as possible to complete plans. Think it desirable to defer sending experienced personnel until plans more fully tested here but will hasten the matter every possible way. Meantime

suggest you mature plans to furnish by cable as of 1st and 15th of each month following indispensable data for period: Your receipts from European sources principally articles each Bureau of Supply. Orders placed in Europe with promised deliveries by months. Any important changes in such delivery schedules. We must know status of reserves of important articles to plan quantities tonnage we must provide to bring reserves up to required amounts. These data should be cabled as soon as practicable.

6. Referring to your 739, paragraph 1D. Before metal parts could be furnished, necessary we receive explicit designs, specifications or information where these obtainable here. Since metals constitute large percentage tonnage involved proposed transactions, consider alternative erection either by your force or Bordeaux firm or Middletown Car Company or more U.S.A. cars than you now planning handle. These can be embarked as rapidly as ships available. The 2400 car repair men authorized with hand tools will shortly be moved. Middletown Car Company has 1400 boxes and gondolas for French State Railway finished, packed, ready for shipment. Understood their plants at Saintes and La Garenne with erecting capacity 750 cars monthly practically idle. Is it not better we devote energies having these cars shipped and increase shipment of our own rather than place orders for additional metal parts? [Reply—April 7, P-868-S-8; April 13, P-907-S-2A]
March.

NARA, RG 120, M930, Main Series, War Department to AEF, roll 12.

2

April 1918

April 1

Pershing's Personal Diary

Worked in office in the morning. Had at house to luncheon Mr. [LeRoy] Percy, former Senator from Mississippi, now engaged in Y.M.C.A. work, and another Y.M.C.A. worker called Kerr. Saw also General [P. D.] Lochridge [Bliss's chief of staff at SWC] and Col. R. E. Wood [Director of the Army Transport Service, SOS, who was returning to the War Department to be Acting Quartermaster General]. Worked for some time during the day with General Harbord on recommendations for promotion. Mrs. Lars Anderson of the Red Cross had been invited to house to dinner. She came after we were through, but managed to get something to eat.

LC, Pershing Papers, Diary, May 7, 1917–September 1, 1918, box 4.

Foch, Chief of Staff, General Staff, Ministry of War, to the Minister of War (Clemenceau), in addition to Foch to Minister of War, March 31.

General Staff
No. 34

I have no reason to complain of anyone. I am carrying the heaviest responsibility, the burden of which was placed upon me though I did not ask for it, which implies a commensurate liberty.

However, nowadays, I run up against vexing delays because I have to persuade (which is not always easy) instead of directing. So that, too often, it is somewhat difficult for me to obtain the execution of measures which I hold to be pressing or even immediately necessary.

This is why a power of direction superior to the one I now possess with regard to the Commanders-in-Chief seems to me indispensable to achieve success.

USAWW, vol. 2, p. 272; see also *Les armées françaises dans la Grande guerre, Tome 6,* vol. 1, *Annexes*, vol. 3: *Annexe* No. 1310, p. 5.

Foch, Chief of Staff, General Staff, Ministry of War, to the President of the Council (Minister of War)(Clemenceau).

As far as can be judged today the enemy offensive from Arras to Montdidier and to the Oise seems to be checked; only a few local operations are still being carried out. If the offensive is resumed on a larger scale but with only those means permitted by a rapid advance, the arrival of our reserves, more numerous each day, will enable us to stop it.

To overcome the obstacle facing him the enemy may have recourse to an attack with much heavy artillery. The preparations for such an operation will require considerable time, during which the improvement of our installations and the reinforcement of our artillery will enable us to meet it.

Therefore, from today on, the enemy's initiative can be considered as having been checked.

But the final situation which will result for us from the check of his offensive deserves to be anticipated and given some degree of study.

From certain points of his front the enemy will be able to reach, with his long-range artillery at least, important communication centers such as Amiens, St-Just. Undoubtedly it will be necessary to drive him off, which will bring about local offensives on our part.

A more general offensive would be justified by the necessity of retaking from him the region recently captured before he has had time to effect a systematic and complete defensive organization.

In short, on the Franco-British front it will be necessary to execute either local or major offensives. They will also be governed by the state of our available means and by the forces we and our Allies can devote to them. The operations will have to be considered from the standpoint of comparative results and costs.

At that time also the political situation will come up for consideration. The question may be asked whether, after having checked the German army, it would not be more telling for the dissolution of the enemy coalition, to strike a blow in Austria, in Italy.

The enumeration of these various questions, the answers to which brook no delay, proves the necessity for a comprehensive study of the war of the Entente and for a direction of the war.

It is for this reason that it is not enough to coordinate the actions of the British and French armies as is prescribed in the Doullens Agreement, but that to this function must be added the mission of directing the war in conformity with the views of the governments, with military means adequate for the required efforts, if it is desired to pursue the objectives assigned by politics, and that the directing agency be given sufficient authority over the Commanders-in-Chief.

The agreement of April 1 in Dury, which necessitated the presence of Marshal Haig and General Foch to settle the matter of one division, shows once more the paralysis of our system when this authority is lacking.

USAWW, vol. 2, pp. 272–73; see original at *Les armées françaises dans la Grande guerre, Tome 6*, vol. 1, *Annexes*, vol. 3: *Annexe* No. 1307. pp. 1–2.

Editor's Note—After a review of the situation facing the Allies as the March German offensive waned, Foch analyzed the problems which underpinned his three memoranda to Clemenceau and resulted in the ensuing Allied conference at Beauvais on April 3:

> No matter what attitude the Germans assumed, we ought to act as soon as possible south of the Somme, in order to drive the enemy away from the Paris-Amiens railway and the Amiens rail centre, both essential for our communications and supply. With this end in view the French troops should make an offensive in the Montdidier area, having for its object to throw the enemy back on Roye, and the British troops an attack on both sides of the Somme, in order to free Amiens.
>
> This reasoning implied offensive action on the part of the Allied armies. The purely passive attitude and the work of consolidation to which events had condemned them since March 21st would come to an end and be replaced by an active initiative.
>
> Now, to plan this offensive action, to inspire and direct it, to ensure its being carried on by the commanders in chief, and also to arrive at an equitable distribution of forces, the powers conferred upon me by the Doullens Agreement were plainly inadequate. They were insufficient to cover even the present defensive operations; they would necessarily be all the more inadequate when, in the not far distant future, it became my duty to decide upon the strategic employment of the Allied armies, renewed and strengthened by the cooperation of the Americans, determine, according to circumstances, the point against which these forces should be applied, distribute the offensive and defensive tasks and, perhaps, effect exchanges between the French and Italian fronts.
>
> The simple role of coordinator was not sufficient for the larger programme which would certainly have to be shortly undertaken. It gave far too little play to the *initiative* of the officer who filled it if he was to react rapidly and forcibly to contingencies brought about by a defensive battle, or organize and mount important offensive undertakings. The role should be changed into one of *direction*. If the inter-Allied organ created at Doullens by an effort of mutual confidence was to produce all that was expected of it, its powers must at once be widened, and the strategic direction of the war on the western front entrusted to it. Its authority over the Allied commanders in chief should be affirmed and this authority extended to include all the troops in line from the North Sea the Adriatic.
>
> A few days' experience has been sufficient to expose the inadequacy of the Doullens Agreement. The present as well as the future interests of the Coalition required that it be amended without delay. I placed the question before the French Prime Minister in this light and requested that the decision touching me, taken on March 26th by the British and French governments, be supplemented. Monsieur Clemenceau discussed the matter with me on April 1st and decided to assemble a new conference. To this he

invited the American representatives as well as the British and French. The meeting was held at the Beauvais town hall two days later, April 3d. (Foch, *Memoirs*, pp. 274–76.)

Pershing to Haig, CINC, BAF, in reply to Haig to Pershing, March 23.

As you know, I held three regiments of Engineers at your disposition, in accordance with your request dated March 23rd, until the movement was suspended at the request of your Headquarters on March 27th. [See also April 2, Bacon to CG, GHQ, AEF]

I regret that I have no heavy artillery available. However, I have information that certain heavy artillery personnel is now en route to France. Due to recent events I shall probably be unable immediately to equip two regiments (12 batteries) of this personnel. If you desire to use any of the personnel of these two regiments, they are at your disposal.
[Reply—April 6, Haig to Pershing]

NARA, RG 120, Office of the Commander-in-Chief, Office of the Secretary of the General Staff, Entry 22, Reports of the Commander-in-Chief, folder 34: GHQ War Diary, January 24–April 28, 1918, diary entry April 2, 1918, 297-h, p. 270, box 4.

Bliss, Chief, American Section, and Permanent Military Representative, SWC, Versailles, to Pershing.

Telegram No. 42 [sent].
The following message was received by me over the telephone from London at 3:20 this afternoon:

"The Prime Minister wishes to know whether Mr. Baker and General Pershing and General Bliss can go to London for conference with him immediately after Mr. Baker returns from Italy."

NARA, RG 120, M923, American Section, SWC, file 317: Telegrams sent by the American Section, Jan. 21, 1918–Dec. 5, 1919, roll 19; see also online "WW I Supreme War Council, American records," at https://www.fold3.com.

Bliss, Chief, American Section, and Permanent Military Representative, SWC, Versailles, to Pershing.

Telegram No. 43 [sent].
Colonel Grant tells me you have telephoned that you have not received copy of Resolution of March 27th with the Secretary's recommendation to the President. The

Secretary dictated his recommendation on morning of March 28th and the resolution with this recommendation was coded and sent to Washington late same day. One official copy was made for you and one for the Secretary and inclosed in envelope addressed to Secretary. On your copy I placed a note to the Secretary asked him to hand it to you. This envelope was receipted by Officer of the Day at General Lewis' office on night of Thursday, March 28th, to go to your headquarters by your courier at 8 o'clock, Friday morning. Have directed another copy go to you by your courier tomorrow morning. Also copy of proceedings at your hearing before the Military Representatives on March 27th.

NARA, RG 120, M923, American Section, SWC, file 317: Telegrams sent by the American Section, Jan. 21, 1918–Dec. 5, 1919, roll 19; see also online "WW I Supreme War Council, American records," at https://www.fold3.com.

Bliss, Chief, American Section, and Permanent Military Representative, SWC, Versailles, to Pershing, Chaumont.

I inclose herewith three documents.

The first is a copy of the cable to Washington transmitting the Joint Note No. 18 of the Military Representatives, together with the Secretary of War's recommended action, to the President [see March 28, Bliss to TAG, War Department, cable 67-S]. A copy of this paper was sent to your headquarters by your courier who leaves Paris every morning at, I think, 8 o'clock. As soon as Col. Grant told me that he had learned over the telephone from your headquarters that you had not received it I sent you a telegram a copy of which I inclose herewith [see above, Bliss to Pershing, cable 43]. If the copy of Joint Note No. 18 failed to reach your headquarters, it must have been through some negligence of the courier or some negligence in the Provost Marshal General's Office in Paris where the document was receipted for, for transmission to you, the night before the courier left. I think that it is very important that the missing copy should be located because it would not do to have it fall into alien hands.

The second document which I send is the proceedings of the meeting of the Military Representatives at the time of your statement to it last Wednesday [March 27]. Stenographers are not used either at the meetings of the Supreme War Council or of the Military Representatives. Brief notes are taken by the Secretaries of the different Sections and immediately after the meeting these Secretaries compare their notes and a common draft is made up which is agreed to by all of them. As a matter of fact, the record of proceedings is largely intended to show that the Military Representatives met at a given date and considered a certain subject, showing in the briefest possible terms the persons who took part in the discussion and enough of their statement to show whether they were for or against a given proposition. These proceedings never leave the archives here. If a Resolution is adopted as a result of a meeting that Resolution alone is sent to the different governments for their action. The proceedings in the document herewith which I have marked "2" are brief outlines of proceedings which resulted in Joint Note No. 18 which I hand you herewith in document which is marked "1".

The third document was a suggested reply drafted by the representatives of the Foreign Offices of Great Britain and France and submitted to the Military Representatives for their views. It is a reply to a letter received by England and France (which in due time will doubtless be received in Washington, although none of us here has seen any of them) from the Red Cross Committee in Geneva, on the subject of doing away with the use of asphyxiating and poisonous gases. The Military Representatives approved the proposed draft of the letter, in French, and since then we have not heard, nor do we expect to hear, anything further about it. [*Ed.*—Bliss informed the War Department about this matter in his cable 65 of March 27 (not reproduced), which can be located at NARA, RG 120, M923, American Section, SWC, file 315: Cablegrams Sent to War Department, Jan. 22, 1918–Dec 10, 1919, roll 18; see also online "WW I Supreme War Council, American records," at https://www.fold3.com.]

I repeated to you this afternoon, by wire, the message which I received from London about the desire of the Prime Minister to have a conference there with Mr. Baker, as soon as he returns from Italy, and you and myself [see above, Bliss to Pershing, cable 42]. I have no doubt that what he wants to talk about is this same old subject, of the use of American manpower in the English and French armies. That makes me think that the Ambassador in London has not received information from our State Department that the President approves Mr. Baker's recommendation as to Joint Note No. 18. As soon as the Prime Minister receives the official information of the President's motion through his Foreign Office, he may call off the proposed conference. On the other hand he may, for all I know, want to talk on some entirely new subject. Of this I know nothing. At any rate, the Secretary of War is not here, and the matter will have to rest until he does come, if he returns here at all.

Inclosures 1, 2, 3, herewith.
[Enclosure 1—see March 28, Bliss to TAG, War Department, cable 67-S.]
[Enclosure 2—Document 1 referred to by Bliss is an unnumbered copy of Bliss to Pershing, cable 43. Document 2 is "Draft of Extract of Minutes of the Meeting of the Allied Military Representatives at the Supreme War Council 27 March 1918," which contains Pershing's statement and comments until he left that meeting. This can be found at March 27 in SWC/153, SWC (MR) 24, so it is not reproduced again here.]
[Enclosure 3 (not reproduced)]

LC, Pershing Papers, folder: Supreme War Council, February–April 1918, box 193; see also LC, Bliss Papers, folder: American Expeditionary Forces and American Forces in France, January–December 1918, box 248.

Foulois, Chief, Air Service, SOS, AEF, to CS, GHQ, AEF, in addition to Foulois to Logan, ACS, G-1, GHQ, AEF, March 20.

Subject: Air Service Program.

1. Attached herewith is copy of a memorandum for the Chief of Staff, dated February 6, 1918, Subject: "Estimate Air Service possibilities latter part of 1918" [See Vol. 3, February 6, Foulois to Chief of Staff, AEF], and a Memorandum to Assistant Chief of Staff, G-1, dated March 20, 1918, Subject: "Priority for Aviation Personnel and Material" [See Vol. 3, March 20, Foulois to Logan, ACS. G-1, GHQ, AEF].

2. The Chief of Air Service has not, as yet, received any information as to the approval or disapproval of these memorandums.

3. If it is contemplated that the Air Service shall organize and equip any additional aero squadrons for front line service, prior to June 30, it is urgently requested that the Chief of Air Service be given some definite information as to the plans of the General Staff.

NARA. RG 120, M990, Gorrell's History of the American Expeditionary Forces Air Service, 1917–1919. Series A, Vol. 1: Foulois, Air Service Lessons Learned during the Present War, January 29, 1919, roll 1; see also online "Gorrell's History—AEF Air Service," at https://www.fold3.com.

Benson, CNO, Washington, to Sims, Commander, U.S. Naval Forces Operating in European Waters, London, in reply to Sims to OpNav, March 27, cable 5635.

Cable 4475.
Very Secret.
Opnav, 4475. "Situation regarding USS *Leviathan* most unsatisfactory as regards routing to Liverpool England. Unless active steps are taken nothing will be accomplished. Necessity for actually putting troops into France is one which will admit no delay or temporizing over difficulties attendant thereupon. If USS *Leviathan* runs to Brest France she can make round trips in from 18 to 20 days. On present schedule she takes over 40 days besides going through a more dangerous zone. All of difficulties cited your 5635 can be met except coal and the Army can handle troops. Divert for the purpose of building up coal reserves sufficient to coal U.S.S. *Leviathan* either the USCT *Crowell* or 1 of the 2 ships of Lake type assigned to mine operations northern barrage. Make best arrangements possible for berth U.S.S. *Leviathan* for on next voyage she will be routed to that port. Matters of converting a few boilers to burn oil under consideration." Acknowledge.

NARA, RG 45, ONRL, 1803–1859, T829, Miscellaneous Records of the Navy Department, Miscellaneous Materials, 1–6/1918, 7–12/1918, Miscellaneous Material Printed Files, World War, roll 408; see also Naval History and Heritage Command, website:

April 1918   121

The U.S.S. *Leviathan* rides at anchor in the roadstead at Brest after arriving on May 2, 1918, following its initial voyage from Hoboken, New Jersey (New York harbor). Because of its draft, no pier at Brest could then accommodate the large ship, so lighters had to transfer passengers and cargo to piers for unloading. Two lighters are tied up alongside the ship in this photograph. Source: NARA, Still Pictures Branch, RG 111, 111-SC-13431.

Wars, Conflicts, and Operations, World War I, Documentary Histories, April 1918, OpNav to Sims, April 1, 1918; original document at NARA, RG 45, DNA, Entry 517B.

Editor's Note—As Benson instructed, the *Leviathan* made its initial voyage to Brest departing from New York on April 24 and arriving on May 2. On this trip it carried 9,352 passengers—8,925 Army personnel (8,238 soldiers, 97 NCOs, 361 officers, and 229 nurses), 413 Navy, and 14 civilians. Through October 17 it made 7 more round trips between New York and Brest before another trip to Liverpool and Brest on October 27, and then made additional round trips after the Armistice. On its trips to Brest, the *Leviathan* carried more than 10,000 Army personnel on 5 occasions (May 22, June 15, July 8, August 3, and August 31), reaching its largest number of 10,881 on the August 3 voyage from New York. During the war (April 1917-November 11, 1918), the *Leviathan* transported a total of 96,804 passengers to France and England. After the Armistice, it returned 93,746 from France back to New York until it completed its final voyage on September 8, 1919. Among its many passengers on that trip, it carried Pershing and his GHQ AEF Staff, who were returning to the United States. See *History of the U.S.S. Leviathan, Cruiser and Transport Forces, United States Atlantic Fleet* (Brooklyn, NY: Brooklyn Eagle Job Department, 1919), table: "U.S.S. Leviathan Statistics of Numbers Carried," following p. 218; Gleaves, *A History of the Transport Service*, pp. 248–49; "Report of the Secretary of the Navy," Appendix F: Troop Transportation, pp. 209–10, in *Annual Reports of the Navy Department for the Fiscal Year 1919* (Washington: GPO, 1920).

The passengers and cargo from the *USS Leviathan* had to be landed at Brest by lighters. Here a lighter carries soldiers from the 61st Infantry Regiment, 5th Division, to a pier for disembarkation. They were then moved to a nearby camp for rest prior to continuing inland by rail to the divisional training area at Bar-sur-Aube. Source: NARA, Still Picture Branch, RG 111, 111-SC-13436.

On its initial run to Brest, the U.S.S. *Leviathan* carried Army nurses of the 30th Base Hospital who were on their way to Royat to set up their new hospital. The professional medical personnel of the 30th Base Hospital were organized from the University of California, San Francisco, Medical School and Center. Here the nurses are disembarking on May 5, 1918, from the lighter that had carried them ashore. Source: NARA, Still Picture Branch, RG 111, 111-SC-13438.

Pershing to TAG, War Department, in part in reply to TAG, War Department, cables A-995-R, March 27, and A-1014-R. March 31.

Cable P-834-S.
1. For Chief of Staff. 1A. With reference to paragraph 6, your cablegram 1014. Storage construction proceeding in preference to all other work except dock construction. Arrangements made to handle for the present all property arriving. Non-perishable property will be put in place and covered with sheds later if necessary. All perishable property can be stored. Will keep you advised as to situation.

1B. Question of cars and locomotives most pressing need because of demand for troop movements.

1C. With reference to paragraph 4, your cablegram 1014. Your statement of policy is understood to be that line officers on duty in staff Departments will not be promoted therein as rule ahead of officers of their permanent arm. This policy is concurred in by me but it is hoped that the administration of it will be the same for officers in France as in America, otherwise injustice is done. Following seem to be exceptions to this policy as per paragraph 6, your cablegram 895 [not reproduced], following detailed Ordnance Officers pass officers in their own arm. In Coast Artillery: Colonel Casad, 180 officers; Colonel Jenks, 160 officers; Lieut. Col. John B. Rose, 199 officers; Lieut. Col. Kenneth B. Harmon, 377 officers; Major Prentiss, 318 officers. Field Artillery: Major W. C. Young, 74 officers. Other instances can be added.

1D. With reference to paragraph 4, your cablegram 995 [requesting Pershing's recommendations for General Officers]. Following are recommended for promotion Major General, National Army: Willard A. Holbrook, James H. McRae, Peter E. Straub, George B. Duncan, Edward M. Lewis, Ernest Hinds, Charles S. Farnsworth, James W. McAndrew, Edward F. McGlacklin, Jr., William Lassiter. Following recommended for promotion Brigadier General, National Army: Arthur Johnson, John M. Jenkins, Guy H. Preston, George T. Langhorne, Harry E. Smith, Lutz Wahl, John L. Hines, Robert J. Fleming, Joseph C. Castner, Samuel D. Rockenbach, Julian R. Lindsey, Lincoln C. Andrews, Dwight E. Aultman, Paul B. Malone, Charles C. Smith, Albert E. Sexton, Johnson Hagood.

NARA, RG 120, M930, AEF to War Department, roll 2.

TAG, War Department, to Pershing.

Cable A-1020-R.
6C. Signal Corps is considering equipment first 200 Handley Page airplanes for taking British-type drop bombs. Does prospective supply bombs from British source justify this action? Desire information existing order in England. Wheeler [Acting Chief of Ordnance]. [Reply—April 24, P-987-S-2; April 30, P-1031-S-6A]

7. Do you desire the present force of Marines in France increased by addition of other units now on trial as infantry and what are your desires in regard to formation

of a Division composed of Marines for infantry and machine gun units with its artillery and auxiliaries taken from Army? March. [Reply—April 3, P-850-S-1C]

NARA, RG 120, M930, Main Series, War Department to AEF, roll 12.

April 2

Pershing's Personal Diary

Worked in office all day. Saw Major Tinant, Belgian representative at G.H.Q. Received word from General Wagstaff that, in view of the present events on the front, Prince of Wales would not visit headquarters on April 4th, as had been planned. In the afternoon saw Colonel [Edward D.] Ardery of the Gas Service with reference to "Lifire," Major Harjes and Mr. Floyd Gibbons of the Chicago Tribune. Had General Ragueneau come to the house after dinner, as he was leaving for French G.H.Q. the next day. Also had Colonel Fox Conner come to quarters after dinner. Had Captain Cutcheon at house to dinner.

LC, Pershing Papers, Diary, May 7, 1917–September 1, 1918, box 4.

War Office to Brig. Gen. C. M. Wagstaff, GS, Chief, British Military Mission with GHQ, AEF, Chaumont, for Pershing.

55540 cipher.
M. O. L. [sent telegram, War Office]. Please convey to General Pershing our appreciation and gratitude for the manner in which he has offered to place American units at our disposal to meet the present grave situation. In some of the British divisions the fighting strength of the infantry has been reduced below 2,000 rifles, and we cannot use them until we have increased their rifle strength though otherwise ready to take part again in the battle. The value of the American troops will depend largely upon the rapidity with which they can be incorporated into the British divisions. I would therefore ask that General Pershing will allow us to use the infantry now being transported through England as part of the monthly quota of 12,000 men for the American army by battalions in accordance with the six-division scheme, if he can do so without affecting immediate reserves for his own divisions which are taking part in the battle.

LC, Pershing Papers, folder: Data for Book *My Experiences in the World War*, folder 11: Extracts from official records of British War Office, *The Progress of the American Army in France*, vol. 2, document no. 111, box 354; *USAWW*, vol. 3, pp. 76–77.

Col. Robert Bacon, Member, American Military Mission with GHQ, BAF, Montreuil, and American ADC to Haig, to CS, GHQ, AEF.

1. In confirmation of my telephone message and telegram of today, I have been called up by General Wigram, O.B., B.E.F., to say that they all appreciate very much the splendid work the engineer units, two companies of the Sixth Regiment, have done during the last ten days. He had heard from General Montgomery, Chief of Staff for General Rawlinson [the new CG of the reassembled British Fifth Army], on the subject, and they hoped it would be possible to allow them to remain and continue their invaluable work of bridge building and not withdraw them as he understood it had been intended. General Wigram also said that he hoped that the two engineer regiments for which they had asked, but for which as yet they had been unable to furnish transportation, might still be available, for if it could be arranged with the French, they would very much like to have them now [see March 23, Haig to Pershing, and April 1, Pershing to Haig].
2. I called up General Harts [Chief, American Military Mission] to report this to him, but finding him absent for the day thought it best to wire as above.

NARA, RG 120, Office of the Commander-in-Chief, Office of the Secretary of the General Staff, entry 22, Reports of the Commander-in-Chief, folder 34: GHQ War Diary, January 24–April 28, 1918, diary entry April 2, 1918, 297-k, pp. 271–72.

Kernan, CG, SOS, to CINC, AEF.

Telegram.

The following submitted by General Atterbury for transmission to you:

"We are in receipt of letters from R. B. Stevens, representative of Allied Maritime Transport Council, to effect that Italian coal situation is so critical that unless every effort is made to deliver coal at once the result will be disastrous. England is making every effort to divert their ships for Italian coal, but it will not be possible for her to supply all required tonnage. Mr. Stevens suggests there are two possible methods whereby we can assist; First, by allowing three or four of largest ships we have employed in transporting coal from England to France, to make one voyage to Italy; Second, by diverting certain American transports now discharging in France to one voyage carrying coal to Italy before returning to the United States. Our position is that we have insufficient tonnage of our own in England-France service to meet our requirements for materials purchased in England, as well as for coal, and that we have been forced to charter a fleet of small Swedish vessels to help out, leaving our own steamers for coal trade as far as possible. While we have a good coal credit with the French, I have not all facts available regarding actual amount of coal in France, but do not believe we are in position to divert temporarily to England-Italian coal trade any of our present coal ships. I see no other course therefore than to divert some of the American transports now discharging in France to one voyage carrying coal to Italy before returning to the United States. I want, however, to call your attention to the fact that even if we were in safe position to divert any of our ships, we are forbidden by orders of the War Department either to requisition American steamers for any purpose, or to divert or transfer any of Army transports in trans-Atlantic service, to other service, without permission from Washington. I would also call your attention to position that had been taken by Admiral Sims in connection with service to Mediterranean ports. In view of foregoing, it seems to me that in any event Washington should cancel its order preventing us, in emergencies, from using ships as we deem best, and that Admiral Sims should be immediately requested to review his determinations on the service to Mediterranean ports. Will you kindly let me have your instructions? Atterbury."

My own view is that because of the delay incident to sea carriage and the increased danger of tonnage losses, transportation of coal to Italy by boat is very undesirable. Therefore every effort should be made, no matter how inconvenient, to send all coal to Italy by rail from France. If that is impossible, and assuming that the coal stocks in France are sufficient for immediate present, diversion of coal ships in transit from England to France through the Mediterranean to Italy seems the next best alternative. The last and least desirable course would be to divert our transports to England for coal carried by water thence to Italy.

LC, Bliss papers, binder 226: February 8–May 4, 1918, pp. 41258–59.

Bliss, Chief, American Section, and Permanent Military Representative, SWC, Versailles, to Pershing.

Telegram No. 47 [Sent].

As requested in your letter April 1 [not reproduced], I have informed Supreme War Council of nomination of Atterbury vice Andrews on Transportation Committee. Mr. Clemenceau says conferences mentioned in my previous telegram today will be at 1:30 P.M. tomorrow. On Sunday I found road somewhat crowded with motor truck trains. It may take a good 2 hours to motor there from here.

NARA, RG 120, M923, American Section, SWC, file 317: Telegrams sent by the American Section, Jan. 21, 1918–Dec. 5, 1919, roll 19; see also online "WW I Supreme War Council, American records," at https://www.fold3.com.

Bliss, Chief, American Section, and Permanent Military Representative, SWC, Versailles, to Pershing.

Telegram No. 48 [Sent].

Mr. Lloyd George and Mr. Clemenceau have telephoned asking General Pershing and General Bliss to meet them at headquarters in Beauvais at noon or a little thereafter tomorrow. If the Secretary of War is with you they would very much like to have him present also. French staff officers here waiting to carry word to Mr. Clemenceau as soon as you have received message. Please acknowledge. [Reply—Harbord for Pershing to Bliss, following]

NARA, RG 120, M923, American Section, SWC, file 317: Telegrams sent by the American Section, Jan. 21, 1918–Dec. 5, 1919, roll 19; see also online "WW I Supreme War Council, American records," at https://www.fold3.com.

Harbord, CS, GHQ, AEF, for Pershing, to Bliss, Chief, American Section, and Permanent Military Representative, SWC, Versailles, in reply to Bliss to Pershing, telegram No. 48, April 2.

Telegram No. 36 [Received].

In reply to yours General Pershing will be at 73 Rue Varennes at noon tomorrow, lunch there, and immediately thereafter go by motor to place named in your telegram. Secretary of War not here. En route from Italy. Expected in Paris tomorrow.

NARA, RG 120, M923, American Section, SWC, file 318: Telegrams received by the American Section, Jan. 1918–Oct. 29, 1919, roll 19; see also online "WW I Supreme War Council, American records," at https://www.fold3.com.

Pershing to Biddle, CG, Base Section No. 3, SOS, AEF, London, for Sims, Commander. U.S. Naval Forces Operating in the European Waters, in reply to Sims to Pershing, March 26, telegram 1721.

Telegram 9379. For Admiral Sims, London.

Reference your 1721. March 27th [26th]. Our request for information was based on information by cable from Washington March 21st stating differences had arisen between British and War Department regarding use of *Mauretania, Aquitania, Olympic,* etc., as expressed to you by my cablegram of March 23rd. We wish to give Washington your understanding of the agreement with a view to settling misunderstanding there. Early reply requested. [Reply—April 4, Sims to Pershing]

NARA, RG 45, ONRL T829, Miscellaneous Records of the Navy Department, Miscellaneous Materials, 1–8/1918, Miscellaneous Material Print Files, World War, roll 411.

Pershing to TAG, War Department, in addition to Pershing to TAG, War Department, cable P-779-S, March 24.

Cable P-836-S.

2. For Chief of Staff. 2B. Recommend appointment of J. G. Harbord as Brigadier General, Regular Army, and request that any existing vacancy in grade of Major General, Regular Army, be held open to be given as a recognition of efficient service to such General Officer as may merit this recognition. [Reply—April 10, A-1077-R-11]

2C. With reference to paragraph 1, our cablegram 779. At least 75% of replacements for combat troops which have arrived have had practically no training. Request that replacements sent hereafter be soldiers with thorough individual training. In view of early service of divisions over here and probably also of succeeding divisions, all replacements should be as well trained as possible before coming here. There will be little time from now on to train recruits. If necessary to accomplish this several divisions should be broken up or converted into training and replacement divisions at home. The value of the short training received in United States is to some extent nullified by lack of disciplinary care and instruction during shipment to port of embarkation and while on shipboard. Recommend that all replacements come completely equipped and classified and with item numbers to show whether automatic, exceptional, et cetera; that all replacements be organized into provisional units with suitable number of trained officers and noncommissioned officers from point of origin in United States to destination in France. If practicable at least 1 officer of experience should command each draft of 250 soldiers throughout the trip for purposes of discipline, instruction, and handling of records.

2E. Request that Shipping Control Committee designate a representative fully acquainted in detail with loading situation in the United States to come to France as soon as possible with the object of familiarizing himself with port and dock conditions here and return to the United States to effect any feasible reforms ship loading methods there. [*Ed.*—On April 6, Maj. Gen. George W. Goethals, Director of Purchase, Storage, and Traffic, War Department, replied in cable A-1057-R-8 that Mr. H. H. Raymond, with a secretary and 2 assistants, will leave "at an early date" to familiarize themselves with port and dock conditions and to effect "closer cooperation in handling transport problems."]

NARA, RG 120, M930, Main Series, AEF to War Department, roll 2, War Department to AEF, roll 12.

April 3

Pershing's Personal Diary

Left Chaumont at 7 a. m. by automobile with Colonel Boyd, Lieutenant Adamson and Lieutenant Hughes. Went via Fontainebleau, arriving at Paris at 11:25 a. m. Had a hasty luncheon and left at once for Beauvais, arriving there at 2 p. m., one half hour after meeting was to take place. However, waited till 3 p. m. before entrance of Mr. Lloyd George and M. Clemenceau. Sat in conference with M. Clemenceau, Mr. Lloyd George, Generals Foch, Pétain, Bliss, Weygand and Sir Douglas Haig. General Spiers acted as interpreter and Lieutenant Colonel Sir Maurice Hankey acted as recorder.

The object of the meeting was to discuss the question of the high command. There was some general discussion without any progress toward a definite conclusion. I made a strong direct statement in favor of a single commander for all the allied armies on the Western front. I stated that we had never had co-operation and would never have until we have a commander-in-chief; that no matter who the commanders-in-chief of the different armies might be, we would never have co-operation unless we have one commander-in-chief of all the allied armies on this front; that it is absolutely essential to the success of the allied cause; that we should adopt such a measure at that meeting; that I was in favor of entrusting this command to General Foch.

An article of agreement was drawn up stating that the British, French and American governments entrusted the co-ordination of military efforts on the western front to General Foch; giving him full authority to direct strategical co-ordination on the Western front, and stating that in case any commanding general considered that, through any order of General Foch his army was placed in danger, he could appeal to his own government. It was at my insistence that the American government was mentioned as one of the parties taking part in this agreement.

LC, Pershing Papers, Diary, May 7, 1917–September 1, 1918, box 4.

Beauvais Conference

Minutes of a Conference Held at the Hotel De Ville, Beauvais, on Wednesday, April 3, 1918, at 3:15 p. m.

Present

France
M. Clemenceau, President of the Council, Minister of War.
General Foch, Chief of the Staff.
General Pétain, Commander-in-Chief of the Armies of the North and Northeast.
Great Britain
The Right Hon. D. Lloyd George, Prime Minister.
Field Marshal Sir Douglas Haig, Commander-in-Chief, British Armies in France.
General Sir H. H. Wilson, Chief of the Imperial General Staff.
United States of America
General J. J. Pershing, Commander-in-Chief, American Expeditionary Force.
General Bliss, Permanent Military Representative, Supreme War Council.

Coordination of the Higher Command on the Western Front

M. Clemenceau said that the subject of discussion was a very simple one and related to the agreement reached by the British and the French Governments at Doullens on March 26, 1918, which had subsequently been accepted by the American Government. Since Field Marshal Haig and General Pétain had succeeded in checking the German attack, this scheme had worked well. The situation now, however, was developing, and a stage had been reached when it was necessary to define, with greater precision, the position of the general of the Coalition, as he would like to call General Foch. Mr. Lloyd George was in London, and he himself was in Paris. The Commanders-in-Chief of the British and French armies were very busy with their own operations. Hence it was necessary to decide on the means for ensuring that the coordination of the two armies was carried out with promptitude and energy. In fact, a decision was required as to whether the Doullens arrangement should stand as it was, or whether it required widening. He suggested that General Foch should explain his views to the conference.

Mr. Lloyd George asked that General Foch, in giving his views, would particularly specify in what respects he considered that the Doullens arrangement conferred insufficient authority on him to coordinate the action of the two armies.

General Foch reminded the conference that the Doullens arrangement stated that he was charged with coordinating the action of the Allied armies on the western front. This implied that if there were no action there was nothing to coordinate. If the French were taking no action, and if the British army were taking no action, it was impossible to coordinate their action. Consequently something more was now wanted. He required the power to imply an idea of action to the Commanders-in-Chief, and to have this action carried out. In fact, before coordinating he must have the power of creating action. For this reason the text of the Doullens arrangement was insufficient, and should be made to include "power for the infusion of an idea of action." Moreover, it was not so much necessary to coordinate the action itself as the preparation of action. In quiet times it was necessary to create an idea around which the preparations should be made in coordination. On March 26, at Doullens, the situation was very different from what it was on April 3, at Beauvais. On the former date it was a question of coordinating action which was in full swing. On the latter date it was a question of coordinating preparation for future action. On March 26 our armies were submitting to a battle imposed on us by the enemy, but today, at Beauvais, we were thinking of our own action. In this latter case the powers of mere coordination of action were insufficient.

General Wilson read the words of the Doullens arrangement, under which General Foch was charged "*de coordonner l'action des armées alliées sur le front ouest*". It appeared to him that, in those words, General Foch would find all the powers he required.

General Foch again insisted that, if there was no action, or no movement, there was nothing to coordinate. His requirements would be met by the insertion of some words such as "order" (*ordonner*), or "or give orders" (*donner des ordres*).

Mr. Lloyd George said that, speaking on behalf of the British public, they were very anxious to ensure that divided counsels should not end in disaster. A real effort had been made to coordinate the action of the Allies by means of the Supreme War Council and the Permanent Military Representatives at Versailles, because it had been realized that the Germans had one army and the Allies had three. Even last year the Allies on the western front had had two strategies: Field Marshal Haig's and General Pétain's.

Field Marshal Haig interpolated that, last year, he was under the orders of General Nivelle.

Mr. Lloyd George said that he did not refer to that period, although he reminded the conference that General Nivelle's strategy had achieved the most valuable results, so far as the British army was concerned, of the whole year's fighting, since it had put the Allies in possession of the Vimy Ridge and the country east of Arras.* What he had referred to, however, were the operations later in the year, when Field Marshal Haig had been fighting in Flanders and General Pétain's army had been carrying out operations with limited objectives at considerable intervals. The consequence was that, although the Allies had had a superiority against the Germans of something approaching 3 to 2, they had, in fact, achieved very little. In their recent offensive, however, the Germans, though probably not superior in numbers, had achieved this very considerable result, and this was mainly due to their unity of control. Versailles had been set up with the object of securing a similar unity of action, but it had not been in full operation when this offensive commenced and none of its decisions had been carried out. Whatever had resulted from the recent actions must be credited entirely to the old system for coordinating the higher command. What he was apprehensive of was that the Allied Governments would today merely reach a new formula without achieving any real unity of command. The British public wanted. and intended, to know whether there was real unity. What we had now to decide was that General Foch should really have all the powers he needed. He said that the British public entirely believed in General Foch, as proved by the way in which his appointment had been received in the press. Of course, if General Foch should put the British army in great peril, Field Marshal Haig would appeal to his own government, and no paper that could be drawn up could prevent this. Consequently, there was no objection to some words being put in to this effect. Unless he had the necessary power, however, General Foch would prove worse than useless. He said he would

---

* In returning the draft minutes, Field Marshal Sir D. Haig asked that the following note might be added to the *proces-verbal*: "With reference to Mr. Lloyd George's statement that 'it (Nivelle's strategy) had put the Allies in possession of Vimy Ridge,' Sir D. Haig interrupted, and stated that the British army attacked and captured the Vimy Ridge contrary to the advice of General Nivelle, who wished that the left flank of the British attack should be on the south of the River Scarpe. Also that the one complaint brought against the field marshal at the famous Calais Conference was that he (the field marshal) insisted in attacking the Vimy Ridge in spite of his (Nivelle's) remonstrance."

much like to hear the views of the American generals on the subject, more particularly as General Bliss and General Pershing now had a special claim to attention, since the army of the United States of America would be fighting side by side with their Allies under President Wilson's recent decision.

General Bliss said that two facts specially struck him. The first was that at Doullens the two Allied Governments principally concerned, namely, those with the greatest stakes on the western front, had come to an agreement which, he understood, had been accepted with cordiality by all concerned. Their agreement had been to the effect that it was necessary to create an organ of command which had not existed before. Under that agreement power was given to one designated officer, who was charged with the responsibility for coordinating the action of the Allied armies on the western front. It was inconceivable that the governments concerned should have given him this great charge without meaning to give him the necessary powers. According to the agreement, the designated officer was to come to an understanding with the Commanders-in-Chiefs concerned, and they were to give him all the necessary information. Why was this latter provision inserted? Evidently in order to enable him to issue instructions based on the information given. The second point which impressed him was that the designated officer now found himself unable to comply with his orders to carry out the duties of coordination entrusted to him. He could not conceive how the responsibility could be imposed on the designated officer without the necessary powers. He believed that a reasonable interpretation of the "Agreement of Doullens," a copy of which he had before him, gave to the designated officer full powers to effect the coordinated military action of all forces on the western front, with the duty of doing which that officer was charged by the Doullens Agreement, both now and for the future, until the Allied Governments rescinded that agreement. But, from what had been said at this conference this afternoon, it appeared that there was some doubt as to the correct interpretation of the powers conferred upon the designated officer by the document accepted at Doullens. His own opinion, therefore, was that if any doubt existed, the terms of the original agreement should be altered so that he should have full powers.

General Pershing said that it appeared to him that we had now reached a point in the war where entire cooperation of the Allied armies should be assured. As a matter of principle, he knew no way to ensure such cooperation except by a single command. It was impossible for two or three Commanders-in-Chief, whose commands were spread over such a huge front, by themselves to coordinate their activities unless the armies were under one head. The experiments in this direction had already gone far enough. They had proved completely that coordination was impossible. Each general had his own responsibilities to think of. Success from now onwards would depend upon the Allies having a single command.

Field Marshal Haig said he was in entire agreement with what General Pershing said. There should be only one head in France. His own instructions from the British Government were to take his ideas of strategy from the French Commander-in-Chief, although he was responsible for the safety of the British army. Consequently, he had always, subject, of course, to the orders of the British Government, looked to the

Commander-in-Chief of the French army for his strategical ideas. It would be very easy to insert in the agreement what General Foch required, and he thought that General Wilson's draft was satisfactory. What was really needed, however, was that the Commanders-in-Chief should work whole-heartedly and willingly in the closest cooperation with General Foch.

M. Clemenceau then read a draft of a new agreement based on proposals made by General Wilson. (See conclusion below)

Mr. Lloyd George accepted this on behalf of the British Government.

General Pétain pointed out that the provision as regards the tactical conduct of the armies could not, in practice, at present apply to the American army, since, under the latest arrangement made with General Pershing, the American army would be working tactically with the British and French armies. He suggested words should be inserted to show that this would not apply to the American army until it consisted of three or four army corps and had assumed autonomy. It was generally agreed, however, that as a practical working proposition it was unnecessary to insert General Pétain's proposal.

Generals Bliss and *Pershing* accepted the agreement, subject to the approval of their government, and asked that words might be inserted to make it applicable to the American as well as to the British and French Government and army.

Conclusion

The conference decided that:

The arrangement for the coordination of the higher command on the western front, concluded at Doullens on March 26, 1918, should be superseded by the following arrangement:

French Text [not reproduced]

English Text:

General Foch is charged by the British, French, and American Governments with the coordination of the action of the Allied Armies on the western front. To this end all powers necessary to secure effective realization are conferred on him. The British, French, and American Governments for this purpose entrust to General Foch the strategic direction of military operations. The Commanders-in-Chief of the British, French, and American Armies have full control of the tactical employment of their forces. Each Commander-in-Chief will have the right of appeal to his Government if in his opinion the safety of his Army is compromised by any order received from General Foch.

* * * * * *

Cooperation of the United States of America.

(At this point Mr. Graeme Thomson entered.)

Mr. Lloyd George informed the Conference that President Wilson had arrived at what was possibly one of the most momentous decisions of the whole campaign, which might not improbably influence the issue of the war more than any other decision that had been taken. The battle might, so far as he could see, continue for months until one or other side was exhausted, or perhaps defeated. Owing to the shortage of shipping President Wilson had decided that the available shipping should be devoted for the present, entirely to the transport of infantry and machine-gunners, and he had promised 120,000 infantry and machine-gunners each month for the next four months. If more shipping could be provided, President Wilson would send more men, and these men would be brigaded with armies already organized. He had thought it right, therefore, to take this opportunity to raise the question when Generals Bliss and Pershing were present, and to put them in personal communication with Mr. Graeme Thomson, the British Director of Transports, who had moved millions of troops during the present war. He himself did not pretend to know what arrangements had been made as regards United States shipping, or how many men were coming in their ships. Mr. Graeme Thomson could tell Generals Bliss and Pershing all about the arrangements for the use of British shipping.

General Pershing said that he had not received instructions in quite the same sense as mentioned by Mr. Lloyd George. The American Government, as he understood the matter, had undertaken to start the shipment of infantry and machine-gunners to meet the present emergency. As yet, however, no particular number of men had been mentioned. The American Government were preparing the infantry of four divisions to start with, and the matter was left for further consideration.

Mr. Lloyd George then read extracts from Lord Reading's telegrams, giving the specific numbers of 120,000 a month [see below].

General Pershing said that he had, as yet, nothing to confirm this. The information in Lord Reading's telegram, however, was so circumstantial in detail that he could not doubt its correctness and would ask for confirmation.

Mr. Lloyd George said that the telegram really admitted of no doubt, since the United States Government had even wanted a general statement of their policy published, without mentioning figures, of course, and this had been done.

General Pershing said he would communicate with his Government on the subject.

(The Conference then adjourned.)

* * * * * *

Specially Secret Addendum.

* * * * * *

Field Marshal Haig said that the present military situation was that the British Army had had to bear the brunt of a very severe attack. Now the enemy was preparing a strong attack on the Arras front. He would, therefore, like the British and French Governments to decide that it was urgent, in order to relieve the situation on the British front, that the French Army should take the offensive as soon as possible.

Generals Foch and *Pétain* agreed with the Field Marshal's proposal, and their view was endorsed by the Conference.

2, Whitehall Gardens, S.W.
April 4, 1918.

Ed.—On April 13, after reviewing the "*Proces-verbal* of the Beauvais Conference," Pershing wrote the following memorandum:

> The enclosed *Proces-verbal* of the Conference at Beauvais April 3, 1918, is substantially correct. The wording in some instances is not exactly as I remember it, but the main facts are there.

LC, Pershing Papers, folder: Conferences and Agreements, Folder No. 1, box 50; NARA, RG 120, M923, Records of the American Section, SWC, folder 376: *Proces-verbal* of the Beauvais Conference. The contents, except for the concluding section on the "Cooperation of the United States," can also be found at *USAWW*, Vol. 2, pp. 274–77.

Editor's Note—The decision reached at Beauvais for the future unified Allied conduct of the war on the Western front was of the greatest importance. For the first time, a single commander-in-chief was empowered to plan and conduct operations for the British, French, and American forces. Lord Hankey, the secretary of the British War Cabinet and an active participant in these meetings, wrote of it as follows:

> At Beauvais Foch explained that the situation had now changed. On March 26th, at Doullens, it was a question of co-ordinating action in full swing. At Beauvais on April 3rd it was a question of the future strategy and co-ordinating preparation for future action. For this he felt his powers to be insufficient—and no wonder when the obstructiveness of some of the generals is taken into account. So long as there was no action either by the French or British armies Doullens gave him no powers of co-ordination. Now he wanted the power of creating action, or, as he put it 'powers for the infusion of an idea of action', round which the preparations should be made in co-ordination. This was the more important because at the time of the Doullens Conference we were submitting to battle imposed upon us by the enemy, but at Beauvais we were thinking of our own action. In a word, Foch wanted it to be clear that the strategy was in his hands.... The Beauvais Agreement, therefore, extended into the strategical field the powers given to Foch at Doullens. As yet, however, his authority did not extend beyond the Western Front. (Lord Hankey, *The Supreme Command, 1914–1918*, vol. 2, pp 791–92.)

Memorandum of the Conference of the Allied Representatives at Beauvais, April 3, 1918

Present—

Mr. Lloyd George,
M. Clemenceau,
General Foch,

Marshal Haig,
General Pétain,
General Henry Wilson,
General Bliss,
General Pershing.

M. Clemenceau, presiding, said: We have come together to settle a very simple question regarding the functions of General Foch. I think we are all in agreement as to the coordination of allied action, but there is some difference in the understanding of General Foch's powers as conferred upon him at the Doullens conference of March 26th. General Foch will explain his difficulties.

General Foch, in substance as follows: The powers conferred by the Doullens conference were limited to the coordination of action between the Allies. They were conferred upon him while the action was on. The power to coordinate has been construed to be limited to the times the Allies were in action. That was March 26th at Doullens. Now we are at April 3rd. Now that the two armies are no longer in action but have stopped and are facing each other, there is nothing to coordinate. There should be authority to prepare for action and direct it. So that we are right back where we were before and nothing can be done until an action starts again.

Mr. Lloyd George: We have had more than 3 years of this war, and we have not had unity of action during that time. During the last year we have had two kinds of strategy, one by Haig and another by Pétain, both different, and nothing has been gained. The only thing that was accomplished was by General Neville when he was in supreme command (Marshal Haig endeavored to interrupt him.) The Germans have done exactly what General Neville tried to do. The Supreme War Council that met in February adopted a plan for handling a general reserve but through the action of those concerned nothing has come of it. It is a nullity. What has happened recently has stirred the British people very much and must not happen again, as the people will demand why it is happened, and somebody will be called to account. They want some sort of unity of command. General Foch is now empowered to coordinate the action of the allied armies, but this does not go far enough as he has no authority to control except by conferring with the respective commanders in chief. He wants authority to prepare for action. I think the resolution made at Doullens should be modified so that we may have a better understanding. I should like to hear what General Bliss and General Pershing have to say.

General Bliss, in substance: I find here two points (reading the Doullens resolution)

"Le General Foch est charges par les Gouvernements britannique et francais de coordonner l'action des armees allies sur le front oust. Il s'enterdra a cette effet avec les generaux en chef, qui sont a lui fournier tous les renseignements necessaires.

(Signe) Clemenceau
Milner
Doullens, le 26 mars, 1918."

in this resolution. The powers conferred upon General Foch are to coordinate the action of the British and French armies, but he is given no authority to act except in conference with the two commanders. This is one point. He is to be furnished certain information without which he cannot coordinate. This should be given him. That is the second point. (General Bliss went into this discussion rather more fully than indicated above.)

General Pershing: The principle of unity of command is undoubtedly the correct one for the Allies to follow. I do not believe it is possible to have unity of action without a supreme commander. We have already had experiences enough in trying to coordinate the operations of the Allied Armies without success. There has never been real unity of action. Such coordination between two or three armies is impossible no matter who the commanders-in-chief may be. Each commander-in-chief is interested in his town army, and cannot get the other commander's point of view nor grasp the problem as a whole. I am in favor of a supreme commander and believe that the success of the allied cause depends upon it. I think the necessary action should be taken by this council at once. I am in favor of conferring the supreme command upon General Foch.

Mr. Lloyd George: I agree fully with General Pershing. This is well put. (Mr. Lloyd George then called upon Marshal Haig.)

Marshal Haig: We have had practically complete unity of action. I have always cooperated with the French, whom I regard as in control of the strategical questions of the war. I was placed directly under the command of General Neville, and General Pétain and I have always worked well together. I agree with General Pershing's general idea that there should be unity of command but I think we have had it.

(The proposed resolution was then read but it referred only to the British and French Armies.)

General Pershing: I think this resolution should include the American Army. The arrangement is to be in force, as I understand it, from now on, and the American Army will soon be ready to function as such and should be included as an entity like the British and French armies.

General Pétain: There is no American army yet as such, as its units are either in training or are amalgamated with the British and French.

General Pershing: There may not be an American army in force functioning now but there soon will be and I want this resolution to apply to it when it becomes a fact. The American government is represented here at this conference and in the war, and any action as to the supreme command that includes the British and French armies should also include the American army.

The following resolution was then read and adopted:

Beauvais, April 3, 1918.

[English version from *Process-Verbal*]

General Foch is charged by the British, French, and American Governments with the coordination of the action of the Allied armies on the Western Front. To this end all powers n necessary to secure effective realization are conferred on him. The

British, French, and American Governments for this purpose entrust to General Foch the strategic direction of military operations.

The Commanders-in-Chief of the British, French, and American armies have full control of the tactical employment of their forces. Each Commander-in-Chief will have the right of appeal to his Government if, in his opinion, the safety of his army is compromised by any order received from General Foch.
Signed the following

Lloyd George	G. Clemenceau	General Pershing
Field-Marshal Sir D. Haig	General Foch	General Bliss
General Sir H. H. Wilson	General Pétain	

An exchange of signed copies of the above resolution then took place and the meeting adjourned. [*Ed.*—Signed copy in the folder.]

LC, Pershing Papers, folder: Conferences and Agreements, Folder No. 1, box 50.
Lloyd George, Memorandum, April 3, 1918. (See above, Beauvais Conference minutes, "Cooperation of the United States of America.")

Mr. Lloyd George stated that he had a cable from Lord Reading, the British Ambassador, to the effect that the President had said he would do all he could to help the Allies, and that the President had acceded to his request to send over American infantry and machine gun units to the number of 120,000 per month beginning in April provided the shipping necessary could be obtained. And that the disposition of these troops should be left to the American Commander-in-Chief in Europe.

Mr. Graeme Thompson afterwards said the same thing in detail:—

1. That the President had agreed to send over 120,000 troops per month and more if possible.
2. That the British had made arrangements to send over 60,000 per month.
3. That the Americans would send over 52,000 per month.
4. He requested that the Americans make arrangements to send over the remaining 4,000 per month.
5. And he hoped additional numbers not specified be brought over if shipping could be found, and suggested that all available space on passenger steamers be utilized for this purpose.

LC, Pershing Papers, folder: Conferences and Agreements, Folder No. 1, box 50.

Editor's Note—Lloyd George's manipulation of the facts in his statement during the discussion "Cooperation of the United States of America" in the Beauvais Conference became a very serious issue with the American political and military leaders.

Writing to Secretary Baker on May 4 after the Abbeville Conference, Bliss declared in his postscript:

> In the printed text of the *Procès-verbal* of the Conference held at Beauvais on April 3, please note the words of Mr. Lloyd George under the heading "Cooperation of the United States of America." These words are "Owing to the shortage of shipping, President Wilson had decided that the available shipping should be devoted, for the present entirely to the transport of Infantry and Machine-gunners each month for the next four months. If more shipping could be provided, President Wilson would send more men, and these men would be brigaded with armies already organized." When General Pershing and I told you of this statement, at General Pershing's house in Paris, you telegraphed to the President to ascertain what engagements he had made. He replied, as I remember it, to the general effect that he had made no such specific engagement as to numbers and time. Mr. Lloyd George's statement was based on a telegram from Lord Reading in Washington which he read to the Conference at Beauvais. As long as the statement made by Mr. Lloyd George at Beauvais remains uncorrected and, on the contrary, is given official circulation, it will be the cause of misunderstanding. It seems to me that it would be well if Lord Reading were himself to send a communication to Mr. Lloyd George correcting this statement. (LC, Bliss Papers, folder: General Correspondence—Bliss to Newton Diehl Baker, December 1917–May 1918, box 250.)

Kernan, CG, SOS, AEF, Tours, to Pershing, reply to Pershing to Kernan, March 20.

Your letter of March 20th [see Vol. 3] regarding the S.O.S. as seen during your recent inspection trip came to my headquarters after I had started on an inspection of several base ports. Col. Hagood read it to me over the long-distance phone, and steps were taken at once to mend some of the things mentioned.

The congestion at St. Nazaire had ceased when I got there and but two or three ships were at the docks. However, it is a recurrent condition dependent upon the relation of incoming ships and outgoing freight trains and to care for the excess periods we must have the storage planned for Montoir [see Editor's Note following]. Genl. Langfitt [Chief of Utilities, SOS] at my request is down there now and the construction will be pushed as fast as material and labor permit.

At Brest I found not a single transport in harbor but 3 arrived just as I was leaving. The requirements at Brest do not cover extensive storage areas, but require ample hospital arrangements and sufficient barracks to care for our incoming troops pending train assembling. The facilities have kept pace with our needs and will continue to do so. An immediate increase in the available hospital beds is the most pressing need and is being attended to. All the barracks were dirty and gave no evidence of a proper standard of police. An experienced officer to command immediately all the troops, as respects police, and discipline, has been sent there this week.

At Cherbourg the English are building camps to accommodate about 6000 troops. It was shown to me by the base commandant and is well situated just outside the city—good water is available and the drainage is fine. A French hospital of 300 beds has been placed at the disposal of the English for the care of our troops.

Col. Kean of the Med. Dep't. accompanied me and he inspected the hospital (empty now) and discussed with the English the need of some isolation wards for those certain to arrive with contagious disease.

In regard to Is-sur-Tille I was on the point of relieving Col. Farmer and assigning Col. Hilgard to the command when it was learned that G.O. 73 G.H.Q. 1917 was in process of revision and I understood Col. Connor to suggest that action be deferred in this matter till the new order was out. The situation therefore remains as it was at that point.

I am getting data as to all officers in the S.O.S., not on duty directly with troops; that is, all on staff duties and detached services of various kinds. The surplus will be disposable with the combatant troops or elsewhere.

I have not heard of any serious friction or trouble in S.O.S. since the new organization went into effect and I believe affairs are moving on reasonably well.

LC, Pershing Papers, folder: Gen. Francis J. Kernan, box 111.

Editor's Note—Kernan's comment to Pershing above on Montoir (Montoir-de-Bretagne, *Loire-Inférieure*) reflected the importance of this port and general storage depot to the AEF's logistical and strategic plans. In 1917, the Director General of Transportation developed plans for a large base storage, railroad, and pier complex to be built at Montoir, adjacent to St. Nazaire, the AEF's primary port of entry in France. As approved in January 1918, the planned complex would eventually contain 138 50 x 504-foot warehouses with 4,215,000 square feet of covered storage, an additional 9,812,000 square feet of open storage, and 236 miles of trackage. However, the war ended before all of the facilities were completed. Main rail lines across France linked the ports of St. Nazaire, Montoir, and Nantes on the Loire River to the AEF's headquarters, training, and concentration areas in northeastern France where the AEF was to be employed (see Map 4). Montoir became a critical initial point on the primary line of communications which carried supplies and equipment forward 202 miles to the Intermediate Section's large general supplies storage depot at Gièvres (near Villefranche) for storage. From there shipments moved another 200 miles to the regulating station and storage depot at Is-sur-Tille and other forward depots for distribution to the subdepots in the Advanced Section and combat and support units in the Zone of the Advance (area of active operations). Wilgus, *Transporting*, pp. 254–59.

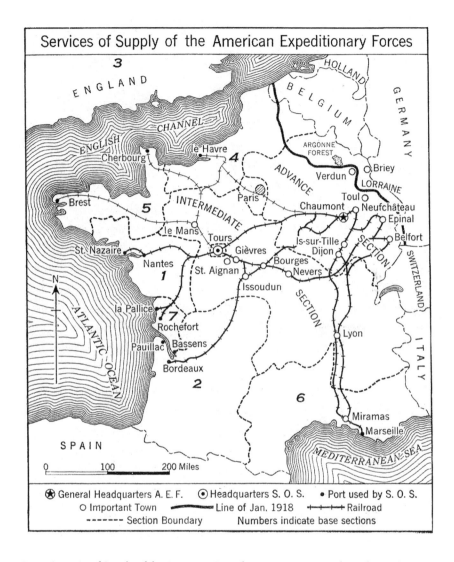

Map 4. Services of Supply of the American Expeditionary Forces. Pershing devoted a great amount of time and effort to planning and building the Services of Supply into an efficient and effective organization that would fully support the requirements of the AEF's strategic plans. The successful development and operation of the primary line of communications from the St. Nazaire–Montoir–Nantes port complex to the AEF's concentration, training, and probable operational areas in northeastern France were absolutely vital to the achievement of this objective. Source: American Battle Monuments Commission, *American Armies and Battlefields in Europe*, p. 438.

The AEF's General Storage Depot at Montoir-et-Bretagne (Montoir) was the main storage site for general supplies, materials, and equipment arriving at St. Nazaire and the newly opened pier there. In April 1918 the large storage depot was still under construction and just beginning its operations. This photograph shows just the part of the area used to store Engineer materials, in this instance primarily railway tracks intended for numerous critical projects on the line of communications to the east. Source: NARA, Still Picture Branch, RG 111, 111-SC-10173.

This photograph of the Engineer storage area at Montoir-et-Bretagne General Storage Depot was taken in February 1919, when the depot was in full operation. A comparison with the previous photograph of Montoir in April 1918 clearly indicates the immense volume of materials still being received for the AEF and stored at the partially completed depot. Source: NARA, Still Picture Branch, RG 111, 111-SC-53034.

Edward M. House, Counsellor to the President, Washington, to Pershing.

This letter will introduce to you my good friend Mr. Peter Clark Macfarlane who is going to Europe for the purpose of writing articles for the *Saturday Evening Post* about the work of American soldiers and sailors is Europe.

I am particularly interested in Mr. Macfarlane's work and I consider it exceedingly important that the splendid work now being done by our Army and Navy in Europe should be kept graphically before the American public. I know of no one better able to help do this than Macfarlane, and I trust that so far as you properly can, you will make it possible for him to do his work in a thorough manner.

Edward Mandell House Papers, Manuscripts and Archives, Yale University Library, Series 1: Correspondence, folder 3072: John J. Pershing, box 89.

Bliss, Chief, American Section, and Permanent Military Representative, SWC, Versailles, to TAG, War Department.

Cable 76-S.

For Acting Chief of Staff.

Confidential and not to be made public.
1. French and British Great Headquarters report only local actions to noon today. No important changes in lines. Junction of British and French forces has been moved northward to a point 1,300 meters southeast of Thennes.
2. For the President, Secretary of War and Acting Chief of Staff. In the conference at Doullens on March 26th General Foch was charged with the responsibility of coordinating the military action of the Western front but he was not specifically given full power to do this. The result has been what might have been expected. He has been obliged to persuade the allied commanders when he ought to have had the power to give them orders. Yesterday General Pershing and myself were requested by Mr. Lloyd George and Mr. Clemenceau to attend a conference at Beauvais at about noon today. There were present Mr. Lloyd George, Mr. Clemenceau and Generals Haig, Pétain, Foch, Wilson, Pershing and Bliss. The following agreement was made with perfect unanimity and cordiality. "General Foch is charged by the British, French and American governments with the duty of coordinating the action of the allied armies on the Western front; and with this object in view there is conferred upon him all the powers necessary for its effective accomplishment. For this purpose the British, French and American governments entrust to General Foch the strategic direction of military operations. The Commanders in Chief of the British, French and American armies *shall* exercise in full the tactical conduct of their armies. Each Commander in Chief shall have the right to appeal to his government if in his opinion his army finds itself placed in danger by any instructions received from General

Foch. Signed by Mr. Lloyd George, Mr. Clemenceau, Pétain, Foch, Haig, Wilson, General Bliss and General Pershing." I was not in favor of the right of appeal of any Commander in Chief to his own government. Nevertheless there was cordial agreement by all to the above quoted document.

3. The English and French at above conference expressed belief that Germans are about to deliver another heavy attack north of Arras.
Bliss.

NARA, RG 120, M923. Records of American Section, SWC, Cablegrams Received Sent to War Department, Nos. 13 to 100, January 22, 1918, to April 27, 1918.

Pershing to TAG, War Department, in part in reply to TAG, War Department to Bliss, American Section, SWC, Versailles, cable 40-R, March 30, and Bliss to TAG, War Department, cable 67-S, March 28.

Cable P-844-S. Confidential.
For the Chief of Staff.

1. Reference recommendations of Supreme War Council which the Secretary of War approved in cablegram sent the President by General Bliss [March 28, cable 67-S,] and your cable of March 30 to General Bliss [March 30, cable 40-R]. Have made preliminary arrangements for training and early employment with French of such units of infantry as may be sent over by our own transportation. This infantry will be placed in quiet sectors with French units as far as practicable unless they are urgently needed for more active service elsewhere. It is not intended that our units shall replace losses of British or French organizations and therefore our artillery should be held in readiness to follow when called for in order that our divisional organizations may be completed as soon as possible when the opportunity offers. In the meantime, the artillery should receive the most thorough training possible and should be rushed on any transportation that can be so used especially if there should be any delay in preparing infantry or getting it to seaboard.

2. Further reference your cable to General Bliss, March 30, infantry of divisions for training with British. They should be started as early as arrangements can be made. Situation may become so serious that some of our infantry units will be forced to serve with British temporarily. But Americans must not lose sight of the purpose to build up divisions and corps of their own, even though both British and French should be compelled to reduce the number of their divisions. And any aid we give in this manner must be considered temporary only and in order to meet the present emergency.

3. It is recommended that you start by sending over the infantry of the two British divisions, holding the artillery and auxiliary troops at ports and in readiness to be shipped on any available transportation. Also that you send the infantry of two divisions by our own transports, holding the artillery and auxiliary troops in like manner for shipment when possible. It is not believed that plans should look further into

the future than this as we must avoid the tendency to incorporate our infantry into British divisions where it will be used up and never relieved. Any such general policy would be disastrous to us. I firmly believe our own divisions will be as good after one month training here as any British division in existence. Although Allies are now demanding infantry, it is my belief that they will both be asking for artillery personnel in the near future.

4. 18,500 replacements needed now. Estimated 27,000 additional replacements needed in next three months. This total of 45,000 replacements should be echeloned and the last of them should arrive with the last of the infantry of the 4 divisions.

5. Recommend that plan outlined in your cable of March 30 to General Bliss be followed, limiting priority of infantry to 4 divisions for the present and adding the replacements noted in paragraph 4 above.

6. In this connection you are advised that in a discussion of this subject with the military representatives of the Supreme War Council, it became known that the French representative wanted the same concessions made to his government and the Italian representative asked whether his government might expect same assistance by our infantry units. So that we must stand firm on this matter and after the action indicated in the foregoing paragraphs is taken we must take over our infantry as soon as practicable and form our own divisions. [In addition—April 8, P-876-S]

NARA, RG120, M930, Confidential Series, AEF to War Department, roll 7; see also LC, Pershing Papers, folder: Training and Employment of American Troops with British, box 198.

Pershing to TAG, War Department.

Cable P-845-S.

3. For Chief of Staff. 3B. Transport Montrose actually at La Pallice well adapted for cross-channel service. Carries 5500 tons coal on 22-foot draft. Request authorization to requisition her immediately. [Reply—April 8, A-1066-R-8]

4. For Chief of Staff and Chief of Ordnance. Situation of Ordnance supplies for reserve and replacement is very critical. Supplies have been properly ordered in due time from the states. Supplies so ordered have been proper to provide for depot reserve and replacement supply in kind and quantity. Of practically none of these articles are the specified reserves in depots. Few of these items are available in needed quantities for replacement. Additionally considerable quantity of such limited supplies as have been received were issued to provide for shortages of initial equipment. For all of these items frequent cables have been sent stating urgency. Everything possible must be done to relieve this situation at once. Urgently request that following cables in this subject be brought to you personally for your information: [hereafter list of 10 AEF cables, not reproduced]. [Reply—April 16, A-1110-R-2E]

NARA, RG 120, M930, Main Series, AEF to War Department, roll 2.

Pershing to TAG, War Department, in part in reply to TAG, War Department, to Pershing, cable A-1020-R, April 1; in addition to Pershing to TAG, War Department, cable P-133-S, August 31, 1917 (Volume 1).

Cable P-850-S.

1. For Chief of Staff. 1C. With reference to paragraph 7, your cablegram 1020. Please see paragraph 14, my cablegram 133. My views as expressed in last sentence of that cablegram are unchanged. The larger the force of Marines in France the more complicated will be the system of supply, accounts, promotions, et cetera. The Marine Brigade here gives such representation as might for the sake of sentiment be desired for that Corps in France. They are a fine Corps, officers and men. If more can be spared from their statutory duties they should be discharged from the Navy and taken over by the Army.

NARA, RG 120, M930, Main Series, AEF to War Department, roll 2.

TAG, War Department, to Pershing.

Cable A-1034-R. Confidential.

16. Information received through Operations Navy contains the statement that the French have 20 passenger liners not at present profitably employed. Also that 10 of these could be obtained with accommodations for at least 20,000 troops. Please investigate and advise promptly if French have any passenger liners not at present in use. March. [Reply—April 10, P-887-S-1B]

NARA, RG 120, M930, Confidential Series, War Department to AEF, roll 18.

TAG, War Department, to Pershing, in addition to Bliss to TAG, War Department, cable 67-S, March 28, and TAG, War Department, to Bliss, cable 40-R, March 30.

Cable A-1036-R. Confidential.

The following extract of a cablegram from the British Ministry of Shipping to their representative in the United States is repeated for your information:

"We have informed War Cabinet that in shipping provided by Great Britain we shall be able embark in America in April some 60,000 men, Admiral Sims' estimate of carrying power of American troop fleet is 52,000 per month. In addition there is certain Dutch tonnage available for use by America and we are obtaining use of certain Italian tonnage. In total it is considered that 120,000 American troops can be embarked in April and if anything rather more in following months. In view of urgent military needs Lord Reading had approached the President with the view of obtained dispatch of 120,000 infantry per month to Europe between now and July. Infantry and machine gun units only. Men to be brigaded with British and French divisions on the same basis as in case of 6 division plan. This means using all troop-carrying ships to carry American infantry without reference to recent controversies. The President agrees that all possible measures must be taken to insure maximum use of troop tonnage."

This program would practically stop all shipments of artillery, technical units, service of rear, Army and Corps troops. It is requested that you cable at once what arrangements, if any, you have made with British and French for the supply and maintenance and land transportation of the infantry and machine gun units that are now being given preferential transportation as far as practicable in accordance with General Bliss's cable number 67. Your attention is invited to my cable Number 40 to General Bliss [see March 30] which was requested to be repeated promptly to you. Repeat promptly to General Bliss.
March.
[Handwritten note: *"Phoned CinC who is to forward copy to Gen Bliss."*]

NARA, RG 120, M930, Confidential Series, War Department to AEF, roll 18.

[GHQ AEF reaction to cable A-1036-R]

April 6, 1918

Conner, ACS, G-3 (Operations), GHQ, AEF, to CS.

1. This cable 1036-R shows that the British are endeavoring to extend the principle of priority of infantry until July. The cable also indicates that the British hope that their shipping and our own will be able to transport 120,000 infantry and machine-gun personnel per month during the three months involved.

2. The cable does not indicate that the French and Italians are cooperating with the British in insisting on this project. Based on past experience, however, it may be assumed that both the French and Italians have joined the British in the representations made by the latter.

3. The phrase in the cable "The President agrees that all possible measures must be taken to insure maximum use of troop tonnage" appears clearly to indicate not only that our government is not yet wholly committed to this project, but that the administration desires the recommendations of its military advisors before formulating its course of action.

4. It is known that the incorporation of Americans in British units is the only alternative to an early reduction in the number of British units. The gradual reduction in the strength of their units which the British foresaw last spring was undoubtedly one of the causes which led to their written proposal to draft our men under their colors.

It is well to inquire whether or not the present project will not in the end accomplish what was proposed and rejected last spring.

5. The British have already lost not less than 250,000 men in the present battle. Even before the present battle the British units were below strength. While by combing the manpower of Britain it may be possible to replace the present losses it is impossible that Britain can replace the further losses which she is to suffer.

As a consequence we may expect the British to attempt to hold any of our units incorporated under their colors; for only by so doing can they avoid reducing the number of British divisions.

The natural conclusion appears to be that from the standpoint of forming our own forces it is at least as easy to resist incorporating our soldiers with the British as it will be to secure the return of our units once we have brigaded them with the British.

6. The 360,000 infantry and machine-gun personnel which are involved in the present project represent the contingents of those arms required for 21 divisions. To complete the organization so that we may bring these 360,000 officers and soldiers together with American forces, we must bring over [542,592]* other troops including army corps, army and service supply troops. In addition, we are now 22,120 short in these latter categories. The total excess required over the 360,000 infantry and machine guns is thus 564,710 officers and soldiers.

In addition, before all these troops can be brought over the replacements which we shall need will amount to about 158,000.

It will thus be not less than 7 months after July 1 before we could completely reassemble our forces if the project is accepted.

7. But the delay in assembling our troops is not the most serious side of the question. Should we accept the plan it must be with the fullest realization that we will be totally unable to supply our troops or to exercise anything more than a purely fictitious control over these officers and soldiers for many months after July 1, 1918. Instead of relieving us from a burden, acquiescence in such a plan delivers over 360,000 officers and soldiers to foreign commanders, down to include the regiment, but leaves us unable to evade ultimate responsibility. There is no precedent for such a plan in all the history of equal nations. Great Britain did not even follow such a course with her dependencies, Canada, Australia, and New Zealand, but formed the contingents from those countries in complete divisions and army corps.

8. If the proposed plan be adopted, only continuous success could avoid the resentment of our people at seeing our soldiers incorporated on a wholesale scale under other colors. It is understood that the press representatives have shown a tendency to formulate criticisms that after nearly a year we have no independence.

---

*[Bracketed change in figures appears in pencil on document, and following 3 sentences are lined out in pencil.]

These moral factors cannot be neglected and there is no certainty, and in fact little probability, that 360,000 infantry and machine guns can definitely turn the present Allied situation into a decisive victory.

9. Infantry alone cannot stop the German. However, much we may need the tutelage of the British and the French, we need not fear to assert that troops of all arms are as essential in the defense as in the attack.

10. The only hope of really winning this war lies in an American army. The formation of that army is a paramount consideration and any scheme which postpones the organization of our army, and which virtually eliminates the possibility of carrying on the training of our higher officers and staffs in conjunction with that of the troops, is fundamentally unsound.

11. In developing the army not the least essential element is the development of the service of supply, including its staff. That service is already short of its proper ratio of troops. We are even now unable to operate the trains which feed our troops.

The present project stagnates the service of supply and, in short, means that not until the summer of 1919, if then, could we hope to handle our own supply.

12. The present call upon us may be likened to the calls made by local commanders for reserves during battle. The commander who accedes to all these local calls uses up his reserves piecemeal and prematurely, and is beaten. America possesses the only potential reserve. Even though that reserve should not be exhausted its use piecemeal is nonetheless a grave mistake. Even though such piecemeal employment of our forces should against all precedent result in a tactical victory, America would not accomplish her object. America must have a voice in the peace councils if a peace satisfactory to her is to be formulated. She will have no such voice if her forces are used up by putting her battalions in French and British units.

13. Familiarity with past events forces us, willingly or unwillingly, to the conclusion that both the British and the French are determined to delay in every possible way the organization of a purely American force under American command. Although such a belief is mortifying, the undersigned believes that in acting thus the British and French, actuated by the highest motives, are convinced that we are incapable of handling large forces. If we are incapable, then the war is lost, for neither our people nor our soldiers will consent to the indefinite virtual drafting of our men under foreign colors.

14. The method of pushing this project is very similar to that adopted in other cases. First an opening is obtained here or in Washington and then a further development is sought at the other end.

15. The execution of the present project ends any hope of forming even a single army corps this year, if indeed it does not end all hope of seeing an American army in this war.

16. No action in rejecting this proposal can be too energetic.

[In addition—April 8, Pershing telephone conversation with Conner.]

USAWW, vol. 2, pp. 283–85.

April 4

Pershing's Personal Diary

At Paris. Worked in quarters. Saw Mr. Elmer Roberts [Associated Press]. Did some shopping; bought some ties for Warren. Had talk with General Bliss; had him, his son Captain Bliss, and Major [Arthur] Poillon [Bliss's aide] to lunch. Talked into phonograph to make propaganda record for Columbia Phonograph Company. The Secretary of War and his party arrived from Italy in the afternoon and stopped at house.

LC, Pershing Papers, Diary, May 7, 1917–September 1, 1918, box 4.

Brig. Gen. Benjamin D. Foulois, Chief, Air Service, SOS, AEF, to Maj. Gen. Sir Hugh Trenchard, Chief of Staff, Air Ministry, London.

B.D.F. 169.

Due to recent changes in the military situation in France, as regards its effect on bombing operations in the Nancy area, to the consolidation of the Allied Armies under a Supreme Command, and to radical changes in the organization of the American Expeditionary Forces which also affect the American Air Service, I find that certain changes in my assignments of officers for bombing operations in the Nancy area will, I believe, result in more efficient future cooperation.

I find that on account of the present widely separated fields on which General Salmond, General Newall, and myself are working, that it is absolutely necessary that I have an officer specially designated to act as a traveling liaison officer between British Air Service Headquarters in the field, your Headquarters in London, and my Headquarters here in France. I have therefore thought that the most suitable American officer who is available is Major Harold Fowler, who has heretofore been working in connection with the bombing operations in the Nancy area.

Major Fowler had considerable previous field service with the Royal Flying Corps before coming into the American Air Service, and I sincerely hope his assignment to this duty will meet with your approval. Major Fowler will be especially charged with the duty of keeping me informed at all times as to the progress of our combined bombing program, and will travel back and forth between the three headquarters for the purpose of keeping me more promptly informed of the plans of yourself, General Salmond, and General Newall.

Pending the resumption of British activities in the Nancy area, I have issued instruction to Colonel Van Horn, my representative in the Advance Section, to rush work on aerodromes in that area and in the Chalons area.

We have now an opportunity to secure a considerable number of labor troops for this work, and I have placed Colonel [Ambrose] Monell (under Colonel Van Horn) in special charge of this work with instructions to push it as rapidly as possible. This action I hope will also meet with your approval.

As you probably know, our Handley Page parts will not be coming out of production in the United States much before June, on account of numerous delays in production, so this will set back our schedule on Handley Page squadrons for at least two months.

Am using every effort to build up the Caproni Night-Bomber factories in Italy, and hope to get a few squadrons built up, using these Italian machines.

Also, as I have fully expected, our production of Bristol Fighters, De H 4's, and De H 9's from the United States will not begin to reach us to be of any use before July 1. If shipping is made available, however, I believe that these machines will come very fast during the last half of 1918.

As you may know, I have been designated as the American Air Service representative to work with the American Section of the Supreme War Council at Versailles, and also am the American representative on the Inter-Allied Aviation Committee. In these various positions I feel that I can be of some assistance to the British and American Air Services in connection with their present or future needs in raw, semi-finished, and finished materials, and I hope the British Air Service will feel free to call upon me at any and all times to assist in carrying our any plans which they or you may have in view for General Salmond or myself.

I don't know what your views are in connection with the Supreme Air Service command, but I will frankly state that I believe either yourself or General Salmond should be selected for the command, if a Supreme Air Service command is contemplated.

I hope that the steps which I have taken toward a more efficient coordination of our combined operations in the Nancy area will meet with your approval, and if there is anything also that I can be doing in that area at the present time, I wish you would so inform me.

I am sending a copy of this letter to General Salmond, in the event that he may have something for me to look after in that area while we are waiting for instruction from the Supreme Command regarding the use of the American Air Service.

Our American squadrons are eating their hearts out because they have no machines with which to get in and take their share in the present work, and I hope that we won't have to wait much longer for an opportunity to get into action.

[copy to Maj. Gen, J. M. Salmond, General Officer Commanding, RAF in the Field.]

LC, Foulois Papers, folder 14: AEF, Air Service, Operations—Bombing General, 1918, n.d., box 9.

Dawes, GPA, AEF, SOS, Paris, to Pershing.

[Handwritten]
These are the hardest days I have had. I just want to write to relieve my mind, and as if I had your helpful presence with me. I do so miss seeing you from time to time.

Am getting labor first as fast as I can wh. [which] I understand is what you want. This results in my getting a bit of stress and criticism at points when I send labor—that we do not amount to anything, and send labor before it is wanted and with undermanned (officered) units. This comes because it seems a physical impossibility for the S.O.S. to give us officers & men as fast as we get the labor. But I would be derelict in duty if I let any of this labor get away. And just as soon as I can get my officers I will have no trouble in straightening it out. You know it would be very easy *to go slow*, and not allow my labor recruiting to go ahead fast.—But I know you want the men—and I am going to get them and slow up this temporary attack. Kernan & Patrick are, I believe, my faithful friends—but I am making, without even knowing them, active opponents who seem to resent everything I try to do. There is nothing I want you to do—it is a relief in the midst of anxious effort to skip for a moment, and write to a helpful old friend like you. But don't you get it into your head for a minute that I am weakening.

I was never more certain of success in my life than I am now in this labor work. But when you remember that we are dealing including the Italian preparations with 25,000 men—and that they are not under military discipline, and I do not have but a fractional part of the men requisite to handle them, you must be prepared to hear things that I do not know my business, etc., for a little time. The great thing now is to get the men. This it was predicted we could not do—and now, for instance, after furnishing over 4000 men to a local commander (who, the men, are doing good work), he is so belittling me and my organization that I have had to ask officers detailed to me to be sent to Paris instead of Gièvres for fear he will demoralize them. Headquarters S.O.S. are all right. They are workers like you and me, and of course getting hell probably on that account.

This letter is not a complaint. I do not need your help. When I do, I should not hesitate to ask for it—for I am only trying to faithfully carry out your plans.

I hope you keep well. These are the critical times. I thank Heaven that a man like you commands us, and represents his country here. Don't let me worry you just because I care for you so much I can't help writing you once in a while in this personal way.

LC, Pershing Papers, folder: Gen. Charles G. Dawes, 1918, box 59.

Sims, Commander, U.S. Naval Forces Operating in European Waters, to Pershing, in reply to Pershing to Biddle for Sims, April 2, telegram 9379.

Telegram 1815.

For General Pershing. Ref. your cable of 2 April. I have never been informed in any way as to agreements under which troops were to be carried. I have twice requested information from Navy Department but was informed in each case that matter was being handled by the War Department.

NARA, RG 45, ONRL, T829, Miscellaneous Records of the Navy Department, 1–8/1918, Miscellaneous Material Print Files, World War, roll 411.

Pershing to TAG, War Department, in part in reply to TAG, War Department, to Pershing, cable A-984-R, March 25; in addition to Pershing to TAG, War Department, cable P-669-S, March 2.

Cable P-856-S.
    3. For Chief of Ordnance. With reference to paragraph 2B, our cablegram 669, and paragraph 1A, your 984. Orders being placed with British Government for 41 8-inch howitzers and 176 9.2-inch howitzers. This provides for Army Artillery to be armed with equal numbers of each caliber of howitzers. Proportion of Mark I and Mark II howitzers will be cabled later. In addition to small quantity of British ammunition the following 9.2-inch howitzer ammunition is required in France for estimated consumption July 10,000; August 35,000; September 35,000; October 50,000; November 50,000, December 80,000. Total for balance of calendar year 260,000 rounds. In addition to above 250,000 rounds are required for reserve of 3 months' supply. This reserve should be accumulated at the most rapid rate possible. Paragraph 1A, your cablegram 984, indicates that the importance of furnishing this ammunition is not appreciated. No further aid can be expected from the British. Request that you give the supply of this ammunition your personal attention and that you inform me what deliveries can be made. [*Ed.*—On April 20 in cable A-1141-R-1, the Ordnance Department replied that its best present estimate was "possibly 5,000 additional in July. We are taking active steps to place new orders and will advise later." When the Ordnance Department finally answered the GHQ AEF on July 10 in cable A-1690-R-20D, it stated "Delayed completion of loading plant prevents fulfillment of delivery estimates 9.2-inch Howitzer ammunition." It now estimated "best possible seaboard deliveries" as 1,500 rounds in July, 12,000 in August, 27,000 in September, 45,000 in October, 48,000 in November, and 52,000 in December.]

NARA, RG 120, M930, Main Series, AEF to War Department, roll 2, and War Department to AEF, rolls 12 and 13.

TAG, War Department, to Pershing.

Cable A-1035-R.
    1N. Attention Air Service. We desire brought to the United States a small quantity single-seater pursuit machines training purposes. This should be the same

machines as single-seater used on front. What is considered best single-seater now in use on front? [Reply—April 14, P-913-S-1F]

NARA, RG120, M930, War Department to AEF, roll 12.

TAG, War Department, to Pershing, in part in reply to Pershing to TAG, War Department, cable P-790-S, March 27.

Cable A-1039-R. Confidential.
   1. It is at present estimated that production of Liberty engines up to June 30th will amount to 3,256, including those already delivered. Of this amount 734 have been allotted to Navy, leaving 522 [*sic*: 2,522] to be divided between Army Aviation Service, British, French, Italian and Ordnance Department for tanks. It is estimated that probable production of combat planes requiring Liberty engine up to June 30th will amount to 1,439, including 525 Bristol fighters, 904 DeHaviland 4's, 10 Handley-Page. To equip these planes will require 2,174 Liberty engines.
   1A. Great Britain has requested 980 engines, France 6 engines, Italy 5 engines, Ordnance Department for tanks 500 engines to be delivered at the factory prior to June 30th; total requirements 3,665, total shortage 1,143. French and Italian representatives here state that they will make additional request for Liberty engines as soon as tests now being made in France are completed. British representative states that if a total allotment of 980 engines be given them they can probably furnish certain fully equipped machines for our squadrons in France. Request that you advise us what allocation we should make of available engines between our Allies, Ordnance Department for tanks and United States Army air service. Cable your decision without delay. In the event that our output of planes is limited by shortage of engines, we will take action looking to redistribution of raw materials between ourselves and Allies. [Reply—April 12, P-904-S; in addition—April 12, A-1088-R; April 13, A-1101-R-1; May 3, P-1043-S-1, 1A]
   3. Operations Navy cabling Admiral Sims the following: "Situation here regard *Leviathan* most unsatisfactory as regard route to Liverpool. Unless active steps are taken nothing will be accomplished. The necessity for actually putting troops into France now is one which will admit of no delay or temporize over difficulties attendant thereupon. If the *Leviathan* runs to Brest she can make the round trip in from 18 to 20 days. On present schedule she takes over 40 days besides going through a more dangerous zone. All of the difficulties cited your recent cable can be met except the coal and the Army can handle the troops. Diverting for purpose of building up the coal reserve sufficient to coal *Leviathan* either the USCT Crowell or one of the 2 mine ships of the lake type assigned to mine operations northern barrage. Make best arrangements possible for berthing *Leviathan* for on west voyage she will be routed to that port. Matter of converting a few boilers to burn oil under consideration." [See April 1, Benson to Sims, cable 4475.]

In your opinion do you foresee any difficulty not covered by Navy in carrying out the plan suggested? March. [Reply—April 10, P-887-S-1A]

NARA, RG 120, M930, Confidential Series, AEF to War Department, roll 12.

April 5

Pershing's Personal Diary

At Paris. Worked in quarters. Left for Chaumont with Colonel Boyd and Lieutenant Adamson at about 11:30, leaving the Secretary, and his party at the house, Rue de Varenne. Left Lieutenant Hughes and Colonel Mott to look out for them. Stopped at Mrs. Boyd's house at Fontainebleau for luncheon. Reached Chaumont at about 5:30 p. m. Saw Colonel McCoy, Acting Chief of Staff, and Colonel Fox Conner. General Harbord left for 1st Division.

LC, Pershing Papers, Diary, May 7, 1917–September 1, 1918, box 4.

Foch, Chief of Staff, French GHQ, to Minister of War (Clemenceau).

Headquarters Allied Armies,
General Staff.
No. 92

I have the honor to ask you to be kind enough to let me have a copy of the Beauvais agreement, dated April 3, confirming my mission as set forth by the Doullens Agreement and adding the necessary powers enabling me to fulfill it.

I would like to avail myself of the present opportunity to request that you let me know in an official letter the title I am to assume with the armies in official written communications. The only title I hold at present, that of Chief of the General Staff of the army, whose functions are set forth in Paris by executive decree and for whose duties no provisions are made in the armies, is insufficient to justify certain orders or instructions which I have occasion to give.

The title could be replaced by that of commander of the Allied armies.

At the same time the position of my general staff with the armies could be set forth * * *
[In addition—April 14, Foch to Minister of War]

USAWW, vol. 2, p. 281; see also *Les armées françaises dans la Grande guerre, Tome 6*, vol. 1, *Annexes*, vol. 3: *Annexe* No. 1461, pp. 169–70.

Pershing to Secretary of War Newton D. Baker (then in Paris).

[Handwritten]
I noticed the other day that one of the British papers, in referring to the fact that plans had been made to send American troops to the assistance of the allies, stated that this would relieve the British of the necessity of depleting the strength of the forces kept at home for defensive purposes.

This suggests to my mind a certain political phase of the British situation which may give us additional explanation as to why Mr. Lloyd George and British representatives are so urgent in their appeals for assistance from America. The train of thought leads me to conceive the existence of a condition that may be fraught with danger to the cause in that it indicates a serious lack of cooperation between the civil and military authorities of Great Britain, as was also indicated to you in some of the things I repeated to you yesterday. All these together give me the idea of a national half-hearted determination, and no more, on the part of the British civil control to do all they can to win the war.

Following this farther, may I suggest that you give the matter serious thought. There is so very much at stake for us that it seems to me that very frank representations should be made to the British government as to the urgency of their putting into the army every possible man that can be mustered to meet the immediate emergency. It need not be pointed out that there is a limit to the rapidity with which our troops can be brought over, and there seems to me to be a very real danger of the British political world allowing itself to be lulled into inaction upon the theory that the Americans are in a position to meet all possible contingencies that may arrive.

It may be that you would think it advisable to go to London, or else to intimate to the President the urgency of Great Britain's putting into the ranks every possible man to withstand the present German onslaught, even if they have to promise to withdraw them in six months, and of their doing so without waiting on us or counting on us in the slightest degree. There will be few enough men even with the best we all can do. It will be time enough for Great Britain to consider the defense of England after she has put forth every possible energy on the continent. Here is the place to beat Germany, and not on British soil. In writing this I have in mind what you told me regarding available men in England.

I give you the following from General Sir William Robertson in a letter to me dated January 17th:

" * * * The British Government has given the most anxious consideration to the question of the maintenance of the armies in the field during 1918, and, by making every effort, there will become available for service at the front 449,000 men now under training, plus 100,000 men to be called up. In addition, there will be called up 100,000 men of lower category who are not fit for the first line, plus 120,000 lads of 18 years of age, who will not be available for service at the front till 1919. Please keep these figures strictly secret."

It may be that some of these have already been called out, but I am informed that large numbers of men are held for home defense.

LC, Pershing, folder: Newton D. Baker, January–June 1918, box 20.

Pershing, Paris, before departing 73 rue de Varenne for Chaumont, to Secretary of War Newton D. Baker.

I am leaving for Chaumont, thence to our own front, and shall return here on Sunday on my way to the British front in connection with our in-coming units, so I shall see you before you leave.

In the meantime it will give me the greatest pleasure to have you consider this house as your own.

Col. Mott will remain in Paris, and Lieut. Hughes will stay here at the house to be of any service they may be needed for.

I have arranged to send Sergeant [Frank] Lanckton to the States with you, my first thought being to have him look after you, and the second being to give him a trip. He has not been any too strong for some time and the voyage will do him good. I trust that this will be satisfactory to you and that he will not be in your way, but that he will be really useful.

LC, Pershing, folder: Newton D. Baker, January–June 1918, box 20.

Editor's Note—Frank G. Lanckton was a career Army enlisted man who served as Pershing's enlisted orderly and personal driver from Pershing's time as Military Governor of the Moro Province in the Philippines (1909–13) through the expedition into Mexico (1916–17), the World War (1917–19), and as Chief of Staff (1921–24), and well into Pershing's retirement and his tenure as chairman of the American Battle Monuments Commission. Lanckton had a close relationship with Pershing's only surviving child, Francis Warren Pershing. He retired as a Master Sergeant.

Secretary Baker, then in Paris, to the President.

For the President.

Returned from Italy Thursday. Spent one day at the front and one in Rome as Mr. Page feared misunderstanding if I failed to visit Capital after having been in Paris and London.

Military situation continues stationary with very heavy artillery duel more or less continuously. Believed here that the Germans have still thirty divisions of fresh troops and plan another attack in force near Arras. Plans for defence along the whole line are made and allies have much larger and better placed reserves than on March 21. If estimate of thirty divisions is correct Germans have used up more than half of their first quality attack troops. Our first division begins to move out of the trenches tomorrow to become a part of the battle reserve and will probably be in action in a week or ten days. This division about equals two British divisions in numbers and is regarded as fully trained. The men are full of enthusiasm and pride. They are also completing one of the replacement divisions so that we will have four in the trenches and one in battle. Our four because of larger numbers release six French for reserve.

Our contribution is thus important and helpful. Counterattack in preparation which may modify whole recent situation.

The original appointment of General Foch was hesitating and powers given him largely advisory. At meeting yesterday whole matter was reviewed and practically supreme command given him over British, French and American armies on West front.

So far as I can see there is nothing else for me to do here now and unless you advise otherwise I will leave on Tuesday, April ninth, for home. No available ship sails earlier. Reply will reach me care Ambassador Sharp.
Baker.

Link (ed.), *The Papers of Woodrow Wilson*, vol. 47: *March 13–May 12, 1918*, pp. 261–62.

Gen. Louis Ernest de Maud'huy, CG, 11th French Army Corps, to Pershing.

I have the honor of thanking you for the flattering mark of esteem which you have been kind enough to give me and for which I shall ever remain most grateful.

We shall always be proud to have had the 26th Division under my orders, having recognized in these splendid troops, from their Commander to the last enlisted man, an absolute devotion to duty and the finest qualities of the soldier.

I hope to have the good fortune of again meeting with the Division on the field of battle.

I beg to convey to you, General, together with my thanks for your kind attention, my heartfelt wishes for the glory of your arms and the success of your Army.

[*Ed.*—Pershing had met with de Maud'huy on March 8 at his headquarters at Soissons and had a long and frank discussion about the 26th Division. See Vol. 3, Pershing's Personal Diary, March, 8, for details.]

LC, Pershing Papers, folder: General de Maud'huy, box 125.

Pershing to CG, SOS, AEF, Tours.

1. The Chiefs of the various services under your command have in their organizations excellent material in officers from civil life, many experienced in corporation management, whom perhaps they may not be using to full effect.

2. You will direct them each to select such an officer, especially experienced in the handling of personnel and the building up of new enterprises, and after thoroughly instructing him in the existing organization that he be detailed to visit all parts of the particular services; living with and getting to know its personnel, informing himself as to just what these officers are doing and how they are doing it, absorbing their ideas of the machine as a whole and as to how their particular part may be improved; to thoroughly study all ideas so obtained in relation to their effects on the other parts

of the Service and on its existing organization. Those officers should work in close harmony and sympathy and in every way under the orders of their respective chiefs.

3. Chiefs of Services should in this way obtain valuable ideas for the continual improvement of their Services and much information regarding the detailed working of their machine, which the time factor does not allow them to obtain completely for themselves. If properly chosen, these officers should tend to create a close and sympathetic liaison between the different elements of an organization and its Chief, and tend to obviate criticism similar to that of some of the departments at home during the recent investigations.

4. You will inform these Headquarters of the selections made in each instance. [Reply—April 24, Kernan to CINC, AEF]

NARA, RG 120, Office of the Commander-in-Chief, Office of the Secretary of the General Staff, entry 22, Reports of the Commander-in-Chief, folder 34: GHQ War Diary, January 24–April 28, 1918, diary entry May 3, 1918, 328-a, p. 312, box 4.

Lt. Col. George S. Simonds, CS, II Corps, with BEF, to CS, GHQ, AEF.

1. Newspaper reports dated Washington have for the past two days dwelt somewhat on the service with the British of our battalions in their brigades. I have assumed that this was simply making public some of the features of the arrangements which we have been making here for the service of the six divisions on this front in accordance with the terms laid down by the C. in C.; and in my arrangements with the authorities here we are still proceeding along these lines.

2. However, it is very evident that in the minds of the staff at British, G.H.Q., there is an idea that the plan of bringing over the divisions has been or is about to be changed, and that battalions of infantry are to be rushed over and put into the line with British troops with the least possible delay.

3. They are showing great anxiety over their manpower in the coming weeks. This lull now is giving them a breathing spell, but I believe they feel that it is within possibility that the Germans can repeat this last performance of theirs one or more times during the coming summer and that if this be so there is very grave danger even though it be on a smaller scale. They seem to have plenty of everything else, but manpower is their vital need. Another thing that is impossible to visualize accurately from the newspapers and the ordinary report is the losses they have suffered. Great claims are made as to the German losses and they undoubtedly have been great, but from what I have personally seen of the organizations that have been and still are in the fight, and from my talks with officers, I am convinced that the British losses in the first days of the fight were very heavy and above the normal of the defensive.

NARA, RG 120, Office of the Commander-in-Chief, Office of the Secretary of the General Staff, entry 22, Reports of the Commander-in-Chief, folder 34: GHQ War Diary, January 24–April 28, 1918, diary entry April 7, 1918, 302-b, pp. 280–81, box 4; *USAWW*, vol. 3, pp. 80–81.

Bliss, Chief, American Section, and Permanent Military Representative, SWC, Versailles, for Baker to TAG, War Department, for the President. Copy to General Pershing.

Cable 79-S.

1. The Secretary of War directs that you hand his following message to the President as early as practicable and cable his reply direct to me for the Secretary: The reply should reach here by Saturday evening, April 6th.

2. "To the President: Mr. Lloyd George read to General Bliss and General Pershing on Wednesday April 3 a cablegram from Lord Reading which reported that in an interview with him you agreed to the transportation in American and British ships, of infantry and machine gun units to the extent of 120,000 a month for 4 months. I have General March's cablegram Number 39 informing me of your approval of Resolutions of Supreme War Council as recommended by me in Bliss Number 67, March 28th, but no numbers of troops are stipulated in those resolutions. As I am to confer with British and General Pershing on Sunday morning [April 7] to arrange details, it would be helpful if I could have particulars of any agreements reached with Lord Reading and particularly numbers of infantry and machine gun units per month and for how many months, if such details were definitely arranged. Baker." [Reply—April 6, cable 45-R]
Bliss.

LC, Pershing Papers, folder: Supreme War Council, February–April 1918, box 193; NARA, RG 120, M923. Records of American Section, SWC, Cablegrams Received Sent to War Department, Nos. 13 to 100, January 22, 1918, to April 27, 1918.

TAG, War Department, to American Section, SWC, Versailles. Copies to Secretary of War Baker and General Pershing by General Bliss, and to Chief of Staff, British Army.

Cable 43-R.

1. Acting upon the call of the Interallied Supreme War Council for the fullest possible immediate American military participation the President has decided after consultation with representatives of England and France and heads of Government Departments to increase our military efforts as follows:

(1) A minimum of 91,000 troops will be shipped oversea monthly commencing April 1st. Every available American transport, the transports loaned by the British, and American and British liners will be used for this movement. We understand England to have guaranteed besides sufficient additional tonnage to carry at least 29,000 additional troops per month. This makes a total of 120,000 troops per month as a minimum.

(2) A cargo movement will be carried out consisting of the necessary engineering materiel for ports and lines of communication, such parts of the aviation and ord-

nance program as will be ready for shipment, including replacement materials, 438,000 long tons for France and 250,000 long tons for England, Quartermaster, Medical and miscellaneous supplies for monthly increments of 91,000 men, plus maintenance of our troops now in France and the establishment of Reserves. Great Britain to furnish the materials and supplies for the additional troops according to her agreement as fully stated in Pershing's Cablegram Number 596 dated February 12th and Number 705 dated March 10th.

A. After careful study of all tonnage requirements of the United States it is clear that this movement can be carried out, but only with the greatest difficulty. The execution of the undertaking is subject to the provision that we retain all neutral tonnage now employed in the service of the United States, that the submarine sinkings do not develop to an unusual extent above the present losses, that the Emergency Fleet Corporation's promised deliveries of ships be carried out, and that the import reductions now planned be not impeded. All tonnage owned or controlled by the United States will be required by the Shipping Board to meet the military program and other imperative needs and command of ships loaned to France and Italy will not now be disturbed but we must utilize all Dutch ships requisitioned in our harbors to meet our present program. We cannot divert any additional tonnage without impairing the military program to which we are thus definitely committed. British and French Ambassadors notified. Send copy of this cable by officer to General Pershing.
March.

LC, Pershing Papers, folder: Supreme War Council, February–April 1918, box 193; NARA, M923, American Section, SWC, file 316: Cablegrams received from the War Department, Jan. 23, 1918–Nov. 19, 1919, roll 18; see also online "WW I Supreme War Council, American records," at https://www.fold3.com.

Editor's Note—Although cable 43-R from March at the War Department to Secretary Baker appears to confirm the British contention that Wilson agreed to ship 120,000 troops per month, cable 45-R of April 6 from Wilson to Baker seems clearly to contradict the British claim. See below.

TAG, War Department, to Pershing, in part in reply to Pershing to TAG, War Department, cable P-799-S, March 27.

Cable A-1043-R.
3. With reference to paragraph 3, your 799 (A, B and C). You are authorized to commission as 2nd Lieutenants graduates of the Army Candidate Schools in number not to exceed vacancies now existing in forces under your command. Successful graduates in excess of that number may be commissioned as vacancies occur in forces under your command. (D) Commissions to be temporary and subject to confirmation by the War Department. Commandant Marine Corps desires 16 soldiers mentioned be not commissioned in Army. Authority will later be given Doyen to

commission in Marine Corps more than that number and it is desired to hold the 16 Marine graduates for these vacancies. (E) Under present policy graduates born in Allied countries cannot be commissioned. In accordance with existing law, soldiers under 21 cannot be commissioned in National Army. March. [Reply—April 22, P-977-S-1]

NARA, RG 120, M930, Main Series, War Department to AEF, roll 12.

TAG, War Department, to Pershing, in reply to Pershing to TAG, War Department, cable P-808-S, March 29.

Cable A-1045-R. Confidential.
 Reference 1C, your 808. This requirement is not in accordance with latest international agreement to give priority to Infantry and machine gun units. Aero squadrons are being shipped to England now whenever there is any available space after Infantry is assigned. Report how many men aviation corps now training in England. March. [Reply—April 14, P-913-S-1L]

NARA, RG 120, M930, Confidential Series, War Department to AEF, roll 18.

April 6

Pershing's Personal Diary

Went with General Alvord, Colonel Boyd and Captain de Marenches by motor to see 1st, 26th and 2nd Divisions. Left Chaumont at 7 a. m. Saw part of 1st Division on road going to entrain for the Somme. Saw General Bullard in Sebastapol hospital north of Toul where he was confined with neuralgia or a kind of sciatica. He will be out in a few days. Saw General Edwards, commanding 26th Division, at his headquarters at Boucq. Talked with him about the defensive plans of his sector. Went from there to headquarters 2nd Division. Stopped en route for luncheon at Ligny-en-Barrois and at Souilly to see General Hirschauer, commanding 2nd Army. He spoke in the highest terms of the American soldiers and stated that he had as much confidence in the regimental and higher commanders as he had in his French commanders. Saw General Bundy [CG, 2nd Division] at P. C. Toulon, which is about 5 kilometres forward of Sommedieue. Talked with him about the organization of the sectors in which his troops are serving. Returned to Chaumont about 9 p. m. and after dinner had the Chief of Staff and Colonels Conner and Fiske [Harold B., ACS, Training (G-5), GHQ, AEF] in to house.

LC, Pershing Papers, Diary, May 7, 1917–September 1, 1918, box 4.

Following the massive German offensive of March 21, 1918, on the British front, Pershing worked closely with the Foch and Pétain to free the combat-ready 1st Division for use and to position available AEF divisions to replace French frontline units to free them for redeployment to threatened sectors. One of the divisions that had completed its familiarization training with the French at the front was the 26th Division. It was repositioned from the Chemin des Dames sector near Soissons to the Toul sector of the St. Mihiel salient in Lorraine to replace the 1st Division. These movements often took a number of days to complete because many of the 26th's divisional elements still relied on animal-drawn transportation for road movements. Here elements of the 101st Ammunition Train are passing through the village of Soulosse-sous-Saint-Élophe north of Neufchâteau on April 10 on their way to the new sector. Source: NARA, Still Picture Branch, RG 111, 111-SC-10452.

Haig to Pershing, reply to Pershing to Haig, April 1.

OB/2196/1

I am very much indebted to you for your ready response to my request for Engineer Regiments, and I only regret that owing to the rapid development of the situation, and the calls made on the Transportation Service by French troop movements, I was unable to avail myself immediately of your permission to employ these Regiments.

Two of them have now arrived at Abbeville and are being immediately forwarded to points at which I anticipate that their services will be of great value. I am the more confident of this in view of the distinguished services already performed by the two Companies of your 6th Engineer Regiment, which were in action with the Fifth British Army during the recent operations. [On this matter, see also April 2, Bacon to CS, GHQ, AEF]

I have to express my thanks also for your offer of the personnel of the two Heavy Artillery Regiments now en route to France. This personnel will be a valuable reinforcement of which I shall be very glad to avail myself.

Doubtless you will let me know in due course when the Artillery personnel is likely to arrive and at what port, and what amount of training it has had and with what weapons.

LC, Pershing Papers, folder: Field Marshal Sir Douglas Haig, 1917–1918, box 86.

Maj. Gen. Peyton C. March, Assistant Chief of Staff, War Department, to Pershing.

This will introduce to you Mr. H. H. Raymond, a member of the Shipping Control Committee, who is leaving for France to familiarize himself with the conditions existing in French ports so as to assist in the drive which is now in progress to increase our personnel and supplies in France.

You will find Mr. Raymond an expert in his business and certain to be of value in the work which is before us.

LC, Pershing Papers, folder: General Peyton C. March, box 123.

TAG, War Department, to Bliss, Chief, American Section, SWC, Versailles. General Bliss personally gave copies to Secretary of War Baker and General Pershing.

Cable 44-R.

The actual monthly cargo movements involved in the Military Program of the United States as approved by the President April 3rd and set forth in Cablegram Number 43 to you is estimated as follows:

In thousands of long tons	April	407,
	May	463, (442?)
	June	488,
	July	633,
	August	747,
	September	710,

	October	727,
	November	743,
	December	<u>748,</u> (727?)

Making a total movement
April to December inclusive of   5,687,

Total shipments by Departments will be in thousands of long tons
    Engineers   1,783,
    Quartermasters   1,853,
    Ordnance   1,648, including about 480 replacements
    Signal   278,
    Medical   64,
    Miscellaneous   62,

    Recent and possible changes in composition and disposition of Expeditionary Forces may change above departmental estimates but will not reduce totals. Send copy to General Pershing,
March.

LC, Pershing Papers, folder: Supreme War Council, February–April 1918, box 193; NARA, M923, American Section, SWC, file 316: Cablegrams received from the War Department, Jan. 23, 1918–Nov. 19, 1919, roll 18; see also online "WW I Supreme War Council, American records," at https://www.fold3.com.

TAG, War Department, to Bliss, Chief, American Section, SWC, Versailles, reply to Bliss to TAG, War Department, cable 79-S, April 5. Copy to General Pershing.

Cable 45-R.
    With reference to your Number 79, following received from President:
    "Please cable to the Secretary of War that I agreed upon no details whatever with Lord Reading. I told him that I had agreed to the proposition of the Supreme War Council in the formulae proposed to me by the Secretary of War by cable and that I would assure him that we would send troops over as fast as we could make them ready and find transportation for them. That was all. The details are left to be worked out and we shall wish the advice of the Secretary of War as the result of his consultations on the other side. Woodrow Wilson."
March.

LC, Pershing Papers, folder: Supreme War Council, February–April 1918, box 193; NARA, M923, American Section, SWC, file 316: Cablegrams Received from War Department, Jan. 23, 1918–Nov. 19, 1919, roll 18; see also online "WW I Supreme War Council, American records," at https://www.fold3.com.

Pershing to TAG, War Department, in part in reply to TAG, War Department, to Pershing, cable A-839-R, February 27; in addition to Pershing to TAG, War Department, cable P-635-S, February 22.

Cable P-865-S.
    2. For Chief of Staff. With reference to paragraph 1, our cablegram 635, and paragraph 1D, your cablegram 839. In order to meet conditions mentioned in above cables with reference maintaining full complement officers and soldiers with combat organizations at all times and in order to meet conditions that have already arisen and to provide for those that may arise in the present emergency affecting the operations of our replacement system it is requested First, that authority be granted to organize such provisional replacement units as may be necessary from time to time. Second, to maintain all replacement organizations at such strength in officers and noncommissioned officers and soldiers as the military necessity may demand. Every effort will be made to keep replacement organizations at authorized strength. This practically covers again the request and the authority granted in cables mentioned. The request is renewed in a more detailed and complete manner in order to insure sufficiently broad authority to enable us to operate the replacement system in most efficient manner. Conditions now arising necessitate a prompt reply. [*Ed.*—On April 12 in cable A-1090-R-4, the War Department granted Pershing the authority to organize and maintain provisional replacement units as requested.]

NARA, RG 120, M930, Main Series, AEF to War Department, roll 2.

TAG, War Department, to Pershing, in part in reply to Pershing to TAG, War Department, cable P-836-S, April 2.

Cable A-1048-R. Confidential.
    It has been necessary for the War Department to give positive assurances that you will be able to unload promptly monthly shipments April to December inclusive aggregating 5,680,000 tons. All estimate of cargo movements based upon 60-day turn around. Tonnage in Army cargo service to be increased by 140,000 tons deadweight of Dutch ships. Further increase will be made therefore to meet your increasing requirements as set forth in the schedule of cargo movements. This procedure will entail many sacrifices and some hardships which cannot possibly be justified except by most efficient use of the ships turned over to Army service. If Army cargo ships are delayed in French ports for an average period exceeding which the utmost difficulty will be experienced in securing from month to month the required number of additional ships. I realize fully the difficulty confronting you but hope that in the light of a complete understanding relative to our position you will be able to secure assistance from the French and British that will be required in order to meet rapid increasing demands which will be made upon you. Hereafter your Priority Schedule covering monthly shipments from our ports should equal in the aggregate the

monthly shipments set for in the cable Number 43 to Bliss. In accordance with your request [see April 2, P-836-S-2E], H. H. Raymond, Member of Shipping Control Committee, leaves New York on Wednesday [April 10] for France. Send copy to Bliss [done by hand on April 7]. March. [Reply—April 10, P-887-S-1C; May 5, P-1057-S; May 26, P-1194-S-2]

NARA, RG 120, M930, Confidential Series, War Department to AEF, roll 18.

April 7

Pershing's Personal Diary

Left Chaumont at 8 a. m. for Paris. Lunched at Fontainbleau and arrived in Paris at 1:30 p. m. Secretary of War and party still stopping at house. Had talk with Secretary; then with him had talk with Generals Whigham and Hutchison of the British Army on the subject of American troops that are to be brought over by British. They apparently expected a large number. After some discussion we came to an agreement which is covered in document. Had talk with Colonel Simonds [Chief of Staff, II U.S. Corps, with the British] and Generals Ford and Dawney of British G.H.Q. on arrangements concerning American troops to be trained with British.

The Secretary and party left at 8:08 p. m. for Brest. I sent Sergeant Lanckton with the Secretary.

LC, Pershing Papers, Diary, May 7, 1917–September 1, 1918, box 4.

Editor's Note—A note prepared by Bliss on April 8 provides the background for how the meeting with Generals Whigham and Hutchison came about and the questions raised on his own staff about building an American Army in France:

> The rough pencil notes attached hereto [not located] were made by me in connection with a telephonic conference on Friday afternoon, April 5, 1918, with General Wilson, C.I.G.S., in regard to certain difficulties being encountered in the British War Office in carrying out the proposition as to the use of American manpower by bringing over for the present only infantry and machine guns units. This telephonic conference resulted in the agreement that General Wilson would send over General Wigham [Whigham] and Hutchison to confer with General Pershing and his staff officers while Mr. Baker, the American Secretary of War, was still here, on Sunday morning, April 7th. In the evening of April 5, just at the moment of my leaving Versailles for Paris in order to inform Mr. Secretary Baker of the coming conference, the attached memorandum signed "S.D.E." (Colonel Embick), was handed to me. I carried it with me and showed it to Mr. Baker and told him that the American Section with the Supreme War Council

were a unit in believing that in view of the present situation the time had come to make quite a radical change in the American Military Program, both with a view to utilizing in the most effective way in the shortest time our available manpower and also with a view to securing the largest trained independent American army in France by a given date. In a general way Mr. Baker expressed himself to me as coinciding in this general view. He committed himself to no details but stated that he would defer action until conference with General Pershing.

Notes attached [not located].

[Attachment]

American Section, Supreme War Council, Versailles

April 5, 1918.

Memorandum:

  1. In cablegram No. 67 [see March 28, cable 67-S] of the American Military Representative, the Secretary of War outlined the present adopted project as to preferential transportation for American infantry and machine gun units during the present emergency. In his cablegram No. 40 [see March 30, cable 40-R], the Acting Chief of Staff stated that in following out this plan every effort will be made to carry out the shipping schedule of October 7, 1917, as regards the completion of each division and phase as shipping space becomes available and as far as consistent with new instructions as to preferential transportation of infantry and machine gun units.
  2. Assuming that preferential transportation for infantry and machine gun units be continued through the months of April, May and June, 1918, using for this purpose both American and British controlled shipping, it is estimated that there can be brought to France the infantry and machine gun complements of 20 American divisions, or approximately 320,000 men, plus monthly replacements of 10%. That amount of infantry would correspond to the infantry components of approximately 40 French or British divisions.
  3. Assuming that American controlled shipping only will be available subsequent to July 1, 1918; that its monthly personnel capacity will amount to about 91,500 men; and that monthly replacements for combatant infantry in France will equal 10%; then there will be available a surplus personnel capacity after July 1st of about 53,000 monthly. If this capacity be used as indicated in cablegram No. 40 of the Acting Chief of Staff, it will be sufficient to complete only about 1.8 divisions per month, as the present American division includes about 11,000 troops other than infantry, and the complement of corps and army troops for each division under the project of General Pershing amount to about 8,800 men, and the complement of

service of the rear troops per division under the same project amounts to about 10,000 men.

4. It is not believed that the assignment of surplus capacity to the carrying out of the schedule of October 7, offers the best solution of this problem, or that of the rapid creation of an American Army. This belief is based upon the following:

(a) Such action would result in the utilization of a large part of the transport capacity above that required for replacements, for the shipment of non-combatants. It is believed that many of these non-combatants would not be necessary if the plans for the service of the rear for American forces are made to dovetail with those of the French and British forces, and to supplement the latter only where necessary. Wastage in the service of the rear is but a small percentage of that of the infantry. The French and British forces have each built up elaborate organizations behind the lines, the impairment of which is but slight in comparison with the depletion of their combatant forces, as is illustrated by the fact that these organizations are prepared to furnish service of the rear for all American infantry units that may be incorporated in the Allied forces.

(b) Assuming that the final phase of the training and use of American infantry units in Allied forces will be that in which an American infantry brigade will constitute the entire infantry component of an Allied division, it will be noted that the withdrawal of each infantry component in order to complete a purely American division will leave an unbalanced military unit, which unbalancing will extend into the corps, army and service of the rear troops, and will vary in amount in direct proportion to the wastage in the several arms of the service. The wastage in the infantry may be assumed to be roughly three times that of the artillery, seven times that of the engineers, and from ten to twenty times that of the service of the rear.

(c) The rate at which auxiliary troops could be provided under this plan would permit of the completion of only about eleven additional purely American divisions during 1918, and the infantry components of the nine remaining American divisions, or eighteen Allied divisions, would not be completely absorbed until May, 1919. Under this plan, therefore, the majority of the American infantry would remain with the Allied forces during the active season of 1918.

5. The following plan appears preferable to that of October 7th and is presented for consideration:

(a) Modify the project for the service of the rear for the American forces so as to call for American personnel and materiel only to the extent necessary to supplement the corresponding services of the French and English in meeting the needs of the entire Allied military force to be maintained on the Western front during 1918.

(b) Transport American divisional artillery, engineers, and auxiliary and corps and army troops to the respective numbers required to meet irreplaceable Allied wastage in those arms in divisions in which American infantry has been incorporated, and to provide such components for divisions to be brought over and trained as complete American divisions.

(c) When the training of American infantry units with the Allies reached the stage at which the entire infantry component of some of the Allied divisions is composed of American infantry, assign to the American Army and to American divisional commander, one-half of such divisions. (The ratio of infantry to total combatants is approximately one to two in each of the several belligerent forces.) S.D.E. [Stanley D. Embick]. (NARA, RG 120, M923, American Section, SWC, file 30: Correspondence, Reports, and Charts relating to Transportation of U.S. Troops and Supplies to France. Documents 30-105 and 30-106, roll 2.)

Secretary of War Newton D. Baker and General Pershing—Conference in Paris with Major Generals Robert Dundas Whigham, Deputy Chief of the Imperial General Staff, and Robert Hutchison, Director of Organization, British War Office, Regarding Transportation of American Troops.

General Whigham stated that he had come to discuss arrangements for carrying out the agreement of the Supreme War Council dated March 27th [Joint Note No. 18] whereby American infantry and machine gun units are to be given priority of shipment, according to the present understanding the British will be able to ship 60,000 troops per month and the Americans 60,000 making a total of 120,000 men per month beginning with the month of April.

The *Secretary of War* brought out that no figures were mentioned in the Versailles Agreement [Joint Note No. 18, March 27].

General Whigham suggested that a certain proportion of infantry would necessarily have to be kept apart as replacement troops and that these replacements would probably be landed in England, whereas the fighting troops could be sent directly to France.

The *Secretary of War* asked why these replacements should not be sent to France and left with General Pershing for training until needed.

General Whigham stated that there would be difficulty in railroad transportation from the American sector to the British in northern France.

General Pershing stated that the American idea had been that this infantry should go to British units for training and, as soon as trained, was to be replaced by other infantry and that he had not considered the subject of replacements for troops while on this period of training.

The *Secretary of War* stated that he had understood that the infantry and machine gun units were to be sent to the British for training and that as soon as trained they were to be replaced by others; that in the event of an emergency, they were to fight and that, in this case, he saw no necessity for replacements.

A discussion followed as to the recommendation of the Versailles Conference [Joint Note No. 18, March 27].

General Whigham insisted on the necessity for replacing at once small losses while American units are with the British troops; he suggested having a small proportion of the reserves in France and the remainder in England. He stated that the British did [it] this way and they would handle the American reserves in the same way; and shipping across the channel is very uncertain and therefore a small proportion of reserves should be in France.

The *Secretary of War* inquired as to the origin of this figure of 120,000 troops per month, and called attention to the fact that there had been no obligation on the part of the Americans to send any number of troops or for any particular period. He did not think it was clear that the original 6 division decision was annulled by the Versailles Agreement [Joint Note No. 18, March 27]; that the Versailles Agreement [Joint Note No. 18, March 27] simply was to the effect that American infantry and machine gun units should be given priority of shipping until further orders and this further order might come tomorrow.

General Whigham stated that interpretation of the British War Office was that the Versailles Agreement [Joint Note No. 18, March 27] wiped out all previous agreements and that it is now a question of sending infantry and machine gun units be trained with the British, French and Americans, the proportion to go to each army to be decided later.

The *Secretary of War* stated that what is pertinent to the present discussion is American troops going to the British for training; that he did not want the British public or the British Army, or the French public or French Army, to have an exaggerated idea that this scheme provides or will provide a means by which their losses are be made up in the future; that he does not want any feeling of disillusionment when General Pershing calls for the return of the troops entrusted to these armies for training.

General Whigham stated that this was thoroughly understood by the British. He then outlined a scheme for placing American battalions in line, later uniting them as American regiments and still later as brigades and so on.

General Pershing asked what would become of the British divisions when, in a month or so, American troops serving with them are withdrawn.

General Whigham stated he hoped these troops would not be withdrawn so soon; that when this does happen, some British divisions will be broken up; that they also hope to get 400,000 or 500,000 troops through conscription. He talked of the gradual increase of American personnel in divisions to such a point when all the infantry might be American and the artillery British. He stated that at some such period the division would be considered an American division and that there was no reason why British artillery should not serve in American divisions.

General Pershing stated that if the 120,000 men, infantry and machine gun units, per month were shipped for 3 months, this would make 360,000 men. He called attention to the fact that it would take several months to bring over the additional men and build up divisions around these infantry and machine gun organizations, as more than that many additional personnel would be required to make complete divisions; that the proposition for bringing over infantry and machine gun units should have to be considered as a temporary measure and also that other units would have to be brought over.

The *Secretary of War* stated that he wished the British to understand that when the Americans decide to discontinue the Versailles Agreement [Joint Note No. 18, March 27] that the British will be notified.

General Whigham ask what proportion of the first 60,000 men to be brought over by the British might the British count on having for the present.

General Pershing stated that they should have all of them.

General Whigham insisted on the necessity of bringing them over in organized units; he stated that it is understood that these men are to come over as completely clothed and equipped as possible; that what is necessary to make up any deficiencies in clothing and equipment will be supplied by the British.

The *Secretary of War* insisted that the uniforms must be American.

It was also stated that land transportation furnished for use of these troops will be kept by them and passed over to the Americans by the British when these troops are replaced in American divisions.

The *Secretary of War* résuméd the conclusions of the meeting as follows:

That it is agreed by General Pershing that the 60,000 men to be brought over by the British in April will be turned over to the British; the disposition of troops to be brought over in the month of May will be determined later; that the 60,000 troops to be brought over in April and turned over to the British shall include 20,000 replacement troops; that these troops are to be trained in accordance with the agreement between General Sir Douglas Haig and General Pershing; and the disposition of all troops to be brought over by the British shall be fixed by General Pershing and the British War Office; that the land transportation to be turned over by the British to the American troops is to be kept by these troops; that clothing for these troops is to be furnished by the Americans as far as possible and any deficiencies are to be made up by the British; that the British are to furnish machine guns for the machine gun units and any units which they cannot supply with machine guns will be turned over to General Pershing.

LC, Pershing Papers, folder: Training and Employment of American Troops with British, box 198; see also *USAWW*, vol. 2, pp. 286–88. The AEF sent a somewhat different version of the meeting's minute to the Secretary of War on April 19 in cable P-955-S. NARA, RG 120, M930, Confidential Series, AEF to War Department, roll 7. See April 19 below for cable.

Editor's Note—Pershing recalled the conference with Generals Whigham and Hutchison in his *My Experiences in the World War*:

> On the day of the Secretary's departure Generals Whigham and Hutchison came over from the British War Office to discuss arrangements for the transportation of American troops, in accordance with the provisions of Joint Note No. 18. The conversation indicated that the British understood

that we were to send 60,000 men per month to train with them and that they were to bring over the same number, making a total of 120,000 per month beginning with April. They held that the President's approval of Joint Note No. 18 had superseded agreements previously made, including the six-division plan. General Whigham said:

"The interpretation of the British War Office is that the Versailles agreement (Joint Note No. 18) wipes out all previous agreements and it is now a question of sending infantry and machine gun units to be trained by British, French, and Americans, the proportions to go to each to be decided later."

The whole tenor of the conversation showed that the British then regarded it as certain that our troops were to be used to build up the French and British armies. But neither Mr. Baker nor I had received any intimation that the President had agreed to the British proposal mentioned in the above cable [see April 3, cable A-1036-R], and his qualified approval of Joint Note No. 18 did not commit us to any such program as the British claimed. Moreover, I was opposed to any commitment that would tie our hands and make it impossible to form an American army. My attitude toward the proposal was made perfectly clear. Mr. Baker knew nothing more than the declaration contained in the joint note, which stated no figures.

The British conferees entirely ignored the specific condition that the final arrangements as to training and disposition of all our units were to be left in my hands. Their error was pointed out and Mr. Baker then said:

"What is pertinent to the present discussion is American troops going to the British for training; that he did not want the British public or the British Army, or the French public or French Army, to have an exaggerated idea that this scheme provides or will provide a means by which their losses are be made up in the future; that he does not want any feeling of disillusionment when General Pershing calls for the return of the troops entrusted to these armies for training."

The conference ended with the understanding that 60,000 American infantry and machine gun units to be brought over by the British in April should go to them for training. It was also understood that the disposition of other troops would be left for later decision. Certain deficiencies in land transportation, clothing and machine guns were to be provided by the British. While they accepted this at the moment and declared that they thoroughly understood, that was not to be the last of it, as the whole question was taken up again in conference in London later in the month. (Pershing, *My Experiences in the World War*, vol. 1, pp. 383–84.)

Pershing's comment "that was not to be the last of it" played out almost immediately in meetings of the British War Cabinet on April 8 and 9 when Major Generals Robert Hutchison, Director of Organization, War Office, and Robert Dundas Whigham, Deputy Chief of the Imperial General Staff (Operations), reported the results of their meeting in Paris with Baker and Pershing on April 7 to Lloyd George and his ministers. Hutchison found that Pershing's "attitude towards incorporation of American battalions in British divisions was unsatisfactory." According to Lonergan in his *It Might Have Been Lost!* Whigham's comments to the War Cabinet were "very nearly a distortion of the facts" (p. 132) that "could have left no other impression with the War Cabinet than that General Pershing, alone, constituted the aggravating interference with its endeavors. . . . One figure had remained aloof and unassailable, yet powerful enough to block successful accomplishment. It was necessary to employ drastic pressure immediately lest the entire project fail" (p. 134). This led to Foreign Secretary Balfour dispatching a most unsavory cable No. 2017 on April 8 to Lord Reading in Washington that he approach President Wilson about the meeting with Pershing on April 7 from which it was clear "that General Pershing's views are absolutely inconsistent with the broad policy which we believe the President has adopted. . . . I am very unwilling to embarrass the President, who has shown such a firm grasp of the situation, with criticisms of his officers. But it is evident that the difference of opinion between General Pershing on the one side and what we conceive to be the President's policy on the other is so fundamental and touches so nearly the issues of the whole war, that we are bound to have the matter cleared up." All of this was clearly another effort to undermine Pershing and convince Wilson to remove him from command of the AEF.

LC, Pershing Papers, folder: Data for Book *My Experiences in the World War*, folder 11: Extracts from official records of British War Office, *The Progress of the American Army in France*, vol. 2, document no. 116-A, box 354; Lonergan, *It Might Have Been Lost!* pp. 122–24, 132–34. Lonergan provides a detailed account of these events in pp. 120–37. In addition, Whigham's comments to the War Cabinet are at Appendix No. 10, pp. 288–90, and in LC, Pershing Papers, folder: Data for Book *My Experiences in the World War*, folder 11: Extracts from official records of British War Office, *The Progress of the American Army in France*, vol. 2, document no. 119, box 354.

Pershing to Secretary of War Newton D. Baker [then in Paris], in reply to Baker to Pershing, April 5.

I wish to thank you for the very kind personal letter you wrote and especially for the one you enclosed for publication after your departure. It is a splendid message to our forces and will be the greatest encouragement to everyone as it is to me.

I am more than delighted that you have come to see the work that has been done in organization, training and construction, but most of all that you have felt the true spirit that stirs us all and makes it possible to give everything we possess to the great cause in which the great country that we represent is engaged.

I feel sure that upon your return we shall see added enthusiasm and energy given by our people to their part in the war, and I am confident that there will be no thought of any outcome but victory by force of arms.

Thanking you again for the personal encouragement of your visit and the assurance it gives that the country and the War Department are doing everything possible to make our cause a success, I can only renew our own pledges to you and the President.

May I ask you to convey to the President my most loyal greetings, and will you please accept my warmest and most sincere greetings yourself, both official and personal.

I trust that it will be possible for you to return within a short time. It will be of the greatest value to the army and the country to have you come frequently.

LC, Pershing Papers, folder: Newton D. Baker, January–June 1918, box 20.

Pershing to TAG, War Department, in part in reply to TAG, War Department, to Pershing, cables A-872-R, March 6, and A-1018-R, March 31; in addition to Pershing to TAG, War Department, cable P-621-S, February 20.

Cable P-868-S.

8. For Felton. With reference to cablegram DGT 60 [not located] and DGR 75, paragraph 1 [A-872-R-1] [see March 31, A-1018-R-6]. Relative to car building plant, we intend requisitioning from you all metal parts standard with French steel cars which can be utilized in construction of cars with wooden underframe. Uniform design is now being perfected here in connection with contract 6,000 wooden cars to be constructed near Bordeaux. Will shortly send full details metal parts wanted. Will cable definitely later. Will probably require complete powerhouse equipment for driving planing mills but only limited blacksmith shop equipment required if metal parts shipped from America. Conference with Belgian Government called covering questions of labor, electric current and other principals involved.

NARA, RG 120, M930, Main Series, AEF to War Department, roll 2.

TAG, War Department, to Pershing.

Cable A-1062-R.

1. For Air Service. 1H. British Air Board advise they can supply at least 200 SE 5 planes without engines. We can arrange production of 180-horsepower Hispano Suiza engines for the same at rate of 5 per day within 30 to 60 days. Shall we arrange engine supply? If so, will you arrange contract for planes? [Reply—April 21, P-973-S-1]

NARA, RG 120, M930, Main Series, War Department to AEF, roll 12.

April 8

Pershing's Personal Diary

At Paris. Worked in quarters all day and saw General Kernan and Rogers and Colonel Madden. Had Colonel Dawes to house for luncheon. In afternoon worked in quarters and saw General Williams, Major Harjes, General Foulois and Major Ward.

LC, Pershing Papers, Diary, May 7, 1917–September 1, 1918, box 4.

Editor's Note—General Foulois met with Pershing to discuss the content of the recent cable A-1039-R of April 4, which proposed what Foulois considered to be an unacceptable allocation of Liberty engines to the Navy in the coming months. He outlined the results of this meeting with Pershing and his objections to the cable in the following memorandum:

Foulois, Chief, Air Service, SOS, AEF, to Chief of Staff, GHQ.
April 10. 1918
Subject: Answer to Cablegram No. 1039.
   1. Herewith is a copy of cablegram No. 1039. Par. 1 estimated production of Liberty Engines in the United States and subparagraph A, which refers to allocation of same.
   2. This matter was taken up a few days ago, in Paris, with the Commander-in-Chief and he announced as his policy that, in the existing emergency, every effort should be made to maintain the Allied Air Services even at the expense of temporarily delaying the air program of the United States. The Commander-in-Chief further stated that the United States Tank Service should not be given priority on Liberty engines over our own Air Service or the other Allied Air Services.
   3. I have just had a long conversation with General Brancker [Maj. Gen. Sir Sefton, then Controller-General of Equipment], of the British Royal Air Forces, who informs me that the British aeroplane production program for the next six months is absolutely dependent upon promises made in the United States, that a certain specified number of Liberty engines will be allocated to Great Britain. General Brancker further states that the British Air Service has diverted a large proportion of the Rolls-Royce "Eagle" type engine for Anti-submarine work. In view of the probable delay in production of aeroplanes for the United States Navy he can see no logical reason for diverting such a large number of Liberty engines (734) to our Navy at the present time. I fully concur in this opinion and believe that the best interests of the Allied Air Services in the field will be served if our Aircraft Board in Washington is fully and finally impressed with the fact that for the next three months, at least, the Air Service program of the Unites States Army and Navy should not be allowed to interfere in any way with the

needs of England, France and Italy. I therefore recommend that the attached answer to cable No. 1039 be sent. [For the AEF's response to A-1039-R incorporating Foulois's view, see April 12, P-904-S.] (NARA, RG 120, M990, Gorrell's History of the U.S. Army Air Service, American Expeditionary Forces, Series B, Air Service Activities with the French, British, and Italians, Vol. 9: Development of the Handley Page Program in England, roll 3; see also online "Gorrell's History—AEF Air Service," at https://www.fold3.com.)

Bliss, Chief, American Section, and Permanent Military Representative, SWC, Versailles, to Pershing, Chaumont.

I inclose for your information a copy of a memorandum which I have just received from the Inter-Allied Transportation Council.
[Enclosure]
Maj. Gen. C. Sackville West, Acting British Military Representative, British Section, SWC, to Permanent Military Representative, American Section, SWC.

The attached letter from the Secretary of the Inter-Allied Transportation Council is forwarded for your information.

It is pointed out that the position is perhaps a little better since the attached letter was actually written, but every effort is necessary to increase American rolling stock in France. The American Expeditionary Force require 20,000 wagons. They are at present using 11,000 British ones. They have 1,000 of their own. The 11,000 British are urgently required elsewhere.

Gen. Atterbury, the American Representative on the Inter-Allied Transportation Council, has asked the American Government for:

60 wagons per day and 75 locomotives per month.
These number are considered absolutely essential.

[Enclosure]

10, Place Edouard VII
Paris
2nd April, 1918.

The Secretary
Supreme War Council
Versailles.

The Inter-Allied Transportation Council desires to call the attention of the Supreme War Council to the congestion of traffic for the American Expeditionary Force at ports used by the latter in France, which is occasioned by an insufficient supply of railway equipment.

The following represents the average tonnage unloaded *daily* by the American Expeditionary Force at ports:

December	4,500 tons
January	5,000 "
February	6,600 "

and in March it is anticipated that the average will be at least 10,000 tons daily. This considerable and satisfactory increase has created a constantly greater demand for wagons, which has not been satisfied, notwithstanding the admirable effort of the French Railways and an active co-operation in the repair of wagons. The average number of wagons loaded at American ports in France is now about 488 per day representing a loading of approximately 5,000 tons. Of the tonnage unloaded from ships (10,000 tons), 70% or 7,000 tons per day must be moved by wagons, but as wagons can apparently be provided for only about 5,000 tons, traffic is now accumulating at the rate of about 2,000 tons per day. This can be tolerated for about two weeks longer, at the expiration of which time, unless relief is found, importations will have to be materially reduced.

The Transportation Council points out that to furnish the transport necessary—either in whole or in part for the American Expeditionary Force—from the resources now available in France places a dangerous burden on an already overstrained machine and its continuance is to court disaster.

In view of this and the position above reviewed, the Council urges the Supreme War Council to take such steps as will assist and augment in every way the importation of railway equipment by the American Expeditionary Force to France, in order that the *American Armies may be made self-sustaining in transportation at an early date.*

For the Inter-Allied Transportation Council:
[signed]
H. W. Thornton, R. E.,
Provisional General Secretary.

LC, Pershing Papers, folder: Supreme War Council, February–April 1918, box 193; see also LC, Bliss Papers, folder: American Expeditionary Forces and American Forces in France, January–December 1918, box 248.

Report of telephone conversation between General Pershing at Paris, and Colonel Conner, ACS, G-3 (Operations), GHQ, AEF, Chaumont. 11 a. m.

General Pershing said that he was sending Col. Simonds [George S., Chief of Staff, U.S. II Corps, with the British] down to Chaumont to talk over the question of handling the British troops and Col. Fiske [Harold B., ACS, Training, GHQ, AEF] is going back to Chaumont also. He also stated that he went over the memorandum submitted by Col. Drum giving the requirements of replacements and service of the rear and artillery, and said it seemed to him that Col. Drum was a little off in his estimates. He had tried to make it look a little more than it is, on the total requirements for everything except combat troops.

Colonel Conner stated that Col. Drum's figures were in accordance with the priority schedule.

General Pershing stated that Col. Drum was calculating on a basis of 300,000 already here.

Colonel Conner stated that the estimate was made on the basis of what combat troops were here and 360,000 more, and that on the replacements the estimate was rather under if anything because we took as basis for replacements the 3,500 men per corps per month.

General Pershing stated that what we wanted to get at was the following:

We have now to meet the situation here that confronts us. My idea is to bring over as many combat troops as possible and as few service of the rear and other troops as possible, to fill this emergency.

I want to calculate on bringing over 60,000 infantry and machine-gun units as planned and then hold up for the next month until we can bring over such proportion of other troops, especially the artillery, and then perhaps get started in on more infantry and machine-gun units for the succeeding month, we need not go by months, but the movement of troops could be regulated by the amount of transportation available. I would like to have some new figures made out on this so that we can present them to the War Department.

I want to encourage, just as far as possible to do so, the bringing over of combat troops. For the time being the English will take care of a good many of these troops while they are being trained there, for a couple of months, and we can probably reduce the number of service of the rear troops, and maybe cut down some of our corps and army troops a little, postpone them a little, but the idea is to revamp our personnel schedule and priority schedule with the idea of pushing as fast as possible combat units, divisional units, mixing the other troops in with successive waves of combat troops, without sitting down and saying we need so many service of the rear and other troops. I don't think that attitude is the correct one to take even if those troops of the rear are more or less delayed two or three months. I would keep putting them a little further on in the future in order to enable them to bring over as many combat troops as we can.

The British want to take care of the first 60,000 that the British bring over. We are going to be pushed by our Allies to continue that as fast as possible, but I want to insist that instead of having 60,000 infantry and machine gun units, that we bring over immediately the personnel of the artillery so that they will not be far behind and can be training and they will be ready about the time the infantry is ready, and we can call out these units and bring them in to our own organization.

Colonel Conner then said:

What you want done is to make a study to see what can be done in the way of reducing everything except combat units and especially divisions, to eliminate as far as possible service of supply and also corps and army troops to the advantage of bringing over divisions.

General Pershing stated that the question had been presented yesterday of replacements. He said:

I admit that as far as the first 60,000 are concerned, one-third of them may be replacements and they will probably be brought in behind the British lines, and possibly into England. I much prefer to have them brought here to give them immediately 40,000 combat troops with 20,000 replacements standing by. Of course, this looks as if those men were going right into the fight but this cannot be avoided. We cannot get away from that.

We can of course keep up replacements and this in a much shorter time than we have figured, and we can pull them out and put others in for training. We will probably keep a flow through the British ranks without allowing it to accumulate to any great extent.

USAWW, vol. 2, pp. 290–91.

Pershing to TAG, War Department, in addition to Pershing to TAG, War Department, cable P-844-S, April 3.

Cable P-876-S. Confidential.
For Chief of Staff

In conference yesterday between two representatives of British War Office and Secretary of War and myself, it was agreed that the 60,000 troops to be brought over in April by British tonnage should go to them under the same conditions as previously agreed upon for the six divisions, one third of which are to be for replacements. Further allocation of units brought over by the British was left for future consideration. The new plan to give priority to certain infantry and machine gun units makes it necessary to readjust entire Priority Schedule which is now being prepared. Propose to postpone shipment of all noncombatant troops to the utmost extent possible to meet present situation and at same time not make it impossible to build up our own army. Will cable you full report in two or three days [see April 11, P-891-S]. Meanwhile request you follow recommendations made in my 844.

NARA, RG 120, M930, Main Series, AEF to War Department, roll 2; see also LC, Pershing Papers, folder: Training and Employment of American Troops with British, box 198. (This cable was actually Confidential, but was filed in the Main Series at GHQ, AEF.)

TAG, War Department, to Pershing, in part in reply to Pershing to TAG, War Department, cable P-845-S, April 3.

Cable A-1066-R.

8. With reference to paragraph 3B, your 845. Requisition transport Montrose approved. Will it be practicable for you to relieve 1 of the larger vessels now in cross-channel service? The assignment of transport Montrose necessarily reduces our cargo capacity unless you are able to release vessel in her place. [Reply—April 19, P-958-S-1]

NARA, RG 120, M930, Main Series, War Department to AEF, roll 12.

TAG, War Department, to Pershing.

Cable A-1067-R.
2. Attention Air Service. 2A. Captain Northrup has sailed with partial lists machinery equipment and supplies for Air Production Center Number 2 [Romorantin]. Also complete reports with equipment lists and shop plans for assembling DH 4 aeroplanes and other miscellaneous reports. Sending Burgess and Farwell with DH 4 planes and spares to bring back report on boxing and sending Crow with shipment to assist in plane assembly. [Reply—May 18, P-1142-S-8C]
2D. Communicate Foulois. Reference London HQ 25, paragraph 4. Handley Page work well underway. Shipments should be freighted 10 June, 50 July. Monthly deliveries at the rate of contract thereafter. Spare parts with machines. [Reply—April 16, P-933-S-4A]

NARA, RG 120, M930, Main Series, War Department to AEF, roll 12.

April 9

Pershing's Personal Diary

Worked in quarters in morning. Left after luncheon for Chaumont, arriving at 6:30 p. m.

LC, Pershing Papers, Diary, May 7, 1917–September 1, 1918, box 4.

Editor's Note—Although Pershing was certainly occupied with many pressing issues, it is difficult to understand that in his Personal Diary he made no mention of the beginning of the second large German offensive of that spring: Operation Georgette, against the British and Portuguese forces of the British First and Second Armies in Flanders south and north of Armentières on the Lys River (see Map 5). The Germans once again made substantial gains but achieved no major breakthrough as they had in the first offensive of March 21. Pershing briefly mentioned the Lys offensive in his memoirs:

> The German offensive on the Lys was another formidable attempt to break the British lines. The attack was made to the north and south of Armentières on a front of twenty-four miles by twenty-seven German divisions. The exhausted British, though they fought with most commendable courage and skill, were forced again to yield, with heavy losses to themselves and the division of Portuguese that was with them. . . . Although several French divisions were hurried to the front, it was a week after the attack before they were put into the line. They then relieved British divisions at the famous Kemmel Hill, only to be surprised and defeated themselves on April 25th,

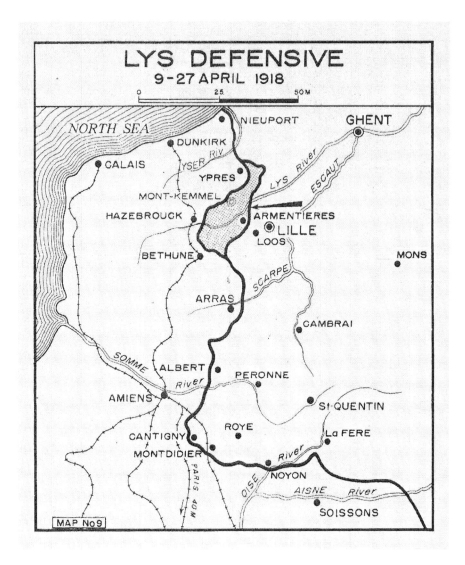

Map 5. Lys Defensive, April 9–27, 1918. The second German blow of 1918 fell along the Lys River to the north of the Somme area. Although not nearly as successful as the initial offensive of March 21, it did inflict significant losses on the British and Portuguese forces holding the line. Source: *The United States Army in the World War,* vol. 4, p. 59.

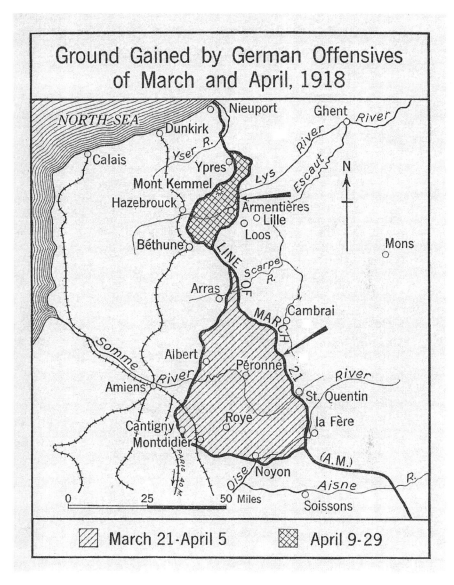

Map 6. Ground Gained by German Offensives of March and April 1918. Combined, the two German offensives of March and April 1918 had dealt severe damage to the British forces on the northern section of the Allied front. The British had suffered heavy losses in men and material, which would be difficult to replace in the short term. While inflicting major losses on the British and gaining considerable ground, the Germans had also suffered significant losses and had not achieved their strategic objectives. Source: American Battle Monuments Commission, *American Armies and Battlefields in Europe,* p. 27.

much to their chagrin. The battle was practically ended by the last of the month with a gain by the Germans of ten or eleven miles, but they failed in their effort to capture the important objective of Hazebrouck [see Map 6]. (Pershing, *My Experiences in the World War*, Vol. 1, pp. 395–97.).

Conner, ACS, G-3 (Operations), GHQ AEF, to CS.
1. General Ragueneau stated that he had come to obtain certain information concerning which he had intended seeing General Pershing today.

2. General Ragueneau first asked as to the availability of the 32d Division, the infantry of which, he stated, the Commander-in-Chief intended to place in French divisions.

I informed General Ragueneau that the concentration of the 32d Division was underway, as well as the process of bringing the regiments up to a strength of approximately 200 men per company; that certain arms and equipment would have to be issued and a certain amount of instruction given; and that at least three weeks must elapse before the 32d Division could be available.

In response to a question from General Ragueneau, I informed him that as far as I knew there had been no change in the plans of the Commander-in-Chief with reference to the 32d Division.

3. General Ragueneau took up the question of infantry units in French divisions and intimated that it would be necessary to leave the infantry units placed in French divisions as an integral part of those divisions for an indefinite period. He stated that of course when a calm period, such as next winter, arrived it would be possible to withdraw these units.

I informed General Ragueneau that as far as I knew the Commander-in-Chief had no idea of leaving infantry units indefinitely incorporated in French or English divisions.

4. General Ragueneau asked what arrivals of infantry could be depended on for the next three months. I informed him that that matter was being studied at the present time. I further informed him that, as far as I could see, the actual arrivals in France in the next three months would not exceed six or eight divisions, together with the indispensable auxiliary troops.

5. General Ragueneau stated that France had no men left but that she had the trained staffs and that was what was needed.

He further stated that he did not see the possibility of our obtaining competent staffs for divisions and higher units.

I informed him that there was no doubt in my mind as to the possibility of our forming our own divisions under our own commanders.

6. General Ragueneau insisted upon the necessity of leaving our infantry units in French divisions.

I informed him that, as far as I knew, the Commander-in-Chief had no intention of leaving units indefinitely in foreign divisions, and called General Ragueneau's attention to the fact that German papers had already commenced a propaganda to the effect that our men were being incorporated in British and French divisions.

USAWW, vol. 3, pp. 282–83.

Conner, ACS, G-3 (Operations), GHQ, AEF, Chaumont.

Memorandum for Chief of Staff:
 1. The principles which the Commander-in-Chief has enunciated are understood to be:
 (a) That priority shall be given to the transportation of a certain number of infantry and machine-gun units.
 (b) That infantry and machine-gun units will serve for a period not to exceed two to three months in the divisions of our Allies; especially the British.
 (c) That artillery and other combat troops be given such priority as will ensure our being able to form our infantry into divisions promptly at the expiration of the period mentioned in (b) above.
 (d) That arrivals of corps, army and service of supply troops be postponed to as late a date as practicable consistent with being able to take care of the divisions to be united as outlined in (c) above.
 (e) That plans formulated at this time be limited to a period of the next three months.
 2. Considering the number of troops yet to come in the first phase and those belonging to the second phase it is apparent that the plans for the next two or three months will involve only the remainder of the 1st Phase, the 2d Phase and such elements of the succeeding phases as must be considered on account of the fact that certain units belonging to those phases have already arrived.
 3. Based on Par. 2 this study will then be limited to a rearrangement of the priority schedule for the remainder of the 1st Phase and for the 2d Phase, and will concern itself very little with succeeding phases.
 4. Since difficulties of obtaining materiel render it impossible to hope to equip them within the next three months, we may at once postpone the arrival of all tank personnel and army artillery.
 5. In aviation we have more personnel than can be equipped in the next three months. Except that we require two additional balloon companies, we also have now a greater proportion of aviation personnel than will be required to balance our forces at the end of June.... Aviation, except for two balloon companies, may therefore be eliminated.
 6. A detailed consideration of the 2d Phase appears to justify us in postponing the arrival of a total of 78,747 officers and soldiers until after the end of June 1918....
 7. Since we are already obligated to furnish 3 additional Negro regiments for service with the French, those regiments are retained in the revised schedule.
 On the other hand, the remainder (7,786) of the motor mechanics for service with the French have been dropped.
 8. According to the information available there is sufficient tonnage, equally divided between that which we control and that controlled by England, to transport 120,000 men per month. This gives a possibility of 360,000 men during the months

of April, May, and June. This number corresponds to the number of troops remaining after making the deductions referred to in the preceding paragraphs.

9. In view of the former agreement with the British concerning the 6 divisions and the desire to assist the British by putting as many as practicable of our infantry units temporarily with British divisions, it appears logical for the British to transport all infantry units plus such auxiliaries and replacements as make up the numbers needed to fully utilize British shipping.

10. Based on the idea expressed in Par. 9, Table I [see below] has been prepared showing the assignment of troops between our own and British shipping. It will be noted that the majority of the army and S.O.S. troops retained in the revised schedule are assigned to American shipping.

11. Under the priority schedule the greater part of the army and S.O S. troops of the 2d Phase appear at the beginning of that phase. Under the revised schedule these troops are echeloned; the bulk of them coming however in May; that is, at the middle of the revised schedule.

12. It will also be noted that under the revised schedule the artillery should complete its training by the time the several infantry units are relieved by the British.

13. While it is estimated * * * that up to the end of June, 60,022 replacements will be required, it has only been possible to provide for 44,000 in the revised schedule.

* * * * * *

15. It may be anticipated that the proposed schedule will not please the French since they seem more than ever anxious to incorporate our units in their divisions.

16. It is recommended that after final decision has been reached a written agreement be drawn up between the Commander-in-Chief and the British commander in France and also between the Commander-in-Chief and the British War Office.

In this way the misunderstanding which arose with reference to the 6 divisions should be avoided.

H.A.D. (G-3)

Table I Troop Shipments								
	British Ships			United States Ships				
	April	May	June	April	May	June	Totals	
Inf. and M. guns II Corps	53,553	53,553					107,106	This equals infantry, etc., of 6 divs., II Corps
Inf. and M. guns III Corps			a 17,891	b 35,702			53,553	This equals infantry, etc., of 3 divs., III Corps

Artillery, etc., II Corps				10,990	32,970	21,980	65,940	This equals artillery, etc., of 6 divs., II Corps
Artillery, etc., III Corps				10,990		10,990	21,980	This equals artillery, etc., of 2 divs., III Corps
1st Phase	3,000				9,652		12,652	This completes 1st Phase
2d Phase (less divs.)		3,000	6,000		17,300	6,465	32,765	This completes 2d Phase (less 18,000 laborers)
3d Phase (less divs.)			12,149			1,500	13,649	
Replacements			24,000			20,000	44,000	
Negro Regts. 3	3,000	3,000		3,000			9,000	
Totals	59,553	59,553	60,000	60,682	59,922	60,935	360,645	

Recapitulation

Troops—275579—8 complete divs. and infantry of 1 div. Complete II Corps, and 2 complete divs. and 1 infantry of a div., III Corps and 3 colored regts.

Phase troops—59066—Complete 1st and 2d Phases (Less 18,000 laborers) and 13649 on 3d Phase.

Replacements—44000—Note: July mostly needed for 3d Phase and Replacements
    (b) This is infantry of the 1st and 3d Divs. of III Corps
    (a) This is the infantry of the 2d Division

USAWW, vol. 2, pp. 292–95.

Editor's Note—Fox Conner's memorandum lays out an overall readjustment of the GHQ's carefully worked out Priority Schedule of October 7, 1917, for the sequenced preparation and shipment of personnel, units, and equipment for the buildup of a balanced American Army in France. The incessant demands of the British and French for more and more American infantry and machine-gun units to plug holes in their ranks to stem the German March offensive scrambled the existing plans of Pershing and his staff for an orderly development of American divisions into corps, and corps into armies, provided with all of the necessary supporting corps, army, and SOS units and personnel.

Col. Carl Boyd, ADC to Pershing, to Maj. Gen Francis J. Kernan, CG, SOS, AEF, Tours.

General Pershing desires me to inform you that he has directed Lieutenant Colonel F. E. Pope to turn over to you for your official use a Locomobile limousine.

The General has been very well pleased indeed with the Locomobile he has been trying for the last two weeks, and he hopes you will find the one he has assigned to you both useful and pleasant.

LC, Pershing Papers, Correspondence with Francis J. Kernan, box 111.

TAG, War Department, to Pershing, in part in reply to Pershing to TAG, War Department, cables P-345-S, December 6, 1917, P-655-S, February 27, and P-760-S, March 21,

Cable A-1069-R. Confidential.

1. With reference to your paragraph 1C, your 760. As far as consistent with new Priority Schedule effort will be made to keep up shipment of aviation personnel as indicated in paragraph 16 and 16A, your 276 [November 8, not reproduced], and paragraph 1, your 345, that is 30 service squadrons, 8 balloon companies, and 20 park squadrons with photographic and meteorological sections monthly. This personnel will only be partially trained and not complete with pilots or observers. [Reply—April 16, P-933-S-4A]

1A. Chief Signal Officer of the Army states monthly maximum output present schools in United States now authorized 750 pilots and observers. This figure will probably not be reached before July or August.

1B. With reference to equipment Chief Signal Officer of the Army says with reference to paragraph 2, your 655, estimated here that manufacturing program will enable us to deliver at port of embarkation in United States 106 squadrons by November 1st. Type of machines and dates of arrival there as follows: 28 Bristol fighter squadrons, 1 in May, 4 in June, 9 in July, 9 in August, 3 in September and 2 in October. 24 observation DH Squadrons, 1 in May, 4 in June, 6 in July, 7 in August, and 6 in September. 44 Day bomber DH 4 squadrons, 8 in June, 11 in July, 13 in August and 12 in September. 10 night bomber Handley Page squadrons of which we hope to deliver 3 in July and 7 in August. The foregoing includes replacements. This is exclusive of the 14 pursuit squadrons for which it is assumed you can supply the airplanes from European source. Our manufacturing program now in operation will produce 3 times as many De Haviland per month as Bristol fighters. [Reply—April 30, P-1031-S-6; in addition—April 16, A-1107-R-7, May 2, A-1224-R]

1C. Foregoing statements of Chief Signal Officer of the Army will be verified by thorough investigation and in case there is any change you will be immediately notified. In view of the state of equipment as indicated herein do you desire any change in shipment of aviation personnel? Cable your recommendations. It is desired that in future no agreements with Allies be made as to furnishing men and material from here without first referring the matter to us. Every effort being made to meet your wishes but manufacturing program of equipment, shipping, et cetera, has not advanced as rapidly as was hoped for in the beginning. March. [Reply—P-898-S-3D; April 30, P-1031-S-6]

NARA, RG 120, M930, Confidential Series, War Department to AEF, roll 18.

April 10

Pershing's Personal Diary

Worked in office all day. Saw General Bethel and General Hinds, also Colonels Fox Conner, Fiske, Logan, W.D. Connor and Colonel Nolan.

LC, Pershing Papers, Diary, May 7, 1917–September 1, 1918, box 4.

Pétain, CINC, Armies of the North and Northeast, to Pershing.

No. 9667

During your visit to my Headquarters on March 25th last, you spontaneously offered to put at my disposal, due to the great battle going on, all the American forces disembarked in France, as well as those which be sent you by American tonnage upon their arrival.

We agreed to send your 1st Division to participate in the battle as soon as possible and to establish in sectors on quiet parts of the front the 3 other divisions of the Ist American Corps, which could relieve French divisions thus made available for the battle.

The second part of your proposals contemplated putting later on at my disposal American units, by regiments or battalions, on their arrival in France. I am ready to receive them immediately by battalions or regiments in the French divisions occupying quiet sectors, and I will appreciate your informing me, in as precise a manner as possible, the number of the units you anticipate putting at my disposal and the schedule of the dates of their arrival.

Nevertheless, however considerable it may be, the aid that you will bring us will remain strictly limited and far from compensating for the using up of our units in the battle. On the other hand, the effectives which we possess as reinforcements are equally limited; therefore, as I anticipated, we must contemplate shortly the disbanding of a certain number of our divisions.

This disbanding is of such a nature as to considerably influence the result of the 1918 campaign. I see only one way of avoiding it: that is to obtain from America, who alone has the necessary resources in men, a sufficient support to compensate for our losses.

It is for infantry that the needs are imperious and urgent; it would be suitable then that priority were given to the transport of American Infantry during the following months so as to maintain the effectives of our divisions during the battle, which may be prolonged during the entire summer of this year.

If, following the request addressed to this effect to the U. S. Government, the tonnage assigned to military transportation can be immediately and measurably increased, it is to the shipment of American Infantry that it would be most important to assign this supplement of tonnage, at the same time, if necessary, a part of the tonnage actually used for the transport of the American Army.

If the tonnage assigned to the transport of the American Army cannot be measurably increased, the plan of transport now in effect should be changed to give a larger part to the transport of infantry.

In effect it is not necessary to contemplate the shipment of the other arms and services in numbers corresponding to that of the infantry since our units are provided with all the other means of combat and all their services, and since they lack, to continue the campaign, only infantry and machine gun units.

I permit myself to make this suggestion to you because I see the solution of the grave problem of effectives in the present campaign only in the aid of American Infantry. I thus ask that you pay every attention to my request.

I must tell you, my dear General, that the decision in this matter may have the greatest influence on the course of present events and even on the decisions which we will have to make in the conduct of the battle engaged in. Because of its urgency I would appreciate your letting me know, as soon as possible, what you have decided.

Copy to: Minister of War, 3rd Bureau.
          Supreme War Council of Versailles.
          General Foch at Sarcus.
          General Ragueneau.

[Reply—April 12, Ragueneau to CINC, Armies of the North and Northeast]

LC, Pershing Papers, folder 14: Translations of various French and German documents by Maj. Rayner and Maj. Koenig: Annex No. 2, Pt. 3, The Defensive Campaign, March 21–July 18, 1918, Marshal Pétain's Report as CINC, Armies of the North and Northeast, box 355; for a different translation, see also *USAWW*, vol. 3, pp. 283–84; *Les armées françaises dans la Grande guerre, Tome 6*, vol. 1, *Annexes*, vol. 3: *Annexe* No. 1588, pp. 325–26.

Dawes, Chief, GPA, SOS, AEF, Paris, to Pershing.

Personal

I found the enclosed article about port facilities in France in the New York Tribune of March 5th. Have you any idea as to who filed this alleged information? It would seem to me that this article is perhaps the beginning of an attack on us over here. It has evidently been carefully prepared. It only shows what we both have had in mind, that is, that when any serious congestion occurs at the ports our critics will see that the attention of the world is directed toward it irrespective of the fact that everything possible has been done to avoid it. The only thing necessary is of course to prevent congestion and I am very glad that you have a man like Moore [Maj. Hugh B. Moore] in charge of the docks. No one knows better than yourself, who are possessed of so much of it, that there are some emergencies, which are only met by nervous energy. This is one and Moore has it. The newspaper writer falls into the usual custom of damning the Quartermaster Corps.

[Handwritten]

Am just leaving for Tours to round up my labor organization. May go over to La Courtine & possibly to St. Nazaire for a day in seeing that our assignments for handling situations are adequate. By the end of the week we will have furnished 12,000 laborers.

Enclosure.

New York Tribune, March 5, 1918

U.S. Supplies Piling Up on Piers Abroad

Congestion Threatens to Interfere Seriously with Army Shipments

Terminals, Started Late, Incomplete

Vessels Slow in Unloading: 40 Per Cent of Cargoes Held Back

(Staff Correspondence)

Washington, March 4—Failure of the quartermaster's department of the army to develop adequate facilities at the French ports to handle supplies shipped overseas to Pershing's army has already choked the docks and the partly completed terminals and is seriously interfering with the army supply programme, according to reliable information laid before members of the Senate Military Affairs Committee.

While the United States could find use for additional tonnage in other channels, a well-informed member of the Senate stated today that even if the Shipping Board doubled the tonnage at the disposal of the War Department at once it could not be used by the army authorities. This Senator declared that the much mentioned "neck of the bottle" was not at the docks and terminals into which American supplies are being shipped. The army quartermaster's corps is not able to move into the interior more than 60 per cent of the supplies being poured daily into the French ports by American vessels, he stated, and there is already a congestion which matches that of the Port of New York at its worst.

Terminal Work Delayed

Reciting the causes which have brought about this situation, the Senator declared:

"When the army commenced to develop its organization and administrative machinery in France, later last summer, it first turned its attention to the construction of supply depots in the interior. Then it undertook the construction of several hundred miles of railroad, meantime casually commencing the construction of port and terminal equipment. This latter equipment, which, with seaboard storage facilities, was the most important of all, was left until the last.

"Interior supply depots, which could have waited, were rushed. Railroads, of course, necessary, but not so essential as port facilities, were also rushed. The port improvements and installations waited. The existing congestion, which is effectively blocking "the neck of the bottle," is the result.

Must Be Stored Here

"If the War Department had rushed the construction of docks and terminal storehouses in the French ports, American supplies could be advanced as rapidly as ships could make the round trip. Any quantity could be stored at the French seaboard terminals, to be drawn upon as rapidly as the facilities for moving them into the interior and the needs for their consumption arose.

"However, as things stand now, the supplies must be stored in America, 3,000 miles away, until the existing chaos at the terminals is cleared away. Already this chaos has slowed down the transport operations of the too few ships available for overseas transport. Vessels are compelled to wait for docking, which reduces the efficiency of our tonnage tremendously. If they do not wait for docks they are compelled to unload to barges and lighters, which involves double handling of the cargoes and involves delays equally as bad.

"It is impossible to lighten the burden at the French ports by diverting some of the supplies to English ports for transport across the Channel, because every square inch of docks and terminals in England is monopolized by the gigantic port operations necessary to keep the British army in France supplied.

Definite Programme Lacking

"One of the greatest shortcomings of the War Department has been its failure to call into consultation, early in the war, officials of the Shipping Board and map out a definite programme for the overseas transport of men and materials.

"Not until we had been at war for over six months did the War College first undertake systematic cooperation with the Shipping Board. Before that the quartermaster's department made a practice of presenting extravagant demands for tonnage as the needs arose. The entire overseas programme until lately has been one which has ignored the future.

"Now the War Department is reaping the ill harvest [of] its short-sightedness planted, and the country is confronted with the anomalous situation, borne out by statements from responsible sources that the War Department if it had double its present tonnage, could not use it on account of the lack of terminal facilities in France."

LC, Pershing Papers, folder: Gen. Charles G. Dawes (1918), box 59.

Pershing to Harbord, CS, GHQ AEF, then visiting the 1st Brigade, 1st Division.

We have had no word from you since you left, nor are we hearing about the First Division in general.

Am quite anxious to know just what sort of work they are doing in preparation for entering the line. Please drop me a note the first opportunity. I am going to establish a daily courier service between here and there.

Nothing very much going on here.
[Reply—April 11, Harbord to Pershing]

LC, Harbord Papers, folder: Correspondence with John J. Pershing, box 11; copy in LC, Pershing Papers, folder: General James G. Harbord, 1910–1918, box 87.

Pershing to Kernan, CG, SOS, AEF, Tours.

Despite repeated instructions from my headquarters regarding uniformity and neatness in dress, I have had called to my attention and have personally observed that not enough attention, even on the part of general officers, has been paid to this important matter.

The conspicuous position in a foreign country that our officers and men occupy makes every slouchy officer and man a reflection on the whole American army.

I therefore desire that you give this subject your personal attention to the end that all the officers and men of your command may be impressed with the necessity for a more scrupulous observance of all regulations regarding neatness, uniformity and smartness in personal appearance.

LC, Pershing Papers, folder: Gen. Francis J. Kernan, box 111.

Pershing to Sims, Commander, U. S. Naval Forces Operating in European Waters, London.

[Handwritten]
We have reached a point in handling tonnage that make it necessary to consider the possibilities of other ports besides those we are now using. Our port facilities and the increase in rail transport are going to be delayed beyond the time when large additional tonnage is to be available. While realizing the objections, I think we shall be forced to seriously think of using Marseille, but before making a positive recommendation I would like to have your views.

Col. Logan will present this letter and will explain our situation to you. I shall be glad if you can give me the benefit of your opinion after hearing what the problem is that we have to solve. [Reply—April 13, Sims to Pershing]

LC, Sims Papers, Special Correspondence: John J. Pershing, box 77.

Pershing to Brig. Gen. James W. McAndrew, Commandant, Army Schools, AEF, Langres.

Despite, repeated orders from my headquarters regarding the importance of neatness in dress and personal appearance, I have had called to my attention and have personally observed that sufficient stress has not been laid upon this important matter.

As Commandant of the Army Schools I desire that you make every effort to impress upon all the instructors and students at your schools the importance of rigid observance of all regulations regarding neatness and uniformity in dress to the end that when they return to their organizations for duty they may, by precept and example, inspire their men with new standards regarding dress and personal appearance.

LC. Pershing Papers, folder: Gen. James W. McAndrew, box 126.

Pershing to TAG, War Department, in part in reply to TAG, War Department, to Pershing, cables A-609-R, January 7, and A-1022-R, April 2 (not reproduced); in addition to Pershing to TAG, War Department, cable P-787-S, March 26.

Cable P-884-S.
  3. For Chief of Ordnance. 3B. With reference to your cablegram 609. Only 3699 cases ammunition for 75-m.m. has been received to date. French Government may not be able to meet promised deliveries this type ammunition purchased from them. What quantities this type ammunition can you positively ship weekly beginning immediately? Promised deliveries for March behind schedule date. Also what deliveries can be made on anti-aircraft ammunition projects 4 and 5?
[Reply—April 22, A-1154-R-1G]
  4. For Felton. Large quantity of beef now afloat which cannot be promptly moved until we receive portion of refrigerator cars requested for April delivery in paragraph 1H, cable 787. Of the 375 refrigerator cars thus ordered for April, can you assure us of early delivery of 150? [Reply—April 17, A-1118-R-1E]
  4A. With reference to paragraph 1J, your cablegram 1022. See paragraph 1H, our cablegram 787, and paragraph 3, our cablegram 796. When the entire order of 80-pound rail has been shipped we wish rail shipments to continue with the 67½-pound Russian rail so far as standard gauge allotment allows and when possible as

base load in addition to this not to interfere with shipping light railway material in paragraph 1N, our cablegram 787. [Reply—April 17, A-1118-R-1A]

NARA, RG 120, M930, Main Series, AEF to WAR Department, roll 2.

Pershing to TAG, War Department, in addition to Pershing to TAG, War Department, cables P-319-S, November 27, and P-601-S, February 14 (see February 3, A-730-R-1, for note on P-601-S).

Cable P-885-S.
5. For Chief of Staff. 5B. With reference to paragraph 4, my cablegram 601, and paragraph 1A, my cablegram 319. Inequalities mentioned have become more pronounced due to arrival of officers from United States drawing extra flying pay who are on duty with Artillery Observers doing exactly the same work but who do not get the extra pay. I again recommend that steps be taken to correct this injustice to other arms of the Service. [Reply—April 22, A-1155-R-1]

NARA, RG 120, M930, Main Series, AEF to War Department, roll 2.

Pershing to TAG, War Department, in part in reply to TAG, War Department, to Pershing, cables A-1034-R, April 3, A-1039-R, April 4, and A-1048-R, April 6.

Cable P-887-S. Confidential.
For the Chief of Staff. 1A. With reference to paragraph 3, your cablegram 1039. Our understanding is *Leviathan* is manned, provisioned, coaled and operated by Navy and that Navy is to concentrate at Brest reserve supply coal for *Leviathan* using naval vessels therefor. Is this correct? Army is prepared to discharge and forward troops and cargo of *Leviathan* at Brest. [Reply—April 14, A-1100-R-1]

1B. With reference to paragraph 16, your cable 1034. Baker, United States Navy, Paris, advises this matter already investigated with Minister of Merchant Marine. 6 large ships available for transporting troops but French Government has planned to use these ships for transporting 150,000 troops from Algiers. Recommend that French High Commissioner, Washington, be approached with a view to our obtaining priority of use these vessels. [Reply—May 26, A-1400-R-1]

1C. With reference your cablegram 1048. The subject of handling aggregate tonnage mentioned is being given serious study. The output with present port facilities will be increased to maximum and the use of additional ports is being taken up with the French and British authorities. Have no doubt of our ability to handle the amount of tonnage mentioned. Further detailed recommendations will be sent on the subject of systematic loading, reductions in existing requisitions and priority of shipments after study has been completed. [In addition—May 5, P-1057-S]

NARA, RG 120, M930, Confidential Series, AEF to War Department, roll 7.

Editor's Note—Following the dispatch of P-887-S-1C to the War Department, Pershing put the General Staff to work on the problem of obtaining additional port facilities in France. On April 10 Pershing wrote to Adm. Sims and sent Col. James A. Logan Jr., his ACS, G-1, to London to deliver the letter and to discuss the matter with Sims and his staff. As a result of these discussions, Sims sent his letter of April 13 to Pershing outlining his proposals. More discussions with the British and French followed.

On April 23, Sims reported to Operations, Navy Department, on Logan's visit to London and their discussions:

> Staff officers from General Pershing's staff have recently come to London for consultation with this staff concerning movements of army troop and supply ships. The principal new feature presented by them is a desire to use Marseille in case necessity arises. It is understood that at present the principal difficulties on the French Coast arise from lack of rolling stock [i.e., railroad materials] which has been required by the French since the beginning of the German offensive. It is also understood that a considerable amount of rolling stock returning from Italy might be utilized from Marseille north. The west coast ports of France would seem to be able to meet the demands of the next few months, but to prepare for emergencies, the army desires to investigate the possibilities of using Marseille in case the necessity should arise. The increased distance involved in using the latter port, and the lack of adequate escort craft renders the use of Marseille a difficult problem. It is possible that certain of the faster ships might be diverted to that port from time [to time] depending upon submarine activity and other circumstances. (Naval History and Heritage Command, website: Wars, Conflicts, and Operations, World War I, Documentary Histories, April 1918, Sims to Operations, Navy Department, April 23, 1918; original document at NARA, RG 45, DNA, Entry 517B.)

On May 1, Logan sent the following letter to the CG, SOS, outlining the issues involved in the use of Marseille and the Mediterranean route:

> With reference to the question of the use of the port of Marseille, referred to in telephone conversation this morning with your C. of S., this letter is transmitted to confirm the C. in C's. instructions, which were communicated to Gen. Hagood. The question of the use of Marseille has been taken up with the French, through M. Ganne, and also with Sir Sam Fay, who have both expressed their consent to the use by the A.E.F. of the port of Marseille. General Atterbury, it is understood, has discussed the details as to the ten berths that the French will immediately assign for the use of the A.E.F. at Marseille, and also as to the use of certain storage facilities now

existing at Miramas. It is also understood that he had full and detailed information as to both of these points, and, as a matter of fact, it is understood that a preliminary reconnaissance has already been made of these points by his representatives as well as the French.

2. The following is a quotation from a letter dated April 13, 1918, from Admiral Sims to the C. in C., which is self-explanatory: [hereafter he quotes extensively from Sims's letter.]

3. Subsequent to writing this letter, during a conference between Col. Logan and Commander Long, of Admiral Sims' Staff, it was considered advisable for these Headquarters to make recommendations direct to the War Department at the proper time that Marseille be used as a port of debarkation for supplies only of the A.E:F., stating at the same time that Admiral Sims had taken up directly with the Navy Department the question of the characteristics of the particular vessels which would be used in our Marseille trade. [see May 5, P-1057-S] The sea trip to Marseille from New York as compared with Bordeaux or Brest may be put down as 700 miles longer, or, in the round trip, 1400 additional miles steaming, this meaning perhaps five days additional for the turnaround as applied to ships discharging at Marseille, as compared for example, with Bordeaux. During the conference, it appeared to be the Navy Department's opinion that A.E.F. cargo transports to Marseille should be selected from amongst our fastest ships especially armed for this service. The German submarines which threaten these ships are reported to be of the largest type, which cannot do much submerged. These submarines, however, carry 6-inch guns and come to the surface and shell ships with the same. It also was the Navy's idea that cargo ships sent to Marseille should make the run from the U. S. to Gibraltar without convoy. They would be convoyed from Gibraltar to Marseille and return to Gibraltar where arrangements would have to be made for recoaling, and that then they would be convoyed out to sea. There would be a certain loss in freight capacity incident to the additional coal that would have to be carried. The Navy were of the opinion that the time lost by these ships in making this extra mileage over and above the time necessary to go to the Bay of Biscay ports would be nearly offset by the extra time gained in making the Atlantic Ocean trip without convoy.

4. The great improvement which has been made, and is continuing to be made, at our existing Bay of Biscay ports leads to the belief that ultimately we will have no difficulty whatsoever in handling the tonnage referred to in confidential cable No. 1048, of April 6th, a copy of which is hereto attached and indeed much more. However, every effort must be made to attain the minimum turn-around possible in our ships as soon as possible. We may be somewhat hampered at our existing Bay of Biscay ports by the additional coal which will be thrown into these ports by the French and British, owing to the complete suspension of coal shipments from the northern French coal mines and the consequent water shipments of coal from England. This particular phase has been completely investigated by Gen. Atterbury.

In view of the foregoing, it appears necessary for us to at once proceed with the use of the port of Marseille and on this account you are requested to prepare and submit as soon as practicable a proposed cable to be transmitted to the War Department, requesting the War Department to load certain ships designated by the Navy with certain classes of supplies up to tonnage limits recommended by you for Marseille. In view of the somewhat increased risk incident to the shipment of supplies to Mediterranean ports, it is believed advisable that these shipments for the present should be limited to classes of supplies which are readily replaceable from the stocks on hand or in transit, and that they should not include classes not replaceable. The C. in C. desires that your recommendations be submitted quickly but that no definite action be taken until further orders from him. (NARA, RG 120, Office of the Commander-in-Chief, Office of the Secretary of the General Staff, entry 22, Reports of the Commander-in-Chief, folder 34: GHQ War Diary, folder 35: April 28–June 12, 1918, diary entry May 19, 1918, 344-a, pp. 349–51, box 4.) [In addition—May 5, P-1057-S.]

Pershing to TAG, War Department.

Cable P-889-S.

5. For Chief of Staff. Present class at General Staff College numbers 162 representing all divisions in United States and France except 4th, 5th, 6th and 7th. Course completed about June 1st. For next course at Staff College beginning probably about June 15th recommend selected officers be sent to France as follows: By each division 1 officer for each of 3 sections General Staff. Request early information of action taken in order that arrangements may be made for class consisting of officers referred to above and like contingents from divisions in France. [Reply—April 25, A-1173-R-1C]

NARA, RG 120, M930, Main Series, AEF to War Department, roll 2.

TAG, War Department, to Pershing, in part in reply to Pershing to TAG, War Department, cable P-836-S, April 2.

Cable A-1077-R.

9. For Nolan [ACS, G-2]: Reference message brought by General Glenn concerning information contained in press reports this country which you desire cabled. Just what class of information do you wish and with how much detail? Do you want any English-speaking papers as well as foreign covered? Do you want daily or weekly cables? [Reply—April 20, P-965-S-5]

11. With reference to your 836, paragraph 2B. Your recommendations Harbord filed for future considerations. No appointments Major General or Brigadier General, Regular Army, being considered at present. March

NARA, RG 120, M930, Main Series, War Department to AEF, roll 12.

April 11

Pershing's Personal Diary

Worked in office all day. Talked with General Hinds on question of a Chief of Artillery. Sent Colonel Logan on mission to Admiral Sims. Talked with Major Frederick Palmer who is just leaving for short stay with 1st Division. Saw General Brewster, also Mr. McKenzie, a newspaper man representing a Canadian syndicate, and Mr. Clothier, representative of the Adjutant General of the Army. Rode with Colonel Boyd.

LC, Pershing Papers, Diary, May 7, 1917–September 1, 1918, box 4.

Maj. Gen. Sir Hugh Trenchard, Chief of Staff, Air Ministry, London, to Foulois, Chief, Air Service, SOS, AEF, reply to Foulois to Trenchard, April 4.

T. 438.

I was very glad to get your letter of April 4th, B.D.F. 169, which was very clear and useful to me at this present juncture.

Taking your paragraphs as you have written them:

I quite agree with your suggestion of appointing Major Harold Fowler [later served as Chief, Air Service, U.S. Third Army, in 1919] as a travelling liaison officer between R.A.F. Headquarters in France, your Headquarters in France and my headquarters in London. Major Fowler will do admirably, and I shall be able to keep him informed of everything that goes on.

I am pressing on hard with the D.H. 9's for the Nancy area. I hope with luck, if the weather clears, to be able to get out two squadrons this month and three or four next. I am afraid the Handley Pages will be a bit late, but I hope to fill up the squadrons down there and perhaps send another squadron by June.

I am very glad to hear you are pushing on with the aerodrome work because this is most essential.

I have heard a certain amount about your Handley Pages being delayed and also your D.H. 4's and D.H. 9's.

I would like to say that I am very glad to hear you have been appointed American Air Service representative to work with the American Section of the Supreme War

Council at Versailles, and also the American representative in the Inter-Allied Aviation Committee. At present we only have a liaison officer at Versailles, and when the Air Committee meet it was intended that I or my representative should go out I believe, but this matter, owing to the battle now being fought, has been hung up. I am certain you would be of great use in helping to allocate the raw material necessary for the different Services. Sir William Weir is our representative on the Inter-Allied Aviation Committee, but as he is under Munitions I think it had better remain that way.

With regard to the Supreme Air Services command, it is very kind of you to say you would accept me as Supreme Commander, but this is a matter which I think is barely ripe until we get more squadrons for bombing purposes in France.

I am certain the steps you are taking will lead to a more efficient coordination of our combined work in the Nancy area, and the only thing I would like to ask you to do is to put one squadron with General Newall as early as possible so that we may all begin to work on the same sort of principle. I am certain it would be better for all of us.

I saw a lot of your American Squadrons divided amongst our squadrons the other day, and it struck me they were very keen to get their own machines going. I believe it is chiefly a question of engines, as I understand we offered you 200 S.E.s without engines the other day, but owing to the engine difficulty it was not possible to take them. Of course, we are suffering from engine shortages ourselves.

Next time I go to France I shall make a point of trying to come and see you.

LC, Foulois Papers, folder 14: AEF, Air Service, Operations—Bombing General, 1918, n.d., box 9.

Bliss, Chief, American Section, and Permanent Military Representative, SWC, Versailles, to Pershing.

Telegram No. 1264 L.R. Urgent.

General Foch urgently wishes to know whether the First American Division now in the vicinity of Gisors is at his disposition for service in battle. He particularly wishes to know the following points first, is the Division ready to go; second, is it at General Foch's complete disposition; third, will another commander be designated in place of the present one who he understands is ill? He wants to feel that the high command of the division is thoroughly familiar with his troops and conditions existing within the division before committing it to battle. I have told him that you will answer his questions direct.

LC, Pershing Papers, folder: General Tasker H. Bliss, 1917–1918.

[GHQ, AEF Action]
April 12, 1918

With reference to the above telegram, the following was sent this date to the Commanding General, 1st Division, A. E. F.:

[Telegram No. 934 L.S.]

[Commanding General] 1st Division, A. E. F., Chaumont-en-Vexin.

Please send an officer to General Foch with the following message:

General F. Foch, Commanding Allied Forces. Reference your inquiry regarding 1st Division, transmitted through General Bliss, I consider the 1st Division ready for active service. This division has received thorough training and has had considerable experience in the trenches. A brief program of exercises in open warfare is now being carried out at its present station. The permanent division commander, General Bullard, has been temporarily ill but is now on his way to join the division. Upon his arrival and upon the completion of the brief program of instruction in open warfare, there is no reason why this division should not take its place actively wherever you desire to place it. In case you consider it urgent, the division could go in at once.

Pershing.

Acknowledge receipt.

Conner
Acting Chief of Staff.

USAWW, vol. 3, p. 490.

Harbord, CS, GHQ AEF, then visiting the 1st Brigade, 1st Division, to Pershing, reply to Pershing to Harbord, April 10.

Your note just received. I have not sent any word of any kind, because there has been nothing of note to report.

The rail movement does not seem to me to have been very well planned by the French. The principal town around which our people are billeted is Gisors, the use of which, however, is not permitted to any of our troops and at which none of them were detrained. General Duncan's Headquarters detrained Saturday night at a point twenty miles distant from here. One battalion of his Brigade detrained at a distance of about thirty-five miles from its billeting place. Other units throughout the Division have been detrained one or more marches from their billets.

The result has been that the last units of the Division did not arrive in the area until yesterday. The weather was rainy and the marches wearisome. Under the orders from G.H.Q., one day was to be allowed for rest and cleaning up and then the programme was to begin. That was the programme dated March 31. I have seen a copy of a programme from G.H.Q., however, dated March 30, which allowed two days for cleaning up. In the 18th Infantry the later programme was not received and units started to take two days' rest. The uneven arrival of units will result in an inequality of opportunity for training.

The Division forms part of the 5th French Army under General Micheler. Day before yesterday Division Headquarters published a notice that General Micheler would prescribe the open warfare training which was to be followed. Three or four days of open warfare training culminating in a terrain exercise, that the details would follow later. The details have not arrived and General Duncan's Brigade, with which I have spent my time, has been working on our G.H.Q. schedule. Company and battalion problems; attack formations, close order drills. Some drills with gas masks on, all drills to be attended by men carrying gas masks and taking the full pack to the drill fields. The French authorities evidently selected the training area from the map without a knowledge of the country, for the terrain selected cannot be used, due to the fact that it is all covered with growing crops. That is the reason why the Division maneuver, which was to be the culmination of the training, is now to be a terrain exercise instead.

The march under condition of rain and mud brought in a number of men with sore feet, reaching as high as fifteen percent in some units. There is a little complaint of the French ration but not very much. It includes a good deal more bread than our ration which the French dip in their wine. With us the wine ration not being issued the quantity of bread seems unnecessarily large.

The troops are looking well; seem to be in good spirits and are attacking the training schedule with vigor. General Duncan sees all parts of his Brigade daily and I have been constantly with him. We go mounted half of the day and in automobile the other half. According to the programme, if followed out, the training should culminate probably Sunday or Monday [April 14 or 15]. Unless otherwise directed I shall remain with the 1st Brigade until after the training culminates in the terrain exercise.

General Duncan and I paid our respects to the French Army Commander, but did not meet him. He is said to be very cordial and expresses himself as pleased with the American Troops. The Division suffered a little by General Bullard's absence, sick. I understand he returned last night, but have not seen him. Will go there this afternoon.

The postal authorities are just now getting their post office in operation. In the meantime there has been no mail service for the Command.
[Over]
[Handwritten]

I enclose a copy of Gen. Micheler's preliminary order for the terrain exercise which has just come [not reproduced]. I'll send the exercise outline, which is rather long, when it has been copied—probably tomorrow.
JGH
Later—On arriving at Div Hdqrs I find that Gen. Bullard has not yet arrived, The Chief of Staff has heard nothing from him since day before yesterday when he was reported much better.
JGH

LC, Pershing Papers, folder: General James G. Harbord, 1910–1918, box 87.

Biddle, CG, Base Section No. 3, London, to Pershing.

During the last week it has seemed to me that the seriousness of the situation in France has had more effect upon the people at large than previously, both among the army officers and also among the civilian population. The almost constant successes of the Germans are making, naturally, a very serious impression. There is, however, still no real depression, nor any weakening of the morale.

I heard the speech of the Prime Minister a day or two ago in the House of Commons, and while he praised the Army very highly, at the same time what he stated about the Army situation was much to my mind as to leave an unsatisfactory impression. At all times both in the newspapers and as conversation with officers, acts of individual bravery are being dwelt on, and the great events passed over, which in itself indicates uneasiness on their part.

The arrival of American troops and the placing them promptly in the line was continually dwelt upon in the Prime Minister's speech, and that is also the constant talk of the War Office.

At the same time, as stated above, the general morale in England remains excellent.

LC, Pershing Papers, folder: John Biddle, box 25.

Maj. Paul H. Clark, American Military Mission to French GHQ, Compiègne, to CINC, AEF.

[Handwritten]
No. 40. 6 pm.
Subject: Military Situation.

2. This morning Gen. de Barescut [Chief of Operations] phoned requesting that I come to his office immediately. I went. He began by saying that the French were very much satisfied with the present status of the 1, 2, 26 and 42 U.S. divisions, that everyone at French GQG appreciated very profoundly the noble sentiment that had actuated the American Commander in placing the four divisions named in the great battle now in progress or in the trenches, "but events move so rapidly and the French, already short of divisions, may momentarily find themselves seriously embarrassed for troops."

"In looking about for more troops the 32 div. U.S. was perceived and the question naturally occurs to the French staff, will the Americans immediately send that division forward."

Gen. de B requested that I present the request that so much of the 32 Div as can be sent, be sent at once, i. e. inside of 3 days, to draw very near to the line. He explained that the Fr. would like to place this 32 div. with the 21st Corps in 7th Army and that by company and battalion they would be inserted in the line for instruction purposes as fast as they were sufficiently advanced for such instruction—and until they were sufficiently advanced they would be held in reserve thus relieving French troops to go to the Great battle.

He pointed to the attacks delivered in the last two or three days on the British and said any day the French may have to take over more front to assist the Br. and consequently the French must have more troops at their disposal and one way to get perhaps a Fr. division soon was to place the 32d Am. in the line.

I assured the General that I would present the matter in the same length and with the same urgency that characterized his conversation with me and would transmit to him any reply that might be confided to me.

3. I asked the Gen. for his view of the situation and he said that very likely without doubt the present missions of the German Army is the destruction of the British Army, that the French X Army is moving north and is actually, today, north of Amiens, that the French would very likely take over Br. front as far as the Somme. At this juncture, Gen. Anthoine (Chief of Staff) sent for him so our conversation ceased...

LC, Paul H. Clark Papers, folder: April 1–30, 1918, box 1.

Pershing to TAG, War Department, in addition to Pershing to TAG, War Department, cables P-844-S, April 3, and P-876-S, April 8.

Cable P-891-S. Confidential.
For the Chief of Staff.

1. Reference my cablegrams numbers 844 and 876 relating to priority of combat troops and allocation of units to British. Readjustment of Priority Schedule, based on agreement indicated in above cablegram and the availability of shipping for 120,000 men per month (equally divided between British and U.S.), provides for total shipment in April, May and June of 8 complete divisions, the infantry and machine guns of 1 division, 3 colored regiments for French, 44,000 replacements and 59,000 Service of Rear troops.

1A. As indicated hereinafter the revision provides for shipment on British shipping of infantry of 3 divisions in April, same in May and for the infantry of 1 division in June. While present plan contemplated holding each of these divisions with the British in France for about 2 months, when, unless circumstances demand otherwise, they will be withdrawn and join their artillery in rear of French front, existing agreement with British covers only the month of April. Decision as to the training and employment of other units transported by British held in abeyance for the present. The employment of our own shipping provides for the entire 3rd Division and 1 other complete division in April, the artillery and auxiliaries of 3 divisions in May and the artillery and auxiliaries of 3 divisions in June. This arrangement should result in the progressive training, etc. of the various divisional units so that when infantry is withdrawn from British the complete division will shortly thereafter be available as a unit. Considering the number of our troops now with the French, the 3 colored regiments and those mentioned above, the French phase of the situation should be satisfactory.

1B. In order to accomplish the foregoing and as indicated below, it has been necessary to postpone the sailing of about 78,000 Service of Rear troops of the 1st and 2nd Phases and all Air Service except 2 balloon companies and all tank personnel. The postponement of the latter 2 services is practicable and desirable as necessary equipment will not be available, and as needs of our forces in aviation can be met by the addition of the 2 balloon companies to that now in England and France. [In addition—April 12, P-898-S-3D; April 17, P-942-S-4]

1C. The reduction of Service of Rear troops is practicable with the possible exception of 18,000 laborers. However, if necessary this shortage can be met by employment of combat troops which otherwise will be available for active service.

1D. Recommend investigation as to employment of space on cargo transports and commercial liners for some of our Service of Rear troops. Indications here are that several thousand per month could be sent in this way, especially during the summer.

1E. In addition, the sailing of remaining motor mechanics, about 7,700 for the French, will have to be postponed.

1F. Plans for months subsequent to June will depend on future conditions and will be held in abeyance until about the end of May.

[*Ed.*—Subsequent subparagraphs 1G, 1H, and 1I contain detailed information on troop and unit shipments from April through June and identifies the AEF's Priority Schedule, and the breakdown of units of the 6 divisions going to be shipped in British ships. See April 13, P-911-S-1.]

1J. Request you cable as soon as practical action taken in this connection and also a plan for shipment showing the organizations and services by month by both British and our shipping.
[Reply—April 13, A-1102-R; in addition—April 18, A-1122-R]

NARA, RG 120, M930, Confidential Series, AEF to War Department, roll 7.

Pershing to TAG, War Department.

Cable P-894-S.

9. Colonel R. C. Bolling, Signal Corps, U.S. Army, has been missing since March 25th. Last seen near Amiens driving his own car in direction of enemy. Every effort is being made to ascertain his whereabouts and any interaction obtained will be cabled. [In addition—April 17, P-941-S-4]

Editor's Note—Col. Raynal C. Bolling was killed in a shootout while traveling behind the British front on March 26 when penetrating German forces stopped his car near Estrées. A complete account of the effort to discover what happened to Bolling, his encounter with the Germans, and his death is at LC, Foulois Papers, folder 15: AEF, Officers, Bolling, box 10. See especially "Statement of Private Paul L. Holder, 22nd Aero Squadron, U.S.A.," January 14, 1919. Holder was Bolling's driver and was captured at the same time that Bolling was killed. He witnessed the entire event.

NARA, RG 120, M930, Main Series, AEF to War Department, roll 2.

TAG, War Department, to Pershing.

Cable A-1080-R.
1N. 4 DeHaviland planes and 6 Liberty engines floated in charge of Lieutenant Farwell. Suggest you arrange for 1 of 4 Captains who are experts on Liberty engines be present when the planes and engines are prepared and flown.

NARA, RG 120, M930, Main Series, War Department to AEF, roll 12.

April 12

Pershing's Personal Diary

Worked in office all day. Talked with Major Shannon about decorations. Saw General Ragueneau [see below]. Rode in the afternoon.

LC, Pershing Papers, Diary, May 7, 1917–September 1, 1918, box 4.

Ragueneau, Chief, French Military Mission with the American Army, Chaumont, to CINC, Armies of the North and Northeast.

[Meeting with Pershing regarding Pétain's letter to Pershing, no. 9667, April 10]

No. 9468/O. I.
I have the honor of reporting to you an interview which I had this afternoon with General Pershing, who for the first time answered the questions raised in your letter No. 9667 of April 10.
I. Regarding the shipping of troops from the United States, the General informed me that the infantry and machine guns of four divisions will be embarked between now and April 20, a total of 64,000 men, by British as well as American shipping.
The General estimates that the infantry of 4 or 5 other divisions will be shipped during May and June, bringing the total of infantry to that of 8 or 9 divisions for the

present quarter. Nevertheless, this second series of shipments will include the minimum proportion of artillery and auxiliary troops so as to bring the 8 or 9 divisions gradually up to their regulation strength in troops of all arms and services.

That would total 128,000 infantry whose shipment could be counted on during the current quarter.

The General has asked that shipments of army and zone of communication troops, which will preferably be loaded in small groups on cargo ships, be reduced to the minimum so as to save the passenger ships for the infantry.

II. The American infantry, once having arrived, will be divided, in accordance with a proportion which the General cannot specify exactly and which he judges should be about half and half, among French and British divisions for its period of training.

This attachment to Allied divisions will be made as soon as possible after debarkation, as soon as the shortages in equipment have been made up.

While they are being trained the regiments placed with French divisions will do trench duty in quiet sectors.

III. The General, obviously taken up with forming large American units as soon as possible, asks if France will be able to furnish all the necessary artillery materiel. He has no worries regarding the 75, but he is afraid that the materiel for the 155 cannot be furnished within the desired time.

He suggests, as has been recommended to him by General Pétain, changing, by substitution of personnel, French divisions into American divisions which would take over French materiel. Two French divisions could be consolidated into one in such a way as to make available the materiel of one division.

I pointed out to him that General Pétain's idea was gradually to substitute American units for French units within the framework of the French divisions, and that as far as the substitution of the commanders and their staffs is concerned, it would be best to wait for a period of calm. He asks me to designate an officer of the mission to proceed, in agreements with the operations section of American G. H. Q., to the study of the conditions under which this substitution could take place.

IV. At my question relative to the increase of tonnage desired for the shipment of American troops, General Pershing told me that he did not know what the amount of this increase in shipping could be and that the shipping board itself probably knew nothing of it. All available boats are being taken and loaded, as fast as they can be gotten, to the maximum of their capacity.

V. As regards the 32d Division, its regiments scattered along the lines of communication are now assembling in the Prauthoy zone.

The General hopes to put them at the disposal of the French High Command in a very short time.

VI. I reminded the General of your proposal to send the 26th, 42d, and 2d Divisions into battle in several weeks after having withdrawn them from sector and returned them for several days' training. The General accepts the proposal. However, he insists that these divisions can be sent into battle at the side of the 1st Div., so as to form the I Corps of the American army.

I have informed him that I shall submit his proposition.
The interview ended on this last question.
I have informed the General that I shall transmit to General Pétain this first answer to the latter's question until such time as he will be able to give him more detailed information in writing.

Les armées françaises dans la Grande Guerre, Tome 6, vol. 2, Annexes vol. 1: Annexe No. 31, pp. 82–83; see also USAWW, vol. 3, pp. 285–86.

Bliss, Chief, American Section, and Permanent Military Representative, SWC, Versailles, to Pershing, in addition to Bliss to Pershing, telegram No. 1264 L.R. (GHQ, AEF), April 11.

Telegram No. 55 [sent]. Very Urgent.
General Foch has just sent me a message at noon begging for immediate reply from you to message from him telegraphed to your headquarters from here 5:30 yesterday afternoon. He says he is losing most valuable time.

NARA, RG 120, M923, American Section, SWC, file 317: Telegrams sent by the American Section, Jan. 21, 1918–Dec. 5, 1919, roll 19; see also online "WW I Supreme War Council, American records," at https://www.fold3.com.

Pershing to Bliss, Chief, American Section, and Permanent Military Representative, SWC, Versailles, reply to Bliss to Pershing, March 18.

Your letter of the 18th ultimo, concerning the offer by the Italian Commissioner General of Aeronautics, is at hand, but I regret to state that it is impossible, at the present time, to send American Aero Squadrons to Italy for duty on the Italian front. I have, however, directed the Chief of the Air Service, A.E.F., to discuss with the Italians, and to submit for my approval, terms whereby we can increase the number of student pilots which Italy is training for us and, in return, permit these pilots so training to serve temporarily on the Italian front in existing Italian Bombardment Squadrons.

Will you please have the kindness to express to General Giardino my sincere appreciation of his distinguished considerations and to request him to express to the Italian Commissioner General of Aeronautics my regrets that it is impossible, at the present time, to place American Aero Squadrons on the Italian front, but that I have instructed the Chief of the Air Service, A.E.F., to take up for me the question of training additional American pilots in Italy and of then using them temporarily on the Italian front. [*Ed.*—On April 16, 1918, as requested, Bliss forwarded a copy of Pershing's letter to the Permanent Italian Military Representative.]

LC, Bliss Papers, folder: American Expeditionary Forces and American Forces in France, January–December 1918, box 248; see also NARA, RG 120, M923, American Section, SWC, file 97: Memorandums relating to the assignment of American Air Service Personnel in Italy, Sept. 1917–June 1918, roll 6; see also online "WW I Supreme War Council, American records," at https://www.fold3.com.

Pershing to Bliss, Chief, American Section, and Permanent Military Representative, SWC, Versailles, in reply to Bliss to Pershing, April 8.

Permit me to acknowledge the receipt of your note of April 8th, enclosing a copy of a memorandum from the Inter-Allied Transportation Council.

The facts set forth in this memorandum are, of course, well known to me and have been the subject of serious consideration and discussion for some time. The situation has also been urgently presented to the War Department which is no doubt giving the matter every attention.

Under the new arrangement of allotting tonnage monthly to various departments we shall be able to control the shipment of cars and engines better than before.

I am urging constantly that our port works be pushed and that all arrangements for handling freight be expedited with the especial purpose of increasing our storage facilities at ports. The outlook is more and more promising.

LC, Pershing Papers, folder: Supreme War Council, February–April 1918; box 193; LC, Bliss Papers, folder: American Expeditionary Forces and American Forces in France, January–December 1918, box 248.

Maj. Paul H. Clark, American Mission with French GHQ, to CINC, AEF.

[Handwritten note: *"The French Aide Major General (Chief of Operations) asked me very particularly to present to you the following questions and to try to obtain your answers thereto:"*]
No. 41.

Subject: Questions upon which French Aide Major General for Operations would like to have answers.

1. May the 26th U.S. division be sent, upon French initiative, to relieve the 1st U.S. division, should the latter become fatigued or use in battle?

2. Does the answer to the first question apply in principle to the 2nd and 42nd divisions; if the answer does not apply, may the 2nd and 42nd divisions, one at a time, under French initiative, been sent to relieve the 1st U.S. division?

3. Will the 32nd division be loaned to the French?

4. Without waiting for the complete assembly of the 32nd division will so much of it as is now assembly in vicinity of Langres or elsewhere in northeast France, be immediately, i.e., within 2 or 3 days, loaned to the French?

5. What is the earliest date on which the 32nd division will be loaned to the French?

6. If none of the questions asked elicit answers indicating American attitude toward 32nd division under what circumstances and conditions will 32nd division be loaned to the French?

7. Will the 3rd and 5th divisions, as fast as they arrive in France, be loaned to and sent to the French by battalion, or regiment or brigade; if not when and under what conditions and circumstances will the 3rd and 5th divisions be loaned to the French?

8. How much and what kinds of artillery have the Americans now in France, or coming, soon, not belonging to a division, which the Americans will loan to the French for the present emergency?

This includes: Heavy, Coast, Field, Marine or other kind of artillery.

LC, Paul H. Clark Papers, folder: April 1–30, 1918, box 1.

Editor's Note—After speaking with Maj. Gen. de Barescut on April 11 and with these questions in hand, Clark headed to Chaumont on the late morning of April 12 to meet with Pershing. See April 14 for his report to Pershing on his meeting with de Barescut on his return to French GHQ.

Pershing to Brig. Gen. W. W. Atterbury, DGT, SOS, AEF.

I have just received a letter from the American military representative of the Supreme War Council, enclosing a communication from Colonel Thornton urging, on behalf of the Inter-Allied Transportation Council, that the Supreme War Council take such steps as will augment in every way the importation of railway equipment by the American Expeditionary Forces. [*Ed.*—See April 8, Bliss to Pershing.]

Of course you know, as well as I do, that everything has been done that can be done to get railway equipment from the states, and it really seems to me a waste of time on the part of the Inter-Allied Transportation Council, to write letters of this sort on subjects which are being handled promptly and completely by these headquarters, as you, of course, must know.

If, in the light of knowledge in its possession, the Inter-Allied Transportation Council is spending valuable time urging this question, it seems to me that some of the members thereof might better be attending to their own affairs. What do you think the Inter-Allied Transportation Council is accomplishing anyway?

In this connection, I see you have called for 1500 cars and 100 engines in April and suppose you will call for as many as possible in May, when the available tonnage is known. In the meantime get behind the repair question with all possible energy.

LC, Pershing Papers, folder: W. W. Atterbury, box 18.

Pershing to TAG, War Department.

Cable P-898-S.
  3. For the Chief of Staff. Recommend that every effort be made to supply troops sent abroad with as many Regular Army officers as possible. With the possibility of open warfare being substituted for trench warfare experience, previous training and the sound knowledge of tactical principles possessed by our Regulars will be more and more valuable. At present less than 1% of our Captains have had 1 year's service, while I understand that Infantry officers of less than 10 years' service in the Regular Army are still Captains. Is it not possible to relieve for service abroad all suitable Regular officers now on recruiting, remount or duty of a similar nature in the United States? The percentage of Regulars on duty with the First Corps including its Headquarters is 7%, and while that may be a higher percentage than similar organizations in the States believe the fact should not be lost sight of that there now exists an extreme emergency which may be regarded as the critical period of the war. Earnestly recommend that this be given immediate and most serious consideration. [Reply—May 4, A-1243-R-4]
  3B. Unable to procure any further cessions of tractors and motor equipment for 155-m.m. G.P.F. regiments from French. French materiel obtained for 2 regiments G.P.F. for 1st Corps only. Request that Ordnance Department immediately ship all motor equipment required for 2 regiments 155-m.m. G.P.F. Corps Artillery and 1 Brigade 155-m.m. G.P.F. Army Artillery to equip troops now arriving and that they be prepared to ship tractors and motor transport for Corps and Army Artillery hereafter in time for equipment of troops as they arrive. As need for this material has arisen unexpectedly request special tonnage allotment for such part as can be shipped in April without disturbing Ordnance Priority as stated in our cablegram 787. Cable what can be shipped immediately. [*Ed.*—Pershing's cable emphasized the serious situation that the AEF now faced with the continuing lack of cars, trucks of all types, heavy wheeled- and tracked-tractors (caterpillars), and all sorts of equipment from the United States that was badly needed to outfit units arriving in France. The exchange between the AEF and the Chief of Ordnance continued throughout the summer as the pace of combat operations accelerated and placed even heavier demands on the AEF.]
  3C. Request authority to exercise power of the President to assign an officer to command without regard to seniority in rank in the same grade as given in the first clause of the 119th Article of War. [Reply—May 3, A-1235-R-1]
  3D. With reference to paragraph 1C, your cablegram 1069. Request views expressed in paragraph 1B, my cablegram 891, be followed.

NARA, RG 120, M930, Main Series, AEF to War Department, roll 2.

Pershing to TAG, War Department, in part in reply to TAG, War Department, to Pershing, cables A-1039-R, April 4.

Cable P-904-S. Confidential.
For the Chief of Staff and Chief Signal Officer.
    With reference to paragraph 1A, your cablegram 1039. In order to hold the supremacy of the air on the western front, it is absolutely necessary that the United States keep France, England and Italy fully provided with raw semi-finished and finished aircraft materials even at the expense of temporarily delaying the United States Army and Navy air programs. The allotment of 734 Liberty engines to our Navy is not understood in view of the present critical needs of the England and French land Air Services. England, owing to her trust in the American allotment of Liberty motors, has allotted her Eagle Rolls Royce output to Big America Flying Boats for anti-submarine work and so is dependent on America for a large proportion of her Army's long-range Reconnaissance and bombing aeroplanes. England's request for 980 engines should therefore be given full priority and that 850 be dispatched to England before June 30th. The allotment of Liberty engines for tanks is not approved at the present time for the same reasons. The allotment of 2,174 Liberty engines for an estimated production of 1,439 aeroplanes is considered excessive in view of the present critical needs of the French and English Air Services. Recommend that the request of England, France and Italy as outlined in Subparagraph A, your 1039, be given priority over all other needs. Request reasons for priority of deliveries of Liberty engines to Navy and Ordnance Department over Army Air Service in order that we may advise regarding allocation of Liberty engines. Request information regarding the suitability of the Bristol Fighter equipped with Liberty engine. Recent information received here that Bristol Fighter equipped with Liberty is not satisfactory. Reference redistribution of raw materials between ourselves and Allies, this should be done regardless of our own needs for the next 3 months in order that England, France and Italy may be kept fully supplied until our aircraft production capacity in the United States is sufficient to take care of our own needs without imperiling the air activities of our Allies. Above conclusions based on necessity of meeting present emergency on western front. [Reply—April 13, A-1101-R-1; May 9 – A-1271-R-23; in addition—May 3, P-1043-S-1, 1A]

NARA, RG 120, M930, Confidential Series, AEF to War Department, roll 7.

TAG, War Department, to Pershing, in part in reply to Pershing to TAG, War Department, cable P-790-S, March 27; in addition to TAG, War Department, to Pershing, cable A-1039-R, April 4.

Cable A-1088-R. Confidential.
    For Air Service. With reference to your 790, paragraph 2. English have placed with us order for 3,000 Liberty engines. Deliveries to be made in England March 10, April 20, May 150, June 300, July 300, August 600, September 700, October 720. We

have delivered 10 for March. We have also delivered in United States to French 6 high-compression and to Italians 3 high-compression engines. We have made no definite commitment to English and are awaiting your decision as to manner in which engines available to July 1st should be allocated. We have no further definite orders or contracts for engines. Italian mission states they understand their order for 3,000 engines with deliveries July 150, August 300, September 450, October 600, November 740, December 750, still stands, but contract is awaiting action Italian Government, and test of Liberty engine. French have placed no definite order, but they are waiting tests of Liberty engine when they state they will place large order. With our factories just getting into production, and with uncertain labor conditions, it is difficult for us to make any absolute schedule of promised deliveries. We are delivering 70 engines this week mostly from Packard, and with only slight assistance from Lincoln, which will increase rapidly. Ford and possibly Buick and Marmon may give us small production in April, increasing thereafter.

NARA, RG 120, M930, Confidential Series, War Department to AEF, roll 18.

April 13

Sims, Commander, U. S. Naval Forces Operating in European Waters, London, to Pershing, in reply to Pershing to Sims, April 10.

This morning Colonel Logan presented your letter of April 10, 1918, and we have had a pow-wow over using additional ports for certain supply ships whose cargoes cannot in the near future be handled in the ports now available.

In five minutes we reached a conclusion in principle, based upon the entire willingness of the Navy to do anything to help along the Army in every possible way.

The case in point seems perfectly clear:

1. The ports now used cannot handle all the supplies that will soon be coming in.
2. The army needs the supplies, therefore they must be brought in somehow.
3. Hence an additional port or ports must be used.
4. It is only a question of which ports can be used to the greatest advantage.
5. The question is being studied by your people and mine, and doubtless Marseille will be recommended.
6. They will also recommend the kind of vessels to use and the kinds of supplies they will carry.
7. That settled, it will be up to the Navy to do the best they can to protect them— the degree of protection depending upon the number of vessels available. Unfortunately, the supply of new destroyers is away behind the promised schedule.
8. However, as you say, the supplies must be landed, even though there is some risk. This risk will not be great if the vessels are reasonably fast and well armed.

This is not a definite reply to your questions. That will be communicated to you by Colonel Logan when he and my people have completed their study. I am writing only to assure you that I am, and at all times have been, in complete sympathy with you in your many complicated duties and heavy responsibilities, and that I am always more than anxious to help out in every possible way.

We sailors recognize that the enemy's Navy is not making war against the allied navies. On the contrary, they take pains to avoid our military ships in order the better to attack the lines of communication of the allied armies – the ships bringing our troops and supplies.

So it is the sailors' function (1) to protect these lines and (2) to attack the Hun pirates whenever we can find them.

Unfortunately the former requires so many of our destroyers, etc., that there are not enough to be very effective against the latter.

However, conditions are improving all the time. More destroyers are coming out, forty-eight submarine chasers (hunters of 110 ft. with hydrophones) are on the way and a hundred more to follow, and we are destroying a considerable number of submarines—about twenty-five since January 1st.

We will win out soon if the armies can hold the enemy on the Western Front. But even if they can't hold him at present, we will win out all the same.

I thoroughly recognize that our nautical stunt, both in administration and operation, is very simple compared to yours; that our primary mission is to aid the armies; and that our success is bound up with yours.

There is not a day, and hardly an hour of the day, that I do not think about what you soldiers are up against, and my heart is with you all the time.

I am looking for ways to help out. Would it not be desirable for you to have a competent naval officer actually with your staff at all times? He could often answer nautical questions or give information that your people would otherwise have to write about.

I have no such officer available just now, but if you should ask for one, I believe I could get one from home.

For example, if you should telegraph me: "It has become apparent that the efficiency of cooperation between my forces and yours regarding the rapidity and safety of transporting troops and supplies would be augmented if a competent naval officer were permanently attached to my staff," I would at once apply to Washington, and I believe that, with your support, I could get one.

There is another point that is none of my particular business, but concerning which I believe a mistake has been made.

A few days ago the British proposed that some of our troops should be sent over on what are called Medium Speed transports. These are relatively small vessels carrying all the way from fifty to a few hundred troops. They would come in 9-knot convoys. Both the War and Navy Departments turned this down because of the speed.

I did not butt in, but I believe this decision to be a mistake, because I believe that a small number of troops on a slow ship are in less danger than a large number on a fast one, because in case the vessel is torpedoed, the small number can probably all be saved—and this can seldom be the case with a large number. The Tuscania was a marked exception in that the ship did not sink for two or three hours, and the sea was smooth enough for destroyers to go alongside. One of them took away 900 troops.

If you should recommend that troops be sent on these vessels, I believe that both the War and Navy Departments would change their decisions. I am informed that it is a question of getting over about 10,000 more troops per month.

If I make any recommendations that you do not approve of, don't hesitate to turn me down hard. I don't profess to know anything about fighting off the water.

Don't waste any of your own time answering my communications. I have time to burn compared to what you have, and you should not waste any of it writing me an autograph letter, or even signing your name. A letter signed "By Direction", or a simple memorandum will receive just as prompt and earnest attention. We sailors will do anything we can to help out and get on with the war. [Reply—April 23, Pershing to Sims—see below, April 23, P-960-S]

LC, Sims Papers, folder: Special Correspondence: John J. Pershing, box 77.

Harbord, CS, GHQ, AEF, then at Foch's GHQ, to Pershing,

I find General Foch absent from his headquarters and no one here who can speak for him, so I am going to stay until he returns, about 6:30 p.m. I left Paris this morning as directed and went to General Bullard's headquarters and had a little conversation with him. He had a long hard ride yesterday but looks well, and says he has recovered. He believes he suffered from the effect of the anti-tetanus injection which they gave him when he smashed his fingers in the motor car door. He says what I supposed he would—that while more time would perfect the training of the Division he thinks it is now ready to do its part as soon as you desire it. He informed me that the telegram to General Foch was forwarded this morning. I find here that it was delivered about 11 a.m.

I was under the impression that General Foch had his Headquarters at the place where you met Messes Lloyd-George and Clemenceau, but on arrival there found he had moved. The Town-Major (French) gave us the name of the new location, but after travelling fifteen miles to the place it developed that he misinformed me, and the real Headquarters are forty kilometers in the opposite direction. So at 2:30 p.m. I am here to wait until 6:30. No one here knows whether General Foch will use the Division at once, or later, or in open or trench warfare. When he gets here I will communicate his statement in separate letter.

With the foregoing preliminary I will get to the purpose of this letter.

1. When I left G.H.Q. I left in my basket a memorandum for you with recommendation that you establish liaison with General Foch. The only American here is Colonel B. H. Wells, representing General Bliss. As long as that is true all your business will probably take the Versailles route. I believe you should have with General Foch one of our very best officers,—Eltinge, Drum, Birnie, Moseley or Grant, or some one of that caliber. #

[Handwritten insertion from the left margin: "# *The British have a general officer who messes with Gen. Foch. The Italians have a Lieut. Col. and Wells is a Colonel. Only Generals mess with Gen. Foch. Perhaps you might wish to send a General. If all your recommendations are made you will have some extras.*"]

2. The more I see of the 1st Division, the more numerous appear to me to be the reasons that would justify my assignment to the 1st Brigade if General Duncan is promoted.

I have been with him constantly since his Brigade left the old area.

I know what units he considers strong and which weak.

I have seen every part of the brigade a number of times.

I know the state of its training.

I know all the field officers, and some of the juniors, and know what General Duncan thinks of them.

I know intimately General Duncan's methods of handling the individuals and the units.

I happen to know the Artillery Commanders of the Division, with whom the Brigade will work, as well as the Commander and Staff of the Division.

I have studied the method of liaison which has been worked out for use between the Infantry and Artillery.

The foregoing is true of no other Brigadier under your command, unless Hines should be promoted.

If you thought it best to assign me I could if necessary stay right here with the Brigade, sending back for any of my stuff which I have not brought with me.

Please do not think me insistent or inconsiderate of conditions at G.H.Q. As I have so often said I am entirely at your disposition to use as you think best, but this Brigade looks mighty attractive to me, and the chance of going in with this 1st Division is one that any man might covet. I believe I can deliver the goods if you give me the chance. I also believe that the assignment would be acceptable to General Bullard. In fact he has this morning asked me why I do not try for it, and said when he heard I was with the Brigade he had hoped that was what was in the wind. [Ed.— When Duncan was promoted to major general and appointed to command the 77th Division early in May, Col. John L. Hines, CO, 16th Infantry, became commander of the 1st Brigade on May 4.]

3. If Hines is promoted there is no one who can take the regiment. Reed is doing well. Hines has him in charge of the animals. He is keeping straight and is all right, but I do not think is yet equal to the command. Freeman, the infantry Lieutenant Colonel with the 16th is recovering from a broken leg and not equal to field service. I understand he is senior to Reed though I cannot be positive about that. General Duncan says neither of the majors is up to the regimental command. Bash is the only officer who occurs to me. He is A.G. S.O.S., and according to Col. Dawes, is most unfortunate in his manner to various civilian-bred officers with whom as a principal staff officer he comes in constant contact. He stood white-haired Cutcheon up for some admonition recently, and Dawes says is making enemies for the regular army. As a Colonel perhaps his vinegarish disposition might not be so out of place. Of

course some man like Nolan, Fiske, McCoy, Davis, Conger, Shannon or that type would be splendid if he could be spared. With Hines' promotion imminent I think some man should be in mind.

4. Last spring at the War College General Bridges [Military Member of the Balfour Mission] said the British never think of sending a division to the attack without first withdrawing about twenty-five percent of the best officers and men to form a nucleus for training, esprit, traditions, etc. in case the losses are very heavy. I am told the French do the same thing, sometimes going as high as thirty percent. I spoke of this to Gen. Bullard who agrees that it should be done. We were both of the opinion that it is a matter for him to take up with the General under whom he goes in,— probably Gen. Debeney.

I dined with Colonel Dawes last night and we afterwards went to the theater program but the program was interrupted by an air Alert, and the performance closed. Two planes flew over and dropped a few bombs, killing 11 and wounding 50 I believe. Dawes is very keen about pooling all our resources with the French and English as he conceives you have done with the human element. Thinks if French and British were told that our supplies were at their disposal we could stop building port facilities, storehouses, etc. His plan is Christ-like in its unselfishness, and a very broad highminded conception, almost Utopian it seems to me. He speaks of sinking personal considerations, matters of national identity, etc., as he conceives you have done by placing troops at the disposal of our Allies. I told him I thought there were practical difficulties in the way, and that while we must get along with our Allies I thought they ought to do part of the "getting". I said with a minority of the stock it was probably proper that we play a minor part on the Board of Directors, but that we were hoping to acquire a majority of the stock later, and with it there should come the rights usually accorded to the owners of the majority stock in a corporation. Without undue suspicion, I should think it a trifle risky to throw money, men, supplies and facilities of every kind into a pool, with British and French or even American human nature what it is.

This letter is very long. I had my typewriter in the motorcar, and with nearly four hours to wait thought I would improve the opportunity to write to you.

LC, Pershing Papers, folder: General James G. Harbord, 1910–1918, box 87; copy, LC, Harbord Papers, folder: Correspondence with John J. Pershing, box 11.

Dawes, GPA, SOS, AEF, Paris, to CINC, AEF, Chaumont.

Subject: Military Control, Allied Service of Supply.

From the time that you landed in France you have exerted an influence for coordination of effort and centralization of authority in inter-Ally activity which has had the most far-reaching results. You have exerted this influence among the Allies during the time that you were creating a coordinating and centralizing system in your command. To carry out the purpose of the centralization of purchase and supply in your own army, to become connected with which effort you called me from St. Nazaire, you have as a matter of fact devised the plan the extension of which to the entire Allied operations would seem now vitally essential to Allied success in the war. What I am to suggest to you arises from conclusions based upon knowledge and experience gained in the position in which you have placed me. Even with the conviction which I have of the vital importance of the matter I would hesitate to call it to your attention, were it not for your constant demonstration of the desire to subordinate everything, including your own personal authority as an independent commander, to the common purpose of an Allied victory. To willingly sacrifice individual authority and individual prestige in time of emergency for the sake of a common cause is the highest test of greatness and one which, in all your actions over here, you have stood. The power and influence of the great people of the United States and their assets in men and material with which to secure victory are in the hands of the President and yourself, and you have rightly interpreted their spirit when you notified General Foch to do with you and your army as he might desire. In this offer you have already taken the step, the proper carrying out of which I am going to suggest in this letter. The peculiar position of the United States in this situation, including your own relation thereto, is such that upon the initiative of our Government alone is it possible to accomplish it.

The general proposition is this: that just as there is now a unified military command of the Allies at the front, in other words a merging and consolidation of three distinct independent military authorities into one military authority (General Foch), there must be a corresponding merging of all separate individual authority of the Allies in reference to the Service of Supply into one military authority responsible to the corresponding military authority at the front. One is just as necessary as the other. In fact, for every argument for the necessity of the Foch command at the front, there exist two arguments for a similar authority for supply and transportation in the rear. I mean by this supplies from America, supplies from England, supplies from France, and the land and sea transportation therefor, warehousing and handling thereof. The Foch command at the front necessitates similar control of the rear, and in this case the rear means France, England, the United States, and perhaps Italy. Before discussing the method of accomplishing this let me illustrate in a manner which has no doubt often occurred to you its overwhelming importance. The United States is at this time using an immense amount of tonnage for the purpose of building enormous warehouses and dockage facilities. It is doing this notwithstanding the warehouses of France and England are being emptied and will continue to grow emptier. The French Government has used to a very large extent private warehouses for storing of supplies. Owing to the steadily lessening amount of supplies there is a large amount of French warehouse capacity now idle, and at the same time we are proceeding, at the heavy expense of current tonnage, on plans to immensely increase our warehouse facilities. Who is there, with authority to act, to determine from a bird's-eye view the relation of existing English and French warehouse capacity in France to the present warehousing and transportation projects of the A.E.F.? It cannot be done, except in a haphazard and inefficient way, unless by one man with military authority extending over all the Allies. This man, for the same reason that led to the selection of General Foch, must be a Frenchman and England and the United States must accept him. He must be given exactly the same authority toward the ocean and land transportation, engineering, and supply activities of the entire Allied forces which you have given me in connection with purchase and supply and certain other activities of the A.E.F., his authority being created by the same method. The position of General Purchasing Agent, A.E.F., you built up by a system of compelling the partial cession of independent authority. The weight of your own great powers and personality was thrown into the effort of compelling the creation of this authority, and when any independent head showed signs of not recognizing the necessity for it or bending to it, you broke him on the cross. What has made the success of the organization of my office is its now unquestioned power and authority over independent agencies. I never have had a meeting of the General Purchasing Board except on minor matters such as the distributing of office space or matters relating to the collection of information – never on the determination of action. Our organization is military. The reason why our Allied Boards fail is because action has to be by a board and not by an individual. The organization of the entire transportation and supply of the Allies must be military in its nature and not based upon the principles of either oligarchy or democracy. I do not have to argue this to a man like you. Some time after this war is over get Herodotus and read the discussion of the seven Persian generals when they were riding horseback on their way to Persia discussing the best form of government for them to set up in the place of the monarchy of an assassinated king. If we do not have military management and military control we may fail and a German army at the ports may save us the trouble of unloading some of our engineering material from ships, thus devoted, which should have been bringing men and food to have stopped our enemies where they are now. It may be that our present plans may not have to be abandoned or materially altered, but the point I make is that it is impossible with this great multiplicity of civil boards, crisscross authority between the Allies, and lack of coordination in supply effort to properly determine the matter or properly act after its determination. Take the question of joint supplies. Impelled by the same emergency pressure that compelled unity of command at the front, the French and the English are calling upon me for information as to supplies of our army, with intimations of the necessity of pooling, etc. I am working the best I can in coordination with the French and English in all these matters, but I am in a position where I realize that these questions can be settled, in time to be of avail, only by military authority which, gathering its information, acts, and does not discuss. Who knows today, considering the Allied forces as one army, whether or not the great supplies of steel, oil, barbed wire, rubber tires, chloroform, sugar, picks and shovels, forage, clothing, etc., existing in France, England, and the United States are being marshaled in Foch's rear by the quickest routes to proper points, to warehouses built or to be built, considering both present and future needs and the present military emergency? In this present great military emergency shall we again pursue the time-worn policy of appointing an Allied Board to secure this information, and then, after long delay, subject the self-evident conclusions arising therefrom to the discussion of three separate authorities, influenced by personal or national considerations, personal ambitions, and counter-purposes?

In writing this way I almost feel as if I were insulting your intelligence, who have been the chief leader and have made the greatest personal sacrifice in the effort to apply remedies for this sort of business. If the suggestions herein you cannot force into adoption with the weight and prestige of your country and your own personal power, then we must go back at this time to a new effort to concentrate authority in a new Board of the Allies to do by common consent and town-meeting methods that which should come at once from central military authority extending over all. No one knows better than you what this means in delay, and what delay may mean in a time like this, in a war like this. Can you not force the Allies to agree to adopt immediately the principles involved in the relations of your own Military Purchasing Board to the entire Service of Supply of your own army through which this entire Allied supply and transportation situation shall be placed in the hands of a French military officer with the same kind of authority over the Generals in command of the different services of the rear of the Allies that your General Purchasing Agent has over the separate purchase and supply services of the American army? The authority for the French command of these services could be created by the same method through which you have placed authority in me for our purchase and supply situation in the A.E.F. The three Generals in command of the Allied rear should be coordinated and controlled by French military authority as are the members of the General Purchasing Board by the General Purchasing Agent. As in the case of the purchasing board of the A.E.F., this does not mean the radical interference with the conduct of current activities. It does not even mean the lessening of current activities. It means their proper coordination and intelligent direction, and above all it means that when once a necessity is determined, the authority is in existence to compel its immediate relief. The influence of such unified military command of the service of the rear of the Allies upon the question of tonnage, use of material, economy of construction, and general betterment of conditions, must be self-evident. To go with unified military action at the front must come unified military support at the rear. You are the only man that can bring this about. If it was anybody else than you, even under the tremendous pressure of the present emergency, I should hesitate to suggest it; for human nature is weak. Nothing but the weakness and ambition of human nature prevented the unification of military command which you have always advocated until the death of hundreds of thousands and continued military failure brought individual and national ambition under the yoke of a common necessity involving existence itself.

General Harbord took dinner with me last night and spent the evening and I presented these views to him. He did not express himself, but I judge from his demeanor that he was not entirely unimpressed. I understand from Harbord that you may be here within the next few days. I had intended to come to Chaumont to present verbally what I am writing here. There is probably nothing in this letter which has not already been considered by you. However, now that unification of military command at the front has been secured, I am sure that the application of your General Purchasing Board idea to the service of the rear of the Allies is that which will go farther just now in bringing a successful conclusion to this war than any other thing.

Dawes, *A Journal of the Great War,* vol. 1, pp. 84–90.

Maj. Frederick Palmer, Special Assistant to the CINC, to Pershing.

[Handwritten]

As our army is being infiltrated into the British and French why not do a little infiltrating on our own account? Why not make trained American officers working members of British and French Army, Corps, division and brigade staffs? Then when we are ready to form, our own corps from the scattered units we can meet any argument that we have not trained but to be right in the thick of the work.

Your position is such now that any decision of yours may play a great part in the future of our country's military and political policy. The metal is at white heat & set to mould. For forty years British policy has been to keep Canada estranged from us as a part of retaining her loyalty to the Empire. Why not put our regiments in Canadian brigades (Australian, too) as well as British. The answer will be that the Canadian brigades are full (for the British, politically will not favor the plan); but in that case increase the number of Canadian divisions by one intermixing Americans. Rightly approached Currie and the Canadians would be flattered. It would mean hands across the border—unity of the English-speaking people of North America. Consider if we had a regiment on Vimy Ridge with the Canadians. The Canadians and Americans are more alike. They can work together if our fellows are diplomatic, and one extra division with the Canadians keeps up the number of divisions against the Germany just as well as if we were mixed with the British.

LC, Pershing Papers, folder: Col. Frederick Palmer, box 153.

Pershing to TAG, War Department, in part in reply to TAG, War Department, to Pershing, cables A-861-R, March 2, and A-1018-R, March 31; in addition to Pershing to TAG, War Department, cable P-789-S, March 27.

Cable P-907-S.

2. For Chief of Staff. Rigid inspection of troops before embarkation absolutely essential. Men arriving European ports badly infested with lice. Disinfection of ships and adequate bathing facilities necessary to reduce this evil. Every effort should be made to properly disinfect outer clothing, launder underclothing and insure cleanliness among troops. Recommend Surgeons of units be instructed to spread information concerning dangers of lice. Strongly urge most energetic action. [*Ed.*—On April 18, in cable A-1133-R, paragraph 9, Goethals informed Pershing that "definite and positive action will be taken on your recommendations reference lice."]

2A. With reference to paragraph 1, your cablegram 861. We can now erect 100 standard gauge locomotives per month. With improved facilities expect ultimately can erect 150, but cannot now state when it will be possible to erect more than 100. Can now erect 1000 cars monthly, and can arrange with Middletown Car Company for erection of 500 to 750 additional. See paragraph 2 R, our cablegram 789. By August we should be able to erect as many freight cars as you can ship, up to 2500 per month. With reference to paragraph 6, your cablegram 1018. We desire to supplement car erection as above by making suggested arrangements with Bordeaux firm as regards metal parts, this saving, so far as concerns the 500 cars per month which we could obtain from them, about 2/3 in bulk shipping space. Detailed plans can be mailed in about a week and preliminary information cabled at that time. The Middletown plants at Saintes and La Garenne are at present idle, but we are negotiating with them for the use of these shops, with which we expect to erect the 500 to 750 cars monthly mentioned above. Think shipments of Middletown Car Company for French State Railways should be hurried. With reference to paragraph 2R, our cablegram 789, we are anxiously awaiting your reply regarding tools for Nevers shops and for 35th Engineers. [Reply—April 20, A-1143-R-8A]

NARA, RG 120, M930, Main Series, AEF to War Department, roll 3, and War Department to AEF, rolls 12 and 13.

Pershing to TAG, War Department, in addition to Pershing to TAG, War Department, cable P-891, April 11.

Cable P-911-S.
1. For the Chief of Staff and Chief of Ordnance. Reference our cablegram 891 proposing schedule for shipments of troops during April, May, June. Possibility of equipping 155 m.m. howitzer regiments of 6 Artillery Brigades sailing May and June and 75 m.m. regiments of 3 Artillery Brigades sailing June as well as all units of these calibers sailing thereafter until deliveries from U.S. begin dependent upon fulfillment by French of promises for deliveries to be made during those months and subsequent thereto. Although French have not said they will not be able to meet their promises in this regard consideration must be given to this possibility on account of present situation and possible present and future losses of artillery materiel and every effort must be made to increase speed and production in U.S. and to advance dates for deliveries especially on calibers mentioned. Should this contingency arise what deliveries in France of 75 m.m. guns and 155 m.m. howitzers before May 31st and before June 30th can be made? As our schedule provides for no more army gun or howitzer brigades to sail during April, May or June our needs in 155 m.m. guns and 8.0-inch and 9.2-inch howitzers are met to July 1st but failures by French and British of future deliveries on these calibers will be felt after that date. Every effort should therefore be made to attain rate of production and of deliveries of these calibers in France to meet our needs after July 1st. [Reply—April 28, A-1199-R-1]

NARA, RG 120, M930, Main Series, AEF to War Department, roll 3.

Pershing to TAG, War Department, in part in reply to TAG, War Department, to Pershing, cable A-984-R, March 27.

Cable P-912-S.
　1. For Chief of Ordnance. 1A. With reference to paragraph 1L, your cablegram 984. Do not hold up shipments of Vickers machine guns needed for immediate use by Air Service. After 4000 Vickers guns have been shipped those that follow should be sent altered. It is assumed that all aeroplanes shipped from United States to Europe will come completely armed. . . . [Reply—April 30, A-1203-R-1B]
　1B. Is Marlin gun adapted for tanks the same as Marlin aircraft? If not what modifications have been made? Are these guns provided with pistol grip? Request 60 these guns be shipped at once with full equipment, especial belt holders, loading tools and accessories. Are you planning to equip 2333 light tanks with this gun or only the 840 pertaining to United States allotment? Will tank mounting take either Hotchkiss gun or Marlin mentioned your cable? [Reply—April 22, A-1154-R-1J, May 3, A-1233-R-1K]

NARA, RG 120, M930, Main Series, AEF to War Department, roll 3.

TAG, War Department, to Pershing.

Cable A-1094-R.
　1. For Air Service. Indications are that the 300-horesepower Hispano will begin to come from production in October. What type(s) should be built to receive it? Would the other Bristol fighter equipped with this engine be of value? It could be put into production without great difficulty. That would give us 2 types of Bristol fighters, 1 equipped with the 300-horsepower Hispano and the other equipped with the Liberty motor. [Reply—May 5, P-1059-S-7E; Vol. 5, May 26, P-1192-S-5; June 2, P-1229-S-6; June 8, P-1271-S-2A]
　1I. British War Mission advises that the British Government can furnish 200 S.E. 5 planes without engines at once, and within 60 days could supply 30 per week without engine. We could within 4 weeks begin to supply 180-horsepower high-compression direct-drive Hispano Suiza engine with vertical magneto drive same as now used on 150-horsepower or by July 1st could supply 180-horsepower high compressed motor with horizontal magneto drive same as used by the British. These engines to be shipped to England to be installed in the planes by the plane manufacturers. Would this type of fighting machine be of value to you, and if so shall we proceed to provide the engines for you? We are advised that this type is in successful use by the British on the front. Would it be advisable for us to put either the SPAD [XIII] or S.E. 5 in production for use with the 180 Hispano? [Reply—April 21, P-973-S-1; Vol. 5, June 2, P-1229-S-6; in addition—April 24, A-1165-R-1; May 1, A-1214-R-2]

NARA, RG 120, M930, Main Series, War Department to AEF, roll 12.

TAG, War Department, to Pershing, in reply to Pershing to TAG, War Department, cable P-904-S, April 12.

Cable A-1101-R. Confidential.
    1. With reference to your 904. British representative here has been notified that they have been allotted and we will deliver to them 980 Liberty Engines at United States factories prior to June 30th. Have notified Ordnance Department that we will not deliver them the 500 engines required prior to June 30th. Our total estimated output to that date is still 3,256; 734 have been allotted to Navy, making total allotted 1,714, and leaving 1,542 available for French, Italian and United States Air Service. French and Italian representatives here have notified us informally that they will make a request for engines after certain tests now going forward have been completed. Their desires will be to have the earliest possible deliveries. If they should be allotted a portion of the 1,542 available, we should like to have advice of it at once. We will arrange distribution of spruce and dopes accordingly we will then continue the manufacturing output of planes as far as available spruce will permit and store them awaiting supply of Liberty motors and dopes. Request that you confer with French and Italians, and if possible, cable us your recommendations as to the numbers to be allocated to them. We will meet your wishes, but wish to inconvenience our factories as little as may be in order that ultimate output may not be seriously jeopardized. Answering requests for information in regard to suitability of Bristol fighter equipped with Liberty engines, preliminary tests have just been started and will continue regularly. Tests made so far cast some doubt upon its quick maneuvering abilities. Judgment should be withheld until tests have gone considerably further. Will report progress and advise you as to ultimate results shown. [Reply—May 3, P-1043-S-1, 1A]

NARA, RG 120, M930, Confidential Series, War Department to AEF, roll 18.

April 14

Pershing's Personal Diary

    Worked in office in morning and until 4 o'clock in afternoon. Saw Generals Bradley [Chief Surgeon, AEF], Atterbury and Ragueneau. Left for Paris at about 4 p. m. with Colonel Boyd, Captain de Marenches and Lieutenant Adamson.

LC, Pershing Papers, Diary, May 7, 1917–September 1, 1918, box 4.

Foch, GHQ, Allied Armies, to Minister of War (Clemenceau), in addition to Foch to Minister of War, April 5.

Headquarters Allied Armies.
Operations, General Staff
No. 176

At the Beauvais Conference of April 3 I was given adequate powers for conducting the war of the Allies. Subordinates know nothing of them. Hence indecisions, delays in execution.

To remedy the situation I had the honor of asking you in my letter of April 5 to be kind enough to let me know the title I should assume for my new functions.

I suggest that of Commander-in-Chief of the Allied Armies.

As the direction of operations brooks of no delay I beg of you to forward my request to the British Government immediately so it can give its answer at once.
[Reply—April 14, Clemenceau to Foch]

USAWW, vol. 2, p. 324; see also *Les armées françaises dans la Grande guerre, Tome 6*, vol. 1, *Annexes*, vol. 3: *Annexe* No. 1707, p. 324.

Clemenceau, Minister of War, to Foch, GHQ, Allied Armies, in reply to Foch to Minister of War, April 5 and 14.

No. 149/H. R.
Coded telegram.

By dispatch of this date Mr. Lloyd George informs me that he agrees with me to give you the title of: General Commander-in-Chief of the Allied Armies in France.

USAWW, vol. 2, p. 324; see also *Les armées françaises dans la Grande guerre, Tome 6*, vol. 1, *Annexes*, vol. 3: *Annexe* No. 1707, p. 324.

Editor's Note—Elizabeth Greenhalgh commented in her *Foch in Command* that while Foch was involved in critical meetings with Haig, Wilson, and Milner at Abbeville on April 14 on actions to be taken to hold the most recent German offensive (Georgette) on the Lys River:

> Foch found time in the midst of everything else to press both Poincaré and Clemenceau for a title (Lloyd George agreed to 'Général en Chef des Armées Alliées' on 14 April) and for an official letter of appointment. He received the letter as a brief presidential decree dated 22 April, countersigned by Clemenceau. The letter makes no mention of to whom Foch was

responsible, hence by whom he could be sacked. Presumably it was thought that the matter could be left in abeyance while the fighting continued. (Greenhalgh, *Foch in Command*, p. 316.)

On April 15, Clemenceau passed this information on to Pershing and requested that he obtain official American approval for Foch's new title. Pershing immediately informed Bliss of Clemenceau's telegram and that day dispatched cable P-923-S to the War Department for the Secretary of War and Chief of Staff seeking the requested American approval. See April 15 below.

Maj. Paul H. Clark, American Military Mission with French GHQ, to CINC, AEF.

[Handwritten]
No. 43. Sunday, 3.00 pm
Subject: Military Situation

1. I called on General de Barescut [Chief of Operations] this a.m. and said: Upon being informed of my arrival at Chaumont General Pershing directed that I should come to his office in order that he might learn the latest information from French G.Q.G. He received me a few minutes after General Ragueneau had finished a conversation with him.

General Pershing manifested a very profound interest in the events that are taking place, and after he had questioned me he gave me an opportunity to offer him the questions to which you charged me to obtain his replies.

With regard to the relief of the 1st U.S. div., should it become used or fatigued, I understood General Pershing to say that he is disposed to send either the 26, 42 or 2 U.S. div. to relieve the 1st U.S. It would be necessary only for the proper representations to be made to him for him to cause the appropriate orders to be issued.

With regard to the 32d div., which you desired as soon as possible, immediately in two or three days, General Pershing comprehends very well your urgence for the 32d div. and is therefore disposed to send it to you by battalion or regiment or brigade, as soon as possible.

General Pershing took occasion to express his very great interest in what is now transpiring and to say that while having clearly in mind the formation of an American army, he is never-the-less glad, during this crisis, to lend to France such aid as he can and he feels a serene and calm confidence that—"that the Boche cannot win a decision."

I continued.

At this point the General said with great earnestness and apparent conviction, "He is right, the Boche cannot obtain a decision, he cannot do it"—emphasizing his words by punching his right fist into his left hand—"he cannot do it"—he almost shouted. The French and British and American armies will not permit it. 'J'en suis convaincu' (of that I am convinced)." Continuing he said "How soon will General

Pershing give me the 32d div? I understand that it has been used as laborers and is much in need of certain kinds of instruction, but do not fear, we will give them the instruction they need before they actually go into the line. Our line, you must remember is thin and for our troops to see some American units arriving in their rear, even for training, is calculated to hearten them considerably. The French will see that reserves are close to them and in case of trouble the Americans can come to their aid and later replace them in the trenches."—with earnestness—"If Gen. Pershing will give me that division now I will gain one month—I will have another French division to go to the battle one month earlier than would otherwise be possible. When will he give it to me?"

Clark: "He did not find it practicable to name a particular date but said he would give it as soon as possible."

de B: "Urge him to give it now. It is very important."

Clark: "I will do so, General; I will relate to him exactly what you have told me. What is the situation this morning?"

de B: "Things are very much improved. The tired British troops are holding well. We have sent troops to succor them. Two divisions (French) have already gone to the scene of the present fight and it heartens the British to see our troops coming to help them, and rest assured it will hearten the French to see the 32d arrive, even though they do not immediately go into the trenches. The French are ready to fight anywhere anytime. It is really only one battle."

Clark: "I would like to take a copy of this map to Gen. Pershing. May I have one the next time I go to see him? (A map showing location of French, British and German units—combined order of battle.)

de B: "Yes indeed. I will have one made and thanks very much for conveying my questions to Gen. Pershing. We shall always rely on you." . . .

7. British losses are 200,000.

Their reinforcements 150,000.

They have little left in rear and will not have much replacements before October. 33 Divisions have been reconstituted of which 32 have been reconstituted twice. There are 5 divisions which await arrival of the Americans before they can be reconstituted. The British have made a very considerable transport effort and have succeeded in completely replacing all losses of material. . . .

13. Gen. Ragueneau was here yesterday.

14. The French staff here are studying the scheme of reconstituting their divisions. The scheme favored is the gradual introduction of Americans. For instance, when it is not practicable to reconstitute a division, put all that remains of one regiment into the other two regiments and introduce one American regiment and the staff and Commander of an American division thus. . . .

[Diagram omitted]

This plan, he said, had many advantages over the plan of reaching the final stage abruptly and immediately without the intermediate gradual stages; it, the first plan, assured that the American comdr. and staff, working side by side, like comrades, with the French staff, would enable the Americans to acquire rapidly and most effectively the instruction of which they stood in need, so that when the division should be composed exclusively of Americans, and the French comdr. and staff had departed, the American comdr. would be fully competent and *have* beside him a skillful staff. . . .

I called at British Mission. Gen. Clive was busy phoning. I talked to Majors Benson and Smythe. Benson said: "Everything looks very much better. We feel we can hold the Boche now. We had only the remnants of about 6 or 7 tired divisions around Armentieres when the Germans attacked and still their progress was much less slow than when they advanced on the 5th Army. We have repulsed repeated attacks along the line Wvtschaete-Neuve Eglise-Steenwerck and I believe we can hold there. Kemmel, about 300 feet high, is the most important point in the region and though the Germans now have village of Messines, the British expect to hold the two ridges which run approximately: [diagram] . . .

Gen. Clive came from inner office and said he was going to lunch with 3d Bureau so I asked permission to walk with him. He said: "Things look much better. We now hope to hold the Boche. We have done much execution. We estimate German losses at 350,000 to 380,000. Our losses are about 250,000, French 50,000. Germans have used thus far 130 divisions and still have 30 or 40 for another battle. We think Germans at start of this battle did not plan so considerable an action but they made such good progress that they kept it up. All our troops were tired. . . .

22. I recall, now, that Gen. de Barescut also said: "I fully agree with Gen. Pershing that he should build up an American Army, but tell him that this year is a year of defense, next year will be "American Army year", when the three armies Fr., Br., and Am. will resume the offensive. This year we will fight to the last in defense and we will succeed in stopping and holding the Boche."
       [signed] Paul H. Clark
       7.30 p.m.

LC, Paul H. Clark Papers, folder: April 1–30, 1918, box 1.

Pershing to Brig. Gen. Edward M. Lewis, Commanding, U.S. Troops, Paris.

Despite repeated instructions from my headquarters regarding uniformity and neatness in dress, I have had called to my attention, and have personally observed, that not enough attention, even on the part of general officers, has been paid to this important matter.

The conspicuous position in a foreign country that our officers and men occupy makes every slouchy officer and man a reflection on the whole American Army.

I therefore desire that you give this subject your personal attention to the end that all the officers and men of your command may be impressed with the necessity for a more scrupulous observance of all regulations regarding neatness, uniformity and smartness in personal appearance.

Please make report to their respective division commanders, by my direction, the case of each officer presenting a slouchy appearance or guilty of misconduct, and send to me a report of any officer of the grade of field officer or above.

LC, Pershing Papers, folder: HQ District of Paris, box 154.

Pershing to [Lt.] Col. George S. Patton, Jr., Tank Service, AEF.

I have been intending for several days to write you a line of sympathy at the loss of Mrs. Patton's mother. This is going to be a very hard blow for Beatrice on top of her father's death. I feel too sorry for words. I cabled her as soon as I heard the sad news, but you know cabled words or written words or even spoken words mean very little at such times as this. I only hope that Anne is with her and that she will get some comfort from that.
Please accept for yourself my sincere sympathy.
[Reply—April 16, Patton to Pershing]

LC, Patton Papers, folder: Chronological File, April 18–30, 1918, box 8.

Pershing to TAG, War Department, in part in reply to TAG, War Department, to Pershing, cables A-1035-R, April 4, and P-1045-S, April 5.

Cable P-913-S.
1. For Chief Signal Officer. 1F. With reference to paragraph 1N, your cablegram 1035. Preparing to ship you following single-seater pursuit machines. 1 each, Morane A1C1, Nieuport 28, Martinsyde F 3, Vickers 16E; also 2 150 Gnome engines used in the Morane and Nieuport and 3 ABC engines. Martinsyde and Vickers take Rolls Royce Falcon 250 or Lorraine Dietrich 275 or may take 300 Hispano if successful. Propose to send you new Béchereau SPAD and drawings for 300 Hispano later. Best single-seater fighters now in use on front are SPAD 13C by French and SE 5 by British, both equipped with Hispano 180 or 220 engines. Morane is wonderful but engine uncertain. [Reply—April 24, A-1165-R-1; May 15, A-1318-R-3; Vol. 5, May 26, A-1399-R-1D]
1I. Send full information any proposed U S program construction Liberty engine 8 cylinders. Also your opinion of this engine for use in single fighter about 225 to 275 horsepower required. Only other engines appeared suitable are Lorraine 275 and Hispano 300 and they cannot be obtained in sufficient quantity here. [Reply—April 26, A-1181-R-2F]
1L. With reference to your 1945, there are now in England 82 Squadrons as follows: Service 69, construction 8, supply 3, repair 2 squadrons and about 1304 bricklayers.

NARA, RG 120, M930, Main Series, AEF to War Department, roll 3.

Pershing to TAG, War Department.

Cable P-916-S.
    3. For Chief of Ordnance. British deliveries of 8-inch and 9.2-inch howitzers not sufficient to arm heavy artillery troops now arriving. Because of existing conditions have not yet been able to obtain definite information as to future deliveries. Ordnance delivery sheets show that over 40 8-inch howitzers have been completed. 24 of foregoing will be listed on our May priority statement. Request that you give your personal attention to the early shipment of this material. [Reply—April 27, A-1191-R-1E]
    9. For Chief Signal Officer. 9A. The United States should make immediate preparations for the production of single-seater machines to supplement those we may receive from France and England. To this end we are sending a Martinsyde which should be fitted with the Liberty 8, and upon completion of tests drawings and data of and if possible a Vickers for the Liberty 8 and a Sopwith Dolphin for the 300 Hispano. Due to lack of information we cannot tell which will be the best for you to produce. The Martinsyde was built for the Falcon 275, the Vickers for the Lorraine 275, and the Sopwith for the 200 Hispano but has been modified for the 300 Hispano. Cable in full your advice so that we can make final decision. [As modified by April 19, P-958-S-2D] [Reply—April 24, A-1165-R-1; May 15, A-1318-R-3]

NARA, RG 120, M930, Main Series, AEF to War Department, roll 3.

Pershing to TAG, War Department, in part in reply to TAG, War Department, to Pershing, cable A-687-R, January 24.

Cable P-922-S.
    2. For Chief of Ordnance. Drawing 58-15-1 received showing new model 8-inch gun, 35 calibers long. Understand that 25 guns in accordance with this drawing have been ordered manufactured for use as spare guns on railroad mounts. Cannot more Navy guns be secured as spare guns and manufacturing facilities be held available for other guns? If not, why cannot 8-inch guns, 50 calibers long with corresponding increase in power be manufactured? Understand that study of such a gun has been completed in Ordnance Office. It is desired that any guns now manufactured be of the modern design and of greatest practicable power. [Reply—April 30, A-1211-R-1B]
    3. For Chief of Staff. With reference to paragraph 4, your cablegram 687. Request that you obtain from the Navy Department complete set of drawings of the railway mounts to be furnished by them for 14-inch guns, 50 caliber, and for 7-inch guns. Also complete drawings and lists of accessory material, fire control instruments, etc. Request that cable information be furnished as to general characteristics of 14-inch gun railway mount. [Reply—April 24, A-1163-R-1]

NARA, RG 120, M930, Main Series, AEF to War Department, roll 3.

TAG, War Department, Pershing, in part in reply to Pershing to TAG, War Department, cables P-868-S, April 7, and P-887-S, April 10.

Cable A-1100-R.
1. With reference to paragraph 1A, your 887. Your understanding with reference to *Leviathan* is correct.
1A. The question of obtaining priority in use of 6 large French transports will be taken up with French High Commission. You will be advised on the result.
1B. If the present flow of troops abroad is maintained, the aggregate cargo tonnage necessary to maintain them increase rapidly between now and August. With the tonnage now available and that in sight, it will be necessary to reduce the number of days in ports abroad to 14 or better. Cargo vessels are now averaging 20. [Reply—Vol. 5, May 25, P-1185-S-2; May 26, A-1400-R-1]
1C. We should be advised definitely what arrangements you have made with British relative to maintaining troops operating with them. The number so assigned from time to time so that provisions can be made for the necessary cargo tonnage to maintain balance of force abroad. Goethals. [Reply—Vol. 5, June 11, P-1284-S-8]
4. With reference to paragraph 1, your cablegram 868. Matter of claim legislation. You are informed that Act passed the House April 6th and Senate April 9th. Awaits now only signature of President of the United States. March. [Reply—April 16, P-930-S-1]

NARA, RG 120, M930, Main Series, War Department to AEF, roll 12.

TAG, War Department, to Pershing, in reply to Pershing to TAG, War Department, cable P-891-S, April 11.

Cable A-1102-R. Confidential.
With reference to your 891. Divisions will be shipped as follows: By British ships during April, Infantry, etc., of 77th, 82nd and 35th Divisions. During May, Infantry, etc., of 28th, 4th and 30th Divisions. During June, Infantry of 27th Division. By United States ships during April, 3rd Division complete, Infantry, etc., of 5th Division, Artillery, etc., of 77th Division, during May, Artillery, etc., of 82nd, 35th and 28th Divisions. During June, Artillery, etc., of 4th, 30th and 5th Divisions.
A. Corps assignments changed as follows: to 2nd Corps, 77th, 82nd, 35th, 28th, 4th and 30th Divisions. To 3rd Corps, 3rd, 5th, 27th, 6th, 78th and 33rd Divisions.
B. All colored regiments have already sailed. Their places in schedule will be filled by Service of Rear troops. Information about shipment of Service of Rear troops will be cabled later. March. [In addition—April 18, A-1122-R; see also letter, April 16, Hill to CG, AEF]

NARA, RG 120, M930, Confidential Series, War Department to AEF, roll 12.

April 15

Pershing's Personal Diary

At Paris. Received telegram from M. Clemenceau, telephoned from headquarters, informing me that Mr. Lloyd George accepted M. Clemenceau's proposition to confer upon General Foch the title of Commander-in-Chief of the Allied Armies in France, and asking if I agreed to this proposition, subject naturally to the approval at the American government. I answered at once, through the headquarters and by a personal note to M. Clemenceau, informing him that I was in full and complete agreement with this proposition, subject to the confirmation of my government, which I had no doubt would be immediate. I left Paris at 11:15 a. m. for Chaumont-en-Vexin, headquarters of the First Division. Witnessed there a problem in attack, executed by the officers and liaison element of the First Division. Met there General Micheler, commanding the 5th French Army with whom the First Division is serving; also General Crepy, commanding the army of the division. Found General Bullard a little weak from his recent illness. Met there also General Harbord. Returned to Paris about 6:00 p. m. Had dinner with Colonel Dawes and Colonel Boyd, and talked with Colonel Dawes about having a single commander for all services in the interior of France, as now exists for the allies at the front. Saw at the Ritz the Duke of Connaught, also Miss Mary [Mabel] Boardman. Colonel Dawes and Colonel Boyd went to the theatre. I returned to my quarters to work soon after dinner.

LC, Pershing Papers, Diary, May 7, 1917–September 1, 1918, box 4.

Editor's Note—Charles Dawes provided valuable details on his discussion with Pershing concerning the recommendations made in his letter of April 13 advocating a unified Allied supply organization:

Paris, Monday, April 15, 1918 (11.10 p.m.)

> I am tired, but I know that if I do not make some notes of this time of crisis I shall always regret it.
>
> Colonel Boyd called me up and arranged for General Pershing to come to the hotel for dinner with him and me. We discussed my letter of April 13 relative to placing—or rather having the United States make an effort to place—all the Allied service of the rear under one (French) military command to correspond with the military unification of the front, already accomplished chiefly through General Pershing's insistence and self-effacement.
>
> I feel that the General can now, with the prestige of our country and his own prestige, successfully initiate military control of the rear—and the rear means England, France, and the United States, and perhaps Italy. My contact is very close with the whole supply and transportation system of the Allies behind the front. Emergency is forcing us to joint action now reached incompletely through a common perception of necessity all along the line

of command. The time has come for joint action compelled by one military authority. National and personal ambition must make way. A unified front necessitates a unified rear. Our backs *are* against the wall. England is fighting not only for Calais, but for Paris and a free New York. The time has come to abolish Supreme War Councils, Allied boards, town-meetings, and common consent discussions, and relegate discussions and diplomacy to their proper place—substituting military consideration and action. One man must control the rear, subject to one man who controls the front—a General, not a civilian, even though he be a prime minister.

I am sure that John agrees with me that for the Supreme War Council should be substituted a French General. I believe that John can and will bring it about and that he must bring it about if we are to win the war. He has devised in his own army, in my position, the plan which the Allies must now adopt for the control of their entire service of supply, including transportation. These matters are so important that I know what I write here must hereafter be discussed. I hope that my use of the personal pronoun may not create the impression that these ideas are more mine than John's. They are his ideas—for which ever since he has been here he has fought, for which he willingly sacrificed his independent command, for which today, if necessary, he would step aside. He is a great leader. I love and revere him. Whatever may be the outcome his country has had his best—unselfishly and unconditionally. Surely greatness requires no harder test than the willingness in an historical crisis to suggest supreme power for others at the expense of our own. But John never thinks of that—only the best way to accomplish it for victory's sake. He arrived from Chaumont last night. Sergeant Kilkenny delivered him my letter of the 13th on Sunday the 14th (yesterday noon). It contains a discussion of the steps which should be taken. Tomorrow I am going with John and Boyd to the front, where John will address the officers of the 1st Division before they go into battle. (Dawes, *A Journal of the Great War*, vol. 1, pp. 90–91.)

Pershing's thorough discussion and acceptance of Dawes's concept for the coordination of the Allies logistical organizations (services of the rear or supply) was based on his personal and difficult experiences with building the AEF's Services of Supply since June 1917 and with the French supply system. He now became the major advocate for this concept of "pooling" supplies and actively discussed it personally and in writing with the British and French political and military leaders in the following weeks in meetings with Clemenceau in Paris on April 18, Haig at Montreuil on April 19, Lloyd George, Lord Milner, and Henry Wilson in London on April 23, and Foch at Sarcus on April 28, letters to Clemenceau on April 19 and May 3, Peyton March on April 23, Lloyd George and Foch on April 28, and cables to March on April 19 (P-953-S) and Secretary Baker on April 27 (P-1007-S). At the Supreme War Council meetings at Abbeville, Pershing had further discussions with Clemenceau, Lloyd George, and Orlando on the Allied pooling of supplies which resulted in the decision for representatives of each government to meet in Paris on

May 6 to begin detailed negotiations on how to establish such an Allied coordinating body (see May 6, Pershing to TAG, War Department, P-1064-S-3).

Clemenceau to Pershing.

Telegram.

    Mr. Lloyd George informs me that he accepts my proposition to bestow upon General Foch the title of Commander-in-Chief of the Allied Armies in France. I hasten to ask if you agree to this proposition, subject naturally to the approval of the American Government. [Reply—see following.]

USAWW, vol. 12, p. 85.

Pershing to Clemenceau, in reply to telegram, Clemenceau to Pershing, April 15.

    In reply to your telegram, repeated to me this morning, I hasten to express my full and complete agreement with your view and that of Mr. Lloyd George as to conferring on General Foch the title of Commander-in-Chief of the Allied Armies in France. This is subject to the confirmation of my government, which I have no doubt will be immediate.

LC, Pershing Papers, folder: Georges Clemenceau, box 47.

Pershing to Bliss, Chief, American Section, and Permanent Military Representative, SWC, Versailles.

    I am enclosing herewith a copy of a telegram sent today to the War Department which explains itself.
    I am glad to see the Allied Governments at last thus completely recognize the necessity of the cooperation that this final action indicates we are going to have. [Enclosure—See below, Pershing to TAG, War Department, P-923-S.]

LC, Bliss Papers, folder: American Expeditionary Forces and American Forces in France, January–December 1918, box 248.

Kernan, CG, SOS, AEF, Tours, to Pershing, reply to Pershing to Kernan, April 10.

    Acting on your letter à propos of the conduct and dress of our troops, I am sending instructions today to each section commander as shown by the enclosed copy.

The carelessness of American troops in respect to matters of saluting, niceties of dress, etc., is due, I think, partly to a wrong view of the meaning and importance of these things and partly to imperfect instruction.

The mass of our officers appear to have no better standard than the enlisted personnel. I think instructions and insistence by letters, rather than by an order, more likely to bring some improvement and thence I am resorting to that form of endeavor.

Regarding the number of officers on duty at these headquarters, I am sending forward today the collected data. Some twenty odd have been relieved since those reports were received and others, from time to time, will follow.
[Enclosure (not located)]

LC, Pershing Papers, folder: General Francis J. Kernan, box 111.

Pershing to Senator F. E. Warren, U.S. Senate, Washington, in reply to Warren to Pershing, March 18 (confidential letter apparently destroyed).

I have just received your confidential letter of March 18th, which was delivered through Mr. Frazier, Mr. House's friend. I was, of course, very glad to get it, and shall destroy it as soon as I answer some of the points you bring out.

. . . I am glad you had a chance to talk with General March, and am still of the opinion, as expressed in a former letter, that he is going to do well. Of course he came in after the Secretary of War left and has not had a chance to have the Secretary's full backing. I believe he will get this and that, together, they will make an excellent team.

You speak of sending over a letter by Mabel Boardman. I do not know whether she has arrived, but assume from this that she is expected here shortly. I suppose, of course, this is in connection with the Red Cross and that I shall see something of her and perhaps get on the good side of her.

With reference to Griscom, I fear that he will fall into the same category as Colonel Bacon. Having once been an ambassador to Europe, one is always an ambassador, and an ambassador in uniform is something of a difficult person to handle. His being "Ambassadeur ancient" entitles him to be shown every consideration by these people, while his rank places him down considerably below many others in his own service. So that fact alone would mitigate against him, no matter what his other qualifications might happen to be. So there we are. I do not see anyone in the field who will quite fill the bill that Colonel House and I had in mind, so for the present I shall let it drift along.

I am glad you found Colonel House such a pleasant and attractive gentleman. I was more than pleased with him, and feel that he is going to do everything he can to make things go so far as I am concerned, and I am glad that he expressed to you the same opinion of me and how things here gone here as he did to me.

Mr. Baker has just been here for a long visit and I got very well acquainted with him. We started in with the ports, all of which we visited and thoroughly inspected. We then came up the line of communications and inspected the various aviation fields, storehouses, salvage plants, regulating stations, and, finally, spending an entire day at my headquarters going through the general staff organization, of which I am very proud. Then two days at the front, which gave him the experience of his life. A Boche shell landed within 25 yards of him and made him feel that he was quite in the war, which he really was. I explained to him, while traveling about, the reason for the selection of the ports and the line of communications and the probable front. I explained to him also the difficulties we had had in getting materials and pushing our construction, and went into the details of training and preparation of our men for actual fighting. I then went with him to the French G. H. Q. in the field and went over the details of our relations, both civil and military, with both the French and British. I was pleased to have him express himself as pleased with what had been done. He said to me—

> "General Pershing, I selected you because of your fighting qualities, and have been very surprised and pleased to know that you also possess such high diplomatic talent. Both the President and myself have been most gratified at the way you have conducted things here in Europe. You have the President's entire confidence, as you have my own. We will back you in every possible way."

The Secretary spent some days at my house as my guest while waiting for the outcome of the German offensive conducted against Amiens. He then went to Italy and returned to my quarters in Paris, staying a couple of days and sailed for home on the 8th.

I see that our mutual friend, General Wood, has succeeded in putting it over on the medical board and has been declared fit for active service. How in the hell any board could bring itself to believe that General Wood is fit for active service is more than I can understand. He is a cripple and that is all there is to it, and there is no use in sending cripples over here to do men's work. I have no doubt he will use this as ground for propaganda and will keep that up as long as he has breath.

The matter of the publication of our losses has given me great concern. We are going to have some heavy losses before long, and it seems to me that if we undertake to publish them, we are going to have all the newspapers in the country filled with lists of names of our casualties. I am rather of the opinion that the rule followed by the French is the best, and that these lists should not be published except perhaps in local papers after the War Department has notified the relatives. I am recommending to the War Department that in case they should decide to publish these lists, they should be published under the title of "Roll of Honor," as I think this would be very good propaganda and would be a consolation to the friends and relatives of those who are killed, and would hold up to the public the idea that everyone on the list lost his life in a cause which is worthy of every sacrifice.

I shall be very glad to have you take Warren out with you to the ranch this summer, because, as you know, I want Warren to see as much of you and you as much of him as is possible. I think his association with you will make him much more manly, and I desire to have him impressed with his mother's father. Warren is a fine boy and

I am wrapped up in him, of course. It is terrible to be separated from him in this way, and I hope that matters may take such a turn that I may have him over here during his summer vacation. Secretary Baker, of his own volition, suggested that on his next visit he would be glad to bring Warren over with his own little boy and leave Warren here with me. I think this was a very kindly thought on the part of Mr. Baker and it touched me very deeply. My brother Jim also wants to come over and bring Warren, but all this depends upon the turn affairs take.

As to Magoon's fears, I think he is just a little bit overly-anxious. Bullard has been perfectly splendid and I have no misgivings at all about him, either as a soldier or a friend. I fear, however, that his health is not going to hold up. He has already been in the hospital just at the time his division was going into the line, and I am more or less anxious about him.

As to Edwards, I have had to call him down two or three times. Edwards is given to shooting off his face and criticizing everybody. I sent word to him that if I heard any more of it he would be relieved, and he promised to discontinue it. He has not any too much sense anyway as to the ordinary proprieties and is more or less a loud-mouthed ass.

As to the military situation, it looks more or less precarious. We hope to help both the French and the British by lending them as many troops as we can put in the line, having due regard for our future organization into units as parts of an army to fight under our own flag. While the Germans are making hard drives and the French and British are having heavy losses, I believe the unity of command we now have under General Foch is going to give us such cooperation that we shall be able to keep the Boche from breaking through the line and separating the two armies.

Incidentally, I was, myself, instrumental in bringing about the Unity of control which we now here. Without going into detail, I will say that at our last council of war I stood firmly for unity of command and I said I did not think we had ever had it since the war began and that the success of the war depended upon having unity of command. My position was highly approved by Mr. Lloyd George and, I think, convinced some of our allies that they had better get into line and accept a solution of the problem which they had never heretofore been able to agree to.

Mr. Frazier sent me your telegram and I shall use the method of cabling to you through him. I think he is perfectly safe and I do not think we should have any particular reason to fear him or Auchincloss.

LC, Pershing Papers, folder: Senator F. E. Warren (1918), box 394.

Pershing to TAG, War Department. Copy to Bliss, enclosure to Pershing to Bliss (see above).

Cable P-923-S. Confidential.
For Secretary of War and Chief of Staff.

The following letter from Mr. Clemenceau has just been received:

Mr. Lloyd George informs me that he accepts my proposition to bestow upon General Foch the title of Commander-in-Chief of the Allied Armies in France. I hasten to ask if you agree to this proposition, subject naturally to the approval of the American Government.

To which I replied as follows:

In reply to your letter to me this morning by telephone, I hasten to express my full and complete agreement with your view and that of Mr. Lloyd George as to conferring on General Foch the title of Commander-in-Chief of the Allied Armies in France. This is subject to confirmation of my Government, which I have no doubt will be immediate.

[Reply—April 16, A-1113-R]
Copy to Bliss.

NARA, RG 120, M930, Confidential Series, AEF to War Department and War Department to AEF, roll 7, and War Department to AEF, roll 18; NARA, M923, American Section, SWC, file 316: Cablegrams received from the War Department, Jan. 23, 1918–Nov. 19, 1919, roll 18; see also online "WW I Supreme War Council, American records," at https://www.fold3.com.

TAG, War Department. to Pershing, in addition to TAG, War Department, to Pershing, cables A-468-R, December 3, A-522-R, December 16, A-797-R, February 17, and A-913-R, March 13, in part in reply to Pershing to TAG, War Department, cable P-818-S, March 29.

Cable A-1105-R.

5E. With reference to your 818, paragraph 1C. Estimated deliveries 4.7-inch and 6-inch guns revised since our 797, paragraph 1E, 522, paragraph 3, and 468, paragraph 1. Seaboard deliveries 4.7-inch unchanged since our 913, paragraph 1G. Expected seaboard deliveries 6-inch guns as follows: May 18, June 1, July 9, August 32, September 32.

NARA, RG 120, M930, Main Series, War Department to AEF.

TAG, War Department, to Pershing, in part in reply to Pershing to TAG, War Department, cables P-745-S, March 18, and P-812-S, March 29; in addition to TAG, War Department, to Pershing, cable A-845-R, February 28.

Cable A-1106-R.

2A. Drop bomb schedule as outline in our 845, paragraph 1A, B, C, D, E, F, was accepted by you in your 745, paragraph 8G [not reproduced]. Your 812, paragraph 2, appears to be at variance with this acceptance and does not clearly indicated program of active squadrons of different types at the front. Very necessary we should have clearly defined reasonable maximum program active squadrons different types month by month as basis for drop bomb and aeroplane machine gun program. Until further advised will continue both programs on basis indicated in our 845, paragraph 1A, B, C, D, E, F. [Reply—April 30, P-1031-S-6]

NARA, RG 120, M930, Main Series, War Department to AEF, roll 12.

April 16

Pershing's Personal Diary

At Paris. Left for headquarters of the First Division at 9:00 a. m. with Colonel Dawes, Colonel Boyd, Captain de Marenches and Lieutenant Adamson, arriving there about 10:30 a. m. The officers of the division were assembled in the garden of the chateau where General Bullard had established his headquarters. I gave them a talk which Lieutenant Adamson took down as I made it, the record of which is in my private file, document no. [ ]. [A copy is in *My Experiences in the World War*, vol. 1, pp. 393–95.] After this I went to General Duncan's headquarters, Tyrie Chateau, for luncheon. Then I went to see General Foch at his headquarters at Sarcus, to the west of Grandvilliers. Had a talk with General Foch in which I told him that when the Secretary of War was in France, he had expressed the opinion, to which he adhered firmly, that as soon as practicable there should be formed in France an American army; that the Secretary stated that this was also the opinion of the President of the United States; and also that it was my opinion. I stated that the President, the Secretary of War and I were of the opinion that this is of the greatest importance in order to sustain the interest of the people of the United States in the war; that now, as the big battle is on and the first American Division is to be engaged, the people will be all the more interested in seeing an American army, operating as such, in the war; that as soon as two, three or four divisions can take their part together in the war, it is my intention to assume command of them and that this is of the greatest importance for the reasons stated above. General Foch agreed to the principle of this idea and stated that its execution would depend upon the time when the other divisions could be placed with the First Division. I stated that the 26th and 42d Divisions might at any time from now on be ready to go into the fight; that they would naturally have to be withdrawn from the front which they are now holding and given a short time to rest and recuperate, as had been given the First, before going into battle. That soon after this, the Second Division will be ready to follow the others. I also stated that the 32d will, within a few days, take its place in the line. The understanding on this subject was definite. The only thing that was left indefinite was the date as to when the American army will be formed. I also told General Foch that I wished to place at his headquarters a representative from my headquarters who would be there to act as liaison officer between General Foch and myself and also to perform any duty which General Foch might see fit to assign him. I suggested Lieutenant Colonel T. B. Mott for this duty. General Foch stated that he knew Colonel Mott and that Colonel Mott would be entirely agreeable to him. Received a telegram from Sir Douglas Haig, inviting me to spend several nights at his headquarters to study operations.

LC, Pershing Papers, Diary, May 7, 1917–September 1, 1918, box 4.

Editor's Note—Robert Bullard, the CG of the 1st Division, recorded his impressions of Pershing's impromptu speech to the officers of his division in his wartime memoirs:

> General Pershing witnessed the test manoeuvre. After it he had the officers of the division assembled at my headquarters and spoke to them. All non-American officers were excluded. He was going to talk to Americans only. It was not oratory. He is not, or at least was not then, an orator. He halted in his speech, after every few words saying "eh, eh, eh." But he had a message and he gave it. It was an earnest but not a dramatic speech, as many, after the stirring events that followed, tried to make it out. I am told that General Pershing himself now, in 1921, says that on this occasion he was deeply moved by the import of impending mighty events. If so, then I am inclined to believe that he, too, sees more in the occasion by backsight than he saw by foresight. His message, given in his terse, business-like way, was simple enough. It was, in substance: "You have just had a test of efficiency and met it. I am gratified. I am confident that you will likewise meet every test put upon you. You have been observed by a high French commander and other high French officers and been commended. You are now to go against a victorious enemy under new and harder conditions. All our Allies will be watching to see how you conduct yourselves. I am confident that you will meet their best hope and my expectation for you. In your training you have been made by my orders to adhere to American traditions and methods. You must hold to these in your fighting and in all your future action against the enemy. They are ours, right, sane, reliable, and will win."
>
> These were all natural things to say. They were hardly new to his hearers. His training methods had long before this brought their minds in line with his; his thoughts were their thoughts on this subject. In after months the occasion appeared more historical than it at the time seemed, and men were asking what General Pershing had said. Few could remember. The very naturalness of what he said kept it from being especially marked for memory by his hearers. (Bullard, *Personalities and Reminiscences of the War*, pp. 181–82.)

On April 16, 1918, Pershing visited the Headquarters of the 1st Division at Chaumont-en-Vexin, where he spoke to the division's officers assembled in the chateau's garden. He especially wanted to speak to the officers because the division was soon to enter full frontline duty and combat for the first time. Robert L. Bullard, the 1st Division's commanding general, recently returned from the hospital and wearing a heavy winter fur coat, faces Pershing. Source: NARA, Still Picture Branch, RG 111, 111-SC-10910 and 111-SC-10911.

Bliss, Chief, American Section, and Permanent Military Representative, SWC, Versailles, to Pershing, in reply to Pershing to Bliss, April 12 (two letters), and April 15 (Copy of Pershing to TAG, War Department, cable P-923-S).

I am just in receipt of your two notes of April 12, one of them about the copy of the memorandum from the Inter-Allied Transportation Council on rolling stock, and the other about the suggestion of the Italian Commissioner General of Aeronautics in regard to sending American aero squadrons to Italy for duty on the Italian Front.

In accordance with your request I have prepared a note to General Giardino requesting him to 'express to the Italian Commissioner General of Aeronautics your regrets that it is impossible, at the present time, to place American Aero Squadrons on the Italian front, but that you have instructed the Chief of the Air Service, A.E.F. to take up for you the question of training additional American pilots in Italy and of then using them temporarily on the Italian front.'

[Handwritten: *"P.S. Have just received your note with copy of your telegram to Washington about Gen. Foch's designation as Commander in Chief. It is fine and will produce the best of results. T.H.B."*]

LC, Pershing Papers, folder: Supreme War Council, February–April 1918, box 193; see also LC, Bliss Papers, folder: American Expeditionary Forces and American Forces in France, January–December 1918, box 248.

Maj. Gen. Hunter Liggett, CG, I Corps, AEF, to Pershing.

I want to thank you for your great kindness in sending me the fine motor car I found here for my official use upon my return from inspecting the Corps Artillery.

It will facilitate my getting around as I find I must do as much as possible to keep things in the Divisions moving. I found everything in excellent shape with the Corps Arty—a fine clean soldiering outfit—somewhat handicapped by need of 800 replacements but otherwise seems to be fit for service about May 10. Gen'l McGlachlin is very efficient.

LC, Pershing Papers, folder: Gen. Hunter Liggett, box 117.

Bradley, Chief Surgeon, SOS, AEF, to Pershing.

In view of our conversation on Sunday [April 14], I have this day forwarded an official letter asking that decision on any report which may be rendered by the Board may for the time being be deferred. I have given in the application my reasons therefor and requested the privilege of a re-examination later. I have had no leave since I have been in Europe, now a matter of nearly two years, and the days lost this past week in hospital have been the only days I have not been actively on duty since the arrival of your headquarters last June.

Hoping for your favorable consideration and your personal action on my official request, I beg to remain . . .

[Enclosure]

April 16, 1918

Brig. Gen. Alfred E. Bradley to CINC, AEF.
Subject: Physical examination.

1. Under Paragraph 3, Special Orders 89 March 30th I have recently undergone a physical examination.

2. From information given me by the Board I have reasons to believe that its findings will be an unfavorable report.

3. I desire, therefore, to state that on April 6th I received telegraphic orders to report on April 7th for physical examination at Chaumont. I had just arrived in Paris from a trip to England which had been very exhausting with irregular hours and meals, involving almost constant travel. During this trip I had contracted a hard cold and on reporting at G.H.Q. was suffering from a severe laryngitis and bronchitis and was acutely and seriously ill. The Board, however, proceeded with my examination and on its completion directed me to enter the hospital at Chaumont. This I did at once and remained one week when certain portions of the examination were repeated with the results stated in Paragraph 2.

4. It is my belief that the conditions on which the findings will be made by the Board were largely transitory and that when entirely recovered from the acute conditions, with a period for a much-needed rest and recuperation, it is fair to expect a different report.

5. I, therefore, request that decision in my case be deferred and that I be granted a reexamination at a later date.

[Reply—April 30, Pershing to Bradley]

LC, Pershing Papers, folder: Bradley, box 33.

Patton, Jr., CO, 1st Light Tank Center, Bourg, to Pershing, reply to Pershing to Patton, April 14.

Please accept my sincere thanks for your very nice letter to me in regard to the death of Mrs. Ayer [Patton's mother-in-law]. I appreciate your thoughtfulness more than I can say.

Anne was with Beatrice at the time of her father's death and I think was still there when Mrs. Ayer died. I hope this was the case as it would have been a great help to Beatrice.

There is one good feature connected with the death of Mrs. Ayer, namely that now Beatrice will be able to stay in California which will be a comfort to both she and Anne. Mrs. Ayer's health was so bad that she would have been a constant worry to herself and family so that my statement is not as heartless as it sounds.

LC, Pershing Papers, folder: Col. and Mrs. Geo. S. Patton, box 155

Col. Roy A. Hill, Office of the Adjutant General, War Department, to CG, AEF, France, in reply to Pershing to TAG, War Department, cable P-891-S, April 11; in addition to TAG, War Department, to Pershing, cable A-1102-R, April 14.

No. 322.03

1. Confirming my cablegram of April 13, 1918 [received April 14], the following reassignment of divisions to corps has been made:

II Corps—for training with British: 77th, 82d, 35th, 28th, 4th, and 30th Divisions.

III Corps: 3d, 5th, 27th, 6th, 78th, and 33d Divisions.

2. The reassignment was necessary by reason of the fact that upon receipt of your Cablegram No. 891, parts of several divisions were either on transports or at ports and concentration camps near the port. In order to carry out your wishes and agreement as to shipping the infantry of the II Corps by British ships, this reassignment had to be made.

3. Of the above divisions, the 82d is a training division and the 33d, 35th, and 77th are replacement divisions.

4. As it was impossible to avoid these assignments here, it is thought that you can make the necessary reassignments and reorganizations of artillery regiments after all the divisions reach France and after the infantry has been released by the British.

5. Your attention is also invited to the fact that until the receipt of your 891 the assignment to corps was as follows, and the model of rifle in possession of divisions is noted after each:

II Corps		III Corps	
Division	Model	Division	Model
77th	1917	3d	1903
82d	1917	5th	1903
28th	1917	35th	1903
80th	1917	4th	1903
78th	1917	6th	1903
30th	1917	33d	1903

To facilitate shipment without the delay incident to rearming and to take advantage of troops at or near the ports of embarkation the rearrangement of divisions in corps became necessary, one division, the 80th being removed and its place being taken by the 27th which was better prepared to meet the requirements of the amended program. The result is as follows:

II Corps		III Corps	
Division	Model	Division	Model
77th	1917	3d	1903
82d	1917	5th	1903
35th	1903	27th	1917
28th	1917	4th	1903
4th	1903	78th	1917
30th	1917	33d	1903

It is well understood that it is not desirable to have divisions of the same corps armed with a different model rifle, but to avoid delay in shipment it is believed that this is a matter that can be easily adjusted by you by the transfer of the 35th and 4th Divisions from the II to the III Corps and the transfer of the 27th and 78th Divisions from the III to the II Corps, the result being that all divisions of the II Corps will have the 1917 rifles and the III Corps the 1903 rifles, as follows:

II Corps		III Corps	
Division	Model	Division	Model
77th	1917	3d	1903
28th	1917	5th	1903
82d	1917	35th	1903
27th	1917	4th	1903
78th	1917	6th	1903
30th	1917	33d	1903

By order of the Secretary of War:

USAWW, vol. 2, pp. 325–26.

Editor's Note—Needless to say, these paper assignments of divisions to corps did not last long once the divisions were transported to France, trained, and ready for their actual combat assignments. In fact, as the AEF withdrew divisions upon completion of their training with the British during the summer of 1918, the II Corps was reduced to only the 27th and 30th Divisions, which remained with the British through the remainder of the war. While a total of nine corps were organized in the

AEF as more divisions arrived and were prepared for active operations, only five of those corps (I, II, III, IV, and V) were engaged in active combat operations, two (VI and VII) held quiet sections of the line to the east, and two others (VIII and IX) were more postarmistice administrative organizations. GHQ, AEF, repeatedly juggled the actual divisional composition of its corps during the war based on combat requirements and the combat readiness of its divisions, especially following periods of heavy combat and the need for rest, recuperation, and refitting.

TAG, War Department, to Bliss, Chief, American Section, and Permanent Military Representative, SWC, Versailles.

Cable 47-R. Confidential.
    The President has approved for the United States the designation of General Foch as Commander in Chief of the Allied Armies in France. March.

Copy furnished to Gen. Pershing Apr. 19.

NARA, M923, American Section, SWC, file 316: Cablegrams received from the War Department, Jan. 23, 1918–Nov. 19, 1919, roll 18; see also online "WW I Supreme War Council, American records," at https://www.fold3.com.

Pershing to TAG, War Department, in part in reply to TAG, War Department, to Pershing, cable A-1100-R, April 14.

Cable P-930-S.
    1. For Chief of Staff. With reference to paragraph 4, your cablegram 1100. Request authority to make and publish necessary regulations to give effect to claim legislation. Also request that full text of law be cabled in order that same, together with regulations may be published at earliest possible date. [Reply—April 27, A-1197-R-2]

NARA, RG 120, M930, Main Series, AEF to War Department, roll 3.

Pershing to TAG, War Department, in part in reply to TAG, War Department, to Pershing, cables A-1067-R, April 8, A-1069-R, April 9, and A-1074-R, April 9 (not reproduced), in addition to Pershing to TAG, War Department, cable P-868-S, April 29.

Cable P-933-S.
    3. For Q.M. General. 3E. The question of loading from 5 to 8 locomotives aboard ships is up for discussion as to whether it would not be advisable to practically utilize

whole ship for cargo locomotives or heavy lift articles; further, no storage space available for small cargo at points where heavy cranes are located. Suggest may be used for the blocking of heavy lifts, to expedite and facilitate unloading. One ship recently arrived with locomotives which were blocked with small heavy cases of steel weighing 250 to 350 pounds each. Considerable difficulty experienced working these small cases out between framework of lift and stanchions of ship. Estimate saving 4 or 5 days in discharge if our recommendation in loading ships complete with heavy lifts is followed. [Reply—April 23, A-1158-R-5]

4. For Chief Signal Officer. 4A. With reference to paragraph 2, your cablegram 1067, and paragraph 1, your cablegram 1069. What is actual number Bristol fighters airplanes to be floated in each month April, May and June? Give some information regarding DH 4 and DH 9, give Handley Page figures for July and August.

NARA, RG 120, M930, Main Series, AEF to War Department, roll 3.

TAG, War Department, to Pershing, in addition to TAG, War Department, to Pershing, cable A-1069-R, April 9.

Cable A-1107-R.

7. Our 1069, paragraph 1B, give the number of DH 4 and Bristol aeroplanes and sets of Handley Page parts which will be delivered to port of embarkation up to October 1918. These deliveries will practically complete all orders for these types. In order to keep continuous production it is necessary you inform us as soon as possible as to your prospective needs for aeroplanes for fall and winter of 1918 and spring of 1919. Cable this information giving quantity of each type needed monthly. [Reply—April 23, P-981-S-3]

14. Information and recommendations desired as follows. Number of artists other than camouflage now attached to American Expeditionary Forces. How and when will their work be made available to the public? Are any artists accredited with permission to send their work to any in United States? Are any officers or enlisted men permitted to send painting or drawings to United States? [Reply—April 23, P-981-S-2A]

NARA, RG 120, M930, Main Series, War Department to AEF, roll 12.

TAG, War Department, to Pershing, in part in reply to Pershing to TAG, War Department, cable P-845-S, April 3.

Cable A-1110-R.

2E. With reference to your 845, paragraph 4. Situation as to Ordnance supply for reserve and replacement thoroughly appreciated. Utmost efforts being made to stimulate production of needed items and to expedite shipment oversea. Your previous cables have received attention and shipments have been made as rapidly as material became available. Material enumerated our cables 766, paragraph 1, 767, paragraph 1, and 914, paragraph 6 [not reproduced], should when received operate to relieve situation somewhat. Special and vigorous attention being centered on automatic supply shipment during the coming month(s) in order to insure adequate replacements and reserves.

NARA, RG 120, M930, Main Series, War Department to AEF, roll 12.

TAG, War Department, to Pershing.

Cable A-1111-R.
1. War Department being importuned to modify restrictions as to relatives of soldiers being given passports to France. Claims are made that you had stated to Mr. Carter that you had no objection to sisters of soldiers coming as workers provided they would agree not to ask to visit or attend their relatives whether well or otherwise. Department has advice from you on this subject and if you have modified your attitude request that we be informed promptly. March. [Reply—April 18, P-946-S-3A; Vol. 6, July 28, P-1525-S-1D]

NARA, RG 120, M930, War Department to AEF, roll 12.

TAG, War Department, to Pershing.

Cable A-1113-R. Confidential.
1. The President has approved for the United States the designation of General Foch as Commander-in-Chief of the Allied Armies in France. March.

NARA, RG 120, M930, War Department to AEF, roll 12.

April 17

Pershing's Personal Diary

Worked in quarters all day. Suffering somewhat from pain in chest and bad cold. Saw Mr. Frazier, Colonel Fries [Chief, Gas Service] and General Sackville-West [British Permanent Military Representative, SWC]. Sent telegram to Sir Douglas Haig stating that I would go to his headquarters tomorrow. Received word from headquarters that cablegram had been received from the President confirming my action in agreeing to appointment of General Foch as Commander-in-Chief of the

Allied Armies in France [April 16, cable A-1113-R]. General Harbord came yesterday afternoon from the First Division and left this morning for Chaumont. Asked him to have study made as to the best disposition to make of officers who are found unsuited for service at the front; that something should be done with them other than sending them to the United States, as some worthless officers are liable to take advantage of this means of getting back home.

LC, Pershing Papers, Diary, May 7, 1917–September 1, 1918, box 4.

Editor's Note—An unmentioned visitor was Charles Dawes, who had accompanied Pershing on his trip to the 1st Division and to visit Foch at his GHQ before they returned to Paris on the 16th. In his diary, Dawes related the substance of his discussions with Pershing on the evening of their return, in which he focused on the key issues of his upcoming visit to Field Marshal Sir Douglas Haig, the British CINC:

Paris, Wednesday, April 17 (Night, 11 P.M.)
I think I should keep notes, for General Pershing's sake, of what he is considering and the environment under which he plans. Upon some of his decisions, soon to be made, depends the outcome of the present war, in all probability. Whatever may be the result of his decisions, this contemporaneous record of what confronts him should be made by some one. It cannot be made by him, for a man cannot be General and historian at the same time.

In the General's bedroom tonight (Rue de Varenne)—he is suffering from a cold contracted on our trip yesterday—he went over matters fully. Haig is calling him for a conference. What Haig wants is men—Americans—to be fed into his hard-pressed army. He maintains that unless he has a minimum soon of 150,000, and more later, his army may not be able to withstand the tremendous onslaught of the numerically superior enemy. He is being pressed in around the Channel ports. General Pershing must decide for himself Haig's real situation, and the full nature of the apparent emergency. The rate of destruction of men is so great that once in, the American 150,000 will be so reduced in numbers by counter-attacking that the foundation of the American military organization now forming will be largely destroyed. If the emergency is such that it seems necessary, the men will be fed in; if the emergency seems less acute than represented, more care can be had for the relation of present American losses to the future military effectiveness of the American section of the Allied forces. The General, and he alone, must decide in the next few days to what extent immediate amalgamation of American forces into the English army is necessary. With the natural intense desire of an American and an army commander for the preservation of national and personal independence, he yet will fearlessly make any decision inconsistent with their preservation which is necessary to ultimate victory or the escape from an immediate Allied defeat. If the emergency, in his judgment, does not involve immediate Allied disaster (after a personal inspection of the battle area), he must preserve from unnecessary destruction, as far as possible for the future of the war, the existing vital germ now here of the future vast army of the United States. This is what he tells me—and whatever his action, these are the principles which will control it. It is due to him to state them now "*in medias res.*" His head is very cool. His judgment will be formed from conditions and facts uninfluenced by emotionalism, politics, ambition, or personal considerations of any kind. After three hours of a visit with him alone, all of which were devoted to a discussion of the situation, I came away knowing that he is the one American to be in his present place. He says again that Foch is very confident.

Am a little worried for fear of pneumonia attacking him, and made him promise to get a doctor tomorrow if he did not feel better. He wants to start for Haig's headquarters tomorrow. John expects to have fifteen divisions by June. Men are coming rapidly. But of the men now going into the English and French battle lines it can be said that, though their numbers may be comparatively few, they may yet determine which way the balance of the nations shall swing. (Dawes, *A Journal of the Great War*, vol. 1, pp. 94–95.)

Pershing to TAG, War Department, in part in reply to TAG, War Department, to Pershing, cable A-891-R, March 9.

Cable P-939-S.

1. For the Chief of Staff. With reference to paragraph 7, your cablegram 891. Careful study has been made. In view of the fact we have already purchased over 2,500,000 tons material not subject to replacement, the open market in Europe is stripped. However constant energy uncovers unsuspected sources of supply. General Purchasing Board estimates as available from Europe during next 6 months not subject to replacement as follows: vegetables 2,000 tons, other quartermaster supplies 20,000 tons, all coal necessary, motor supplies 20,000 tons, all horses necessary, Belgian locomotives 60,000 tons, all cement necessary since we replace coal for this from England, all incandescent lamps necessary, miscellaneous supplies 50,000 tons, Signal Corps 2,000 tons, practically all lumber necessary for all services, air service supplies 3,000 tons, medical service negligible in tonnage. Should be understood that even with careful study estimates cannot be accurate. Cable being sent to Chief Signal Officers on French inability to make further deliveries of aeroplanes and other equipment. [*Ed.*—No such cable has been located.] [Reply—April 28, A-1200-R-1A]

NARA, RG 120, M930, Main Series, AEF to War Department, roll 3.

In his cable P-939-S to the Chief of Staff, Pershing emphasized the numerous steps that the AEF had taken to obtain supplies and materials in France and Europe to relieve as much of the burden as possible from the limited trans-Atlantic cargo tonnage. One of the most important statements he made was that the AEF was now providing "practically all lumber necessary for all services." Initial American plans in France envisioned an enormous demand for all types of rough and finished lumber products for a wide variety of construction projects as well as for railway ties and heavy pier lumber. Realizing the magnitude of the requirements for lumber products, Pershing in 1917 pushed for access to French forests for lumber and to bring Army forestry units to France to cut trees and process lumber to meet all the AEF's needs. By April 1918, Engineer forestry units in France were fully engaged in logging, operating sawmills (such as this one in the Pontenx area southwest of Bordeaux), finishing lumber products, and shipping them throughout the AEF. Source: NARA, Still Picture Branch, RG 111, 111-SC-10210.

Pershing to TAG, War Department, in part in reply to TAG, War Department, to Pershing, cable A-1014-R, March 31; in addition to Pershing to TAG, War Department, cable P-894-S, April 11.

Cable P-941-S.

1. For the Chief of Staff. With reference to paragraph 6, your cablegram 1014. Following are quantities in square feet of covered storage now in use and available at each port:

St. Nazaire	215,000
Montoir	284,000
Bordeaux	275,000
Bassens	257,000
Saint Sulpice	411,000
La Pallice and La Rochelle	36,380
Brest	<u>104,000</u>
Total	1,582,280

Following additional will be available by May 1st:

St. Nazaire	23,000
Montoir	440,000
Saint Sulpice	261,000
Brest	<u>10,000</u>
Total	734,000

Reference second question of above-mentioned cable asking whether we will be able to unload steamers at maximum capacity before additional storage recommended is provided, answer is yes.

4. Reference to paragraph 9, my cablegram 894. Following reported from Berne, Switzerland, through British intelligence. "Major Raynal Cawthorne Bolling, ORC, killed, shot through the heart on or about 29th March in small Fiat car on road between Estrées and Feukencort,"

NARA, RG 120, M930, Main Series, AEF to War Department, roll 3.

Pershing to TAG, War Department, in addition to Pershing to TAG, War Department, cables P-569-S, February 4, and P-891-S, April 11.

Cable P-942-S.

4. For Chief of Staff. With reference to paragraph 5B, my cablegram 569, temporarily suspended by paragraph 1B, my cablegram 891. Desire selection of personnel and organization 12 heavy and 24 light tank companies without delay. Give 1 months intensive training as Infantry then pistol practice and Machine Gun training, varied from usual training by firing from a slow-moving truck. [Reply—May 27, A-1406-R-2; in addition—June 6, P-1258-S-2C]

NARA, RG 120, M930, Main Series, AEF to War Department, roll 3.

The port of St. Nazaire on the Loire River remained the primary base port for the AEF throughout the war. Other French Atlantic ports were also developed during the war, and the AEF identified certain ports for specific cargo to facilitate unloading and the turnaround of ships. AEF units at St. Nazaire (Base Section No. 1) had developed and manned facilities for assembling automobiles and trucks from the crated and broken-down components arriving from the United States. The motor assembly buildings, such as the one pictured here, reassembled the components into functioning vehicles, tested them, and then stored them in vehicle parks (next photograph) for later shipment by rail to depots throughout France for distribution. Source: NARA, Still Picture Branch, RG 111, 111-SC-10150 and 111-SC-10398.

The American port and facilities at Bassens (Base Section No. 2) were located five miles below Bordeaux on the east side of the Gironde River. The entire complex had to be built from scratch one mile downstream from the existing French Bassens and included plans for fifteen new berths plus warehouses and trackage with a daily total capacity of 12, 600 tons of cargo. A large amount of construction was required at the American Bassens, which began in 1917. By the spring of 1918, construction continued throughout the complex while unloading and storage operations were fully underway in the completed sections. Source: NARA, Still Picture Branch, RG 111, 111-SC-10236 and 111-SC-10244.

TAG, War Department, to Pershing, in part in reply to Pershing to TAG, War Department, cable P-884-S, April 10.

Cable A-1118-R.
 For General Atterbury:
 1A. Your 884, paragraph 4. Have requested depots at ports of embarkation to ship rail as you wish.
 1E. Your 884, paragraph 4. 100 refrigerator cars now being floated. [Reply—May 7, P-1066-S-2]
 2. Am required to submit at once estimates covering railroad equipment and supplies that will be required to meet military program up to March 31st, 1920. Fully realize difficulty of estimating requirements especially at the present time but some reasonable data necessary here to formulate . . . a war program. Will you not cable best estimates you can now make of your requirements for machinery including cranes, pile drivers, steam shovels, derricks, grinders, track layers and tractors; water stations; iron and steel products including structural steel and corrugated iron; hardware and hand tools; push cars; hand cars; motor cars; railway rolling stock; railway motive power; lumber; track materials and fastenings including rail; horse drawn transportation and supplies; building materials and supplies; railway repair shops; floating plants including barge derricks, pile drivers and tugs. We are entirely in the dark and have no data on which to make estimates here. We are working on estimate that you will have to move from ports in June average of 16,000 tons per day and in August average of 25,000 tons and that daily tonnage will continue to increase as our forces are augmented. If these estimates are right and unless you have much more equipment in sight than we have any knowledge of will you not be extremely short of locomotives and cars especially the latter? Should you not have at least 40,000 cars for the locomotives now ordered? Have you in sight the balance over and above our 19,000 cars? Felton. [Reply—Vol. 5, June 6, P-1259-S]

NARA, RG 120, M930, Main Series, War Department to AEF, roll 12.

TAG, War Department, to Pershing, in part in reply to Pershing to TAG, War Department, cable P-823-S, March 30.

Cable A-1120-R.
 3. With reference to paragraph 4A, your 823. Bill authorizing Chaplains 1 for each 1200 men, grade from 1st Lieutenant to Lieutenant Colonel without command, passed the House of Congress. Instructions being issued that Chaplains will not wear insignia of rank. March. [*Ed.*—President Wilson vetoed this particular bill, and it took another month before the issues were resolved and chaplains were officially authorized in all branches of the U.S. military at 1 per 1,200 men with rank, pay, and allowances authorized by law. However, Pershing's request on insignia was retained and incorporated into Army Special Regulations in May 1918. After his retirement

in 1924, the War Department officially rescinded this provision in June 1926, and insignia of rank were returned to chaplains. See Earl F. Stover, *Up from Handymen: The United States Army Chaplaincy, 1865–1920* (Washington: Department of the Army, Office of the Chief of Chaplains, 1977), pp. 205–206; Roy J. Honeywell, *Chaplains of the United States Army* (Washington: Department of the Army, Office of the Chief of Chaplains, 1958), pp. 177–78.)]

NARA, RG 120, M930, Main Series, War Department to AEF, roll 12.

TAG, War Department, to Pershing.

Cable A-1122-R. Confidential.
    1. Urgent. Cable complete for information Secretary of War who is now here your memorandum containing record of conference held between Secretary of War, yourself and 2 British representatives reference shipment of American troops to France during coming months in both English and American tonnage. Disregard our 1102. Detailed information as to priorities will be sent you later. March. [Reply—April 19, P-955-S]

NARA, RG 120, M930, Confidential Series, War Department to AEF, roll 18.

TAG, War Department, to Pershing.

Cable A-1123-R. Confidential.
    The Secretary of War has this date accepted the offer of the Secretary of the Navy to furnish in this emergency the infantry and machine gun platoons belonging to one brigade of Marines, it being understood that the transfer of these units will be in Navy transports and that the replacements for the Marines will continue to be furnished by the Navy. March.

NARA, RG 120, M930, Confidential, War Department to AEF, roll 18.

April 18

Pershing's Personal Diary

    At Paris. Worked in quarters and saw Colonel Dawes, Mr. Chappel of the National Magazine, Mr. Brown of the Washington Post and Major Palmer. In afternoon Lord Milner came to see me. He has just been appointed Secretary of War and was on his way to London. Saw M. Clemenceau.

LC, Pershing Papers, Diary, May 7, 1917–September 1, 1918, box 4.

Editor's Note—Charles Dawes, the AEF's General Purchasing Agent, who had proposed a unified approach for the Allied supply systems in his lengthy letter of April 13, had been with Pershing on his recent visit to the 1st Division and Foch's GHQ. During their travels, they had thoroughly discussed Dawes's ideas. Dawes provided additional background on Pershing's meetings with Clemenceau and Lord Milner in his memoirs:

> *Paris, Thursday night, April 18, 1918 (10.30 P.M.)*
> General Pershing sent word (telephone from Colonel Boyd) this evening to come again to his house. I had had another conference with him at his house this noon on the subject of military unification of the entire Allied service of supply along the lines of my April 13 letter. Pershing in the afternoon called on Clemenceau (also Milner). He is to meet Haig tomorrow evening, but has not yet seen him in the matter of the new plan. General Pershing announced to me this evening that he had finally and definitely settled on a demand for the central military control of the Allied supply and transportation system; that he had proposed it to Clemenceau this afternoon; that the latter had immediately accepted it in principle, wondering (he said) why some one had not thought of it before; that Clemenceau had asked for a written statement of the idea for study which he (John) was preparing [see April 19, Pershing to Clemenceau]; that he (John) proposed to name me in his letter to the French to represent him in the formulation of the plan; that Clemenceau and he had agreed to pool for the French and Americans whether the English would come in or not (subject, of course, to approval of the President and War Department); that he (John) would see Haig tomorrow, but whether Haig approved or not would leave for England to urge it on the Government immediately after seeing Haig; that he (John) was preparing a cable to the War Department which he would send tomorrow stating his intentions and reasons and asking approval of the extension of his General Purchasing Board principle (devised by himself) to the Allied service of supply and transportation and of his demand for it [see April 19, Pershing to TAG, War Department, cable P-953-S].
>
> We discussed the matter further. The idea is to put a military control and military methods in the place of civil control and civil methods which have failed. The Supreme War Council has been a supreme failure. Our idea is that a General—one man—must take the place of the Supreme War Council. The latter never gets anywhere. Every reason in the world exists for the creation of an authority sought to be reached by the Supreme War Council. It has failed to exercise it effectively. Therefore its authority must be placed where it can be properly wielded. When this plan goes into effect, it means that military authority must practically control civil activities and civil bodies; that we shall control tonnage as a necessary result of the condition created; that order will come out of this chaos at the rear, and that we shall commence to win the war. (Dawes, *A Journal of the Great War*, Vol. 1, pp. 96–98.)

Alfred Lord Milner became a member of Lloyd George's War Cabinet in December 1916 and soon was a trusted adviser whom the Prime Minister employed on numerous critical diplomatic and military missions. He played a particularly important role after the German spring offensive began. At the Doullens Conference he convinced his friend Georges Clemenceau to support the appointment of Foch as commander-in-chief of the Allied Armies. On April 18, Lloyd George appointed Milner as Secretary of State for War. Source: Library of Congress, Prints and Photographs Division, Bain News Service Collection (LC-DIG-ggbain-31907).

Pershing memorandum.

Conversation with Lord Milner.

Paris, April 18, 1918.

The conversation ran along the general subject of the war. Lord Milner inquired how many divisions we had, mentioning the fact that the First Division was now about to enter the lines near Montdidier. I replied that we had three other divisions in Lorraine serving in the trenches with the French—the 26th, and 42d as complete units, and the 2d by regiments with French divisions. I further stated that the 32d was being assembled and would soon go to a sector for training by regiments. He said that the question of manpower was a very important one just now and would be for the next three months; that they had filled up practically all their losses but would have only about 30,000 replacements per month from now on until August but he (as the Secretary of State for War) would try to increase this to 50,000; their losses had been about 200,000, this in one month, and normally from now on would be 100,000 per month. I asked what number of men he expected from the new law advancing the age for service and including the Irish. He replied that after July they would have altogether about 450,000 men, including the number they could obtain from Ireland in the conscription, and that they must depend upon the United States to keep up their divisions to full strength until that time. He said "You know, I have always approved of your view that you must build up an American army, taking the units you train with us and uniting them with your artillery for that purpose, and you must do that. But in the meantime you can send over your units to help us out until we can get hold of our new reservoir of men. I always approved of Sir Douglas Haig's view that we could build up our depleted divisions with American divisions, by adding American units until the entire division should be American."

"We should probably have to reduce the number of our divisions until the new supply of men becomes available."

[*Ed.*—Lord Milner was a member of Lloyd George's War Cabinet and was appointed Secretary of State for War on April 18 while in Paris replacing Lord Derby, who became British Ambassador to France.]

LC, Pershing Papers, folder: Training and Employment of American Troops with British, box 198.

Secretary of War Baker to Pershing.

... We arrived safely in New York on Tuesday morning at 8 o'clock [April 16], and had a delightful and uneventful voyage. The entire party has the happiest recollections of its visit in France, and I personally cherish the opportunity I had to be with you and to see the wonderful work you and our Army are doing.

The news from France yesterday and today seems quite disconcerting and the situation most serious; but having been through the daily anxiety of the big drive I am now look[ing] for a turn in the tide which seems to come when these great movements have spent their initial force.

LC, Pershing Papers, folder: Newton D. Baker (1918), box 19.

Pershing to TAG, War Department, in part in reply to TAG, War Department, to Pershing, cable A-1111-R, April 16.

Cable P-946-S.
    3. For the Chief of Staff. 3A. With reference to paragraph 1, your cablegram 1111. It is not recommended any change be made in policy heretofore fixed by me. Sisters of men serving in American Expeditionary Forces not desired as workers in any capacity either Y.M.C.A., Red Cross or similar organizations. [Reply—Vol. 6, July 28, A-1525-S-1D]

NARA, RG 120, M930, AEF to War Department, roll 3.

TAG, War Department, to Pershing, in part in reply to Pershing to TAG, War Department, cables P-399-S, December 20, P-465-S, January 9, and P-718-S, March 12 (not reproduced).

Cable A-1128-R.
    1. With reference to your 399, paragraph 4, and 718, paragraph 1J [not reproduced] and 465, paragraph 1, relative to super-heavy artillery program. Ordnance Department has been directed by War Department to furnish you with following material:

    28 Army 5-inch guns and 28 wheeled carriages no spare guns
    92 Army 6-inch guns and 92 wheeled carriages no spare guns
    62 Army 8-inch guns and railway mounts plus 40 spare guns and 22 more will be ordered
    13 Navy 8-inch guns and railway mounts plus 5 spare guns
    54 Army 10-inch guns and railway mounts plus 54 spare guns
    9 Army 12-inch guns and railway mounts plus 3 spare guns
    3 Navy 12-inch guns and railway mounts plus 1 spare gun
    90 12-inch mortars and railway mounts plus 6 spare mortars. . .

Estimated number of rounds that can be fired before relining becomes necessary is as follows:

    5-inch gun 2,000
    6-inch gun 1,800

8-inch gun 1,500
10-inch gun 1,000
12-inch gun 500
12-inch mortar 2,500
14-inch 300

NARA, RG 120, M930, Main Series, War Department to AEF, roll 12.

TAG, War Department, to Pershing, in reply to Pershing to TAG, War Department, cable P-922-S, April 14.

Cable A-1130-R. Confidential.
    1. With reference to paragraph 3, your 922. The 14-inch naval guns railroad mount project consists of 6 locomotives and following cars: 5 gun mounts, 10 ammunition, 5 anti-aircraft, 5 battery headquarters, 5 kitchens, 15 berthing, 5 fuel, 5 workshops, 1 staff, 1 staff kitchen and dispensary, 1 staff radio and spares, 1 staff commissary, 6 construction, 5 crane, 5 sand and timber. Organization of 6 separate trains—5 trains each to include 1 gun car and 1 train to accommodate battery commander and staff.
    1A. Each gun car mounts 1 14-inch, 50 caliber, gun, 2800 F S. [feet per second]. Weight of gun 100,100 pounds, elevation 45 degrees, maximum range 23,000 yards, can fire from regular track up to 15 degrees elevation and range of 23,000 yards.
    1B. Projectile weight 1400 pounds, loaded with 79 pounds TNT, base fuse, 1000 being supplied.
    1C. Weight of gun car complete 475,000 pounds. Ammunition car each accommodates 50 rounds.
    1D. Two guns for each mount available for replacement, anti-aircraft cars mount 2 3-inch guns each, 100 Lewis machine guns, 400 rifles and 400 pistols with full outfit of ammunition and spares being furnished.
    1E. Entire project will be entirely complete and ready for shipment June 1st. Can ship first 14-inch gun mount and sufficient equipment for action May 10th, any [as] necessary. Port of debarkation not yet assigned. March. [Reply—May 6, P-1063-S-1B; in addition—May 8, A-1264-R-7]

NARA, RG 120, M930, Confidential Series, War Department to AEF, roll 18.

TAG, War Department, to Pershing, in part in reply to Pershing to TAG, War Department, cables P-823-S, March 30, and P-907-S, April 13.

Cable A-1132-R.
    1A. With reference to your 823, paragraph 1A [not reproduced]. Increase in troop movements overseas alters situation as indicated in our 834, paragraph 1I.

Factory delivery schedule Browning-Colt light machine rifles as follows: delivered 1400, April 1600, May 2500, June 6000, July 7500, August 10,500, September 12,500, October 12,500, November 12,500, December 10,000. In view of above we request further recommendations regarding prospect of Chauchat caliber 30 cancellation. [Reply—May 6, P-1063-S-3]

NARA, RG 120, M930, Main Series, War Department to AEF, roll 12.

April 19

Pershing's Personal Diary

At Paris. Worked in quarters with General Harbord till 3:30 p. m. Sent letter to M. Clemenceau concerning unity of command in rear [see below]. Also sent cable to Washington re promotions [see below cable P-954-S]. Left Paris at 3:35 with General Harbord and Colonel Boyd. Arrived at Sir Douglas Haig's headquarters at about 8 p. m. After dinner had long talk with Sir Douglas.

LC, Pershing Papers, Diary, May 7, 1917–September 1, 1918, box 4.

Editor's Note—In his *My Experiences in the World War*, Pershing provides more details on his lengthy meeting with Haig:

> While at Sir Douglas' headquarters, he and I reached an understanding as to the training and administration of American troops that were to be temporarily with the British [see April 19, Lawrence, Memorandum of Conversation between Field Marshal Sir D. Haig and General Pershing, Commander-in-Chief, U.S. Army]. In the first place, they were to be allocated by regiments to British skeleton divisions under such a schedule as might be agreed upon. The training staffs of British divisions were to be at the disposal of these regiments, especially for instruction in the use of the rifle and machine gun, and in the handling of gas. After that, and with the approval of their American division commander, each regiment was to be attached to a British division in line, so that each of its three battalions would have the opportunity of serving with one of the British brigades. Our battalions were to be commanded by our own officers, and our regimental staffs were to be attached to those of British brigades. In the next stage, each of our regiments, with its three battalions under the regimental commander, was to act as a brigade in a British division. The final stage would find the four American regiments reunited to form the division under its own officers, with British artillery until the arrival of its own artillery brigade.

In carrying out this scheme, the tendency at first was for British officers actually to assume command of our units in training. Our officers in most cases permitted this to be done until it was checked by my orders, which directed that "American units must be commanded in training by officers and noncommissioned officers who are to command them in battle," and further, that American troops would in all cases be commanded in battle only by Americans.

The program probably expedited preparation in some respects, but questions of food, transport, and methods of instruction arose which demonstrated that any attempt at permanent amalgamation would have surely led to friction and inefficiency. Because they were needed elsewhere, none of the divisions sent to train with the British, except the 27th and 30th, remained long enough to carry out the prescribed course.

The subject of coordination of the supply systems of the armies on the Western Front was also taken up with Sir Douglas. I explained my idea of pooling supplies, and pointed out that he was already committed to the principle, as illustrated by his providing certain equipment and transportation for our divisions that were to serve behind his lines for training. But the proposition of relinquishing control of his supplies, even partially, did not appeal to him. He was afraid that if it should be given general application it would be a one-sided affair. To a certain extent this might have been the result, as we would probably have been the greatest beneficiaries. But if by pooling certain things common to all armies, more tonnage could have been saved to transport our troops and supplies, it would have meant that much more aid to the Allied cause. (Pershing, *My Experiences in the World War*, vol. 2, pp. 3–5.)

Pershing to Clemenceau.

Referring to our conversation of yesterday, permit me to confirm my suggestion that all supplies and war materials that are used in common by the Allied armies be pooled and that the principle be extended as far as possible to the civil populations of the Allies in Europe.

After many disappointments in Allied endeavors to secure coordination in the operation of the Allied armies, we have finally come to recognize the absolute necessity for the appointment of Commander-in-Chief of the Allied armies, with full power to give all necessary directions for unity of command.

The defects of present methods of handling supplies have long been recognized in similar manner, but each of the Allied armies continues to think only in terms of its own requirements independently of the other armies. While it is fully realized that there are many classes of supplies that are used by all the Allies which could be pooled and issued to a particular army as required, a practical solution to the problem has not yet been reached.

I consider this subject of vital importance. The next three or four months are going to be difficult and combatant units from the United States should have every possible ton of shipping that can be saved by utilizing available Allied supplies and materials. The A.E.F. has recently reduced or postponed its requirements in tonnage to the lowest limit to save sea transportation, and a study of the subject leads to the conclusion that our Allies could also do much more than is now being done.

While some attempt has been made through coordinating Allied committees, including the Supreme War Council, these bodies are only advisory and hitherto each has considered only one subject. A bird's-eye view of the whole problem of supply is lacking, and the authority to order the allotment and distribution of supplies to the different armies does not exist. This authority should be vested in a military chief.

The classes of supplies and material that are common to all armies are many, but too much detail should not be undertaken. The subject should be viewed broadly. The following classes of supplies, naturally, would be included: aviation materials, munitions as far as practicable, horses, oats, hay, meat, flour, coal, gasoline, wagons, harness, motor transport, depots, warehouses, lumber and timber. Such concentration or control of supplies would probably result in economy of port construction, especially in storage facilities.

To meet the situation in question, I propose to you the designation of one military chief occupying a position as to supplies and material similar to that of General Foch as to military operations, who shall have authority to decide just what supplies and materials should be brought to France by the Allies and determine their disposition.

May I urge that this matter be given early attention? Permit me to suggest that Colonel Dawes, Purchasing Agent of the A.E.F., be called into consultation with such officers of the French Army as you may designate to discuss this important subject.

Dawes, *A Journal of the Great War,* vol. 1, pp. 280–81; a heavily edited version is at Pershing, *My Experiences in the World War,* vol. 1, pp. 398–99.

Secretary Baker to the President.

Memorandum for The President:
Prior to March 28, 1918, various negotiations had been entered into between the British Government and the United States with reference to the transportation of American troops by Great Britain, in addition to those possible to be transported in American tonnage, and on that date the arrangement substantially stood that Great Britain had agreed to transport the full personnel of six (6) complete divisions (American Army standard size of division) in such a way as not to interfere, by the use of ports or otherwise, with the continuity of the American program of shipping in its own tonnage its troops at a rate not less than two (2) complete divisions per

month. On the 28th of March, 1918, the permanent military representatives with the Supreme War Council adopted unanimously a joint note reviewing the military situation in Europe proceeding from the German concentration and attack, expressing the opinion that "it was highly desirable that the American Government should assist the Allied Armies as soon as possible by permitting, in principle, the temporary service of American units in Allied Army corps and divisions, such reinforcements must however be obtained from other units than those American divisions which are now operating with the French, and the units so temporarily employed must be eventually returned to the American Army." [See March 28, cable 67-S.]

In execution of the foregoing, the permanent military advisers recommended that "until otherwise directed by the Supreme War Council, only American infantry and machine gun units . . . be brought to France, and that all agreements and conventions hitherto made in conflict with this decision be modified accordingly." [See March 28, cable 67-S.] This joint note was submitted to the Supreme Military Council, and the President approved it in the following language:

"The purpose of the American Government is to render the fullest cooperation and aid, and therefore the recommendation of the military representative with regard to the preferential transportation of American infantry and machine gun units in the present emergency is approved. Such units when transported will be under the direction of the Commander-in-Chief of the American Expeditionary Forces and will be assigned for training and use by him in his discretion. He will use these and all other military forces of the United States under his command in such manner as to render the greatest military assistance, keeping in mind always the determination of this Government to have its various military forces collected as speedily as their training and the military situation will permit, into an independent American Army, acting in concert with the armies of Great Britain and France, and all arrangements made by him for their temporary use, training, and service will be made with these ends in view." [See March 29, cable 39-R, reference March 28, cable 67-S.]

Thereafter, March 30, Mr. Lloyd George dispatched to Lord Reading a cable directing him to present to the President urgently the view of the British Government that for a period of four (4) months American infantry and machine gun units should be preferentially transported, and setting up an estimate of the combined capacity of British and American shipping for such transportation aggregating 120,000 troops per month. The arguments by way of inducement for this consisted of a discussion of the available reserves in Great Britain and the length of time necessary to prepare them for replacement use with the existing British divisions. In the language of Mr. Lloyd George's dispatch, he directs Lord Reading to urge that "as the American regiments arrive in France their battalions should be brigaded with the British or French divisions on the same basis as that planned for the infantry of the six (6) divisions," and refers to the recommendation of the military representatives with regard to the preferential shipping of infantry and machine gun units, and concludes: "In the case of the above 120,000 troops, just as was agreed in that of the six (6) divisions, battalions as soon as trained can be re-formed in regiments and sent to General Pershing as he may require."

Thereafter a study of the shipping possibilities was made, and by direction of the Chief of Staff of the War Department the determination of the President with regard to the stimulation of our dispatching of troops was conveyed to the Supreme War Council under date of April 5, which determination covered the shipping of 91,000 troops monthly, beginning April 1, in American transports, British-loaned transports, and British liners; in addition to which Great Britain was to carry 29,000 troops per month, aggregating the total of 120,000. Certain arrangements with regard to cargo tonnage were also set forth in that dispatch, a copy of which was handed to the British and French Ambassadors in the United States and a copy sent to General Pershing.

At a meeting in Paris between General Pershing, Sir Robert Whigham, General Hutchison, and me, the question was raised as to how many troops of those to be transported were to be trained with the British, and an agreement was reached satisfactory to all present, covering only the troops transported in the month of April, of which 60,000 infantry and machine gun personnel were assigned for training with the British; the other 60,000 to be transported in the month of April to be otherwise disposed of by General Pershing; and leaving the question of troops to be brigaded and trained with the British, out of those transported in May, June, and July, to be subsequently disposed of by General Pershing on the theory that he would either continue this basis of division and assignment if the situation continued to justify it, or modify the distribution as the exigencies of the situation require.

Lord Reading, by the direction of Mr. Lloyd George, desires to have definite assurance that the program of 120,000 American troop personnel per month will be maintained for four months, and that the recommendation of the Versailles permanent military representatives with regard to the preferential shipment of infantry and machine gun personnel will be adhered to throughout that period.

By the action of the President upon the joint note of the permanent military representatives, the United States is committed to the preferential transportation in the present exigency of infantry and machine gun personnel. The recommendations of the permanent military representatives, however, stipulated no time for the continuance of that preference, nor do they stipulate numbers.

I recommend that I be authorized to say to Lord Reading:

"Pursuant to the direction of the President and in conformity with his approval of the joint note of the permanent military representatives at Versailles, the United States will continue, throughout the months of April, May, June, and July, to supply for transportation both in its own owned and controlled tonnage, and in that made available by Great Britain, infantry and machine gun personnel. It is hoped, and on the basis of study so far it is believed, that the total number of troops transported will be 120,000 per month. These troops when transported will, under the direction and at the discretion of General Pershing, be assigned for training and use with British, French, or American divisions as the exigencies of the situation from time to time require; it being understood that this program, to the extent that it is a departure from the plan to transport and assemble in Europe complete American divisions, is a concession to the exigencies of the present military situation and is done in order to bring into useful cooperation at the earliest possible moment the largest possible number of American personnel in the military arm most needed by our Allies.

It being also understood that this statement is not to be regarded as a commitment from which the Government of the United States is not free to depart when in its view the exigencies upon which the concession is made no longer require it; and also that the preferential transportation of infantry and machine gun units here set forth as a policy and principle is not to be regarded as so exclusive as to prevent the Government of the United States from including in the troops carried by its own tonnage from time to time relatively small numbers of personnel of other arms as may be deemed wise by the United States, as replacements and either to make possible the use of a maximum capacity of ships or most efficient use of the infantry and machine gun units transported, or the maintenance of the services of supply already organized and in process of construction for the American Army already in France.

These suggestions are made in order that there may be neither any misunderstanding either of the intention of the United States or misconstruction of the execution of that intention, and they are not stipulated as indicating any intention on the part of the United States, until the situation has in its judgment changed, to depart from as full compliance with the recommendation of the permanent military representatives as the nature of the case will permit." [See April 26, cable A-1184-R, and Editor's Note following; also letter, Baker to Pershing, April 29.]

Link (ed.), *The Papers of Woodrow Wilson*, vol. 47: *March 13–May 12, 1918*, pp. 372–76.

Editor's Note—The memorandum that Baker proposed to send to Lord Reading soon became known as the "Baker Memorandum." It grew out of meetings among Wilson, Baker, Chief of Staff March, Lord Reading, and British General Hutchison after the Secretary's return from France on April 16. Lord Reading raised these issues with Wilson on the prompting of Lloyd George and the British War Cabinet earlier in April in an effort to undermine Pershing and his opposition to incorporating American units into British divisions [see Editor's Note following April 7, Baker-Pershing conference with Whigham and Hutchison]. Frederick Palmer, in his biography of Baker, explains how this memorandum came about and its important consequences:

> After Baker's vivid experience of Allied relations in France, a new crop of Allied difficulties formed a part of the accretion of problems on his desk which he could consider in the light of his observations abroad. That ghost of an integral army, which would not down, had been haunting the White House. The President had given no encouragement to Lord Reading that we would continue for three months the program of 120,000 infantry a month to be trained with the British. It had even been reported back to Washington that Baker had agreed to this with British representatives in Paris. Baker had a transcript of his talk at the conference cabled to him [see April 17, cable A-1122-R, and April 19, cable P-955-S]. It showed that he had not

agreed. Baker at once gave Lord Reading what came to be known at the "Baker memorandum."

By this we agreed to go on shipping infantry and machine-gun personnel at the rate of 120,000 a month in April, May, and June, if the British supplied enough additional shipping....

Lloyd George's reply on the same day that Reading transmitted Baker memorandum to him was that "we accept Secretary Baker's memorandum as it stands. Pershing is here [in London] and arranging details with the War Office." Pershing, ambassador on the move as well as general in command, made what was known as the Pershing-Milner [see April 24, cable P-961-S] agreement with Lord Milner, by this time British Secretary of State for War. This was practically the same as the offer that Haig had made four months previously. Six divisions were to be trained with the British. On April 29, after the second German offensive had been stopped and the British were apparently secure in their line in Flanders, Pershing, relentlessly pursuing his object in and out of crises, had the principle of the mobilization of all American divisions into an American Army at the earliest practicable moment accepted at the Abbéville Conference [see below], at which Clemenceau, Milner, Foch, Haig, and Wilson, Chief of the British Staff, were present....

By this time it should have become clear to all concerned, premiers, war ministers, ambassadors, members of Allied missions and generals, that the President and the War Department consistently supported Pershing. There was no other course in principle or policy. (Palmer, *Newton D. Baker*, vol. 2, pp. 168-70.)

Baker later wrote to Pershing and Bliss on April 29 concerning the situation he found upon returning to Washington after this trip to France and Great Britain (see below). In his letter to Pershing, he included a copy of his memorandum to Lord Reading. Writing on June 6 in reply to Pershing's lengthy report of May 9 on the Abbeville Conference (see below), Baker explained in detail the outcome of the sometimes-heated discussions with the British and French on the Milner-Pershing London Agreement and the often confusing back-and-forth among Washington, London, Paris, and Chaumont on these major issues. The outcome was that President Wilson had decided that Pershing would have the final word on troop shipments. In his letter to Pershing, Baker described how this decision came about:

When you and Lord Milner made the so-called London Agreement, the French adopted a more or less concerned attitude, on the ground that the Milner-Pershing agreement was solely for the benefit of the British and made no provision for aid to the French. This, however, is fully set forth in the memorandum which you sent me. Lord Reading and I had had a good deal of conference on this subject and he was constantly pressing upon the President representations from Mr. Lloyd George for larger and larger shipments of infantry. As the result of these various conferences, the President and I drew up the memorandum which I sent you on the subject as being an expression of the intention of the Government of the United States, communicated to the British Government through Lord Reading. Before that reached you, you and Lord Milner negotiated your London agreement. Lord Milner had a copy of the Baker-Reading agreement in his pocket while he was conferring with you, but you had not received your copy at the time. Lord Milner's feeling was that the Baker-Reading statement merely outlined the intention of the American Government in the matter of shipments of troops, but made no definite allotment of any troops to the British. He therefore preferred to work out an independent arrangement with you. We were, therefore, all more or less working without full knowledge of what the other was doing, a situation which I think is inevitable when we are separated by so great a distance, and as soon as I discovered how much confusion was being created I recommended to the President strongly that further agreements on this subject be made only by you, and I said to Lord Reading and Mr. Jusserand [the French Ambassador in Washington] that I would myself make no further agreements on the subject and would suggest that they communicate with Mr. Lloyd George and Mr. Clemenceau, suggesting that Lord Milner and General Foch be asked to confer with you if they had any further suggestions to make on the subject, so that we would have one agreement made at one place, rather than several agreements made in several places which were more or less irreconcilable in some of their terms. (LC, Pershing Papers, folder: Newton D. Baker, January–June 1918, box 20.)

Sims for Raymond B. Stevens, Vice-Chairman, U.S. Shipping Board, U.S. Representative, Allied Maritime Transport Council, London, to Chief of Naval Operations (OpNav), for Edward N. Hurley, Chairman, U.S. Shipping Board, Philip Franklin, Chairman Shipping Control Committee, and Benedict Crowell, Acting Secretary of War. Copies to Bliss, SWC, and Pershing.

Serial No. SM-132.
Very Secret
Ship Mission Number 132. For Secretary of War, Hurley and Franklin only.

We are advised this afternoon by both British and French Governments that the movement of troops and supplies in the Arras District now requires the entire use of the railroad facilities in that region. As a result it is necessary for the present that all shipments of coal from that District be stopped. As stated in our Ship Mission 110 [not reproduced], these mines have been producing 900,000 tons of coal per month. The coal reserves of France are near exhaustion and at least 500,000 tons of coal per month must from now on be shipped to France from England in addition to the amounts heretofore carried. This enlarged movement of coal from England to replace in part the stoppage of coal supply from Northern France is absolutely essential in carrying on the military movements in France.

In our opinion it is not likely that steamers from England will be able to make more than one round trip to France per month with coal although the Ministry of Shipping estimate that they can be turned around in three weeks, which is about the present turn-around. This additional coal movement will therefore require at least 350,000 and possibly 500,000 deadweight tons of shipping. It will be impossible for the British and French to supply the necessary tonnage and in our opinion it is inevitable that help come from American shipping. Any additional ships from America will have to be available for loading in England beginning May 1st. This will require the ordering of American steamers as fast as they complete discharge in France to England in order to load coal.

I expect to get in touch with General Pershing tomorrow either directly or through the French military authorities and you will receive a further message direct from France or from me here. In making your plans, however, you should be prepared to receive a call that cannot be disregarded for tonnage for this most important purpose. Stevens. 22320. SM-132. Sims.

Naval History and Heritage Command, website: Wars, Conflicts, and Operations, World War I, Documentary Histories, April 1918, Sims to CNO, April 20, 1918, original document at NARA, RG 45, DNA, Entry 517B.

Editor's Note—In the copy that Sims sent to Bliss as Serial No. 1981 on April 20, Stevens added the following after quoting the above cable:

> The foregoing cable was sent by me to Washington last night April 19. I am also sending a copy to General Pershing. Stevens 23420. (NARA, RG 120, M923, American Section, SWC, file 30: Correspondence, Reports, and Charts relating to Transportation of U.S. Troops and Supplies to France, document 30-118.)

Pershing's response to the War Department concerning the contents of Stevens cable can be found at April 27, P-1009-S.

Pershing to TAG, War Department, in part in reply to TAG, War Department, to Pershing, cables A-963-R, March 22, A-989-R, March 26, A-995-R, March 27, and A-1077-R, April 10; in addition to Pershing to TAG, War Department, cables P-758-S, March 20, and P-764-S, March 22.

Cable P-950-S.

2. For Chief of Staff. In order to meet immediate requirements of Transportation Department it has been necessary to detach from other organizations large number

of men who are now necessarily carried on rolls of their old organizations as on detached service. This is causing much difficulty when such organizations are moved. As these men will be permanently assigned to Transportation Department it is essential that they be organized into organizations of railway troops. To meet the requirements of the present and of the near future request authority to organize 4 additional battalions of standard gauge railway operation troops of same organization as authorized for 39th, 52nd, 53rd, and 54th Engineers; also 1 standard gauge Transportation Battalion of same organization as authorized for 36th Engineers. In order to enable us to forecast our future requirements, and to determine whether or not it will be possible, in view of the above organizations, to omit certain railway organizations from the later Phases of the Priority Schedule, request you furnish full information as to what railway organizations are already organized in U.S. and which remain to be organized. In view of importance of getting men now on detached service with Transportation Department organized as indicated above, request immediate reply approving organization of units herein requested. [*Ed.*—On May 3 in cable A-1231-R-2, the War Department approved the AEF's request to organize the new units as the 58th, 59th, 64th, and 65th Engineers and the 67th Transportation Battalion without additional personnel.]

2A. Personnel for operating and maintaining our Lines of Communication imperatively needed so that we may supplement serious shortage of men on French railroads and thereby secure more active movement of French rolling stock with corresponding relief in existing car shortage. Cable approximate dates when we may expect Priority Schedule items first phase E 435, E 453A, E 456. Second Phase E 457, E 459, E 460. Also cable if necessary hand tools and other tools and machinery without fail will precede or accompany these troops, giving approximate dates when we may expect them. We are still without roundhouse equipment Item 29 requisition Number 6 of last July, although other branches of service have received and are using shop tools ordered subsequent to our requisition Number 6. Until these arrive and are set up we are unable to furnish assistance so essential to French in handling our troops and supplies. Also cable definitely when we may expect remainder of tools and machinery for Nevers heavy repair shop and for 35th Engineers car erecting shop, large portion of which has not yet reached France. Nothing so imperative as personnel, tools and equipment on order for many months dating back to last July, in the absence of which we are unable to transport our growing volume of troops and supplies. [*Ed.*—On April 28 in cable A-1200-R-1E, 1-F, not reproduced, the War Department reported that the tools and equipment mentioned had been sent to France already or were being ordered or prepared for shipment as quickly as possible.]

2D. With reference to paragraph 1, 2 and 3, your cablegram 963. See paragraph 1C, our cablegram 764. Purchase of animals proceeding satisfactorily.

NARA, RG 120, M930, Main Series, AEF to War Department, roll 3.

Pershing to TAG, War Department, in addition to Pershing to War Department, cables P-228-S, October 19, 1917, P-348-S, December 7, 1917, and P-408-S, December 22, 1917.

Cable P-952-S.
    1. For the Chief of Staff. Conditions found among troops recently arriving in France indicate insufficient attention being paid in United States to training in open warfare relatively too much time being devoted to trench warfare.
    1A. With reference to paragraph 16, my cablegram to 28, paragraph 4, my cablegram 348, in paragraph 1, my cablegram 408. Again strongly urge absolute necessity of making open warfare prime mission training in United States and that training in United States for trench warfare and for specialties for use in trench warfare be keep distinctly in subordinate place.
    1B. Training for trench warfare relatively short process best completed in France in atmosphere of front and with instructors who are familiar latest developments. While trench warfare somewhat complicated so far as work of Staffs is concerned, it makes relatively small demands upon initiative and resource of subordinate commanders and troops. Incidents trench warfare, both in attack and defense, largely foreseen and provided for, so trench warfare assumes character carefully rehearsed routine.
    1C. Open warfare on other hand demands initiative, resource, and decision upon part of all commanders from highest to lowest, requires that all organizations be made into highly developed flexible teams capable rapid maneuvering to meet swift changes in situation.
    1D. Construction efficient divisions for trench warfare therefore relatively short process. On other hand sufficient training to make handy divisions for open warfare matter considerable time. Areas lacking in France for extensive maneuvering and time will not be available after arrival in France. Moreover, greater part special weapons for trench warfare issued troops after arrival in France.
    1E. During this war successful operations across trenches have again and again been nullified because training in open warfare had not been sufficient to give officers and men resource and initiative required for exploitation success.
    1F. Great battle now raging makes certain that too much trench warfare militates against successful conduct great operations. Morale troops long accustomed duty in trenches lowered thereby. When driven into open men have feeling nakedness and helplessness. Current great battle also emphasizes extraordinary value highly trained rifleman and machine gunners.
    1G. Recommend therefore following outline for training United States: Thorough instruction in marksmanship to include known distance firing for all men to 600 yards and battle practice after methods school musketry. Production excellent close order drill to further high discipline. Thorough instruction both officers and men in open warfare. Small units should be thoroughly grounded in patrolling, in all forms of security, and in attack and defense of minor warfare. Problems for such should customarily be prepared by next higher commander.

1H. In training Field Artillery following considered most important: Perfection of mounted instruction over difficult ground and at increased gaits, care of horses, accurate laying by frequent verification and competition, observation of fire with most stress on fundamentals and some advance and lateral observation, manipulation of sheaf, rapid preparation and conduct of fire without maps, rapid reconnaissance and occupational positions under tactical situation, changes of position by echelon, ammunition resupply, telephone. Map laying and refinements of position warfare best taught in France and should be subordinated at home to points emphasized.

1I. During training of small units commanders of divisions, brigades and regiments should be engaged in a series of training exercises involving use brigades and divisions in open warfare. Director for such exercise should be carefully chosen for this competency and should freely criticize. Advisable frequently to conduct these training exercises with framework system of liaison or communication, including infantry and artillery aeroplanes, signal battalion, liaison groups of brigades and regiments. By painstaking use these means considerable progress will be made toward development of brigade and division teams before troops are trained to point where large maneuvers are of value. Finally complete division should be worked out in a series of carefully thought-out maneuvers to accustom all parts and arms to function together.

1J. By means these exercises a maneuvers determination should be obtained as to ability commanders exercise their functions. Prompt elimination of unfits should follow.

1K. Suggest further for education higher commanders establishment at suitable geographical points centers of instruction to which should be sent division brigade commanders infantry and artillery for instruction after methods of Leavenworth, laying stress upon terrain exercises in command and communication or liaison similar several those outlined in preceding paragraphs. By demonstration and practice these centers of instruction should familiarize artillery and infantry with best means for production highly developed teamwork these arms required in modern battle.

1L. Recommend that production staffs be considered function Staff College in France. Plant now operating here working along best lines with assistant excellent instructors Allied Services. Not wise to establish another plant in United States since almost certain teachings 2 institutions would soon diverge.

1M. Suggest further that matter of increasing responsibility and training sergeants be considered. Sergeants need habit command, schooling, and prestige to be able at once replace officer when down. Suggest among means schools be established for sergeants and sergeants be messed separately in organizations and their intercourse with other soldiers be minimized.

1N. Major Requin of French Mission enroute United States has memorandum which in general agrees my idea proper coordination training between United States and France. Broadly France complete training for trench warfare and educate staff; United States train for open warfare and production tactical commanders reducing training trench warfare to distinctly secondary phase and attempting nothing in trench warfare beyond battalion in defense.

[Reply—May 15, A-1317-R-2]

NARA, RG 120, M930, Main Series, AEF to War Department, roll 3.

Pershing to TAG, War Department, in addition to Pershing to TAG, War Department, cable P-904-S, April 12.

Cable P-953-S.
For the Chief of Staff.
   1. The matter of tonnage is so vital to success of Allies that every possible ton is being cut from our requirements during the next 3 or 4 months as already indicated by reductions reported. A careful study of Allied demands for tonnage as a whole makes it evident that further reductions can be made if we pool our supplies that are in common use by Allied armies and certain reductions could also be made in supplies for civil populations of Allied countries. We have at last combined military forces under the supreme command of one man and should do the same thing as to supplies and war material. The appointment of many coordinating boards has led to confusion and loss of positive action. Strongly urge that supply question be placed in the hands of one military head with power to determine and decide on disposition and distribution of Allied supplies in Europe and determine what shall be shipped from United States. Much information necessary for prompt action is already available but no one has power to decide. Supreme War Council comes in the same class with other boards in its lack of power. One man in military control of Allied supplies is necessary. Principle involved is foundation of A.E.F. Purchasing Board. The next 3 or 4 months should at least be covered by this arrangement. The class of supplies such as: Aviation (which has been taken up my cable No. 904); munitions (as far as possible considering different calibres); coal, horses, gasoline, notes, hay meat, flour, shoes, sugar, wagons, tentage, demountable barracks, lumber, timber, supply depots, and warehouses are the principal items that could be pooled. Such pooling would affect material saving in our construction program including railroad construction. Have presented this suggestion to Mr. Clemenceau who approves. Shall go to London Sunday to adjust questions relative to handling our troops that go to British. While there shall submit pooling plan to Mr. Lloyd George. Have designated Colonel Dawes, who made this study, to confer with French representatives to be named by Mr. Clemenceau. Shall report progress later. [Reply—May 3, A-1231-R-4]

NARA, RG 120, M930, Main Series, AEF to War Department, roll 3.

Pershing to TAG, War Department.

Cable P-954-S. Confidential.
   With reference to recent list of promotions to Major General and Brigadier General the policy of the War Department is not understood. It is highly important that

this be made known to the service in general but more especially to those who are called upon to make recommendations. In making my recommendations, efficiency and length of service were both taken into account. The entire list of both brigadier generals and colonels of the line were studied and the views of disinterested officers sought. In pursuance of this policy which is considered the only just one, such men as Eltinge, W. D. Connor, McCoy, Fox Conner and Nolan, whose services here with the A.E.F. stand out preeminently, were not reached for the present because others senior to them were believed efficient and these men were held for later consideration. It is not thought possible that these men are considered by the War Department as less efficient than their juniors who have been promoted. The list shows that the above rule was not followed by the War Department. Such promotions do not make for contentment nor for efficiency and it is earnestly urged that the tasks before us make it imperative that promotions be just and fair and that special cases for promotion of juniors be made only for exceptional efficiency with troops in active service here. It is observed that 25 brigadiers were promoted and that only 17 recommendations were called for from here. Reference to promotion of brigadiers to rank of major general, consider General Traub the best brigade commander in this command and believe him superior to most of the present major generals. It is requested that the above views be brought to the attention of the Secretary of War without delay and that confirmation be suspended until an additional list of deserving officers on duty here whose names were not considered for reasons stated can be submitted. [Reply—April 23, A-1159-R-2]

NARA, RG 120, M930, Confidential Series, AEF to War Department, roll 7.

Pershing to TAG, War Department, in reply to TAG, War Department, to Pershing, cable A-1122-R, April 17.

Cable P-955-S. Confidential.
For the Secretary of War.
Reference your cable No. 1122, paragraph 1.

Following is report of conference [April 7, 1918]: General Whigham stated that he had come to discuss arrangements for carrying out the agreement of the Supreme War Council dated March 27th whereby American infantry and machine gun units are to be given priority of shipment, according to the present understanding the British will be able to ship 60,000 troops per month and the Americans 60,000 making a total of 120,000 men per month beginning with the month of April. The Secretary of War said that no figures were mentioned in the Versailles agreement [Joint Note No. 18]. General Whigham suggested that a certain proportion of infantry would necessarily have to be kept apart as replacement troops and that these replacements would probably be landed in England, whereas the fighting troops could be sent directly to France. General Pershing stated that the American idea had been that this infantry should go to British units for training and, as soon as trained, was to be replaced by other infantry and that he had not consider the subject of replacements for troops while on this period of training. Secretary of War stated that he had understood that the infantry and machine gun units were to be sent to the British for training and that as soon as trained they were to be replaced by others; that in the event of an emergency, they were to fight and that, in this case, he saw no necessity for replacements. A discussion followed as to the recommendation of the Versailles conference [Joint Note No. 18]. General Whigham insisted on the necessity for replacing at once small losses while American units are with the British troops; he suggested having a small proportion of the reserves in France and the remainder in England. He stated that the British did [it] this way and they would handle the American reserves in the same way; and shipping across the channel is very uncertain and therefore a small proportion of reserves should be in France. Secretary of War inquired as to the origin of this figure of 120,000 troops per month, and called attention to the fact that there been no obligation on the part of the Americans to send any number of troops or for any particular period. He did not think it was clear that the original 6 division decision was annulled by the Versailles agreement [Joint Note No. 18]; that the Versailles agreement simply was to the effect that American infantry and machine gun units should be given priority of shipping until further orders and that this further order might come tomorrow. General Whigham stated that interpretation of the British War Office was that the Versailles agreement [Joint Note No. 18] wiped out all previous agreements and that it is now a question of sending infantry and machine gun units be trained with the British, French and Americans, the proportion to go to each army to be decided later. The Secretary of War stated that what is pertinent to the present discussion is American troops going to the British for training; that he did not want the British public or the British Army, or the French public or French Army to have an exaggerated idea that this scheme provides or will provide a means by which their losses are be made up in the future; that he does not want any feeling of disillusionment when General Pershing calls for the return of the troops entrusted to these armies for training. General Whigham stated that this was thoroughly understood by the British. He then outlined a scheme for placing American battalions in line, later uniting them as American regiments and still later as brigades and so on. General Pershing asked what would become of the British divisions when, in a month or so, American troops serving with them are withdrawn. General Whigham stated he hoped these troops would not be withdrawn so soon; that when this does happen, some British divisions will be broken up; that they also hope to get 400,000 or 500,000 troops through conscription. He talked of the gradual increase of American personnel divisions to such a point when all the infantry might be American and the artillery British. He stated that at some such period the division would be considered an American division and that there was no reason why British artillery should not serve in American divisions. General Pershing stated that if the 120,000 men, infantry and machine gun units, per month were shipped for 3 months, this would make 360,000 men, that it would take several months to bring over the additional men to build up divisions around these infantry and machine gun organizations, as more than that many additional personnel would be required to make complete divisions; that the proposition for bringing over infantry and machine gun units should have to be considered as a temporary measure and also that other units would have to be brought over. Secretary of War stated that he wished the British to understand that when the Americans decide to discontinue the Versailles agreement [Joint Note No. 18] that the British will be notified. General Whigham ask what proportion of the first 60,000 men to be brought over by the British might the British count on having for the present. General Pershing stated that they should have all of them. General Whigham insisted on the necessity of bringing them over in organized units; he stated that it is understood that these men are to come over as completely clothed and equipped as possible; that what is necessary to make up any deficiencies in clothing and equipment will be supplied by the British. The Secretary of War insisted that the uniforms must be American. It was also stated that land transportation furnished for use of these troops will be kept by them and passed over to the Americans by the British when these troops are replaced in American divisions. The Secretary of War resuméd the conclusions of the meeting as follows: "That it is agreed by General Pershing that the 60,000 men to be brought over by the British in April will be turned over to the British; the disposition of troops to be brought over in the month of May will be determined later; that the 60,000 troops to be brought over in April and turned over to the British shall include 20,000 replacement troops; that these troops are to be trained in accordance with the agreement between General Sir Douglas Haig and General Pershing; and the disposition of all troops be brought over by the British shall be fixed by General Pershing and the British War Office; that the land transportation to be turned over by the British to the American troops is to be kept by these troops; that clothing for these troops is to be furnished by the Americans as far as possible and any deficiencies are to be made up by the British; that the British are to furnish machine guns for the machine gun units and any units which they cannot supply with machine guns will be turned back to General Pershing".

NARA, RG 120, M930, Confidential Series, AEF to War Department, roll 7.

Pershing to TAG, War Department, in part in reply to TAG, War Department, to Pershing, cable A-1090-R, April 12.

Cable P-956-S.
2. For Chief of Staff. With reference to paragraph 12, your cablegram 1090 [*Ed.*— Cable A-1090-R-12 asked for details about press reports that German propaganda "alleges Americans poor fighters, distrusted by Allies"]. German propaganda has used such stories persistently in effort to stir up distrust and dissension among Allies. In some case facts have been distorted as for example when unarmed working parties were captured and this was played up as capture of combat troops. In most cases stories are completely false. Following are examples of German wireless news "March 5th the Americans recently captured had been placed with French troops in the Front lines for training purposes. They were caught in the attack of Badenese and Thuringian assault troops which was made after a short drum fire and surrendered without offering much resistance. They came from the state of Connecticut. They are

strong young fellows but do not seem to have much desire to fight. They have no understanding of the war. To them it is an enterprise undertaken by New York financiers. They hate but respect the English. With the French they are on good terms. They have not slightest idea of military operations and seem stupid and fatalistic in comparison with the war accustomed French men. They were badly shaken from the violence of the German attack and were glad to escape further fighting. March 29th French officers do not conceal their disillusionment over the value of the veteran American troops and are using them by battalions and larger units among the English and French infantry. They are entirely incapable of carrying out independent operations. April 5th That American troops are being distributed by regiments among the English and French troops shows the slight confidence which the Entente places in the fighting ability and leadership of the Americans. While Belgians, Portuguese, and Colonial troops are fighting in larger independent units the Americans must serve merely as filling for French and British units."

Distribution of propaganda is attempted by small balloons sent across with favoring wind also printing of cleverly imitated Italian papers for distribution back of Italian front also circulation of stories by enemy agents. These efforts having scant success.

NARA, RG 120, M930, Main Series, AEF to War Department, roll 3; War Department to AEF, roll 12.

Pershing to TAG, War Department, in part in reply to TAG, War Department, to Pershing, cable A-1066-R, April 8.

Cable P-958-S.
    1. For Chief of Staff. With reference to paragraph 8, your cablegram 1066. Montrose sailed before requisition was approved. She is too large for our cross-channel purposes. Navy authorities advise that it is dangerous to sail large or fast ships in this service. We require slow small steamers for this service. Shipping Board in Washington have details of our requirements. Please confer with them and advise us any definite steps taken to fulfill our needs. [Reply—April 26, A-1182-R-5]

NARA, RG 120, M930, Main Series, AEF to War Department, roll 3.

Pershing to TAG, War Department, in part in reply to TAG, War Department, to Pershing, cable A-1009-R, March 30, in addition to Pershing to TAG, War Department, cable P-608-S, February 16.

Cable P-964-S.
    4. For Chief Signal Officer. With reference to paragraph 2D, your cablegram 1009. Reasons for putting into production in the United States 2 types of night bombers were fully set forth in paragraph 6, our cablegram 608, which decision was

approved by the Inter-Allied Aviation Committee and Joint Army and Navy Aircraft Committee. England has gone to great expense in preparing to assemble in England our Handley Page parts for 30 squadrons during 1918 and 1919 and no change should be made in these plans which have been approved by the Commander in Chief, A.E.F. We plan to assemble at Air Production Center Number 2 [Romorantin] Handley Page parts which are shipped as spares direct to France. We also plan to assemble complete Caproni aeroplanes from parts shipped from the United States. Recommend that the Italian order for 1,000 sets Caproni parts be taken over by us it being understood that these planes are to have Liberty motors. We recommend that first 10 be assembled in States and defects corrected. That after these have been assembled shipments begin in groups of 10. First shipment should be preceded or accompanied by at least one man familiar with each stage of assembly work. By July we expect to be able to take care of 10 per month and 20 in August. Cannot make an estimate beyond that time as output here depends on too many unknown factors. Recommend your production try for output in States of at least 20 by end of May, 35 in June and increase as rapidly as possible up to 75 per month. Advise fully what your plans are and what your output for overseas can be. Will advise fully concerning equipment, material and personnel after Allen returns from Caproni plant in Italy and after receipt of your statement of the output in America. Your estimate for overseas should be based on minimum probable output otherwise we will divert energy that should be used for other purposes. This item is very important as we have concentrated labor and the materials on projects to take care of deliveries expected from your estimates and as a result other important features of Air Service have been gravelly handicapped. [Reply—May 6, A-1249-R-2]

NARA, RG 120, M930, Main Series, AEF to War Department, roll 3.

April 20

Pershing's Personal Diary

At British G.H.Q. Left at about 10:30 a. m. with General Harbord, Colonel Boyd, Colonel Bacon and Captain Morton, A.D.C. to Sir Douglas. Stopped at Fruges and had talk with Colonel Simonds, Chief of Staff of 2nd Corps. He explained the dispositions taken with reference to the arrival of the Corps. The 77th Division has already almost 5,000 men landed. Saw there Colonel Waldron and Captain Aleshire.

From there went to Nordausques area, Recques, the Château de Recques (Cocove), Headquarters 77th Division. Saw General [Evan M., Jr.] Johnson temporarily commanding brigade and his Chief of Staff, Colonel [Ewing M.] Booth. Stayed there for luncheon. General Johnson, who seems to have great confidence in this National Army Division, stated that he had had some 58,000 men assigned at some time or other to the division and was bringing over some 30,000. He called attention to the labor and delay to instruction occasioned by having men thus pass through the division instead of having two or more divisions designated to furnish details, odd men, etc., so that the other divisions might go on uninterrupted with their instruction.

From there we went to Chamblain l'Abbe, where I met General Sir A. W. Currie, K.C.B., K.C.M.G., commanding the Canadian Corps. I also met his Chief of Staff, General Weber, and his Chief Engineer Officer, General Lindsay. General Currie spoke with considerable feeling over the fact that Passchendaele is now being given up so easily when last year he was told it must be taken at any cost, and it cost 16,000 good Canadians, but they took it. He thought the Boche capable of making another formidable push, but did not seem to think it dangerous. He said the Canadians are holding 9,000 yards front, about, per division; that if they would give him 7,000 or less per division and one-third of his forces in reserve he did not believe the Germans capable of breaking through his front. He seemed very kindly disposed toward Americans and speaks like an American. We returned to Sir Douglas Haig's headquarters at about 7 p. m. After dinner I had a talk about American troops to serve with British units with Sir Douglas, his Chief of Staff, General Lawrence, General Harbord, and Lord Derby, who had just been relieved as Minister of War. General Harbord made notes of the agreements reached.

LC, Pershing Papers, Diary, May 7, 1917–September 1, 1918, box 4.

Editor's Note—Pershing does not mention that when he and Harbord visited the 77th Division, which had arrived late in March 1918 and was now training with the BEF, he spoke with his old friend, Maj. Lloyd C. Griscom. At that time Pershing clearly was considering Griscom to be his liaison officer to the British and/or French, but he had not yet finally decided and did not offer him such a position. Griscom, *Diplomatically Speaking*, pp. 383–84.

Memorandum of Conversation between Field Marshal Sir D. Haig and General Pershing, Commander-in-Chief, U. S. Army.

Lt. Gen. H. A. Lawrence, Chief of General Staff, BAF.

O. B./2196

It was agreed that American troops arriving in France should be disposed of as follows:

On arrival, American divisions would be allocated for training as agreed upon by the respective staffs to English cadre divisions. The training staff of the English divisions to be at the disposal of the American regiments for instruction in English rifle, Lewis and machine guns, gas precautions, and details of various kinds.

As soon as approved by the American divisional commander, each American regiment will be attached to an English division in the line so that one American battalion will be attached to each of the 3 brigades of the English division. The American battalion will be commanded by its own officers and will work as part of the

English brigade. The staff of the American regiment will be attached to the staff of an English brigade for instruction. In the next stage the American regiment (3 battalions) under its own commander will be attached as a brigade to an English division. Finally, the American regiments will be grouped again as a division under their own commander. The Field Marshal will be prepared when this stage is reached to place the artillery of an English division, up to 6 divisions at present, at the disposal of the C-in-C, American army, until such time as either the American divisional artillery arrives or the English cadre divisions are made up to full strength.

[*Ed.*—This agreement between Field Marshal Haig and Pershing is repeated almost verbatim in paragraph 3 of Pershing's cable P-961-S, April 24, from London to the Secretary of War and Chief of Staff laying out the Lord Milner-Pershing London Agreement.]

LC, Pershing Papers, folder: Conferences and Agreements, Folder No. 1, box 50; see also *USAWW*, Vol. 3, pp. 90–91.

Bliss, Chief, American Section, and Permanent Military Member, SWC, Versailles, to Secretary of War Baker.

[Weekly Letter No. 2]

Since sending my last letter by courier to Brest a week ago today not much has happened of which you have not been kept advised by cable. . . .

You have learned from General Pershing's despatches about the movement of the First American Division (Bullard's) which for a few days was in reserve at Gisors, southeast of Beauvais. I have been informed from Foch's headquarters that it now going to take position on the French line with their Third Army at Fontaine sous Montdidier, near Montdidier. It was yesterday morning reported in the vicinity of Froissy en march to its final position. I believe this division will give a good account of itself.

The transfer of this first American Division, with the possibility that it may be followed by others, to a point north of Paris, brings up what the Inter-Allied Transportation Council thinks may be a rather serious question in regard to the supply system for our army. M. Clemenceau sent for me a few days ago to speak about it, in connection with a proposed temporary suspension or check in the movement of our troops pending the transportation of additional American rolling stock. I told him that I thought that the suspension of bringing troops to France, at least our infantry and machine gun units, even for a month would be unnecessary and unwise provided the French could supply us with temporary billets at or in the immediate vicinity of our ports of debarkation on the Atlantic coast. If necessary, they would wait in those places, where the minimum of rail transportation would be required, until a crisis should develop—if it does develop—when there is no doubt that these troops would be moved to the front to meet such a crisis regardless of any difficulties in the way of rail transportation. The French and English both think that if a real crisis would come it will be at the end of perhaps four or five weeks from now, provided the Germans are able to continue their heavy assaults which, although costly to themselves, are also costly to the Allies. If the crisis comes it will be solely due to the lack of men to make up for casualties. If we could have a considerable force of fairly well-trained infantry on the coast when such a time should come, it will be a thing greatly to be desired.

Last Wednesday I took lunch with General Spiers (head of the British Mission in Paris) and Mrs. Spiers and there learned of the death of Major Bolling who had been missing for the past two weeks. It seems that sometime late on March 28 he left Amiens in a small motor car which he drove himself and alone. News came from the Hague, on information received from the Germans, that they had found Major Bolling on the 29th—being presumably enroute to Paris—at a point where he had come under machine gun fire, and was dead, shot through the heart. It seems they buried him there but, having learned from papers on his person who he was, they sent word as indicated. . . .

LC, Bliss papers, folder: General Correspondence—Bliss to Newton Diehl Baker, December 1917–May 1918, box 250.

Bliss, Chief, American Section, and Permanent Military Representative, SWC, Versailles, to March, Acting Chief of Staff, Washington.

* * * * * *

You already know from the urgent requests of our Allies that what they now want is men, men, and still more men. I am fully convinced, and it is the unanimous opinion of the American section here, that the quickest and most effective way for us to bring our manpower to bear is in the way now proposed, to wit: To send over our infantry and machine-gun units for an indefinite time. I believe they can very soon be formed into brigades and will in the near future constitute the complete infantry of a certain number of British and French divisions. From the brigade commanders who will thus gain their experience and be tried out, we will get the commanders for American divisions to be formed out of our troops loaned to the British and French as soon as the present emergency is over, provided this emergency is to be followed by another campaign. If another campaign follows this one, I believe that in that way we will secure most quickly and effectively a well-trained and independent American army, and if this campaign is not followed by another one, we will have avoided the horrible conclusion of having the war end without our having taken an effective part in it.

The war as now conducted is a matter of brutal arithmetic. One side defends and the other attacks. The defense losses 50,000 men and the attack 75,000. In the old days, after such a result, one side would pack its baggage and return to Berlin and the other would return to London and Paris. Today they simply gain their breath while bringing up replacements to fill up the vacancies. Tomorrow there is again a loss of 50,000 on one side and 75,000 on the other. If a time should come when the defense has used up its last 50,000 men while the attack still had 50,000 or 75,000 men left, the latter has a walkover. That is all there is to it. The British and French seem to think that the crisis will come in four or five weeks, when the former say they will have used up practically all their replacements.

This question of the ability of England to supply more than a certain number of replacement troops is a rather burning one. I have urged the British Military Representative here to represent to his Government the necessity for furnishing the Government in Washington with an absolutely accurate and reliable statement of the disposable forces still in the United Kingdom. Last February, when we were studying the question of the proper strength and organization of an Inter-Allied General Reserve, the British Section here furnished me with the following statement:
"Secret
British Army at Home.
Jan, 28th, 1918.
Total number of men with columns in United Kingdom   1,416,658
Made up as follows:

1. In office at headquarters		
Of which "B" men	1,285	1,579
" " "D" men	6	
2. Preparing for Overseas		12,389
Of which "B" men	2,405	
" " "D" men	272	
3. Home Service		483,954
Of which "B" men	345,682	
Of which "D" and "E" men	25,403	
4. Reserves under training		593,340
Of which "B" men	139,194	
Of which "D" and "E" men	64,521	
5. Depots		216,674
Of which "B" men	18,144	
Of which "D" and "E" men	175,945	
6. Command Depots		61,563
Of which "B" men	326	
Of which "D" and "E" men	57,913	
7. Administrative		77,159
Of which "B" men	32,025	
Of which "D" and "E" men	3,431	

Total by Categories:	"A"	550,025
	"B"	539,061
	"D" and "E"	327,481

Of the "A" men 171,036 are A.iv youths under 19 years.

"A"—Fit for general service.

"B"—Not fit for general service, but fit for service at home (and abroad in the case of men passed fit for service Overseas).

"D" and "E"—Either temporarily unfit for service in Categories "A" or "B" but likely to become fit within six months *or* unfit for Categories "A" and "B" and unlikely to become fit within six months.

Approximate number of "A", "B", "D" and "E" men serving in Ireland:

"A"	10,619—	4,753 are A.iv men.
"B"		8,889
"D" and "E"		<u>1,412</u>
		20,920"

I am not authorized to communicate the foregoing to you officially, nor do I suppose that at this moment it is at all correct; but I am quite sure that a new statement will not show a larger number of effectives available for service on the continent, nor will it so, show until the new manpower bill has had time to operate. General Hutchinson of the British Army must have reached Washington about the time that the Secretary of War did and you could ask him to supply the statement desired.

* * * * * *

NARA, RG 120, M923, American Section, SWC, file 342: Letter of Apr. 20, 1918, discussing American and Allied manpower.

Pershing to TAG, War Department, in part in reply to TAG, War Department, to Pershing, cable A-1077-R April 10.

Cable P-965-S.

5. For Van Deman [G-2]. With reference to paragraph 9, your cablegram 1077. The Commander in Chief and Staff here have no means of keeping in touch with American sentiment and public opinion except from newspapers received 4 to 6 weeks after publication. This is unfortunate from many aspects particularly as regards press censorship which cannot be exercised intelligently without full knowledge of conditions at home. Knowing them we could often assist in strengthening the position of the Government. Kind of information desirable will be found by reference to our General Staff Press Review, copies of which can be had at War College in articles reviewing American Press written here. Suggest semi-weekly cable along

those lines. In addition enterprising American Newspapers often print important articles on Russia, Allied, Neutral and enemy countries which European newspapers do not secure. Clippings should be sent by mail. It should be remembered that all European press is under strict censorship and that news printed here of America as well as all other countries is the news the respective governments want published and nothing else. [Reply—May 3, A-1235-R-3]

10D. With reference to paragraph 2, your cablegram 1106. Your interpretation is correct.

NARA, RG 120, M930, Main Series, AEF to War Department, roll 3.

Pershing to TAG, War Department, in part in reply to TAG, War Department, to Pershing, cable A-1001-R, March 28.

Cable P-970-S.

1. For Chief of Staff. With reference to paragraph 4, your cablegram 1001. We concur advisability using smaller and slower vessels for channel coal service. Recommend such suitable vessels be given us in place Kerwood, Kerkanca, Jupiter, Frederick Luckenbach and Louis K. Thurlow. Our maximum average monthly coal requirement will soon aggregate 150,000 tons. We should prepare accordingly. We are required transport coal to France April 65,000 tons, May 75,000 tons, June 90,000 tons. [Reply—April 30, A-1205-R-2B]

NARA, RG 120, M930, Main Series, AEF to War Department, roll 3.

TAG, War Department, to Pershing, in part in reply to Pershing to TAG, War Department, cable P-907-S, April 13.

Cable A-1143-R.

3. Chief Signal Officer requests authority to organize and send to France a permanent Intelligence Department to supply him with "accurate and dependable information regarding aeroplane designs, construction and other important and necessary information". Your views on this proposition are desired. March. [Reply—April 28, P-1016-S-3D]

8. For General Atterbury. 8A. Your 907, paragraph 2A. Hanson advises that capacity of plant(s) at Saintes and La Garenne is 25 cars per day each which would give total of 1500 cars per month erected by the 2 plants. [Reply—May 9, P-1080-S-7]

NARA, RG 120, M930, Main Series, War Department to AEF, roll 12.

April 21

Pershing's Personal Diary

At British G.H.Q. Went to British Headquarters and had talk with General Lawrence [Chief of Staff] and General Coxe [Chief of Intelligence, BAF] and Colonel Nolan who happened to be visiting headquarters at same time. Visited office of Colonel Bacon and Major Quekemeyer. Lunched with Colonel Bacon and left for London via Boulogne with General Harbord and Colonel Boyd. Lieutenant Adamson joined us at Boulogne. Left Boulogne on regular boat at 2:30 p. m., and arrived at Folkestone at about 4:15. Were met there by General Biddle and Colonel [Harry] Rethers [Chief Quartermaster, Base Section No. 3]. Arrived London at 7 p. m. Stopped at Savoy Hotel. Had dinner there. Was somewhat annoyed because orchestra struck up "The Star Spangled Banner" as I entered restaurant; every one stood up and made me feel conspicuous. A very gay place and little like anything I have seen in France—people very dressed up and no signs of food shortage. We had oysters, soup, salmon, chicken, asparagus and soufflé, all on a regular menu card. Met at Folkestone Mr. Stevens and Mr. [L. H.] Shearman of the Shipping Board. They are much excited over coal situation and are disposed to interfere with shipping of troops in order to send coal from England to France. [See April 19, Sims for Stevens to Hurley, et al., cable Ship Mission 132.]

LC, Pershing Papers, Diary, May 7, 1917–September 1, 1918, box 4.

Foch, CINC, Allied Armies, to President of the Council and the Minister of War (Clemenceau).

No. 316.

I have the honor of submitting to you a memorandum attached hereto which sums up:

1. The existence of the available American forces in France.
2. The program of arrivals of American divisions.
3. The measures to be taken to have more infantry arrive than our artillery resources allow to be utilized immediately and fewer American artillery or service troops.

If you share in the view considered in this memorandum, I request you to take it up with the American Government at once.
[Enclosure]

General Staff	Headquarters Allied Armies
No. 314	*April 21, 1918.*

April 1918   287

Memorandum of the American Army
I. As of April 20:
The American Army has the following troops in France:
The I Army Corps, complete, comprising 6 divisions, of which: 4 are at the front, the 1st in Debeney's army, 3 others (Nos. 2, 26, 42) in quiet sectors:

1 (No. 32) will have its 4 infantry regiments assembled in the region of Is-sur-Tille on April 22,[1] where they will enter French divisions in turn to complete their training and participate in the employment of the divisions.

1 (No. 41) is just a depot; responsible for the maintenance of the others, it cannot be considered as a combatant force.

To sum up, 5 divisions are used:
4 of which are employed as divisions (infantry and artillery), nucleus of the American Army, representing a strength of	108,000
1 whose infantry will reinforce French divisions (provisionally at least)	16,000
In addition, 2 Negro regiments are serving in the French divisions	7,000
	131,000

Thus, of a total strength of 335,000 Americans[2] present in France on April 1, 131,000 are combatant troops, and of these, 23,000 infantry are reinforcing French divisions for the time being.

II. 3 divisions are in the process of being shipped:

1 of the II Army Corps, which is being shipped in British bottoms and whose 6 divisions, as far as the infantry is concerned, are intended for employment in the British army. This is the 77th Div., 5,000 men of which have already arrived.

2 of the III Army Corps, being shipped in American bottoms and intended for the French front. These are the 3d Div., whose entire infantry has landed in France, and the 5th Div., just announced. The infantry of these two divisions will be placed in French divisions[3] within 3 to 5 weeks.

According to information received from General Pershing's staff, the artillery and services of these divisions would be shipped immediately after the infantry.

Such is the program for April. As can be seen, probable shipments totaling 100,000 men will only give the combined British and French armies the infantry of 3

---

1. The artillery of this division will receive its training at Camp-de-Souges.
2. The remainder is comprised approximately as follows:

Artillery, engineers, aviation, etc.	76,000
Noncombatants	107,000
Miscellaneous serving in the British and French Armies	23,000

3. Under the conditions indicated above for the American 32d Div.

divisions or: 16,000 x 3 = 48,000 infantry, without counting the complements in artillery and services, for which there is little need.

III. Program for the following months:

If, as information from the American General Staff seems to indicate, the same method of shipment continues to be used, each of the months of May and June will permit the shipment of 3 divisions under similar conditions: Infantry first, then artillery.

Just as the method used in April, it will only supply the combined British and French armies with 48,000 infantry, in addition to complements in artillery and services which are of no use for the time being.

Thus, the second quarter of 1918 will only add 48,000 x 3 = 144,000 infantry to the Allied armies.

Consequently, there will be 60,000 to 70,000 men for the British and French armies each.[4]

These results, taken in the light of the momentous crisis in numerical strengths which the Allied armies face, are too ineffective for words.

First of all, the British army, which has lost 220,000 men and which already lacks the resources to replenish 9 of its divisions, will not benefit before September by the new laws that have been passed, and meanwhile the only aid they would receive during the three months of battle to come would be 70,000 American infantry; and the same applies to the French army, the bulk of whose forces will enter the battle in its turn.

Therefore, the matter of prime importance today is for the American army to furnish immediately a quantity of infantry sufficient to bridge this crisis.

This result can be attained if the order of shipments is changed, if priority is given to shipments of infantry and machine-gun units and if this principle of priority is applied not to a period of one month (that, in reality, is of no advantage, since the advance in infantry gained during the first half of the month is lost during the second because of the shipment of artillery), but to a period of 3 months, that is to say, if during the 3 months to come only infantry and machine-gun units are shipped.

The results obtained by this procedure can be calculated as follows:

Thanks to the means of shipping available, British as well as American, 59,000[5] men were shipped from America to France during the first half of April—this permits us to count on shipping 100,000 to 120,000 men per month.

---

4. And still, in the mind of General Pershing, this aid is momentary, since he has the intention of regrouping these infantry units in divisions as soon as possible; it is for this purpose that he has them followed by artillery. Nevertheless, it does not seem advisable at the present time to enter into a discussion on the question of the time during which this infantry will remain in the Allied divisions; the important thing is for it to be there.

5. But the number of infantry shipped is greatly reduced proportionately:

Last week of March 1,800 infantrymen out of 17,000
First week of April 4,500 infantrymen out of 21,000

[*Ed.*—This document has been slightly rearranged to facilitate its publication.]

Thus, in the period of three months a total of 300,000 to 350,000 infantry would be obtained, which would allow an addition of 150,000 to 200,000 infantry to be made to the British and French armies each.

The Allies need these troops if they are to win the battle. Moreover, they have sufficient artillery and ammunition.

In the attached Joint Note No. 18 of March 27, by the military representatives of the Supreme War Council, General Bliss, permanent military representative at Versailles, has already considered and recommended to his government this manner of serializing shipments.

The American Government seems to have adopted these recommendations on March 31, as General Bliss' memorandum of April 2, attached hereto testifies.

However, General Pershing, his mind set on commanding a large American army as soon as possible, without thoroughly examining present necessities and wishing to have fully constituted divisions, urges that the artillery and services of each group of 3 divisions be shipped as soon as the infantry of these three divisions is transported.

This being the case and to put an end to any doubts in the matter, it is necessary to inform the American Government of our needs and the manner in which they can be met more fully.

After having explained to the American Government:

That the measures recommended are necessary in order for America to give her Allies the proper military aid which they need at this time;

That these measures will not interfere with the autonomy of the American army in the future, but will only retard its realization;

That it will in no way impede the American army's organization of bases and transportation lines, as the army now has at its disposal a sufficient number of men of the various services to assure this organization.

Therefore, it is expedient that the American Government be requested at once that during the coming three months there be transported to France in British as well as American bottoms, only *infantry and machine-gun units.*

USAWW, vol. 2, pp. 337–39; *Les armées françaises dans la Grande guerre, Tome 6*, vol. 2, *Annexes*, vol. 1: *Annexe* No. 43, pp. 107–10 (No. 314), and *Annexe* No. 44, p. 110 (No. 316).

Pershing to TAG, War Department, in part in reply to TAG, War Department, to Pershing, cables A-1062-R, April 7, A-1094-R, April 13, and A-1096-R, April 14.

Cable P-973-S.

1. For Chief Signal Officer. With reference to paragraph 1H, your cablegram 1062, and paragraph 1I, your cablegram 1094. Will the production of 180-horsepower Hispano Suiza engines be interfered with by contracts placed by French

or English? If not, we strongly recommend production of this motor for our needs this year on following basis: June 200, July 225, August 234, September 273, October 237, November 361, and December 300, total 1830. Paragraph 1I, your cablegram 1094. Guarantee should be obtained from British Mission that the 200 SE 5 planes offered will be held for us if we arrange to furnish these engines. Believe that most satisfactory method is for production of engines to be provided for on basis of quantities given in above and that we make contracts monthly as engines are freighted. This will enable each shipment of engines to be delivered by us to either French or English as status of plane manufacture renders most desirable. Our contract for 300 Sopwith Camels which has been reduced 45% by British due to delay in French deliveries of motors for same and the British requirements indicates that it will be more desirable for us to place motors month by month in accordance with conditions existing at the time motors are ready for shipment. The situation with reference to single-seater fighters for the remainder of 1918 is as follows: Both France and England have a plane production in excess of their engine production and as the 180-horsepower Hispano Suiza is already in production in the States in small quantities, our only practical means of securing the necessary number of single-seater fighters will be for the production of this engine for overseas duty to be increased so as to provide the numbers indicated and for us to distribute these engines here month by month as conditions require. The entire question of the provision of single-seater airplanes for 1918 and 1919 is being thoroughly investigated and a comprehensive report will all necessary data will be forwarded by an officer familiar with the entire situation. [Reply—May 1, A-1214-R-2]

2. For Chief of Ordnance. With reference to paragraph 1L, your cablegram 1096. Replacements of losses occurring on the 50 improvised 75-mm anti-aircraft guns can be secured in France. Replacements of losses on the 51 75-mm anti-aircraft guns on truck mounts must come from America. 30 rounds is the present calculated expenditure per fire a day for all 75-mm anti-aircraft guns in service with AEF. Additional quantities of anti-aircraft gun equipment may be required in the future because of expansion in our operations, we cannot discount these requirements at present.

NARA, RG 120, M930, Main Series, AEF to War Department, roll 3.

TAG, War Department, to Pershing, in part in reply to Pershing to TAG, War Department, cable P-739-S, March 16.

Cable A-1151-R.
   3. For General Atterbury. We now understand that you wish us to provide a complete car building plant including dry kiln, powerhouse for planing mill and with limited blacksmith shop equipment including hand tools for wooden underframe 20-ton box cars with a capacity of 30 cars per day, to be operated by the Belgian Government, we to furnish all metal parts for which you will send us drawings and lists

that you are preparing ad that the original order will cover 10,000 cars. [Reply—May 11, P-1094-S-7]

3A. We also understand in addition to these that you will have constructed near Bordeaux 6,000 20-ton wooden underframe box cars and that we will be expected to furnish all metal parts at rate of 500 cars per month; we will not be required to furnish any hand tools or shop equipment. Your 739, paragraph 1D, indicates we are to immediately order these metals parts which have previously been furnished by several American firms. We cannot locate firms who have furnished metal parts for wooden underframe cars; can you give us their names? The Standard, the Pressed Steel, and American Car and Foundry Company have all furnished metal for steel underframe box cars. If you cannot give us names of companies who have furnished metal parts for wooden underframe cars, send Vandykes [proofs] or blueprints of parts required. Is this understood? Are we correct in all these details? [Reply—May 4, P-1052-S-4; May 13, A-1306-R-1D; Vol. 5, May 22, P-1163-S-11.]

NARA, RG 120, M930, Main Series, War Department to AEF, roll 12.

April 22

Pershing's Personal Diary

At London. Called on Ambassador Page in morning. He talked at length of the appreciation of the high British officials for my offer to General Foch [March 28]. He said that they have not yet ceased their very sincere expressions of praise and admiration for the stand I took. I impressed on the Ambassador the importance of having as soon as possible an American army in the field. Saw also at Embassy Mr. Laughlin and Colonel Slocum [Military Attaché]. Went also to see Admiral Sims. He stated that the Navy are getting the submarine under control and was very optimistic on this question. He proposed sending a liaison officer to my headquarters. We also talked about the decision of the War Department to not take advantage of passenger space on small boats which could afford passage for from 50 to a few hundred troops at a time. We both think these accommodations should be used and I promised to send a cable on this subject [see April 23, P-960-S]. Had on the whole a very satisfactory talk with the Admiral.

Had to luncheon at Officers Club, General Biddle, General Wagstaff, Major Maitland Kersey, Captain Biddle and my own party. In afternoon had a conference with General Sir Henry Wilson [CIGS] and one with Lord Milner [Secretary of State for War]. General Harbord was with me at these conferences and made notes on them. Went also to the office of General Biddle. Saw there Colonel Sam Jones, Colonel Raymond, M.D., and Major Darrow of the Purchasing Board. Sent telegram to General Kernan asking report as to why my instructions re cancellation contract in England for steel huts have not been complied with. Went with General Biddle to dinner with Mrs. Whitelaw Reid. After dinner went to the Gayety Theatre and joined General

Harbord, Boyd and Captain Biddle. Saw a very amusing show entitled "The Beauty Spot." Met General and Mrs. Wagstaff at the show.

LC, Pershing Papers, Diary, May 7, 1917–September 1, 1918, box 4.

Memorandum of General Pershing's Visit to the British War Office, and Interview with General Sir Henry Wilson, and Lord Milner.

By appointment General Pershing called on General Sir H. Wilson, Chief of the Imperial General Staff, at 3 p. m., April 22.

General Wilson opened the conversation by reading a telegram or memorandum from Hankey, the British shipping man. [*Ed.*—This was probably from J. P. Maclay, the British Minister of Shipping, and not Hankey. See April 24, Maclay to Milner.] This stated that a review of the shipping situation indicated that the British would be able to produce enough tonnage to bring to Europe by July 31, three-quarters of a million men (750,000).

This statement was questioned somewhat by General Pershing as being greatly in excess of anything previously considered, also stating that it was necessary to consider a moment the disposition and supply of such a force if it could be brought.

The conversation then took the form of taking stock as to what troops the British may expect from the American shipping program for the next two months. General Pershing read the cablegram 901-S [*Ed.*—In the original document on the Savoy Hotel, London, letterhead, this cable number is overwritten twice and not clearly readable, but it is definitely neither P-901-S nor A-901-R as cited in the *USAWW* document below. More likely it is P-891-S, April 11, in which Pershing summarized decisions on shipment of troops to the AEF.] and portions of the agreement between Secretary Baker, Generals Whigham and Hutchison and himself, showing that while the shipping program might call for a certain number of troops to come, the only actual obligation to the British was to give them for training approximately 60,000 infantry, including replacements. [See April 7, Secretary of War Newton D. Baker and General Pershing—Conference in Paris with Major Generals Robert Dundas Whigham, Deputy Chief of the Imperial General Staff, and Robert Hutchison, Director of Organization, British War Office, Regarding Transportation of American Troops, and P-876-S, April 8, which specifically refers to the April 7 meeting.] General Pershing then read the memorandum by General Lawrence of the conversation between Field Marshal Haig and General Pershing, including the offer of Sir Douglas Haig to turn over the artillery of six divisions with which American infantry should constitute American divisions. [See April 20, Memorandum of Conversation between Field Marshal Sir D. Haig and General Pershing, Commander-in-Chief, U. S. Army, O. B./2196.]

The conversation with General Wilson was adjourned at 3:30 p. m. to the office of Lord Milner, Secretary of State for War.

After a few explanatory remarks as to what the conversation had been in the office of the Chief of Staff, General Wilson said that he had been trying to ascertain just where the British stood on the matter of American infantry.

Lord Milner referred to the original Versailles agreement which he styled Plan B, which called for the infantry of six divisions or about 96,000 men plus necessary replacements. That number was to have come by British tonnage in April and May. The plan for bringing over 750,000 by July 31 was referred to with some doubt as to whether that number existed in the United States. It was pointed out that it was about the infantry of 45 divisions, the original number raised last year, of which six divisions and a part of two others are already in France. Lord Milner and General Wilson referred to a supposed promise of the President to Lord Reading to send over 480,000 infantry. General Pershing stated that no such promise had been made, and it was admitted that possibly Lord Reading had misunderstood the President or the war office had misunderstood Lord Reading.

It was admitted that the agreement is for the infantry of six divisions to be trained by the British and brought over by them, but Lord Milner said it was very important to know whether concurrently with their bringing of the infantry the U.S. tonnage would be bringing artillery, etc., or more infantry. He thought it should be nothing but infantry for the present. General Pershing quoted Sir D. Haig as in favor of building up an American army at the earliest moment, and his offer to lend artillery for the present, but stated that when the British replacements required their artillery in perhaps July or August, the American infantry would then be without artillery unless America had brought it over. He pointed out the necessity for artillery to build up American divisions. Lord Milner continued to emphasize the urgent necessity of continuing to use all transportation to bring infantry. He considered the crucial moment of the war to be here, and that if the Germans reached Calais and the channel ports, the American divisions would be too late. Complete divisions were no doubt the best in the long run – if there is to be any long run. He thought Haig's plan would give us the necessary artillery until ours could come. General Pershing agreed that such use of artillery would permit American tonnage to bring over some more infantry, but thought it was about as broad as long, as the British artillery could if necessary be used as infantry. Lord Milner did not agree and continued to urge more infantry: Men! Men! Men! General Pershing thought our American artillery could train with British guns. He stated the war would undoubtedly be fought out on the Flanders front, and pointed out the great moral and psychological effect of an American army fighting side by side with the British. Lord Milner stated that such an army would eventually turn the scale and win the war. He pointed out that the Germans are counting on beating the Allies before the American army can be made. Time is needed to set up such an army, and in the meantime every possible man must be flung in during this emergency, just as Foch has relinquished his cherished plans, to send French divisions to the north behind the British lines. No doubt Foch bitterly hated the necessity of doing it, as Lord Milner hated to urge this. Allusion was made to General Pershing's recent offer to General Foch of all our American resources [March 28].

The interview terminated by General Pershing agreeing to study the matter and submit a proposition as to what he believes can be done, at 4 p. m. April 23.

LC, Pershing Papers, folder: Conferences and Agreements, Folder No. 1, box 50; see also *USAWW*, vol. 2, pp. 340–41.

Col. U. S. Grant, 3rd, Secretary, American Section, SWC, Versailles, to Brig. Gen. W. W. Atterbury, DGT, SOS, AEF, Paris.

Subject: Joint Notes Nos. 22, 23 and 24.

1. Enclosed please find copies of Joint Notes Nos. 22, 23 and 24, passed by the Military Representatives on April 18, 1918, and based on reports received from the Inter-Allied Transportation Council. I also enclose a copy of resolution of the Military Representatives on the subject of the Railway Lines in the Region Amiens-Abencourt [not reproduced]. [*Ed.*—Bliss forwarded these resolutions to the Acting Chief of Staff in cable 94-S on April 20 (not reproduced).]

[3 Enclosures]

Joint Note No. 22, Transport Between France and Italy. 18 April 1918 [not reproduced].

Joint Note No. 23. Utilization of Belgian Railway Resources. 18 April 1918 [not reproduced].

Joint Note No. 24. Shipment of Rolling Stock from the United States.

Supreme War Council
Versailles, France
April 18, 1918

Joint Note No. 24
Shipment of Rolling Stock from the United States.
From: The Military Representatives.
To: The Supreme War Council.

1. The Inter-Allied Transportation Council has called the attention of the Military Representatives to the congestion of traffic of the American Expeditionary Forces at ports used by the latter in France, which is occasioned by an insufficient supply of railway equipment. That Council shows that to furnish the transport necessary either in whole or in part for the American Expeditionary Forces from the resources available in France, places a dangerous burden on an already overstrained machine, and its continuance courts disaster.

2. In view of the grave situation reported by the Inter-Allied Transportation Council, the Military Representatives urgently recommend that action be taken to assist and augment in every possible way the importation of railway equipment by the American Expeditionary Forces into France, in order that the American Armies may be self-sustaining in transport at an early date. [Reply—May 5, Pershing to Bliss]

NARA, RG 120, M923, American Section, SWC, folder 196: Correspondence, memorandums, and notes relating to the organization, function, and transactions of the Inter-Allied Transportation Council, March 1918-August 1919, document 196-7; and folder 330: Joint Notes 23 and 24 and related correspondence on railroad transportation to support the American Army, April 1918, document 330-1.

Pershing to TAG, War Department, in part in reply to TAG, War Department, to Pershing, cables A-704-R, January 28 (not reproduced), and A-1043-R, April 5.

Cable P-977-S.

1. For the Chief of Staff. With reference to paragraph 3, your cablegram 1043, in which authority was given to commission graduates Army Candidates School only as vacancies occur in forces here. Imperative to have reservoir of surplus lieutenants in France from which to send to United States the 150 per month ordered by paragraph 8, your cablegram 704 [not reproduced]. Also to allow attachment to divisions upon arrival. This permits training of troops to proceed rapidly from moment of arrival while their own officers are at Corps School learning the new weapons. Believe it also good policy to commission graduates Army Candidates School so as to provide ample reserve for replacement of casualties. Candidates after proving leadership in service at front have been carefully tested and selected at school and constitute best officer material. Desirable not to repeat mistake of Allies in keeping good officer material in ranks until needed as this results in undue losses and serious shortage such material as war is prolonged.

1A. Therefore request authority to commission graduate Army Candidates School as second lieutenants in reserve corps and to order them to active duty immediately. These commissions to be temporary and to be confirmed by the War Department. Prompt action requested as desire attach these officers to divisions now arriving. Pershing. [Reply to 1 and 1A—April 30, A-1206-R-4]

5. For Chief of Ordnance. 5D. With reference to paragraph 1, your cablegram 984. Deliveries of 155-millimeter gun ammunition are not satisfactory. It is impossible for the French to meet their own demands let alone supply us. It is absolutely essential that we meet our requirements and help the French. Request that no efforts be spared in expediting the prompt manufacture and delivery of this caliber of ammunition. [In addition—April 28, P-1015-S-1E]

NARA, RG 120, M930, Main Series, War Department to AEF, roll 3.

TAG, War Department, to Pershing, in part in reply to Pershing to TAG, War Department, cables P-884-S, April 10, and P-912-S, April 13.

Cable A-1154-R.

1G. With reference to your 884, paragraph 3B. Expected seaboard deliveries 75-millimeter shell 50,000 weekly June, 500,000 during month of July, 1,000,000 August, 2,000,000 September. 3,000,000 monthly thereafter. Large shipment shrapnel this month and expected factory production 725,000 each month April, May and June. Expected deliveries anti-aircraft ammunition not yet determined but will be cabled at an early date. [Reply—May 9, P-1083-S-1C; Vol. 5, May 22, P-1164-S-3]

1J. With reference to paragraph 1B, your 912. Marlin gun adopted for tank use is not same as Marlin aircraft. It has modified heavy barrel similar to old Colt barrel, pistol grip and old Colt sights without windage. Will arrange for production of 60 of these guns with full equipment to be shipped to you as soon as possible.

NARA, RG 120, M930, Main Series, War Department to AEF, roll 12.

TAG, War Department, to Pershing, in part in reply to Pershing to TAG, War Department, cable P-885-S, April 10.

Cable A-1155-R.
 1. With reference to paragraph 5B, your 885. Two schools for aerial observers have been established in the United States. These are attended largely by Artillery officers. About 30 or 40 officers are graduated from these schools per week. The ones graduating are detailed in the Aviation Section, Signal Corps, and thus are embraced in that part of Section 13, National Defense Act, authorizing an increase of 25% for aviation officers participating regularly and frequently in aerial flights. The aerial school in France, which you have established, should have been included in this scheme. You are authorized to detail graduates of your aerial school to the Signal Corps of the Army and thereby obviate the discrimination between fliers. So far as concerns the general discrimination the War Department submitted a draft of a bill repealing all laws granting increased pay and grade to fliers. Your recommendation was placed before the Committee of Congress and in the hearing the War Department explained why the discrimination should cease. But the Congress refused to concur and nothing further can be done at present. March. [Reply—May 16, P-1134-S-1L]

NARA, RG 120, M930, Main Series, War Department to AEF, roll 12.

April 23

Pershing's Personal Diary

In London. Went to Ministry of Munitions to see Mr. Winston Churchill. He had nothing special to say. Stated that he has enough guns to replace another loss like they had in the recent offensive. He stated that they were well ahead on ammunition; that the German attacked one month later than they were expected to, therefore the British were one month ahead on ammunition. Saw in afternoon Lord Milner and General Sir Henry Wilson. Later saw Mr. Lloyd George.

LC, Pershing Papers, Diary, May 7, 1917–September 1, 1918, box 4.

Editor's Note—Once again Pershing provided additional details of these critical meetings and discussions in his wartime memoirs:

> Following the suggestion of Lord Milner, I went to London to consider further the shipment of American troops. At our first meeting there were present Lord Milner and General Sir Henry Wilson, who had succeeded General Robertson as the Chief of the General Staff, Harbord, and myself. The main point of difference that had developed in previous conferences was to just how far the Americans should be committed to serve in active operations was again considered. I stated that the principal thing was to get our units trained, and that while I was opposed to amalgamation, yet if during the period of instruction the British units with which they were serving should be attacked, or if another great emergency should arise, of course our men would go in. Naturally, the British wanted unlimited infantry and machine gun units, but I could not go further than to consider a limited extension of the six-division plan.
>
> During the conference, a cable from Lord Reading to the Prime Minister was brought forth which stated that the President had agreed to the amalgamation of Americans with the British. [*Ed.*—For the cable of April 20, Lord Reading to Lloyd George, forwarding the Baker Memorandum, see Lonergan, *It Might Have Been Lost!* pp. 149–51; Link (ed.), *The Papers of Woodrow Wilson*, vol. 47: *March 13–May 12, 1918*, pp. 386-88.] I had nothing official at hand later than the President's conditional approval of Joint Note No. 18 as suggested by Mr. Baker, so I promptly said that it could not be possible that any such concession had been made, and that the classes of our troops to be shipped over and their disposition must be left to me. Of course, we knew that the British were pressing this point by constant appeals to the President and that they were insisting that he should agree to the shipment of 120,000 infantry and machine gun units per month for four months, to the exclusion of all other personnel. While the British conferees had concluded from Lord Reading's cable that their case was won, I took quite another view and declined to consider the information as conclusive.
>
> As a result of these discussions, we reached an agreement which provided for the shipment in, the month of May, by British and American tonnage, of the infantry, machine gun, engineer, and signal troops, together with the various unit headquarters, of six divisions for training with the British Army. It was provided that any shipping in excess of the amount required for this number of troops should be utilized to transport the artillery of these divisions, and that such personnel as might be required to build up corps organizations should then follow; it being understood that the artillery regiments would train with the French and join their proper divisions when the training of the infantry was completed.
>
> In order to meet any emergency which might require an excess of infantry after the completion of this program, it was agreed that all the American

and British shipping available for the transportation of troops was to be used under such arrangement as would insure immediate aid to the Allies, and thereafter as far as possible provide other units necessary to complete the organization of our divisions and corps. It was further agreed that the combatant troops mentioned in connection with May shipments should be followed by such service of supply troops and other contingents as we ourselves might consider necessary, inasmuch as the shipment of such troops had been postponed; and that all these troops should be utilized at my discretion, except that the six divisions which the British were to transport would be trained with them. (Pershing, *My Experiences in the World War*, vol. 2, pp 5–7.)

Harbord, who was with Pershing throughout these discussions, cryptically commented, "This agreement lasted without change until the next time there was an opportunity to discuss it" (Harbord, *The American Army in France*, p. 255).

Just as in his meeting with Pétain on December 23 and during the recent Beauvais Conference (see above, April 3 and Editor's Note following Lloyd George's Memorandum), Pershing was surprised and put at a severe disadvantage during a critical meeting when this time Lord Milner presented him with important information on decisions made by the President and the War Department that had not been communicated to him in a timely manner but which the Allies had received from their Ambassadors in Washington well in advance. In this instance, Lloyd George, Lord Milner, General Wilson, and the War Office all had copies of the Baker Memorandum in hand in London on April 22 while Pershing only received his copy in cable A-1184-R of April 26 (see below) when he returned to Chaumont on April 29. Baker finally had March send this cable to Pershing with a copy of the Baker Memorandum of April 19 to Lord Reading. Baker then followed up this cable with a lengthy letter on April 29 outlining the decisions leading up to this memo and its significance for Pershing and the AEF. As it turned out, Lloyd George later wrote that "Reading advised us that these were quite the most favourable terms we could hope to obtain, and strongly urged their frank acceptance," which the War Cabinet then did on April 23 [Lloyd George, *War Memoirs*, p. 1823]. Milner and Wilson thus completed the detailed discussions with Pershing and Harbord resulting in the Milner-Pershing London Agreement that was signed on April 24 [see April 24, cable P-961-S].

Another important and unfortunate consequence of this whole Baker Memorandum situation was the development in the postwar years of a nasty feud between Pershing and March regarding the matter. (See March 30, Editor's Note following Storr to Bliss.)

Like Lloyd George, Henry Wilson, the CIGS, who met with Pershing on April 23 and would meet with him again the next day to continue discussions, was no admirer of the American CINC. In his private diary, Wilson had earlier described Pershing as "'a beaten man already' and 'worried and out of his depth'" (January 9) and a "d_____ fool" (April 8). Following these meetings, Wilson maintained his previous view of Pershing, seeing him as "a hopelessly stupid pig-headed man" (April 23) and "so stupid, so narrow, so pig-headed" (April 24) (as quoted in Spencer, *Wilson's War*, pp. 142, 144, 145).

Pershing, then in London, to Sims, Commander, U.S. Naval Forces Operating in European Waters, London, in reply to Sims to Pershing, April 13.

Confidential.

Referring to your personal letter of recent date regarding additional ports for our supply ships, I wish to express my very cordial appreciation of the spirit of cooperation you have constantly shown in all our relations. I shall advise you later as to the conclusion reached in this matter, after consultation with the French authorities upon my return to Paris.

Following our recent conversation, I think it may secure still further efficiency of cooperation between our land and naval forces regarding the transport of troops and supplies if a competent naval officer were permanently attached to my staff. I hope you may see your way to let me have such an officer at an early date.

With reference to the proposal of the British to send over some of our troops on what are called "medium speed transports," the matter was discussed in a general way between the Secretary of War and myself during his recent visit. I see no reason why such vessels should not be used, especially in view of the fact that you, yourself, consider them quite as safe as the larger class of transports. I have therefore sent to the War Department a cablegram on this subject, copy of which is enclosed.
[Enclosure (not reproduced)—see below, April 23, P-960-S]
[Reply—May 8, Sims to Pershing]

LC, Pershing Papers, folder: Sim (Adm. Sims document misfiled), box 184.

Pershing, then in London, to the Secretary of War, in addition to Pershing to TAG, War Department, cable P-954-S, April 19.

With reference to my cablegram No. 954 regarding the question of promotions, copy of which is enclosed, I sincerely trust that it may not be considered in any other light than as an endeavor to aid in placing the policy of the War Department with reference to promotions upon such a basis that we shall always be sure to get the best men and always have due consideration for their length of service. The number of regular officers is small and it seems to me that, at this early period of the war, we should not overlook men who have the ability that places them well up on the list of availables.

It is difficult always to draw the line and some men may be considered as possessing greater ability than some of their seniors, but unless we intend to permanently jump them their length of service ought to be considered. The opposite theory will soon lead us down to the grade of company officers in making selections for the higher grades. I have given this matter serious thought, and in studying the list of colonels for the recent promotions a great many were omitted who I did not regard as available or at least who have not fully demonstrated their abilities. In giving thought to efficient men and considering their length of service, many men well known for ability, some of whom I mentioned in my cablegram, were not recommended at this time. So it has been made to appear that I am overlooking good service and adhering too much to the question of seniority when such is not the case.

I think, Mr. Secretary, that it is essential that a well-defined policy be adopted by the Department and that an exchange of cables might level up promotions so that men over here may not be overlooked. I should prefer that selections made from my forces here should not be made without opportunity to comment on such proposed promotions and it was my understanding that this would be done. I am only saying these things in the best interest of the service as I see it, and in no way intend to imply a criticism of the War Department. Our different points of view can without doubt be coordinated to the benefit of general efficiency.

1 inclosure [Copy of cable P-954-S, April 19 (not reproduced).]
[Handwritten note]

P.S. The above was written before the receipt of your cable [see April 23, A-1159-R] which meets with my entire approval in principle. My original cable mentioning the names of Connor, W.D., Eltinge, etc., was intended to draw attention to these men who are very efficient but who were passed over by Westervelt, who is a part of my command and was not recommended by me, and McIntyre, some years their juniors. I fear General March has lost sight of the principle that I have attempted to emphasize and which has guided me in making recommendations.

LC, Pershing Papers, folder: Newton D. Baker, January–June 1918, box 20.

Pershing, then in London, to March.

I am glad to see that the Secretary has returned, and naturally presume that you will soon get settled down under a new order of things, with his view of the latest phase of the war from our standpoint at your back. Mr. Baker's visit was satisfactory to me in every way. It was his wish to make a thorough inspection of all our projects, our organization and training, beginning at the ports and ending with the trenches. This he did and seemed pleased with what he saw. In fact, he said so several times.

Our port work has been progressing well of late, especially when we take into consideration the delays that held us back in the earlier stages of our work. The construction of storehouses has, generally, progressed fairly well. At present I am laying particular stress upon the question of storage facilities at the ports to relieve any congestion that may be ahead of us.

If it should turn out that we are to have tonnage now estimated, it will push us some to handle it, so I am casting about for another French port, and think we shall be able to utilize Marseille. The Navy have agreed to undertake to escort our troops in case we should decide to send certain classes of tonnage around into the Mediterranean. The reasons for looking toward the Mediterranean port are found in our lack of dock facilities and also in the railroad situation which is at present very congested.

Cars and engines are being absorbed rapidly on account of the urgency of shifting troops to meet the military situation at the front. By utilizing Marseille, if it should become necessary to do so, we shall be able to take advantage of rolling stock returning from Italy which usually comes back empty. While this matter has not been definitely settled, I think there would be no trouble in using Marseille if we should see fit. The port facilities there are practically unlimited.

The Germans have made a very hard drive against the Allies, but with the new arrangement for unity of command under General Foch I believe the Allies will be able to hold. The French are of this opinion, and so are the British, although not quite so strongly. We have, as you know, the First Division near Montdidier as a part of General Debeney's army and this division is likely to be in the fight at any moment. The other three divisions, the 26th, 42d and 2d are still in Lorraine, but will be drawn out before very long and probably sent farther to the west. I have just visited General Foch and Field Marshal Haig on my way over here, and also inspected the early arrivals of the 77th division, which is to be located behind the British lines for training and service.

After a thorough discussion of the subject with Marshal Haig, I find him of the opinion that the earlier we get American troops organized as divisions the better it will be and he is now apparently quite strong for the original plan that I advocated, instead of the plan of feeding our contingents permanently into British divisions, so we are in a fair way to arrive at a satisfactory agreement.

There are several British divisions which are practically reduced to artillery alone, and with these it is proposed that we shall build up American divisions until our artillery can be got over and put into shape.

I have come over to London to discuss this matter with the British authorities, and also to talk over the pooling of bulky supplies, as indicated a few days ago [see April 19, cable P-953-S]. I shall leave here tonight or tomorrow (Wednesday) and return to my own headquarters.

Let me say a word, March, with reference to the recent promotions. I am really very anxious about our policy in this matter, as I consider it one of prime importance. It is essential that both you and I appear before the army at large as being in accord on this question of promotions, and we must reach a thorough understanding so that there may be a very clear policy. You will agree with me that we must not hurry too rapidly down to the lower grades in seeking our general officers. While I do not for one moment mean to recommend anyone not considered efficient, I think that, other things being equal as to efficiency, that men of longer service should be first promoted. It occurs to me that in future it would be well for us to exchange cables and adjust any difference of opinion as to promotions. I hope you may take this view.

As there have been several people cabling different things on this infantry question, I am trying to get it settled so far as the next two or three months are concerned. After that it will depend upon events. I am firmly of the view that we must not destroy our own plans nor, indeed, interfere with them more than is necessary to meet any present emergency. Will cable you in a day or so—long before you get this letter. [see April 24, P-961-S]

LC, Pershing Papers, folder: General Peyton C. March, box 123.

Pershing, Paris, to TAG, War Department.

Cable P-960-S. [This cable is out of the AEF's numerical sequence because it was sent from London.]
  Confidential for the Chief of Staff and Secretary of War.
  Have discussed with Naval authorities the question of using medium speed transports for shipment of troops to France. Admiral Sims believes that use of these ships would not involve any greater danger than use of larger transports. Concur in this view and recommend that matter be given further consideration by War Department in order to expedite shipment of personnel.
[In addition—see also, May 5, P-1056-S]. Copy to Sims.

NARA, RG 120, M930, Confidential Series, AEF to War Department, roll 7.

Pershing to TAG, War Department, in part in reply to TAG, War Department, to Pershing, cables A-1107-R, April 16.

Cable P-981-S.
  2. For Chief of Staff. 2A. With reference to paragraph 14, your cablegram 1107. 8 artists commissioned Engineers have been ordered to report for duty with Historical Section. 3 have arrived and are now at work with troops. Some sketches will be forwarded to Chief of Staff leaving here in 2 weeks and shipments monthly thereafter. Recommend distribution through Committee Public Information recognizing sole object to give American public all possible pictures of Expeditionary Forces. Recommend distribution be arranged so that maximum use of pictures in metropolitan and country papers alike and all magazines be assured. Colliers has 1 artist enjoying privileges of visiting correspondents but so far as known there are no others working with definite connections. Colliers artist is permitted to send work to United States after censorship but plans to hold it and take it back with him next month. Officers and men are permitted send drawings home after censorship but none have yet submitted to censorship. [*Ed.*—Replying to Pershing on May 7 in cable A-1253-R-3, March approved these recommendations concerning "the distribution for publicity purposes" of all cleared sketches prepared by AEF artists to be furnished.]
  3. For Chief Signal Officer. With reference to paragraph 7, cablegram 1107. You have the General Organization project approved by the Commander-in-Chief July 11th, 1917, as amended by Service of the Rear Project approved by Commander-in-Chief,

September 18, 1917. These projects as modified by the Burtt, Drum, Barker Board approved by the Commander-in-Chief, January 5, 1918, and the Handley Page agreement give the only program that we can have. Our needs for aeroplanes are thereby fixed and should govern in your production calling the 14 squadrons to be equipped in Europe pursuit squadrons. Europe cannot be depended on for further equipment. Total squadrons provided in these projects include the 30 Handley Page squadrons.

NARA, RG 120, M930, Main Series, AEF to War Department, roll 3.

TAG, War Department, to Pershing, in part in reply to Pershing to TAG, War Department, cables P-669-S, March 2 (not reproduced), and P-933-S, April 16.

Cable A-1158-R.
5. With reference to paragraph 3E, your 933. Locomotives are now being loaded on vessels suitable for carrying largest numbers thus practically utilizing whole ship space. Project now under way to load 20 or more locomotives set up complete on special vessels equipped for this purpose. This project well under way and shipments in such manner expected to commence on or about May 20th. [Reply—Vol. 5, May 23, P-1173-S-7B]
5A. Are you able to handle all shipments of frozen beef? Information here indicates refrigerator ships will be unduly delayed in your ports. Paragraph 7E, your 669 [not reproduced], advises us to make full shipments frozen beef, but due to urgent need for refrigerator vessels their use to full capacity is essential. [Reply—April 30, P-1031-S-3]

NARA, RG 120, M930, Main Series, War Department to AEF, roll 12.

TAG, War Department, to Pershing, in part in reply to Pershing to TAG, War Department, cable P-954-S, April 19.

Cable A-1159-R.
2. Your 954 has been personally shown Secretary of War who directs you be informed accordingly as follows: The American Expeditionary Force is only a part of the American Army and whatever promotions to the grade of Major General and Brigadier General are necessary will be made by him from the entire Army. You were directed to submit recommendations as were other general officers. These instructions did not limit your recommendations in any way. Your recommendations are regarded as especially valuable as far as they are limited to the American Expeditionary Force, but the efficiency of senior officers at home is determined by what is actually accomplished here, based upon specific reports of inspectors and division commanders. The Secretary of War demands the utmost efficiency in his generals

and is going to get it, regardless of rank and seniority and appointments. There will be no change in the nominations already sent to the Senate.

NARA, RG 120, M930, Main Series, War Department to AEF, roll 12.

Editor's Note—In his biography of Baker, Palmer writes about cable A-1159-R that:

> Later, Baker wrote this note underneath the copy of the foregoing cable that is in his files: "An excellent illustration of the way *not* to send a message. March's manners were not always considerate, but he did get results." (Palmer, *Baker*, vol. 2, pp. 209–10.)

April 24

Pershing's Personal Diary

In London. In morning had another conference with Lord Milner and General Wilson, and came to an agreement which we drew up and I signed and sent over by General Harbord in the afternoon [see below, Pershing-Milner (London) Agreement, and cable P-961-S]. Lunched with Major and Mrs. Astor. Worked in quarters till late in afternoon. Called on Sir William Robertson, but found him out. Dined at St. James Palace with the Duke of Connaught.

LC, Pershing Papers, Diary, May 7, 1917–September 1, 1918, box 4.

Pétain, CINC, Armies of the North and Northeast, to Foch, CINC, Allied Armies. Sarcus.

No. 25973.
I have the honor of submitting to you the proposals outlined below concerning the use of the American troops during the present operations.
  I. <u>Trained Divisions</u>.
The present situation of the 4 combat divisions of the I U.S. Corps is as follows:
The 1st U.S. Division, withdrawn from the Menil-la-Tour sector and transported to the region of Chaumont-en-Vexin, is in rear of the front of the I Army into which it is ready to enter.
The 26th U.S. Division relieved on April 3rd the 1st U.S. Division in the Menil-la-Tour sector. It came from the front of the XI A.C. on the Ailette, where it had finished its training by regiment. It holds 17 kilometers of front with 3 regiments in line and 1 in reserve. P.C.: Boucq.

The 42nd U.S. Division on March 30th entered the sector of Baccarat after having finished its training by regiment in the divisions of the VII A. C. It holds 13 kilometers of front with three regiments in line and 1 in reserve. P. C.: Baccarat.

The 2nd U.S. Division: on March 20th entered the front of Les Hautes Meuse by regiment in the II C. A. C. divisions (52nd and 33rd I. D.). Will have finished this training about April 25th and will be able to take a division sector.

I think that the American divisions ought to form part of the general chain of our divisions, that is to say that the 26th, 2nd and 42nd U. S. divisions should be relieved by French divisions and come to the battle. These reliefs should be made in the near future.

The American Divisions wear themselves out quite quickly in sector (lack training, useless fatigues, poor feeding due to lack of knowledge of cooking, etc.). The 26th US Division was already fatigued when it left the front of the Ailette, it has had to relieve the 1st U.S. division without a period of rest, it has just undergone the attack of the Bois de Remières [Seicheprey]. The 2nd and 42nd U.S. divisions, at the end of the present month, will have nearly a month at the front.

The 3 divisions, it thus seems should be relieved shortly in the following order: 26th, 2nd, 42nd.

The 26th and 42nd are in principle better trained than the 2nd since a latter has only finished its training by regiment at the front, but the American G.H.Q. seems to consider this division as of better composition than the two others (Division of the regular army while the 26th and 42nd are of the National Guard) and consequently it considers that this 2nd U.S. Division is as suitable for combat as the two others.

The American Command will perhaps wish to maintain the 26th U.S. Division in the Menil-la-Tour sector with the idea of placing there at a later date the 1st U.S. Division, returning from battle, either to relieve the 26th, or even to introduce it alongside of this latter and form the American front.

But on the one hand it does not appear to be advantageous to await the return of the 1st U.S. Division to relieve the 26th which risks using itself up prematurely prior to entering battle, and, in addition, there would be serious inconveniences in creating too soon an extended American front, which might tempt the enemy.

Consequently the best solution seems to be to relieve in a short time, the 26th U.S. Division by a French division. The 2nd and 42nd U.S. Divisions should also be relieved by French divisions. As soon as the 1st U.S. Division has returned to the east, it can retake the Menil-la-Tour sector.

As for the autonomous sector of the I U.S. Corps, it should be formed later on when the divisions of this Corps have taken part in the battle and have thus proved themselves.

II. Regiments to introduce on the front and the cadre of French divisions.

a) 32nd U.S. Division. The regiments of this replacement Division were disbursed length of the lines of communications, they are now regrouping in the zone of Prauthoy to the south of Langres.

Two regiments (125th and 126th) had reduced strength and whose training is fair are to be given us towards the 5th of May.

The two other regiments (127th and 128th) will be ready only at about the 20th of May.

The four regiments will be entered by brigade on the present front of the XXI A. C. (Vosges) (at the request of General Pershing). Each will have at least a battalion on the front.

The entry of these 4 regiments should be hastened in order to help our troops who are holding very much extended sectors.

b) 3rd and 5th U.S. Divisions. These two divisions are now disembarking, the 3rd is almost complete. They are assembling, one in the zone of Bar-sur-Aube. The other in that of Châteauvillain (west of Chaumont).

It is understood that the regiments of these two divisions will, as soon as possible, go to the front in the cadre of French divisions. But General Pershing has made reservations, to General Ragueneau, concerning the sending of all the regiments of these divisions to the front.

A precise date cannot it be said for the entry on the front of these regiments.

III. <u>Colored Regiments</u>.

a) The 369th Regiment has been assigned to the 16th I. D. for over a month (Sector of the VIII A. C. Ville-sur-Tourbe, Massiges). The companies are on the front mingled with the French companies. The regiment will be soon considered as trained and will take a subsector similar to a French regiment.

b) The 370th and 371st expected shortly are assigned to the XIII A. C.

c) The 372nd, due to closely follow the 370th and 371st, is assigned to the XL A.C.

d) Two colored depot regiments are stationed in the region of Saint Florentin (northwest of Tonnerre).

Summing up, there remains to be taken up with the High American Command the following questions:

1. The principle of the relief of the 26th, 2nd, and 42nd U.S. Divisions, and their participation in the general chain.

2. The dates in order of these reliefs.

3. The hastening of the putting at our disposal of the regiments of the 32nd U.S. Division, then those of the 3rd and 5th U.S. Divisions.

If you concur in my point of view I will be able to regulate these questions with General Pershing, either directly, or through General Ragueneau.

LC, Pershing Papers, folder 14: Translations of various French and German documents by Maj. Rayner and Maj. Koenig: vol. 3, Pt. 3, Annex No. 44, *The Defensive Campaign, March 21–July 18, 1918: The Battle of Flanders (9 April to 20 May)*, in Pétain, *Report of the Commander-in-Chief of the French Armies of the North and Northeast on the Operations in 1918*, box 355; *Les armées françaises dans la Grande guerre, Tome 6, vol. 2, Annexes, vol. 1: Annexe No. 57*, pp. 137–39; for an edited version, see *USAWW*, vol 3, pp. 289–91.

J. P. Maclay, Minister of Shipping (Shipping Controller), to Lord Milner, Secretary of State for War.

The estimated figures for troops to come from America are as follows:

	British Ships	American Ships
April	60,000	58,000
May	130,000	70,000
June	150,000	70,000
	340,000	198,000

Total 538,000

To the end of July it is thought that a total of 750,000 can be provided for between British and American ships.

These figures have been fully cabled to Washington.

LC, Pershing papers, folder: Training and Employment of American Troops with British, box 198.

Editor's Note—Maclay's estimate to Milner was immediately seized upon by Harbord in his memorandum to Pershing (paragraph 4) in Editor's Note following Pershing and Milner (London Agreement) to question seriously the validity of earlier British estimates of their available shipping. Indeed, Pershing cited the figures in this note in his cable P-961-S-5 (below). The copy of Maclay's note in the folder cited above has a penciled annotation in the margin "*Par. 5*," referring to P-961-S, paragraph 5, and lined out the phrase "between British and American ships," which was accordingly not included in the cable. Pershing also used this new information on shipping in his meeting with Foch at Sarcus on April 25.

Pershing and Lord Milner, Secretary of State for War, London (The London Agreement).

Transportation of American Troops

It is agreed between the Secretary of State for War, representing the British Government, and General Pershing, representing the American Government, that for the present American troops be sent over in the following order:

A. That only the infantry, machine guns, engineers and signal troops of American divisions and the headquarters of divisions or brigades be sent over in British and American shipping during May for training and service with the British army in France up to six divisions and that any shipping in excess of that required for these troops be utilized to transport troops necessary to make these divisions complete. The training and service of these troops will be carried out in accordance with plans already agreed upon between Sir Douglas Haig and General Pershing, with a view at an early date of building up American divisions.

B. That the American personnel of the artillery of these divisions and such corps troops as may be required to build up American corps organizations follow immediately thereafter, and that American artillery personnel be trained with French materiel and join its proper divisions as soon as thoroughly trained.

C. If, when the progress outlined in paragraphs A and B is completed, the military situation makes advisable the further shipment of infantry et cetera of American divisions, then all the British and American shipping available for transport of troops shall be used for that purpose under such arrangement as will insure immediate aid to the Allies, and at the same time provide at the earliest moment for bringing over American artillery and other necessary units to complete the organization of American divisions and corps. Provided that the combatant troops mentioned in A and B be followed by such service of the rear and other troops as may be considered necessary by the American Commander-in-Chief.

D. That it is contemplated American divisions and corps when trained and organized shall be utilized under the American Commander-in-Chief in an American group.

E. That the American Commander-in-Chief shall allot American troops to the French or British for training or train them with American units at his discretion, with the understanding that troops already transported by British shipping or included in the six divisions mentioned in paragraph A are to be trained with the British Army, details as to rations, equipment and transport to be determined by special agreement."

Signed	Signed
Milner	John J. Pershing, General, U.S. Army
London	
April 24, 1918.	

LC, Pershing Papers, folder: Training and Employment of American Troops with British, box 198, which has an original copy signed by Milner and Pershing; see also LC, Bliss Papers, folder: Military Papers, January–July 1918, box 249.

Editor's Note—Within days of returning from London with Pershing, Harbord sent him this undated memorandum on the arrangements worked out with the British to bring American troops to Europe:
Harbord, CS, GHQ, AEF, to Pershing.

Memorandum

1. Any material alteration of the present agreement for priority of infantry troops to be turned over to the British for training, and use while so training, should be in view of the future employment of such troops. How long will the present emergency which threatens the Channel ports probably last? How long before the troops brought over in any particular month can be of use in withstanding such threat? Granting that the Allies successfully resist the present German offensive, what beyond that is necessary to win the war?

(a) How long before troops brought over in any month can be used in the lines?

The bad management in the United States which has resulted in deranging the personnel of the National Army Divisions to fill up the National Guard has passed through each National Army Division from 25,000 to 50,000 men, and now leaves all of them with a large proportion of recruits—men of less than two months service. The 77th Division, now landing at Calais, has several thousand men who at time of embarkation had but three weeks service. It is not conceivable that on the average these divisions can be used under one month after arrival in France. Troops arriving in June will not be available until August; May in July; April in June.

(b) The present emergency has lasted one month, during which time the Germans have used over one hundred divisions. They have half their force on the front of the present offensive. The remainder of the line can hardly be further shorn of its strength. They are presumed to have had about 600,000 for replacements of losses in this offensive. A very conservative estimate of their losses is 350,000 men. (The French estimate 400,000). It seems then that the zenith has been reached. By the end of June the present emergency will have been ended.

(c) Assuming that a crop failure in Germany has not happened; that there have been no political disturbances resulting from the failure of their offensive; the end of June should find them dug in on the lines they then hold and the two enemies confronting each other in a practical impasse. Surely if the war is to be won by the Allies, plans must look farther than mere resistance of the present menace to the Channel ports. With waning manpower in Great Britain and France it is obvious that any offensive to be carried on by the Allies must contemplate an army from America.

2. Based upon the foregoing it is evident that there is no good reason for planning <u>emergency</u> measures in priority of troop shipments beyond the month of June. It may be doubtful whether it is desirable to plan such measures beyond the units to embark in May.

3. Based on the Versailles conference with Secretary Baker, emergency priority shipments were planned to include June. It was intended therein to postpone the arrival of Service of Supply and army troops and to give the infantry and machine gun units a six weeks advance over other divisional units. This plan also contemplated the then existing estimate of tonnage available as for 120,000 men per month, equally divided between British and American shipping.

4. According to present estimate the British shipping available could bring over 750,000 men by July 31st, or 250,000 per month. The difference between the former but recent estimate and this present estimate is so great as to be astounding. Certainly there is nothing in past records of troop transportation which justifies the present estimate. It would mean 25 ships carrying 10,000 each, or their equivalent, each month. Where has such an

amount of shipping been? Why has it needed a German menace to the Channel ports to make it available? It is believed that if the estimate of 60,000 men for May be doubled we will probably have covered the maximum possibilities of British tonnage during that month.

5. It is now stated that the British will be able to furnish at least six of their divisional artilleries for use with American divisions. Considering the difference between the British and American establishments this artillery would suffice for but three American divisions.

6. Unless it is maintained that the war must end with the present emergency it is only possible to give additional priority to troops, other than artillery, for which the British can furnish artillery, i. e.—for three divisions. It is not conceded that the end of the present emergency will be the end of the war. To secure a satisfactory peace the war must continue and American forces must be built up to that end.

7. The use of British artillery in American divisions is objectionable in that it complicates ammunition supply; introduces another system of artillery, and retards the development of American artillery. Nevertheless it is believed wise, on the theory that British tonnage can bring over 60,000 troops in addition to those already scheduled for May, to give priority to other troops than artillery for three additional divisions, amounting to 68,664 men.

8. It is therefore proposed that British shipping be scheduled to bring over in May three divisions less artillery in addition to the present schedule. Further, that after May any British tonnage available to bring troops in excess of that now already scheduled, be devoted to bring over entire American divisions. American tonnage will be understood to be free to proceed on its own Priority Schedules after June.

9. It is suggested that much confusion and probably some actual delay to the actual shipment of troops has resulted from the activity of British representatives in Washington working along lines differing from those agreed upon between British War Office and ourselves in Europe. Highly necessary that it be understood that after the agreement of this date there will be no further similar activity in Washington on their part. (LC, Pershing Papers, folder: Training and Employment of American Troops with British, box 198.)

As the AEF's Chief of Staff, Harbord's comments about British shipping in paragraph 4 were based on his knowledge of which nation was then carrying the heavier burden of transporting American troops to Europe. From May through December 1917, 77 American ships had carried 121,664 troops compared with 75,500 in 53 British ships. In 1918 through March, 60 U.S. transports had carried 121,918 troops while 27 British ships carried 57,399. Only in April, after the first two German offensives had smashed into their front in Flanders, would the British begin significantly to accelerate their movement of American troops as a result of the agreements at the

Beauvais conference and the Pershing-Milner Agreement of April 24. ("Report of the Secretary of the Navy," Appendix F: Troop Transportation, p. 206, in *Annual Reports of the Navy Department for the Fiscal Year 1919.*)

TAG, War Department, to Bliss, Chief, American Section, SWC, Versailles. Copy furnished to Pershing.

Cable 49-R.

1. When I was in Italy I was urged by everybody with whom I talked to bring about the appearance of American troops in that country for the purpose of showing America's interest in the Italian situation and strengthening the Italian morale. The present situation in France obviously makes such a thing not justifiable, and General Pershing gravely doubts its advisability for two reasons; first, all American troops are needed in France, and second, any small contingent sent would create expectations of larger forces to follow, which it would be difficult to satisfy. I would like to have your opinion whether something could not be done by sending a single regiment or, as an alternative, require the British or French to brigade some of the infantry troops assigned to them with their divisions on the Italian front. If neither of these plans is promising, have you any suggestions? It seems important to do anything we can to stimulate morale and show American interest. Baker, Secretary of War. [Reply—April 29, cable 101-S]

NARA, M923, American Section, SWC, file 316: Cablegrams received from the War Department, Jan. 23, 1918–Nov. 19, 1919, roll 18; see also online "WW I Supreme War Council, American records," at https://www.fold3.com.

Kernan, CG, SOS, AEF, Tours, to CINC, AEF, in reply to Pershing to CG, SOS, AEF, Tours, April 5.

1. Immediately upon receipt of your letter of April 5th, 1918, on the above subject, I took up the question with the Chiefs of the various departments of the Services of Supply to whose department the provisions of your letter apply. The spirit of your letter is being complied with by all and I am sure good results will be obtained. Three of the departments have, for the present, no officer who is suited to this duty. When one is available in their personnel he will be designated.

2. The selections that have been made in each department are as follows:

Chief Quartermaster, Captain Franklin d'Olier, Q.M.U.S.R.
Chief Surgeon, Major J. M. T. Finney, M.R.C., Director General of Surgery.
  Major W. S. Thayer, Director General of Medicine.
Chief Ordnance Officer, Major E. S. Toothe, O.D., U.S.N.A.
Chief of Gas Service, Captain R. Mayo-Smith, Sanitary Corps, N.A.
Chief of Air Service, Colonel Ambrose Monell, A.S.S.C.

Director General of Transportation, Lt. Col. H. M. Waite
Director, Motor Transport Service, Major Barrett Andrews, Q.M.R.C.

Chiefs of the departments who will have to defer until later the selection of such an Officer are:
Chief Engineer Officer,
Director, Department of Construction and Forestry.
Chief Signal Officer.

NARA, RG 120, Office of the Commander-in-Chief, Office of the Secretary of the General Staff, entry 22, Reports of the Commander-in-Chief, GHQ War Diary, folder 35: April 28–June 12, 1918, diary entry May 3, 1918, 328-a, pp. 312–13, box 4.

Pershing, then in London, to TAG, War Department.

Cable P-961-S. Confidential. [This cable is out of the AEF's numerical sequence because it was sent from London.]

    For the Chief of Staff and Secretary of War.
    1. The following memorandum regarding the shipment of American troops has been agreed to as indicated:
[Here the above Milner-Pershing London Agreement on April 24 is reproduced.]
    2. The plan seems to meet the situation as it appears at present and leaves shipment of services of the rear troops and other necessary contingents for our own determination as may be required. It also provides for and is understood to cover the question of bringing over artillery with very little delay to complete our divisional and corps organizations. There now seems to be a real desire on the part of Sir Douglas Haig and Lord Milner to do this as early as practicable.
    3. Memorandum of agreement between Field Marshal Sir D. Haig and General Pershing:
"It is agreed that American troops arriving in France for service with British be disposed of as fellows: American divisions will be allocated for training as agreed upon by the respective staffs to English cadre Divisions. The training staff of the English divisions to be at the disposal of the American regiments for instruction in English rifle, Lewis and machine gun, gas precautions and details of various kinds. As soon as approved by the American Divisional Commander each American regiment will be attached to an English division in the line so that one American battalion will be attached to each 3 brigades or the English division. The American battalion will be commanded by its own officers and will work as part of the English brigade. The staff of the American regiment will be attached to the staff of an English brigade for instruction. In the next stage the American regiment (3 battalions) under its own commander will be attached as a brigade to an English division. Finally the American regiments will be grouped again as a

division under their own commander. The Field Marshal will be prepared when this stage is reached to place the artillery of an English division, up to 6 divisions at present, at the disposal of the Commander in Chief, U.S. Army, until such time as the U. S. Divisional artillery arrives or the English cadre divisions are made up to full strength."

4. It is confidently asserted by the British shipping authorities that the shipment of personnel by both British and American shipping can be very much expedited which if possible of accomplishment will enable us without doubt to bring over whole divisions and all other personnel necessary for organization of units and for various other services. In this connection it should be remembered that England has Irish conscription question on her hands. Numbers of British troops will probably be sent to Ireland to enforce conscription. The possible political effect on American troops of Irish origin fighting under British flag even temporarily should not be lost sight of. This only emphasizes the desirability of our organizing American units as such and uniting the into an American Army at the earliest date possible.

5. The following estimate as to troop transportation from America is made by the British: "British ships: April 60,000, May 130,000, June 150,000 total 340,000. American ships: April 58,000, May 70,000, June 70,000, total 198,000, grand total 538,000 men. To the end of July it is thought that a total of 750,000 can be provided for" [see above, Maclay to Milner].

[In addition—April 29, P-1024-S-1J; April 30, P-1031-S-1C]

NARA, RG 120, M930, Confidential Series, AEF to War Department, roll 7.

Editor's Note—On April 29, Baker sent Pershing's cable to President Wilson with the following note:

> I enclose a copy of a confidential memorandum received by me today from General Pershing.
> Clearly, General Pershing, Lord Milner, and Sir Douglas Haig have had a conference and agreed among themselves upon a plan for the shipping of American troops which differs widely from the arrangement we worked out with Lord Reading, and is very much more favorable to the early building up of complete American divisions.
> Lord Reading called on me today with a copy of the same agreement, which had been transmitted to him by Lord Milner. Lord Reading said that he was mystified and disturbed at the modification which had been made in the plans. I told him, however, that I felt he and I were too far from the situation to see this as clearly as those in Europe and that so far as I was concerned I felt it my duty to cooperate to carry out the arrangement which plainly seemed wise to Lord Milner and General Pershing.
> The modification really is not so serious when one remembers that the total number of infantry and machine gun units which would have been shipped under this program is as great as we could in any case have ready for

shipment by the last of July, while the increased tonnage made available will carry over artillery and other personnel, making total shipments of troops by the last of July very much larger than were contemplated in the memorandum submitted by Lord Reading to which I made reply a week ago. (Link (ed.), *The Papers of Woodrow Wilson*, vol. 47: *March 13–May 12, 1918*, p. 455.)

In his *Pershing*, Don Smythe laid out in detail the conundrum Baker faced in making this recommendation to Wilson. His memorandum of April 19 was substantially at odds with the Pershing-Milner Agreement. In it he had agreed to the shipment of 480,000 infantry and machine gunners from April to July, while the Pershing-Milner Agreement provided for only 126,000, and those only in May.

The question now was, which agreement would the United States honor?

By all rights, it should have been the Baker Memorandum of April 19, made by Pershing's superior, the Secretary of War. But Baker, once he learned of the April 24 London Agreement, decided to support it, perhaps thinking that, if the British were willing to agree to it, things were not as bad as they seemed. (In point of fact, the second German offensive petered out by April 26 and, although it had advanced about ten miles, was not as serious as the earlier one in March.) Furthermore, Pershing was on the scene. His London Agreement preserved American freedom of action, kept future options open, and did not so drastically postpone the formation of a separate American army.

The fact that two separate and contradictory agreements had been made (the Baker-Reading Memorandum of April 19 and the Pershing-Milner London Agreement of April 24) brought home to Secretary Baker the inevitable confusion of trying to carry on negotiations simultaneously on both sides of the Atlantic. Accordingly, he strongly recommended to President Wilson that any future arrangements be made by Pershing, "so that we would have one agreement made at one place, rather than several agreements made in several places which were more or less irreconcilable in some of their terms." To their great vexation, the British and French ambassadors were told that Baker would make no further agreements with them concerning troop shipments; on this question the man to see was Pershing. (Smythe, *Pershing*, p. 110; the Baker quote comes from his June 6 letter to Pershing in which he discusses this entire issue in paragraphs 2–4.)

Pershing to TAG, War Department, in part in reply to TAG, War Department, to Pershing, cables A-610-R, January 7 (not reproduced), and A-1110-R, April 16 (not reproduced).

Cable P-986-S.

8. For Chief of Ordnance. Understand negotiations being made for procurement of 8-inch, 10-inch and 12-inch Navy guns of various lengths of bore. For railway

mounts extremely important that 8-inch, 10-inch and 12-inch guns have maximum possible range. Recommend procurement from Navy of guns of 50 caliber if possible, otherwise 40 caliber.

8B. With reference to paragraph 8, your cablegram 610, and deliveries promised in paragraph 2, your cablegram 1110 [neither reproduced]. Will not place orders for additional Hotchkiss tripods. Our plans contemplate replacement Hotchkiss guns by Brownings between October and December 1918. Will Browning guns be furnished to meet these requirements? If this can be done no additional deliveries of Hotchkiss tripods will be required. [Reply—May 3, A-1233-R-1N]

NARA, RG 120, M930, Main Series, AEF to War Department, roll 3.

Pershing to TAG, War Department, in part in reply to TAG, War Department, to Pershing, cable A-1020-R, April 1.

Cable P-987-S.

2. For Chief of Ordnance and Chief Signal Officer. With reference to paragraph 6C, your cablegram 1020. Prospective supply of British bombs justifies placing orders for equipment for taking British bombs on first 200 Handley-Page airplanes. Orders are now placed in England for 4500 20-lb. bombs for delivery 1500 June 1st, 1500 July 1st, 1500 August 1st; 36750 50-lb. bombs delivery 12250 June 1st, 12250 July 1st, 12250 August 1st; 3600 112-lb. bombs delivery 1200 June 1st, 1200 July 1st, 1200 August 1st; 1200 230-lb. bombs delivery 400 June 1st, 400 July 1st, 400 August 1st. Suspensions and releases for these bombs also ordered for delivery in advance of bombs, quantities as follows: 300 sets 20-lb. bombs, 900 sets 50-lb. bombs or 112-lb. bombs, 150 sets 230-lb. bombs. Suspensions built into fuselage to carry either 16 20-lb. 16 50-lb., or 16 112-lb. bombs; in addition 2 suspensions for 2 230-lb. bombs each under each wing and 2 suspensions for 2 230-lb. bombs each under fuselage; 4 suspensions for 500-lb. bombs may be placed under fuselage in place of 230-lb. bomb suspensions. [In addition—April 30, P-1031-S-6A]

NARA, RG 120, M930, Main Series, AEF to War Department, roll 3.

Pershing to TAG, War Department.

Cable P-990-S.

1. Have learned from division commanders and staff officers recently arrived from the United States that large numbers of recruits have been assigned to divisions designated for service in Europe. The same lack of training is found in replacements as already reported in previous cables. In view of the urgency of the situation here there is no time to drill raw recruits in France in elementary work. To send them into the trenches or into battle without requisite training would mean useless and

unwarranted loss of life. Therefore urgently recommend that no men be sent over who have not at least 4 months intensive training and who have not also had full and thorough instruction in target practice and that a limited number of divisions be broken up to accomplish this if necessary. Attention invited to original project which contemplated organization of 7th division for training recruits.

2. Reference target practice have been informed that none of our troops have had practice above 300 yards. Consider this very grave oversight that should be corrected as soon as possible. Target practice should embrace instruction in skirmish firing and practical application of the principles of fire direction, control and discipline with especial emphasis upon instruction of younger officers in musketry as applied to tactical problems in open warfare. Request advise as to action taken upon above recommendation and also information regarding what instruction has been carried out in divisions to come over within the next 3 months.

3. Regard it most imperative that there be no delay in calling out a new draft and the entire summer season devoted to instruction and training so that new troops may be thoroughly and systematically trained without disturbing organization when formed. Believe German offensive will be stopped but Allied aggressive [?] must be undertaken as early as possible thereafter and American forces must be in position to throw in their full weight. Recommend that a call be issued at once for at least 1 million and a half men. Having in mind large replacements of losses that are sure to occur, and the delays of organization, equipment and training of new drafts this is the smallest number that should be considered.

4. Attention invited to reports from reliable sources that Germans contemplate using Russians to build up larger army. There is little doubt that German influence in Western Russia is rapidly becoming effective and that peasants may easily be led to believe their future lies with Germany. Every means at hand to combat this movement should be exerted by the Allies but especially by our country.
[Reply—May 7, A-1259-R]

NARA, RG 120, M930, Main Series, AEF to War Department, roll 3.

татар, War Department, to Pershing, in part in reply to Pershing to TAG, War Department, cable P-922-S, April 14.

Cable A-1163-R.
1. With reference to paragraph 3, your 922. Drawings for 14-inch gun received from Navy Department and will be sent by courier. No drawings available for 7-inch gun. Following data reference 7-inch gun and mount 45 calibers long: Muzzle velocity 2700 F.S. [feet per second], weight of projectile 165 pounds, weight of powder charge 62 pounds, weight of gun, yoke, and breech mechanism, 30,050 pounds, total weight of mount, 64,000 pounds approximately, hydro-pneumatic recoil system, maximum angle of elevation 40 degrees.

NARA, RG 120, M930, Main Series, War Department to AEF, roll 12.

TAG, War Department, to Pershing, in part in reply to Pershing to TAG, War Department, to Pershing, cables P-913-S, April 14, and P-916-S, April 14, in addition to TAG, War Department, to Pershing, cable A-1094-R, April 13.

Cable A-1165-R.
1. Attention Air Service. Referring to your 913, paragraph 1F, your 916, paragraph 9A. In connection refer to our 1094, paragraph 1I. We can contract with British Government for SE 5 planes at rate of 30 per week beginning July 1st. We can supply from here 180-horsepower high-compression Hispano Suiza motors for these planes, shipment from here at rate of 30 per week beginning July 1st, engines to be installed in planes in England. Advise quickly if you desire us to make this arrangement which will permit quickest possible delivery of single-seated fighting machines on the front. We can also place this same machine in production here and begin shipment in September. Advise if that is desirable. We expect to have Hispano Suiza 300 in production in October. Will design single seater for it here and will also expect to receive from you drawings and samples of Béchereau SPAD for this motor. SE 5 equipped with Hispano is the only single-seater pursuit machine we can produce quickly. [Reply—May 4, P-1052-S-2A]
4. I have just had a conference with Postmaster General with reference to proposal to take over distribution of mail in France, leaving money orders and registered mail to be handled by postal agents. The Post Office Department has no objection, but feels certain from its experience that military men will find the problem difficult and full of embarrassments, particularly if we do not take over a substantial part of the trained postal personnel into the organizations created by us for handling the matter. Please cable me as fully as you can just how you expect to organize for the assumption of this work and whether you would desire trained personnel transferred to you either from those already in France or sent from the United States for your use. Baker. [Reply—May 10, P-1084-S-1C]

NARA, RG 120, M930, Main Series, War Department to AEF, roll 12.

TAG, War Department, to Pershing.

Cable A-1170-R.
President of the United States date of April 18th issued following proclamation:
"An enemy who has grossly abused the power of organized government and who seeks to dominate the world by the might of the sword challenges the right of America and the liberty and life of all the free nations of the earth. Our brave sons are facing the fire of battle in defense of the honor and rank of America and the Liberty of Nations. To sustain them and to assist our gallant solders in the war, a generous and patriotic people have been called upon to subscribe to the Third Liberty Loan. Now therefore I, Woodrow Wilson, President of the United States of America, do appoint Friday, the 26th day of April 1918, as Liberty Day. On the afternoon of that day, I

request the people of the United States to assemble in their respective communities and liberally pledge anew their financial support to sustain the Nation's cause. A patriotic demonstration should be held in every City, Town, and Hamlet throughout the land under the general direction of the Secretary of the Treasury and the immediate direction of the Liberty Loan Committees organized by the Federal Reserve Bank. Let the Nation's response to the Third Liberty Loan express in unmistakable terms the determination of America to fight for peace, the permanent peace of Justice. For the purpose of participation in Liberty Day celebrations all employees of the Federal Government throughout the country whose service can be spared may be excused at 12 o'clock noon, Friday, April 26th." Liberty Day will be observed by troops in your command to the extent that you deem wise but wherever patriotic programs are presented public reading of President's message will be included.

NARA, RG 120, M930, Main Series, War Department to AEF, roll 12.

April 25

Pershing's Personal Diary

Left London 11:20 a. m. via Folkestone and Boulogne. Landed at Boulogne about 4:15 p. m. Met by Colonel Mott who went with me to Sarcus where we took dinner with General Foch. Had talk with General Foch after dinner. Present at the conversation were Generals Bliss, Harbord and Weygand, Colonel Boyd and Lieutenant Colonel Mott. Thrashed out with General Foch the question of American troops that are to be brought over for service with British and French. General Foch seemed to think more of transportation of Infantry for service with the French and British than of the formation of an American army. I insisted that we must prepare for the latter. After showing him that I would not consider any other policy than one looking to this end, I showed him the proposition adopted by the English on this subject and he finally agreed that if the British are capable of bringing over as many troops as they state it would be satisfactory to bring over entire divisions. I also discussed with him the coal situation of which he appeared to have but little knowledge. Returned to Paris at about 1 o'clock in the night.

LC, Pershing Papers, Diary, May 7, 1917–September 1, 1918, box 4.

Report of Conversation between General Pershing and General Foch at Sarcus, April 25, 1918.

Present at the conversation were:

> General Bliss
> General Harbord

General Weygand
Colonel Boyd
Colonel Mott and a French captain who made notes on the conversation.

General Foch referred to General Pershing's offer of March 28 and asked for some details as to the state of preparedness of the American divisions now in France. *General Pershing* told him that these divisions should go in in the following order: 1st, 26th, 42d, 2d, and that the 32d would follow as soon as possible. (Some regiments of this division are ready now, and others within a few weeks.) That the 26th and 42d could go now at any time and the 2d very soon afterwards; that naturally these divisions would have to be withdrawn from the front they now occupy for a short period of rest and instruction before going to the battle front.

General Foch called attention to the very great need of infantry, on account of the present emergency, and requested that America bring over, especially for the English army, as much infantry as possible. He referred to the Versailles recommendation that America, for the present send to Europe only infantry and machine-gun units, and stated that he supposed General Pershing agreed with the principle of this.

General Pershing stated that he did not agree with this; that he could not commit himself to such a proposition; that we must in every step we take prepare for the formation of an American army in France; that the tonnage facilities for the next three months would bring at least 360,000 men; if these be of infantry and machine-gun units, it would be October or November before the corresponding artillery and auxiliary troops could be brought over, and that we may not foresee the formation of an American army before next spring.

General Foch found this estimate a little pessimistic and stated that if we brought infantry during May, June, and July, the artillery could be brought over in August, and that in October the formation of the American divisions could begin.

In view of General Pershing's disagreement with the Versailles recommendation, *General Foch* asked what he would propose in this connection.

General Pershing stated that he thought we should bring over infantry for the month of May. This would amount, according to the estimates of experts, to more than 120,000 infantry; that the artillery and auxiliary troops for this infantry should follow in the month of June; that he was not willing to have artillery and auxiliary troops arrive more than one month later than their infantry.

General Foch stated that, assuming that 100,000 men can be brought over per month and if we brought infantry, we could have 100,000 by the end of May, 200,000 by the end of June, and 300,000 by the end of July; that this would be a factor worth considering in the present battle where the need for infantry is so urgent; that if in the month of May we could bring over 120,000 infantry this would still lack 100,000 of making up the losses which the British have already suffered; that taking into consideration the losses which they will suffer in the meantime, the Allied forces would rapidly be declining; that if in the month of June we brought over no infantry we would still have no more infantry than at the end of May; meanwhile the infantry of the Allied forces would be still further declining.

General Pershing stated that the proposition of bringing over 120,000 infantry in May and following them by the artillery, etc., in June had been agreed to by the British; that he had just spent three days in London talking this matter over with Lloyd George, and General Wilson, and Lord Milner, and that he was in full accord with them on this proposition. He stated further that Sir Douglas Haig is very anxious to have an American army in the line as soon as possible and fighting on the right of the British; that we must not lose sight of the importance of having this American army.

General Foch stated that he wanted to see an American army—as soon as possible, as large as possible, as well instructed as possible—taking its place on the Allied front, but that if we did not take steps to prevent the disaster which is threatened at present the American army may arrive in France to find the British pushed into the sea and the French back of the Loire, while they try in vain to organize on lost battlefields over the tombs of Allied soldiers. He stated that we must look to the present needs, without considering propositions agreed to before we become engaged in the present struggle.

General Pershing stated that he wished to make himself as clearly understood as possible; that he favors bringing over American troops as rapidly as possible; that these troops are to go with the British or the French for a period of training; that during this period of training they will follow the sort of troops with which they are serving, but that we must foresee and prepare an American army fighting as such under American commanders.

General Foch asked General Bliss to explain the reasons which led the Versailles Council to adopt the measure referred to as the Versailles proposition.

General Bliss gave the only reasons which he knew. [*Ed.*—According to Pershing's version of the discussions, Bliss said the following: "The collective note recommended to the United States to send only infantry until the Supreme War Council should give instructions to the contrary. The Government of the United States in conformity with this note and with the recommendations of Mr. Baker consented to this plan. As far as the employment of the units on the front is concerned, the question should be decided by General Pershing according to agreement with the Commander-in-Chief to whose army they may be attached." (Pershing, *My Experiences in the World War*, vol. 2, p. 12.)]

General Pershing asked General Foch how he contemplated employing American units assigned for temporary duty with the Allied forces.

General Foch replied that he thought by regiments or by brigades. Finally, four American regiments might be united with French or British artillery and called an American division,

General Pershing asked how long he thought they would have to serve as regiments before being united into brigades and as brigades before being united into divisions.

General Foch thought it not possible to say, except that this would depend on General Pershing and on the troops themselves.

General Pershing outlined the system agreed upon by himself, General Pétain, and General Haig, and stated that it worked very satisfactorily with the troops we had

had with the French. None have yet had an opportunity of trying it with the British. He stated that he wished his brigade and division commanders during the periods of instruction of the troops to be attached to the headquarters with which their troops are serving, so as to learn something of their own duties, and that he wanted the regiments united as soon as possible into divisions under American commanders.

General Foch agreed to the principle but stated that the time for forming American divisions could not now be stated. He still further insisted on its not being necessary for the Americans to have an artillery, but they could use French or British artillery.

General Pershing stated that the proposition is as long as it is broad, and that if American artillery is brought over to serve with American infantry, the British and French artillery thus not needed can be used by the British and French as they see fit.

General Foch stated that to bring over 120,000 troops in the month of May is a splendid effort, that this effort should be continued in June in the same way, and that in June we should certainly not contemplate bringing over any artillery.

General Pershing stated that the plan which he had outlined was one which had been drawn up by Lloyd George, Lord Milner, General Wilson, and himself, and that the procedure had been agreed to by Sir Douglas Haig. He further stated that an examination of the British shipping facilities made by Sir Joseph Maclay revealed, according to Sir Joseph, that the British have more shipping than has been thought which they can place in the troop transport service; that they are going to put all of their available shipping to this use, and that they have reported that they can bring within the next three months 750,000 men.

General Pershing had read to General Foch part of a statement made by the British on the shipping situation; that he had agreed with the British to bring over 120,000 infantry and machine-gun units in May, these to be followed then by their artillery, etc., and that the British were disposed to bring over any other American units; that toward the end of May it is to be decided what shall be the shipping program for the month of June. This is to be dictated by the situation at that time.

General Foch stated that if the British had this much shipping to place in the troop transport service that it would be a wonderful asset, but we must still foresee the needs in infantry for the month of June.

General Pershing asked General Foch if the British were capable of bringing over troops as stated, would he (General Foch) agree to their bringing over entire units as planned.

General Foch agreed, but he still insisted on planning for the transportation of a large amount of infantry for the month of June.

The conversation ended with mutual assurances of confidence and cooperation.

General Pershing asked General Foch if he had heard anything of the reported situation as to shortage of coal.

General Foch appeared not very familiar with this situation and no decision was taken in the matter.

LC, Pershing Papers, folder: Conferences and Agreements, Folder No. 1, box 50; a copy of this report version is at *USAWW*, vol. 2, pp. 348–50; for the much more detailed Foch memo to Pershing (No. 420, undated) on the meeting, see *Les armées françaises dans la Grande Guerre, Tome 6*, vol. 2, *Annexes*, vol. 1: *Annexe* No. 59, pp. 141–46; Pershing, *My Experiences in the World War*, vol. 2, pp. 10–13, has a partial version somewhat similar to the French one but with some significant differences. The version used here is significantly different both from the French and Pershing versions mentioned above.

Editor's Note—Tasker Bliss, who participated in the above meeting with Foch and Pershing, wrote about it in his weekly letter no. 3 to Secretary of War Baker on April 27 (see below). However, he confuses the date, placing it on April 26 rather than April 25. Pershing puts the meeting on April 25 in his personal diary, as does *USAWW*, the report in Pershing's papers, and the French minutes in *Les armées françaises dans la Grande Guerre, Tome 6*, cited above.

General Foch wrote extensively about this meeting with Pershing in his postwar memoirs:

> The evident feebleness of this result [*Ed.*—The slow arrival of American troops in France] demanded that the mistakes which up to the present had been made in the matter of transporting the American Army to France be corrected. What was needed above all was that during several months the United States should send the Allies only infantry, to the exclusion of all other arms. By this means only could the British and French armies procure the 300,000 to 350,000 infantry which were needed to get through their existing crisis in effectives. In a detailed memorandum to the French Prime Minister, I presented these views and asked him to appeal to the American Government to put them into effect. [See April 21, Foch, No. 316.]
>
> This government, in fact, was already informed and seemed disposed to accept the proposition of the Commander in Chief of the Allied armies. It remained to convince General Pershing, who was full of the idea of commanding a great American army as soon as possible, although he was not, it is true, fully aware of the urgency of our present necessities.
>
> He and I readily fell into accord regarding this point, in the course of a conference held at Sarcus on April 25th, which was also attended by General Bliss. After a close discussion it was decided that the American troops to be brought over in May and June should, in principle, consist first of all of infantry. For the month of May, the question was settled there and then. For the month of June, it was agreed that a definite decision would be taken a little later; but from now on it was understood that the Government at Washington would prepare to send the infantry of at least six divisions to France.
>
> This meeting at the same time disclosed the urgent necessity for directing and coordinating to the advantage of the Coalition the effort being put forth by the United States, directing it so as to adapt it to necessities as they arose, co-ordinate it so as to prevent personal arrangements, such as that

concluded between General Pershing and Lord Milner and revealed in the course of the conference on April 25th, from having the effect of frittering away that effort. In a word, what ought to be done was for the Allied governments to study the question of American effectives as a whole and whatever decisions were taken, take them together. (Foch, *Memoirs*, pp, 307–8.)

Lt. Col. T. Bentley Mott, whom Pershing appointed as his liaison officer with Foch and his Allied Headquarters on April 16 and who acted as his interpreter during meetings with Foch thereafter, later wrote of this meeting at Sarcus:

> Pershing was fresh from his fight in London over this very phase of the question, Foch was tormented by daily contact with two armies in imminent peril, and the atmosphere grew tense. In vain the latter pointed out that if the present battle was lost the British might be driven back to the sea and the French behind the Loire. "The American Army would be formed," he went on, "but it seems to me you would find it easier to help us defend the Seine than to be obliged to reconquer all the territory lying between the river and the Loire."
>
> Foch was not only brilliant, he was methodical, and to study and understand Pershing had become a duty which he carefully pursued. It was evident to me on this occasion, when I served as interpreter, and on many others. He would try Pershing out on different lines to get his reaction and find the best approach. As time went on he came to understand the fire and generosity that were hidden beneath a grim exterior which, at first, had seemed to him, as to many others, like an unrelenting obstinacy, and he would deftly play upon these chords.
>
> No one who had not assisted at such interviews can imagine the heart-breaking difficulties that arose when two such men, both bent upon understanding each other and upon whose mutual comprehension so much depended, were forced to talk through an interpreter. Their minds could haltingly get into contact, but their souls would be groping in the void. What was said could be translated, but what was so behind the words could not be rendered it could only be guessed at by the other, and frequently the guess was wrong.
>
> The talk ended late at night with Pershing unconvinced and Foch disappointed. (Mott, *Twenty Years as Military Attaché*, pp. 242–43)

James Harbord, Pershing's Chief of Staff, who was also present at the meeting, had the following observation on Foch's attitude during the discussions:

> We returned from London by way of Folkestone and Boulogne. The motor-cars had been waiting for us at Boulogne, and we left at once for Sarcus to see General Foch. General Bliss was there and, after dinner that evening, we

discussed with him and Foch the arrangement made with Lord Milner. The Allied Commander-in-Chief, from whom General Pershing for the moment withheld the information that we were to have some British shipping, seemed to see in our agreement something which the British had accomplished to the disadvantage of the French. The troops to come in May were to be trained with the British, and he was not enthusiastic about it. His strong face lighted up, however, when General Pershing told him that the troops were coming in British shipping and he seemed to agree without further parley to the number of troops and the character of the organizations and their promised disposition. I state his agreement in that tentative form because the date was April 27th [25th], and he had changed his mind by the first of May. (Harbord, *The American Army in France*, p. 256.)

Pershing to TAG, War Department, in part in reply to TAG, War Department, to Pershing, cable A-877-S, March 7, in addition to Pershing to TAG, War Department, cable P-891-S, April 11.

Cable P-993-S.
4. For Chief Signal Officer. With reference to paragraph 4, your cablegram 877. In view of paragraph 1B, our cablegram 891, no additional personnel can now be sent. The total of 270 squadrons allowed in that program to include December 31st, 1918, is total personnel now authorized for Air Service. That includes the English training agreement, but does not include the Handley Page agreement which is not complete until spring of 1919.

NARA, RG 120, M930, Main Series, AEF to War Department, roll 3.

TAG, War Department, to Pershing.

Cable A-1172-R.
6. On account of the large number of colored men that are being drafted to comply with established quotas, it is urgently necessary that more colored combatant troops be sent to oversea service. The Infantry and Machine Gun units of the 92nd Division colored, are now in fairly good state training and can be made ready to embark in May and June. An early movement is desirable in order to clear certain camps at the ports. Your recommendation as to sending them to France is requested. March. [Reply—April 29, P-1024-S-1J; May 8, P-1074-S-1C]

NARA, RG 120, Main Series, War Department to AEF, roll 12.

TAG, War Department, to Pershing, in part in reply to Pershing to TAG, War Department, cables P-582-S, February 8, and P-889-S, April 10; in addition TAG, War Department, to Pershing, cable A-852-R, March 1.

Cable A-1173-R.

1. With reference to paragraph 1B, your 582. Following personnel Historical Section can sail immediately if you desire: Major R. M. Johnson, National Army, Harvard University, Lieutenant Lawrence Higgins, National Army, Lieutenant William E. Moore, Pictorial Section, Signal Reserve Corps, Major H. H. Sargent, retired, physically fit except quite deaf, and 6 trained clerks and translators. [*Ed.*—Pershing replied on April 30, cable P-1025-S-6, recommending "that personnel indicated for historical section sail at an early date. March replied in cable A-1257-R-5, on May 7 that the "officers and clerks for Historical Section will be sent without delay."]

1C. Reference your 889, paragraph 5. As only approximately 19 divisions will be left in United States on June 1st and because of urgent need of all available officers with these divisions here not practicable to designate officers from them for next course. It is expected now that about 10 General Staff Officers on duty at the War Department here can be designated to take the course. No other officers from United States can be spared for this purpose. March. [*Ed.*—On May 2 in A-1227-R-10, March designated the officers who would be going to France to attend the course.] [Reply—May 4, P-1051-S-3]

NARA, RG 120, M930, Main Series, War Department to AEF, roll 12.

April 26

Pershing's Personal Diary

At Paris. Saw in the morning members of the Shipping Board, Messrs. Stevens, [Dwight W.] Morrow, [George] Rublee and [L. H.] Shearman, with General Atterbury and Colonel Logan. Talked with Lieutenant Colonel Percy Jones about the relations of the ambulance service with the French authorities. Lunched with General Harbord and Colonel Boyd at Foyots. After luncheon saw Colonel Dawes. Had a talk with Mr. Loucheur about the coal situation, heavy artillery and airplanes. Saw Dr. Hamilton Holt, Editor of the Independent. Saw Mrs. Bliss at her house.

LC, Pershing Papers, Diary, May 7, 1917–September 1, 1918, box 4.

Editor's Note—The American members of the Allied Maritime Transport Council were in Paris for a meeting of the Council and met with Pershing on April 26 and 27 for a thorough review of the Allied and American shipping situation. Pershing had always taken great interest in these matters because shipping was the lifeblood of the

AEF, whose existence was problematic without it. In his memoirs, he discussed the results of their meetings:

> The shipping situation as brought out in conference with the American members of the Maritime Transport Council did not appear so favorable as we had been led to believe. Only two of our newly built vessels had been delivered and our shipbuilding program was not yet far enough along to count as an important factor, although prospects were that the rate would soon begin to increase. A full study made by our delegates to the Council of the demands to be made upon Allied and neutral tonnage for military, naval, and general needs showed an estimated shortage of nearly 2,000,000 tons. It was obvious that the program for strengthening the Western Front must be carried out if possible. Therefore, all practicable measures for the economical employment of every available ton of shipping, especially for freight, were given consideration at our conference.
>
> It was thought, in the first place, that the Allied navies could reduce their requirements of merchant tonnage by a joint examination of the naval programs; second, that considerable shipping could be saved by suspending or reducing military and naval activities in theaters of war other than the Western Front; third, that further reductions in Allied civilian imports might be made temporarily; and, finally, that insistence upon the adoption of unified action in the supply services by the Allies on the Western Front, already suggested, would result in a material saving of tonnage.
>
> I heartily approved of the above recommendations and sent a cable to Washington to that effect [see April 27, P-1007-S]. . . .
>
> Of course, certain agreements as to raw materials had to be maintained in order to keep production of ammunition and airplanes going and these required at least 30,000 tons monthly. In general, as with the question of unity of supply, to which all agreed in principle, so it was with sea transportation, but action in the latter case presented serious difficulties. As a matter of fact, in the broad sense the two were intimately connected. It seemed to me that the control of Allied supplies could well be vested in a board (with executive powers) consisting of a representative from each Government. It appeared logical that this board, in consultation with the Allied Maritime Council, should be authorized to allot Allied tonnage. This was fully stated in my cables, but Washington did not wholly accept my views. (Pershing, *My Experiences in the World War*, vol 2, pp. 13–15.)

Dwight W. Morrow, a former partner in J. P. Morgan and Company and then member of the U.S. Shipping Board, later became a member of the Executive Council of the Allied Maritime Transport Council. He was instrumental in working with Pershing and Dawes to resolve many of the shipping and tonnage problems confronting the AEF in 1918. He subsequently served as a member of the Military Board of Allied Supply.

Pershing to Foch, CINC, Allied Armies.

I am sending you through Colonel Mott a copy of the memorandum agreement signed by Lord Milner and myself regarding the transportation of American infantry, et cetera, for training with the British army.

While a liberal construction of this memorandum contemplates the completion of the provisions contained in paragraphs A and B, I shall, nevertheless, when the time comes, stand ready, in accordance with our recent conversation, to make recommendations to my Government with reference to further transportation of infantry, et cetera.

However it is my earnest hope and belief that the additional tonnage now reported as available will entirely remove any further anxiety as to the flow of American troops to Europe and make it unnecessary to consider the shipment of infantry troops alone.

[Enclosure—For the text of the London Agreement signed by Lord Milner and Pershing, April 24, 1918, see April 24.]

LC, Pershing Papers, folder: Training and Employment of American Troops with British, box 198.

Maj. Gen. William M. Black, Chief of Engineers, U.S. Army, to Pershing.

Personal and Confidential.

As I supposed the Secretary has already told you, we arrived safely on this side, after a very pleasant and comfortable voyage. I spent a great deal of my time on my back trying to recover from the strain received in France, and I am still suffering from the effects, though it is gradually wearing away.

I am back on duty, and Wednesday, accompanied by Colonel [Herbert W.] Alden of the Ordnance Corps, I inspected the flame throwing devise of which I spoke to you when in France. I believe that we have developed a weapon which will be very effective within its sphere of usefulness, and with which a loop-holed village or other like inclosed strong point can be cleaned up on short order. I recommended to the Chief of Staff that the apparatus on hand be sent to France immediately together with the inventor, Major Henry Adams, Engineer Reserve Corps, and three other men who have been working with him in the development. You will find that the space taken up by the apparatus is small enough to permit its use in the largest size of our and the British tanks. In its performance, it surpassed anything of its kind which either Colonel Alden or myself had seen, or of which we had read.

I think the feeling of all of our party on our return, was one of confidence in the final outcome of the war and a firm resolve to do all that is possible to assist you who are over in France. Personally, I am greatly indebted to you for many kindnesses while I was on the other side, and very particularly for the opportunity of seeing both of my sons.

With best regards for you and the members of your staff who did so much for us, and every desire to do everything for you that is possible to assist you in your great work....

LC, Pershing Papers, folder: Gen. William M. Black, box 26.

TAG, War Department, in part in reply to Pershing to TAG, War Department, cable P-913-S, April 14.

Cable A-1181-R.
    2. Attention Air Service. 2F. Reference your 913, paragraph 1I. Liberty 8-cylinder engine has never been placed in production and would require 4 to 5 months to do so. It has been tested to limited extent at Dayton, Mineola and Pikes Peak for altitude, but we would not recommend it unreservedly without further experience. According to tests already made and Major E J Hall's opinion this engine could be made satisfactory for single-engine fighting planes and we can put it in production if so directed by you. However recommend you give consideration to the fact that we have 180-horsepower Hispano engines in production by July and 300-horsepower Hispano by October. These engines are smaller in bulk and size and for all these reasons might be better for this purpose. Advise us your conclusions. [*Ed.*—On May 12 in cable P-1101-S-3A, the AEF informed the War Department that a Board of Officers was studying the engine question and that it would be informed as to its conclusions. In cable P-1203-S-5 on May 28, the AEF advised the War Department that it "omit Liberty 8 from further consideration for single-seater fighter at this time."]

NARA, RG 120, Main Series, War Department to AEF, roll 12, and AEF to War Department, roll 3.

TAG, War Department, to Pershing, in part in reply to Pershing to TAG, War Department, cable P-958-S, April 19.

Cable A-1182-R.
    1. With reference to paragraphs 5, 5A and 5B, our cablegram 914. Remains of Officers and enlisted men and civilian employees of the Army who die in British Isles will be buried there under the same conditions as for those who die in France. Instruct General Biddle.
    5. Reference paragraph 1, your 958. Shipping control committee advise this date that 1 lake steamer will be ready to sail within the next few days and should arrive abroad before May 16th. This vessel will immediately be followed by 14 additional lake steamers due to arrive in France prior to June 1st. 10 additional lake steamers have been requisitioned for your use and definite steps are being taken for their early delivery. Advise as to what port(s) these vessels should be sent. [*Ed.*—For back-

ground on this issue, see Vol. 1, September 19, 1917, Editor's Note following P-167-S.]
[Reply—April 27, P-1009-S; May 4, P-1051-S-6A; Vol. 5, May 26, P-1195-S-6B; in addition—May 10, A-1282-R-8]

NARA, RG 120, M930, Main Series, War Department to AEF, roll 12.

TAG, War Department, to Pershing, in addition to letter, Secretary of War Newton D. Baker to Pershing, April 29.

Cable A-1184-R. Confidential.
  1. Following notes have been furnished British Ambassador to the United States:

"April 19, 1918. Pursuant to the direction of the President and in conformity with his approval of the joint notes of the Permanent Military Representatives at Versailles, the United States will continue, throughout the months of April, May, June, and July, to supply for transportation both in its own owned and controlled tonnage, and in that made available by Great Britain, infantry and machine gun personnel. It is hoped, and on the basis of study so far it is believed, that the total number of troops transported will be 120,000 per month. These troops when transported will, under the direction and at the discretion of General Pershing, be assigned for training and use with British, French, or American divisions as the exigencies of the situation from time to time require; it being understood that this program, to the extent that it is a departure from the plan to transport and assemble in Europe complete American divisions, is made in view of the exigencies of the present military situation and is made in order to bring into useful cooperation at the earliest possible moment the largest possible number of American personnel in the military arm most needed by our allies. It being also understood that this statement is not to be regarded as a commitment from which the Government of the United States is not free to depart when the exigencies no longer require it; and also that the preferential transportation of infantry and machine gun units here set forth as a policy and principle is not to be regarded as so exclusive as to prevent the Government of the United States from including in the troops carried by its own tonnage from time to time relatively small numbers of personnel of other arms as may be deemed wise by the United States as replacements and either to make possible the use of a maximum capacity of ships or the most efficient use of the infantry and machine gun units as such transported, or the maintenance of the services of supply already organized and in process of construction for the American Army already in France. These suggestions are made in order that there may be a clear understanding of the intention of the United States and of the mode of execution of that intention, and they are not stipulated as indicating any intention on the part of the United

States, until the situation has in its judgment changed, to depart from as full compliance with the recommendation of the permanent military representatives as the nature of the case will permit."

In connection with foregoing General Hutchison of the British Army has suggested to the Secretary of War the feasibility of placing American Infantry in British divisions where the largest number of such infantry can be utilized with the idea that in a comparatively short time such divisions would consist entirely of American Infantry with British field artillery and that at that time they should be turned over to you as American divisions. It is understood that General Hutchison has cabled these suggestions to his Government. Your views are desired.

March.

NARA, RG 120, M930, Confidential Series, War Department to AEF, roll 18.

Editor's Note—In volume 2 of his wartime memoirs, Pershing commented at length about the significance of this memorandum and Lloyd George's maneuvering:

> Upon reaching Chaumont [upon his return from London and Paris], I found a cablegram, dated April 26th, transmitting a memorandum, dated April 19th, that had been sent by direction of the President to the British Ambassador at Washington in conformity with his approval of Joint Note No. 18 of the Supreme War Council. In this memorandum the shipment of only infantry and machine gun units for four months was conceded, and it was hoped and believed that the number would be 120,000 per month. Their assignment for training and use was to be left to my discretion. The memorandum went on to say that the United States, until the situation changed, had no intention of departing from as full compliance with the recommendation of the Permanent Military Representatives as the nature of the case would permit.
>
> This was the first official information I had received that the Administration had agreed to send any specific number of infantry and machine gun units to France.
>
> [*Ed.*—Paragraph 1 of cable A-1184-R repeated.]
>
> This concession went further than it was necessary to go and much further than I had expected. Realizing the complications that might arise from commitments so far in the future and the delay in forming an American army that would follow, I did not agree in later discussions at the Supreme War Council with all that the Allies now felt justified in demanding. I was opposed to the action of the Council in assuming the power to dispose American troops under any circumstances. Moreover, it was not in any sense a prerogative of this body.

There can be little doubt that even before the President's memorandum was issued Lord Reading received the distinct impression that infantry and machine gun units would be sent to France at the rate of 120,000 men per month for four months, beginning with April. That the President agreed to this "in principle" is practically certain. It need not be further emphasized that such a concession, even though prompted by the most generous impulses, could only add to the difficulties of our task of building up an army of our own. It is probable that Lord Reading, skilled advocate that he was, did more while Ambassador at Washington to influence the Administration to grant Allied requests than any other individual.

The Secretary of War upon his return caused the Administration's position to be somewhat more clearly defined through the President's memorandum, but the statement still left much to be desired in the way of a positive declaration of our purpose to have our own army. It left a very definite notion in the minds of the Allies that the Administration at Washington was favorable to amalgamation and that the main obstacle to be overcome was the military head of the American forces in France. This is doubtless that reason why all the Allied verbal "heavy artillery" was often turned in my direction.

The agreement made in London, as actually drawn, while insuring the shipment of largely increased numbers of troops, did not commit us to sending infantry and machine gun units exclusively beyond June 1st. It provided a reserve of the classes of troops that might be needed by the British until their new drafts should be available, and offered the possibility of our getting other classes of troops to complete our plans of organization for the auxiliary arms and Services of Supply. The British thought that this program could be very much exceeded and believed it might be possible to transport entire divisions besides a number of corps and S.O.S. troops. The concession we made for May was a radical departure from the wise policy of bringing over balanced forces in complete organizations, but the clamor was so great and the danger of the absolute defeat of the Allies seemed so imminent that it was thought to be warranted as a temporary expedient.

The question of applying conscription to Ireland was then under consideration by the British and it appeared probable, according to views expressed more or less guardedly, that British troops would be required to enforce it. Inasmuch as such a measure would more than likely have affected the attitude of American troops of Irish origin toward service with the British, our argument was strengthened regarding the desirability of keeping our own troops together and organizing them into an American army at the earliest possible date. (Pershing, *My Experiences in the World War*, Vol. 2, pp. 7–9.)

Harbord, who was personally involved in these matters, provides his assessment of the impact of the Baker Memorandum and cable A-1184-R:

The cabled Memorandum conceded the shipment only of infantry and machine-gun detachments in numbers hoped to reach 120,000 per month for the four months, and it committed the United States during the current situation to as full compliance as the nature of the case permitted, with the recommendation of the Permanent Military Representatives. That meant not General Pershing but Bliss, Foch, Wilson and Cadorna. The Memorandum was safeguarded by some qualifying provisions, but they were not strong, and included a voluntary limitation of the troops to be carried on our own ships "to relatively small numbers of personnel of other arms, etc., etc." It was a concession that cut the ground from under General Pershing's feet. It was the first definite official information that the Administration had agreed to any specified numbers of infantry and machine guns. It confirmed what Lord Milner had told us in London, but which we had been unable to bring ourselves to believe was true. . . .

The Allies interpreted the action of the President to mean that the Administration was out of sympathy with General Pershing's contention against amalgamation or the incorporation of American soldiers in French and British units. It added to General Pershing's burdens. (Harbord, *The American Army in France*, p. 259.)

With this observation in mind, it is most enlightening to read Lloyd George's vitriolic attack on Pershing in volume 2 of his *War Memoirs*, which follows a short quotation from the above-cited Pershing comments. The Prime Minister writes, "Thus the decision of the President of the United States proved of insufficient value in face of the stubborn intransigence of the American Commander-in-Chief. He could see no further than the exaltation of his own command, the jealous maintenance of his own authority." (*War Memoirs*, vol. 2, p. 1823).

April 27

Pershing's Personal Diary

At Paris. Saw in morning members of Shipping Board; also had talk with Miss Birkhead. In the afternoon got off cablegram on shipping situation [see below, P-1007-S] and saw General Foulois and Colonel Burtt about proposition of Mr. Loucheur tending toward better cooperation with French for turning out more airplanes [see below]. Talked with Colonel Jordan [Harry B., Acting Chief Ordnance Officer] about proposition of Mr. Loucheur for cooperation with the French in turning out long-range guns. Did a little shopping. Had Colonel Mott come down from General Foch's headquarters and talked with him before dinner [see April 28, Mott memorandum, for details]. Had to dinner at Foyots Mr. Crosby, Colonel Dawes, Colonel Mott and Colonel Boyd. At dinner talked about possibility of getting Italian laborers. After dinner saw in quarters Major Clark [Pershing's Liaison Officer with

Pétain's GHQ] who informs me that M. Clemenceau has sent a telegram to General Ragueneau informing him that I have promised to give the British eight divisions in the month of May and nothing to the French. I told him to let them understand this is the same proposition agreed on with them for six divisions to which M. Clemenceau had agreed. He also stated that the French think the British still have about 1,000,000 men in England in the depots, 700,000 of which are good for service in France. I told him he could say that I had just returned from England and believe the British have practically no reserves at all in England.

LC, Pershing Papers, Diary, May 7, 1917–September 1, 1918, box 4.

Editor's Note—Although Pershing discussed the London Agreement with Foch in general terms on April 25, he soon discovered that Foch was not pleased with the arrangement. Accordingly, he called in Lt. Col. Mott, his liaison officer with Foch at Sarcus, and after a lengthy discussion, sent him back to see Foch and Weygand about this agreement. While Pershing notes further French interest in the agreement in his diary entry above, he mentions nothing either here or in his memoirs of the meeting that the British and French leaders held at Abbeville on the morning of the 27th. In attendance for the French were Clemenceau, Foch, and Weygand, and for the British Lord Milner, Douglas Haig, and Generals Henry Wilson (CIGS), H. A. Lawrence, J. P. Du Cane, and E. L. Spiers. One of the subjects brought up was the London Agreement. In his excellent study, *It Might Have Been Lost!* Lonergan describes the meeting thusly:

> On the same day in France, there was held a Conference at Abbeville, attended only by French and British representatives, during which, the French Prime Minister introduced the subject of the London agreement, expressing surprise that it should have been consummated without the knowledge or representation of the French Government and suggesting that it be supplanted by an entirely new measure, which he evidently considered would be more effective....
>
> M. Clemenceau complained that the British and Americans had made an agreement without consulting the French, and that General Pershing had gone to London to discuss this matter without any French representative being present. By the agreement come to the American contingent for the French Army was to go to British formations. M. Clemenceau did not dispute the desirability of the arrangement made, but he could not understand how such an agreement could have been arrived at without the French being present. M. Clemenceau said he understood General Pershing was against American infantry and machine guns preceding other arms to France. What General Pershing wanted was to form a great American Army. M. Clemenceau asked that a French and British General should go to Washington and present a Joint Memorandum in favor of the view that infantry and machine guns should be sent to France. The agreement with

General Pershing, dated 24th April, (i.e., the London agreement) was read. M. Clemenceau and Lord Milner agreed that this paper should be submitted to the Supreme War Council. [See below, May 1, Abbeville Conference, at which the London Agreement was brought up during the first day and thoroughly discussed.]

Lord Milner explained his policy as follows:

Every month the first 120,000 men should be infantry and machine-gunners, certainly for the first three months, and if possible afterwards, and that all surplus tonnage in any one month should be for the purpose of carrying Artillery and Administrative units at the disposal of the Americans. This was agreed to....

The complications that might have ensued, had M. Clemenceau been able to force the fulfillment of his request, may be easily conjectured. It was certain, nevertheless, that the British would have opposed strenuously the course of action he had suggested, because of the disaster it would have wrought with the results of the efforts they had exerted so untiringly, since December 1, 1917, with Colonel House and General Pershing in France and, through Lord Reading, with President Wilson and the Secretary of War in Washington. The acceptance by M. Clemenceau of Lord Milner's alternative, that the London agreement be submitted to the Supreme War Council instead, must have afforded the British contingent considerable relief.

For the second and last time a move [for the first attempt, see Editor's Note following April 7, Baker-Pershing conference with Whigham and Hutchison], which might have jeopardized the retention of command of the A.E.F. by General Pershing, was frustrated. The gesture had been restrained before the ictus [sharp blow] could be delivered. It is true the restraining force had been applied in this instance by the British, who, themselves, not long before had entertained a somewhat kindred sentiment. Not that a direct appeal to President Wilson, for General Pershing's removal had been deliberately contemplated in either case.

Rather that the representation by the British, or the French and British Governments jointly, to the President of a seemingly stubborn disinclination on the part of the American Commander-in-Chief to execute the Washington commitment in the matter, might engender in the mind of the President a fear as to General Pershing's suitability to retain command, because of the latter's express adverseness to adjust, fully and harmoniously, the provisions of that commitment with the Allies thus making operation, through lack of co-operation, difficult in the common enterprise.

The accumulating incidents of the first four months of 1918 bear convincing testimony to the loyal purpose and unswerving determination of General Pershing. From the very beginning he had not been left free to organize, train and fight his soldiers, but had been charged with all details in France including, as Sir William Robertson had told the British War

Cabinet, the responsibilities of a political character. This last charge would not have been so oppressive, had he been completely upheld in the final decisions which he had been authorized to make, or at least had the Administration refrained from making concessions incompatible with his decisions, and nearly always without his counsel or knowledge. (Lonergan, *It Might Have Never Been Lost!*, pp. 160–63; the proceedings of this conference can be found at *USAWW*, vol. 2, pp. 355–56.)

Louis Loucheur, French Minister of Armament and War Fabrications, and J. L. Dumesnil, Under-Secretary of State for Military and Naval Aeronautics, Paris, to Pershing.

Memorandum on the Co-Operation that is Necessary between the Production Departments of the American and French Air Services.

It is essential to coordinate more closely the production resources of each of the two countries, America and France.

Just at present, America wishes to build complete new airplanes immediately, which (undertaking) requires long experience which France has only acquired at the cost of heavy sacrifices.

Our idea is as follows:

Take from each country that which it can produce, at the present time and with the least effort, either in the way of engines or of planes, and assemble the complete airplanes in France.

1. Pursuit Aviation. French factories are at present very well equipped to produce in very large batches—and in even bigger batches if this became necessary—Hispano Suiza engines. These motors are now being used in SPAD planes, but, for use with the new 300 H.P. engines, we contemplate a new plane, the tests of which will be completed very quickly.

Not only should the production of 300 H.P. Hispano engines be developed in France—but this production should also be developed in the U.S. Moreover, the production in France of the corresponding airplane bodies, should be increased; this with the help of raw materials from America, in order to be able to satisfy, as fully as possible, the requirements of American Aviation in pursuit machines.

2. Army Corps Aviation (Observation and Reconnaissance). We are examining the use of Liberty engines in Breguet bodies. We think this engine will be satisfactory.

If this proves to be the case, we can surely supply the Breguet bodies, which will be fitted with Liberty engines, received from America, and which will constitute the Army Corps, or reconnaissance aviation of the American Army.

We could even, if the U.S. wishes, make a swap and trade a certain number of Salmson airplanes for the Breguet-Liberty units.

3. Day-Bombing Aviation. Always with the reservation that the Liberty engine gives satisfaction and proves to be as good as the Renault, we have from now on

made our plans for doubling the output of the Michelin factory at Clermont-Ferrand, which manufactures Breguet day-bombing plane bodies.

It would therefore only be necessary to send us the necessary Liberty engines in order to enable us to supply the American Army with a considerable number of day-bombing planes.

On the other hand, if Liberty engines are given to French Naval Aviation, as has been requested, it would be possible for us in this way to withhold a certain number of Renault engines, which would make it possible to still further increase the number of day-bombing planes which are to be manufactured.

4. Night-Bombing Aviation. We have just produced on an industrial basis some remarkable types of night-bombing planes.

We can foresee the production of the plane bodies; we will only be embarrassed in their production by the lack of engines.

By making certain changes in Liberty engines, we could bring about a much greater production of night-bombing airplanes, to the benefit of the allied armies.

Furthermore, there is nothing to prevent the U.S. also from undertaking large-scale production of airplane bodies, selected from among the best types perfected by us. Indeed the U.S. must do this if she is to realize the Great Aerial Fleet which the Allies are expecting her to produce. By the time that French factories have reached their full output, with the help of engines and raw materials coming from the U.S., she (the U.S.) should be completely organized for the rapid and perfect manufacture of the biggest and latest airplane types. The U.S. should also be able to use the necessary tonnage to transport these airplanes to France, in addition to those which she is already sending us.

The manufacture in the U.S. of an airplane (without motor) conceived in Europe is not an easy matter.

We are often obliged to begin quantity production even before the final detail drawings have been made; to enable the U.S. to begin quantity production of a given type it is necessary to send over these detail drawings, it is necessary to add the time required for transmission, the time necessary in acquiring an exact understanding of the drawings, time for studying the tool equipment, and by the time that the American manufacture of airplane bodies is completely perfected and transportation working on a normal basis so much time will have elapsed as a result of inevitable delays that the airplane made in this way is nearly sure to be "out of style" (semi-obsolete) by the time it arrives in France.

If, on the other hand, the U.S. in agreement with us, immediately concentrates its effort on a definite number of 300 H.P. Liberty's and perhaps also on a certain number of accessories or component parts of the planes, we would, between us, work up to a tremendous production, benefitting both armies as a result.

In this connection it would appear eminently advisable for the U.S. to undertake the immediate manufacture of the Canton-Unne Z.18 500 H.P. which we have just tested out and the quantity manufacture of which is beginning immediately in France. It is essentially two Z.9 motors coupled together. The Z.9 motor has given perfect satisfaction to the French Army; it is easy to manufacture; it gives the biggest output in proportion to the weight of raw material used. If the U.S. produces the Z.18

along with us the result will be an altogether remarkable flexibility in the production of corresponding airplanes.

Indeed, we contemplate the use of this Z.18, 500 H.P. motor for two-seater and multi-seater combat planes, for day and night bombing planes, for hydroplanes, and it is an engine which we think it will be possible to use on almost all types of planes. Its actual employment will certainly increase our present lead on Germany – for we repeat it – in three months, this engine will be produced in quantity in France.

If necessary, we are ready to send a man to America with the sole object of giving all information relating to the manufacture of this engine and to take with him all the necessary data.

We have at our service the necessary experts for working out the corresponding airplane bodies. We have an organization here which enables us to do this work quickly, and at the same time we will put the airplane bodies into quantity production, for the American Army as well as for the French Army, particularly if we receive assistance in the way of raw material, and provided tonnage priority for aviation is effectively granted in accordance with agreements already entered into.

[*Ed.*—Pershing referred this memorandum to Brig. Gen. Benjamin D. Foulois, Chief, Air Service, SOS, AEF, for comment and recommendations. See Foulois's answer on April 28.]

LC, Foulois Papers, folder 12: AEF, Air Service, Allied Air Service, box 7; see also LC, Pershing Papers, folder: Data for Book *My Experiences in the World War*, folder 1: Foulois, "Air Service—American Expeditionary Forces (1917–1918)," Encl. H: "Efforts of the French to establish a Joint Aircraft Production Program with the United States, to the exclusion of England. and Italy," pp. 1–3, box 351.

Arthur H. Frazier, Counselor, assigned to Supreme War Council, U.S. Embassy, Paris, to Pershing.

Confidential.

I hope you will forgive my temerity in writing to you about military matters but the gravity of the situation in Italy was called so emphatically to my attention this morning that I venture to send you these few lines.

An American, just back from the Italian front and having the full confidence of the Italians, told me that if we do not send American troops to Italy within the next few weeks it will be too late; he claims that their presence in a place like Turin would have a very great moral effect. The same man informed me that the Italians have prepared successive positions to fall back upon as far as the river Po; he pointed out that the loss of Venice would be a disaster for the Italian navy and would seriously embarrass the Allied navies in the Mediterranean.

With apologies for taking up your time. . . .

LC, Pershing Papers, folder: Arthur Hugh Frazier, box 78.

Bliss, Chief, American Section, and Permanent Military Representative, SWC, Versailles, to Secretary of War Baker.

[Weekly Letter No. 3]

On Thursday night [April 25], and again on Friday morning, I received an urgent request from General Foch to go to his headquarters in order to have a conference on Friday night with himself and General Pershing. [*Ed.*—Bliss is incorrect on the date. See Editor's Note following April 25.] I left here at noon and it required six hours to make the trip which ordinarily could be done in 2½. The roads were encumbered with countless ammunition and supply motor trains, hospital trains, etc., all moving toward the battlefield. I had taken a very round-about way, much further to the west than on any of the previous trips I have made to General Foch's Headquarters, but it seems impossible at this stage of the game to get beyond the region of moving troops and supply trains.

The Conference illustrated one of the peculiarities of the French mind. Their military men seem unwilling to act except upon a definite agreement drawn up in black and white, with every "i" dotted and every "t" crossed, and then signed. General Foch has noted that the Resolution of the Supreme War Council, approved by our President, relating to the sending of American infantry, says that this movement is to continue only while the emergency demands it. General Foch is convinced that the emergency will last until at least the end of July. The object of his Conference was to get General Pershing to accept this view and to agree that American infantry would have precedence, to the exclusion of all other units, until at least that date. As this was a matter which concerned General Pershing alone, I said nothing. After a long discussion without, apparently, getting anywhere, General Foch appealed to me as to what the Military Representatives meant when they prepared the Joint Note in regard to the movement of American infantry. I replied that they meant just what the Resolution said, to-wit: that in view of the existing emergency American infantry should have precedence in transportation to France, with the assumption that this movement would continue as long as the emergency continued. I said that so far as I could see he and General Pershing were in substantial accord except as to a mere form of words which did not in reality amount to anything; that he, General Foch, wanted General Pershing to agree that the emergency would last to at least a fixed date, which General Pershing was unwilling to do because no one could tell what might happen tomorrow that would relieve the emergency; that he, General Pershing, agreed that the movement should continue as long as the emergency existed; in other words, that General Pershing was, in reality, more liberal in his view than General Foch demanded, because General Pershing's attitude was that the movement should continue as long as the emergency lasted, even if it lasted longer than the month of July; and that he, General Foch, had secured an understanding with General Pershing that went even further than General Foch had asked. The Conference broke up with, apparently, that general understanding.

LC, Bliss Papers, folder: General Correspondence: Bliss to Newton Diehl Baker, December 1917–May 1918, box 250.

Editor's Note—Baker forwarded Bliss's entire letter to President Wilso on May 8. Link (ed.), *The Papers of Woodrow Wilson*, vol. 47: *March 13–May 12, 1918*, pp. 563–66.

Edward M. House, Counsellor to the President, New York, to Pershing, in reply to Pershing to House, February 27.

Thank you for your letter of February 27th. I have delayed answering because I have been ill with grippe for about six weeks.

I hear from you practically every day through cables and I feel that I am in almost daily touch with what you are doing.

Major General Hutchison of the British Army has been with me today and has outlined the suggestion which he has made to Secretary Baker and in which he hopes the British Staff will concur. If the British will consent, and I am sure they will, to turn over to you at the end of this crisis their ordnance and engineers which are now to help complete our divisions, it will be a fine solution of a difficulty and will tide over the period of disappointment which our lack of ordnance would otherwise bring about. It will also give us an American Army under your command much sooner than if we had to supply all units ourselves.

His idea as you will now know is for us to replace their artillery and engineers with ours when we are able to do so.

I do not feel at all depressed over the news which comes from the Western Front. The fact that the Germans made this offensive is pretty good evidence that they were compelled to do so by conditions not so much in Germany as in Austria, and if we can send a sufficient American force to make good the Allies' losses during the Spring and summer, I believe Germany will see the end of her ambitions.

I may say to you in confidence that there are constant efforts in certain directions antagonistic to the Administration to discredit you, but I am sure they will fail for the reason that you will give them no opening where a thrust can be effective. However, the Administration from top to bottom and the American people are back of you and will give you that loyal support which is not only due you, but which is so necessary for success.

LC, Pershing Papers, folder: Col. E. M. House (Confidential Notes), box 97; copy at Edward Mandell House Papers, Manuscripts and Archives, Yale University Library, Series 1: Correspondence, folder 3072: John J. Pershing, box 89.

Pershing, Paris, to TAG, War Department, in addition to Pershing to TAG, War Department, cables P-953-S, April 19, and P-960-S, April 23.

Cable P-1007-S. Confidential.
For the Secretary of War.

A. Mr. Stevens, the American delegate to the Allied Maritime Transport Council, has handed me a copy of the statement of the tonnage position of the Allied and neutral world for 1918 and the various demands upon that tonnage for military, naval and general transport needs. A full copy of that statement has been forwarded to the President by Mr. Stevens. It shows an estimated tonnage deficit for 1918 of almost 2,000,000 deadweight tons unless some of the existing programs can be reduced. Obviously the military program on the Western front cannot be reduced. In fact it must be increased, especially the participation of the United States therein. But it is strongly believed by the Council and by me that much more efficient service from the tonnage available for supplying this front can be obtained if the following suggestions be approved: First, that the use of merchant tonnage by Allied navies might be materially reduced by joint reconsideration of naval programs; Second, that considerable tonnage might be saved by suspending or reducing military activities in theatres of war other than the Western front. (While we have no direct interest in campaigns other than on the Western front, we have a decided indirect interest therein because of a withdrawal of tonnage from the common store for such purpose may actually paralyze our own efforts in the common cause of the Western front); Third, that further reductions in civilian imports carefully considered by inter-allied criticism can release additional tonnage; and Fourth, that the insistence upon the part of our government of the adoption by all the Allies of a unified action in supply services on the Western front by some such procedure is suggested in my cable No. 953.

B. I therefore heartily approve the recommendation made by the Allied Maritime Transport Council (which, it is important to note, as a body upon which French and English ministers are sitting) that all of the military programs of the Allies be brought under joint review by the appropriate military authorities to the end that effort may be concentrated on the Western front. While this is of vital importance to the common cause, it is of peculiar and of almost supreme importance to our own rapidly growing Army. If programs are allowed to remain in effect which call for more tonnage than is in existence, the calls for diversion of our ships for food supplies, coal, nitrates, and other things essential to our Allies would become more and more insistent. They will tend to converge more and more upon our program because our program is rapidly expanding and the others are comparatively rigid. Therefore a cutting down of all military programs that do not directly contribute to the common cause and a greater unity in the prosecution of those plans that do contribute to the common cause are essential during the next few months if we are to avoid the disaster that will come from haphazard curtailments of absolute essentials at the 11th hour.

C. The naval authorities are of the opinion that the defense against the submarine is becoming more and more effective and there is ground for expecting that it will be under control during the present summer. The tonnage situation should therefore improve rapidly after the next 6 months. During those 6 months when tonnage will be at its lowest point we must use every effort to avoid putting a greater strain on existing tonnage that it can possibly bear.

D. Question of tonnage transportation is naturally intimately connected with that of pooling supplies referred to in my cable No. 960. Both should be equally under military control as far as possible. The necessity for the use of all supplies and facilities, including sea transportation, for the common military end is realized and agreed to in principle by both the French and British and presumably by the Italians. In order to get this complete concert of action allotment of shipping and supply should be under military control. Have suggested appointment of a military expert by each government would together form a board with executive powers that should determine all questions of allocation of general supplies and, in consultation with the Allied Maritime Transport Council, would direct the allotment of Allied tonnage. Such a board could at least consider ways and means of bringing about this concert of action and would be the first step out of which it is believed joint control under one executive head would probably grow.

NARA, RG 120, M930, Confidential Series, AEF to War Department, roll 7.

Pershing to TAG, War Department.

Cable P-1008-S.
8. For Chief Signal Officer. 8B. With reference to paragraph 9, your letter March 23 [not located] to Foulois. Handley Page contract calls for supply by the United States of the personnel for 3 aircraft acceptance parks aggregating 1314 workmen of various trades given in detail in table attached to contract. As you will also see from contract this personnel is for erection of planes and testing at acceptance parks and not for assembly of planes in factories from parts shipped from United States. [Reply—May 7, A-1260-R-1C]

NARA, RG 120, M930, Main Series, AEF to War Department, roll 3.

Pershing to TAG, War Department, reply to TAG, War Department, to Pershing, cable A-1182-R, April 26.

Cable P-1009-S.
Reference Stevens cable no. 132, April 19th [Sims for Stevens to Secretary of the Navy (Operations), SM-132]. We have gone into coal situation with following result: England can meet present emergency with her tonnage but we must be prepared to help out. We now have approximately 60,000 deadweight tons our shipping working in the cross-Channel coal trade to which can be added the 25 lake steamers referred to in paragraph 5, your cablegram No. 1182. Assuming capacity these latter vessels as 3,000 tons each this would give us 135,000 deadweight tons total for this trade. These vessels will be made available for the common stock of coal in France as and when necessary. If situation is found so pressing as not to permit awaiting arrival lake steamers and if England and France cannot meet the emergency we shall be required to divert for a single cross-Channel voyage some of our trans-Atlantic steamers while

on this side. We had relied upon all of these lake steamers for our own cross-Channel trade. The strong probability that they will be absorbed for some time in supplementing the French coal requirements emphasizes anew the great importance of your requesting for service over here any small vessels useful for channel service. It would be a great misfortune if we should be compelled to divert any of our existing trans-Atlantic fleet for this purpose as any diversion of latter can only result in slowing up our military effort. Stevens board concurs. [Reply—May 7, A-1261-R-2]

NARA, RG 120, M930, Main Series, AEF to War Department, roll 3.

Editor's Note—Raymond Stevens and several members of the U.S. Shipping Control Board visited with Pershing, Brig. Gen. W. W. Atterbury, Director General of Transportation, SOS, AEF, and Col. Logan of the AEF staff in Paris on April 26 and 27 for a thorough discussion of the entire issue of the cross-Channel coal trade. Stevens, a member of the U.S. Shipping Board and the American representative on the Allied Maritime Transport Council in London, was a major player in the entire business of American and Allied maritime shipping requirements and resources and was well known to Pershing.

TAG, War Department, to Pershing, in part in reply to Pershing to TAG, War Department, cable P-818-S, March 29.

Cable A-1189-R.

1A. Reference to paragraph 1D, your 818. Making special effort ship 6 batteries 4.7-inch early June. 2 regiments 35th Division equipped with 4.7-inch which it is understood will accompany that division. Making special effort for shipment in July 24 4.7-inch guns complete. Production 4.7-inch and 155-millimeter guns being pushed utmost speed. [Reply—June 12, P-1292-S-4A]

NARA, RG 120, M930, Main Series, War Department to AEF, roll 3.

TAG, War Department, to Pershing, in part in reply to Pershing to TAG, War Department, cable P-916-S, April 14.

Cable A-1191-R.

1E. With reference to paragraph 3, your 916. Will ship in May 24 8-inch howitzers, probably without firing platforms. Could ship in May in addition to foregoing 53 howitzers and carriages, 36 limbers, 33 limber boxes, but probably will have no sights and firing platforms. British War Mission suggest sights could be obtained from England. Part of tractors will have to be 15-ton. Instructions requested. [Reply—Vol. 5, May 20, P-1154-S-2]

NARA, RG 120, M930, Main Series, War Department to AEF, roll 12.

TAG, War Department, to Pershing.

Cable A-1192-R.
5. Attention Air Service. Captain Mackenzie advises that it is contemplated to send pieces for Handley Page spares directly to France for assembly at Air Production Center Number 2 [Romorantin] instead of to England as per understanding between Waldon and Sir Henry Fowler. We are still working on your original instructions January 9th to Waldon and London Conference decision that all Handley Page assemblies of planes and spares to be made in England. Believe difficulties in laying out plant and providing equipment including duplicates all jigs and fixtures used in assembly in England will be greater than difficulties in transportation of finished spares from England. We are making layouts for two types for Caproni work as per Allen report March 15th but making no provision Handley Page assemblies at APC 2. From our point of view, we believe the above arrangements should not be changed, particularly for wing assembly as all wing ribs will be made and assembled in England. Please cable us further. [Reply—May 9, P-1083-S-6C]

NARA, RG 120, M930, Main Series, War Department to AEF, roll 12.

TAG, War Department, to Pershing, in part in reply to Pershing to TAG, War Department, cable P-930-S, April 16.

Cable A-1197-R.
2. With reference to paragraph 1, your 930. You are authorized to make in the name of the Secretary of War and publish necessary regulations to give effort to legislation in Public Number 133. Copy as follows: "An Act to give indemnity for damage caused by American forces abroad.

Be it enacted by the Senate and House of Representatives of the United States of America in Congress assembled, that claims of inhabitants of France or any other European country not an enemy or ally of an enemy for damage caused by American military forces may be presented to any officer designated by the President, and then approved by such an officer shall be paid under regulations made by the Secretary of War.

Section 2. That claims under this statute shall not be approved unless they would be payable according to law or practice governing the military forces of the country in which they occur.

Section 3. That hereafter appropriations for the incidental expenses of the Quartermaster Corps shall be available for paying the claims herein described.

Section 4. That this statute does not supersede other mode of indemnity now in existence and does not diminish the responsibility of any member of the military forces to the persons injured or to the United States.

Approved April 18th 1918."
March

NARA, RG 120, M930, Main Series, War Department to AEF, roll 12.

April 28

Pershing's Personal Diary

At Paris. Saw Colonel Logan on Red Cross matter; Colonel Jordan [Acting Chief Ordnance Officer] about proposition of Mr. Ganne concerning big guns; talked with General Foulois and Colonel Burtt about Mr. Ganne's proposition for cooperation in production of aviation material [see below, Foulois to Pershing], and with General [William] Crozier on Italian situation [Chief of Ordnance, then in France]. Also had talk with Colonel Mott [see Mott memorandum below]. Had to luncheon General Crozier, Colonel Dawes, Colonel Mott and Colonel Boyd. Left Paris about 6 p.m., stopping at Fontainebleau for dinner. Arrived at Chaumont about 1:30 in the night.

LC, Pershing Papers, Diary, May 7, 1917–September 1, 1918, box 4.

Pershing to Lloyd George, Prime Minister, London.

Referring to our recent conversation, permit me to confirm my suggestion that all supplies and war materials that are used in common by the allied armies be pooled and that the principle be extended, as far as possible, to the civil populations of the Allies.

After many disappointments in efforts to secure cooperation and coordination among the allied armies, we have finally come to recognise the absolute necessity for the appointment of a Commander-in-Chief of the Allied Armies in France, with full power to give all necessary directions for unity of military command.

Similarly, the defects of present methods of handling supplies have long been recognised, but each of the allied armies continues to think in terms of its own requirements independently of the other armies. It is apparent that there are many classes of supplies used by all the allies which could be pooled and issued to a particular army as required, but a practical solution of the problem has not yet been reached.

I consider this a matter of vital importance. The next three or four months are going to be difficult, and in order that combatant units and their necessary supplies can be brought from the United States every possible ton of shipping that can be saved by a communal system of allied [supply] should be made available. The A.E.F. has recently reduced or postponed its requirements in tonnage to the lowest limit to save sea-transportation, and even a casual study of the subject leads to the conclusion that our allies could also do considerably more than is now being done.

While some attempt has been made through coordinating allied committees, including the Supreme War Council, these bodies are only advisory. A bird's-eye view of the whole problem is lacking and general authority to order the allotment and distribution of supplies to the different armies does not exist. It is believed that this authority should be military.

The classes of supplies and material that are common to all armies are many, but too much detail should not be undertaken. The subject should be viewed broadly. The following classes of supplies, naturally, would be included: Aviation, materials, munitions as far as possible, horses, oats, hay, meat, flour, shoes, blankets, coal, gasoline, wagons, harness, motor transport, depots, warehouses, lumber and timber. Such concentration or control of supplies would probably affect a saving in American rail and port construction, as well as construction of storage accommodations.

May I also refer in this connection to the question of allied shipping? As you are no doubt aware, a very careful study shows that for the year 1918, there will be a deficit of 2,000,000 tons dead weight tonnage unless some of the programmes can be reduced. Obviously the military programme on the Western Front must be given first consideration and cannot be reduced. Actually it will be increased as American participation increases.

It would seem possible as recommended in substance by the Inter-Allied Maritime Council.

(1) That the use of merchant tonnage by allied navies might be materially reduced by joint reconsideration of naval programmes;

(2) That considerable tonnage might be saved by suspending or reducing military activities in theatres of war other than the Western Front;

(3) That further reductions in civilian imports carefully considered by Inter-Allied criticism can release additional tonnage.

It would seem desirable that these two subjects of pooling supplies and shipping control should be under Inter-Allied Military management and that one executive head be given control of both. It is believed that a very great increase in efficiency will result from the centralised executive management suggested.

I have already written M. Clemenceau on the question of pooling supplies which he approves in principle.

[*Ed.*—The above copy of Pershing's letter is drawn from a British War Cabinet document, hence the English spelling, which the British Permanent Military Representative to the SWC provided to Gen. Bliss.]

War Cabinet.

G. T. 4430   Pooling of Supplies for the Allies

Copy of letter from General Pershing to the Prime Minister

Note by the Secretary.

I append a copy of a letter dated April 28th addressed by General Pershing to the Prime Minister. I find that an almost identical letter was addressed by General Pershing to M. Clemenceau on April 9th. While at Abbeville the Prime Minister arranged with Monsieur Clemenceau, Signor Orlando, and General Pershing that a small Committee should be formed in Paris for the purpose of examining this question. The Secretary of State for War has selected the Quartermaster-General to attend the Committee, which will meet at Paris on Monday, May 6th, 1918, at 3 p.m.

[Signed]
M. P. A. Hankey

2 Whitehall Gardens, S.W.
May 4th, 1918

LC, Bliss Papers, folder: Military Papers, January–July 1918, box 249; copy of both documents at Edward Mandell House Papers, Manuscripts and Archives, Yale University Library, Series 1: Correspondence, folder 3072: John J. Pershing, box 89.

Lt. Col. T. Bentley Mott, Chief, American Mission to CINC, Allied Armies, Sarcus, to CINC, AEF.

[Handwritten in pencil]
Memorandum of Conversation between General Foch and Lt. Col. T. B. Mott at Sarcus April 28, 1918. Also present Gen. Weygand and Col. Destecker.

I went to Paris April 27, dined with Gen. Pershing & Col. Dawes, Mr. Crosby & Col. Boyd being present. Before dinner and the next day, Gen. Pershing talked to me concerning his interview the evening of April 25 with General Foch and gave me with considerable detail his views as to the method of engaging American troops on the line after their arrival in France.

During these conversations he charged me with informing Gen Foch on certain matters as they occurred to him; at other times when Gen Pershing made certain interesting statements to me I asked him if I was authorized to repeat them to Gen. Foch, and to this he several times assented.

On my return to Sarcus at 7:30 PM April 28 I asked, after dinner, to see General Foch & upon his receiving me I informed him as follows:

> I first gave a brief history of the Convention recently signed in London between Gen. Pershing and Lord Milner, starting with the various negotiations between the former and the British authorities, looking to the employment of British tonnage for the transport of American troops. I stated that Mr. Clemenceau and Gen. Pétain were informed of these negotiations and both had given their approval of the result finally arrived at.

General Pershing went to London for the purpose, amongst other things, of examining personally with the American & British authorities & experts there, the question of tonnage available for transporting American troops & supplies. During these interviews he was surprised & pleased to learn that Sir Joseph Maclay, after careful examination on both sides of the water, gave it as his opinion that 250,000 men could be brought over each month, beginning now. Desiring to seize the opportunity to intensify the transport of American troops, Gen. Pershing came to an agreement with the British Government, whose terms are set down in the Convention of which a copy had been already furnished Gen. Foch. There was nothing new in this Convention, nothing which departed from the arrangements already known to Mr. Clemenceau &

Gen. Pétain & approved by them, except that it secured from the British a greater amount of tonnage for transporting American troops than was contemplated in the original agreement. Indeed the amount devoted to this purpose far exceeded any expectations which Gen. Pershing had when he arrived in London, and it was with the desire of announcing this news to General Foch and of receiving his approval, that General Pershing had decided to stop on his way to Paris & see the latter.

I then referred to Gen. Weygand's question, during the Conference of April 25, as to the apparent conflict between the words "during May" in Par A of the Convention and the opening words of Par C, and to General Pershing's reply thereto at the time. I had brought this matter again to Gen. Pershing's notice and he authorized me to confirm what he had said April 25th, viz, that during the month of May only Infantry, Machine Guns, Engineer & Signal troops of divisions & HQrs of divisions & brigades, would be sent over, that Gen. Pershing had also referred to his statement made at the conference of Apr 25, concerning the continuance of this arrangement, decided upon for May, as applying during June or even July. He had directed me to again explain to Gen. Foch that if the emergency now confronting him continued to exist, that if the battle now engaged continued during May to offer the same or similar danger to the Allied Armies, he would see that, in sufficient time, orders were given for continuing to send over only infantry, et cetera, during June.

I said that I knew that General Pershing was most anxious that there should be no possible doubt in the mind of Gen. Foch or of anyone else as to his desire and his determination to constitute complete American divisions, corps and armies, at the earliest possible moment, but this understood and fully agreed to by all concerned. I felt myself justified in saying that from the whole tenor of General Pershing's long conversations on the subject it was visibly his intention – an intention manifested more than once with passionate earnestness – to bring to General Foch's aid, in the supreme task now confronting him, every available American soldier to throw into the line, every resource that he could command to help win the battle.

I said that General Pershing realized that in making his plans for meeting the enemy's effort now apparent or to be anticipated., General Foch was anxious to know what he could count upon, what losses he could consent to, what numbers of American regiments he could rely upon for filling the gaps made while this battle lasted, and this for as long a time ahead as possible; that we had talked of this factor in Gen. Foch's calculations, and that General Pershing had said to me "You know very well that I am not going to make any narrow interpretation of my offer to General Foch; I am going to put into this battle every American soldier I can lay my hand on; I am this minute stripping my line of communications to get men for this purpose."

General Foch here interrupted me for the first time, saying "Let me open here a parenthesis. I have in General Pershing an entire, an unqualified, confidence. I know that his intentions are lofty, pure and generous. I want you to tell him that. Now please proceed."

I here ventured to say to General Foch that I had heard General Pershing discuss with Colonel Dawes and Mr. Crosby the means whereby the Italian Government could be induced to send Italian workmen for the American lines of communication;

that he had said "This will enable me to send just that many more men up to the front, and they are already over here and will not absorb any tonnage." This, I remarked, is only one indication of the efforts General Pershing is making in every direction to bring up into the present battle every possible man. Another was his statement that if the British divisions with which our contingents were training were put into battle these American troops would go in with them.

I then said to conclude this part of my subject, when I left General Pershing he charged me with his kindest regards to you and added, "I want General Foch to know, I want you to make him feel, not only that I meant, and mean now with all my heart, every word that I said to him on March 26 [28], but that I am thinking all of the time of how I can help him in his great task; I want him to feel that without his asking me I am trying to devise every means in my power to aid him to win this battle. I have only one thought & that is, how can we beat the Germans."

General Foch said "Tell General Pershing for me that I know this. His coming to me that day in March was a spontaneous and generous act. Whatever he may do I shall always feel perfectly sure that his intentions are conceived in the same fine and generous spirit. At present we must both think of nothing but beating the Boche; when that is over and if he feels like it, we will pull each other's hair to our heart's content."

I then opened the subject of the control of tonnage and supplies, saying that Gen. Pershing desired Gen. Foch to think over the following points and let him know his ideas regarding them. General Pershing considered that all Allied tonnage should be under military control and similarly all staple, bulky supplies – such as oats, coal and such articles – should be considered as one common stock to be apportioned among the various armies on a percentage basis; but that the control of this stock should be under one man or body of men, preferably a soldier, to be selected if possible by Gen. Foch and to be under his orders. General Pershing considered that supplies for the Allied Armies & the tonnage to transport them should be treated as a strictly military question & by military methods.

General Pershing had already talked of this matter with Mr. Clemenceau and with Mr. Lloyd George as well as Mr. Nash. They all approved of this pooling in principle, but nothing had yet been said about military control and that control being exercised by an agency under Gen. Foch. The tonnage of the Allies is already 2,000,000 tons short of requirements for 1918 & the curve will not begin to ascent till August. I also stated Gen. Pershing's belief, founded on assurances from fully qualified sources, that the U-Boat menace could be considered as met, the problem really solved.

I then told Gen. Foch of General Pershing's conviction that it was of the highest importance for the Allied cause that the Italian Army be placed under his Supreme Command; I told him that General Pershing had that day prepared a telegram for his Government recommending that President Wilson exercise his influence, directly with the Italian Government, or else through the British & French Governments, to bring this about; that he had suggested that the Italians felt the greatest confidence in Gen. Foch and it would seem that the moment for securing this entire unity of command was auspicious. General Pershing had authorized me to say that he was sending a telegram conveying these ideas.

General Foch made notes of these last two matters, and after some further cordial expressions toward Gen. Pershing he allowed me to leave.

P.S. General Foch's whole attitude during this interview, the earnestness & deliberation with which he twice expressed his feelings toward General Pershing, his belief in him, his faith in him, combined with the nods of approval from General Weygand, produced upon me the impression that any disappointment which there is no doubt he felt at the outcome of the interview of April 25, has disappeared, and that he is satisfied that General Pershing is going to do all that is humanly possible to help him with the present battle.

LC, Pershing Papers, folder: Col. T. Bentley Mott (1910–1918), box 141.

Maj. Paul H. Clark, American Mission to French General Headquarters, to Pershing.

[No. 57] 8:00 P.M.

Subject: Military Situation.

1. I called on Comdt. Rozet today who said that Boche still have 208 divs, of which 139 have been engaged, there have been 184 "passes" or "*entrées*" (entries) of divisions from which it is apparent that some divisions have gone to the battle more than once.

2. The Allies have engaged 91 of their divs.—55 British and 36 French.

3. 32 Boche divs. have already received replacements of the 1919 class.

4. New report from Roumania indicate that Mackensen [German Commander] is in course of sending the 216th div. to France and that the 216th will be followed by others of his force which it was believed would remain indefinitely in Roumania. This movement of divisions from Roumania is taken as a further evidence of severe Boche losses during their offensive.

5. Another confirmation of German losses is report that recently in conversation Gen. Wille, Chief of Staff, Swiss Army, Germanophile, married to German woman, said there was fear in Germany that the offensive could not be persisted in on account of the severe German losses.

6. The retirement of the British and Belgians from the line in front of Ypres to behind the Canal, which was accomplished night of Apr 26–27, was perceived by the Boche who have followed.

7. We have sent the 32d div., being the last element of the 16th Corps to go, to join the D.A.N. [*Détachement l'armée du Nord* (Detachment of the Army of the North)], Gen. de Mitry. That gives de Mitry 8 divisions and 1st Cav. Corps.

8. The 168, 42 and 121 divs. now being withdrawn from our trench front to go to battle.

9. The 28 div. French, engaged at Mount Kemmel, has only 2,000 infantrymen left. The 28th abandoned 20 of their cannon, having first destroyed them.

10. The British now asked that 2 new corps be sent to the north to take over a front between the Belgian and British armies.

11. The relief of divisions is beginning to be very difficult (*trés dur*).

12. Yesterday at Abbeville there was a meeting between Clemenceau, Lord Milner, Gen Foch and Gen Haig with a view to determining the degree and nature of the effort that should be made by the French and by the British. The subject was to be treated "*carrément et franchement*" (squarely and frankly).

13. There will be an Inter-Allied Aviation conference May 9th, probably at Paris, with a view to "pooling" aviation personnel and materiel—at least to arrange a distribution of effort proportioned to capacities.

14. The D.A.N. (Mitry's group) await a new attack. The British have suffered very severe losses.

15. Q. Yesterday I (Clark) stated that while the D.A.N. was under Gen Plumer (Brit. II Army) nevertheless Gen de Mitry (D.A.N.) is acting quite independently; is that a statement founded on fact?

A. "Yes, Mitry is under Plumer, but Mitry's force is a formidable one and he does act very independently."

16. I saw several officers—Gen. de Barescut. Col. du Chesne. Capt. LeBleu, Comdt. Bourgine, but it was reported to be a calm day. I read the "Compte Rendu" (The Report Submitted) but saw nothing to extract therefrom.

17. Independent of each other, Col. Rozet and Comdt. Bourgine both asked me whether it is planned to give to the British the American troops that arrive by American transports, or whether troops so arriving in France would continue to go to the French Army. Rozet said the answer would be very interesting to all at French G.Q.G. as Gen. Foch has informed them that all American troops arriving in France in May would go to the British Army. I promised to gain a categorical answer as soon as possible.

18. Gen. de Barescut asked if the date for turning over the 32d div. to the French could not be advanced, say, to May 1st.

19. I called on General Pétain and, following your instructions of last night, said:

Yesterday I saw General Pershing at Paris. It has been said to him that there are French officers who manifest a certain restlessness on the subject of the decision taken to give the British army about six divisions which will be transported to Europe by the English during the month of May.

Well, General Pershing is very desirous that this decision should be well understood. He charged me to say to you that the decision taken concerning these divisions is in conformity with the discussions which took place at the Supreme War Council toward the end of January, or at the beginning of February, and also, he added, M. Clemenceau and you had been informed and that you had acquiesced.

General Pershing invites attention to the very important fact that these divisions will be transported on English ships and that without this means of transport they could not arrive in reach France at present.

General Pershing has also learned that there are French officers who are convinced that the English hold in England about one million soldiers of whom the major part are capable taking part in the present operations; General Pershing has directed me to say to you that he is convinced that that conviction (belief) is not at all well founded, he is sure that the English have done their best to find all the soldiers possible and that they have already sent them to France. General Pétain did not wait for me to speak the last three words. He interrupted me with:

I will reply separately to your two propositions. With regard to the first if General Pershing or the American Government see fit to send those six divisions to the British Army, it is not my affair. There is no doubt but that those divisions will contribute to the general need of the Allies. As for the second question General Pershing has believed stories that are not true. I know what I am talking about. The British should have a million more men in France now than they have. Why did Gen. Robertson resign? Because his government would not send over the 500,000 men asked for by Gen. Haig and Gen. Haig would have resigned at the same time if he had known . . . (I did not catch several words). Look at the map. Here is the French front (indicating); here is the British front (indicating). The British have 48,000,000 people in England, Scotland, Wales and Ireland, and we French have 39,000,000 in France, and think of all the British colonies, and yet France can put 1,000,000 more men on the front than Britain. Why? Because we make more effort, because in England a man is excused from service upon slight cause whereas in France he is not excused for slight cause.

But General, I interrupted, I think General Pershing employed the word soldier which is the word I used, in quoting him; do you think that there is a large number of soldiers in England who should properly be sent over to France to fight?

To which he said:

If they are not soldiers they ought to be. The men are there, but Lloyd George and the others are afraid to act. Ask Gen. Pershing if he does not recall the day at the Supreme War Council when Gen. Foch made a comparative statement of the effort made by the 2 countries. It was illuminating, even Mr. Lloyd George said it was convincing. No "*Jamais, jamais, jamais*" (with emphasis) England has not made the effort that France has made. She has produced only about 1/2 of the soldiers that France has produced, though she has 10,000,000 more population and her colonies to draw from. The General spoke with emphasis, even feeling, and while perfectly polite gave the impression of one who is profoundly sure of what he said. He looked in perfect physical and mental condition.

I plan to come to Chaumont tomorrow a. m.

LC, Pershing Papers, folder: Paul H. Clark, Letters from Colonel Paul H. Clark, American Military Mission, French G.H.Q., to The Commander-in-Chief, A.E.F., March–April 1918, box 44; see also a handwritten copy in LC, Papers of Colonel Paul H. Clark, folder: Dispatches to CINC, GHQ AEF, April 17–28, 1918, box 1; an extract of paragraph 19 of this dispatch with a slightly different translation can be found at *USAWW*, vol. 3, pp. 92–93.

Foulois, Chief, Air Service, SOS, AEF, to Pershing.

Subject: Joint memorandum of the 27th of April, 1918 from French Minister of Munitions and Under-Secretary of State for Aeronautics.

With reference to the attached memorandum, the following is submitted:

1. There is nothing in the entire memorandum which will assist either the French Government or our own Government in placing a single additional aeroplane on the Western Front, before July 1st, 1918.

2. The entire memorandum has chiefly to do with the production of new and modified types of aeroplanes and engines, both in the United States and France, the production of which cannot possibly become effective until the latter part of 1918.

3. The entire memorandum is in my opinion, a well-planned effort to avoid future political and industrial difficulties which may arise, if the Liberty engine, and the American-built aeroplane, enter into competition with French engines and French aeroplanes.

4. The memorandum is also indirectly an effort to slow up the present development of the aeroplane engine and aeroplane industry now under way in the United States, with a view to transferring a large part of the industry to French manufacturers.

5. Suggested answer to memorandum is enclosed herewith. [See May 4, Pershing to Minister of Armament.]

[*Ed.*—At his meeting with Foulois, Pershing had some questions concerning the French proposal and asked Foulois to meet with Dumesnil about these issues. Foulois accordingly met with the French Under-Secretary in Paris on April 30. The minutes of this meeting are at that date.]

LC, Foulois Papers, folder 12: AEF, Air Service, Allied Air Service, box 7; see also LC, Pershing Papers, folder: Data for Book *My Experiences in the World War*, folder 1: Foulois, "Air Service—American Expeditionary Forces. (1917–1918)," Enclosure H: "Efforts of the French to establish a Joint Aircraft Production Program with the United States, to the exclusion of England. and Italy," p. 3.

Editor's Note—Pershing later commented in his memoirs on the entire issue of obtaining airplanes from the French and British:

> We were never quite sure of obtaining airplanes from the Allies, as material and expert labor for their manufacture were never fully up to requirements. While advices from home and the frequent promises of the French kept us hopeful, the cancellation by the latter of our early contract for airplanes created an uncertainty that made it difficult to plan either for the training of our aviation personnel or their participation in operations. So far we had received no planes from home and none from the French except a few for training purposes.

My conference with General Foulois was to consider a proposition purporting to bring about closer cooperation with the French, emanating from their Minister of Munitions, M. Loucheur. In a letter from the Undersecretary for Aeronautics, it was suggested that the French should increase their output of airplane bodies of various types and that we should confine ourselves to the production of Liberty engines, and possibly also undertake the manufacture of a particular type of engine which they recommended. Analysis of the proposal showed that, if adopted, we should have to abandon our plans for the manufacture of planes at home, and furnish the French additional raw material, and probably expert labor. We were always keen for cooperation that would advance the common cause, but production would not have been hastened under this plan. Our experience so far had not been such as to give confidence in their fulfillment of an agreement of this sort, so the suggestion was politely rejected. (Pershing, *My Experiences in the World War*, vol. 2, pp. 17–18.)

Pershing to Maj. Gen. John Biddle, CG, Base Section No. 3, SOS, AEF, London, for Henry P. Davison, Chairman, American Red Cross.

Telegram.

Please have following message delivered to Mr. Henry P. Davison of the American Red Cross now in London at 40 Grosvenor Gardens:

"Very much disappointed to find upon my return to Paris that you had left for London as I had looked forward to having a long talk with you. I hope you may find it convenient to come back for this purpose. You will understand how difficult it was for me to see more of you during Secretary of War's visit. I particularly regret not having seen you before your departure and hope that I may yet see you as I want to express to you personally my keen appreciation of the splendid work the Americas Red Cross is doing not only for the American soldiers but also for the Allied soldiers. Permit me to congratulate you on the splendid work that Major Perkins and his colleagues of the American Red Cross are doing here in Europe. Their work is exceedingly useful. If I do not see you as I hope I will, I wish you a pleasant voyage home and hope that you will come over again very soon and that during your next visit we will see much more of each other than during your recent visit. Pershing"

Have a colonel or lieutenant colonel of your staff detailed for service with Mr. Davison as my personal representative to remain with him and be constantly at his disposition the remainder of his staff in Europe. Also arrange in every to facilitate Mr. Davison in his work.

[Reply—April 30, Davison to Pershing, telegram]

LC, Pershing Papers, folder: Red Cross—Statement by Gen. Pershing, box 170.

E. R. (Elmer Roberts, Associated Press Correspondent, Paris), to Pershing.

Jules Cambon told me on Wednesday that the French General Staff considers that the American private soldier takes instruction and becomes a disciplined and efficient man more quickly than the British private soldier. Consequently, the feeling at French Headquarters is that the American forces in France will season rapidly.

The French Foreign Office has taken note of the fantastic descriptions published in German newspapers of the conditions of living in France and especially in Paris, where it is said life has become insupportable on account of the daily bombardment of German guns, that the capital can no longer be adequately provisioned, that business is suspended, that German prisoners taken from the camps (not prisoners recently captured) are marched through the streets of Paris to deceive the Parisians into the belief that the French have had victories. Stories such as these have been published by the most responsible newspapers of Germany such as the Kölnische Zeitung, Berlinertageblatte, Berlinerlokal-Anzeiger. They have been emitted also by the Wollf semi-official agency.

The fictions printed by German official inspiration have never been so exaggerated at any time since the war began as they are now. This is looked upon in the French Ministry of War as symptomatic of a depression in public opinion Germany which needs to be restored by describing the woeful conditions in which Germany's adversaries exist. The German believing these semi-official outgivings would believe that France was on the point of collapse and that Germany need hold out only a few days or a few weeks longer to win the war.

LC, Pershing Papers, folder: Elmer Roberts—Confidential Reports, box 175.

Pershing to TAG, War Department, in addition to Pershing to TAG, War Department, cable P-977-S, April 22.

Cable P-1015-S.
    1. For Chief of Ordnance. 1E. With reference to paragraph 5D, my cablegram 977. Your attention is invited to the fact that 2 regiments of Corps Artillery now organized and 3 regiments of Army Artillery being organized with 155-millimeter GPF [Filloux] materiel will not be able to go into action until sufficient ammunition is delivered in France from the United States to meet all needs with the exception of training requirements. The estimated requirements are 18,000 rounds per regiment per month for consumption, plus 50% of this amount per month to build up a 90 days reserve during the first 6 months. It is informally understood that the French desire 50,000 rounds per month from the United States for their own use in addition to the above. [Reply—May 15, A-1323-R-1B]

NARA, RG 120, M930, Main Series, AEF to War Department, roll 3.

Pershing to TAG, War Department, in part in reply to TAG, War Department, to Pershing, cable A-1143-R, April 20.

Cable P-1016-S.
3. For Chief Signal Officer. 3D. With reference to paragraph 3, your cablegram 1143. It is not desired that permanent Intelligence Department be sent to France. Board of experienced officers has been appointed to consider and report upon all airplane designs. Organization now formed is able to obtain accurate and dependable information on all matters concerning aviation, is in close touch with foreign governments on all aviation matters. The formation of a new organization which is not familiar with the details of European problems would not be in best interest of the service and would tend to complicate matters rather than to better conditions.

NARA, RG 120, M930, Main Series, AEF to War Department, roll 3.

TAG, War Department, to Pershing, in part in reply to Pershing to TAG, War Department, cable P-911-S, April 13.

Cable A-1199-R.
1. With reference to your 911, paragraph 1. There are now 76 guns and carriages 75-millimeter Model 1917 British type at training camp here; 62 additional will be completed by end of May and 60 per month thereafter. Estimate deliveries at factory 75-millimeter guns and carriages Model 1916 as follows: April 15, May 25, June 25. Factory production 75-millimeter guns and carriages Model 1897 French will not begin until July. If emergency demands shipment overseas of Model 1916 and Model 1917 British type during these months practically nothing will be left for training purposes in this country except 3-inch materiel. One month should be allowed for shipment of materiel mentioned above for factory or training camp to seaboard. Every effort will be made in production 155-millimeter guns, 8-inch and 9.2-inch howitzers; 60 unit 8-inch howitzers now freighted or at port of embarkation without sights, limbers and firing platforms, 24 complete to be ready for floating late May or early June. [Reply—Vol. 5, May 20, P-1154-S-2]

NARA, RG 120, M930, Main Series, War Department to AEF, roll 12.

TAG, War Department, to Pershing, in part in reply to Pershing to TAG, War Department, cable P-939-S, April 17.

Cable A-1200-R.
For Atterbury. 1A. Your 939, paragraph 1. Estimate 60,000 tons Belgium locomotives available. Does this mean that you have or will purchase 600 to 800 Belgium locomotives? [Reply—May 15, P-1119-S-8]

1E and 1F [not reproduced]. [*Ed.*—In these paragraphs, the War Department reported extensively on the tools and equipment already sent to France or that were being ordered or prepared for shipment as quickly as possible.]

NARA, RG 120, M930, Main Series, War Department to AEF, roll 12.

April 29

Maj. Gen. François Paul Anthoine, Chief of Staff, GHQ, Armies of the North and Northeast, Provins.

No. 31449.
Memorandum Concerning Policy which, under the Present Circumstances, Should Govern the Utilization of the American Forces
   I. During the course of the great battle now in progress, the armies are entering a critical phase, marked by an intense attrition due to the violence and continuousness of the struggle. Hence the decision may spring from the fact that one of the two parties may become powerless to maintain sufficient effectives in the battle.
   The present military situation is also characterized by an apparent state of equilibrium between the forces. But one must consider the fact that the English divisions, which have been severely tried, are experiencing difficulty in reorganizing; moreover, their number will be even sensibly reduced thereby. On the other hand, the French divisions are being brought in to take over the battle gradually, against an enemy who still has fresh divisions and well-filled depots at his disposal. In order to maintain the present situation—something which, while awaiting a more favorable turn of events, must have our entire attention—we must at all costs avoid reducing the number of large units whose employment enables the High Command to meet the situation through proper functioning of reliefs.
   Being unable, at the rate at which troops are now being expended, to depend solely on French reinforcements to keep the infantry of our divisions up to full strength, it is then absolutely necessary that we have all possible American aid assured us at once.
   II. This help can be given in two forms:
   (1) Either by replacing French divisions that it might be necessary to dissolve, due to the lack of sufficient reinforcements, by complete American division as they arrive.
   This method would present the grave problem of throwing into the battle larger units not ready to engage in it. The task of organizing the Higher Command and divisional headquarters as well as the combined training of the corps and divisions in liaison between infantry, artillery, and aviation, and in cooperation of the different arms, etc., prohibit this method. This is apparent in the case of the American 1st Division recently assigned to the [French] First Army after 6 months of intensive training. The serious deficiencies which have been observed in that division in this

connection would all the more likely be found to exist in units hastily thrown into battle to meet the needs of the moment.

Moreover, this method would not permit us to make use of existing cadres of French divisions which have been dissolved.

Thus there would be, on one hand, a poor use of very good American troops and on the other hand failure to make use of excellent French cadres of the higher units.

Finally, it is essentially infantry which will be lacking in our organizations and the speediest possible measures to provide reinforcements must be applied solely to the infantry.

Therefore, at a time when the battle exacts a rational and maximum use of all the Allied military forces, it does not appear possible to adopt a solution so contrary to the interests of the common cause.

(2) Or this help can be given by maintaining the command, staff, artillery, and services of the French divisions as a permanent cadre and by limiting reinforcements for troop units to the infantry, by means of American infantry, which can on the whole be considered sufficiently trained for use within regimental formations.

This plan would present all the advantages not offered by the preceding plan. It seems to be the only one which can meet the exigencies of the present hour.

Methodically applied to a certain number of our large units with a view of maintaining the strength thereof, this does not obligate the more distant future—a future in which the use of fully organized American units is in no way precluded.

III. Under this plan, it may be assumed that the French divisions chosen by the Commander-in-Chief, as much as possible from among those selected to occupy a sector and then to go to active fronts, would each receive at the start an American infantry regiment in addition to its 3 organic regiments. It would be important, in this case, that the meeting of the American regiment with the French division be effected in a rest area, as this would provide a favorable situation for the first contact, for the amalgamation and, if possible, for the training of the American units.

IV. A division thus organized going to an active front would furnish its own reinforcements, insofar as its French effectives are concerned.

Hence it would be necessary to foresee the time when such a division would be reduced from 3 to 2 French regiments. In the case of the American regiment it would be reinforced, if necessary, by American units which would enter into the composition of the divisional training centers. Later this same division would be reduced to one French regiment and 2 American regiments: later still, it would consist, in the final analysis, exclusively of 3 American regiments.

V. It should be thoroughly understood that this plan, which provides for the progressive transformation of a French division into an American division must not result in a decrease in the number of large units, but that, on the contrary, by means of American additions, endeavor should be made to increase this number. Therefore the application of this plan should be limited to the number of French divisions strictly necessary, this number to be determined by the possibilities of reinforcing the other French divisions by means of the existing national resources. It should be added that this reduction in the number of French divisions, if it is forced on us by future circumstances, must only be considered as a temporary expedient and that it will be of the greatest importance to bring this number up to the present figures as soon as it is possible to do so.

VI. The commander, the staffs and the American services would be placed alongside similar French elements of the division, close to which they would develop, as a result of close collaboration in the action, essentially the product of experience. During this time, the regimental commanders and the higher commanders, being in close touch with actual warfare, would become the best source for obtaining future American higher commanders and staffs.

VII. As for the artillery, it would be necessary first of all to arrange for debarking units to receive technical instruction on a firing range. As the artillery battalions complete this training, they could be placed alongside of artillery of French divisions under conditions similar to those just set forth above for the infantry. The possibility of increasing the proportion of field artillery in the new divisions should be examined if the resources of the Allies – presumably pooled – permit.

During this time the American heavy artillery and the American aviation would be working in close collaboration with similar French units.

Thus outlined in its major aspects, the proposed plan permits maintaining the necessary numbers of divisions at the front with all of their means, under a command and within a framework which permits continuity of effort and reduces to the minimum the risks attending any change in the organization of the forces.

In short, we must know whether, in this grave and perhaps decisive period through which we are passing, the High Command can count on American help.

If the answer is yes, the proposed plan is the only possible one.

Later, when the enemy has been brought to a standstill—and even before that time, should the flow of American infantry units become greater than the decrease in our own infantry effectives—then it will be time to start forming large American units by regrouping all of their organic elements.

These units, added to the existing units, should later insure us that superiority of organized means toward which we must strive tirelessly to guarantee success.

USAWW, vol. 3, pp. 287–89; *Les armées françaises dans la Grande guerre, Tome 6*, vol. 2, *Annexes*, vol. 1: *Annexe* No. 71, pp. 166–69.

Secretary of War Baker to Pershing.

I enclose a copy of cablegram sent by the Permanent Military Representative of the Supreme War Council on March 28 with the memorandum attached by me as the result of our conference, for the President's information. On my return to Washington I discovered that the President, in acting upon this, merely notified General Bliss that he concurred in the recommendation of the Permanent Military Representatives in the sense suggested by me for his action, so that in this copy you have the full text of the recommendations of the Military Representatives and the language of the President's action.

I think it important for you to have this paper on file, because the question is constantly being raised as to just what the President and the War Department have agreed upon in the matter of the preferential dispatch of infantry and machine gun units, and this paper is the beginning of the whole negotiations on that subject.

When I returned to the United States I found that Lord Reading was pressing upon the President the earnest wish of Mr. Lloyd George to have a definite agreement entered into by the United States to the effect that infantry and machine gun personnel at a rate of 120,000 per month should be shipped for four months to the exclusion of all other personnel. I conferred with the President about the matter and finally conveyed to Lord Reading a memorandum which stipulated exactly what the intention of the United States is in this matter, and I directed that a copy of the memorandum be sent you by cable, for your information [see April 26, 1918, cable A-1184-R]. I am enclosing herewith another copy, in order that you may have the exact text, as I have discovered that there are some variances between the cabled copy and the original text, due to error in transmission. What I have endeavored to do in the matter is to express the present intention of our Government without binding ourselves to a bargain from which we should not feel free to depart if the conditions in our judgment so changed as to justify a departure, and you will observe that I have also stipulated in the memorandum that we reserve the right to send in relatively small numbers during these four months other personnel. I have a very strong feeling that we ought not to make any such definite and obligatory promise as will permit representatives of the British Government to feel that they have a right to watch what we do and sit in judgment on our action.

There seems at present to be a strong likelihood that the rate of shipment for troops will be made substantially to exceed 120,000 per month, and I this morning had a conference with Lord Reading, and later with General Hutchison, in which both of them produced figures showing that in four months we might succeed in sending over as many as 700,000. I at once notified them that when 480,000 men have been sent I shall regard myself as entirely free to discontinue further shipments of infantry and machine gun personnel and to use all available American tonnage for the transportation of other arms as you may advise.

Lord Reading and General Hutchison both pressed upon me the desirability of some assurance to the British Government in the matter of the assignment of infantry and machine gun personnel for May and June to the British, as our Paris agreement covered only the 60,000 to be assigned for the month of April. I declined to discuss the question and told them that they had better cable Sir Henry Wilson to get into communication with you on the subject as the whole determination of that subject rests in your sound discretion.

General Hutchison told me that he was cabling Sir Henry Wilson advising that American contingents be not spread out through a great many British divisions, but consolidated into as few British divisions as possible, with the purpose in view of arriving rapidly at a situation in which the majority of the personnel in these divisions would be American. Upon the attainment of this situation, he advised that such divisions be turned over to you as American divisions with their British artillery contingents, engineers, etc., with the understanding that you would replace the British elements as soon as convenient, but that in the meantime the composite division would be regarded as an American division, commanded by an American division commander and under his direction as a part of your Army. This seemed to me a very wise suggestion, and I told him so. It is wise not only from our point of view but from theirs; for if they spread our troops out through a large number of British divisions and when they are trained we take them away, they will have a correspondingly large number of incomplete divisions on their hands, while if our troops are with a relative few divisions they can use their replacements to keep full those divisions which they are permanently to keep.

General Hutchison is to remain in this country only ten days, he tells me, and I am inclined to think that you will find him helpful, as he seems to have quite an intelligent view of the difficulties which we find so trying to overcome in this whole question.

[Handwritten: *P. S. This will be brought you by Sergeant Lanckton who has been most helpful and efficient while with me. Really I cannot speak too highly of his spirit or his service. His visit home has been beneficial to his health and his family were overjoyed to see him again.*]

[Enclosure 1: See March 28, 1918, cable 67-S]

[Enclosure 2: See above, April 26, 1918, cable A-1184-R,]

[Enclosure 3: Copy of Baker's April 19 note to Ambassador Reading]

War Department

Washington

April 19, 1918.

Pursuant to the direction of the President and in conformity with his approval of the joint notes of the Permanent Military Representatives at Versailles, the United States will continue, throughout the months of April, May, June, and July, to supply for transportation both in its own owned and controlled tonnage, and in that made available by Great Britain, infantry and machine gun personnel. It is hoped, and on the basis of study so far it is believed, that the total number of troops transported will be 120,000 per month. These troops when transported will, under the direction and at the discretion of General Pershing, be assigned for training and use with British, French, or American divisions as the exigencies of the situation from time to time require; it being understood that this program, to the extent that it is a departure from the plan to transport and assemble in Europe complete American divisions, is made in view of the exigencies of the present military situation and is made in order to bring into useful cooperation at the earliest possible moment the largest possible number of American personnel in the military arm most needed by our allies.

[*Ed.*—When Pershing read this last sentence, he wrote in pencil on the copy "*If this isn't amalgamation, what is it? JJP.*"]

It being also understood that this statement is not to be regarded as a commitment from which the Government of the United States is not free to depart when the exigencies no longer require it; and also that the preferential transportation of infantry and machine gun units here set forth as a policy and principle is not to be regarded as so exclusive as to prevent the Government of the United States from including in the troops carried by its own tonnage from time to time relatively small numbers of personnel of other arms as may be deemed wise by the United States as replacements and either to make possible the use of a maximum capacity of ships or the most efficient use of the infantry and machine gun units as such transported, or the maintenance of the services of supply already organized and in process of construction for the American Army already in France.

These suggestions are made in order that there may be a clear understanding of the intention of the United States and of the mode of execution of that intention, and they are not stipulated as indicating any intention on the part of the United States, until the situation has in its judgment changed, to depart from as full compliance with the recommendation of the permanent military representatives as the nature of the case will permit.

LC, Pershing Papers, folder: Newton D. Baker, January–June 1918, box 20.

Secretary Baker to Bliss, Chief, American Section, and Permanent Military Representative, SWC, Versailles, in reply to Bliss to Baker, March 28.

No. 1.

. . . On my return to the United States I found that Lord Reading was urging to the President a request from Mr. Lloyd George that a very definite engagement be entered into by the United States to ship infantry and machine gun personnel at the rate of 120,000 per month for four months, and that no shipping be used to dispatch any other personnel. The resolution of the Permanent Military Representatives of the Supreme War Council, to which the President had given his assent, was regarded as in substitution for all previous plans for military cooperation from the United States; that is to say, the two division a month program was regarded as replaced by a plan for the exclusive shipment of infantry and machine gun personnel. I had the very strong feeling that we ought to adhere to the recommendation of the Permanent Military Representatives, shipping both in British and American controlled tonnage infantry and machine gun units until the situation in Europe so alters as to justify a diversion of a part of the tonnage to other uses; but I did not believe and do not believe that our action in this matter should be made the basis of a binding agreement which would authorize the British Government to regard itself as justified in keeping watch over our movements and complaining of our conduct if in its judgment our compliance with the recommendation of the Versailles conference was not absolute. In other words, I prefer to follow the recommendation of the Versailles conference as a matter of choice, rather than a matter of promise to Great Britain. I could easily see that in order to make the maximum use of ships there will be many opportunities to send here and there small elements of other personnel when we have not infantry enough assembled at the port of embarkation to make complete shiploads, or action which would be misunderstood or at least require explanation if we were under constant observation and bound by a literal promise. The President concurred in my view of the matter, and I therefore handed Lord Reading a statement, which he has transmitted to Mr. Lloyd George, expressive of the intention of the United States and rather explicit as to some of the exceptions which are quite likely to become apparent in the execution of that intention. I think the whole question is now more or less definitely disposed of, satisfactorily. Meantime, both the British and the United States are finding additional tonnage available, and we are rapidly increasing the number of troops transported, so that when the figures for the month of April are completed I shall be quite surprised if we have not actually gotten the total number up to 120,000; and I should not be much surprised if in May we actually went substantially ahead of that number. Recent events on the Western Front justify the course of action recommended by the Permanent Military Representatives in this regard, and I am hopeful that the large shipments of American infantry and machine gun units will really and in fact prove a substantial aid in the battles of this Summer, even if the present great battle should come to any sort of a temporary halt.

I sent you a cablegram on the 25th with reference to the Italian situation [*Ed.*—See April 24, cable 49-R]. When I was in Italy everybody emphasized the importance of the appearance of the American flag on the Italian front. The arguments used were those which are already familiar to you. In the first place, it was said that the people of Italy have more knowledge of the United States than they have of either France or Great Britain, more of their people having been here than in either of those countries and more of them having relatives and friends here. In addition to that, we are sufficiently far away to make it quite certain that we have no political interests; and again it was suggested that everything which tended to make the Italians feel a complete unity of interest between them and the Entente Allies (including ourselves in that phrase) would have the effect of stimulating and preserving the Italian morale. Of course I realized that the appetite for American soldiers, when once aroused, is insatiable, and that sending a small contingent to carry the flag is a promise of more to come, no matter what sort of statements are made at the time they go; and yet we have had one costly experience of the effect of trouble in Italy, and I suspect it is true that if the weakness of the Tagliamento line had been foreseen and the British and French had been sent before that battle the divisions which they sent after it, the disaster would have had far less proportions. If another such blow were to fall in Italy, or at least if any such blow, having fallen, could be at all attributed to a depressed morale in Italy, we would all blame ourselves for not having done everything possible to strengthen and stimulate that morale, and as the appearance and presence of American troops is the one thing upon which all Italians have set their hearts, I am persuaded that we ought to make any possible effort to satisfy them. No doubt I shall have had an expression of your views on this subject by cable long before this letter reaches you, but I am referring to it here to give you a better view of the problem than was possible in a cablegram. [*Ed.*—Baker was correct, as Bliss replied this day to his earlier cable, 49-R of April 24, concerning the issue.] General Pershing's view on the subject is most natural and military, and I do not think sentimental considerations ought to allow us sensibly to weaken our strength in France, so that the whole inquiry really is whether we can do something effective in Italy without doing anything which will render us appreciably less effective in France. I confess I am thinking too of the situation after the war is over, when the struggle for international friendships will begin again and when there will be those who will desire to woo Italy away from us by pointing out that we gave her no military assistance when she deemed herself in great need of it. This situation doubtless is important for commercial reasons, but I am not thinking of commerce, but rather of the sort of alliance of sentiment and confidence which will group together the nations whose task it will be to preserve the peace of the world and maintain the sanity of its thinking on the whole subject of international relations.

In your letter of March 28, which did not reach me in Paris but came to me by mail from General Pershing's Headquarters, I noted that General Nash asked you whether M. Claveille had taken up with me the question of railroad cars and engines. I neglected to tell you that Mr. Claveille did take the subject up with me at our Embassy the day before I left Paris to return to America. He presented me a very elaborate study on the subject, made by General Nash, and a memorandum of his own which was supplementary to that of General Nash and of more recent date. I placed them both in the hands of General Black for his guidance, and immediately upon my return here I inquired about the shipment of cars and engines, with the gratifying result that I learned of a very much larger shipment in continuous progress now and a fair prospect of our being able to make a substantial contribution of this sort of equipment from now on. I have no doubt that many cars and engines are already in France as the result of this accelerated program. The difficulty heretofore seems to have been that our erecting shops in France were not ready to take up many engines or cars and we would simply have congested our storage facilities at the ports of debarkation if we had sent over either cars or engines in large numbers before those erecting shops were further along in their facilities. I would be glad if you would let me know anything that you may hear further on this subject, as it is of course of very great importance.

There is a great deal of talk in this country regarding the size of the army which we should plan ultimately to have in Europe. Five million men seems to be the favored unofficial estimate, for what reason I cannot say. I have not as yet been able to convince myself that we could maintain so large a force with any shipping yet in prospect, nor do I believe those who speak of five million men have the faintest idea of what the subsistence and supply of such a force would require. I do think it necessary to have a great army, but I do not want to permit a repetition of the disillusionment which comes from exaggerated expectations and therefore am having the General Staff study the problem in a thoroughly practical way, and when all the data are at hand I will lay them before the President for his final determination. If you have any views on this subject I would be most happy to have them, although I suspect it is difficult to form a settled judgment because there are some elements in the strength of our adversary difficult if not impossible to forecast.

You will be interested to know that General March is making a most favorable impression as Acting Chief of Staff. I find his judgment quick and sure, and he seems to have an ability to inform his judgment by a study of details which is rather rare in so quick a mind. I talked several days ago with Senator Chamberlain and Senator Thomas of the Senate Committee on Military Affairs about a plan I have to relieve you from the embarrassment which you feel over the retention of the rank of Chief of Staff while you are absent in Europe. I found them both sympathetic, but apparently they felt it necessary to consult the other members of the Committee before they could give any assurance of the Senate's acquiescence. I shall not write you the details of the plan as some other course may present itself and be adopted even before this letter can reach you, but in general my thought is to have the President nominate and the Senate confirm you for brevet rank of General in recognition of the service rendered by you as Permanent Military Representative. Upon the confirmation of such brevet rank and new designation as Permanent Military Representative under the brevet rank, General Crowder tells me, entitle you to all the rights, insignia, emoluments of the rank so long as the detail to Versailles lasts. Should this plan work out and the confirmation be secured from the Senate, I would ask the President to at once accept your resignation as Chief of Staff, if that be necessary to complete the legal record; and if not, in any case I would ask him to nominate General March to succeed you in that office. [*Ed.*—Baker's plan was pretty much executed as he laid it out here, and on May 20 March succeeded Bliss as the Chief of Staff.]

LC, Bliss Papers, folder: General Correspondence—Newton Diehl Baker to Bliss, March 1918–March 1920, box 250.

Bliss, Chief, American Section, SWC, Versailles, to TAG, War Department, in part in reply to TAG, War Department, to Bliss, cable 49-R, April 24.

Cable 101-S.

1. For the Secretary of War. With reference to paragraph 1 signed by you in telegram number 49, I report the following. In my weekly letter to you dated April 20, which left Brest on transport America, I stated that General Giardino had represented to me on April 18 view of Italian Government about sending American military units to Italy. He said they did not expect a large unit but only a brigade or even only a regiment. They propose to put them in training behind the line near the Swiss frontier. I told Giardino I did not favor dispersion of our military efforts but that I would write to you sympathetically about suggestion of sending small unit solely for moral effect if it should prove possible. Danger is that demand would follow for more troops. This morning had interview with Italian Civil Representative with War Council and learn

Upon his return from France to Washington, Major General Peyton C. March became the Acting Chief of Staff of the War Department on March 4, 1918. He remained Acting Chief of Staff until Bliss formally retired in May, when March was promoted to Chief of Staff and the rank of full General. A forceful person, March soon set about restructuring the War Department and its General Staff. Not all of March's reforms appealed to Pershing and Harbord in France, and relations between Pershing and March steadily deteriorated during the rest of the war and thereafter. Source: Library of Congress, Prints and Photographs Division, Harris & Ewing Collection (LC-DIG-hec-10481).

that his view is that we would send at first small unit and then establish a base in Italy with view to having eventually large force there. I told him emphatically that I did not believe my government would send any troops except with distinct understanding that it would be a small unit for moral effect and not to be followed by others. I think your proposition is only practicable solution. Let British or French or both send some of the infantry that we are loaning them to be brigaded with their divisions now in Italy relieving equivalent number British and French troops that can be sent North. I think this plan would be gladly accepted by British and French and do for the Italians all we can do. Number of troops sent to Italy should be small, not more than one or two regiments. Personally I do not favor sending troops to Italy because of the certain demand that will be made for more. The trouble in Italy is not so much the morale of the army as it is the morale of the country at large. The common people will soon complain that more Americans are not coming in order to relieve them from the burden of the war and the final moral effect may be bad instead of good.

NARA, RG 120, M923, American Section, SWC, file 315: Cablegrams Sent to War Department, Jan. 22, 1918–Dec 10, 1919, roll 18; see also online "WW I Supreme War Council, American records," at https://www.fold3.com.

Editor's Note—On May 1, Baker sent a copy of paragraph 1 to President Wilson with the following note:

> After conferring with you several days ago about the possibility of sending an American military unit to Italy, I sent a confidential cablegram to General Bliss [see April 24, cable 49-R], stating the whole case, and asking for an expression of his views. Incidentally, I pointed out to General Bliss the danger of our creating expectations of further forces which it would be difficult for us to meet, and proposed as one solution of the problem that we get the British or French, or both, to brigade some of the American troops which we are sending for training with them with their divisions in Italy. I have just received a cablegram from General Bliss which reads as follows: [*Ed.*—hereafter the above paragraph 1 is quoted in its entirety.]
>   If this meets with your approval I will cable General Pershing, asking him to suggest to General Foch or General Pétain and to Sir Douglas Haig the sending of some American troops to be brigaded with their several divisions in Italy, explaining to General Pershing that our object is the appearance of American soldiers on the Italian Front under circumstances which will not create expectations of further forces at the present time of a kind which would be created if an independent American force made its appearance there. (Link (ed.), *The Papers of Woodrow Wilson*, vol. 47: *March 13–May 12, 1918*, pp. 486–87.)
>   President Wilson replied on 3 May:
>   Thank you for your letter of the first about sending men to Italy. General Bliss's message about the matter seems to me singularly just and compre-

hensive in its appreciation of the many things involved, and I hope that you will take the action which you suggest, namely, ask General Pershing to suggest to General Foch, or General Pétain, and to Sir Douglas Haig, that some of the American troops be brigaded with their several divisions in Italy with the explanation that our hope is that American soldiers may appear on the Italian front under the circumstances which will not create the expectation that we can send further forces at the present time or an independent American force at a later time. (Link (ed.), *The Papers of Woodrow Wilson*, vol. 47: *March 13–May 12, 1918*, p. 501.)

[*Ed.*—On May 5, Baker sent cable A-1248-R to Pershing outlining the decisions made above and requesting his views on the matter.]

Pershing to Foulois, Chief, Air Service, SOS, AEF.

Personal and Confidential

It has occurred to me that questions of supply concerning the Air Service and negotiations with our Allies on these matters might, to advantage, be entrusted to some officer who has had experience in civil life which would qualify him for this kind of work.

I have thought that some such officer as Lieutenant Colonel Philip L. Spalding, of your service, now stationed at Headquarters, S.O.S., formerly of the New England Telegraph and Telephone, might fulfil the requirements.

I wish you would think this matter over and give me as soon as possible a frank expression of your opinion on the subject.

Editor's Note—Early in April, Foulois had decided to familiarize Lt. Col. Spalding of his Supply Section staff with how the British organized supplying the RAF with aircraft and equipment from the factories to the front. On April 6, he sent Brig. Gen. Livingston of the Air Ministry a letter requesting his support for Spalding's study and the reasons for his mission:

April 6

I am sending Colonel Spalding of the American Air Service to England for the purpose of studying the way you handle your supplies and equipment from the factory to the front.

Colonel Spalding is one of our big industrial men in the United States and as soon as he has made a thorough study of your methods he will return to the States to put your methods into effect. He had been with me in France for the past five months and is quite familiar with our needs from French ports to the front. I am now very anxious to have him familiar with the link between the manufacturer, the factory and the steps from the factory to the shipping points in England.

Hope you can assist him in this matter.

Spalding was assigned to special duty with the British in France and England from April to late June 1918, when he was returned to the United States for duty with the Director of Aircraft Production. For more on Spalding, see Vol. 5, May 24, P-1178-S-4, and Editor's Note following.

LC, Foulois Papers, folder 16: AEF, Air Service—Personnel, Officers, Miscellaneous, box 10.

Harbord, CS, GHQ, AEF, to CINC, AEF.

It is generally known and frequently remarked both by the military and non-military people, that nearly every new and effective change in warfare in the past three years, tactics, materiel, and scientific warfare, has been initiated by the Boches. Such uniform success is not the result of chance, but of a very systematic and intelligent use of a branch of the greater general staff, which is not tied down to routine work, nor casual details. There is no such organization in any of the Allied Armies, including our own. So far our General Staff has had to content itself with learning from the experience and mistakes of others and we are all still trailing the Germans. Every section of the General Staff at G.H.Q. is entirely occupied with the present and near future conditions, and has gotten in a frame of mind of meeting the initiative of the Germans, rather than trying to think ahead and prepare for aggressive action on some new and unexpected lines to them.

To counter the Germans and over-reach them on what is generally accepted as their own game, I suggest that in each of the Services there be a committee of men, who will see and think ahead, who are not afraid to suggest and criticize, and that the coordination and supervision of this work in the Gas, Ordnance, Engineering and other Services be by a committee from the G.H.Q. General Staff of not more than three members, one from each of the First, Third and Fifth Sections. This committee should report directly to the Chief of Staff, not tied to desk, telephone nor paperwork and not subject to use by Assistant Chiefs of Staff for any work other than this important prevision; that this committee have full power to travel and visit all parts of the Front, especially any part in action, to find out methods of offense and defense from the men who are using them. I think these men should still remain members of their Sections to keep in close touch with what is going on, but in no sense be bound by the limitations of the daily work. [Note] The Chief, of Staff on April 30th referred the above memorandum to the Assistant Chiefs of Staff, G-1, G-3 and G-5, informing them that the C.-in-C. has had the above ideas in mind for some time and desires that they recommend an officer from each of their respective sections for detail on a committee which will make a study for practicable work and action.

NARA, RG 120, Office of the Commander-in-Chief, Office of the Secretary of the General Staff, entry 22, Reports of the Commander-in-Chief, GHQ War Diary, folder 35: April 28–June 12, 1918, diary entry May 3, 1918, 328-c, pp. 313-14, box 4.

Theodore Roosevelt, Oyster Bay, N. Y., to Pershing.

[Handwritten]

My son Kermit has been very anxious to get into our army, in the line, at the front, under you; and as the active operations in Mesopotamia were over for the season, and he had won his spurs in actual service, I told him that he could apply to his superior for permission accordingly.

I received from Lord Derby the following cable "Glad to inform you General Marshal reports Kermit to have done excellently both with light armored cars with which he has been in action twice and as engineer and suggests sending him to France with view employment with United States army there. How do you view suggestion." I at once cabled my thanks, and put cable before General March, who notified me that "Mr. Kermit Roosevelt be appointed Captain Field Artillery National Army effective April 28th, 1918, and that he be directed to report Commanding General American Expeditionary Forces for assignment to duty. Mr. Roosevelt should be addressed care American Ambassador Madrid Spain," and he requested me to cable Kermit to go to Madrid to get his orders, which I have just done, addressing him at Bagdad.

Kermit was at Plattsburg last spring and was recommended for a captaincy in the National Army. He had served as Captain in the British Army in Mesopotamia, first as engineer, and then, by transfer, as Captain of a light armored motor battery of machine guns which he has taken into action twice. I would suppose that he could do best with machine guns; but of course I do not know what the needs of the situation will demand when he reaches France. I shall tell him to see General Harbord or Colonel McCoy or Col. Moseley.

I am exceedingly proud that all of my four sons are now under you in our expeditionary army; Quentin is the only one who has not been in action, and I suppose he will be sent to the front from his aviation camp as soon as they get armed fighting planes.

LC, Pershing Papers, folder: Col. Theodore Roosevelt and Family, box 177.

Pershing to TAG, War Department.

Cable P-1020-S. Confidential.
For the Chief of Staff and Secretary of War.

Realizing that the President approves of unity of command of the Allied forces and that the principle is now accepted by the Allies in France, recommend the extension of the principle to the Italian Army. General Foch has the confidence and even the affection of the Italians, grateful for his energetic help after their disaster last autumn. It is suggested that the President might with propriety make an appeal to the Italian Government to complete the unity of command of all Allied armies by placing its army under the same control. No one is so qualified to make this request no one would be listened to with such respectful attention. This suggestion coming from France or Great Britain might excite suspicion; coming from the President only the highest motives touching the general good would be ascribed. It seems possible that the Italian Cabinet is already willing to take this step if it felt able to protect itself from hostile criticism in the Italian Parliament and the Italian opposition press. This protection would be amply furnished by the fact that the suggestion came from the President. Both the Italian Government and the people would see in his action only a desire to serve the common cause. Should the President not wish to make the recommendation directly to the Italian Government the next best solution would then be to communicate his views to the French and British Governments and authorize them to present it to the Italian Government. I am making this recommendation on my own initiative and have consulted no one. Its realization would strengthen us with the Italian Government and would have a happy effect in France and Great Britain. [In addition—May 3, P-1043-S-3]

NARA, RG 120, M930, Confidential Series, AEF to War Department, roll 7.

Editor's Note—Pershing was a consistent advocate for Allied unity of command and remained concerned about Italy's reluctance to accept Foch as Allied Commander-in-Chief. This led him to send cable P-1020-S to Baker in the days leading up to the next Supreme War Council gathering at Abbeville in the first days of May. His reasons for this were explained in his memoirs:

> In discussing unity in general, the failure of the Italians to place their armies under the Supreme Command on the Western Front was frequently mentioned, and it was feared in high places that there might arise another dangerous situation similar to Caporetto, but all hesitated to take action. From the military standpoint the Western Front really extended to the Adriatic Sea, and support for the Italians in case of necessity would have to come, as before, from the armies in France.
>
> The question was a delicate one, but it occurred to me to suggest to the Secretary of War that the President might intimate to the Italian Government the propriety of completing the unity of command by placing its armies under the same control as the others. It was believed that the Italian Cabinet might be willing to take the step if it could be done in such a way as to prevent hostile criticism among their own people. It was thought that if the suggestion should come from the British or the French, especially the latter, it would very likely be regarded with suspicion, whereas none could ascribe any but the highest motives to Mr. Wilson in making such a move. However,

the question came up for discussion at the next meeting of the Supreme War Council, which was held at Abbeville, and the authority of General Foch was extended to include the Italian armies [see May 2, Abbeville Conference (Day 2)]. This completed the unity of command from the North Sea to the Adriatic. (Pershing, *My Experiences in the World War*, vol. 2, pp. 18–19.)

Pershing to TAG, War Department, in part in reply to TAG, War Department, to Pershing, cable A-1172-R, April 25.

Cable P-1024-S.

1. For Chief of Staff. 1D. With reference to Army-Navy article of agreement of March 27th 1918, concerning transportation of sick and wounded to home territory, it is absolutely essential, in order to insure an efficient evacuation service and not embarrass Army hospitalization facilities at base ports here, that Army and Navy Departments, through their Surgeon Generals, agree on and communicate to their transport officials the principle that the number and kind of patients to be transported to the United States by the Navy will be determined by me and governed only by the capacity of the ship and ability of the Army Medical Department to furnish such additional medical attendance enroute as may be deemed necessary. We are prepared to furnish these attendants as required. It is understood that the Navy has issued instructions that not more than 5 insane cases shall be received on any ship. As this restriction particularly hampers our evacuation problem I request that it and any others in conflict with the policy above proposed be removed.

1F. Following Brigadier Generals National Army have been found incapacitated physically for further duty in France, namely: Brigadier Generals Benjamin Alvord, Alfred E. Bradley, Peter Murray, R. D. Walsh. Orders are made returning these Officers to the United States. While physical condition would doubtless justify action of retiring board in their case, the excellent reputation and faithful service of these officers justify their being given an opportunity for service in the United States with their present rank. [*Ed.*—Although Robert D. Walsh was deemed medical unfit for frontline service, he was not returned to the U.S. and remained in command of Base Section No. 1 at St. Nazaire until July, 1918. He then was assigned to the Director General of Transportation until November 1918 when he assumed command of Base Section No. 2 at Bordeaux until March, 1919. Peter Murray was returned and served on the War Department General Staff from June 1918 until October 1921 and then was Chief of Staff, II Corps Area, until his retirement in November 1924.] [In addition—April 30, P-1025-S-1C]

1G. Medical Board has found Brigadier General Charles A. Doyen, U.S. Marine Corps, physically incapacitated for further service in France. General Doyen is an excellent Officer, has rendered most valuable service and had brought his Brigade to high efficiency. I very reluctantly return him to the United States and hope that he may be suitably employed there. Pursuant principle I have adopted of rotating Staff Officers shall relieve Brigadier General Harbord as Chief of Staff for a tour of duty

Brig. Gen. Charles A. Doyen, U.S. Marine Corps, was commanding general of the 4th Marine Brigade, 2d Division. In this photograph, taken on March 22, 1918, Doyen is inspecting trenches recently occupied in the Troyon sector of the front east of the Meuse and north of St. Mihiel. Accompanying him are Maj. Holland M. Smith, Brigade Adjutant (on Doyen's right and behind him), and Lt. Col. Frederick M. Wise, commanding officer, 2nd Battalion, 5th Marine Regiment (on the left). Smith gained later fame in World War II as commander of the V Amphibious Force (later designated Fleet Marine Force, Pacific) in the Central Pacific in 1943–45 and earned the nickname "Howlin' Mad" for his fiery disposition and disputes with the U.S. Army. Doyen's continuing ill health resulted in his removal from command in late April and to his replacement by James G. Harbord in early May. Source: NARA, Still Photo Branch, RG 111, 111-SC-12162.

with the line and assign him to command the Marine Brigade. In the event that a Brigadier of the Marine Corps is sent from the United States to replace General Doyen it will be necessary to assign him to a unit not actively engaged in the line [see April 30, Doyen to Pershing]. [*Ed.*—Brig. Gen. John A. Lejeune, then commanding the Marine Barracks at Quantico, Virginia, was eventually assigned to replace Doyen, and temporarily assumed command of the 4th Marine Brigade, 2nd Division, on July 26, before replacing James Harbord as division commander two days later. Doyen died of influenza at the Marine Training Station, Quantico, Virginia, on October 6, 1918.]

1J. With reference to paragraph 6, your cablegram 1172. Recommend 92nd Division be sent as one of the divisions mentioned in paragraph 1, my cablegram 961 [see April 24, P-961-S]. [In addition—May 8, P-1074-S-1C]

NARA, RG 120, Main Series, AEF to War Department, roll 3.

TAG, War Department, to Pershing.

Cable A-1201-R.
9. Scheduled production tanks is 1500 this year. Initial United States requirements are 365 to be completed August, in addition to 60 per month thereafter as replacements. This will leave available British and French 135 August, 240 per month September, October and November and 40 December. Will that suffice for those Governments and can they agree on satisfactory distribution? French High Commissioner here objects to our tank agreement with England stating French requirements as 600 tanks by November 1st and 400 more by February 1, 1919. He wants clause providing first 600 to U. S. dropped and allocation made by agreement between the 3 Governments. Chief of Ordnance recommends manufacture here and shipping assembled of 500 large tanks additional to the 1500 above if necessary to meet situation. March. [Reply—Vol. 5, June 7, P-1264-S-2A]

NARA, RG 120, M930, Main Series, War Department to AEF, roll 12.

April 30

Pershing's Personal Diary

Worked in office. Saw Colonel Nolan, Bishop Brent, Colonel Fries [Chief, Gas Service, AEF], Colonel Rockenbach [Chief, Tank Corps, AEF] and General Bethel. Left for Paris at 3 p. m. with Colonel Boyd.

LC, Pershing Papers, Diary, May 7, 1917–September 1, 1918, box 4.

Pershing.

Memorandum:
Without giving consideration to the conduct of individual officers in this Seicheprey affair, the following defects are noticed and should be remedied without delay. Some of them are traceable to defects in our methods of instruction.
    1. Liaison. Too much emphasis cannot be placed upon giving specific instruction to all units in this important feature. Unless the various units on the battlefield are connected up by all of the various methods of communication, then only disaster may be expected. This subject should be given special attention by both the operations and training sections and defects along these lines constantly pointed out to division commanders and their subordinates. Separate reports should be rendered periodically to the Chief of Staff, regarding other divisions, showing defects in this regard.
    I desire to have prepared some special instructions on liaison work based upon its failure in this particular action.

2. As I have pointed out a number of times to various division commanders, including the Commanding General of the 26th Division, I think the front lines are too strongly occupied. This is, at this stage of the war, a serious oversight on the part of the higher command. These lines need only to be held lightly at any time, but more especially at night and during the fog.

3. The third lesson to be learned is that the safety of a command depends upon the information regarding the movements of the enemy; and to sit quietly in trenches during a heavy fog and allow a surprise attack to be sprung on men who are unprepared is, to mind, inexcusable, and will not be tolerated in this command. Necessary instructions will be prepared covering the subject of outposts to be equipped with telephonic or sound communication of some sort so that no such trap may be sprung upon our men again in future.

Whatever instructions are prepared on this subject should be prepared immediately, and I desire them submitted to me before they are issued.

LC, Pershing Papers, folder: vol. 2: Memoranda, A.E.F., 1918, box 133; see also *USAWW*, vol. 3, p. 621.

Editor's Note—When the German attack on Seicheprey took place, Pershing was visiting Haig's GHQ and inspecting British training areas and incoming American divisions while on his way to London. Once he had returned to Chaumont, he familiarized himself with what occurred and had much to say about this episode in his memoirs, in which he somewhat moderated his initial assessment:

> On the night of April 20th–21st, the Germans made a raid on the 26th Division in the vicinity of Seicheprey. The attack covered a two-miles front extending west from the Bois de Remières. It came during a heavy fog and was a complete surprise to our troops, who were considerably outnumbered. The fighting at Seicheprey was violent, causing heavy losses on both sides. The town was taken by the enemy. The success of the raid may be attributed largely to the destruction by the German artillery of the divisional system of communications, which naturally resulted in some confusion in the division. Although cooperation among the units was difficult under the circumstances, it was finally established and the original front was reoccupied the following day. (Pershing, *My Experiences in the World War*, vol. 2, p. 16.)

For more information on the 26th Division at Seicheprey, see Maj. Gen. C. R. Edwards, CG, 26th Division, "Report of Enemy Raid of the 26th Division at Seicheprey, April 20/21, 1918," April 23, 1918 [Extract], *USAWW*, vol. 3, pp. 613–17; May 6, Frederick Palmer to CINC, AEF, "Notes of Observation with the 26th Division"; and Shay, *The Yankee Division in the First World War*, pp. 78–89.

General Harbord, in his *The American Army in France*, added an important footnote to this matter, which Pershing himself did not mention. He noted that Pershing "was considering some minor disciplinary action, when news came that the French

Corps Commander with whom the 26th were serving, had considered the occasion as calling for a liberal distribution of the Croix de Guerre, and had acted accordingly." Of course this prevented any such disciplinary action from being taken and moved Pershing "to send a rather chilly letter to each Allied Commander-in-Chief requesting that no decoration be awarded to any member of his command without his approval first obtained." (Harbord, *The American Army in France*, p. 199.)

Foulois, Chief, Air Service, SOS, AEF, Paris.

Memorandum of General Foulois' Conference with Sous-Secretaire Dumesnil, on April 30, 1918, at Ministry of Aviation—5:20 P. M.

1. *General Foulois* beginning the conference stated that he had discussed with Gen. P. letter recently addressed to General Pershing by Mon. Loucheur and Mon. Dumesnil, and that General Pershing desired him to talk over several of the points raised in their letter. Also that General Pershing was heartily in accord with their desire to cooperate in every possible way in coordinating production between France and the United States.

Mon. Dumesnil, in reply, explains that he and Mon. Loucheur had had an occasion to visit General Pershing in connection with other matters but that the question of Aviation came up at the same meeting. This fact explained why their communication was addressed directly to General Pershing instead of, in the usual way, to General Foulois.

2. *Pursuit Aviation. General Foulois* informs Mon. Dumesnil that the 300 H.P. Hispano Suiza engine will be in production in the United States by next October.

3. (a) *General Foulois* asks Mon. Dumesnil when the French Government will be ready to make a definite decision on the suitability of the Liberty engine for use in Breguet cellules.

Mon. Dumesnil replies that the tests of the Liberty engine in France have, as yet, been entirely tentative and inconclusive, owing to the fact that they have been conducted with an engine which is admitted to be inferior to the improved type; that he is impatient to receive samples of the improved engine in order that the necessary complete and final tests may be made. He states it as his opinion that the low compression Liberty (4.8 compression, as used for Navy engines) will be a more conservative choice and even ultimately may prove superior to the high compression Army type engine. This remark raises a question as to what Liberty engines have been ordered by the French and whether they have placed any separate order for 300 low compression Liberties to be used in hydro-airplanes for the French Navy. Mon. Dumesnil has the question looked into and finds that the 300 low compression engines which he expected to allocate to the French Navy formed part of the single big French order for 1500 low compression Liberties.

(b) Referring to the increased production of Breguet Observation Planes, *General Foulois* asks what production may be expected in the near future.

Mon. Dumesnil states that he is unable to give any exact figures as to quantities or dates but that he will be glad to have the question examined and will send a letter shortly to General Foulois, giving him definite data on this point. He wishes to emphasize the fact that the letter addressed to General Pershing dealt purely with questions of principle and did not pretend to go into detail as to definite numbers or dates.

(c) As the question of knowing the date when Liberty engines will be needed for installing in Breguet machines depends on the time which it will take the Breguet Company to increase their production, the question as to the date by which Liberty engines will be needed in France does not arise until this information has been gathered.

4. *Day Bombing.* (a) The question of using Liberty engines in Breguet Day Bombing Cellules depends, as in the case of Breguet Army Corps Observation Planes, on the arrival of improved Liberty motors with which final tests may be conducted.

(b) In reply to General Foulois' question, *Mon. Dumesnil* states that he will obtain information and within a few days write him a letter giving data as to the number of day bombing Breguet cellules which the Michelin Factory will be able to turn out under their increased production schedule. The number or percentage of output of these planes which the French Government will be willing to sell to the United States is a question of detail, which he can only take up after the broader question of principle has been mutually agreed to.

5. *French naval Aviation.* *Mon. Dumesnil* states that. the 300 low compression Liberty engines destined for the French Navy are included in their lump order for 1500 low compression engines. These 300 engines are to be installed in French hydro-aeroplanes, used on coast patrol service in connection with submarine protection. The request for these engines has not been made the subject of a separate order. His decision to use 300 out of their total order of 1500 motors for Navy planes was, however, arrived at about 2 months ago.

6. *Canton-Unne Motors. Z 18 - 500 HP.* (a) *General Foulois* asks what type of cellules are being designed for this engine. *Mon. Dumesnil* replies that several builders, including SPAD, Breguet, and Morane-Saulnier, have designed planes to take this motor which can be used in 2-place and multi-place combat machines, in day bombers, and probably even in night bombers and observation. He thinks that in 1919 practically all planes will be driven by engines of about 500 HP. The tests of experimental planes designed to take this engine are expected to take place within the next month. The engine itself is already in production, having completed its test. It consists of 2 - 250 Canton-Unne motors coupled together, an engine which has given satisfactory service for some time. The uncertainty of coupling 2 of them together to make one larger unit is not therefore as great as would be the case if an entirely original design had been attempted. This new 18-cylinder 500 HP motor is, he states, the simplest airplane engine to manufacture, it requires the smallest quantity of raw material in proportion to its power, and is very compact and well suited to installation in cellules. *Mon. Dumesnil* emphasizes the desirability of starting the production of this engine in the United States. He states his belief that France will always be able to build the cellules but will need assistance when it comes to engines, that it would

be very desirable if she could depend on getting additional supplies of this same motor from the United States. As such a supply, combined with our own production, would mean a sufficient number of high-powered engines, all interchangeable and capable of being installed in a number of different types of planes. He believes that American facilities are much better suited to working in metals and producing engines than to working in wood, etc. Furthermore, that types of airplanes change quicker and more frequently than types of engines and that the time elapsing between the development of a new airplane in France and its output on a large scale in America and shipment back to France would mean that such planes would probably be out of date on their arrival in France. He hopes that the United States will concentrate mainly on the production of engines.

(b) The *General* informed Mon. Dumesnil that he is glad to accept the latter's offer to send a Canton-Unne engine to the United States with complete drawings, data, and the necessary engineer experts to enable the authorities in Washington to investigate the possibilities of producing the engine in the United States.

7. *Night Bombing*. In reply to General Foulois' question, *Mon. Dumesnil* states that at least one of the new French Night Bombers has been tested out, namely, the Caudron Type C-23, which has proven far superior to any other existing night bomber (it uses 2 - 250 HP engines, has a speed of 150 kilometers an hour at 2,000 meters, carries 5 hour's fuel, and 500 kilos of useful load). He thinks the Liberty engine, if successful, might be used in connection with these machines. He expects to get an output in this type beginning in May, with 10 or 12 machines, and increasing up to a considerable output in the month of August.

The question of standardizing on this machine for night bombing work will be brought up for discussion at the next meeting of the Inter-Allied Aviation Committee.

LC, Foulois papers, folder 12: AEF, Air Service. Allied Air Service, box 7.

Foulois, Chief, Air Service, SOS, AEF, to CINC, AEF

Subject: U.S. Navy Air Operations on the Western Front.

1. I have recently learned that the U.S. Navy is planning to carry out a bombing offensive on the Western front, against enemy submarine bases.

This project involves several vital points, as follows:

(a) Independent air operations by the U.S. Navy, operating from land bases with land airplanes, on the Western front.
(b) Priority of U.S. Navy over U.S. Army Air Service and Allied Air Services in Europe, as regards airplanes and engines shipped from the United States.
(c) Priority of U.S. Navy over U.S. Army Air Service as regards airplanes and engines on order in Italy.

2. "Independent Air Operations, etc."

Independent air operations by the U.S. Navy on the Western front, without reference to the Commander in Chief, A.E.F., is, in my opinion, a matter which should be settled at once, if intelligent and effective co-operation on air operations by the United States Air Forces is desired.

3. Priority of U.S. Navy over U.S. Army and Allied Air Services regarding airplanes and engines shipped from the United States.

An immediate decision should he obtained from the War and Navy Departments in Washington as to whether the initial, output of airplanes and engines, built in the United States shall be allotted to the United States Navy or the United States Army, and the Allied Armies if needed.

In this connection attention is invited to cable no. 1039 [see April 4] received from the War Department regarding the allotment of Liberty engines to the U.S. Navy, regardless of the needs of the Allies or the American Air Service in France.

Attention is also invited to cable No. 904 [see April 12] sent in answer to 1039, and proposed cable of April 23rd, 1918, sent in connection with the same subject [not sent, but rewritten and sent on May 3 as P-1043-S].

It is apparent that the U.S. Navy is receiving priority on Liberty engines over the Air Service, A.E.F., which in my opinion is not justified under the present military emergency.

4. The U.S. Army Air Service placed with the Italian Government over six months ago an order for 200 Caproni type, Night Bombing airplanes. The Italian Government has steadily insisted that these airplanes cannot be supplied until the United States Government supplies Italy with a certain amount of raw materials. Several urgent requests by cable have been made by the Commander-in-Chief to the War Department, requesting that raw materials for Italy be expedited, and the final result has been as outlined in cable No. 974 and 1035 herewith attached [not reproduced]. In spite of the fact that the U.S. Army has an order placed with the Italian Government for 200 airplanes, I am informed that the U.S. Navy has a representative now in Italy negotiating for 60 or more Caproni Night bombing airplanes. I further am informed that the U.S. Naval authorities have offered to bring to Italy a certain amount of raw materials on U.S. Naval vessels, and in exchange for such materials they expect to receive finished airplanes of the type now on order for the Air Service, A.E.F.

The Air Service, A.E.F., is in no position to compete with the United States Navy in matters of this kind, and it is therefore recommended that the entire question of naval air operations on the Western Front be settled, in order that the Air Service, A.E.F. may know where it stands in reference to its priority on airplanes and engines from the United States and Italy.

5. Attached herewith is a proposed cablegram which I recommend be sent in order that the situation in France may be clearly understood by the authorities in Washington.

[*Ed.*—No draft cable was attached, but it was noted that Pershing sent cable P-1043-S, May 3, after the discussions on this matter.]

LC, Pershing Papers, folder: Data for Book *My Experiences in the World War*, folder 1: Air Service, AEF, box 351.

Brig. Gen. Charles A. Doyen, USMC, CG, 4th Marine Brigade, 2nd Division, AEF, to Pershing, reply to Pershing to Doyen (not located).

I wish you to know that I highly appreciate your very kind letter and your opinion as expressed in the copy of cablegram sent and I thank you for your good wishes.

Of course, I regret giving up my command, but I am entirely of the opinion if there is any defect in an officer whereby he is liable to break down at a critical time, that he should be relieved and I accept the dictum of the medical board without complaint and under the circumstances shall be very glad to return to my home and family.

Thanking you once more for your many kindnesses and your good opinion of the Marines. . . . [P. S.] I request that I may be allowed to take my personal orderly with me. He has been with me for the past 12 years.

LC, Pershing Papers, folder: Charles A. Doyen, USMC, box 66.

Pershing to Brig. Gen. Alfred E. Bradley, Chief Surgeon, S.O.S., A.E.F., reply to Bradley to Pershing, April 16.

I have your note of April 16th with reference to your recent physical examination. While I appreciate to the very fullest extent your desire to remain in France in your present position, which is probably the most important one in the medical world today, I do not feel that one who is not entirely well could do justice to the strenuous duties of the office. I can only repeat what I said to you at our recent conversation that I think you would not want to remain unless you were entirely capable, physically, of meeting every requirement that would be expected of you. Moreover, every man with a family owes it to himself to prolong his years as far as possible and to continue such useful work as he may be fitted for.

While you may not be up to a high enough standard, physically, to carry on the arduous work that you are called upon to perform, I think you will be able to render a very distinct and beneficial service in the Surgeon General's office as your presence there will place us in direct touch as to our requirements.

May I express to you my most sincere appreciation of the splendid monument you have left to your ability and industry. Whoever follows you will have a very solid foundation upon which to build, with which your name will be associated for all time. I am deeply sensible, personally, of the loss your departure will bring to me.

Please carry with you the most cordial appreciation of all members of the American Expeditionary Forces, especially those of the staff who have had the pleasure of working with you and the efficient department you have created. [Reply—May 13, Bradley to Pershing]

LC, Pershing Papers, folder: Bradley, box 33.

HQ, Base Section No. 3, SOS, AEF, London, for Henry P. Davison, Chairman, ARC, London, to Pershing, reply to Pershing to Biddle for Davison, April 28.

Telegram. HQ 2666.

It was a disappointment to me not to see more of you while in France but perfectly understood the pressure upon you and therefore would have regretted taking any of your time when possible to avoid doing so. Notwithstanding my desire for a visit with you, your most thoughtful telegram appreciated. If I understood that you wished especially to discuss matters with me I should at once give up my sailing plans and return to France. But not so understanding your message, I am arranged to sail as planned on Saturday subject to any further word from you. It will always be a source of greatest satisfaction to me if the Red Cross can in any way serve you and your army and thus possibly lighten in some slight degree the burden upon you. I am sure you realize that we have but one thought and one purpose. Your helpful attitude from the beginning has enabled us to make some progress and I am confident that you will call upon us at any and all times to render any service within our power. Davison.

LC, Pershing Papers, folder: Red Cross—Statements by Gen. Pershing, box 170.

Bliss, Chief, American Section, and Permanent Military Representative, SWC, Versailles, to TAG, War Department.

Cable 102-S.

For Acting Chief of Staff. I leave 7 A.M. Wednesday for Abbeville for session Supreme War Council which will probably last two days. I learned from a Mr. Clemenceau that one question for consideration will be agreement signed by Lord Milner and General Pershing about transportation American troops. The French strongly oppose this agreement. Other questions will be withdrawal of more troops from Italy and Salonika, and extending General Foch's powers as Commander-in-Chief to include Italy. These questions are liable to produce friction.

NARA, RG 120, M923, American Section, SWC, file 315: Cablegrams Sent to War Department, Jan. 22, 1918-Dec 10, 1919, roll 18; see also online "WW I Supreme War Council, American records," at https://www.fold3.com.

Pershing to TAG, War Department, in addition to Pershing to TAG, War Department, cable P-1024-S, April 29.

Cable P-1025-S.
1. For Chief of Staff. 1C. With reference to paragraph 1F, my cablegram 1024. Have announced Colonel R. C. Davis as Adjutant General, AEF. Recommend that services of Brigadier Generals Benjamin Alvord and Alfred E. Bradley be utilized in the departments to which they belong. Consider that their experience with this Expedition would be an invaluable asset to both of these departments. [*Ed.*—After returning to the United States, Alvord was hospitalized until July 1918, when he was appointed Acting Chief of Staff, Southeastern Department until May 1919 and then held the same post in the Western Department until April 1922. He was appointed Assistant to The Adjutant General (with rank as Brigadier General) in August 1922 and he retired in May 1924. Bradley was also hospitalized after his return, but his physical condition prevented any additional service assignments until he retired in March 1920.]

1E. Recommend promotion to Colonel, National Army, of Lieutenant Colonel T. B. Mott retired. This officer is head of the mission established with General Foch, Commander-in-Chief Allied Armies in France, a most important duty requiring the rank requested. [*Ed.*—The War Department confirmed Mott's promotion to Colonel on May 4 in cable A-1241-R-5]

NARA, RG 120, M930, Main Series, AEF to War Department, roll 3, and War Department to AEF, roll 12.

Pershing to TAG, War Department, in part in reply to TAG, War Department, to Pershing, cables A-929-R, March 15, and A-1169-R, April 24 (not reproduced); in addition to Pershing to TAG, War Department, cable P-709-S, March 12.

Cable P-1027-S. Confidential.
For the Chief of Staff.
Referring to paragraph 13, your cablegram 1169 [not reproduced] and our cablegram 709. Present situation politically entirely favorable to us in view of our government's agreement for allocation and shipment of wheat to Switzerland and favorable impression created by shipments already made.

The fact that present German offensive is so far removed from Swiss frontier has relieved for time being Swiss fears of German invasion. Swiss Government on April 5th gave confidential instruction to Swiss press to abstain from hostile criticism toward Germany. These have been followed for most part, but have not prevented criticism of Germany's action in doubling price of German coal sent to Switzerland beginning May 1st. Swiss investigations of possibility of securing grain shipments from Ukraine, through Germany, in case of failure of American deliveries have shown that the Ukraine will be unable to supply Swiss needs this year. This fact, together with German agreement to safeguard under certain conditions ships carrying wheat for Switzerland, have greatly relieved tensions.

NARA, RG 120, M930, Confidential Series, AEF to War Department, roll 7.

Pershing to TAG, War Department, in part in reply to TAG, War Department, to Pershing, cables A-845-R, February 28, A-1020-R, April 1, A-1069-R, April 9, A-1106-R, April 15, and A-1158-R, April 23, in addition to Pershing to TAG, War Department, cables cable P-961-S, April 24, and P-987-S, April 24.

Cable P-1031-S.
 1. For the Chief of Staff. 1B. With reference to paragraph 3, your cablegram 1120. Recommend that Charles H. Brent be appointed Chaplain with grade of Lieutenant Colonel. Bishop Brent is an international figure in church work, his influence exercised officially as a chaplain would be a powerful factor in maintaining high standards desired in this command. He is 56 years of age. If this is over the age limit, recommend such limit be waived. Recommendations for appointment of 17 other chaplains will follow in a few days.
 1C. With reference to my cablegram 961. Request to be informed in agreements therein quoted are approved and if the number of troops referred to for the month of May and subsequent months will be available. It is important to know this in order to reach agreements with British and French as to details and to make adjustment of supply matters, et cetera.
 3. For Quartermaster General. With reference to paragraph 5, your cablegram 1158. The cold storage plant at Gièvres will be running to 3,000 tons capacity by May 1st which will double capacity of all refrigerator cars owing to short time required for turn around. There are also 100 refrigerator cars floated. During April when we have been unable to get refrigerator cars the French have in every case taken at ports the frozen beef we were unable to handle. Anticipate no reasonable delay in unloading refrigerator vessels during May provided ships arrive at intervals.
 6. For Chief of Ordnance and Chief Signal Officer. With reference to paragraph 2A, your cablegram 1106. Following estimate of explosive bombs American manufacture is recommended for planes built in United States and equipped with American suspensions. Latest program based on paragraphs 1B and C, your cablegram 1069, and used as latest basis for plane deliveries from United States will result according to best advices here in the following squadrons American-built planes to be equipped and maintained at front. Observation squadrons in service: July 2, August 10, September 25, October 41, November 50, December 52. Day Bombing squadrons: July none, August 8, September 19, October 32, November 44, December 44. Night Bombing squadrons: July none, August none, September 3, October 10, November 10, December 10. This program assumes planes will be at front 2 months after delivery from port of embarkation. Recent information from front indicates

average number of raids per bombing plane each month will be 12 instead of 10. Recommend therefore 20% increase in allowance for explosive bombs per plane per month over schedule given in your cablegram 845, paragraph 1C and D. Reference subparagraph B, experience in present battle shows greatly increased use 20-pound fragmentation bombs by observation and pursuit planes. Recommend therefore allowance 20-pound fragmentation bombs for pursuit and observation planes be increased 300%, and deliveries be increased in amount accordingly.

6A. If you cannot furnish American bombs and American suspensions to carry them on Handley Page machines and plan to use English suspensions and English bombs as suggested in paragraph 6C, your cablegram 1020, and paragraph 2, our cablegram 987, the supply of British bombs now ordered will be sufficient to meet needs of night bombing squadrons indicated in program given in preceding paragraph during September and October. Should you propose to continue use of British bombs for these squadrons beyond that time it will be necessary to negotiate with British for further supply.

6B. We plan to furnish French planes with French bombs and suspensions and Italian planes with English suspensions and English bombs if Italian planes are secured.

NARA, RG 120, M930, Main Series, AEF to War Department, roll 3.

TAG, War Department, to Pershing, in part in reply to Pershing to TAG, War Department, cables P-621-S, February 20, and P-912-S, April 13.

Cable A-1203-R.

1B. Reference paragraph 1A, your 912. We have followed suggestions contained in paragraph 1A, your 621, in distributing Vickers Machine Guns. In view of advance in dates of embarkation of Infantry Brigades and Machine Gun Battalions ordered overseas, Divisions beginning with the 13th to arrive in France and up to and including the 25th Division will have to be equipped with Vickers Machine Guns before embarking overseas. To equip these latter 13 Divisions with Vickers Machine Guns it will take the production of these guns up to June 1st. After that date the Vickers guns will be available for Air Service and can be modified in this country before shipment overseas if you so desire. Browning Machine Guns will be available first issue as divisional equipment in the latter part of June and the production will be ample to cover all requirements. [Reply—May 16, P-1123-S-1, May 16, P-1133-S-1; in addition—May 3, A-1233-R-1D; Vol. 5, May 27, A-1406-R-1C]

NARA, RG 120, M930, Main Series, War Department to AEF, roll 12.

TAG, War Department, to Pershing, in part in reply to Pershing to TAG, War Department, cable P-970-S, April 20.

Cable A-1205-R.
1. French Government demands payment certain port dues and tolls in ports used by us. War Department accepts in principle and desires to settle whole matter by payment of lump sum. Confer with French authorities and determine proper amount of such sum due in each case. Will forward by mail copies of French notes and pamphlets, giving detailed information regarding port charges. Notify War Department of details of agreement arrived at. March [Reply—May 16, P-1134-S-1A]
2B. Reference paragraph 1, you 970. The colliers now in your service appear sufficient to take care of coal requirements for April and May. By June it is anticipated that at least 10 lake steamers will be available for such service. At that time, action on your recommendations relative to withdrawal of vessels named by you can be taken. Goethals.

NARA, RG 120, M930, Main Series, War Department to AEF, roll 12.

TAG, War Department, to Pershing, in part in reply to Pershing to TAG, War Department, cable P-977-S, April 22, in addition to TAG, War Department, to Pershing, cable A-1043-R, April 5..

Cable A-1206-R.
4. Reference paragraph 1A, your 977. Authority granted you to commission for reserves surplus Lieutenants not to exceed 500 graduates Army Candidate Schools as 2nd Lieutenants in Reserve Corps and order to active duty immediately, commissions to be temporary and to be confirmed by War Department. These 500 to be in addition to those necessary to replace vacancies contemplated in paragraph 3, my 1043. Plan has been proposed to send as many as practicable of graduates third and subsequent officers training schools of divisions through your schools and commission certain proportions of them after graduating therefrom with a view to assigning where most needed. Your views desired. March. [Reply—May 11, P-1094-S-1]

NARA, RG 120, M930, Main Series, War Department to AEF, roll 12.

TAG, War Department, to Pershing, in part in reply to Pershing to TAG, War Department, cable P-922-S, April 14.

Cable A-1211-R.
1B. With reference to your 922, paragraph 2. Present status of 8-inch gun situation as follows—62 carriages for Army 8-inch guns are under order. 77 Army 8-inch guns

are in existence and available for above carriages, 25 Model 1918 8-inch guns are under order and order is being placed for 38 additional guns of same model. 13 carriages for Navy 8-inch guns are under manufacture with 18 8-inch Navy guns in existence and available for same. Additional Navy guns cannot be obtained. 50 caliber 8-inch guns can be manufactured in place of present design. Design of 50 caliber gun is in an advanced state. These guns would require manufacture of new carriages as they will not interchange with any existing gun. Order for about 25, 8-inch carriages can be canceled so that there will be approximately 100% spare guns available. This cancellation will not involve loss of material. It will however delay final production of carriages. It will also decrease guns on firing line for a time since it involves taking spare guns from those now in existence instead of from new manufacture as has hitherto been contemplated. Prompt relay to this cablegram is urgently requested as manufacture of - - - is being interfered with pending definite decision. [Reply—May 11, P-1096-S-3]

NARA, RG 120, M930, Main Series, War Department to AEF, roll 12.

TAG, War Department, to Pershing, in part in reply to Pershing to TAG, War Department, cable P-973-S, April 21, in addition to TAG, War Department, to Pershing, cable A-1094-R, April 13.

Cable A-1214-R.
    2. Attention Air Service. With reference to your 973, paragraph 1. Production 180-horsepower Hispano Suiza engine will not be interfered with by French or English contracts as Wright Martin Company which manufactures these engines has no contracts with French or English. Refer to our 1094, paragraph 1I signed.... We can ship you high compression 180-horsepower Hispano Suiza engines as follows: 100 in July, 200 in August, and 250 per month thereafter. We are making these arrangements for you. You should make your own arrangements with British Air Service to deliver SE 5 planes commencing latter part of July. Advise us shipping instructions early in June to cover shipment of engines above mentioned. [*Ed.*—The War Department added on July 4 in cable A-1655-R-1J that the first shipment of engines would be the second week of July.] [In addition—Vol. 5, June 24, A-1596-R-1; July 4, A-1655-R-1J.]
    2A. Place order with British Air Board for 4 SE 5 planes arranged for 180 Hispano Suiza high-compression recited type. 2 planes to be fully equipped with engines and all accessories, 2 to be planes only. Expedite shipment in every way possible and cable name boat and date sailing. Large number these planes being put into production here. Have no samples this type and drawings here not enough complete to be understood by our engineers. Early production depends absolutely upon how soon samples are received. British War Mission also cabling Air Board urging shipment. Cable immediately reply. Similar cable sent to Harms London. [Reply—Vol. 5, May 27, P-1197-S-4B]

NARA, RG 120, M930, Main Series, War Department to AEF, roll 12.

3

May 1–May 19, 1918

May 1

Pershing's Personal Diary

Left Paris at about 10 a. m. with Colonel Eltinge and Colonel Boyd. Arrived at Abbeville at about 2:30. Sat in meeting of Supreme War Council held at that place. The principal question discussed in the afternoon was the transportation, employment and allocation of American troops. It looks as though the French became somewhat envious when they learned that the infantry and machine gun units of six American divisions are to be allocated to the British for a short period of training and service, and wish to get a similar allocation from the United States. I very clearly pointed out that it was with the expressed consent of M. Clemenceau and General Pétain that I had made this six-division agreement with the British. (General Foch had not his present position when this agreement was made.) I also pointed out that if the infantry of six divisions is to go with the British, the French have or will have seven American divisions with them and if it is merely a question of dividing up American troops, the French have already what might be called their share. There was no reply to these statements.

LC, Pershing Papers, Diary, May 7, 1917–September 1, 1918, box 4.

Abbeville Conference (Day 1)

First Meeting, Fifth Session, Supreme War Council,
Abbeville, Somme, May 1, 1918—2:45 p. m.
Supreme War Council

[Extract]

Minutes of the first meeting of the Fifth Session of the Supreme War Council, held in the *Chambre des Notaires,* at Abbeville, on Wednesday, May 1, 1918, at 3:30 p.m.

Present:

France
M. Clemenceau, President of the Council, Minister of War (in the Chair).

Great Britain
The Right Hon. D. Lloyd George, Prime Minister
The Right Hon. the Viscount Milner, Secretary of State for War.

Italy
His Excellency Signor Orlando, Prime Minister.

United States of America
Mr. A. H. Frazier, First Secretary, United States Embassy in Paris.

The following also attended:

France
General Foch, Commander-in-Chief, Allied Armies in France.
General Pétain, Commander-in-Chief of the Armies of the North and Northeast.
General Belin, Permanent Military Representative.
Admiral de Bon.
General Mordacq.
General Weygand
Commandant Lacombe

Great Britain
Field Marshal Sir Douglas Haig, Commanding-in-Chief, British Armies in France.
General Sir H. H. Wilson, Chief of the Imperial General Staff.
Major General the Hon. C. J. Sackville-West, Permanent Military Representative.
Lieutenant General the Hon. H. A. Lawrence, Chief of Staff, British Armies in France.
Admiral Sir Rosslyn Wemyss.
Lieutenant Colonel Sir M. P. A. Hankey.
Sir William Wiseman.

Italy
His Excellency General di Robilant, Permanent Military Representative.
Colonel Businelli.

United States of America
General J. J. Pershing, Commander-in-Chief, American Expeditionary Force.
General Tasker H. Bliss, Permanent Military Representative.
Brigadier General Lochridge [Assistant to Bliss].
Colonel Eltinge [Deputy Chief of Staff, AEF].
Colonel Boyd [Senior ADC to Pershing].

* * * * * *

M. Clemenceau said that the first item on the Agenda which the Supreme War Council had to consider was that of the employment of American troops. It had been recommended by their military representatives at Versailles in Joint Note No. 18 [see March 27, Minutes of the Meeting of the Military Representatives] that only American infantry and machine guns should be sent to France for the present. He proposed to ask the interpreter to read out the note.

(Professor Mantoux then read out Joint Note No. 18.)

M. Clemenceau said he wished also to draw the attention of the council to the terms of the Pershing-Milner Agreement of April 24, 1918 [see also April 24, cable P-961-S], which altered to some extent the arrangements which had been agreed upon by the military representatives. It had been understood at Versailles that the United States were to send over 120,000 men a month, half of whom were to join the British and half the French army. Under the new arrangement it appeared that none were to join the French. Now, the French had not been consulted in this matter. It might have been supposed that the American troops arriving in June would be allotted to the French, but it now appeared that the arrangements were that these also would join the British forces. He felt bound to protest against this arrangement, as he could not regard it as satisfactory. In order to make the discussion more definite in its character, he was prepared to accept that the 120,000 to be sent in May should go to the British. He wished, however, that he had been consulted in the matter, so that he might have had the opportunity of recording his assent to these arrangements. But he felt he must insist on the French getting a similar number in June. He further wished to point out that although there were about 400,000 American troops now in France, only 5 divisions, or the equivalent of 125,000 men, were combatants. This is not a satisfactory proportion.

Lord Milner asked if he might say a word of explanation. M. Clemenceau seemed to be thinking that the Pershing-Milner Agreement [see April 24, cable P-961-S] was a reversal of a Supreme War Council decision. To his recollection there had been no such decision. There had only been a joint note embodying the recommendations of the military representatives. No such recommendations had any validity until it had been endorsed by the Supreme War Council. M. Clemenceau further was under the impression that it had been decided that half the American troops should go to Great Britain and half to France. He himself could recollect no such decision. All that he and General Pershing had urged had been that infantry and machine guns should be sent to France. Neither he nor General Pershing had any intention of depriving the French of American troops. He did not know that anything had been said as regards their allocation on arrival in France. The one object of himself and General Pershing had been to get these reinforcements over with the least possible delay.

General Pershing said that in making the agreement with Lord Milner he had only the idea of bringing troops as rapidly as possible in order to meet the existing situation. Lord Milner was quite correct in stating that there was no agreement as to the allocation of American troops either to the British or the French armies. There was no agreement between his government or the Commanders-in-Chief and anybody else that any single American soldier should be sent either to the British or to the French. There was in existence an agreement which had been accepted in principle by M. Clemenceau and General Pétain, between himself and Field Marshal Sir Douglas Haig, and signed by Mr. Lloyd George, to the effect that the infantry and machine-gun units of 6 divisions should be brought to Europe, and this agreement had been signed by his government.

Mr. Lloyd George said he wished to ask General Pershing what would be the total number of men in the infantry and machine-gun units of 6 divisions.

General Pershing said that these would amount to about 120,000, which, of course, would include a certain number of auxiliary troops.

M. Clemenceau said that he had an observation to offer. They were not there today to discuss personal matters or to raise personal issues. They were informed that nothing had been decided at Versailles, but evidently something had been decided in London, and France was very intimately concerned in this question. Nothing apparently had been decided on behalf of the French. He wished again to say that he was sorry that the French had asked for certain technical units, but it apparently was not possible to accede to these requests. General Foch had asked General Pershing what American troops would be allocated to the French, and the reply had been that nothing would be given to the French army in May and that it was impossible to say at present what might be allocated in June. He reminded the council that General Foch had been appointed to the Supreme Command in France. This command was not given as a mere decoration. It involved, amongst other things, serious responsibilities, including suitable provision for the future. In conclusion, he said he did not wish to object to what had been arranged about the allocation of American troops in May, but he desired to know what it was intended should be done with troops arriving from America in June.

Mr. Lloyd George associated himself with M. Clemenceau's view that this was not a personal matter. The interests of the Allies were identical and the problem must be approached from this point of view, otherwise the unity of command which they hoped they had achieved had no meaning. What it had to consider was what was best for the common cause. What was the situation today? The British Army had been most heavily engaged and had suffered the most serious losses. All available drafts in depots in England had been sent over to France, and every single man who becomes available in May or June would be sent out. This would be still the case even if they were sure every American soldier who might arrive in Europe in those months would be allotted to the British army. The position was that some of the British divisions had been so severely handled that they could not be reconstituted. General Foch would know the actual number.

General Foch said the number was 10.

Mr. Lloyd George said that as these 10 divisions could no longer be placed in the line they must be replaced by other divisions which must be French. The Germans were fighting with the object of exhausting our reserves. If they could do this without exhausting their own reserves, they might be able to deliver a blow which we could not parry. He suggested that the decision regarding the allocation of American troops in June should be taken when that month arrives, that is to say, the decision whether such troops should be drafted to broken British or French divisions. The decision depended upon who would have to bear the brunt, the British or the French. He thought it was not desirable at this stage to decide how troops from the United States arriving in June should be allocated.

General Foch said that it was incontestable that the situation today so far as the British were concerned was that they were practically exhausted. None disputed this fact any more than they disputed that American troops arriving in May should be drafted to British divisions. The British certainly had suffered very heavily at the start of the present battle, but lately the French had also had grave losses, notable at Montdidier, and both during the last few days and previously the French and English were fighting shoulder to shoulder. American help was now almost as much needed for France as for Great Britain. That, however, was not the point. The American assistance was not wanted for the French or for the British, but for the Allies generally. They agreed that American troops arriving in May should reinforce the British army. In June, too, their first need was for infantry and machine-gun units. They looked to General Pershing to display his customary generosity and breadth of view and for him to admit the justice of this opinion. They merely asked him to extend his May program over the following month.

Mr. Lloyd George said he wished to add a word in support of General Foch. He suspected that the French depots were by this time as much reduced as the British. The new manpower bill in England would only begin to take effect in August. By August the men who became available under that bill as well as the French 1920 Class would be coming in. The American troops arriving in May would not be ready for service till August. This meant that June was the critical month. He appealed to General Pershing to ask that the program for May should be extended over June.

M. Clemenceau said he was in absolute agreement with Mr. Lloyd George and General Foch.

General Pershing said that he did not suppose that he was to understand that the American army was to be entirely at the disposal of the French and British commands.

*M. Clemenc*eau said that, of course, this was not the case.

General Pershing said that he spoke for the United States Government and for himself when he said that they looked forward to a time when the United States would have its own army. He must insist on its being recognized. The principle of unity of command in the United States army must prevail, and that army must be complete, homogeneous, and under its own supreme command. He would like the council to fix some date when this principle will materialize. It was only fair to Lord Milner and himself to remind the council that 4 United States divisions were now with the French, a fifth division would be ready in a week, and two more divisions shortly afterwards. He wished it to be quite clear that all American troops in France were consequently not going to the British. As regards the suggested extension of the May program into June, he was not quite prepared to consent. Troops arriving in June would not be ready for the front until late in July or the middle of August. They had the whole of May before them, and there was sufficient time therefore to consider if the emergency in June was likely to arise. His reasons for declining now to commit the American army to a program so far in advance he had communicated to Lord Milner and to General Foch. If the emergency should arise he would recommend the extension of the program to his government, but he did not recognize that the need for a decision existed at the moment.

Mr. Lloyd George said, speaking on behalf of the British Government, he entirely accepted the principle laid down by General Pershing. It would be unreasonable and impertinent on their part to treat American troops as drafts for the British army. It was to our advantage that the American army as such should take the field as soon as possible, and, speaking as the head of the British Government, he accepted that principle.

We were, however, now fighting what was probably the decisive battle of the war. If we lose this battle we shall have to provide tonnage to take what is left of the British army and the American army back to their homes. How can we best hope to win this battle? The decisive months might well be next September, October, or later. If the United States Army could come in then as an army, this would suit them all. He saw no reason to believe that the two ideas could not be reconciled, but they could not wait until the end of May to decide, as there was the question of tonnage to be considered.

General Pershing agreed.

Mr. Lloyd George thought that we might wait a fortnight. Hitherto the United States Government had objected to sending over troops in slow vessels. Otherwise another 30,000 to 40,000 men per month would be available.

General Pershing said that both he and Admiral Sims had pressed this point with government.

Mr. Lloyd George said he understood the government at Washington was now prepared to consider this point and to send over troops in ships of 9 1/2 knots and over. The British Shipping Controller thought that 150,000 a month was the maximum which British bottoms could take. American ships can bring another 40,000 or 50,000 men. There was no reason, therefore, why they should not be able to transport the infantry and machine guns as desired as a temporary reinforcement, while General Pershing would also be able to bring over the auxiliary services he required to complete his divisions and armies. In August we should be getting over our reinforcements, and thus by September or October General Pershing would be able to take the field with a formed army made up of experienced soldiers. According to the calculations which had been submitted to him, they could transport 200,000 American troops in May in British and American ships, and 220,000 in June, which would enable both programs to be carried out.

General Pershing said that he understood this increase of tonnage would enable America to send over complete units.

Mr. Lloyd George said that this was the case. What was important in view of the urgency of getting infantry was that priority should be given to infantry and machine guns.

General Pershing agreed up to the extent of 6 divisions. The continuance of this program might be discussed on May 10 or 15. This would give him time to consult his government.

Mr. Lloyd George thought that it must be decided sometime before the end of the month.

General Foch said that nobody appreciated better than himself the principle of an American army as an homogeneous unit. This principle applied to every army. There was nothing to compare with a national army under the national flag and national commanders. He supported the principle of the American army as a separate unit. But they had today to face an immediate situation. The best thing to do in this view was to extend the May program. If the tonnage sufficed for both, so much the better, but before the council rose they ought to agree then and there to extend that program. He suggested that Lord Milner, General Pershing, and himself should meet at once to see how this could be done with the least possible delay.

General Pershing said he was glad to hear the French Generalissimo express himself so strongly in favour of the United States army as a unit under its own flag. Nobody appreciated the immediate situation more thoroughly than he did. He was still ready to recommend to his government that all possible assistance must be rendered in France, but he did not think it necessary for the council to commit themselves today to an extension of the program.

General Foch pointed out that he was in supreme command, and that his appointment had been sanctioned not only by the French and British Governments, but also by the President of the United States. In that capacity he felt it his duty to insist on his point of view. There was the Pershing-Milner Agreement [see April 24, cable P-961-S, Pershing, in London, to TAG, War Department]. If, as supreme commander, he were to have nothing to say to such conventions his position was stultified. He again suggested that the three officers he had named should at once prepare a fresh agreement. He could not forget the responsibility devolving upon him in consequence of the powers granted to him by the three governments to control the fighting on the western front.

General Pershing said that he thought General Foch should be a party to the agreement he had made with Lord Milner.

M. Clemenceau said that, of course, this committee would report at once to the Supreme War Council. At first he had been in agreement with Mr. Lloyd George's views, afterwards he had come round to General Foch's opinion.

It was both an obligation and a necessity to form a single great American army. He deeply sympathized with General Pershing's feelings in this matter. General Pershing was rightly impressed with his duty to form a strong and autonomous American army, but he begged General Pershing to consider carefully the arguments of General Foch and Mr. Lloyd George, and to face the immediate situation. The Germans were confronting us at Villers-Bretonneux. If they broke through there they might soon be at the gates of Paris. They were also hammering on our front to the north, and if they broke through by Hazebrouck they might reach the Channel ports. In either case the consequences would be most grave. Hitherto it was the British who had suffered the greatest losses, now it was the French Army's turn. It was essential that both in May and June, when they would be most short of drafts, that they should have men. General Pershing thought it was better to wait before deciding, but time was pressing. Could they afford even a fortnight's delay? Further, the situation might not have changed in any striking fashion in a fortnight, in which case there would be no new basis on which to form a decision. From the point of view of morale it was most important not only to say to our soldiers that the Americans are coming, but to show them that the Americans are actually there. They had, of course, no right to order the United States Government to do anything, but what they could do was to put the situation before the American Government and to point out its gravity. Another point was that a fortnight would make a great deal of difference as regards the training of the men. Let General Pershing reconcile his own principles with the emergent needs of the moment, which were to have American soldiers at once in France, mixing with the British and the French. He proposed to adjourn the council for a short time, in order that the committee suggested by General Foch should meet and examine the question.

(The session adjourned at 5 p. m.)

(The session reopened at 6:10 p.m.)

M. *Clemenceau* said that the discussion on the question of American troops would be continued on the following day, when the report of the committee would be considered. He asked the council to consider item 2 on the Agenda, which was "The Strength of the Allied Forces and the Future Policy to be pursued in Salonika."

* * * * * *

USAWW, vol. 2, pp. 360–65.

Editor's Note—Pershing explained the details of his discussions with Lord Milner and General Foch during the adjournment, which were not reported in the above minutes:

> At M. Clemenceau's suggestion, the meeting of the Council was adjourned at this point in order that Foch, Milner, and I might meet and examine the question, and see if some agreement could be reached. Whereupon we repaired to an adjacent room and went over the whole subject again.
>
> Milner, and especially Foch, insisted that the war would be lost unless their program was carried out. I repeated the arguments presented to the Council and added that I fully realized the military emergency but did not think that the plan to bring over untrained units to fight under British and French commands would either relieve the situation or end the war.[1] I pointed out that, regardless of the depressing conditions and the very urgent need of men by the Allies, their plan was not practicable and that even if sound in principle there was not time enough to prepare our men as individuals for efficient service under a new system, with the strange

---

1. While our units were to be brought for training as a part of larger British or French units, it was thoroughly understood that they were there to fight, in case they were needed.

surroundings to be found in a foreign army. The very lowest limit ever thought of for training recruits under the most favorable circumstances, even for trench warfare, had been nine weeks devoted to strenuous work, counting out the time that would be consumed in travel, the untrained arrivals could not be ready before August, when the trained contingents of the Allies for 1918 would become available.

Here Foch said: "You are willing to risk our being driven back to the Loire?"

I said: "Yes, I am willing to take the risk. Moreover, the time may come when the American Army will have to stand the brunt of this war, and it is not wise to fritter away our resources in this manner. The morale of the British, French and Italian armies is low, while, as you know, that of the American Army is very high. It would be a grave mistake to give up the idea of building an American army in all its details as rapidly as possible."

Then Foch again said that the war might be over before we were ready.

I said that the war could not, in my opinion, be saved by feeding untrained American recruits into the Allied armies, but that we must build up an American army, and concessions for the time being to meet the present emergency were all that I would approve.

At about this juncture, Mr. Lloyd George, M. Clemenceau, and Mr. Orlando, evidently becoming impatient, walked into the room. Milner met Lloyd George at the door and said in a stage-whisper behind his hand, "You can't budge him an inch." Lloyd George then said, "Well, how is the committee getting along?"

Whereupon we all sat down and Lloyd George said to me, "Can't you see that the war will be lost unless we get this support?" which statement was echoed in turn by Clemenceau and Orlando. In fact, all five of the party attacked me with all the force and prestige of their high positions.

But I had already yielded to their demands as far as possible without disrupting the plans toward which we had been striving for over a year, and a continuance of May shipments into June, without any provision for transporting artillery and auxiliary and service of supply troops, could not be granted without making it practically impossible in the future to have an American army. After going over the whole situation again and stating my position, they still insisted, whereupon I said with the greatest possible emphasis, "Gentlemen, I have thought this program over very deliberately and will not be coerced." This ended the discussion in committee and when the Council reconvened M. Clemenceau stated that the question of American troops would be taken up again on the following day. (Pershing, *My Experiences in the World War*, vol. 2, pp. 27–29.)

According to Col. T. Bentley Mott, Chief, American Military Mission with CINC, Allied Armies (Foch), who was present throughout these meetings, what Pershing more diplomatically wrote as "the greatest possible emphasis" was actually as follows: "Pershing finally closed the discussion by bringing his fist down on the table and saying with a glare of determination, 'Gentlemen, I have thought this program over very deliberately and will not be coerced.'" (Mott, *Twenty Years as Military Attaché*, p. 245.)

Col. LeRoy Eltinge, Pershing's Deputy Chief of Staff, attended these meetings and submitted his lengthy "Notes on the Abbeville Conference" to Pershing afterward. He reported his impressions of an exchange between Foch and Pershing as follows:

> *General Foch* announced that he agreed with having an American Army united under the American flag. He then went on in a very long and impassioned harangue on the present stress, and the belief that unless American replacements were used to fill up French and British infantry, that the Allied armies would be driven back to the Loire before the American Army could be formed. (Note: This speech made a very disagreeable impression on me—had all the atmosphere of clap-trap oratory, and sounded more like a "stump" speech than a discussion.) He finally proposed that later during the present Conference, he, Lord Milner and General Pershing hold a conference as a smaller committee.
>
> *General Pershing* brought out and emphasized the fact that Foch had agreed.
>
> *General Pershing* emphasized that General Foch had agreed to the principle of an American Army under the American flag. However, he declined to change his former decision—that he would not decide upon the further bringing over of infantry and machine guns only until toward the end of May.
>
> *General Foch*: He said that the American Government had helped to make him Commander-in-Chief and had agreed to his authority. He practically tried to use his authority as Commander-in-Chief to order General Pershing to agree. It was finally decided to have the small meeting of General Foch, Lord Milner and General Pershing during the evening. General Pershing agreed. (Eltinge, "Notes on the Abbeville Conference, held May 1–2, 1918," n.d., in LC, Pershing Papers, folder: Training and Employment of American Troops with British, box 198.)

Another participant in these meetings was Field Marshal Haig, who confided his observations of this contentious day in his diary:

> At the Conference of the Supreme War Council a great deal of time was wasted discussing the agreement made by Lord Milner and General Pershing regarding bringing 120,000 American Infantry to France in May to join the British Army. I thought Pershing was very obstinate, and stupid. He did not seem to realise the urgency of the situation.

Finally, the arrangement for May is to hold good and Pershing is to decide in a fortnight whether the same arrangement will continue for June. He hankers after a 'great self contained American Army' but seeing that he has neither Commanders of Divisions, of Corps, nor of Armies, nor Staffs for same, it is ridiculous to think such an Army could function alone in less than 2 years' time! (Sheffield and Bourne (eds.), *Douglas Haig*, p. 409.)

Pétain, CINC, Armies of the North and Northeast.

No. 736.
Memorandum on the Training of American Infantry Units Attached to Major French Units.

American units, especially regiments, will be attached, during more or less prolonged periods of instructions, to certain French divisions. As soon as the amount of training they have had permits, these units will participate in the functions of these divisions, so as to lighten the work of the French regiments, and at the same time continuing their own training.

When a division in sector is relieved to take part in active operations, the American units which it is instructing will not be taken along; these units will be turned over to the relieving division. This arrangement does not apply to American colored infantry regiments, who will remain with the French division to which they have been attached.

The importance of duties of French units having American troops attached cannot be exaggerated; the officers and staffs should exert every energy on their work in order to make it possible for our Allies to enter the battle as rapidly as possible at our side.

The following indications given under the heading of instructions, serve for the proper instruction of the Americans as well as to indicate the relationship to be maintained with them.

II. General Instructions: American units arriving in France have only had, up to the present, very incomplete instructions [training]. This instruction was approximately limited, during their stay in camp, in the United States, to gymnastic exercises, close order drill, rifle fire and drill in field warfare, which consisted too much of small operations, having but little relation to actual warfare, such as attack and defense of convoys, requisitions, etc. They have but slight knowledge of specialties (grenades, F. M. [automatic rifle], machine guns, etc.). They submit rather quickly to discipline under a strict commanding officer. The cadres only include a very small number of officers and noncommissioned officers from the regular army, and the majority have either everything to learn, or only possess the elements of theoretical instruction. The officers, a very different class of men, educated, older and temperamental, are usually strong, athletic, intelligent and very ambitious to learn. They have served in the United States in training school camps, passing through a three months' course. A certain number have gone through schools in France. Lacking a solid military foundation, personal temperament dominates, some being very strict and even domineering, others timid and without much energy. In relations with all officers, it should be borne in mind that they have an extremely highly developed sense of amour-propre, based on their pride in belonging to one of the greatest nations of the world. Consequently, an attitude of superiority over them should be assiduously avoided, a fact which in no way prevents the absolute subordination required by the service, nor carrying out the rules of hierarchy. Avoid also a doctrinal form of instruction; rather suggest and advise, citing existing examples; a method which will always be more effective and more valuable than a purely theoretical lecture.

The service within the units, keeping cantonments in order, hygiene of the men and horses, marching discipline, etc., that is to say, all those duties which require the constant and careful supervision of experienced regular officers, are often far from satisfactorily taken care of at first. The best means for improving these conditions is through French troops setting an example, or by tactful suggestions or advice on the part of the French officers. Results obtained, up to the present by these means have usually been satisfactory and rapid. However, in case of necessity, French officers should not hesitate to exercise their authority.

Preparations of food could often be greatly improved. The suggestion might be made to attach a few French monitors to American kitchens. If this is done in a spirit of camaraderie, it would be greatly appreciated and would tend to develop good relations.

A few French officers, who speak English, and who have gone through the finishing course in the army schools, are attached to American units and live with them. It is their duty to explain our methods, to make certain that instructions given by French commands have been understood, and to establish liaison with the French command, as well as with neighboring French units. They are the same as the American units themselves, under the orders of the French command, but it is solely essential to avoid creating the idea that they are detailed by the French command as controlling or supervising agents, for fear of making their position impossible, or at least limiting their sphere of action with the American units. All suggestions made for the purpose of improving the work of the American unit should be sent directly to the commanding officer of that unit by the French command under whose orders it is placed.

III. Objects to be Attained: American units attached to French divisions will ultimately enter into the formation of American divisions.

The preceding statements indicate the objects to be accomplished and the spirit in which instruction is to be given. It can be summed up as follows:

1. To effect a rapid and essentially practical training.

2. To realize uniform training based on American regulations, organization and temperament, so that American divisions can be constituted with units similarly organized and trained.

3. To include a period of training on the front so as to lighten the burden of French units in sector as much as possible.

IV. Composition of the Units: See the table annexes [Basic Tables of Organization and Equipment for an American Infantry Regiment—not reproduced].

V. General Method of Instruction: The general method of training employed up to the present consisted in placing at the disposal of each American division:

1. As explained in paragraph I.

Selected officer instructors, trained in army schools, with a knowledge of specialties as well as knowledge of English.

2. French units, or demonstrating crews taken from the regiments of the division or from its divisional training center.

This system has produced good results. It would be advisable to continue along these lines. It would also be advisable to place the general direction of this instruction in the hands of an experienced corps chief or the commander of the divisional training center, under the superior supervision of the general commanding the division.

Officer instructors attached to American units are advisors and guides in every sense of the word, within the unit. They must strictly conform to official regulations and instructions, so as to obtain a complete unity of principle and theory, and avoid all exposition of personal ideas, which do not conform with the spirit of our regulations.

The experience of regiments having assisted in the instruction of American divisions proves that instruction by example is especially valuable. A French unit executed a maneuver; the American unit then does likewise, commanded by its own officers and non-commissioned officers.

The new conditions under which the instruction of American units will be planned, as indicated in this memorandum, presents the possibility of training by example in another form, namely, placing these units, from companies up, in calm sectors between corresponding French units. A combination of utilization and training will thus be had.

VI. Regulations: At present the American army is making use of, except for close order drill and field service, our regulations translated for its use, and especially the following:

Training on the Offensive Action of Large Units

Training on the Defensive Action of Large Units

Training on Organization of Terrain (being printed April 15)

Training on Liaison for all Arms (being translated April 15)

Manual for Chief of Section (An adaptation was being prepared on April 15)

Training on Offensive Combat of Small Units (Translation and adaptation based on effectives)

Training on the Tactical Use of Machine Guns (being translated April 15).

VII. Program of Instruction: The training section at American G. H. Q. issues to units, detailed programs showing the work to be done in each subject, hour by hour. These programs are too rigid and do not always conform with what we consider the best method of instruction. It should be borne in mind, as much as circumstances will permit, that the work done on this rigid basis has, nevertheless, been good, due to the enthusiasm and interest shown.

Herewith attached is given, under the heading of information, a general program of instruction covering eight weeks, proposed by the colonel commanding the French 32d Regiment, after having assisted in the training of American divisions [not reproduced].

VIII. Remarks on Certain Details of Training:

(a) *Operations in Open Country*: Americans dream of operating in open country, after having broken through the front. This results in too much attention being devoted to this form of operations, which the Americans consider as superior, and in which, our Allies sometimes seem to think, we are incapable of offering them the same assistance which they expect from us in trench warfare. It is essential:

(1) To take discreet measures to counteract the idea that we are inexperienced in open warfare;

(2) To direct into proper channels, or maintain it within proper bounds, the excellent leaning toward open warfare, and to instruct them on this subject for the purpose of instilling an understanding of mass warfare. In this form of warfare the men are usually supported by veterans, interspersed in the ranks, and the small field service operations mentioned above play but a small part in it.

(b) *Evolution, Orientation, Direction*: These are details which should be especially carefully gone into. A knowledge of shifting of units on the field, study of maps, the use of the compass, orientation, direction, all forms of liaison, utilization of approaches, are things which are entirely new and difficult to realize for inexperienced officers.

(c) *The Defensive—Echelonment in Depth, Flanking Movements, Counterattacks*: Echelonment in depth, especially so far as it concerns the use of defensive barrages, successive and fixed, flanking fire of automatic arms (machine guns) and F. M.'s, should be points of very careful consideration.

They will be slow to grasp the idea of flanking movements. It is essential to instill this principle in our Allies, together with that of the counterattack, carefully planned and immediately launched.

(d) *The Rifle—Automatic Weapons, the Bayonet, the Grenade*: The American soldier is drilled in the use of the rifle and the bayonet. The value of automatic weapons and of the grenade is not generally fully appreciated. These are points which should be developed, at the same time being very careful not to diminish the partiality of the American soldiers for sniping (in which they easily excel) and for the bayonet.

(e) *The Machine Gun*: This organization seems to be poorly arranged. Instead of being assigned to infantry battalions, machine gun companies are grouped in the majority of cases in battalions, one battalion of four companies to a brigade, one battalion of two companies for the division, one company to a regiment, making a total of 14 companies in the entire division. This organization results from a tendency toward limitation, in our opinion, a tendency which probably results also from English influence, which favors the use of indirect fire by numerous machine guns formed into large batteries, rather than the use of direct fire.

In practice, when in sector, one company is assigned to one battalion. But the temporary liaison thus improvised with the battalion is too loose. It seems advisable to instruct the corps chiefs for the purpose of making the assignment of one company to a battalion as permanent as possible.

(f) *Liaison—Reports*: To show the development of liaison from its fundamental principles, and also show how it functions, especially in relation to artillery (use of signals, request for barrage, T. P. S., etc.), and with the superior echelon (support). Apparently the Americans do not like to make reports. They must be educated in this.

It is only with great difficulty that they can be shown the necessity of issuing orders and reports in writing.

(g) *Works*: The American soldier, as did ours formerly, resent manual labor. It is necessary from the beginning to develop his hands and muscles, and in the case of officers, to instruct them as to the tactical idea in the execution of works.

(h) *Training of Officers and Noncommissioned Officers:*—Training of Officers: The instruction of officers and noncommissioned officers is long lines paralleling that for the soldiers. All of them seem to be very ambitious to learn.

It is evident that instruction should be essentially practical. An excellent method to obtain this result seems to be to have all troop maneuvers preceded by practice on the field by the officers and noncommissioned officers.

(i) *Practice Trenches*: In the same way it is essential, for maneuvers of position, to have a system of trenches, if not entirely, at least partially completed, with the remainder laid out. The practical mentality of the American does not adjust itself to theoretical and hypothetical explanation, a fact which is all the more accentuated because his lack of previous military training leaves him unprepared and he is unable to imagine things which he has never seen.

IX. *Mode of Procedure to be Adopted with American Officers*: It is essential that the American officer become accustomed to command, and maintain the necessary prestige with his troops.

Consequently, it is of the greatest importance that French instructors carefully avoid assuming his duties or to give the impression that he is taking his place in the command by giving orders.

In this respect, mutual study with American officers, prior to practice with troops, and going through exercises with the cadres alone, produces the best results.

X. *Patience and Tact*: The main purpose of our collaboration in the instruction of American troops is to give our Allies the benefit of our dearly bought experience.

Our officers, instructors as well as officers commanding demonstration units as a result of not speaking the same language, sometimes find it difficult to fulfill their duties in the beginning. Constant patience and extreme tact, together with application will serve to overcome all obstacles.

[Copies to: Army Groups, Armies, French Mission at Chaumont, and U.S. Mission at General Headquarters.]

[In addition—June 19, Pétain to Generals Commanding Army Groups and Armies]

Les armées françaises dans la Grande guerre, Tome 6, vol. 2, *Annexes,* vol. 1: Annexe No. 79, pp. 179–85; see also *USAWW,* vol. 3, pp. 292–95.

J. L. Dumesnil, Under-Secretary of State, Military and Naval Aeronautics, Ministry of Munitions, to Foulois, Chief, Air Service, SOS, AEF.

Pursuant to our conversation of yesterday [see April 30, Foulois memorandum] I have the honor to confirm the proposition approved by the General Commander in Chief of the French Army, which I made to you to incorporate into French Squadrons at the front, not only 100 American pilots as I had advised you in my letter No. 8175 2/12 of April 8, but the greater number of 400.

French Aeronautics will be proud and happy of the honor which your aviators will bring it in fighting in still greater numbers in its ranks.

As I had already said to you at the beginning of last month, American pilots will be used in our squadrons under exactly the same conditions as French pilots, and until such time as the formation of a greater number of purely American squadrons enables you to take them back, if you so desire.

I would be very much obliged if you would be good enough to submit this proposition to General Pershing, and if, as I trust, it has his approval, to so inform me as soon as possible, and to enumerate the trained personnel which you might be able to put at our service and the dates which you suggest for sending these pilots to the groups of divisional training, whence they will be distributed by the French Command among our various squadrons.

This being the case, I am convinced that those of your trained pilots, above and beyond the numbers necessary for the squadrons equipped with the material put at your disposal during the first semester of 1918, will, (during some time to come), be able to do useful work, without waste of time, as a result of close coordination of our strength.

I avail myself of the opportunity to express to you, and to beg you to be good enough to convey to the attention of General Pershing, the great satisfaction given to the Commander of Aviation of the Garrison of Paris and to me, by your placing at our disposal, some time ago, the American pilots for cooperation in the aerial defense of the capital.

I beg you to accept, my dear General, with the assurance of my high consideration the expression of my cordial sentiments.

P. S. Also, I wish to point out to you that the American Mechanic Companies which we are now using in factories or Aviation Schools are giving us the greatest assistance, not only as the result of the technical ability of the men who make up these companies, but also as the result of their great willingness to work.

I wish to express to you, in this connection, my very lively thanks, and I can immediately point out to you that the French factories and Aviation Schools would have much to gain if they could obtain the services of a new group of about 1200 mechanics which we could use immediately, as soon as the War Committee of Versailles approves of the sending of new American mechanic regiments to France.

I would be greatly obliged if you would kindly look into the question immediately in order that you may be able, without loss of time, to put at the disposal of French Aeronautics these workmen, whose assistance will be particularly valuable to us and will enable us to accentuate still more the effort being made to achieve our common purpose. [Reply—May 9, Foulois to Dumesnil; in addition—Harbord to Chief, French Military Mission, May 4]

LC, Foulois Papers, folder 12: AEF, Air Service, Allied Air Service, box 7.

Col. Dutilleul, CS, for Ragueneau, Chief, French Military Mission with the American Army, Chaumont, to CINC, AEF, CS.

No. 690-01, 7733-3.

I have the honor to confirm to you that in accordance with the verbal understanding reached this morning, the French command counts:

1. That the French 127th Infantry Division, which will entrain at Void beginning on May 4, will relieve from its present sector, after two days of rest, the American 26th Infantry Division, probably beginning on the 8th or 9th.

2. That the American 26th Infantry Division will be regrouped in the zone of Lafauche with the object of taking part in active operations after a period of instruction under conditions which are yet to be determined.

The General commanding the Group of Armies of the East has given orders to the Eighth Army to submit plans for the relief, the echeloning and the duration of movements. He proposes that the movement of the American 26th Infantry Division be made by march.

I have the honor to request you to be kind enough to prescribe that all details of execution be adjusted directly with the Eighth Army.

Note: The original contains a pencil note as follows: "This was not accepted by us and statement in first paragraph is incorrect. F. C." [Fox Conner].
[GHQ AEF Action]

May 2, 1918

Conner, ACS, G-3, GHQ AEF, to CS.

1. The proposition to relieve the 26th Division by a French division about May 7 or 9 was made yesterday by the Chief of Staff, French Mission. The 26th Division was apparently notified at the same time that the division would be relieved on the date indicated.

2. The French propose to concentrate the 26th Division in the 4th area and to give it open warfare training either in that area or elsewhere, with a view to the division being sent to the present battlefront.

3. It is believed that the 42d Division is in better condition, especially with reference to command and staff, than the 26th Division and that the 42d should be sent to the battlefront before the 26th.

4. There are additional considerations which, in the opinion of this section, should be carefully weighed before final decision is reached with respect to the 26th Division.

5. There is no good reason to believe that a final decision in favor of the Allies will be reached on the present battlefront.

6. Our original conceptions of the proper region in which finally to employ our forces are still believed to be correct.

7. Both from the standpoint of training and of the possibility ever to be able to assemble an American force, it is essential that we constantly work toward creating an American sector.

8. By virtue of work done, materiel installed, and hospital and supply facilities created, the present 26th Division sector has gradually been organized to conform to American necessities.

9. In carrying out the work of developing this as an American sector, a considerable number of army troops have been assigned to work in close connection with the sector.

10. In sum, the only nucleus in sight around which to develop the policy of building up an American force is the present 26th Division sector. On account of the extra divisional troops now in the sector, the relief of the 26th Division by a French division will have as its net result a still further dispersion of our forces.

11. It is recommended that the French be informed that we desire to have the available French division relieve either the 2d or the 42d Division and that we do not desire to relieve the 26th.

12. G-5 concurs in the above and in addition remarks that the 2d Division is at least 20 per cent superior to the 42d Division.

[For GHQ AEF reply, see Vol. 5, May 22, McAndrew to Chief, French Military Mission.]

USAWW, vol. 3, pp. 621–22, 622–23.

Pershing to Col. Robert Bacon, Chief, American Military Mission with GHQ BAF.

I have given this day orders to relieve yourself, Colonels Collins, and Shallenberger from duty on my personal staff.

The coming of a Corps Headquarters to the vicinity of the British G. H. Q. with the presence of General Harts commanding the Engineer Troops renders unnecessary the maintenance of a separate office there for the work which you have efficiently performed to my satisfaction since you were detailed as an A. D. C. It is my intention to detail General Harts to take over the work of the American Mission at British Headquarters in addition to his other duties.

I take this occasion to express to you my earnest appreciation of the wholehearted way in which you have constantly performed every duty given you since our departure from New York last May. Your enthusiasm, your willingness and singleness of purpose are an example to all of us.

I have given orders that you be accorded the privilege of a term at the Staff College which will bring you more in touch with the work of the Staff in general and will open for you a new opportunity for increased usefulness.

With best wishes for your future, I remain,

Scott, *Robert Bacon,* pp. 334–35.

Editor's Note—In an unlocated letter to Haig of May 7, Pershing reversed his decision and attached Bacon to Harts's headquarters for duty with the American Military Mission as a liaison officer before assigning him as a member of Haig's personal staff (ADC) on May 31 until he was relieved in March 1919 (see May 16, Pershing to Haig). See Scott, *Robert Bacon*, pp. 335, 337, 444.

TAG, War Department, to Pershing, in part in reply to Pershing to TAG, War Department, cables P-891-S, April 11, and P-961-S, April 24.

Cable A-1217-R. Confidential.

1. With reference to your 961. Present plans contemplate shipment in May of "A" units, that have not already been shipped, of the following divisions: 77th, 82nd, 35th, 28th, 4th, 30th, 3rd, 5th, 27th, 33rd, 80th and 78th. First 6 are our hastily organized original assignment to Second Corps for training with British. Second 6 our assignment to 3rd Corps for training as you direct. These to be followed by "B" units of the same divisions that have not already been shipped. These to be followed by replacements. These to be followed by all other troops of 1st and 2nd Phases. Either replacements or Corps, Army and Service of Rear troops will be interspersed with divisions when necessary to fill space or when specially called for. Do you desire the suspension of shipment of troops mentioned in 1B and 1H, your 891, continued? March. [Reply—May 17, P-1139-S-1B]

NARA, RG 120, M930, Confidential Series, War Department to AEF, roll 18.

May 2

Pershing's Personal Diary

At Abbeville—with Supreme War Council. The deliberations covered the situation in Salonika and withdrawal of troops therefrom—the Czech troops at Vladivostock and the possibility of transferring them to Western Front. As to the question of American tonnage for this transfer, I stated all of this would be needed for shipment of American troops.

M. Clemenceau presented question of acceptance of General Foch as Commander-in-Chief of all Allied forces on Western Front. An agreement with Italy adopted whereby General Foch commands Italian troops in France, and in case of Allied forces in Italy he commands all Allied troops there. A reservation was made in agreement.

The question of American troops was then brought up. General Foch made a dramatic speech outlining the force of the German's onslaught and the dangerous advantage they are taking of the ever-weakening forces of France and England. He then made a strong appeal for 120,000 American infantry and machine gun units in May and June, as he stated the French depots will be empty until August. He requested a recommendation of the Supreme War Council to the President of the United States that for the present only infantry and machine gun units be brought over. He appealed to the governments to express themselves.

Mr. Lloyd George spoke next. He took a stand between General Foch and myself. He agreed with each of us and said that the situation would indeed be precarious if America does not come to the rescue; that if the war is lost it would be lost honorably by France and England, as they would have expended their last for us in the struggle, but that for America to lose the war without having put into it more than Belgium would not be in compatibility with American pride and American traditions. He then came round and talked up to the adoption of an agreement which I had drawn up. He stated he wished to reconcile two interests—1st, to tide the present battle; 2nd, to help General Pershing to form an army. He then outlined the agreement which I had drawn up.

I stated that I agreed fully with General Foch as to the seriousness of the situation; that the American army and American people are all anxious to do their part in the struggle. I called attention to the resentment that would be aroused in the United States if they should get the idea that we have no independent army in France; that already the question is being asked as to where the American army is and under what flag it is fighting; that the American soldier will not do his best under another flag. Warned War Council that day is not far distant when the American soldier and the American government will demand that our soldiers fight under their own flag. I stated I was ready to agree to the proposition just submitted by Mr. Lloyd George.

After some talk the proposition was adopted. It has since been known as the Abbeville Agreement.

Left Abbeville at about 5 p. m. and went to [Le] Mesnil-St.-Firmin, headquarters 1st Division. Had dinner with General Bullard. Went to Paris after dinner, leaving Colonel Eltinge with 1st Division.

LC, Pershing Papers, Diary, May 7, 1917–September 1, 1918, box 4.

Abbeville Conference (Day 2)

Supreme War Council
Minutes of the Third Meeting of the Fifth Session of the Supreme War Council, held in the *Chambre des Notaires,* at Abbeville, on Thursday, May 2, 1918, at 2:45 p. m.

Present:

France
M. Clemenceau, President of the Council, Minister of War (In the Chair).

Great Britain
The Right Hon. D. Lloyd George, Prime Minister
The Right Hon. the Viscount Milner, Secretary of State for War.

Italy
His Excellency Signor Orlando, Prime Minister.

United States of America
Mr. A. H. Frazier, First Secretary, United States Embassy in Paris.

The following also attended:

France
General Foch, Commander-in-Chief, Allied Armies in France.
General Mordacq
General Weygand
Commandant Lacombe

Great Britain
General Sir H. H. Wilson, Chief of the Imperial General Staff.
Major General the Hon. C. J. Sackville-West, Permanent Military Representative.
Lieutenant General Sir J. P. DuCane. [British Liaison Officer with General Foch]
Brigadier General P. P. de B. Radcliffe, Director of Military Operations, War Office.
Lieutenant Colonel Sir M. P. A. Hankey.
Sir William Wiseman.

Italy
His Excellency General di Robilant, Permanent Military Representative.
Colonel Businelli.

United States of America
General Tasker H. Bliss, Permanent Military Representative.
General J. J. Pershing, Commander-in-Chief American Expeditionary Force.
Brigadier General Lochridge.
Colonel Eltinge.
Colonel Boyd.

* * * * * *

M. Clemenceau said that he proposed to invite the Supreme War Council to approve of Joint Note No. 25 of the military representatives regarding the transportation of Czech troops from Russia, and to pass the following resolution arising out of it:

Resolution No. 4:

The Supreme War Council approve Joint Note No. 25 of the military representatives, and agree on the following action:

(a) The British Government undertake to do their best to arrange the transportation of those Czech troops who are at Vladivostock or on their way to that port.

(b) The French Government undertake the responsibility for these troops until they are embarked.

(c) The British Government undertake to approach M. Trotski with a view to the concentration at Murmansk and Archangel of those Czech troops not belonging to the army corps, which has left Omsk for Vladivostock.

(This resolution was formally adopted.)

M. Clemenceau read the following draft resolution regarding General Foch's powers and duties in respect of the Allied forces in Italy. This resolution, he said, had been agreed to by Signor Orlando.

Resolution No. 5:

The extension of General Foch's powers to the Italian front.

(a) General Foch is Commander-in-Chief of the Italian troops in the French front just as he is of the other Allied troops.

(b) The powers of coordination conferred on General Foch by the agreement of Doullens are extended to the Italian front.

(c) Should circumstances bring about the presence on the Italian front of Allied armies fighting together in the same conditions as in France, Signor Orlando would agree that there should be a General-in-Chief of the Allied armies on the western front, and that this General-in-Chief should be General Foch.

It is understood:

(1) That the western front extends from the North Sea to the Adriatic.

(2) That in conformity with the Beauvais Agreement, the General-in-Command of one of the Allied armies can always refer to his government if he considers that the orders received from the General-in-Chief constitute a danger to his army.

Mr. Lloyd George said that he also accepted this resolution.

(The resolution was then formally adopted.)

General Foch then asked permission to make a statement.

[Foch's prepared statement in English is below at Annex E.]

General Foch said that today was May 2, and a great battle was now raging on a front of more than 150 kilometers. The Allied armies had been fighting hard since March 21. Their effectives had been seriously reduced, and their resources were rapidly dwindling. Nobody could say how long this battle would continue.

General Foch said that he had been chosen by the Allied Governments of Great Britain, France, and America to hold the Supreme Command of the French, British, and American forces in France, and his command had now been extended over the

Italian troops in that country. In that capacity it was impossible for him, at one of the gravest moments of the biggest battles of the war, not to give expression to his views on the conditions of the arrival of American infantry in France. He felt very deeply his own responsibility at a time when this great German offensive was threatening Paris on the one hand, and the channel ports on the other. He would now ask each government to realize its own responsibility in the matter of supporting his views or otherwise.

Speaking in the fullest sense of the gravity of the situation, he said it was essential that at least 120,000 infantry and machine-gun units should, during the months of May, June, and July, be given priority of transportation from America over other arms. If tonnage permitted, then this number of infantry and machine-gun units should be increased, for the greater the figure of American troops able to take their place at short notice in the trenches, the nearer and the more decisive the success of the Allies would be.

He wished the council to realize what had been the effect of this last great enemy offensive. It had caused losses in infantry and machine guns out of all proportion to the experiences of the last three years. The British losses in these respects had exceeded in unforeseen proportions any previously suffered. The same applied to the French insofar as they had been engaged. In the coming weeks the scale of loss in infantry is bound to be intensified. It was essential to replace the losses in infantry and machine-gun units without losing a moment. The German reserve resources in these arms amounted to between 500,000 and 600,000 men. On the other hand, the English depots are practically empty, and the French depots would not begin to fill up until next August. General Foch wished most earnestly to beg the Supreme War Council to submit to President Wilson a statement pointing out the gravity of the situation. General Foch fully appreciated the arguments of General Pershing, who naturally desired to bring to France troops of the supplementary services as well as the infantry in order to form as soon as possible the army of which he was the chief. In the formation of that army, the concession of General Foch's demands would cause a delay of a few weeks only. Speaking as a soldier, and as the soldier in supreme command of the Allied troops, he put it to the council that when the German army was making its biggest attack before Amiens and Ypres, and a success at either place might decide the war, it was impossible to hesitate. The huge losses the British had suffered had been sustained with magnificent steadfastness, but as had been stated at the previous meeting, they had been compelled to reduce their army by a whole 10 divisions, and their mere replacement was not enough. New infantry and new machine guns were necessary without delay. His argument in favor of priority being given to their transportation was reinforced by the fact that American troops after landing, would require some training before they could be put into the line. He appealed to the governments at this grave hour to think solely of their common duty to the cause they served. He spoke as the Commander-in-Chief of the Allied troops in France, and his position as such made it imperative for him to submit this request to the governments of the United States of America, France, and Great Britain. The heads of these governments must decide.

Mr. Lloyd George said there could be no question about the urgency of our need. The Germans had not only got a larger number of divisions than the Allies in the west, but they had larger resources with which to replace losses. It was clear that they were reckoning on the numerical superiority. Nothing else could explain their stupendous efforts in order to gain comparatively inadequate territorial results. They counted on gradually exhausting us until they overwhelmed us. The crisis might come either in May, in June, or in July, and would be due to the exhaustion of British and French reserves. Neither France nor Great Britain was in a position to make good their losses. Great Britain had called up her very last men, and was even taking men of 50 years of age. This effort of hers involved the destruction of a great number of industries. The total effort, indeed, amounted to the calling up of six million of men for the army and navy, and this number, if the whole empire were included, amounted to over seven million.

We had now reached the stage when our resources were exhausted. We had taken boys of 18, and, as he had said, we were taking men of 50. The position of France in regard to manpower was the same as our own. Unless the United States of America came to the rescue, there was a serious risk that the German calculations might prove to be correct. If Great Britain and France had to go under, it would be an honourable defeat, because each had put the very last man into the army, whereas the United States would go under after putting in only as many men as had the Belgians. He was sure that the American nation would feel it a matter of prestige and national pride not to accept defeat after, if he might put it so, hardly putting their little finger in the struggle.

Mr. Lloyd George was sure that General Pershing was doing his best to meet this emergency. General Pershing desired that any assistance America might give should not be incompatible with the existence of a separate American army at the earliest possible moment. Mr. Lloyd George said that he counted on seeing such an army formed and taking the field this year, possibly in time to win the war by striking a final blow. In the meantime, the Allies had to makeshift somehow until well into August. He quite hoped that it would be possible to reconcile the two ideas; the assistance of the American troops during the critical period of the battle, and the formation of an American army that would win the campaign. General Pershing had submitted a document which was a modification of what was known as the London Agreement. So far as the month of May was concerned, the original program stood, that is to say, the British Government guaranteed to supply shipping for 130,000 American troops, provided that the United States could find the men. He would remind the council that during April the full numbers promised by America had not been made available. The British Government, therefore, could only undertake to provide ships for 130,000 men if those men were brought on to the quay for embarkation. General Pershing was prepared to extend his May program into June if Great Britain would provide shipping for 150,000 men. He would ask General Pershing whether, in the event of Great Britain, by sacrificing many essential commodities, being able to scrape together shipping for 200,000 men, he would let the extra 50,000 be infantry and machine-gun units only, subject to the same conditions as before. As previously stated, we were already short of the numbers promised by America for April. General Pershing calculated by the end of July he would be short 100,000 men to complete his larger units up to establishment, that is, that if Great Britain could get ships for 280,000 men by the end of June and the United States provide for another 140,000 making a grand total of 420,000, the new American army by the end of July would still have a deficit of 100,000 men on its full establishment. Mr. Lloyd George suggested that America should provide both in May and in June 120,000 infantry and machine-gun units, and an additional 50,000 infantry and machine-gun units for each of these two months if the shipping can be scraped together.

Lord Milner confirmed the fact that only 26,000 men had been despatched in April for brigading with the British forces.

Mr. Lloyd George said that he wished to make another suggestion to General Pershing, that is, that he should undertake at the beginning of June to review the situation with a view to the further extension of the above amended program into July, should the emergency still be great.

General Pershing said that what Mr. Lloyd George now proposed was going far beyond the original agreement.

General Foch inquired what was actually meant by the deficit referred to.

General Pershing replied that it covered corps and divisional and railway artillery, as well as technical troops and rear services.

Mr. Lloyd George asked that the amended agreement suggested by him should be accepted, which would complete the program for May and June, but that if this was found not to be enough, and the situation was still serious, General Pershing should examine it during June with a view to making the necessary timely arrangements for July.

General Pershing said that he agreed with General Foch as regards the seriousness of the situation. They were, in fact, all agreed about this. Speaking for the American army and for the American people, he wished to express their earnest desire to take their full part in this battle and to share the burden to the fullest possible extent. The desire of all of them was the same. They only differed in their methods of attaining that desire. His own views were based on this fact, namely, that the United States entered the war as an independent power, and she must always look forward to fighting the war with an army of her own. There was one important point upon which he desired to lay stress, and that was that the morale of the American troops depended on their fighting under their own flag. Already today America was asking where her army was. Moreover, the Germans were busily engaged in circulating propaganda stating that the British and French had so little confidence in American troops that they parceled them out among their own divisions. The American soldier had his own pride, and before long both the troops themselves and the American Government would demand that they should fight as a separate entity as soon as it were possible to organize them as an American army. The proposal, as he understood it, was that in June the situation should again be reviewed. His own view was that this was as far as they could go at present, and by this arrangement he thought that they were meeting the situation fairly and squarely.

General Foch wished to be quite clear about the new agreement so far as June was concerned.

M. Clemenceau suggested that the draft agreement should be read to the council.

(Professor Mantoux then read out both the British and French texts of the following Draft Agreement.)

Resolution No. 6: Regarding the Cooperation of the American Army:

It is the opinion of the Supreme War Council that in order to carry the war to a successful conclusion, the American army should be formed as early as possible under its own commander and under its own flag.

In order to meet the present emergency, it is agreed that American troops shall be brought to France as rapidly as Allied transportation facilities will permit, and that, without losing sight of the necessity of building up an American army, priority of transport be given to infantry and machine-gun units for training and service with the French and British armies—on the understanding that such infantry and machine-gun units are to be withdrawn and united with their own artillery and auxiliary troops into divisions and corps at the discretion of the American Commander-in-Chief, after consultation with the Commander-in-Chief of the Allied Armies in France.

It is also agreed that during the month of May preference shall be given to the transportation of infantry and machine-gun units of 6 divisions, and that any excess tonnage shall be devoted to bringing over such other troops as may be determined by the American Commander-in-Chief. It is further agreed that this program shall be continued during the month of June, upon condition that the British Government shall furnish transportation for a minimum of 130,000 men in May and 150,000 men in June, with the understanding that the first 6 divisions of infantry shall go to the British for training and service, and that troops sent over in June shall be allocated for training and service as the American Commander-in-Chief may determine.

It is also further agreed that if the British Government should transport any number in excess of 150,000 men in June, such excess should be infantry and machine-gun units and that early in June there should be a new review of the situation to determine further action.

M. Clemenceau said that so far as he could see this agreement might be acceptable, but he would like to examine it with General Foch before finally endorsing it. He enquired whether American tonnage would also be employed.

General Pershing said that it would be so employed for the transportation of personnel.

M. Clemenceau (after a brief discussion of the draft with General Foch) said that he was prepared to accept the resolution.

(The above resolution [The Abbeville Agreement] was adopted by the Supreme War Council.)

M. *Clemenceau* said that he proposed that the three heads of governments present should retire to consider General Foch's statement and to decide whether it should, in its present, or in a slightly modified, form be transmitted to the President of the United States.

(The Supreme War Council concluded its 5th Session at 3:50 p. m.)

* * * * * *

Annex E

Supreme War Council,

Abbeville, Somme, May 2, 1918.

Memorandum from General Foch

I have been designated Commander-in-Chief of the Allied Armies by the Governments of the United States of America, France, and Great Britain; wherefore, it is impossible for me, and in fact incompatible with the greatest battle of the war, to admit that I do not have the right to declare myself on the proposition of the arrival of American infantry in France.

That is why, impressed with the heavy responsibility resting upon me, at the moment when the greatest German offensive today threatens, at one and the same time, Paris and our line of communications with Great Britain via Calais and Boulogne, I am anxious that each of these governments assume its share of the responsibility devolving upon it.

In all conscience, it is of the utmost necessity that there arrive each month in France from America, at least during the months of May, June, and July, on a priority basis, 120,000 American infantry and machine gunners. I am even of the opinion that, tonnage permitting (as we have been led to understand that it will), it would be highly desirable that this figure be exceeded. For, the greater the numbers of American infantry that can speedily appear on the battlefields, the more rapid and more decisive will be the success of the Allied armies.

It must in fact be clearly understood that the nature of the last enemy offensive was such as to carry infantry and machine-gun losses out of all proportion to losses in the war during the past three years. Infantry losses in the British army exceeded to an unanticipated degree all those previously suffered. The same was true of the French to the extent of their participation in the battle, and it is inevitable that during the ensuing weeks infantry losses will grow worse. Losses in infantry and machine-gun troops must therefore be made up without losing an instant, the more so since the resources of the German depots in infantry and machine gunners are estimated at 500,000 or 600,000 men, whereas the British depots are almost depleted and the French depots will be without any resources until next August.

I ask in the most positive manner that the Supreme War Council, composed of the Allied Governments, declare itself on this request and that is submit it to the President of the United States.

It is not that I do not value the views of General Pershing, who justly wishes to bring to France as soon as possible all the auxiliary services needed to bring about at an early date the organization of the great American army that he commands and that we call on most fervently. But, admitting that my request can only cause a delay of a few weeks, my imperative duty as a soldier and as General-in-Chief forces me to declare that, when the greatest German army opens the greatest offensive of this war in front of Amiens and Ypres, so slight a delay cannot be taken into consideration when the very issue of the war may depend on a success of the enemy against the two above named objectives.

After the enormous losses that the English army has sustained with magnificent valor, it has just seen 10 of its divisions made inactive. Replacing them is not enough to check the German armies decisively. What we need without any delay are new infantry forces and machine gunners. And when we consider that American troops, on disembarking, will need a quick period of training to round out their instruction, we can understand how urgent is the decision confronting us on that account. Let each of the governments concerned, in this most critical hour, be inspired solely by its duty to the great cause whose servants we are.

I have here stated the step that my position as Commander-in-Chief of the Allied armies compels me to submit to the Governments of the United States, France, and Great Britain. It is for the heads of these governments to decide. [*Ed.*—The French sent a copy of Foch's memorandum to Ambassador Jusserand in Washington who presented it to President Wilson on May 8. (Link (ed.), *The Papers of Woodrow Wilson*, vol. 47: *March 13–May 12, 1918*, pp. 497–98.)]

USAWW, vol. 2, pp. 366–71; for Foch's memorandum, *USAWW*, vol. 2, pp. 372–73; and *Les armées françaises dans la Grande guerre, Tome 6*, vol. 2, *Annexes*, vol. 1: *Annexe* No. 86, pp. 203–4; for an overview of Foch during the Abbeville Conference, see Greenhalgh, *Foch in Command*, pp. 325–30.

Editor's Note—Pershing wrote thusly of these decisions in his *My Experiences in the World War*:

> My proposal contemplated a largely increased amount of British tonnage, which would permit the transportation of a greater number of artillery and auxiliary units, and a greater proportion of special troops for the Services of Supply than had been previously indicated. Upon consideration, it appeared that this would leave us with sufficient tonnage to provide at least 40,000 men by British shipping and all that could be transported by American shipping and all that could be transported by American shipping of the classes of troops we most desired. M. Clemenceau then read the resolution that I had submitted confirming the London agreement and including the understanding for June, which was agreed to substantially as set forth in the following cablegram to the Secretary of War . . . [see May 3, P-1042-S, and May 6, P-1064-S, both Pershing to TAG, War Department, for the Chief of

Staff and the Secretary of War, and May 9, Pershing to Baker]. (Pershing, *My Experiences in the World War*, vol. 2, p. 33.)

Nowhere in his extensive account of the Abbeville Conference does Pershing mention that Arthur H. Frazier, the U.S. diplomatic observer with the Supreme War Council, and Col. Sir William Wiseman, the Chief of British Intelligence in the United States, played pivotal roles in reaching the compromise between Lloyd George and Pershing that became the Abbeville Agreement. Fowler, in his *British-American Relations,* wrote:

> Wiseman's presence as an observer for Wilson and House perhaps increased Pershing's desire to appear cooperative, but chiefly his contribution was that of a conciliator. Frazier later wrote that Wiseman's "knack at smoothing over rough places" greatly facilitated the negotiation of the Abbeville agreement. (Fowler, *British-American Relations,* p. 147.)

Lt. Col. T. Bentley Mott, Chief, American Mission to CINC, Allied Armies, Sarcus, to CINC, AEF.

General Foch's HQ. Conversation with Officers. [Handwritten in pencil]

General Maistre, Comd'g 10th Army & his Chief of Staff Colonel Hergault (Gen. M. commanded 10th Army in Italy).

Liaison. Liaison through a Mission is not good. The larger the Mission the less intimate, useful & rapid the liaison. There is not only the difficulty of language; suppose that entirely overcome as it often is by officers of any two nations speaking each other's language; there remains the practical difficulty of different systems, different regulations and laws to be met, different customs & habits of thought.

I think the only effective liaison consists in having officers of any 2 nations working side by side in the same office where their specialty is treated. A problem to be solved arises. Each has his idea of how it is to be solved following the regulations of his army & the customary way of going at the matter. But each solution will probably encounter difficulties from the other. A compromise which does not violate the laws or regulations of either country must be found. This can only be accomplished rapidly by two men on the spot working at it together. And the longer they work together the more rapidly all subsequent problems are settled, until finally each is capable of seeing how they must be done.

I believe this applies to all of the bureau of the staff & is the best way to accomplish results through mutual aid and constant contact of two men working at the same job.

I will give you an illustration. When my army & the British took over the Asiago sector in March 1918 our divisions in line were under the command of the Italian general comd'g the Italian 6th Army. This was necessary & acceptable. At the same time under terms of the Rapallo convention I was held responsible for the safety of the French forces in Italy. I therefore asked that some of my officers be placed on the staff of Gen. Tonilli, to work with the Italian officers. Gen T refused to accept them. Gen Diaz then placed another officer in command of this army who was willing to accept this arrangement.

I think this exchange should be mutual & as amongst loyal intelligent officers, all working to one end, viz to get efficiency & avoid mistakes & delays, only good results can come of it.

As to General Foch. You may remember he was a professor at the *Ecole de Guerre* for some years; as was I & I was his subordinate. We had some tremendous fights, for naturally we did not agree always & both of us are rather strong in our convictions & defend them hotly. I never knew him to do a small or disloyal thing. He is an absolutely honest man, and I think I know his character intimately. During this war he has been called upon more than once to show whether he had that rare quality in a chief—self-abnegation. He has proved he possesses it. He has had to accept things & do things which required patriotic self-denial, & he has never whimpered.

General Pershing. I am sorry I do not know General Pershing, but I hope to get a chance to meet him. The impression he had made on us all—us generals, who necessarily must take his personality into our calculations—is admirable. I mean that he inspires confidence; we know where he stands. That at least is the feeling I get from my colleagues. He added, laughing—you have been in Italy & you know what that means amongst chiefs of different nations. If General Foch & General Pershing have absolute confidence each in the other it is worth several army corps.

* * * * * *

Conversation with General [Émile] Fayolle, May 4.

"I have heard something about the Abbeville Conference. It seems to me the conclusions they arrived at there are entirely satisfactory. It is evident that General Pershing has that supreme quality of hard common sense so useful in a chief; and again he has a sense of realities. He sees things as they are and he meets them as they are, and not as he would have them. You know that is the mistake really brilliant men sometimes make—they don't see things as they are but as they prefer to believe them.

I think he has shown an immense generosity in consenting to delay the formation of his army in order to help the British and ourselves in the actual emergency. This is nothing so human, so natural, as for him to want to create his army at once and push it into action as an army, command it, fight it. But this generosity, I repeat the word, is founded on his sense for facts. You Americans are a practical people. He is a practical man. That is evident in all he does. I would much rather that his fine action sprang from this source—a reasoning from facts—than from mere sentimental generosity, as fine as that is. And then, too, he must see, as I see, that what he is doing is not really delaying very much the formation of his army. For when he gets his corps together the separate elements will have already had the experience of battle. That's the thing, that's what makes an army corps, the experience of battle. He ought to put them together as soon as he can. I want to see it but meantime they will all have had their experience—he will have tided us over a very bad time. I don't believe he is going to lose anything by it, and I know all that we gain.

No, he has done the hardest thing a general-in-chief can be called upon to do and he had done it generously. I have a profound respect for him.

Now, the English have never shown this quality of seeing things as they are. I believe in simple & direct solutions. In war they almost always succeed. You know that in every war there is always a principal theatre of operations and then one or more secondary theatres. The wise general concentrates himself on the principal theatre—where the war is really decided. The Boche understand that. You notice he has even taken everything he had in Italy to come up here. He is right. All these campaigns in Mesopotamia and Palestine, all these after-the-war considerations, are a mistake. Right here is where all those things are going to be settled. If the Boche beats us here what good do you think all the victories in Africa, in Asia, in the Colonies will be? Their fate is going to be settled in France—or in Germany, pray God—not in Palestine or Morocco or the Cameroons or on the Euphrates."

I reminded General Fayolle that all the German writers had proclaimed this for ten years before the war, it was no secret. "Why of course, they did, and they were right. No, we have all got just one task & no other—the Boche, the Boche, the Boche, beat him, break him, here where he threatens us, where he is strong. I don't care a hang about the Turks or the Bulgars; when we beat the Boche, they are beaten, and right here in France is where also we can do it. No—the English have never been able to see that, and now they would mighty like to have up north the divisions they had scattered over all those minor theatres.

Amour-propre—Of course one has to consider it. Every nation has got its amour-propre if it is any good. You have got yours, but it does not blind you Americans to realities. You see that we have got to win this battle—and several others; without that we are all done for no matter what happens somewhere else.

The Italian divisions coming to France; well, I don't know how they are going to fight. They have been making a war of a kind for 3 years, but I would rather have in the Armies I command American divisions. I think I know what to expect of them. I have seen enough of the 1st Division to have made up my mind. Give me all you can. I am proud to have them in my Army,

* * * * * *

General Maistre, I forgot to say, drew a parallel between the 30 Years War & other great or prolonged struggles, and this one, adding, "They all have their phases. There was the French phase, the Prussian phase, the Swedish phase (in the 30 Years War). It is the same now. We had the French phase in 1914, French and Russian; then came the English phase and, super-imposed, the Italian phase; then the Russian phase again in her disappearance. Now we have the American phase, just commencing. You are going to finish this now. Your armies will be the final & determining factor."

Sarcus, May 4.

LC, Pershing Papers, folder: Col. T. Bentley Mott (1910–1918), box 141.

TAG, War Department, to Pershing, in addition to TAG, War Department, to Pershing, cable A-1069-R, April 9.

Cable A-1224-R. Confidential.
    Referring to our cable 1069. Not believe it possible to meet Chief Signal Officer's program of 106 squadrons at port of embarkation United States as expressed therein. Many factors are uncertainty of Bristol fighter, which is yet experimental, and available number of Liberty engines. Output of Liberty engines to July 1st is estimated at 3,256. Of these the Navy will receive 733 for flying boats and 124 for De Haviland planes for Navy work. Total 853. Policy of new allocation approved by War and Navy Departments. British have been allotted 980. We have not heard definitely from French and Italians, but are estimated requirements to July 1st at 500 each. Tanks will receive none. Understand all this follows recommendation in your cable 904 [see April 12, 1918] regarding supplying Allies. This leaves 422 Liberty engines available for United States Army Air Service to July 1st. All our calculations are based upon 3 engines for 6 De Haviland or Bristol planes and 2½ engines for each Handley Page plane. In accordance with memorandum from Colonel Gorrell to Colonel Waldon, we estimate replacement requirements at 50% per month to keep squadrons at full strength on front. In determining amount of planes and engines available for service at the front we reserve 5% of available production for losses at sea, 5% for reserve and 10% for training in United States. We base all squadron equipment on 18 planes to squadron, 60 days from port of embarkation to front for Bristols and De Havilands and 3 months for Handley Pages. On this basis we believe that the following squadrons of De Havilands and Bristols can be put on front and maintained at full strength throughout the year: July, 1; August, 2; September, 4. Output of Liberty engines from July 1st to October 1st estimated at 7,500. Of these Navy will demand 1,959. We will make no allocation to Allies or Ordnance as yet. British ask for 2,025. French and Italian requests are estimated at 750 each. Ordnance will also demand engines. Eliminating ordnance as before, if requests of Allies were to be granted, they and Navy would receive 5,479 of our production of these months. On this basis the following De Haviland or Bristol squadrons could be put on front and fully maintained: October 1; November 7; December 13. Handley Page squadrons: November 1; December 4. Total on front January 1st, 1919, 33 squadrons. If allocation of Liberty engines are not made to Allies or a lesser number allotted, a large number of additional squadrons could be put on front by January 1st. Output of Liberty engines is estimated: October, 3,500; November, 4,000; December, 4,000. It is believed that these can be materially increased if orders are placed at once. We are prepared also have at port of embarkation, United States, the following 180 horsepower Hispano-Suiza engines: July 100; August 200; September 250; October 250. We assume that you will secure SE 5 planes for these in England and that they redistribute part of equipment for the 14 pursuit squadrons you expect to obtain in Europe. In view of the above, request that you cable us immediately your recommendations for a program for the first half of 1919. We wish to know the number and type of squadrons to be received from United States equipped with Liberty engines and number of pursuit squadron planes

which should be manufactured in United States and equipped with the Hispano 180 and 300 engines. Your program should be based upon date equipment is needed at front and we will allow for transportation, assembly, et cetera. It is essential that these revised programs be received and authorized promptly. Much squadron equipment has been ordered on the basis of project of rear September 18th. Units of personnel have been organized on this basis and training has been planned to meet new program. Some revision of all these matters will be necessary upon hearing from you. [Reply—Vol. 5, May 20, P-1156-S; May 23, P-1175-S-1A; in addition—May 11, A-1290-R]

NARA, RG 120, M930, Confidential Series, War Department to AEF, roll 7.

Editor's Note—The War Department's cable A-1224-R of May 2 began an intense discussion between the War Department and GHQ, AEF, concerning the exact relationship of the aircraft and engine production program in the United States to the current program of the AEF's Air Service. The series of critical cables that were exchanged over the next month significantly clarified the AEF's program both with the War Department and within the GHQ itself. A key document in understanding what happened was the memorandum of June 5 to Pershing from Brig. Gen. Mason M. Patrick, the recently appointed Chief of the Air Service (see Vol. 5).

May 3

Pershing's Personal Diary

At Paris. Saw General Crozier, Colonel Jordan [Acting Chief Ordnance Officer], Mr. Frazier [U.S. Embassy], Colonel Wiseman [*Ed.*—This was Sir William Wiseman, who was at the Abbeville Conference], British Army, General Foulois, Mrs. Welch, Dr. Hamilton Holt and Mr. Dwight Morrow [U.S. Shipping Board and Allied Maritime Transport Council].

LC, Pershing Papers, Diary, May 7, 1917–September 1, 1918, box 4.

Editor's Note—In his comprehensive study of Wiseman's relations with the Wilson Administration during the war, W. B. Fowler also touched on his dealings with Pershing. He wrote the following summary of Wiseman's activities at Abbeville and his subsequent claims:

> With a sheaf of shorthand notes from his conversation with Wilson [April 1], Wiseman sailed from New York on April 9. He went as a quasi-American observer. . . Serving Wilson as an observer was an unorthodox and complimentary task for Wiseman of which he naturally was proud, but in later years he exaggerated his position at this time to that of an executive

agent for the President. In 1944 he remembered that Wilson asked him to attend the May meeting of the Supreme War Council at Abbeville and there explain to Pershing the President's views on the use of American manpower. When Wiseman, according to his later account, protested that Pershing would surely object to receiving a presidential message from a British officer, Wilson then asked him to brief A. H. Frazier, the American diplomatic observer at the Supreme War Council, who could in turn brief Pershing. This, Wiseman said in 1944, he did. The implication of Wiseman's memory is that Wilson sent him to Europe to instruct Pershing, indirectly, to accede to the Allies' desire for amalgamation. Wiseman did indeed visit Frazier and Pershing and, as we shall see, did play a part in the Abbeville conference, but there is no reason to believe that he delivered directly or indirectly anything like instructions or a reprimand from Wilson to Pershing. Aside from other difficulties with Wiseman's 1944 account, there is the fact that he left the United States prior to Secretary Baker's return from Europe, and Wilson surely would not have vouchsafed any explanations to Wiseman for Pershing before he had heard Baker's report on the war situation. (Fowler, *British-American Relations*, pp. 142–44.)

Pershing to Georges Clemenceau, President of the Council of Defense, Paris, in addition to Pershing to Clemenceau, April 19.

Referring again to my note on the subject of pooling supplies, I wish to say that, after further thought and a full discussion of the tonnage situation with the Shipping Board, it would appear advisable to suggest the consideration of the important subject of control of allotment of tonnage space in connection with the pooling of supplies by the committee of military men that you were kind enough to propose.

I had hoped to have an opportunity to mention it to you in person at Abbeville, but the pressure of other business prevented. I shall, therefore, convey to you in the following paragraphs what I wrote to Mr. Lloyd George on the subject.

As you are no doubt aware, a very careful study shows that for the year 1918 there will be a deficit of 2,000,000 tons dead-weight tonnage unless some of the programmes can be reduced. Obviously the military programme on the Western Front must be given first consideration and cannot be reduced. Actually it will be increased as American participation increases.

It would seem possible as recommended in substance by the Inter-Allied Maritime Council:

(1) That the use of merchant tonnage by Allied navies might be materially reduced by joint reconsideration of naval programmes;

(2) That considerable tonnage might be saved by suspending or reducing military activities in theaters of war other than the Western Front;

(3) That further reductions in civilian imports carefully considered by Inter-Allied criticism can release additional tonnage.

It would appear desirable that these two subjects—pooling supplies and control of shipments—should be under military direction and that one executive head be given charge of both. It is believed that a very great increase in efficiency will result from such centralized executive management.

I would therefore suggest that the officer whom you select as the French representative on Supplies be also instructed to discuss the question of control of shipments.

With renewed expression of esteem and respect, I remain . . .

Dawes, *A Journal of the Great War*, vol. 1, pp. 283–84.

Brig. Gen. William H. Allaire, Provost Marshal General, GHQ, AEF, to Pershing.

Sometime ago you told me that when I wanted anything to write you a personal letter.

In August 1917 a child was born to our Army in France and was named The Provost Marshal General's Department. This child has been growing very fast, but anyone who comes to examine it can see it is not a healthy growth and it is plain that it is suffering from lack of nourishment. The nurses that should have seen to it that this child be given sufficient food have actually taken it away. In other words, troops designated for this Department have never been allowed to reach it. Nevertheless, this child has grown, and in addition to the purely military police work of the combatant troops and in the S.O.S., it is in charge of the circulation in the Zones of our Armies, has established a criminal investigation bureau, particularly valuable at our ports, keeps track of all absentees and deserters and is charged with their apprehension; collects valuable data on crimes and disorders, drunkenness, venereal disease, altercations between French civilians and our personnel, etc. It also has charge of arranging everything concerning leaves, and finally is charged with the care, handling and distribution for work of our prisoners of war.

So, this child has a man's job, but it cannot do this work unless it is given proper tools. I have known this for some time, but have refrained from urging it because of a lack of troops. This condition is improving very fast. The work enumerated above must be done and it might just as well be done properly and efficiently. The organization of this Department, both for the combatant troops and for the S.O.S., will produce satisfactory results if I am supported.

This war is not over yet and all would be lacking in their duty if they failed to think at least a year ahead. I have a concrete proposition concerning the needs of this Department which I would like to submit to you. May I come and see you?

[*Ed.*—In response to Allaire's letter, Pershing wrote on May 7 that "I shall be pleased to see you at any time." There is no clear indication of if and when Allaire met with Pershing or what the outcome of that meeting was.]

LC, Pershing Papers, folder: Gen. William H. Allaire, box 9.

Bliss to TAG, War Department.

Cable 103-S. Very Confidential.
For Secretary of State, Secretary of War, and Acting Chief of Staff.

1. Supreme War Council met for its 5th session at 2:30 p.m., May 1 and adjourned at 4:00 p.m., May 2. Following is the summary of business transacted.

2. First subject taken up was the shipment and employment of American troops, the French Government requesting amendment of agreement made between General Pershing and Lord Milner in London so as to provide for exclusive shipment of infantry and machine gun units not only in May but also in June. After considerable discussion subject was referred to a committee consisting of Lord Milner, General Foch and General Pershing with instructions to draft a form of resolution and submit it at 5:00 p.m. In order to communicate with London for information regarding it, report of subcommittee was delayed until the next day's session when their draft was considered. After impassioned appeals by Mr. Lloyd George, Mr. Clemenceau and General Foch a modified form of General Pershing's proposal was adopted; the essential points of which are:

A. Allied transportation facilities to be used for transportation of American troops, preference being given to infantry and machine gun units, as far as consistent with the necessity of building up an American Army for training and service with French and British Armies subject to provision that they are to be formed into divisions and corps at discretion of American Commander-in-Chief after consultation with Commander-in-Chief of Allied Armies in France.

B. During May infantry and machine gun units of six divisions to be transported and any excess tonnage available applied to transportation of such troops as American Commander-in-Chief may desire.

C. This program to be continued in June, provided British Government furnishes transportation minimum of 130,000 men in May and 150,000 men in June; that, first six divisions infantry go to British for training and service and those brought over in June to be allocated for training by American Commander-in-Chief.

D. If British Government transports more than 150,000 in June, excess will he infantry and machine gun units and situation shall be reviewed early in June with a view to determining program for July...

4. The Executive War Board established by resolution Number 15 of the Third Session Supreme War Council, was dissolved; the main duties having already been transferred to General Foch.

5. Mr. Orlando on behalf of Italy agreed to extension of the powers of General Foch over the Italian troops in France under conditions of Beauvais agreement, April 3. He agreed to General Foch's exercising over the troops on the Italian Front coordinating powers granted to him over British and French by agreement at Doullens, March 26.

6. Formal acceptance was given to Joint Notes Numbers 19 to 24, inclusive of the Military Representatives. Joint Note Number 20 relating to Japanese question was not signed by American Military Representative but was transmitted by me to Washington.

7. Joint Note 25 passed by Military Representatives on April 27th expresses the following conclusions:

"That there is everything to be gained by encouraging the transportation of Czech contingents from Russia; and that, as the greatest rapidity can be ensured by using Archangel and Murmansk, all Czech troops, which have not yet passed east of Omsk on Transiberian Railway should be despatched to these two ports".

Subparagraph A. The Supreme War Council approved the aforementioned note, the British Government undertaking to arrange as far as possible for transportation of Czech troops already at Vladivostok or on their way there, and to request Russian Government to concentrate other Czech troops at Murmansk and Archangel; French Government retaining general charge of Czech troops until embarked. . . .

9. Documents by mail.

[Reply—Vol;. 5, May 29, cable 60-R; in addition—May 22, cable 114-S (not reproduced), and May 29, 119-S]

NARA, RG 120, M923, American Section, SWC, file 315: Cablegrams Sent to War Department, Jan. 22, 1918–Dec 10, 1919, roll 18; see also online "WW I Supreme War Council, American records," at https://www.fold3.com.

Pershing to TAG, War Department.

Cable P-1042-S. Confidential.
For the Chief of Staff and Secretary of War.

Following agreement adopted by Supreme War Council May 2d at Abbeville. Will cable more detail later.

"It is the opinion of the Supreme War Council that, in order to carry the war to a successful conclusion, an American Army should be formed as early as possible under its own Commander and under its own flag. In order to meet the present emergency it is agreed that American troops should be brought to France as rapidly as Allied transportation facilities will permit and, that as far as consistent with the necessity of building up an American army, preference be given to infantry and machine gun units for training and service with French and British armies; with the understanding that such infantry and machine gun units are to be withdrawn and united with its own artillery and auxiliary troops into divisions and corps at the discretion of the American Commander-in-Chief after consultation with the Commander-in-Chief of the Allied Armies in France.

A. It is also agreed that during the month of May preference should be given to the transportation of infantry and machine gun units of 6 divisions, and that any excess tonnage shall be devoted to bringing over such other groups as may be determined by the American Commander-in-Chief.

B. It is further agreed that this program shall be continued during the month of June upon condition that the British Government shall furnish transportation for a minimum of 130,000 men in May and 150,000 men in June with the understanding that the first 6 divisions of infantry shall go to the British for training and service, and that troops sent over in June shall be allocated for training and service as the American Commander-in-Chief may determine.

C. It is also further agreed that if the British Government shall transport an excess of 150,000 men in June that such excess shall be infantry and machine gun units, and that early in June there shall be a new review of the situation to determine further action."

NARA, RG 120, M930, Confidential Series, AEF to War Department, roll 7.

Editor's Note—Baker forwarded a copy of Pershing's cable to President Wilson on May 4 with the following note:

> I enclose a message from General Pershing, which has just come, giving the details of the agreement adopted by the Supreme War Council, May 2, at Abbeville. I understand you have already received the accounts of that conference, sent by Mr. Frazier. In view of the fact that General Pershing, General Foch, and General Haig conferred and, finally recommended this agreement, it would seem to be an authoritative determination of the questions which have been troubling us and now to have the concurrence of Mr. Lloyd George, Mr. Clemenceau, and Mr. Orlando, which relieves us from any possible embarrassment due to a misunderstanding of our execution of the resolution of the Permanent Military Representatives at Versailles.
>
> I confess I was very favorably impressed by the position taken by General Pershing and his bearing throughout the interview, and am glad to see it result in an agreement which apparently has the general concurrence.
>
> President Wilson answered Baker the same day:
>
> Thank you for sending me the full text of the message from General Pershing, giving the details of the agreement adopted by the Supreme War Council, May second, at Abbeville. Personally, I agree with you in thinking the agreement entirely satisfactory and as having been arrived at by just the right sort of conference in the right way. I hope that this will dispose of further indefinite discussions of the particular views of any single government. (Link (ed.), *The Papers of Woodrow Wilson*, vol. 47: *March 13–May 12, 1918*, pp. 517, 535.)

Pershing to TAG, War Department, in part in reply to TAG, War Department, to Pershing, cable A-1039-R, April 4; in addition to Pershing to TAG, War Department, cables P-610-S, February 16, P-904-S, April 12, and P-1020-S, April 29.

Cable P-1043-S. Confidential.

1. For Chief of Staff. Attention is invited to your cable 1039, paragraph 1, and subparagraph A, which indicates United States Navy Air Service is receiving a separate and distinct priority in airplane engines over our own Air Service and that of Allies. My cable 904 requested the reasons for this but no reply has been received.

[*Ed.*—The War Department had actually answered P-904-S in its A-1101-R on April 13.] Information indicates that U.S. Naval Air Service in France is planning a separate bombing offensive against the enemy submarine bases in which they expect to use land types of airplanes and operate from land bases on the Western Front, also that the types of airplanes and engines to be used here by the U.S. Navy will be supplied from the United States and are the same types with the Air Service, A.E.F., seriously needs as soon as they can be supplied. Present military emergencies demand that the Air Services of the Allied Armies be given all priority in advance of the Air Services of the Allied Navies. The air supremacy of the Allies on the Western Front is only held by narrow margin at the present time due to great wastage of material during the present offensive. This wastage must be met as long as the present offensive continues and during this year's crisis. Recommend that least possible number of airplanes and engines be diverted to any service other than to maintain and build up Allied Army Air Services including our own. Urgently request you impress this view on the War and Navy Departments and that I be informed of their final decision. Airplanes and engines now being built in the United States must be distributed to the Allied Army Air Services including our own, as they may determine the outcome of the summer's campaign. [In addition—Vol. 5, June 13, P-1300-S]

1A. Am reliably informed that U. S. Navy representative is now in Italy negotiating for 60 or more Caproni night bombing planes, also that U.S. Naval authorities have offered to bring to Italy raw material on naval transports in exchange for finished airplanes of the type now on order for the Air Service of the Army. The Naval offer would appear to be an inducement to get planes which the Army is not in position to offer. Moreover, it shows an utter lack of coordination and cooperation on the part of the Navy in this regard and places the military authorities at a decided disadvantage. All this is happening at a time when every ton of shipping that can possibly be found is in demand and at a time when every energy is being exerted to coordinate tonnage and reduce supplies. It suggests that an examination be made into the amount of tonnage now in hands of Navy and its proper coordination with world's shipping, especially our own. [*Ed.*—In the War Department's reply on May 14 in cable A-1308-R-4, Goethals said: "Amount of tonnage now in use by Navy will be determined. Naval authorities have from time to time agreed to assist Army with any tonnage under their control should an urgency so require."]

1B. In this connection, attention is invited to the fact that after 3 years' experience the British Army and Navy Air Services hitherto distinct and separate are now united under one head. In as much as the U.S. Naval Air Service in Europe has not in any true sense coordinated their air programs of construction and operation with those of the Army, it is recommended that the matter be given attention with a view either to closer cooperation or to the combination under one single control of both U.S. Air Services in Europe. To go further, there is a strong opinion among Allies that the air services of all Allies, both army and navy, should be under one head. I think this view is sound and hope it may be adopted.

2. For Chief of Staff. Cablegram received from New York dated April 22nd signed Tardieu states that spruce which was to have been allotted to the Allies in accordance

with the distribution made by General Pershing has been almost entirely given to the British by order of American Staff at Washington. Urgently recommend that the allotment of wood recommended in my cablegram 610, paragraph 1, be followed and that France, England and Italy be given equal priority on deliveries. Inter-Allied Aviation Committee meets May 11th. If any readjustment of percentages appear necessary, you will be advised promptly. Please advise Tardieu. [Reply—May 9, A-1271-R-22]

3. Confidential for the Chief of Staff and Secretary of War. Reference my cable 1020 on question of extending to Italian Army the principle of unity of command, resolution adopted by Supreme War Council May 2nd settles question to apparent satisfaction of all concerned and no further action is considered necessary. Text of this resolution will no doubt be cabled by General Bliss.

NARA, RG 120, M930, Confidential Series, AEF to War Department, roll 7.

TAG, War Department, to Pershing, in part in reply to Pershing to TAG, War Department, cable P-953-S, April 19.

Cable A-1231-R.
4. With reference to paragraph 1, your 953. The plan of pooling supplies for all Allied forces, operating under the supreme command of one military commander, is undoubtedly correct in principle but such plan involves certain military, political, and economic features, which will require careful consideration and considerable negotiations. The working details of such plans are not at once apparent, but can be worked out after all phases of the methods of operations, proposed by you, are fully present. The project will be given careful study, awaiting more details from you, after your consultation with Allied representatives referred to in your cablegram. March. [Reply—May 6, P-1064-S-3]

NARA, RG 120, M930, Main Series, War Department to AEF, roll 12.

TAG, War Department, to Pershing, in part in reply to Pershing to TAG, War Department, cables P-705-S, March 10, P-912-S, April 13, and P-986-S, April 24, in addition to TAG, War Department, to Pershing, cable A-1203-R, April 30.

Cable A-1233-R.
1D. Reference our 1203, paragraph 1B. Owing to uncertainty regarding troop shipments it is considered advisable to substitute July 1st as the date after which all Vickers guns will be available for Air Service. [Replies—Vol. 6, August 2, P-1552-S-5]

1K. With reference to your 912, paragraph 1B. Building 4,440 light tanks, all required for United States Army as follows: 1,520 for initial establishment of fighting and signal tanks, 2,480 for wastage at approximately 15% per month, 440 for wastage for overseas shipment. 7/12 of the total or 2,590 will be equipped to take Marlin provided oscillate port shields immediately surrounding gun and weighing 150 pounds are also replaced. Port shields for Marlin only are being made.

1N. With reference to your 705, paragraph 1C. Relative to supplying divisions with Browning machine guns and automatic rifles upon completion of training with Browning light rifles are not interchangeable and will be used in this country. Factory deliveries schedule for overseas shipments as follows: May 2,500, June 6,000, July 7,500, August 10,500, September 12,500, October 12,500, November 12,500, December 10,000. First 750 heavy guns are not interchangeable and will be used in this country. Factory delivery schedule for overseas shipment: June 1,750, July 3,500, August 500, September 7,500, October 9,500, November 13,500, December 7,000. Will the above be sufficient to permit your equipping troops after training as desired? With reference to your 986, paragraph 8B. Will above schedule permit also replacement during October, November and December Hotchkiss by Browning heavy? Cannot determine procedure covering Hotchkiss tripod until replacement program is determined. Williams [Chief of Ordnance]. [Reply—May 16, P-1123-S-1; May 16, P-1133-S-1; P-1134-S-1Q; May 18, A-1341-R-1L; Vol. 5, May 27, A-1406-R-1C]

NARA, RG 120, M930, Main Series, War Department to AEF, roll 12.

TAG, War Department, to Pershing, in part in reply to Pershing to TAG, War Department, cables P-898-S, April 12, and P-965-S, April 20.

Cable A-1235-R.

1. With reference to paragraph 3C, your 898. President authorizes you to assign officers to command without regard to seniority in rank in same grade in accordance with provisions of 119th Article of War. Report of action taken under this authority is to be made in each case without delay. Orders in such case to state "By Direction of the President". March.

3. For Nolan. With reference to paragraph 5, your 965. Semi-weekly wireless will be sent, commencing by Monday, May 6th. March. [*Ed.*—The first of these confidential cables was apparently A-1301-R sent on May 12.]

7. Mr. John D. Ryan, head Aircraft Production reorganization scheme, desires Grayson Murphy as representative of his division in France. Have you any objection? March. [*Ed.*—Pershing replied on May 24 in P-1178-S-4 that "Major Murphy does not consider himself fitted for the position" and recommended Col. Philip L. Spalding, former Chief of the Air Service's Material Division. Spalding returned to Washington in June and joined the Bureau of Aircraft Production but was soon sent back to France. There he served as the Bureau's technical representative with the Air Service's Supply Section until October, when he once again returned to Washington and the Bureau of Aircraft Production. For more information on Spalding, see Holley, *Ideas and Weapons*, pp. 88, 90.]

NARA, RG 120, M930, Main Series, War Department to AEF, roll 12; AEF to War Department, roll 3.

TAG, War Department, to Pershing.

Cable A-1237-R. Confidential.
British Military Attaché reports that British War Office is strongly against the attachment of any colored infantry for training with British. Your views are requested. March. [Reply—May 8, P-1074-S-1C]

NARA, RG 120, Confidential Series, War Department to Pershing, roll 18.

May 4

Pershing's Personal Diary

At Paris. Worked in quarters in a. m. Had luncheon with Colonel Dawes at Colonel Boyd's apartment, and left Paris for Chaumont, via Fontainebleau. Arrived at Chaumont about 7 p. m.

LC, Pershing Papers, Diary, May 7, 1917–September 1, 1918, box 4.

Pershing to French Minister of Munitions, reply to Loucheur and Dumesnil to Pershing, April 27.

Subject: Cooperation between the Production Departments of the French and American Air Service.

Reference your memorandum of 27 April 1918, signed by yourself and the Under Secretary of State for Aeronautics regarding the necessity for more closely coordinating the aeronautical production resources of France and the United States, I wish to state that I am in full accord with your views regarding this very important subject.

As a matter of military policy during the present emergency, the whole production resources of the United States should be employed to insure so far as it can be attained full aeronautical equipment for our Allies, even at the expense of delaying, for the time being, the large air program planned in connection with the operations of the American Army.

1st—Pursuit Aviation

With reference to the production of Hispano-Suiza engines, steps have already been taken to increase the production of this type of engines in the United States.

With reference to the new SPAD aeroplane, we are hoping that you will complete its tests as quickly as possible, in order that we may know whether it is a type of aeroplane which can be satisfactorily used by the American aviation. If this type of aeroplane and engine is satisfactory for pursuit aviation, I will recommend that the necessary additional raw materials be shipped from the United States, in order to replace materials used in the construction of aeroplanes of this type, which may be purchased by the American Air Service.

2nd—Army Corps Aviation.

With reference to the use of the Liberty engine in the Breguet cellule, as soon as you are convinced that the Liberty engine is satisfactory, I would like very much to know the number of *Corps d'Armée* Breguet cellules you would be able to supply to the American Air Service for this work, provided the United States shall furnish the Liberty engines. If the Breguet cellule with the Liberty engine is satisfactory, I will request that a sufficient number of Liberty engines be sent to France, without delay for use by the American Air Service in Breguet cellules.

In the event that the tests are satisfactory I would also be glad to consider the exchange of Breguet Liberty units for Salmson aeroplanes for *Corps d'Armée* and Army Observation Work.

3rd—Day Bombing Squadron.

With reference to the use of the Liberty engine in the "Breguet" Day Bombing cellule, I hope that I may be promptly informed as to the results of any tests with the Breguet Day Bombing Liberty units. As soon as you are satisfied that this unit is suitable for day bombing service, I shall be glad to recommend the immediate shipment to France of the necessary Liberty engines, for installation in such number of Breguet day bombing cellules as may be purchased by the American Air Service. In this connection, it is hoped the tests with the Liberty engine in the Breguet day bombing cellule may be completed and reported upon with the least possible delay, as the present development of day bombing aeroplanes in the United States has progressed so favorably that this type of aeroplane (Breguet-Liberty) would be of no particular service to the American Air Service, unless it can be provided in quantity within the next two or three months.

4th—Night Bombing Aviation.

With reference to new types of night bombing aeroplanes, which you have just produced on an industrial basis, it would appear desirable, in the interests of standardization, that this new type be given a thorough field test with the Liberty engines installed, as quickly as possible, in order that their efficiency may be compared with the two present types (Handley-Page and Caproni) which have been accepted by the Inter-Allied Aviation Committee.

With reference to the use of Liberty engines in these new types of Night Bombing aeroplanes, I will be very glad to request that the necessary number of Liberty engines be sent to France for this purpose, provided you have no Liberty engines available at the present time. If the results of your test prove that these new types are more efficient than the two present accepted types, I would then be glad to consider your suggestion of providing in the United States in larger quantities additional types of Night Bombing aeroplanes which could use the Liberty engine.

I appreciate fully your statement that the manufacture in the United States of an aeroplane (without motor) conceived in Europe, is not an easy matter, and it is, therefore, in my opinion doubly important that all tests of these new types of aeroplanes should be carried out in France without delay, in order that the United States may receive the full benefit of your experience. Detail drawings for such new aeroplanes intended for production in the United States should be most carefully prepared and checked over, by both French and American engineers, before the drawings are sent to the United States. Our past experience has shown that if this is not done, delays will always result. The question of tool equipment and all other manufacturing details should also be studied by American and French mechanical experts before any production plans are put into effect. If these preliminary details are carried out the manufacturing problems connected with the production of new types of aeroplanes in the United States will be greatly simplified and accelerated.

With reference to an agreement between the French Government and the United States, that the United States would concentrate its efforts on the production of a definite number of Liberty engines, accessories and component parts of aeroplanes, it is probable that in view of the shipping situation such an agreement could be made chiefly in connection with the production of additional new types of large night bombing aeroplanes, provided such new types of night bombing aeroplanes are proven equal to or superior to existing types which have been accepted by the Inter-Allied Aviation Committee. It is not considered probable that any agreement could be made at the present time solely in connection with the production in the United States of other new types of aeroplanes, without first making a serious study of the present development of the aeroplane industrial situation, and its capacity to absorb new work, without upsetting the present plans of the United States Government.

With reference to the production in the United States, of the Canton-Unne Z-18 500 H.P. engine, I would be very glad to accept at once your suggestion to send to the United States the necessary engineers, engines, etc., in order that our American engineers may have an opportunity to study the possibilities of this new type of engine, in connection with its general use with two-seater and multi-seater combat aeroplanes; day and night bombing aeroplanes, etc.

If our American engineers are satisfied that it is desirable or practicable to put this new type of engine into production in the United States, I shall be more than glad to assist you in securing the necessary raw materials from the United States, with which to carry on the manufacture of the necessary aeroplane cellules, provided of course that the necessary priority on tonnage is granted by the Allied Maritime Transport Council.

LC, Foulois Papers, folder 12: AEF, Air Service, Allied Air Service, box 7.

Editor's Note—In the report that he sent to Pershing in January 1924, Foulois concluded the following concerning this proposed production agreement and Pershing's letter to Loucheur:

> 4. The foregoing constitutes the only written correspondence of record which is available to the writer of this document. On April 30, 1918, and prior to the despatch of the letter quoted in paragraph 3, the Chief of Air Service, A.E.F., had a conference with the French Under-Secretary of

Aeronautics in Paris, at which time the various questions contained in the memorandum, quoted in paragraph 1, were discussed. During this conference, the Chief of Air Service brought up the question of the effect of such a Franco-American aircraft program on the existing production programs of England and Italy, and asked the Under-Secretary of Aeronautics if this proposed plan for joint production had been discussed with the English and Italian aircraft representatives, to which the Under-Secretary replied in the negative.

The Chief of Air Service, thereupon, suggested that the proposed plan in principle for joint aircraft production between France and the United States, as quoted in paragraph l, of this Enclosure, might be a logical subject for discussion by the Inter-Allied Aviation Committee.

The Under-Secretary of Aeronautics, who at that time was also the Chairman of the above-named Committee, stated that he would take this suggestion into consideration, but so far as the knowledge of the writer goes, no further action was taken toward the establishment of the proposed plan of joint aircraft production between France and the United States.

5. In theory, this proposed plan for joint aircraft production between France and the United States would have resulted in certain mutual benefits to the industries of both countries, but when considered in its entirety, its practical application at any time during 1918, would have resulted in considerable dislocation to the existing aircraft production programs of England and Italy, especially in view of the dependence of these countries, who like France, were also almost entirely dependent on the United States for its raw and semi-finished aircraft materials.

Also the American air production program in the United States was encountering many difficulties at this period, and any new plans which involved any modification of existing production programs would have promptly dislocated the American production program.

Had the war continued into 1919, and had this proposed plan for joint production been submitted for consideration in the Fall of 1918, there is every probability that certain features of the French program could have been adopted, provided, however, that such a program would have been in the joint interests of all Powers concerned, and provided it did not interfere with the common military object of defeating the German Armies in the field. (LC, Pershing Papers, folder: Data for Book *My Experiences in the World War,* folder no. 1: Foulois, "Air Service—American Expeditionary Forces. (1917–1918)," Encl. H: "Efforts of the French to establish a Joint Aircraft Production Program with the United States, to the exclusion of England. and Italy.")

Harbord, CS, GHQ, AEF, for CINC, AEF, to Chief, French Military Mission with the American Army, Chaumont, in reply to Chief, French Military Mission, to CINC, AEF, no. 670/AE and 852/AE (not located).

1. I have the honor to acknowledge receipt of your letter 670/AE in which you ask that American pilots to the number of 80 be assigned to French squadrons in groups of five.

2. I would be extremely glad to see more American aviators on the front but I must insist on their employment in American units and not as individuals.

3. It is doubly important that our available air personnel be utilized to form complete American units, since, in accordance with the French desire, further shipments of air service personnel from the United States has been temporarily delayed.

4. In the event that the French army has available aeroplanes for which it has no pilots I would be very glad to undertake to form at once 4 or 5 complete squadrons. These squadrons would at once be placed at the disposition of the French army, especially in those sectors in which American troops are in line.

5. I have also received your letter 852/A.E. in which you refer to an offer of 53 pilots made on May 2 [not located]. No offer of this kind was actually made. The facts in this case appear to be that a letter was prepared in the office of the A. C. of S., G-1, and a copy of this letter was shown to one of your officers. As G-1 at these headquarters does not dispose of combat troops the A. C. of S., G-1, very properly did not sign the proposed letter but brought the matter to the attention of the Chief of Staff.

6. I regret very much that there should have been any misunderstanding in this matter, but I am sure that on examination you will find the facts as stated.

USAWW, vol. 3, p. 296.

Secretary of War Newton D. Baker to Col. Carl Boyd, ADC to Pershing.

This letter of introduction will be presented to you by Mr. Raymond B. Fosdick, who is chairman of the Commission on Training Camp Activities in the United States and has the President's confidence and mine in the highest degree. The work which Mr. Fosdick and his Committee have undertaken at my request here has been so important for the building up of the morale of the soldiers that I would not be far wrong if I were to characterize it as one of the most important activities of the War Department.

I know that General Pershing feels the necessity of centralizing all the nonmilitary activities of the soldiers in France under the general administrative guidance of the Y. M. C. A., and Mr. Fosdick is not seeking any opportunity to carry the work of his Committee to France, but his trip to France is for the purpose of learning the conditions under which our soldiers live over there so that the work of preparation in this country can be carried forward more effectively.

I will personally appreciate it if you will present Mr. Fosdick to General Pershing, as my friend and valuable aide and adviser, and then without troubling the general with the matter any further equip Mr. Fosdick with any necessary letters or passes which will enable him to see all that he ought to see in France that will be helpful to our work here.

LC, Pershing Papers, folder: Newton D. Baker (1918), box 19.

TAG, War Department, to Bliss, Chief, American Section, and Permanent Military Representative, SWC, Versailles, in reply to Pershing to TAG, War Department, cable P-1020-S, April 29, and Bliss to TAG, War Department, cable 103-S, May 3.

Cable 53-R.
    Reference Cablegram 1,020 from Pershing. The President authorizes you to express the favorable opinion of this Government toward the proposition to include the Italian Army under the same terms as British, French and American Armies now placed under General Foch, the Supreme Commander. Notify Pershing. This approval given before receipt of your 103, paragraph 5. March.
[Annotated: *Copies furnished to Gen. Pershing.*]

NARA, M923, American Section, SWC, file 316: Cablegrams received from the War Department, Jan. 23, 1918–Nov. 19, 1919, roll 18; see also online "WW I Supreme War Council, American records," at https://www.fold3.com.

Pershing to TAG, War Department, in part in reply to TAG, War Department, to Pershing, cable A-1182-R, April 26.

Cable P-1051-S.
    3. For Chief of Staff. With reference to paragraph 1B, your cablegram 839 [not reproduced] and paragraph 1C, your cablegram 1173. Request designation of divisions that will be left in United States on June 1st in order to know what members of General Staff College class should be held here awaiting arrival their divisions. Request that maximum number of officers available at War Department be sent for next course Staff College and desire to strongly renew recommendations in paragraph 5, my cablegram 889, regarding number of officers from divisions remaining in United States. All should arrive not later than June 15th, their orders directing them to report to General Staff College so as to avoid delay in landing. [Reply—May 9, A-1270-R-1]
    6. For Director of Storage and Traffic, Embarkation Branch. 6A. With reference to paragraph 5, your cablegram 1182. When vessels referred to leave States cable contents of cargoes and we will assign destinations through Naval authorities as at present. Should vessels be consigned Great Britain instruct masters upon discharge to report to United States Naval representative Barry Roads, Bristol Channel, for orders. If sailing in ballast also report Barry Roads. Absolutely essential that these ships be in best repair and equipped with both wireless and guns. Material and labor unobtainable this end. [In addition—Vol. 5, July 7, P-1425-S-7]

NARA, RG 120, M930, Main Series, AEF to War Department, roll 3.

Pershing to TAG, War Department, in part in reply to TAG, War Department, to Pershing, cables A-1151-R, April 21, and A-1165-R, April 24, in addition to Pershing to TAG, War Department, cable P-739-S, March 16.

Cable P-1052-S.
 2. For Chief Signal Officer. 2A. With reference to paragraph 1, your cablegram 1165. Your proposed production of 180-horsepower high-compression Hispano approved. Notify us data first shipment of 180-horsepower Hispano can be floated. How many engines in first shipment? Give dates succeeding shipments can be floating and number of engines in each. We will arrange here for contract for planes either English or French as machines are available. It appears now that first shipment of engines should be consigned to Aviation Office AEF London, England, Base Section number 3 for installation in SE 5. Production of SE 5 for 180 Hispano in America disapproved since it appears that necessary planes for this engine can be obtained in Europe either SE 5, SPAD or both. We cannot ask for tonnage priority until we have information above requested. [Reply—May 15, A-1318-R-3; Vol. 5, June 24, A-1596-R] [In addition—May 12, P-1102-S-2C]
 4. For Felton. With reference to paragraph 3A, your cablegram 1151. You are correct in your understanding. For building 6000 wooden underframe box cars by Bordeaux firm will require 6000 car sets following items interchangeable with type K box cars as supplied by Middletown Car Company to French State railways on contract 957. [Hereafter follows list of materials required and measurements.] Advise dates of delivery in United States in order to properly arrange schedule of shipment to France, which should be if possible in accordance with paragraph 1D, our cablegram 739. Cable at once whether there is such certainty of obtaining above materials to warrant us in signing contract. You will not be required to furnish any hand tools or shop equipment. [Reply—May 13, A-1306-R-1D; in addition—Vol. 5, May 22, P-1163-S-11]

NARA, RG 120, M930, Main Series, AEF to War Department, roll 3.

TAG, War Department, to Pershing, in part in reply to Pershing to TAG, War Department, cable P-898-S, April 12.

Cable A-1243-R.
 4. With reference to paragraph 3, your 898. On account of great need of Regular Army officers in United States, impracticable at present to send more to you. With shipment of Regular Army Divisions now proceeding, the quota of Regular Army officers with your command(s) will be greatly increased. March.

NARA, RG 120, M930, Main Series, War Department to AEF, roll 12.

May 5

Pershing's Personal Diary

A very busy day with new Chief of Staff, General McAndrew, and with General Harbord, who is leaving. Saw General [Robert H.] Noble.

LC, Pershing Papers, Diary, May 7, 1917–September 1, 1918, box 4.

Haig to Pershing, with enclosure, Note on Artillery Personnel.

[Handwritten]
I beg to enclose a note showing how I stand in the matter of artillery personnel. You will see that there is a considerable shortage, and consequently if you could arrange to let me have 10,000 American artillerymen, it would be of very great assistance to us.
[Enclosure]
Note on Artillery Personnel
The Adjutant General's branch estimates that on 31st May 1918, the deficits in personnel as regards Royal Horse and Royal Field Artillery, may amount to 3,500, and as regards Royal Garrison Artillery to 1,900.

These net deficits will entail R.F.A. field units being about 6,000 short and R.G.A. field units 4,000 short, owing to the fact that casualties continue to occur while drafts previously demanded are en route.

The Major-General R.A. recommends that the services of 10,000 American Artillerymen should be asked for, two-thirds being field artillery, one-third heavy artillerymen. These men to be attached to British batteries in the first instance and trained as N.C.O.s, Gunners, Drivers, &c.

Subsequently they could be collected to form American batteries to be attached to British Brigades and, finally, these batteries could be organized as American Brigades.

As a rough guide, the following figures indicate the percentages of the various ranks required to meet the estimated casualties:

	Field Artillery	**Heavy Artillery**
N.C.Os.	8%	10%
Gunners.	52%	60%
Drivers.	18%	4%
Signallers.	14%	16%
Layers.	9%	10%

[Handwritten notation: D.H., 5 May 18]

LC, Pershing Papers, folder: Field Marshal Sir Douglas Haig, 1917–1918, box 86.

Maj. Gen. James G. Harbord. With the medical decision to return Brig. Gen. Charles A. Doyen, USMC, commander of the 4th Marine Brigade, to the United States, Pershing selected his Chief of Staff, Brig. Gen. James G. Harbord, to replace him. Harbord assumed command on May 7 and led the Brigade through the difficult fighting in the area of Château-Thierry and at Belleau Wood and Bouresches in June. He was promoted to Major General on July 11 and replaced Omar Bundy as division commander on July 15. Pershing soon moved Harbord, his trusted friend, to command the Services of Supply on July 26. In this staged photograph, apparently from his time commanding the 4th Marine Brigade after his promotion on July 11, Harbord is a Major General wearing the helmet of a French brigadier general. Source: NARA, Still Picture Branch. RG 111, 111-SC-44880.

Maj. Gen. James W. McAndrew. On May 6, Maj. Gen. James W. McAndrew officially assumed the post of Chief of Staff, GHQ, AEF, replacing James G. Harbord, who was assigned to command the 4th Marine Brigade, 2nd Division. McAndrew came to GHQ after serving as commander of the 18th Infantry Regiment, 1st Division, from June through August 1917, when he was promoted to brigadier general (National Army) and assigned to establish the AEF's Corps Schools at Gondrecourt. From there he was moved to Langres in October to be the commandant of the new Army Staff College and Schools, which were to educate the general staff officers needed for the entire AEF. Promoted to major general (National Army) in April 1918, McAndrew was summoned to Chaumont to replace Harbord as Chief of Staff early in May. His considerable administrative, management, and leadership skills were critical to the successes of the entire AEF in the ensuing difficult months leading to the Allied victory. Source: Library of Congress, Prints & Photographs Division, Pershing Collection, Lot 7719.

Pershing to Haig, CINC, BAF, and the same letter to Lord Milner, Secretary of State for War, London, on May 7.

Some time ago I received a cable from my Government to the effect that it was necessary to list one of our colored divisions for early shipment to France. As you know all of our infantry and machine gun units to be embarked in the near future are destined for service, for the time being, with your forces. I accordingly replied to the cable received from my Government to the effect that the 92d Division (Colored) could be included in the troops to be assigned to the forces under your command [see April 29, P-1024-S-1J].

It now appears, however, that the British Military Attaché in Washington had made a protest against including any colored battalions among the troops destined for service with your forces and that he has stated that this protest was made in behalf of your War Office [see May 3, A-1237-R].

You will, of course, appreciate my position in this matter, which, in brief, is that these Negroes are American citizens. My Government, for reasons which concern itself alone, has decided to organize colored combat divisions and now desires the early dispatch of one of these divisions to France. Naturally I cannot and will not discriminate against these soldiers.

I am informed that the 92d Division is in a good state of training and I have no reason to believe its employment under your command would be accompanied by any unusual difficulties.

I am informing my Government of this letter to you [see May 8, P-1074-S-1C]. May I not hope that the inclusion of the 92d Division among the American troops to be placed under your command is acceptable to you and that you will be able to overcome the objections raised by your War Office?

NARA, RG 120, Historical Section, GHQ, AEF, folder: Key Documents II-1, box 2240; see also *USAWW*, Vol. 3, p. 95; Pershing, *My Experiences in the World War*, vol. 2, p. 45, notes that he sent the same letter to Lord Milner on May 7, and *USAWW* notes the preparation of an identical letter to Lord Milner, which was sent to the Chief of Staff, AEF, for action on May 7.

Pershing to Bliss, Chief, American Section, and Permanent Military Representative, SWC, Versailles, in reply to Grant to Atterbury, April 22.

I beg to acknowledge the receipt of your letter dated April 22, 1918, enclosing copies of Joint Notes numbers 22, 23 and 24, passed by the Military Representatives at their meeting on April 18, 1918. These Notes contain matters of great interest and I have gone over them all very carefully.

In reference to rolling stock from the United States, I am enclosing herewith a brief tabulated statement showing what we have, what has been shipped, and what we may reasonably expect in the future. Your attention is also invited to the mechanics whom we have turned over to the French to repair French rolling stock. Our

figures show that up to May 2nd, we have turned over to the French 1530 mechanics to be so employed.
1 Incl
American Locomotives and Cars for Service on the L. of C.

	Locomotives	Cars
Number in Service May 1, 1918	201	733
Number others in France or in Ports	88	681
Number Shipped from U.S. and not yet Received	15	930
Number Authorized for Shipment and not yet Shipped	75	1,500
Proposed Recommendations Relative to Shipments	100 June 100 July 100 Aug. 150 Sept. 151 Oct.	1,800 June 2,000 July 2,500 Aug. 2,500 Sept. 2,500 Oct. 2,500 Nov. 2,186 Dec.
Probable Number in Service	301 June 601 Sept. 980 Dec.	2,233 June 7,533 Sept. 15,033 Dec.
Number Belgian Locomotives in Service	80	

NARA, RG 120, M923, American Section, SWC, folder 196: Correspondence, memorandums, and notes relating to the organization, function, and transactions of the Inter-Allied Transportation Council, March 1918–August 1919, document 196-7, roll 16.

Pershing to Dawes, GPA, AEF, Paris.

With reference to our conversation as to the scope of authority that should be given the executive control of allied army supplies and overseas shipments under the pooling arrangements contemplated, I am of the opinion that, generally speaking, authority should be absolute. However, in its exercise, I do not conceive that there would ever be conflict of authority inasmuch as no radical decision would be likely without the approval of all parties.

So that the real basis of the executive committee's acts is coordination and cooperation founded upon mutual confidence among the controlling allies themselves, and upon the judgment of the committee they have selected. In principle, it should bear the same relation to allied supplies that the Purchasing Board of the A.E.F. bears to the various supply departments in our own Army.

I am firm in my view that the members of this executive control should be military men of as broad business experience as possible, and hope the preliminary conference for the discussion of plans and organization of this committee may take the same view.

As to the duties, there are three main features which have been clearly outlined in our discussions and which fall naturally within the scope of the controlling agency, we hope to create:

1. The pooling and allocation of all bulky supplies that are used in common by all allied armies.

2. The groupment and allocation of military labor and transportation facilities, including motor and field transport.

3. The control of overseas shipments of all allied military supplies and material.

The idea set out in paragraph 3 should be definitely separated from control of shipping by the Allied Shipping Boards, whose authority extends to the allocation of shipping itself, as distinguished from the direction necessary to control shipments of particular classes of supplies and material.

The foregoing is a mere outline, the details of this important work being left to you and those selected to work with you.

LC, Harbord Papers, folder: correspondence on Dawes, box 8, also folder: Military Activity: I, Official War Activity, pp. 4–5, box 8; see also Dawes. *A Journal of the Great War*, vol. 1, pp. 284–85.

Pershing to March.

I am going to give you just a moment during these strenuous days to tell you that I am organizing the artillery along the lines recommended in the memorandum you were kind enough to give me just before you left. I have appointed General Hinds Chief of Artillery and have made him a member of my staff. I think Hinds is the man for the place and am glad he is here and available. Now that Westervelt is a brigadier, he will be available as Hinds' assistant and will add materially to the strength of Hinds' organization.

Most everything these days must be handled by cable or else we would get far behind so you will, before you have received this letter, have settled the question or sending infantry during the month of May. This seemed to me to be the best way to handle the question, instead of committing ourselves to a program covering a number of months. I thought this matter was settled for the time being, as I had taken it up with Foch and explained to him fully my reasons for the action I took with reference to the British, and he seemed to accept it. But the question was sprung again in the Supreme War Council and the new agreement has gone to you. I think we shall find it about as favorable as the one made in May. It was a big fight to get anything out of it. They all wanted to demand only infantry.

As long as this big drive lasts it is going to be difficult for us to get our units into one group, but I have this constantly in mind and shall insist upon it as early as it is possible to do so. I feel that our people are going to demand some positive evidence that America is doing her share under the American flag. I believe you agree with this view and think we must all insist upon it or else lose our identity in this war. The Secretary is also of this opinion, which he expressed to me while here.

According to my idea of rotating the staff, I am sending Harbord out to command the Marine Brigade and am bringing McAndrew ad interim as Chief of Staff. Other members of the staff, including Connor, W.D., and McCoy, are going out for duty with troops and I am bringing Eltinge in for duty as Deputy Chief of Staff and [George Van Horne] Moseley will take Connor's place in G-4.

I am doing my best to select the officers you asked for, although I have not heard from you with reference to the matter of sending over any in exchange. I hope you have made selections of officers for us, as with the formation of these new corps and armies, the demand is going to be greater than the supply. While seemingly there is a large number of staff officers on duty at the various headquarters, they are mostly Reserve Corps or National Army Officers in training and cannot yet be trusted for important work. What gives the impression of a great number is accounted for by the fact that there are so many officers in training for intelligence work under Colonel Nolan.

I am speeding everything up as much as possible for organization of troops for active service. This includes Service of Supply troops, which I hope to replace by labor that will be on a pooling basis as soon as the new pooling arrangements are started.

I hope that I shall be able to get through my proposition to pool all supplies as well as to place the direction of shipments under military control. I think we must do this in view of the apparent shortage of 2,000,000 of shipping for the year 1918. I shall in due time advise you by telegraph of the results.

I hope everything is going well with you, and again wish to say that my sole desire is to establish the fullest cooperation between you and me. You can count on me to do my best to play the game.

[Handwritten: *"P.S. Please extend my warmest regards to the Secretary of War. J.J.P."*]

LC, March Papers, folder: Correspondence File, 1918, box 1.

Pershing to TAG, War Department.

Cable P-1056-S. Confidential.
For the Chief of Staff.

Recommend sending small detachments of from 50 to a few hundred men on each of our medium speed transports. Believed that some thousand additional men per month could come if such ships used. Sims believes that small number of troops on a slow ship are in no greater danger than a large number on a fast ship because in case the vessel is torpedoed the smaller number are more easily saved. Under these circumstances, recommend waiver of speed requirement in these cases and that this space be utilized in sending replacement personnel. [Reply—May 8, A-1264-R-14]

NARA, RG 120, M930, Confidential Series, AEF to War Department, roll 7.

Pershing to TAG, War Department, in addition to Pershing to TAG, War Department, cable P-887-S, April 10, in part in reply to TAG, War Department, to Pershing, cable A-1048-R, April 6.

Cable P-1057-S. Confidential.
For the Chief of Staff.
    Further reference to your cable 1048 and our cable 887, paragraph 1, subparagraph C. We can handle all tonnage indicated your cable with minimum turn around. In addition to existing ports which in themselves will be fully capable shortly handling this tonnage, we have completed arrangements this end for use Marseille which gives us total capacity much in excess your figures. Latter port probably best equipped French port and is now working at less than one half normal capacity. Highly desirable we should have the advantage of Marseille facilities as soon as possible because additional shipments of coal from England to France may throw some extra burden upon the French ports now used by us, which might delay our getting the increasing tonnage out of these ports which we are now confidently expecting. Moreover, Marseille has the great advantage of affording car capacity now not being utilized in as much as shipments for Salonica from England and France and shipments of French coal for Italy result in a back movement of empty cars which we can take advantage of. Have consulted Admiral Sims who agrees to our use Marseille for cargo ships. He will recommend to Navy Department type of ships and armament of same which should be used this movement. Understand his views to be that these ships should be of approximately 7,500 tons, fast and well-armed. Ships to cross Atlantic to Gibraltar without convoy, to be convoyed from Gibraltar to Marseille and return to Gibraltar out to sea. Appreciate that we will lose certain space due to extra bunker coal. However, this loss will be more than compensated by general results in turn around and aggregate cargo delivered. Sims believes that the specially selected ships crossing Atlantic without convoy will require only 2 to 5 days extra in net turn around over and above same ships convoyed all across Atlantic to Bay of Biscay ports. Am having cable recommendations prepared indicating character and amount of tonnage to be diverted to Marseille. In meantime, request matter be taken up with Navy Department so that preliminary arrangements as to particular ships, armament, et cetera for this purpose may be adjusted without delay. Will also incorporate in cable recommendations to effect that cargo consignments for Marseille be limited to replaceable material of current issue so that no embarrassment will be occasioned in the event of loss of steamer. Sims of opinion that additional risk is not substantial. [In addition—May 16, P-1126-S-1]

NARA, RG 120, M930, Confidential Series, AEF to War Department, roll 7.

Pershing to TAG, War Department, in part in reply to TAG, War Department, cable A-1094-R, April 13, in addition to Pershing to TAG, War Department, cable P-1041-S, May 2 (not reproduced).

Cable P-1059-S.
1. For Chief of Staff. With reference to paragraph 1A, my cablegram 1041, notifying you that 30 Staff Officers had left for the United States, urgently request that the 30 officers promised by you to replace them be started at once. The heavy increase of troops will push us to the limit for available Staff Officers. The officers referred to cannot be started too soon. [*Ed.*—On May 15 in cable A-1321-R-2, the War Department listed 21 Staff Officers being transferred to France and stated that 9 more would soon be selected and sent.]
1B. In order that prompt exemplary action may be taken in necessary cases I recommend that 48th Article of War be so amended as to authorize me to confirm all death sentences and order their execution. Full power as to death sentences in French and British Army in France is vested in military authorities. [Reply—Vol. 5, May 20, A-1355-R-4]
7. For Chief Signal Officer. 7E. With reference to paragraph 1, your cablegram 1094. Question being considered by Board of Officers, will cable fully later. [In addition—Vol. 5, May 26, P-1192-S-5]

NARA, RG 120, M930, Main Series, AEF to War Department, roll 3.

TAG, War Department, to Pershing, in part in reply to Pershing to TAG, War Department, cable P-891-S, April 11.

Cable A-1247-R.
1. A. Much confusion has occurred here as to replacements due to your request for replacements from time to time apparently including some of your previous requests which have been ordered shipped but which had not sailed when succeeding requests arrived.
1B. Based on 1G, your 891, following replacement have been ordered shipped in May and June. Infantry, 25,960. Field Artillery, 6,160. Cavalry, 440. Engineers, 3,080. Signal Corps of the Army, Land Divisions, 550. Aviation, 2,640. Quartermaster, 1,320. Coast Artillery Corps, 1,320. Ordnance, 110. . . . In the future make all requests for replacements additional to the above and do not include in any future requests any requests already made. When a request is received from you it is ordered at once but sometimes the personnel is unavoidably delayed. Then if a request arrives which includes those already requested and ordered, it confuses. The above is understood to cover all replacements requested in May and June. Automatic replacements will begin again in July. Is foregoing correct and understood?
March

[*Ed.*—On May 10 in cable P-1089-S, paragraph 3, Pershing replied that "the program of replacements for May and June is understood and is correct. Hereafter, as you direct, our requests for replacements will not include any request already made, but will be additional needs only. However we will cable with each request a statement of balance due according to our account."]

NARA, RG 120, M930, Confidential Series, War Department to AEF, roll 18, and Main Series, AEF to War Department. roll 3.

TAG, War Department, to Pershing.

Cable A-1248-R. Confidential.

After my return I cabled General Bliss with regard to the very urgent request made from many quarters that American troops be sent to Italy [see April 24, Baker to Bliss, cable 49-R], explaining to him that I realized the danger of creating expectations on the part of Italy of more troops to follow, and also our conversations on the subject and suggested to General Bliss that [blank] accomplish the professed object of having American troops make their appearance on the Italian front, by requesting General Pétain and General Haig to brigade some of the American troops allotted to the French and British for training, to their divisions in Italy, this, perhaps, relieving corresponding number for use on the Western front, and also having American troops in Italy.

General Bliss believes this could be done, and is as far as we should go in the matter. I have laid the matter before the President, who has also been urgently pressed to send some troops to Italy. The President regards the suggestion of brigading some Americans with the British and French divisions in Italy as the wisest solution, and asks me to present it to you for your consideration. If you approve, will you kindly take the matter up with General Foch and General Haig? If you do not approve fully take no action. It seems to me that sending Americans under these circumstances would create no expectation that we can send further force at the present time, or an independent American force at a later time. [Reply—May 10, P-1093-S]
Baker.

NARA, RG 120, M930, Confidential Series, War Department to AEF, roll 18.

May 6

Pershing's Personal Diary

A very busy day catching up with back correspondence and seeing people. Major Bowditch reported as Aide. Saw General Bethel [AEF's Judge Advocate General], General [Samuel Tilden] Ansell [Acting Judge Advocate General, U.S. Amy], Major Rand,

General [Albert Hazen] Blanding [CG, 185th Infantry Bridge], Dr. Vincent of the Rockefeller Foundation, Lieutenant Colonel Patterson, M. C., Lieutenant Colonel Churchill, Major Livingston, Bishop Brent and Mr. [Martin] Egan. Had Dr. Mott and Mr. Carter of Y.M.C.A. at house to luncheon, and Colonel Ovenshire at home to dinner.

LC, Pershing Papers, Diary, May 7, 1917–September 1, 1918, box 4.

Brig. Gen. Richard M. Blatchford, CG, Panama Canal Department, to Pershing, reply to Pershing to Blatchford, March 19.

I have your kind letter of March 19th and I thank you for taking a moment of your valuable time to advise me as to the reason for my being relieved from duty with you; needless for me to say that the thought of my being physically unfit could never have entered my head.

I fully agree with you that the personnel of the A.E.F. must consist of men physically fit and that personal friendship should not be permitted to enter into the question of that fitness, and the authorities having assigned you greater responsibilities, than have ever been assigned any other commanding general of the American Army, your opinions must of necessity govern, not only as regards personnel, but all other matters pertaining a the A.E F., both a home and abroad.

Your friendship for me has been demonstrated, and I feel confident I will not jeopardize that friendship when I ask you if you will be willing to reverse your opinion as to my physical fitness, provided the War Department will consent to re-examine me and I pass the board. Knowing you as I do I fully believe you will.

I have this day made application for re-examination, and enclose you copies of the correspondence.

It is with great interest that I read the Panama morning papers, and needless to say, your work on the Western Front makes me feel more than sad the I am not with you, which would not be the case if I could bring myself to believe in the slightest degree that your opinion was the correct one.

I care nothing about the loss of my grade of Major General, but I do know that I am physically fit for any active service in my grade of Brigadier.
[no enclosures]

LC, Pershing Papers, folder: R. M. Blatchford, box 26.

Maj. Frederick Palmer, Special Assistant to the CINC, Chaumont, to CINC, AEF.

[*Ed.*—Pershing sent Palmer, a seasoned war correspondent, to observe the 1st Division April 13–24, as it prepared to take its place in the line. He then went on to the 26th Division. On May 6, his notes were logged into the GHQ, AEF, War Diary, for which he was then acting as the GHQ's war diarist.]

Notes of Observation with the First Division.

1. The movement of the Division from Chaumont-Gisors seemed admirably methodical from stage to stage with little confusion, our forces taking the intervening roads and the main roads kept open for the regular supply traffic.

2. Not only line but Headquarters officers expressed the opinion that our Staff was not capable of handling a division in battle which is encouraged by the various French officers in liaison, who form a system of influence permeating our forces.

3. When we want our army back, the main argument against it here and behind the scenes in Washington will be our inability to command corps and divisions, aside from the one of "losing the war."

4. Perhaps the best way to prove that we can command is to appoint corps commanders and staffs and support them as capable in every way while giving them opportunities for learning. Otherwise, the C-in-C will become a figure-head, and eventually the criticism that he cannot organize a command will be turned on him.

5. The appearance and work of the men of the First Division was splendid; soldierly, disciplined, workmanlike—the finest body of soldiers we ever had—a tribute to our policy of thorough training and our regular officers. The men certainly do not want to fight under the French; and eventually their morale may be affected by integration. What way have you of keeping in touch with the morale of the men aside from the usual channels and their appearance at drill or review? Upon their spirit—upon their determination to kill and the readiness to risk death in order to kill—everything depends. I think their psychology should be studied as thoroughly as the German Staff studies that of its men, and platoon and company commanders, aside from tactical training, should burn into the men's souls the ardor that dies rather than surrenders and the sang-froid that fights shrewdly and savagely to kill for a cause that should arouse a holy fire in any man with a drop of red blood in his arteries. We stand or fall by the way the manhood of America fights.

6. The march up was an excellent drill for more rapid movements in emergency; the fighting in semi-open warfare from individual shelter pits and shell craters and the endurance of increased artillery fire an excellent preparation for more active work. This division should soon have an actual training that will fit it for any action.

7. The best officers are not the most brilliant, but the calm, well balanced, enduring type, who maintain self-control after being up all night. We are a nervous high-strung people. This is a war of nerve-endurance. We must strive for "guts" and "bottom."

8. The relations between our division staff and the French seem to run smoothly.

9. Our men, as they get no wine, should have all possible vidaments, sweets and fats.

10. In the Seicheprey affair we depended upon the French communiques, while the German communiques, I believe, continue to be published in the States. There may be other Seicheprey affairs which will have a bad cumulative effect on psychology at home. Is it permanently inadvisable to leave the forming of our public opinion to French communiques? While issuing no regular communiques, we might give our public a leading with occasional semi-official statement from Headquarters, well-balanced and well-conceived. All leading might look toward developing the war

spirit at home, confidence in this command, our readiness to go the limit in this crisis and the recovery of our army when the occasion warrants.

11. It was noticeable that some of our reserve officers did not look after their men in the approved fashion of regular officers—which does not mean that they are not deserving of the highest praise.

12. It seems evident that the scattered artillery fire of the Germans in the First Division Sector indicated the identification of batteries, which is a reminder, particularly in such a sector, of the care in "digging" and screening requisite against surprise. Training may well be more and more insistent in this respect.

13. The difficult and complicated task of taking over from the French division in a sector of this type was being most successfully accomplished.

Notes of Observation with the 26th Division.
—F. Palmer.

1. There is no French officer at General Edward's mess. The liaison officer comes only to Staff meetings. Sentiment from the Staff down through young lieutenants and the privates is unanimously against French tutelage and restive under it.

2. This division will not be beaten before going into the fight by thinking they do not know how to fight. Everybody wants to get into the big battle. There is more variation in efficiency of officers than with the First, but possibly more fighting spirit than the First, which is more professional. A considerable period of rest and training and tightening of the organization under the new Chief of Staff with the impulse of Edward's personality, ought to put the whole division on it toes for an offensive to avenge Seicheprey. General Edwards, whom we all know, seems in prime physical condition, gets about a great deal and undoubtedly puts spirit into the men by his personality.

3. The Division engineers are working indefatigably on the new defense lines.

4. In view of the fact that the present object is to make our divisions as ready in efficiency and morale as possible for the big battle, the advisability of returning all casualties to their own division as an incentive to spirit of corps, should receive serious consideration. Perhaps we cannot make an ideal replacement system until we have our army united and trained. American human nature must be considered. The men like to be with their own comrades in the fight.

5. If you want to see the best presentation I have seen of the loss of efficiency in infiltrating our army into the French you should read Colonel Shelton's presentation of the subject to General Edwards and forwarded to Corps Headquarters.

6. I have read through every report down to that of platoons about Seicheprey. It would be almost worth your while to read them. They are a wonderful exemplification of our character and system under a strain. It was a platoon commanders' and machine Gunners' fight as all such fights are. The reports of two or three platoon commanders were more soldierly than those of some higher officers. A dozen young lieutenants may go to a test like this on even terms so far as records go. The sudden burst of hell of the barrage at three in the morning, tumbling trenches, cries of the wounded and uncertainty are the real examination of fighting worth. Certain youngsters kept their heads and held their ground and were calmly resourceful and mas-

terly in handling their men. I enclose two reports that might interest you as illustrating what second lieutenants can do. God gave these youngsters "guts" and the "gift". They deserve a recognition different from that of the Distinguished Service Cross for a runner who goes on with his message after being wounded. Upon their recognition and development in a new army depends line fighting efficiency in a war of "strong points" held, or established in an advance to be held; in seizing the advantage of ground and holding it with a soldier's cunning and strength for emergencies.

7. The German system of making machine gunners a corps d'elite seems right. It is the machine gun which is most deadly concentration for success or failure in line fighting. Aviators have perhaps been over honored. Tens of thousands of potentially good aviators vie for the glorious chance of being an Ace, while a good machine gunner sticking alone in face of a charge, breaking it by his coolness, while under shell fire in the mud and shut off from the infantry, or holding out even after the charge is past, is probably harder to develop. Systems of machine gun defense, however excellent, fail if the personnel fails. Excuses have always put the blame on the gun. They did at Seicheprey. As we honored sharpshooters in the past we might honor machine gunners today, specially choosing them and blooding them up to their task, until a machine gunner who has "held" in the midst of hell is the "Ace" of the land.

8. Our aviators are doing surprisingly well. Americans make cracking aviators. There need be no worry on this score if we have the machines.

[Enclosure 1]

Report of Lieutenant Shanahan, Co. E., 102nd Infantry

1. "Their barrage was violent. They destroyed the P C of the Company Commander and obliterated the front trenches, putting all my combat posts out of action and killing five men and wounding sixteen. With the remaining twelve I cared for the wounded and sent a runner back to the commander of B Company to notify him of the situation. I sent another runner back to notify the second platoon to close in and stand to and to guard the right flank. The wounded having been taken to shelter, I sent six wounded men with guard to Seicheprey. With the remaining eight men I had, I took a position forward of the Nantes-Beaumont trench and awaited an attack. The second platoon arrived and these I stationed at various posts with the rest of my men to begin digging out entombed men. The Fourth platoon arrived under orders of Capt. Bissell but not needed at this point and sent back to organize a position farther back. Every man who was killed or wounded was at his post of duty at the time."

[Enclosure 2]

Report of Lieut. H. E. McGlasson, 3rd Platoon, Co. D., First Battalion.

"At three o'clock the enemy's barrage stopped. The boys in it were not nervous. I was greeted by a grin by a number of them as I went up and down the trench. At four thirty the enemy's barrage became a drum-fire of the severest kind. Many direct hits were made in the trench and soon it was impossible to go back and forth. There were no shelters in the trench at all, but everyone stayed at his post until killed or wounded or the barrage let up."

LC, Pershing Papers, folder: Col. Frederick Palmer, box 153; Palmer's report on the 1st Division noted in NARA, RG 120, Office of the Commander-in-Chief, Office of the Secretary of the General Staff, entry 22, Reports of the Commander-in-Chief, GHQ War Diary, folder 35: April 28–June 12, 1918, diary entry May 6, 1918, 331-a, p. 381, box 4.

Brig. Gen. James W. McAndrew, CS, GHQ, AEF, to CS, II Corps, AEF, with the British Armies.

1. Liaison:
(a) Recent experiences of our Allies as well as of our own divisions have emphasized the special importance of a thorough functioning of all methods of liaison.
(b) The essential principles of liaison, as well as most of the necessary details, are set forth in the "Instruction on Liaison for Troops of all arms."
(c) These principles have not however been put into working effect in our divisions. Specific cases which have come to the attention of the Commander-in-Chief indicate a lack of appreciation on the part of division, brigade, regimental, battalion and company commanders of the principles and of the prime importance of liaison. Specific defects have been noted as follows:
1st. Failure to establish liaison with neighboring units.
2d. Failure to provide liaison officers exchanged between larger units with adequate means of communication.
3d. Failure to provide for possible means of communication but trusting instead to a single method which frequently fails at a critical moment.
4th. Failure to realize the importance of frequent messages in critical situations.
5th. Failure to indicate hour at which the situation reported exists.
6th. Failure to realize that effect cooperation between artillery and infantry is above all dependent upon effective liaison and prompt interchange of information between the two arms. So essential is this liaison and interchange of information that it is a rule that each arm must establish its own liaison with the other.
7th. Failure to provide for any but a paper plan of liaison coupled with a failure to realize that no better place than an actual sector can be found in which to perfect liaison instruction. When troops are in sector all methods of transmission of information should be tested daily.
(d) Advantage must be taken of all opportunities for instruction in liaison between infantry and airplanes as well as between artillery and airplanes.
(e) The records of such interception posts as have been established near our divisions show a general lack of proper maintenance of telephone lines and a lack of proper discipline of operators and others using the telephone.
2. Occupation of Front Lines and Observation:
(a) Notwithstanding the information contained in various pamphlets and manuals issued from these headquarters and the instructions given in many cases by the Commander-in-Chief in person, it appears that there is still a lack of understanding as to the principles involved in organizing or occupying a defensive position.
(b) The means available in this war enable the enemy to deliver a blow on the forward trenches which cannot be withstood however densely the most advanced ele-

ments of the trenches may be occupied. To meet this condition and to limit and localize a hostile attack the organization in depth is essential. The occupation in the defense of extreme frontline trenches (observation lines) should be light at all times but especially so at night and in dense fogs.

(c) In certain cases it appears that the cause of too dense an occupation of forward trenches is found in replacing a French unit by one of our own without considering differences in strength. When our divisions are placed in sector under the orders of a French corps commander the latter's orders are of course final as to the method of occupying the trenches. This does not, however, excuse a failure on the part of a division commander to bring to the attention of the French command differences in the strength of American and French units.

(d) In certain recent events involving our own as well as Allied troops there is some reason to believe that units larger than platoons have actually been surprised to the extent that they are engaged in practically a hand-to-hand fight before they were aware of the immediate presence of the hostile infantry. Such surprise is inexcusable. A defensive sector must be occupied in its forward elements by bodies of troops whose organization, distribution and duties are exactly analogous to those of outposts. This again requires organization in depth and it is manifestly impossible adequately to protect from surprise considerable numbers of soldiers by sentinels a few meters to the front. At night or in heavy fogs and when not prevented by intense bombardment, patrols must be constantly active.

(e) A thorough understanding on the part of all concerned must exist as to the methods to be used by patrols and sentry squads in giving the alarm. In addition to rifle fire and the use of messengers advantage must be taken of any other practicable method such as the use of bugle calls, etc.

3. The defects noted above concern fundamental principles and do not relate to new developments. The Commander-in-Chief regrets that it is necessary to call the attention of experienced officers to such glaring errors and expects that division commanders will, by their own action, as well as their supervision of subordinates, render further action unnecessary.

4. The Commander-in-Chief directs that a copy of this letter be furnished each of the division commanders of your corps and to the commandant of the corps school.

USAWW, vol. 2, pp. 381–83.

Pershing to TAG, War Department, in part in reply to TAG, War Department, to Pershing, cables A-834-R, February 27, A-1130-R, April 18, A-1132-R, April 18.

Cable P-1063-S.
    1. For Chief of Staff. 1B. With reference to paragraph 1E, your cablegram 1130. British state 14-inch gun not required now. War Office will advise when shipment is required. [Reply—May 8, A-1264-R-7; May 19, A-1282-R-1]
    3. For Chief of Ordnance. With reference to paragraph 1A, your cablegram 1132, and paragraph 1I, your cablegram 834. Plans here have been based on all troops

arriving after July 1st coming fully equipped with machine guns and automatic rifles and that reserve machine guns and rifles and spare parts would be supplied in sufficient quantity to maintain these arms. Will troops arriving after July 1st be equipped with Browning-Colt machine guns and machine rifles? Will any troops be equipped with Vickers machine guns? It is essential that no new arms be introduced for less than a complete corps and that standard machine guns and automatic rifles be issued to troops departing for France in preference to troops training in the United States. Will this be done? When will Browning machine guns and Browning machine rifles be available for replacing present 8 mm arms in service? Present status Chauchat rifle, caliber 30, as follow: Total accepted 3,350. Average production now 100 per day. Presented last 15 days 2,780, Accepted 1,543. Recommend that the first 6,000 rifles be set aside as emergency supply for Second Corps and remaining rifles not desired by you in United States be cancelled. Full information regarding machine guns, automatic rifles, rifles and pistols has been sent you by Lieutenant Henry who is familiar with manufacturing conditions of Chauchat rifle, caliber 30. [Reply—May 18, A-1341-R-1L]

NARA, RG 120, M930, Main Series, AEF to War Department, roll 3.

Pershing to TAG, War Department, in part in reply to TAG, War Department, to Pershing, cable A-1231-R, May 3.

Cable P-1064-S. Confidential.
For the Chief of Staff and Secretary of War.
    1. Reference conference of Supreme War Council at Abbeville May 2nd. Agreement between Lord Milner and myself seems to have displeased the French notwithstanding their previous approval in February of our sending 6 divisions for training with British. London agreement was principal question of discussion at Supreme War Council. French insisted upon commitment for June and July for exclusive infantry program and would not accept condition London agreement that infantry would be continued for June should situation still appear critical. British were entirely satisfied with London agreement and were willing that decision regarding June program be left until later. After rather warm discussion between French on one side and British and ourselves on the other, Mr. Lloyd George proposed to guarantee to transport 130,000 in May and 150,000 in June by British tonnage alone. Assist offered opportunity for greatly increasing arrival American troops and as arrangement for May was already made, seemed wise to accept British guarantee and extend infantry program for infantry of 6 divisions during June and my memorandum was drawn accordingly. Mr. Lloyd George later proposed that shipment of extra personnel in excess of 150,000 by British shipping for June should be infantry on condition that British should assist us in July to make up other deficiencies caused thereby, to which I agreed. This latter promise by British was not part of my memorandum but was agreed to verbally. The conference ended in good feeling and satisfaction all around and will have good effect on Allies. Also believe that question is now settled definitely.

2. Reference conference with Secretary of War regarding sending small number of troops to Italy. Had conference with Mr. Orlando and outlined proposed plan of sending not more than 1 regiment to begin with and possibly gradually increasing number during succeeding 4 or 5 months up to a division, upon the condition that the Italians furnish transportation which Mr. Orlando thinks can be done. The Italians are immensely pleased over the prospect and the proposition is cordially approved by Mr. Clemenceau and Mr. Lloyd George. Am awaiting cable from Mr. Orlando in regard to transportation before taking any further action. [See also May 9, Bliss cable 107-S, and Telegram No. 66.]

3. Had further conference at Abbeville with Mr. Clemenceau, Mr. Lloyd George and Mr. Orlando on subject of pooling supplies, and a military man business experience has been selected by each government to meet on May 6th to outline plans. The suggestion seems to appeal to all concerned. Believe that considerable can be accomplished although it may not be possible to extend it as far as would be desirable. Believe the plan offers no serious obstacles. It simply means that each Army will share surplus supplies with others, and that general stocks will be regulated not by each Army for itself but by this executive committee for all. Will keep you advised as matter progresses. [For details on Pershing's plans see May 8, Dawes to Jeanneney.]

NARA, RG 120, M930, Confidential Series, AEF to War Department, roll 7.

Editor's Note—On May 8, Baker sent a copy of Pershing's cable to President Wilson:

> I enclose a dispatch which has just come from General Pershing, and which is the last chapter of the conference and agreement about the shipment of troops.
>
> The second paragraph of General Pershing's dispatch I am sure will surprise you, as General Pershing was not in favor of sending troops to Italy when I talked to him about the matter. Apparently, however, the concurrence of Mr. Clemenceau and Mr. Lloyd George, with Mr. Orlando's representations, overcame his feeling in the matter. My own disposition in the situation is to acquiesce in whatever arrangements they feel necessary to make there, because the maintenance of Italian morale is of course of the very greatest importance, and we on this side are never quite in possession of all the information they have over there as to either the need for stimulation of morale or what what [*sic*] will suffice to do the stimulating. In the meantime, I sent General Pershing a cablegram a day or two ago, suggesting the brigading of some of our troops with British and French divisions in Italy as a possible answer to the whole question [see May 5, cable A-1248-R.]. I have not had any reply from him on that subject, and do not know whether the dispatch I am enclosing was sent before or after he received my cablegram. (Link (ed.), *The Papers of Woodrow Wilson*, vol. 47: *March 13–May 12, 1918*, pp. 566–68.)

TAG, War Department, to Pershing, in part in reply to Pershing to TAG, War Department, cable P-964-S, April 19, in addition to TAG, War Department, to Pershing, cable A-1224-R, May 2.

Cable A-1249-R. Confidential.
 1. Secretary of War has authorized shipment on Italian tonnage of 30 sections of the Army Ambulance Service to operate with Italian Army on the same basis as the sections now with French Army. These sections, include Quartermaster personnel attached, 75 officers, 1,207 men, will sail about end of May. Colonel E. E. Persons, M.C., will command and will precede sections to report to you for instructions as to operations, supplies and maintenance.
 2. Replying paragraph 4, your 964. First Capronis produced here will not be available at the front before beginning 1919. Number of these planes which will be available dependent upon production Liberty engines. Situation on Liberty engines fully set forth in our 1224, which also requests your recommendation for program for first 6 months 1919.
March.

NARA, RG 120, M930, Confidential Series, War Department to AEF, roll 12.

TAG, War Department, to Pershing, in reply to Pershing to TAG, War Department, cable P-818-S, March 29.

Cable A-1255-R. Confidential.
 With reference to paragraph 3A, your 818. The rules for handling publicity prescribed therein by the Secretary of War have been rescinded by him after further consideration. It is his desire to give out from the War Department whatever the condition of the public mind of America makes desirable and in order that he may be informed of all the facts of substantial value occurring in the American Expeditionary Forces you are directed to send a communique daily which will contain such matter. In this connection it has been noted, that the information heretofore received has been of less interest than similar information received by the Navy Department from Admiral Sims, and he desires you to make your report as full as may be necessary to give matter of interest to him. Copies of the Stars and Stripes received here indicate that you allow to be published in France articles describing the heroism of officers and men of the American Expeditionary Forces which in his opinion would be of distinct value in keeping up the interest of people at home in our army abroad, and there is no objection to having such facts with names of officers and men who have been mentioned for heroism contained in the daily communique. March.
[Reply—May 16, P-1132-S]

NARA, RG 120, M930, Confidential Series, War Department to AEF, roll 18.

Editor's Note—This cable from the War Department changed the manner in which the GHQ, AEF, reported on its activities as well as on military operations and developments in Europe to the Chief of Staff, War Department, and for public release. For background, see March 23, *Editor's Note* following A-972-R. These previous series of summaries were replaced as per A-1255-R above and in accordance with P-1132-S, May 16, with a new, numbered release entitled "American Official Communique." This update was sent at least daily from May 16 to December 13, 1918, and included more detailed information, much of it on AEF operations and classified as confidential. A total of 227 communiques were sent over these months. These frequently detailed operational accounts also explain to some extent why Pershing sent relative few personal operational updates to the Chief of Staff and Secretary of War during these months.

May 7

Pershing's Personal Diary

Worked in office all day. Saw Mr. [Martin] Egan, Mr. Pomeroy Burton, Lieutenant Colonel Godson, Military Attaché at Berne, Major [Paul H.] Clark [American Military Mission to French GHQ (Pétain)] and General Ragueneau. Talked with General Bethel and Bishop Brent, whom I am sending to London to work with Colonel Ireland on Board considering the venereal question as it concerns our troops in England. Major Quekemeyer reported as Aide. Received a letter from Sir Douglas Haig, written in his own hand, stating that he finds he would need some artillerymen and that if I could have brought over 10,000 of them, he could use them, to good advantage [See May 5]. This is an interesting commentary on all that has preceded on this subject.

LC, Pershing Papers, Diary, May 7, 1917–September 1, 1918, box 4.

Ragueneau, Chief, French Military Mission with the American Army, Chaumont, to Pétain, CINC, Armies of the North and Northeast.

No. 1089/C. A.

I have the honor of giving you a report of the interview that I had this morning with General Pershing.

1. General Pershing, who, at the beginning of the conference seemed a little ill at ease, asked me, right away, without waiting for the questions which I came to discuss with him, when he could hope to see favorable action on his request for the creation of an American sector. It seems to him that, by reason of the situation on the front in Lorraine and the Woevre, which is now very quiet, the time has arrived. He explained to me that the number of American divisions shipped to France is going to increase rapidly and that it is not possible to consider the continued dispersion of these divisions among the French armies.

His preference for the creation of this American sector inclines toward the region north of Toul, a part of which is already held by an American division. It would be desirable, furthermore, in the event that this sector were entrusted to him, to develop the installations already begun insofar as regards the supply depots and the telegraph lines.

I called his attention to the fact that there are no fresh divisions to put in sector in this region now; that on the contrary, the 26th and 42d Divs. will soon be relieved in order to enter the battle and that there is no other division sufficiently trained to take a sector.

The general replied that the 26th Div. can be relieved by the 1st Div. when the latter is tired and withdraws from combat. Furthermore, he would like for the divisions which have just debarked, namely: The 3d and 5th, to have their regiments assigned for their training and tour in sector to French divisions that hold the front in this region, instead of being scattered among the various French armies.

He said that by doing so he saw the advantage that these troops would become familiar with the sector that they will have to take over later on.

I called his attention to the fact that this familiarity with the sector is important to the staffs above all and that, in this connection, it would be highly desirable for the staff of the I Army Corps of the army to come and establish itself at Toul with the staff of the French XXXII Army Corps, instead of remaining at Neufchâteau where it has no unit at its disposal to furnish it information.

The general replied that this step would only be desirable in the event that the commander of the I Corps should actually assume, within the not too distant future, the command of the sector in that region and that, consequently, this question ought first to be decided in a general sort of way.

2. During the conversation of this same subject the general asked me why the regiments of the 32d Div., instead of being sent into the Haute-Alsace sector for their training, could not be with the divisions which occupy the Woevre.

I called his attention to the fact that all the measures for the reception of these regiments in the sector of Haute-Alsace have already been taken, where they are being counted upon to take part in holding the line and where, consequently, the front of the French divisions has been considerably extended. In the assignment of these regiments, allowance, of course, was made for the aid which they were to bring to French elements for the relief of fresh divisions and for sending these latter into battle. At this time the dispositions which have been decided upon for the employment of the 32d Div. cannot be changed.

The general seemed to me to be convinced by my reasoning and did not urge the matter.

Then I reminded him that a week ago he had promised to put these regiments at the disposal of the French command immediately and that I have the mission of insisting that this operation take place without delay.

The general then told me that the inspectors that he had sent to the 32d Div. brought back an unfavorable impression of it and that this division was to remain in its present zone a few more days. Nevertheless, he promised me an answer to this question which I have already put up to him in writing and that he would set the date.

3. I informed the general of plans for the relief of the American 2d Inf. Div. This division will be relieved between the 10th and 15th of May, and will be regrouped in the zone of Combles and Vanault-les-Dames. Immediately afterward, between May 16 and 20, it will be moved to the Reserve Group of Armies in such a way as to clear the regroupment zone on the last date mentioned.

The general raised no objections; he asked about the zone where it is planned to unload the division and the army to which this division will be attached.

He expressed the desire that it might be possible to send it to the army of General Debeney. I told him that the unloading zone had not yet been determined, but that you intended to attach this division initially to the reserve army* of General Micheler, in order to allow it to undergo training like the 1st before going into battle.

The general, as is the custom, asked me for any information that I could give him about the general situation.

From my conversation as a whole I gained the impression that he viewed the present situation with a certain optimism and the modifications in his program that he had consented to under pressure of circumstances six weeks ago no longer seem to him justified to the same extent. I endeavored to combat any undue optimism on his part (or that of his staff) by repeating that the Germans will do everything within their power to obtain a decision this year and that the question of numerical strength continues to be the primary one for us in the operations of the campaign of 1918.

Incidentally, I called the attention of the general to the fact that our front between the Oise and Switzerland is now occupied by only 46 divisions in the face of 55 German divisions superior in strength to ours.

This simple comparison justifies the necessity for American troops to make every effort to aid our divisions in holding quiet fronts.

5. I asked the general if he had any new information to give me on the program of shipments of troops from the United States to France. I was forced to approach this subject cautiously, not having exact knowledge of the results of the Abbeville conference. So I took a position looking at the matter especially from the point of view of the urgent preparations to be made for the installation of these troops in French territory.

The general told me that a study is now in progress at his headquarters and that he will inform me as to its results as soon as it is finished.

The only thing that he could definitely see arrive in May is the infantry of 6 divisions, but he stated that this infantry would be followed immediately by the artillery and other troops and services necessary to complete these divisions.

To sum up, I took away from this interview the general impression that the general is still striving to realize his original plan of forming independent and autonomous

---

*French Fifth Army in reserve in Picardy, in the rear of the French Reserve Group of Armies.

American units and that he has apparently decided to resist more and more any fusion whatsoever of his elements with French or British units.

From information gathered from other sources it is concluded that it would be quite in order to begin a fresh discussion of the arrangements made with the British, in the event that the latter should not carry out to the letter all provisions of past agreements.

[Reply—Anthoine to CS, GAE, and French Military Mission with the American Army, Chaumont, May 9]

Les Armées françaises dans la Grande Guerre, Tome 6, vol. 2, *Annexes,* vol. 1: *Annexe* No. 129, pp. 266–69; *USAWW,* vol. 2, pp. 387–89.

Pershing to Lord Milner, Secretary of State for War, London.

I am glad respond to your call for the conference aimed at joint action by British and American authorities to handle the venereal situation as it affects the Allied troops in England and in France, and to our closer cooperation in measures that it may be deemed wise to take in the future. I am sending to represent the American Expeditionary Forces, General Walter A. Bethel, Judge Advocate of the Forces, Colonel Ireland, my Chief Medical Officer, and Bishop Brent, Senior G.H.Q. Chaplain, who are able to speak with authority on the general situation in America and France as regards the stand and measures our Government has taken to combat the venereal menace.

The Allied military authorities have recognized the necessity of unity of purpose and coordination of effort in this fight in France. Three conferences on this matter have already been held between members of our medical corps and the French authorities with a very helpful outlook for concerned measures. The conference which you have called holds out the same promise as regards cooperation of military and civil authorities in England, without which nothing we can say or do will help.

I have heard also with great satisfaction of the recent decision of the British War Office that the licensed houses of prostitution are to be put out of bounds in the B. E. F. Many of us who have experimented with licensed prostitution or kindred measures, hoping thereby to minimize the physical evils, have been forced to the conclusion that they are really ineffective. Abraham Flexner has argued the case so convincingly that on the scientific side it seems to me there is no escape from the conclusion that what he terms 'abolition' as distinguished from 'regulation' is the only effective mode of combat this age-long evil.

I have the greatest hope that the results of the conference which you have called will be far-reaching in their effect. This menace to the young manhood in the army forces and to the health and future well-being of our peoples cannot be met by the efforts of each Government working apart from the others. It is plain that every day it affects more and more all of the Allied nations now fighting on the Western Front in France. The question long since was an international one, and it is only by an internationalization of our aims and efforts that we can obtain the unity and coordination which will enable us to solve the problem. The gravest responsibility rests on those to whom the parents of our soldiers have entrusted their sons for the battle, and we fail if we neglect any effort to safeguard them in every way.

We have the common ground of humanity, we have the well-considered conclusions of the best scientific minds on our side, and from the fact that, in this war of nations-in-arms the soldier is merely a citizen on war service, we have all the elements which will force cooperation between military and civil authorities. The army can do little unless the citizen at home plays his part in the big scheme. With our nations cooperating hand-in-hand, both in France and at home, we have the brightest prospects of winning the victory.

Pershing, *My Experiences in the World War*, vol. 2, pp. 43–44; copy in NARA, RG 120, Office of the Commander-in-Chief, Office of the Secretary of the General Staff, entry 22, Reports of the Commander-in-Chief, GHQ War Diary, folder 35: April 28–June 12, 1918, diary entry May 11, 1918, 336-a, pp. 332–33, box 4.

Col. Fox Conner, ACS, G-3, GHQ, AEF.

Memorandum for Chief of Staff:

1. After carefully reading the two cables sent by the Commander-in-Chief with reference to the Abbeville agreement [see May 3, P-1042-S, May 6, P-1064-S], I am of the opinion:

(a) That the six divisions referred to as coming in the month of May in this agreement concern a total of six divisions for service with the British.

(b) That the Abbeville agreement in referring to priority for infantry and machine-gun units was not intended to abrogate the London agreement whereby engineer and signal corps units would be included with the divisional infantry and machine-gun units.

(2) On (a) above, the Commander-in-Chief expressed an opposite opinion from that given by me in the verbal conference this morning. As noted above, I am, however, convinced, after a careful reading of the cables, that the British expect six divisions only in May, and do not expect six divisions in addition to units which may have sailed prior to May 1. The further cable which it is necessary to send is dependent upon a correct interpretation of the two points mentioned in 1 above. Before finally drawing the cable I request that I be given definite instructions as to the interpretation to be placed on these questions.

[Penciled note appearing at head of document:] *"C-in-C states through C. of S. that there was verbal understanding that 6 A units must be brought in May."*

USAWW, vol. 2. pp. 383–84.

Secretary Baker to Bliss, Chief, American Section, and Permanent Military Representative, SWC, Versailles.

You perhaps know that Lord Reading and I worked out an arrangement for the preferential shipping of infantry and machine gun units, which was finally reduced to a memorandum setting forth fully the intentions of this Government. Lord Reading sent a copy of that memorandum to Lord Milner and I sent one of General Pershing. My copy, however, did not reach General Pershing until after he had had a conference with Lord Milner at which an entirely different arrangement had been agreed upon. Lord Reading tells me that Lord Milner entered into this kind of arrangement because in the memorandum drawn up by Lord Reading and me the question of the allocation of troops for training with the British was finally made to rest in General Pershing's discretion and Lord Milner, feeling that the whole question would ultimately be decided by General Pershing, determined that it was best to work it out in advance and secure General Pershing's constant cooperation by beginning well with him. Just what the effect of the final conference of the Supreme War Council on this subject is going to be, I don't know. We have already made arrangements for dispatching infantry and machine gun units to the ports of embarkation as substantially to limit our transportation of troops during May to units of that kind. Undoubtedly, under the arrangements finally made the United States is free, so far as our engagements to the French and British are concerned, to ship in our own tonnage artillery and service of supply troops, and the preference for infantry and machine gun units seems largely to apply to troops shipped in British bottoms. The more I look into the matter the less important this question seems to me, since the British are obviously finding a very large increase of troops transport tonnage and it now looks as though the May, June, and July shipments would be so large as to take over practically all of the infantry and machine gun personnel we have sufficiently trained and still room for substantial numbers of others. Indeed, if the present prospect with regard to troop transports holds out, the increase of our Army in Europe by the end of July will be so great as to exceed all expectations entertained by any of us a month ago.

There is just a little disposition on the part of both British and French to feel that they are in a position to demand, or at least to insist, upon the fulfillment of expectations on their part as against a right on the part of the United States to pursue its own policy. For this reason I am very glad that we have from the first insisted upon leaving these questions to the discretion of General Pershing, and in all my conferences with Lord Reading I have insisted that as General Pershing is the American Commander-in-Chief we must continue to be guided by his judgment of the military exigencies in France in the matter of transportation of troops there. This, of course, is only just to General Pershing, upon whom the responsibility for our military operations rests, and it obviates the possibility of trying to settle the same questions in two places at the same time, with discordant settlements as a result.

LC, Bliss Papers, folder: General Correspondence—Newton Diehl Baker to Bliss, March 1918–March 1920, box 250.

Pershing to TAG, War Department, in part in reply to TAG, War Department, to Pershing, cable A-1118-R, April 17.

Cable P-1066-S.
2. For Felton. With reference to paragraph 1E, your cablegram 1118. In April priority statement, paragraph 1H, our cablegram 787, we asked for approximately 375 refrigerator cars. As stated in paragraph 4, our cablegram 884, these cars are urgently needed and we asked for the delivery of 150 early in April. As yet the 100 floated have not been received. Cannot something be done to hurry those cars? If possible advise name of boat and number of cars aboard. [Reply—May 18, A-1342-R-1A]

NARA, RG 120, M930, AEF to War Department, roll 4.

TAG, War Department, to Pershing, in reply to Pershing to TAG, War Department, cable P-990-S, April 24.

Cable A-1259-R. Confidential.
1. With reference to paragraph 1, your 990. Troops sent you have been best available. Divisions became depleted during the winter on account large number being taken for Staff Corps and other unavoidable causes, and lack of equipment for replacements. Conditions will begin improve early July so that eventually only those divisions with at least 6 months training will be sent. Question of breaking up divisions for trained men has been fully considered, as was the one of organizing 7th Division, and it was decided that depot brigades and replacement camps are better solution. Breaking up divisions now would not help situation.
1A. With reference to paragraph 2, your 990. Your information that target practice for troops has not been had above 300 yards incorrect. Course provides instruction to include 600 yards as well as combat firing and practical application of principle of fire control and discipline. School of Musketry established Camp Perry, Ohio, for instruction of officers and noncommissioned officers as instructors in divisions.
1B. With reference to paragraph 3, your 990. 643,198 white and 73,326 colored men, total 716,524 have been drafted since January 1st, including May draft. Draft will be continued monthly to maximum capacity. Impracticable to draft million and half at one time. Draft already called will fill all divisions now organized and all other troops for second and third phases. Question of organizing new divisions under consideration. We now have troops of all classes under training in replacement camps.
1C. Paragraph 4, your 990, noted.
March.

NARA, RG 120, M930, Confidential Series, War Department to AEF, roll 18.

TAG, War Department, to Pershing, in part in reply to Pershing to TAG, War Department, cable P-1008-S, April 27.

Cable A-1260-R.

    1. Attention Air Service. 1C. Reference your Handley Page agreement with British Air Minister, construction troops will be approximately 2 months late. Sets of Handley Page parts will be approximately 4 months late. Shall we forward training depot station and bombardment squadrons according to your agreement; this can be done as available personnel at embarkation ports, or shall we set back their schedule conforming to shipment of materiel in same relation to original agreement. Reference paragraph 8B, your 1008. It is our understanding that aircraft acceptance park personnel can be utilized in spite of delay American Handley Page production, Shall we ship according to schedule? [Reply—Vol. 5, June 1, P-1226-S-6]

NARA, RG 120, M930, Main Series, War Department to AEF, roll 12.

TAG, War Department, to Pershing, in part in reply to Pershing to TAG, War Department, cable P-1009-S, April 27.

Cable A-1261-R.

    2. With reference to your 1009. Shipping Control Committee requested to study means of meeting cross-Channel coal situation. Every endeavor will be made to expedite arrival of lake steamers and place in your service sufficient vessels most suitable for this trade, and thus avoid use of any vessels capable of trans-Atlantic service. Goethals.

NARA, RG 120, M930, Main Series, War Department to AEF, roll 12.

May 8

Pershing's Personal Diary

    Worked in office all day. Saw General Foulois, Colonel Nolan, Colonel Fiske, General Russel and Major [Frederick] Palmer. Also saw Mr. Eyre of the New York World.

LC, Pershing Papers, Diary, May 7, 1917–September 1, 1918, box 4.

Foch, CINC, Allied Armies, Chantilly, to Pershing.

No. 674.

During the course of our interview of April 25, you made it a point to stress your desire that the American 26th, 42nd, and then the 2nd Divisions take part in the battle which we are fighting and you, yourself, indicated to me the order in which these divisions were to be engaged.

I was as deeply touched by this new proof of your energetic and prompt cooperation as I had been by your generous and spontaneous offer of March 28. I might add that the praises which have been received from the Commanding General of the French First Army concerning the American 1st Division, have caused me to hope earnestly for the entry into the line of the American 26th, 42nd and 2nd Divisions.

Since it is necessary that I prepare a dependable estimate of forces on which I can count, I would, therefore, be very grateful to you if you would let me know on what date, in your opinion, each of these three large units will be ready to be moved toward the battle front, and I would be particularly happy if that date were not too distant.

On the other hand, the struggle against the enemy is attaining increasing magnitude. In order to sustain it vigorously and impose our will upon the foe, it is becoming more and more necessary that the French divisions, which are employed from the Oise to the Swiss border, be successively engaged in the battle.

They will not be free to do so unless they can be relieved progressively from quiet sectors by divisions which have already been engaged. But to these latter—tired and worn out—the infantry of the American 32nd, 3rd and 5th Divisions could furnish precious and effective aid.

By means of the addition of American regiments, the French command could extend the front in certain sectors, could relieve in others the burden of occupation which devolves upon our troops.

The infantry of the American 32nd, 3rd, and 5th Divisions and the divisional and brigade staffs would thus have an opportunity to become seasoned rapidly, in close contact with our staffs. The results of this method will certainly be worthwhile on the day when the American 32nd, 3rd, and 5th Divisions, strengthened by the experience thus acquired, are reassembled into organized large units.

It seems to me, if your estimates of April 25 have remained the same, that I should be able to count upon the regiments of the American 32nd Division within a rather short time. Along the same lines I would very much like to know when the regiments of the American 3rd and 5th Divisions will, likewise, appear to you capable of taking over in a quiet sector.

Finally, it certainly cannot have escaped your attention that our aviation squadrons, particularly our attack squadrons, have been obliged to be employed without respite since March 21.

Their very heavy task remains onerous and among all the decisive aids which the American army desires to bring us, that of the aviation permits us to entertain the greatest hopes. The French command is unanimously pleased to acknowledge the skill and fearlessness of the great numbers of pilots in your training camps, all of whom are ready to follow the glorious traditions of the *Lafayette Escadrille.*

If you could detach 4 or 5 pilots per squadron they could complete their training in it to good advantage, they would be of immediate service to us and I would deem it an opportunity for the American army to demonstrate its pioneer spirit once again, in the sky as well as on land.

I have the honor to request you to please let me know your replies to these various questions.
[Reply—May 10, Pershing to Foch]

USAWW, vol. 3, pp. 298–99; see also *Les armées françaises dans la Grande guerre, Tome 6,* vol. 2, *Annexes,* vol. 1: *Annexe* No. 130, pp. 269–70.

Pétain, CINC, Armies of the North and Northeast.

No. 9422.
Confidential Instructions for the Usage of Liaison Officers and Officers Acting as Instructors with the American Expeditionary Forces.

At the moment when the military assistance of our American Allies assumes an importance which will make of it one of the decisive factors in the happy issue of the war, the General, Commander-in-Chief of the French armies, believes it proper to recall to officers of every grade who are employed in connection with the American army certain principles which should guide their action in the accomplishment of the important task which is confided to them.

I. French Officers Should Take into Consideration the Importance of the Military Effort Made by the United States:

In April of 1917, at the moment of their entrance into the war, the United States did not have, properly speaking, an army.

Within a year they have adopted universal and obligatory military service, raised, armed, equipped and sent to France several hundred thousand men, and all of this is only the beginning. They have thus accomplished a task of military organization without precedent in history. They have accomplished and are now accomplishing within the interior of France various works of enormous importance (improvements of the ports of St-Nazaire and Bordeaux, storehouses and ice plants at Gièvres, etc.), which will remain after the war and will enable us to undertake the economic struggle under exceptionally favorable conditions as to equipment.

The American Red Cross is placing at our disposition considerable sums, to relieve people who have met with all kinds of misfortunes.

The General, Commander-in-Chief, desires that during their conversations with American officers the French officers prove to the American that the French fully appreciate the importance of the effort furnished by America and the grandeur of the service rendered to France.

II. In Their Relations with American Officers the French Officers Must Always use the Greatest Tact: The Americans fully recognize the value of our military experience: for our part, we must not forget that America is a great nation, that the Americans have a national self-respect developed and justified by the breadth of vision which they bring to bear upon all the questions which they consider. French officers should treat the officers of their grade, or of a subordinate grade, as comrades who have arrived more recently than they upon the front, and should treat them as little as possible as a master does a scholar. As to officers who are of a higher grade than the French officers, the French should wait to give advice until such advice is requested.

Finally, it is necessary, above all, to avoid giving advice, or to make criticisms in public.

III. French Officers Should Endeavor To Be Personal Friends with American Officers.

Between people who are living constantly side by side, official relations are necessarily very much influenced by personal relations.

The French officers should, therefore, always endeavor to live with their American comrades under the best terms of friendship, and to gain their confidence by demonstrating to them that the advice which they give, and the criticisms which they make, have no other object than the general interest. Such relations are easily realized for the American is by nature cordial and generous.

It is important to ensure in the future, as has been the case in the past, close collaboration between the two Allied armies, a collaboration which constitutes the most certain guarantee of the final success of our common efforts.

Editor's Note—Pershing noted the following on a copy of Pétain's memorandum that was entered in the GHQ AEF War Diary:

> This is truly a letter that signifies true cooperation in a spirit of trust and confidence. Preserve it.
>
> J. J. P.
> May 15, 1918

Les armées françaises dans la Grande guerre, Tome 6, vol. 2, *Annexes,* vol. 1: *Annexe* No. 132, pp. 271–72; *USAWW*, vol. 3, pp. 296–97; NARA, RG 120, Office of the Commander-in-Chief, Office of the Secretary of the General Staff, entry 22, Reports of the Commander-in-Chief, GHQ War Diary, folder 35: April 28–June 12, 1918, diary entry May 26, 1918, 351-j, pp. 362–63, box 4; Pershing, *My Experiences in the World War,* vol. 2, pp. 68–69.

Sims, Commander, U.S. Naval Forces Operating in European Waters, London, to Pershing, in reply to Pershing to Sims, April 23.

This is to inform you that I have finally found an officer that I think will be a good man to give you a lift with nautical matters on your staff.

He is Commander Roger Williams who has been out here a considerable time in successful command of a destroyer doing escort duty.

I will first order him on to London and see that he is thoroughly conversant with all of the methods of handling convoys and supply ships, and then send him over to you.

I am doing this without consulting the Navy Department, and asking them to send a man out to take his place.

LC, Sims Papers, Special Correspondence: John J. Pershing, box 77.

Dawes, GPA, SOS, AEF, Paris, to M. Jeanneney, President, French Council of Ministers, and President, Inter-Ally Conference (called to consider Pershing's proposition and plan for consolidation of Allied Services of Supply).

Subject: Relative to the three questions the conference proposed at its first meeting [held May 6] and in accordance with your suggestion that comments be filed thereon, I submit the following:

General Pershing's plan, in so far as it involves the coordination of military supply, transportation, and construction now located in the immediate Allied rear, is susceptible of adoption by the military commands as distinguished from the civil as a strictly military measure of coordination involving activities now wholly under military control, but as yet not coordinated between the three armies. To this extent the plan may be considered as presented by the Commander-in-Chief, A.E.F., as a measure of military action affecting the immediate rear, and therefore as only necessary in this particular phase to be discussed in its relation to the several existing military as distinguished from civil authorities.

The plan in its more general application, involving the coordination of activities now under civil control, must be first approved by the Government of the United States as well as by England and France. But since the first conference on this subject of prime importance has developed some hesitation as to their authority on the part of members of the conference, I deem it my duty as General Pershing's representative at this conference to place on file the following statement as applying simply to the coordination of the immediate activities of the Allied rear now possible under his plan if approved by the existing military authorities alone.

Before my submission to the conference of General Pershing's plan looking to the military unification of the services of the Allied rear to match the military unification at the front, he had obtained the verbal acceptance of the principle by M. Clemenceau and Mr. Lloyd George. The duty of this conference, therefore, was to devise a plan, not to suggest obstacles to its consummation—to which most of its time was devoted at the first meeting. The letter of General Pershing, addressed to myself and submitted to the conference [see May 5, Pershing to Dawes], considered together with the detailed statement of his plan, indicated that his desire is such to secure military unification of the Services of Supply of the Allied rear, that while he would prefer final authority to be located in one man he would acquiesce in an agreement by which the military authority of the proposed committee could be set in motion only by the unanimous consent of its three members. This suggestion should of itself sweep away the objections raised at this conference to this procedure. General Pershing's contention is that if British and American lives can be trusted to French control so can British and American material. This military central control of Supply Service is as essential to maximum effectiveness of effort against the enemy as unified military control of the front. The recent reverses during the first days of the last offensive were sufficient to sweep away the arguments against Allied military unification suggested by national pride and prestige for the last four years. With the difficult months ahead of us, and the urgency of unity in action and mutual cooperation, minor considerations should not now be raised against a plan involving a principle so indisputably correct that it is immediately adopted upon presentation by those first in authority and committed to us to work out and not to combat.

Given a military control committee of three, one each representing the British, French, and American armies, with authority through military channels to collect full information and then with power to put into effect by military order a unanimous decision improving the coordination of the rear, what harm would result? If it did nothing else this military committee would be a clearing-house of information, thus facilitating the now clumsy efforts, born of overwhelming necessity, to coordinate the activities of the Allied rear. Each Government retaining its control over its member could, through his veto power, save from any possible alteration its entire system of intermingled civil and military control so jealously exploited in the discussions of this conference. So vast are the possible accomplishments of good from the military unification of the Allied Services of Supply, under one man or military committee, extending throughout England, France, Italy, and the United States, properly to be regarded as the "rear" in this effort, that we are instinctively prone to dwell constantly on the impossibility of obtaining it, overlooking the possibilities of obtaining most important advantages in the immediate rear of the armies without necessarily cutting any governmental system of internal red tape and using only existing military authority.

As charged by General Pershing with the duty of making recommendations to him looking toward the coordination with our allies of the army activities of the American rear, if this military committee is formed, and even if contrary to his advice its military authority could not be set in motion except by unanimous consent, I would ask and expect from it unanimous action resulting in the transmission of the necessary orders as follows:

(1) Ordering information from the departments concerned of the three armies as to the status of the present warehouse capacity of the three armies in France, and if it is found sufficient to provide for the present and future requirements of the Allied armies considered as one, an order to the American army not to waste tonnage, material, work, and men in building new warehouses where sufficient empty warehouse space exists.

(2) Ordering information from the concerned departments of the three armies as to the total present unloading capacity of the docks of France (including transportation from the docks to the front of the unified Allied army) and the amount of material now being transported to the front from these docks so that it may be intelligently determined whether the American army is building unnecessary docks and thus diverting material, work, and men from more important service.

(3) Information ordered from the three concerned departments of the total amount of civilian and militarized labor now at the disposal of the three armies, so that if it were ascertained that the present supply, if used in proper coordination, is sufficient, orders be issued for its proper use and for the A.E.F. to cease the continued importation of civilian labor from adjoining countries, thus putting a further tax upon the local resources of France.

(4) Ordering information from the concerned departments of the three armies as to the present status of motor transports in France, and, upon the development of the situation, the issuance of immediate orders preventing any one army from consuming shipping space by bringing camions to France when sufficient are available or can be manufactured here for the unified army at the front.

(5) Information with appropriate orders as to whether central distributing depots for the joint use of the three armies do not now exist to that extent which will render possible an intelligent reduction of American construction projects in this connection.

(6) Information with appropriate orders as to the collective situation of freight cars and locomotives, the use to which they are being put at present, whether economical to that effect as would render it impossible for us to cut down requisitions of this nature from America.

(7) Obtaining information regarding normal supplies common to the three armies with a view to their equitable distribution as needed, in order to prevent unnecessary use of tonnage, to accumulate unusual quantities during the present crisis in shipping.

(8) And many more subjects of importance – the above being only a few important illustrations.

That the members of this conference, instead of devoting themselves to a discussion of the methods necessary to carry out a plan accepted in principle by the Prime Ministers of England and France and proposed by the Commander-in-Chief, A.E.F., confined themselves chiefly to the suggestion of the obvious difficulties in the way of a complete international application of the idea, resulted in this first conference in a comparative lack of discussion of certain practicable steps of greatest importance related to the immediate rear of the armies. General Pershing has made this proposition in no spirit of distrust. It must be realized, however, that if as suggested at this conference the partial pooling of supplies and resources now going on under the pressure of necessity is continued through subordinate or separate controls as distinguished from a military central control, an insuperable obstacle is raised to a fair and complete solution of the problem. This insuperable obstacle to complete perception of the necessities of a common situation and the application of the necessary remedies in connection with it lies in the fidelity of the subordinate in charge of a particular supply to the unit which he supplies. The conception of such a subordinate of a common necessity is determined primarily by its effect upon the need with whose satisfaction he is charged as a matter of military duty.

While the disposition seems to exist to combat the logical extension of the idea of authority in this time of emergency and war to a military dictatorship of the entire

Allied Service of Supply, as suggested by General Pershing, it is well to point out that if that idea was accepted by the three Governments, the central authority being charged with the responsibility for the whole would conceive and carry out these responsibilities in terms of the whole and not in terms of three separate armies. Is it possible that France, England, and the United States will trust under French command their men and hesitate at trusting their material? This question must not be discussed except upon the assumption that if the central control is established it will be impartially administered. Objections to it must be upon the ground alone of the impossibility of creating the machinery.

If I have wrongly interpreted the conservatism in this conference it is not because of any lack of appreciation of the spirit of cooperation, as evidenced by the treatment which the Americans have received from Services of Supply in France. Generosity and quick response to our suggestion of any necessity have ever marked the attitude of our allies. All freely bring to the common cause the limit of resources in wealth and precious lives. The people from the highest to the lowest are one in complete self-sacrifice. The question, therefore, is only one of natural steadfastness and conservatism. But this conservatism and steadfastness should not now be allowed to interfere with the consummation of the common victory. General Pershing has placed his authority over his military Service of Supply at the disposal of the Allies for its proper coordination and to insure the maximum effort against the enemy. This action on his part is the highest expression of his confidence in the justice and fairness of our allies and is the best indication of his belief that the plan which he has proposed, notwithstanding all the arguments raised at this conference against it, is possible of accomplishment if it is met in a similar spirit.

In conclusion, let me say that the matters to which I am calling specific attention and which demand coordination, are matters affecting the immediate military rear of the armies. The authority to create the military central control, absolutely necessary to deal with them effectively, exists or can be made to exist in this conference by the delegation of existing military authority alone.

As military men we have no right to screen our responsibilities for a bad situation as regards coordination in the immediate rear of the armies by raising smoke about civil interference and extending unduly the scope of the discussion of a comprehensive and unquestioned principle. It is our fault and our fault alone if we do not correct the situation. Civil governments have delegated us both duty and a full authority with which to accomplish it. Concessions of independent military authority must be made to a central control. The American Commander-in-Chief in his plan places his at the disposal of the Allies. The present lack of military coordination of the Allied Services of Supply of the immediate rear of the armies prevents the maximum use of our military resources against a thoroughly consolidated enemy. If as military men we fail to correct this we are responsible in blood and lives and possibly defeat – and we alone.

Dawes, *A Journal of the Great War*, vol. 1, pp. 107–14.

Maj. Gen. Henry T. Allen, CG, 90th Division, Camp Travis, San Antonio, Texas, to Pershing.

A telegram has just arrived saying we would sail in June and would go into the Fourth Corps. That gives me the greatest satisfaction and I am psychologically and physically prepared to hustle to the limit with my unit in playing teamwork wherever it be put and whatever be its duty. Above all, I am greatly pleased that the Division is not to be disintegrated.

My divisional staff is thoroughly well adjusted and is operating effectively, though naturally I am reckoning on getting back my officers now at Langres to reinforce us and to add the latest and best from there. The officer in charge of the shooting of the brigade just being relieved at the range tells me that the entire brigade will average marksmen.

It is a pity we have been so decimated by those detachments and require so many new men, for it was my intention to put every man <u>twice</u> through the prescribed firing course. Now that can be done with only about fifty percentum of the war strength. The recruits will get all the gallery practice and target work possible before leaving. Shooting, musketry and minor tactical problems constitute our daily work.

I seem to be a long time in getting into the game, but presumably there will be plenty of work for sometime for all of us.

I sincerely hope you continue to bear so well your burden and am as always cordially and faithfully yours . . .

[P.S. handwritten—*"I note the shifting in your Staff. I forgot to tell you that we have had very high rating on our machine gun work. H.T.A."*]

LC, Pershing Papers, folder: Gen. Henry T. Allen, 1914–1919, box 9.

Pershing to TAG, War Department, in addition to Pershing to TAG, War Department, cable P-1024-S, April 29, in part in reply to TAG, War Department to Pershing, cables A-1172-R, April 25, and A-1237-R, May 3.

Cable P-1074-S.

1. For the Chief of Staff. 1C. With reference to paragraph 6, your cablegram 1172, and paragraph 1J, my cablegram 1024, your cablegram 1237, concerning the 92nd Division. In event Department still desires early dispatch 92nd Division I adhere to former recommendation that Division be included among those to be employed temporarily with British. I have informed British Secretary of State for War that these soldiers are American citizens and that I cannot discriminate against them in event War Department desires to send them to France [see May 5, Pershing to Haig, and note in source citation]. Have also expressed to him my hope that colored soldiers would be acceptable to him and that he will be able to overcome objection of British War Office.

NARA, RG 120, M930, Main Series, AEF to War Department, roll 12.

TAG, War Department, to Pershing, in part in reply to Pershing to TAG, War Department, cables P-582-S, February 8, P-1056-S, May 5, and P-1063-S, May 6, in addition to TAG, War Department, to Pershing, cables A-687-R, January 24, and A-1130, April 18.

Cable A-1264-R.
  7. With reference to paragraph 4, our 687, paragraph 1, your 582, paragraph 1, our 1130 [a detailed description of the Naval guns], and paragraph 1B, your 1063. Entire project for 5 14-inch guns with personnel complete will be shipped by Navy transportation without interfering with other transportation. In view of your report that British do not require 14-inch guns now [see May 6, P-1063-S-1B], they will be sent for use with the American Army. March. [Reply—Vol. 5, May 22, P-1163-S-1]
  14. With reference to your 1056. All available troop space on animal and cargo vessels is now being utilized, 800 troops shipped in this manner during April. Other vessels now being surveyed with view to increasing this method of dispatching troops abroad. Goethals.

NARA, RG 120, M930, Main Series, War Department to AEF, roll 12.

TAG, War Department, to Pershing, in reply to Pershing to TAG, War Department, cable P-1057-S, May 5.

Cable A-1266-R. Confidential.
  With reference to your 1057. The Secretary of War has notified the Navy Department that the War Department will undertake to utilize Marseille subject to proper escort and suggestion is made that it would be desirable to include ships which are scheduled for that port in the present Gibraltar convoy. March. [Reply—May 10, P-1092-S]

NARA, RG 120, M930, Confidential Series, War Department to AEF, roll 12.

May 9

Pershing's Personal Diary

Worked in office all day. Sent confidential letter to Colonel Dawes by Lieutenant McCormick. Saw Colonel Nolan.

LC, Pershing Papers, Diary, May 7, 1917–September 1, 1918, box 4.

Anthoine, CS, GHQ, Armies of the North and Northeast, to CS, Group of Armies East, Miracourt, and French Military Mission with the American Army, Chaumont, reply to Ragueneau to CINC, Armies of the North and Northeast, May 7.

No. 7723/M.

1. In accordance with agreement with the American Chief of Staff, infantry, machine gun units and the signal battalion, 3rd D.I. [Infantry Division] U.S. will be made available to the G.A.E. from 14 May.

2. Units and staffs will be placed in the area at the G.A.E. under conditions specified by letter 7802/3 of 7 May of General Ragueneau.

3. Chief of Staff, Miracourt, will settle the movement of the 3rd D.I.U.S. by direct agreement with Chief of Staff, Chaumont, and will report on the arrangements for stay in sectors of 3rd D I U S on the Upper Alsace front.

Les Armées françaises dans la Grande Guerre, Tome 6, vol. 2, Annexes, vol. 1: Annexe No. 139, p. 285.

Foulois, Chief, Air Service, SOS, AEF, to J. L. Dumesnil, Under-Secretary of State, Military and Naval Aeronautics, Ministry of Armaments, Paris, reply to Dumesnil to Foulois, May 1.

Subject: Request for 400 American Pilots.

Reference your letter of May 1, 1918 requesting the services of 400 American pilots for duty with French squadrons, I am instructed by the Commander in Chief A.E.F. to state that it is not desired to turn over individual pilots or other individuals of the Air Service, but that he would be very glad to form American squadrons for service with the French provided the airplanes for which the French appear to need pilots be placed at the disposal of our squadrons.

LC, Foulois Papers, folder 12: AEF, Air Service, Allied Air Service, box 7.

Pershing to the Secretary of War.

Confidential.

In order that you may be fully advised as to the situation concerning the use of American troops during this crisis, it seems desirable to give you a brief outline of the circumstances, especially of the discussion leading up to the recent resolution adopted by the Supreme War Council.

It appears that the agreement made by Lord Milner and myself at London did not please the French; at least they pretended not to be pleased with it. I am inclined to think they took this attitude simply to strengthen their contention that more infantry should be brought over than the London agreement contemplated.

When the Supreme War Council met, Mr. Clemenceau opened with a discussion of the terms of the London agreement and appeared to feel that this agreement altered arrangements that had already been made by the military representatives and that the British were getting the advantage.

Lord Milner and myself explained that the purpose of the agreement was only to facilitate the arrival of infantry and machine gun units to meet what we all believe to be an emergency and there was no thought of allotting troops to the British in the sense of balancing them against those with the French. I pointed out the fact that the only agreement with reference to the allocation of American troops was the original memorandum that had been accepted by both Mr. Clemenceau and General Pétain when it was arranged in February to bring over six divisions for training with the British.

Mr. Clemenceau appeared to feel that these troops were going to the British in May, but that no answer had been made to the possibility of sending assistance to the French in June.

Mr. Lloyd George suggested that the question of allocating American troops in June be taken up when that month arrived, as they would then know where they were needed most. Then General Foch stated that American assistance was needed for the allies in general and not for the French or British, and he merely asked me to extend the May program into June. This was then supported by both Mr. Lloyd George and Mr. Clemenceau.

I stated in effect that it should be made clear that the American troops were not, generally speaking, to be at the disposal of the French or British commands, but, that we must look forward to having an army of our own; that, I desired that unity of command in the United States army be recognized and that such army must soon be made complete for service under its own supreme command, and suggested that the Council fix some date when this principle would prevail. I also stated that I was not prepared to consent to the extension of the May program into June, and thought that this question could be considered later.

Mr. Lloyd George accepted the principle I stated, but insisted on the necessity of prompt assistance and of having an extended program in order that the tonnage might be allotted, and suggested that September or October would be time for the United States army to come in as an army.

This was followed by a running discussion, during which both General Foch and Mr. Clemenceau agreed to the principle that America should form a great, single army, but that in May and June men were an absolute necessity.

We then adjourned, having agreed to consider the question the next day. The discussion outside of the Council grew a times rather heated. In conference with Mr. Lloyd George, Mr. Clemenceau, General Foch and Lord Milner I stated that I had given my word that, if the situation in June made it still necessary to bring over troops, I would advise my government accordingly; that I was not prepared to commit the government to a June or July program as to the troops which would arrive in June and July could not be used until August or September.

At the meeting the next day General Foch made a statement at considerable length expressing his views on the question of disposal of American troops and his right to indicate whether or not priority of transportation should be given to certain arms. He stated that American infantry and machine gun units were deemed essential during the months of May, June and July and that they should be given priority of transportation over other arms; and that if the tonnage permitted, this number of infantry and machine gun units should be increased.

I again spoke on our position and stated that I thought we all fully appreciated the necessity for bringing over troops but that we differed in the method of attaining the end. The United States had entered the war as an independent power and we must always look forward to fighting with an army of our own; that the morale of the American troops was dependent on fighting under their own flag. I stated that German propaganda had already begun to work and asserted that our soldiers would be very much dissatisfied if they were compelled to serve under either French or British commanders, and that I should organize them as soon as possible into an American army.

At this point Mr. Lloyd George made his proposal to guarantee bringing over a largely increased number of troops in May and June in British shipping, and upon that I agreed to extend the program to include the month of June as indicated in my memorandum.

The agreement is really more advantageous to us than the one drawn up between Lord Milner and myself, and I think will not seriously interfere with our completing a well-rounded program of personnel by the end of June or early July.

I am sending you herewith the copies of the proceedings which will give the details of the discussion. I hope this will end the question of breaking up our units. The British and French drafts will become available late in July, or early in August, and should obviate further requests for our infantry.
[Enclosure (not located)]

LC, Pershing Papers, folder: Newton D. Baker, January–June 1918, box 20.

Bliss, Chief, American Section, and Permanent Military Representative, SWC, Versailles, to TAG, War Department.

Cable 107-S.

I have communicated to General Pershing [see following] the following received from Prime Minister Italy through Italian Military Representative here: "Please communicate to General Pershing that the Italian Government can assign for the transportation of American troops to Italy the steamships Duke of the Abbrussi [D'Abruzzi] and the Duke of Acosta, which are at this moment in New York and are able to carry 4000 men in all. These steamships are part of those that the Italian Government was to consign to the United States and it is therefore understood that should they be utilized for this transportation they will be replaced. In that case the departure of the first American contingent for Italy could be within 15 days. If that solution is not acceptable, the Italian Government will employ for transportation of American troops to Italy the two steamships Taormina and Verona, with a capacity of 6000 men in all, and these steamships will be disposable about the end of the present month and can complete their loading in New York June 20."

NARA, RG 120, file 315: Cablegrams Sent to War Department, Jan. 22, 1918–Dec. 10, 1919, roll 18; see also online "WW I Supreme War Council, American records," at https://www.fold3.com.

Bliss, Chief, American Section, and Permanent Military Representative, SWC, Versailles, to Pershing.

Telegram No. 66 [sent].

The Italian Military Representative asks me to wire you, as a matter of urgency, the following message he has received from Mr. Orlando: "Please communicate to General Pershing that the Italian Government can assign for the transportation of American troops to Italy the steamships Duke of the Abbrussi [D'Abruzzi] and the Duke of Acosta, which are at this moment in New York and are able to carry 4000 men in all. These steamships are part of those that the Italian Government was to consign to the United States and it is therefore understood that should they be utilized for this transportation they will be replaced. In that case the departure of the first American contingent for Italy could be within 15 days. If that solution is not acceptable, the Italian Government will employ for transportation of American troops to Italy the two steamships Taormina and Verona, with a capacity of 6000 men in all, and these steamships will be disposable about the end of the present month and can complete their loading in New York June 20."

Military Representative says that Mr. Orlando asks him for a prompt reply in order that they can immediately assure the availability of the steamships.

NARA, RG 120, M923, American Section, SWC, file 317: Telegrams sent by the American Section, Jan. 21, 1918–Dec. 5, 1919, roll 19; see also online "WW I Supreme War Council, American records," at https://www.fold3.com.

Pershing to TAG, War Department, in part in reply to TAG, War Department, to Pershing, cables A-1143-R, April 20.

Cable P-1080-S.

2. For Quartermaster General. 2B. Account French authorities refusing to allow explosives to unload at La Pallice, railway cars and explosives must not be loaded on same vessel as has been done in case of transport Oosterdyke. Neither should explosives be loaded in any vessel that draws over 25 feet and if you will confine shipments of explosives to small vessels in which you load nothing except French steel and explosives, we will be able to handle these 2 commodities at light draft ports not in general use by us, and the smaller vessel and the lighter the draft, the better for our promptly turning the vessel around. We have 10 vessels here and close by loaded with railway cars and only have 4 berths at La Pallice, where our erecting plant is

located; therefore very serious delay will occur account of loading cars on so many transports. [*Ed.*—In its reply on May 18 in cable A-1346-R-6, the War Department agreed to the AEF's recommendation.]

7. For Felton. With reference to paragraph 8A, your cablegram 1143. Estimate of 500 to 750 cars monthly from Middletown Car Company plants at Saintes and La Garenne maximum estimate for reason that French Railways have claim on these shops and Car Company's representative would not guarantee greater output than stated in our cable. Furthermore, La Garenne shops have apparently been practically abandoned by Middletown Car Company and taken over by Nord Railway account military situation. We are endeavoring to arrange with Middletown Car Company for erection of cars if necessary at another point near one of our ports.

NARA, RG 120, M930, Main Series, AEF to War Department, roll 3.

Pershing to TAG, War Department, in part in reply to TAG, War Department, to Pershing, cables A-1154-R, April 22, and A-1192-R, April 27.

Cable P-1083-S.

1. For Chief of Ordnance. 1C. With reference to paragraph 1C, your cablegram 1154. It is impossible to obtain 75-m.m. anti-aircraft ammunition from French at present time. None of this ammunition available in our depots. Request immediate information as to promised deliveries by months of each type this ammunition. [Reply—Vol. 5, July 3, A-1652-R-1E]

6. For Chief Signal Officer. 6C. With reference to paragraph 5, your cablegram 1192. Endeavoring to arrange with British to make all Handley Page spares in England except wing assembly. Also to have them assemble spare wings for us in their shops in France. All parts for spare to be furnished to England by United States. Will advise results of negotiations. You should made duplicate jigs, etc., for Caproni spares so that we can build such spares in France for Caproni machines as cannot be sent to us complete and which will be interchangeable with your manufacture. [Reply—May 18, A-1347-R-2B; in addition—Vol. 5, June 18, P-1330-S-2D]

NARA, RG 120, M930, Main Series, AEF to War Department, roll 3.

TAG, War Department, to Pershing, in part in reply to Pershing to TAG, War Department, cables P-889-S, April 10, and P-1051-S, May 4.

Cable A-1270-R. Confidential.

1. With reference to paragraph 3, your 1051. Following divisions will be left in United States on June 1st: 6th, 7th, 8th, 29th, 31st, 34th, 36th, 37th, 38th, 39th, 40th, 76th, 79th, 81st, 83rd, 84th, 85th, 86th, 87th, 88th, 89th, 90th, 91st, 92nd. Of the

above, the following are now scheduled to leave during the month of June: 29th, 37th, 83rd, 89th, 90th, 92nd. Impossible at present time to change our action on paragraph 5, your 889. Officers detailed for that purpose will be ordered direct to General Staff College. March.

NARA, RG 120, M930, Confidential Series, War Department to AEF, roll 18.

TAG, War Department, to Pershing, in part in reply to Pershing to TAG, War Department, cables P-904-S, April 12, and P-1043-S, May 3.

Cable A-1271-R.
  22. Replying to paragraph 2, your 1043. Matter of allocation of spruce to Allies arranged to satisfaction of Tardieu and British Mission here. Allocation recommended in paragraph 1, your 610, will be followed until further recommendations are received from you. March.
  23. With reference to paragraph 1, your 904. Allotment of Liberty Engines for large tanks cannot be made prior to October 1st from Signal Corps. Independent production of this engine by Ordnance Department can begin at once, complete engines will begin to come through in September. Is this satisfactory? March. [Reply—Vol. 5, May 25, P-1185-S-3A; June 5, P-1247-S-1B]

NARA, RG 120, M930, Main Series, War Department to AEF, roll 12.

TAG, War Department, to Pershing.

Cable A-1273-R.
  1. As American Government owes to French tonnage in exchange for certain sailing vessels in addition to commitment for certain replacement materials it is important that we be advised whether the steamers operating in Cross-Channel coal service are carrying coal or other supplies for French Government. Goethals. [Reply—Vol. 5, May 20, P-1150-S-1]

NARA, RG 120, M930, Main Series, War Department to AEF, roll 12.

TAG, War Department, to Pershing, in part in reply to Pershing to TAG, War Department, cable P-1043-S, May 3, and in addition to TAG, War Department, to Pershing, cable A-1224-R, May 2.

Cable A-1275-R. Confidential.
  Paragraph 1, your 1043; paragraph 1 and 1A, our 1039; and our 1224. In accordance with dispatches from Sims to Navy Department, priority to U. S. Navy Air

Service for aviation materials necessary to equip and arm sea plane bases was approved by War Department Nov. 14, 1917. On March 17th, 1918, War Department approved request of Navy Department that 80 two-seater pursuit planes be delivered to Navy on or about May 15th, to be used in bombing operations. On May 2nd, War Department acceded to request of Navy that this number be raised to 155 but deliveries distributed over longer period. On April 10th, War Department concurred with Navy Department that operations against submarines in their bases were purely naval work. 734 Liberty engines have been allocated to Navy for delivery prior to July 1st. No allocations have been made after that date. Navy Department for the last year has left matter of engine production entirely in the hands of the War Department and is in this respect wholly dependent for the operations of their aviation service. War Department May 7th carefully reviewed entire matter in view of your cables and has decided that no changes can be made at present in priority decision.

With reference to 1 B, your 1043, matter will be given consideration and results cabled.

NARA, RG 120, M930, Confidential Series, War Department to AEF, roll 18.

Editor's Note—In his 1919 report to Pershing on the Air Service, AEF, Foulois noted:

> This last cablegram [A-1275-R] effectively stopped all further discussion on our part as to the reasons why the U.S. Navy was given priority over the U. S. Army and our Allies, in the allocation of Liberty engines.
>
> 7. The policies as outlined in the cablegram, quoted in the foregoing paragraph, were made entirely without consultation with the Commander-in-Chief of the American Expeditionary Forces, and without full consideration of the needs of our Allies on the Western Front. This same priority for the U.S. Navy directly affected the efficiency of the Air Service, American Expeditionary Forces, in that we had already made tentative arrangements with the French Government to receive an increased number of airplanes in exchange for Liberty engines and had also arranged to install Liberty engines in French aeroplanes which were available and which the French could not use due to shortage of engines.
>
> 8. By reference to the last quoted cablegram (in paragraph 6—No. 1275-R, dated May 9, 1918) it will be noted that the War Department not only allocated a large number of Liberty engines to the Navy, but an allocation of 80 two-seater planes for bombing operations had also been made, with delivery about May 15, 1918. This action showed also an utter lack of appreciation of the priority needs of the military air forces as compared to the naval air forces. Although the number of planes originally allocated was not great, they assume huge proportions when you take into consideration the fact that the American Air Service in France, during the entire war, was never supplied with sufficient planes to meet the needs of the ground troops. (LC, Pershing Papers, folder: Data for Book *My Experiences in the*

World War, folder 1: Air Service, AEF—Foulois to Pershing, "Air Services—American Expeditionary Forces (1917–1918)," January 7, 1924, Encl. E, box 351.)

TAG, War Department, to Pershing, in part in reply to Bliss to TAG, War Department, cable 10-S, December 4, 1917; in addition to TAG, War Department, cable A-614-R, January 9, A-737-R, February 5, and A-790-R, February 15.

Cable A-1276-R.

4F. Reference General Bliss cable 10 from London, our 614, paragraph 1, our 737, paragraph 9, and our 790. Purchase of material authorized in our cables were intended to be sufficient for 24 divisions with 25% replacements. Request that you purchase from French and British such additional quantities as may be needed to equip 30 divisions instead of 24 and provide 25% replacements. It is understood that not all calibers are obtainable. No purchases need be made of 75-millimeter ammunition, 155-millimeter ammunition, 8-inch howitzer ammunition, 9.2-inch howitzer ammunition, 3-inch Stokes mortar ammunition, 9.45-inch trench mortar, 6-inch trench mortar and 6-inch trench mortar ammunition. Proceed at once and cable statement of orders placed and total cost so that necessary reservation of funds can be made. It is understood here that you plan procurement from the British of all the requirements of 4-inch trench mortars and ammunition therefor so that production this material need not be attempted in the United States. Request cable confirmation this understanding. Wheeler [Chief of Ordnance]. [Reply—Vol. 5, May 25, P-1185-S-3]

NARA, RG 120, M930, Confidential Series, War Department to AEF, roll 18.

May 10

Pershing's Personal Diary

Worked in office all day. Had long talk with Major Fiske on subject of Chief of Artillery and other matters. Received a letter from General Foch, brought by his Aide, Captain Miliet. Saw General Patrick whom I had ordered up from Tours. Also talked with Colonel Logan and Colonel Fox Conner. Saw General [Frederick H.] Sykes of the British Air Service [Chief of the Air Staff], and had Colonel Mott and General Patrick at house to dinner. Also saw General Foulois, whom I had ordered to headquarters for consultation.

LC, Pershing Papers, Diary, May 7, 1917–September 1, 1918, box 4.

Editor's Note—In his memoirs, Pershing commented on his meeting with Sykes and Foulois:

> A few days later [after his meeting with Loucheur on April 27] a British air representative [Sykes] also sought joint cooperation with us. The proposal he made was that we should limit our construction, other than for training purposes, to long range strategic bombing aircraft and the manufacture of Liberty engines, and that the British would supply us aircraft for purely American operations. We were asked to send a small staff to London to cooperate along these lines and they would send a strong mission of experts to Washington. When the matter was presented to me along with a prepared telegram to be sent to Lord Reading stating that we and the French concurred, I inquired how it came that the French had agreed to this without consulting us, and it was found that the plan had not yet been taken up with them. I then told the British representative that when the air services of the Allied armies reached an agreement regarding this proposal I would consider it. This was the last we heard of it. Such incidents as these showed the tendency to gain particular advantage and caused us to doubt the sincerity of proposals for cooperation in such matters. (Pershing, *My Experiences in the World War*, Vol. 2, p. 18.)

In his report to Pershing on January 7, 1924, while serving as Assistant Military Attaché in Berlin, Foulois, who was Chief, Air Service, SOS, AEF, from November 1917 to May 1918, provided a detailed account on both his visit to Pershing and their discussion with Maj. Gen. Sykes, the recently appointed Chief of the Air Staff, RAF. See LC, Pershing Papers, folder: Data for Book *My Experiences in the World War*, folder no. 1: Foulois, "Air Service—American Expeditionary Forces. (1917–1918)," Enclosure I: "Efforts of the British to establish a Joint Aircraft Production Program with the United States, to the exclusion of France and Italy," pp. 1–3.

Pershing to Foch, CINC, Allied Armies, in reply to Foch to Pershing, May 8, in addition to Foch and Pershing Conference, April 24.

I just received your letter of May 8 and thank you for the warm feelings that you express.

I am happy to put at your disposal in the shortest time the 2nd, 26th and 42nd Infantry Divisions [see April 24, Foch to Pershing]. The question of the relief of these divisions from the areas occupied by them currently has been agreed with the French Military Mission representing the G. H. Q. of General Pétain. The 2nd Division has already started to withdraw from its sector.

The 32nd Division will come into the line by regiments at an early date.

The training of the 3rd and 5th Divisions has been sped up as much as possible and they will occupy a quiet sector soon. [For locations of American divisions then in France, see Map 7.]

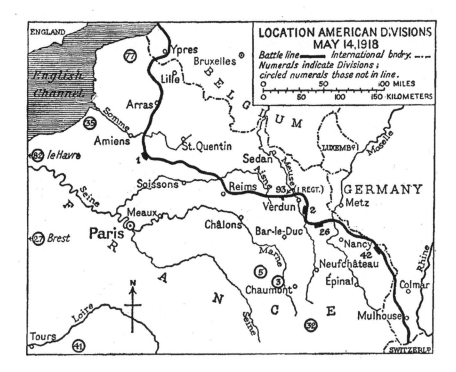

Map 7. Location of American Divisions, May 14, 1918. By mid-May 1918, Pershing had twelve divisions and one infantry regiment available to him in some capacity. Four divisions were on the line—the 1st, 2nd, 26th, and 42nd; one regiment was also on the line with the French—the 369th Infantry (African-Americans); four divisions were either training with the British or had landed and were headed that way—the 27th, 35th, 77th, and 82nd; three divisions were training under the AEF—the 3rd, 5th, and 32nd; and one was a depot division—the 41st. Source: Pershing, *My Experiences in the World War*, vol. 2, p. 47.

As for the matter of aviation of which you asked, I will follow up and let you know as soon as possible its personnel situation. [See Vol. 5, May 21, Foulois to Conner and CS, GHQ, AEF.]

Les armées françaises dans la Grande Guerre, Tome 6, vol. 2, Annexes vol. 1: Annexe No. 150, p. 308.

Pershing to Sims, Commander, U.S. Naval Forces Operating in European Waters, London. Copy to Brig. Gen. Mason M. Patrick, after he became Chief, Air Service, SOS, AEF, on May 24.

With reference to our air services, it seems to me we have wandered far from the idea of coordination and that officers who are handling the Army and the Navy air services are not working together as they should.

In principle, I am of the opinion that there should be but one air service for both the Army and Navy, but there may be obstacles in the way of its realization. However, there is not that close understanding regarding production and operation that efficiency and economy demand.

I understand that there are instances where the two services have actually come into competition in obtaining material. This, of course, can only create an unfavorable impression of our lack of business methods, which affects our efforts to obtain cooperation or unity of purpose in other directions.

I shall be glad, Admiral, if you would give the matter your consideration with a view to a working understanding between the two services which we represent in European waters.
[Reply—May 16, Sims to Pershing]

LC, Pershing Papers, folder: Adm. Wm. S. Sims, box 184.

Kernan, CG, SOS, AEF, Tours, to Pershing.

I am enclosing herewith for your information a memorandum showing troop movement handled by S. O. S. in the past twenty days. I thought it would interest you because it shows the magnitude of the work and the rapid growth of our forces. Upon the whole, although our mechanism back here is not yet perfect and mistakes more or less vexatious are made from time to time, it still is a fact that the essential work is being done and with promptness. This element of promptness I regard as one of our most valuable assets.

It has gratified me very much to have my Chief of Staff made a Brigadier-General in the National Army and I feel no less pleased over the deserved promotion of Arthur Johnson [CO, Intermediate Section, SOS] and I feel that I am indebted to you for both of these.
[Enclosure (not located)]

LC, Pershing Papers, folder: Gen. Francis J. Kernan, box 111.

Foulois, Chief, Air Service, SOS, AEF, Headquarters, Advanced Section, Air Service, Zone of Advance, to CINC, AEF.

Subject: Air Service Organization.
    1. The organization of the Air Service, A.E.F., (General Organization Plan approved by C.-in-C., July 11, 1917) considering heavier than air units only, authorized the formation of a total of 260 squadrons.
    2. The Air Service during the last six months has had official cables of expected deliveries of airplanes for service at the front from the United States alone, varying

from 3000 in June to approximately zero. This record has almost been duplicated in regard to European deliveries for the same period.

3. Each month as new information has been received the organization of the Air Service has been revised, new programs made up and Air Service projects altered.

4. The Air Service fully realizes that the carrying out within less than a year's time of the original "General Organization Plan", under present manufacturing and tonnage conditions and the present exigencies of war, is a self-apparent impossibility. The airplanes and accessories are not available except in very limited numbers.

5. Two conditions now confront the Air Service; first, to utilize and immediately organize to the best purpose, the few available airplanes that are now obtainable from all sources; second, continue the plans in preparation for the future organization in conformity with the wishes and plans of the C.-in-C., so as to make full use of all planes to come from both United States and European sources. Regarding the units requiring immediate organization it is noted the total number of airplanes now obtainable will equip and, it is thought, maintain fifteen squadrons as follows: 6 Corps Observation, 3 Army Observation, 5 Pursuit and one day bombing squadron. These planes are of various kinds of different degrees of efficiency. Of these, two Pursuit and two Corps observation squadrons are organized, assigned to the 1st Corps, and at the front with that Corps. One other Corps observation squadron about ready and can be assigned within a week's time. This will complete units required by G.H.Q. for this Corps.

6. Immediately after the units for the 1st Corps have been provided there will be available for service use, two (2) more Pursuit Squadrons, one Army observation squadron, and at least one and possibly three more observation squadrons. These will be followed shortly by the remainder of the fifteen squadrons. This brings up at once the question of higher organization, tactical use and command.

7. Under the General Organization Project noted in paragraph one, 260 squadrons authorized defined as follows:

Tactical					Strategical				
Corps Obsv.	Army Obsv.	Pursuit	Bombing	Total	Obsv.	Pursuit	Bombing	Total	Agg't
15	24	15	5	59	41	105	55	201	260

8. If the above is to continue to be the approved complete Air Service of an Army, then by the time that army (five corps) is on the line, the Air Service, to keep abreast of the other arms, should have one fifth of the above amount if available. If not available, prior priority of tonnage, etc., should be given to make it available. This, if carried out, would necessitate the organization, as each Corps was formed, of corresponding Air Service, (one fifth of total), distributed as follows:

Tactical					Strategical				
Corps Obsv.	Army Obsv.	Pursuit	Bombing	Total	Obsv.	Pursuit	Bombing	Total	Agg't
3	5	3	1	12	8	21	11	40	52

9. It is fully realized the above program cannot be carried out for the 1st and 2nd Corps quotas. Whether the aggregate can even be attained by the time an army is formed is a question of higher authority. All our present information is that such a project is now unobtainable.

10. The General Staff should decide whether it is desired to alter the original project to conform to the latest advice as to availability of equipment and personnel or to authorize the Air Service to continue to organize such equipment as may be obtained as fast as it is received and with the object, at some time in the future, of catching up with the original project and at the same time to ensure to each Corps as it is formed the tactical air units prescribed by the present tables of organization, viz; 3 Corps Observation Squadrons (with photographic section and Air Park), and 3 Balloon Companies. To this should be added, but placed under orders of superior authority, sufficient pursuit squadrons to ensure protection and sufficient army observation squadrons to do work of heavy army artillery.

11. In this connection it is anticipated a larger number of pilots, observers and bombers will be graduated from schools than can be regularly assigned to organized American air units. If these men will be sent as individuals to French or English squadrons for service work, it should be a policy that they should be assembled whenever practicable, first into a squadron by themselves, then into groups. A senior officer the Air Service, with the necessary staff assistants, should be attached to the Air Headquarters of each nation to exercise the administrative and disciplinary duties and to inspect the equipment and supply. This officer should at the same time study the duties of the various air commanders and so fit himself to exercise tactical command when available.

12. Anticipating the indefinite postponement of carrying out the original Air Service program and authority to continue to organize such personnel as may be available into service units as fast as airplanes and equipment are obtained, it is desired to carry out the scheme and to organize and distribute squadrons as follows:

(a). To the 1st Corps. Three (3) "corps observation" squadrons, (already organized and turned over to 1st Corps).

(b). To organize three (3) more "corps observation" squadrons, under Group Commander who will be under direct orders of G.H.Q., through C.A.S. [Chief, Air Service], (these to be later assigned to the 2nd Corps when that Corps is formed).

(c). To take the two (2) Pursuit Squadrons now organized and turned over to the 1st Corps and the two (2) other new Pursuit Squadrons now ready, organize them into one Pursuit Group, place them under a Group Commander to work directly under orders from G.H.Q., through C.A.S.

(d). To organize immediately one (1) and within a short time, (probably one month), two (2) more "army observation" squadrons. These to be used for "army observation" work with our own troops and similarly to the Pursuit Squadrons under general direction of G.H.Q., through C.A.S.

(e). Organize one (1) day bombing squadron now ready to be used under direction of G.H.Q., through C.A.S.

(f). The one (1) pursuit squadron now with the French, and on account of present emergency to remain as it is. When no longer needed, it will join the other four American pursuit squadrons.

13. In regard to command of air units, it is proposed:

(a) The Air Commander, 1st Corps, will command only the air units of that Corps as prescribed in approved Tables of Organization, viz: 3 Corps Observation Squadrons, 3 Balloon Companies, and, if established separately, an Air Park.

(b) To designated prospective Air Commander for the 2nd Corps. This officer will command the 3 Observation Squadrons destined for that Corps, and will, for the present, act under orders of G.H.Q., through C.A.S.

(c) To assign two Senior Air Service officers, one to the English and one to the French Air Service Headquarters for the purpose as before outlined.

(d) As units and equipment arrive over and above those prescribed for the Army Corps, to organize new squadrons and groups, and to place them for service at the front under orders of G.H.Q., through C.A.S. The nature of equipment received will determine the kind of squadrons to be organized.

LC, Foulois Papers, folder 7: AEF, Air Service, Organization—Chief, Air Service, 1918 (2 of 2), box 10; see also NARA. RG 120, Microfilm Publication M990, Gorrell's History of the American Expeditionary Forces Air Service, 1917–1919. Series A, Vol. 1: Foulois, Air Service Lessons Learned during the Present War, January 29, 1919, roll 1; see also online "Gorrell's History—AEF Air Service," at https://www.fold3.com.

Editor's Note—In his "Lessons Learned" report of January 29, 1919, Foulois added additional thoughts concerning aspects of his memorandum and how the events of the past months and the lack of aircraft, engines, and personnel had so adversely affected the Air Service's overall program:

> In spite of the conditions existing in the Spring and Summer of 1918, and their effect on the organization, equipment, and operations of the tactical and strategical Air Service, there had been organized, equipped, and assigned to duty by the middle of May, 1918, and within the time limited called for by General Headquarters, A.E.F., the necessary Corps Observation Squadrons and Balloon Companies needed for duty with the 1st Corps. In addition to the Corps Air Service units, there had also been organize, equipped, and attached to the 1st Corps, with the time limit specified by General Headquarters, A.E.F., two pursuit squadrons and one Army Observation squadron, which, together with the Corps Air Service units,

included all the Air Service called for by General Headquarters, A.E.F., at that time.

This initial effort to provide an adequate Corps Air Service to meet the needs of the combat ground troops, supplemented by a small nucleus of pursuit units for offensive air work and protective service for the Corps air units, fell far short of the Air Service program as outlined in the General Organization Project, approved by the Commander-in-Chief July 11, 1917, . . . which provided for a tactical and strategical Air Service of 260 squadrons for an Army of 20 combat divisions, which from all information obtainable, would probably be organized into five corps of four divisions each.

By reference to Paragraph 7, 8 and 9 of this Memorandum . . . it will be seen that for each Army Corps there should have been provided 52 aero squadrons of all classes.

The failure to receive personnel and material from the United States, as well as the failure to receive an adequate supply of aeroplanes and engines from the Allies, made it absolutely impossible to organize and equip aero squadrons in the proportion planned. Further, when all priority gave way to infantry and machine guns in March, April, and May, 1918, the creation of new corps due to this priority, rapidly outstripped the organization and equipment of Air Service units, and it was fully realized that the accomplishment of the program planned was an impossibility.

Based on these conditions, it was decided that all our efforts should be concentrated on tactical aviation, with special effort on (a) Corps Observation; (b) Pursuit; (c) Army Observation; (d) Day Bombardment; in the order named, leaving the strategical Air Service units until such time as the personnel and materiel became available.

In view of the indefinite postponement of the original program, the only policy which could be followed, under the uncertain conditions which had to so with deliveries of personnel and materiel, both from the United States and from England, was to strip all projects in the Service of Supplies [Services of Supply] in order to secure personnel for the aeroplanes which at that time we were reasonably certain would be delivered. (NARA, RG 120, M990, Gorrell's History of the American Expeditionary Forces Air Service, 1917–1919. Series A, Vol. 1: Foulois, Air Service Lessons Learned during the Present War, January 29, 1919, roll 1; see also online "Gorrell's History—AEF Air Service," at https://www.fold3.com.)

Foulois, Chief, Air Service, SOS, AEF, to CS, GHQ, AEF.

Subject: Air Service Army Operations vs. Navy Operations.

1. Military operations which involve bombing operations, from the air, against submarine bases in which army or land types of airplanes are used should come under the control of the Military commanders and not the Naval commanders.

2. Naval Air service operations should be confined to operations at sea with Naval vessels, or to operations which require the use of sea-planes at greater distances than 10 miles off shore.

3. Operations against enemy submarine bases, which do not involve going to sea over 10 miles, can be carried out by Army airplanes and Army fliers, equally as well as by Navy fliers.

4. U.S. Navy Air Service plans for securing airplanes and engines are interfering with the requirements of the Allied Army Air Service at the present time.

5. Efforts of Navy Air Services in bombing submarine bases are negligible, and will be negligible until such operations can be carried out on a big and continuous scale. In the meantime the fate of civilization is decided on the Western front by the Armies, and not the Navies, and it is absolutely imperative that the Army Air Services be kept up to maximum efficiency in order that the great wastage of airplanes and engines, caused by the present offensive, be promptly cared for.

6. Air operations against submarine bases are of great importance, but until the present offensive of the Germans on the Western front is conclusively checked, there should be no diversion of personnel or material for bombing submarine bases, which could be more effectively used in connection with Army Air Service operations.

7. If the present plans of the U.S. Naval Air Service, in connection with their requirements for aeroplanes and engines for use in bombing German submarine bases on the Belgian coast, are given priority over the U.S. Army Air Service, the program of the U.S. Army Air Service for 1918 will be reduced at least 50%.

LC, Foulois Papers, folder 8: AEF, Joint Army-Navy Aircraft Committee, Army-Navy Air Competition, 1918–1919, box 8.

Pershing to Bliss, Chief, American Section, and Permanent Military Representative, SWC, Versailles, in reply to Bliss to Pershing, telegram No. 66 [sent], May 9.

Telegram No. 44 [received].

Reference your number 1,515 [no. 66] in relation to sending troops to Italy. I have cabled War Department Mr. Orlando's two proposals recommending acceptance of the second proposal, that is, use of the steamships Taormina and Verona [see May 10, Pershing to TAG, War Department, cable P-1093-S]. [Reply—May 11, Bliss to Pershing]

NARA, RG 120, M923, American Section, SWC, file 318: Telegrams received by the American Section, Jan. 1918–Oct. 29, 1919, roll 19; see also online "WW I Supreme War Council, American records," at https://www.fold3.com.

Pershing to Biddle, CG, Base Section No. 3, SOS, AEF, London, for Sims, Commander, U. S. Naval Forces Operating in European Waters.

Telegram.
Subject: Marseille to be utilized.
Confidential. For Admiral Sims.

Following cable received from War Department, Washington [May 8, A-1266-R] "With reference to your cable 1057 [May 5] the Secretary of War has notified the Navy Department that the War Department will undertake to utilize Marseille subject to proper escort and suggestion is made that it would be desirable to include ships which are scheduled for that port in present Gibraltar convoy". To this cablegram the following reply was sent [May 10, P-1092-S] "For the Chief of Staff. Reference your 1266 Admiral Sims agreed that by using specially selected fast and well armed ships no substantial increased danger exists in their transatlantic movement without convoy. Sending same to Gibraltar in present convoy would probably result in delay turn around some 10 to 15 days on account of loss of time awaiting convoy and slow speed of the same. Sims states ships going to Bay of Biscay ports also require strong convoy on account of activities smaller type enemy submarines in these waters which submarines are particularly effective with their torpedo fire. Enemy submarines operating off Gibraltar of large type which attack usually with gunfire only and not so effective with torpedoes. Recommend matter be taken up with Navy Department as originally outlined. Navy to select vessels to be used in this movement and type of armament to be installed and that they make transatlantic movement without convoys. Have quoted this cable to Sims with request that he transmit similar recommendation to Navy Department". Understood we have not taken any liberty in reference made to you in War Department cable. As the military situation makes it of utmost importance to us to shorten by every possible means time of turn around, cable your recommendation direct to Navy Department as to type of vessel, speed and armament which should be employed in this movement without convoy. [As corrected]

NARA, RG 45, ONRL T829, Miscellaneous Records of the Navy Department, Miscellaneous Materials, 1–6/1918, 7–12/1918, Miscellaneous Material Print Files, World War, roll 409; and Miscellaneous Materials, 1–8/1918, Miscellaneous Material Print Files, World War, roll 411; see also Naval History and Heritage Command, website: Wars, Conflicts, and Operations, World War I, Documentary Histories, May 1918, Pershing to Biddle for Sims, May 10, 1918; original document at NARA, Record Group 45: Naval Records Collection of the Office of Naval Records and Library (ONRL), Entry 517B.

March to Pershing, in reply to Pershing to March, April 23.

Your letter of April 23rd written from London has just reached me, and I am very glad to hear from you.

The Secretary of War has taken hold of things after his return with enthusiastic appreciation of the work being done by the American Expeditionary Forces in France. I have already cabled you the decision of the Department about the use of Marseille [see May 8, A-1266-R].

The work that I have been doing since my return from France has been largely propaganda work with the various organizations that I have found have been created in America for the conduct of the War from a business standpoint. In order to ship across to France the number of men which I desired and which has since become the policy of the Government, a great many conferences were necessary with the Shipping Board, the Ship Control Committee, representatives of the Emergency Fleet Corporation, and other allied bodies. I have tried to give to these bodies the military point of view about the necessity for the increase of manpower in France. All of these matters are now in a reasonably satisfactory state and as you know, the supply of troops is going forward at a very much increased rate.

With reference to promotion to the grade of General Officer, the policy of the Secretary was cabled to you [see April 23, A-1159-R-2]. I will say that the cablegram which was received from you on this subject was a great surprise to the War Department [see April 19, P-954-S], and I had imagined, until your letter reached me, that it was probably sent by Harbord. Of course, it is unnecessary and idle for me to say that appointments of the President are not subject to review. We have instituted in America the practice of requiring specific reports from inspectors who are sent out from Washington to all the camps, upon the efficiency or non-efficiency of General Officers, and the Secretary has relieved from National Army rank, all General Officers concerning whom adverse reports have been submitted. In the same way, those found doing their work efficiently and who are able to pass a physical test, are listed for advancement if so recommended. Division commanders are called upon for reports as to the ability and efficiency of their brigadiers, and in this way I keep accurate check on the performance of the entire list of General Officers in the United States. I agree with you that if there are two officers who are reported as equally efficient, the first advancement should go to the senior within certain limits, those limits being determined by age. The Secretary will not appoint anyone a General Officer who is 62 years of age or over, the policy being to attempt to get men who are not only fit, but have enough service before them to last through the War.

In connection with this subject, the Inspector General's Department has reported a number of officers taken from other arms of the service who have been assigned to the command of Field Artillery Brigades, who, although regarded as competent officers in the arm from which they came, proved total failures in commanding Field Artillery, and whose relief from such command was recommended. This situation has been a matter of great concern to the Secretary, and we are as far as possible, filling the Divisional Field Artillery Brigade with Field Artillery Generals. Heavy Artillery Brigades will be given to heavy Artillery Officers, and in the same way, as far as possible, an attempt will be made to put the round pegs in round holes. With all this policy, I am quite sure that you are in agreement. The Secretary of War has become quite convinced of the futility of making General Officers on what they did twenty years ago. The only thing he wants, as I have cabled you [see April 23, A-1159-R], is EFFICIENCY and EFFICIENCY NOW.

I see Senator Warren frequently and I had a very enjoyable evening in his apartments the other night, where I dined with him and Mrs. Warren. They are both very naturally very much interested in everything they can learn about you and Mrs. Warren seemed to be as affectionate toward you as if she were a real relative.

LC, Pershing Papers, folder: General Peyton C. March, box 123.

Secretary Baker to The President.

Mr. Jusserand [French Ambassador] and Lord Reading [British Ambassador] have both called upon me with reference to the expressions of their Governments in the matter of the preferential shipping of Infantry and Machine Gun units.

There seems to be confusion as to whether the statement of General Foch [w]as made before or after the formal written agreement drawn up by General Foch, Lord Milner and General Pershing as a committee and subsequently approved by the members of the Supreme War Council present at Abbeville. I told both Mr. Jusserand and Lord Reading that it seemed to me quite inadmissible for us here to reach any sort of agreement at variance with the formal written and signed agreement transmitted to us as representing the common belief of the military commanders; that if we undertook to depart from that program General Pershing might well feel disturbed and might come to the belief that so definite an agreement ought not to have been varied by the action of civilians without reference to him.

I, therefore, suggested that if General Foch felt that the agreement made did not really meet the exigencies of the military situation the best course would be for General Foch spontaneously to send for General Pershing, go over the military situation with him, and get General Pershing to agree to whatever modification is proper. We would then have a complete understanding between General Pershing and General Foch, and no possible holdback on General Pershing's part due to a feeling that his Government was not relying upon his judgment.

Mr. Jusserand believes that the wisest course, and told me that he was going to suggest to Mr. Clemenceau that he suggest to General Foch that he send for General Pershing and work out just what they want in a discussion between two military commanders, with full opportunity to weigh from personal observation the military needs.

[*Ed.*—Baker sent Pershing cable A-1297-R on May 11 on this matter.]

Link (ed.), *The Papers of Woodrow Wilson*, vol. 47: *March 13–May 12, 1918*, p. 595.

Pershing to TAG, War Department, in part in reply to TAG, War Department, to Pershing, cable A-970-R, March 23, and A-1165-R, April 24; in addition to Pershing to TAG, War Department, cable P-388-S, December 16.

Cable P-1084-S.

1. For Chief of Staff. Training cablegram number 11. With reference to principles involved in paragraph 2, our cablegram 388, in their application to heavy artillery and in order to provide for a nucleus of trained artillery and mechanical officers and soldiers as mechanics and chauffeurs for tractor organizations with which to facilitate and expedite the training of such units upon arrival here it is recommended that advanced parties of officers and soldiers of Coast Artillery be forwarded as follows: (A) 100 officers, Captain and Lieutenants unassigned Item C A 645 W, preferably drawn from Fort Monroe school, to arrive first each month, beginning July 1st to take courses at Artillery and tractor schools. (B) 20 officers per regiment, Captains and Lieutenants, Item C A 646 W, should arrive in France 2 months in advance of their regiments for course at Artillery and tractor schools. (C) 200 soldiers (sergeants, corporals and privates Item C A 647 W) unassigned, should arrive in France first of every month, beginning July 1st, to take course for mechanics and tractor drivers. (D) 100 soldiers per regiment (sergeants, corporals and privates Item C A 648 W) to arrive in France 1 month in advance of their regiments for courses in (C). The personnel called for under Items A and C will be a continuing demand, and it is calculated that this amount will be absorbed in future replacements and to meet the demand for return of officers to the United States as instructors for troops in training over there. Pershing [*Ed.*—On May 23 in cable A-1379-R-18, the War Department informed Pershing that 100 officers graduated from Fort Monroe would be sent over in July and 200 soldiers in June to take the mechanics and drivers course.]

1A. It is extremely important that officers selected for heavy artillery service in France have a working knowledge of elementary mathematics. 39 of the recently arrived officers who entered the heavy artillery school April 30th were found to be entirely unfamiliar with the elementary mathematics essential to the course and without sufficient educational groundwork to warrant their continuing at the school. All who failed were Coast Artillery National Guard. Officers lacking in this essential cannot become battery officers of heavy artillery, and, until they can be replaced, hold back the instruction and preparation of their units for active service.

1C. With reference to paragraph 4, your cablegram 1165. Organization Military Postal Service provides assumption military responsibility for handling incoming mails, sorted as at present in New York, from ports to troops, and arranging necessary transportation and distribution. Request civilian postal personnel now in France be directed to report to the Military Director, Postal Express Service. A large proportion of such personnel, retaining their civil status in the Postal Department and authorized to wear a uniform similar to that allowed for field clerks, will be assigned by the Military Authorities. To take charge or to serve in Post offices especially requiring technical experience, or for the service of money orders and registered mail. The less technical work will be performed by soldiers detailed for the purpose. Postal personnel not required by Military Authorities may be retained by the Civil Postal Agent for the care of the mail returning to the United States, and the performance of the necessary financial and clerical functions of the Post Office Department. Should it prove desirable to return any of the present civil postal personnel, who may be assigned to the Military Authorities, to the States, it is requested that this be done with the consent of Military Authorities and that they be replaced by others from the Postal Department. It is desired some postal employees be commissioned without prejudice to their ultimate return to present civil service status. Request P. McFarland, superintendent Chicago, be sent to France to study distribution needs in States from military point of view. [*Ed.*—McFarland was not sent.] [Reply—May 16, A-1331-R-1; in addition—Vol. 5, May 28, P-1202-S-2C]

1F. Request authority to confer at once not to exceed 50 Distinguished Service Medals on distinguished officers of our Allied force who have performed extraordinary meritorious service with the American Expeditionary Forces, without reference in each case to the War Department. Believe this will have an excellent effect in promoting good feeling between us and our Allies. It is understood from paragraph 7A, your cablegram 970, that the award of the Distinguished Service Cross and Medal to members of Allied forces is authorized. [*Ed.*—Replying on May 18, in cable A-1346-R-5, March informed Pershing that the President had authorized him "to confer not to exceed 50" DSMs to Allied officers. On June 19, in cable P-1334-S-1B, Pershing requested authority to award 50 additional DSMs to Allied officers and then "to confer limited number of additional" DSMs on November 20, in P-1914-S-3D. Pershing would go on to award many more DSMs to British, French, Belgian, and Italian officers. A partial list of those awardees can be found in P-2123-S, February 12, 1919, at NARA, RG 120, M930, Main Series, AEF to War Department, roll 6.]

NARA, RG 120, M930, Main Series, AEF to War Department, roll 3, and Main Series, War Department to AEF, rolls 6 and 12.

Pershing to TAG, War Department.

Cable P-1086-S. Confidential.
For the Chief of Staff.

1. In order that the War Department may be fully informed as to the present disposition of our Forces in France and of the assistance now being rendered the Allied Armies by these forces, the following summary is given:

1A. On March 19th, 2 days before the German offensive began, there were in France to 296,819 officers and men, of which 167,672 were combatant troops, represented by 4 combat divisions, 1 replacement and 1 depot division and 1 regiment of infantry—colored troops—serving with the French.

1B. At present there are in England and France, 466,412 officers and men, of which 290,765 are combatant troops. To these should be added 21,812 enroute from ports of debarkation giving a grand total of 488,224. The combatant troops are represented by the following complete divisions: 1st, 2nd, 3rd, 26th, 32nd, 41st, 42d, and 77th and the following incomplete divisions: 5th, 28th, 35th, 82d and 93rd. There are also 3 Brigades of Heavy Coast Artillery, the 30th Gas and Flame Engineers, 4 regiments of Cavalry and certain special troops giving a total of 290,765 officers and men.

1C. Organizations serving in American divisional sectors are: 1st Division, 2nd Division, 26th Division, 42d Division, 1 Brigade Heavy Artillery. Total 4100 officers, enlisted men 98,989. These organizations are tactically under the French Corps sector staffs, but for administration, replacement and supply are under our own 1st Corps Headquarters.

1D. The 1st Division is in the Picardy battle near Montdidier; the 2d Division holding a sector near Verdun, but will be withdrawn within a few days (Being replaced by a used French division) and take position on the Picardy front; the 26th Division is holding a sector north of Toul and the 42d Division is holding a sector near Luneville. The 32d Division which, because of the present emergency, has been reconstituted from a replacement to a combat division, will shortly enter line in a quiet sector and relieve further French troops. Our divisions being approximately double the strength in infantry of a French division we are taking over a length of front in proportion to the strength of our troops, thus relieving double the number of French divisions from the line for participation in the Picardy battle.

1E. The Infantry and Machine Gun units of the 77th Division which have arrived in the British area, are receiving preliminary training preparatory to entering the line by battalions in British brigades for initial trench training. The 35th and 82d Divisions are now arriving and will undergo training with the British preparatory to entering line under the same condition as the 77th Division. We have sent to the British the following auxiliary troops: 4 regiments railroad engineers, 1 regiment pioneer engineers, 1 battalion forestry engineers, 1 telegraph battalion Signal Corps and 6 Base Hospitals; also 9,826 officers and men of the Air Service. (4 Aero Squadrons being at the front).

1F. The French have had turned over to them 4 negro regiments of the 93d Division, approximately 5,500 motor mechanics, 6 machine shop truck units and 80 sections of the U. S. Ambulance Service.

1G. To accomplish the above, the A.E.F. Service of Supply has contributed every available unit not absolutely essential to continuing the operation of our supply service.

1H. The following organizations are now undergoing training: the 3rd Division; the 5th Division, less its artillery which had not yet sailed; the 41st Division (Depot) which is composed of necessary personnel only for instruction and administration of newly arriving replacements; heavy artillery, consisting of 31st and 32d Artillery Brigades, which arrived during the past month and is in training and the 54th Heavy Artillery Regiment which has been designated as a replacement for these brigades; the artillery of the 77th Division. Total for training and replacement, officers 5,500, enlisted men 101,600.

1J. Services of Supply troops total 140,049. Combatant troops attached the service of supply include 4 Cavalry and 2 infantry regiments, 1 engineer regiment and 2 ammunition trains. Total 16,885.

1K. Troops with the British in training 34,334, of which 27,960 are infantry, the rest special units. Troops in service with British 11,410, all of which are special units, giving a total of 45,744.

1L. Troops with French in training 8,199, all infantry. Troops with French in service 12,234, all of which are special units. Total 20,423.

1M. Recapitulation. In service. Serving with American Sectors of the line, 103,089; Service of Supply troops 140,049; combatant troops used in Service of Supply 16,885; serving with British 11,410; serving with the French 12,234; total 283,667. In training. In American training areas, including aviation, 133,534; with British forces 34,334, with French forces 8,199; total 176,067. Enroute from ports of debarkation to join A.E.F. and B.E.F. 21,812; sick and detached 6,678; making a grand total of 488,224.

1N. In addition to the assistance being given to the French and British Army in the form of infantry and special troops, as has been enumerated herein, our troops are actually holding 35 miles of the front line. The significance of this fact can be better appreciated when it is realized that this is more than double the front held by the Belgian Army and more than the front held by the British Army during the first year of the war.

NARA, RG 120, M930, Confidential Series, AEF to War Department, roll 7.

Editor's Note—Baker sent Pershing's cable to President Wilson on May 11 with the following note:

> This very specific information will interest you and I think will give you pleasure. It really is the concrete answer to many current doubts and queries. The figures (gross) vary from the half million which I announced the other day because of some troops shipped but not yet arrived in France when General Pershing's study was made. (Link (ed.), *The Papers of Woodrow Wilson*, vol. 47: *March 13–May 12, 1918*, pp. 611–13.)

Pershing to TAG, War Department, in reply to TAG, War Department, to Pershing, cable A-1266-R, May 8.

Cable P-1092-S. Confidential.
For the Chief of Staff.

Reference your 1266. Admiral Sims agreed that by using specially selected fast and well-armed ships no substantial increase danger existed in their trans-Atlantic movement without convoy. Sending same to Gibraltar in present convoys would probably result in delaying turnaround some 10 to 15 days on account of loss of time awaiting convoy and slow speed of same. Sims states ships going to Bay of Biscay ports require strong convoy on account of activity smaller type enemy submarines in these waters which submarines are particularly effective with their torpedo fire. Enemy submarines operating off Gibraltar of large type which attack usually with gunfire only and not so effective with torpedo. Recommend matter be taken up with

Navy Department as originally outlined. Navy to select vessels to be used in this movement and type of armament to be installed and that they make trans-Atlantic movement without convoy. Have quoted this cable to Sims with request that he transmit similar recommendations to Navy Department. [Reply—May 11, A-1292-R]

NARA, RG 120, M930, Confidential Series, AEF to War Department, roll 7.

Pershing to TAG, War Department, in reply to TAG, War Department, to Pershing, cable A-1248-R, May 5, in addition to Pershing to TAG, War Department, cable P-1064-S, May 6.

Cable P-1093-S. Confidential.
For the Chief of Staff.
 1. Reference cablegram from Secretary of War, No. 1248. Have further considered matter of sending troops to Italy and believe wiser policy is to gradually build up a complete division as such unit would more completely represent American than small detachment. It would take its place beside British and French divisions already there and would be considered as generously acceding to Italy's request, which is the impression we should create if we send troops at all. Therefore believe it better, considering all conditions, to look forward to completing 1 entire division. As stated in paragraph 2, my cablegram 1064, both French and British Prime Ministers agree to this plan. Troops need not follow immediately but division can be built up within 3 or 4 months as Italian transportation becomes available.
 2. Italian Government through Mr. Orlando has submitted the 2 following proposals for transporting troops to Italy: (1) Steamships Duke of d'Abbruzzi and Duke Aosta which are at this moment in New York and are able to carry 4,000 men in all. These steamships are part of those that the Italian Government was to consign to the United States and the Italian Government understands that should these ships be utilized for this transportation they will be replaced. In this case the departure of the first American troops for Italy would be expedited; (2) If above solution is not acceptable the Italian Government will employ the 2 steamships Taormina and Verona with a capacity of 6,000 men in all. These latter steamships will be disposable about the end of present month and can complete their loading in New York on June 20. Mr. Orlando desires prompt reply in order to insure the availability of the steamships.
 3. Recommend acceptance to second proposal, that is, use of steamships Taormina and Verona, and the shipment thereby of the following troops to begin with 1 infantry brigade headquarters, 1 infantry regiment, 1 brigade machine gun battalion, 1 ambulance company motorized, 1 field hospital company motorized and 1 outpost company of Field Signal Battalion.
[Reply—May 19, A-1350-R-3]

NARA, RG 120, M930, Confidential Series, AEF to War Department, roll 7.

TAG, War Department, to Pershing, in addition to TAG, War Department, to Pershing, cable A-1182-R, April 26, in part in reply to Pershing to TAG, War Department, cable P-1051-S, May 4, and P-1063-S, May 6.

Cable A-1282-R.

1. Further reference to paragraph 1B, your 1063. To what port should 5 Navy 14-inch guns and carriages be shipped? Heaviest lift 100 tons. [Reply—Vol. 5, May 20, P-1154-S-2A]

8. Our 1182, paragraph 5. 19 lake vessels about 3100 tons dead weight now loading at various Great Lake ports. It is expected most of these vessels will clear from Halifax by end of May, another 10 expected clear Halifax by middle of June. All vessels will be loaded; about one-half with subsistence only, remainder subsistence and auto trucks. As per paragraph 6A, your 1051, all these lake vessels will be given Brest as tentative destination with the understanding that you will order them by wireless through Naval authorities to whatever ports of discharge you desire. Goethals.

NARA, RG 120, M930, Main Series, War Department to AEF, roll 12.

TAG, War Department, to Pershing.

Cable A-1283-R. Confidential.

Vacancies exist for 6 Major Generals and 33 Brigadier Generals in National Guard and Army. Among Brigadier Generals 4 will be appointed from Field Artillery. Colonels to fill vacant Field Artillery Brigades. Other appointments from the Army at large. If you have officers you desire to recommend for these vacancies please submit promptly. As all these vacancies exist in the United States it will be necessary in cases of officers appointed from American Expeditionary Forces that they return to the United States immediately upon their confirmation. Secretary of War will be glad to consider the names of any Colonels of the National Guard whom you think deserving of advancement. March. [Reply—May 15, P-1118-S; in addition—Vol. 5, June 8, P-1266-S-2D, June 27, P-1380-S-7]

NARA, RG 120, M930, Confidential Series, War Department to AEF, roll 18.

TAG, War Department, to Pershing, reference Bliss to TAG, War Department, cable 107-S, May 9.

Cable A-1284-R. Confidential.

3. Reference to statement of Prime Minister [of Italy] . . . sent us by Bliss, which he states he has communicated to you. The Secretary of War desires that any arrange-

ments made with Italy with reference to the supply of American troops should be first submitted to the War Department for approval. The proposition to send American troops direct to Italy has not at any time been considered by the War Department with the exception of the sanitary units which were scheduled to be sent in Steamship Verona. March. [Reply—May 14, P-1115-S]

NARA, RG 120, M930, Confidential Series, War Department to AEF, roll 18.

TAG, War Department, to Pershing.

Cable A-1285-R. Confidential.
    Major General W. A. Holbrook, commanding Southern Department, has recommended that remaining troops of Cavalry Division be placed at his disposal for border patrol work, Situation along the border extremely critical and giving Administration great concern. In view of demands from abroad for infantry and machine gun platoons, impossible to divert such forces for use along the border. As this Cavalry Division was organized in response to your request the Secretary of War directs me to inform you of the necessity for its present use elsewhere than in France so that you may understand why it is taken off your Priority Schedule during present emergency. March. [Reply—May 16, P-1126-S-3]

NARA, RG 120, M930, Confidential Series, War Department to AEF, roll 18.

May 11

Pershing's Personal Diary

    Left Chaumont at 10 a. m. with Colonel Boyd, Colonel Fiske and Colonel Drum. Stopped at the Hotel du Commerce, Bar-le-Duc. In afternoon went out from town to Robert-Espagne and spent the afternoon with General Bundy at headquarters of the 2nd Division. Inspected the 3rd Battalion, 23rd Infantry, which had come out of the trenches in the morning. Their general appearance was very good. Saw Colonel [Paul B.] Malone [CO, 23rd Infantry], General [Edward M.] Lewis [CG, 3rd Infantry Brigade], and Lieutenant Colonel Bessell. Had long talk with General Bundy. Returned to Bar-le-Duc for night.
    Major Shannon came up from headquarters with cable from Washington asking for recommendations in view of appointment of six new Major Generals and 33 Brigadiers [see May 10, A-1283-R]. Sent back to headquarters some notes I had already made on recommendations. Also directed Major Shannon to consult Colonel Eltinge on a new organization table for the headquarters S.O.S. They have too many officers.

LC, Pershing Papers, Diary, May 7, 1917–September 1, 1918, box 4.

Omar Bundy was designated commander of the newly activated 2nd Division in France in October 1917. He commanded the division through spring and early summer of 1918, including the heavy fighting against the Germans along the Marne River and in the area of Château-Thierry and Belleau Wood. Never a strong supporter of Bundy, Pershing increasingly lost confidence in him and by early June decided to relieve him when the time came (see Vol. 5). That time came on July 20, 1918, when Pershing removed Bundy, placing him in command of the VI Corps, which was then largely a training organization. He was returned to the United States early in November. Source: Library of Congress, Prints & Photographs Division, Harris & Ewing Collection (LC-DIG-hec-19236).

Pershing to Haig, reply to Haig to Pershing, May 5.

I am in receipt of your note of May 5th concerning the question of artillery personnel.

Under the recent agreement the shipment from the United States of all artillery personnel other than that pertaining to divisions has been suspended, as you will recall, and infantry and machine gun units have a very considerable priority over even the divisional artillery. [*Ed.*—The agreement at the Supreme War Council meeting at Abbeville on May 2 specifically designated priority for shipment of infantry and machine-gun units rather than supporting arms and services such as artillery and Services of Supply. (See May 3, P-1042-S, and May 6, P-1064-S.)]

I regret to say that all divisional artillery units now in France have either joined their divisions on the front or are on their way to do so, and, of course, will soon be in the line with their units to replace corresponding French divisions.

As to heavy artillery, we have brought over only those units for which equipment was available at the time of embarkation or else promised for early delivery. But as the British War Office has been unable to deliver the heavy howitzers which had been promised for delivery in March and April, there are certain heavy artillery units which as yet I have been unable to equip or train.

While under ordinary circumstances I would much prefer that the training be held at the usual centers, I would be glad, under the circumstances, to send a regiment of six batteries for temporary service provided you have equipment available for them. In the event you desire these troops I would prefer that they be trained and employed as complete units. I shall have the matter further examined and think I shall be able to increase this number.

[Reply—May 15, Haig to Pershing]

LC, Pershing Papers, folder: Field Marshal Sir Douglas Haig, 1917–1918, box 86.

Bliss, Chief, American Section, and Permanent Military Representative, SWC, Versailles, to Pershing, reply to Pershing to Bliss, telegram No. 44 (received), May 10.

Subject: American Troops for Service in the Italian Army.

I beg to acknowledge receipt of your telegram of May 10th relative to the use of steamships Taormina and Verona which I have communicated to the Italian Military Representatives on the Supreme War Council.

Enclosed please find the copy of the original letter on this subject received from the Italian Section.

1 Enclosure [not reproduced]

LC, Bliss Papers, folder: American Expeditionary Forces and American Forces in France, January–December 1918, box 248.

Pershing to CS, GHQ, AEF, Chaumont.

1. I wish you would look into the matter of motor repair shops, etc., now being put in at Dijon. I do not know to what extent this project is being carried out, but should like to know. Please have careful study made regarding its location and magnitude. It seems to me that it is rather out of the way. I should much prefer to see it in the vicinity of Troyes. This should be made the subject of study by the General Staff before we get too far into the project.

2. Reference Is-sur-Tille, the last time I made an inspection there I found the work about half completed; that is, if we are to carry out the entire program as laid down. I am not so sure that we want to push this program at this time as far as originally planned, and with that idea in mind I halted the work there and directed that the question of decreasing the amount of space at Is-sur-Tille [sic] and reported upon. This also should be made the subject of immediate study by the General Staff with a view to a decision as to whether or not it is necessary for us to continue the extensive original work originally planned there.

3. I have heard nothing with reference to the construction of regulating station at Liffol-le-Grand. Here also is a question involving many considerations. The main one, however, is the question of probable front we are going to occupy. As far as I can see now, we shall occupy some front over in this part of the line, even if only for instruction, and will probably need Liffol-le-Grand. In any event, either ourselves or the French are going to need it before the war is over, although not on too extensive a plan.

(Note: The construction at the above three places will be influenced by the location of the sector we expect to occupy or the line of offensive we might assume when the time comes. Meanwhile, we have troops up here which must be supplied and that of itself makes a certain percentage of construction at these three places necessary. The General Staff has already made considerable study, as have I, on the subject of the location of our sector when we enter the line. I wish you would make an examination of this and I will talk with you further on the subject upon my return.)

4. This question of aviation is one that is going to give us a lot of trouble before we progress much further with it. I believe that they are deficient in a great many of the details of their work. For instance, photography, wireless signaling, combat instruction. Desire to have a capable staff officer, possibly of the Inspector General's Department, make a thorough study of aviation matters, especially the details of their instruction in the branches observation and fighting.

5. This question of tanks is another thing that should be given consideration. Our tank program has been worked out theoretically and we have made certain agreements with the French and British regarding construction of tanks and have recommended to the War Department accordingly, but I, myself, am not so sure that we are altogether on the right side of the question. I wish you would have a study made of this question with a view to determining more definitely what is best to do in carrying out this tank program. We have not got so far but what we can retire gracefully. I think an early reconsideration of this matter is essential.

6. The Provost Marshal's office has never been organized to my satisfaction. While they are doing some good work in the towns, especially in Paris, there has never been any system of instruction prescribed for the military police, and I have never found any divisional police that seemed to know what it is for. I would suggest the establishment of a school based upon the British system of handling their military police and that a certain percentage of men be sent from each division to attend this school and get an idea of what their duties are. Please take this up with General Allaire [then AEF's Provost Marshal General], although I have very little hope of getting much out of him.

LC, Pershing Papers, folder: vol. 2: Memoranda, A.E.F., 1918, box 133.

Pershing to TAG, War Department, in part in reply to TAG, War Department, to Pershing, cables, A-1151-R, April 21, and A-1246-R, May 5 (not reproduced).

Cable P-1094-S.
  1. For Chief of Staff. 1B. Believe expedient fill vacancies lower grades in France by promotion only from organizations in France. Can we count on authority to commission successful graduates present class Army Candidate School in Officers Reserve Corps? Course ends June 30th.
  7. For Felton, With reference to paragraph 3, your cablegram 1151, and paragraph 1, your cablegram 1246. Take no further steps in connection with Belgian Car Building Plant. Belgian authorities unable for the present to give any assurance that labor required can be supplied.

NARA, RG 120, M930, Main Series, AEF to War Department, roll 3.

Pershing to TAG, War Department, in part in reply to TAG, War Department, to Pershing, cable A-1211-R, April 30.

Cable P-1096-S.
  3. For Chief of Ordnance. With reference to paragraph 1B, your cablegram 1211. It is recommended that order for 25 8-inch carriages be cancelled, that the number of carriages for 8-inch naval guns be reduced to 9 and that 16 mounts for 50 caliber gun be manufactured and that the orders for 35 caliber, Model 1918 gun, be cancelled. If the execution of the above recommendation will cause a loss of material and a disorganization of the present manufacturing project, it is recommended that sufficient carriages be completed to mount the 77 Army guns plus the number of 35 caliber, Model 1918 guns, now under construction, allowing for 100% replacement and the manufacturing of sufficient mounts for 50 caliber gun to bring the total to 62, allowing for 9 naval mounts. [Reply—Vol. 5, May 24, A-1388-R-1]

NARA, RG 120, M930, Main Series, AEF to War Department, roll 3.

TAG, War Department, to Pershing, in addition to TAG, War Department, to Pershing, cables A-1224-R, May 2, and A-1256-R, May 5 (not reproduced).

Cable A-1290-R. Confidential.
    Referring to our 1256 from Aircraft Board [*Ed.*—This cable was a summary of actual and projected aircraft and engine production, shipments to France, and planned shipments as of May 1], this must not be confused with our 1224. 1256 refers to expected output of planes which may not be equipped with engines if allocation of engines after July 1st is made in favor of Allies and Navy. This production may also be curtailed if raw materials of which there is shortage are insufficient for all needs and available raw materials allocated to Allies. Owing to the uncertainty as to allocation of Liberty engines and raw materials after July 1st it will only lead to confusion to attempt to give production estimates for Inter-Allied meeting in Paris on 11th of each month. In the future will send only actual production results, and such immediate production estimates as known allocation of materials permits to be made.

NARA, RG 120, M930, Confidential Series, War Department to AEF, roll 18.

TAG, War Department, to Pershing.

Cable A-1291-R.
    9. Navy Department has been authorized to send a Brigadier General, Marine Corps, to France to replace Brigadier General Charles A. Doyen. This officer to be assigned to a unit not actually engaged in the line or otherwise as you may see fit, and request for an additional Brigadier General, Marine Corps, to be sent to France for such duty Expeditionary Forces as may be assigned him by you in order that he may be available in case vacancy occurs in connection with the Marines or for such duty as you may deem proper has been approved by War Department. March.
    10. Reference German claim the capture of officers and men amounting to some 183 in the fighting at Seicheprey. Please report if that fact has been verified. March. [Reply—May 16, P-1134-S-1P]

NARA, RG 120, M930, Main Series, War Department to AEF, roll 12.

TAG, War Department, to Pershing, in reply to Pershing to TAG, War Department, cable A-1092-S, May 10.

Cable A-1292-R. Confidential.
    With reference to your 1092. The Marseille proposition was originally taken up with the Navy Department as outlined by you, and approval of the War Department

scheme was based on the concurrence of the Navy. The War Department does not intend to interfere in any way with convoys which are arranged by the Navy. March

NARA, RG 120, M930, Confidential Series, War Department to AEF, roll 18.

TAG, War Department, to Pershing.

Cable A-1296-R. Confidential.

French Commission, having stated they had available here and would be glad to supply information regarding output of their munition plants, following inquiries were made of them:

1. What is present output of French factories of (A) 75-millimeter guns, (B) carriages, (C) recuperators therefor, (D) 155-millimeter guns, (E) carriages, (F) recuperators therefor, (G) 155-millimeter howitzer, (H) carriages, (I) recuperators therefor.

2. Are plants manufacturing guns, carriages and recuperators operating at full capacity, and, to what extent can they be increased? This information is particularly desired respecting plants producing recuperators for 75 millimeter and 155-millimeter guns.

3. What is present output of shells for 75-millimeter, 155-millimeter guns and 155-millimeter howitzers, and are these plants operating to full capacity? If not, to what extent can they be increased?

4. What is percent output of French factories of small arms ammunition, and are these plans operating at full capacity? If not, to what extent can they be increased?

5. If an increase capacity of guns, howitzers, carriages, recuperators, small arms ammunition is contingent upon certain conditions as to replacement of materials in kind or otherwise, what are these conditions?

6. To what extent is the output of French factories producing guns, howitzers and ammunition therefore and small arms ammunition required for French troops, and also to what extent is required to fulfill any obligations to other Allied Governments, not including the United States?

A. French mission now states that they have called abroad for this information, and that under present circumstances they cannot state what part of French output is required for their own troops.

B. While production of artillery in this country is being prosecuted vigorously, nevertheless, having in view probable difficulties and finishing in assembling recuperators for 75-millimeter and 155-millimeter guns, as well as possible delays due to other causes into labor, transportation and <u>fuel</u> supply, it appears desirable to secure as complete a statement as possible regarding output of French factories. As inquiry is before authorities in France it is recommended that efforts be made to secure the information in as complete for as possible, and that it be cabled here in due course.
[Reply—Vol. 5, June 2, P-1231-S]

NARA, RG 120, M930, Confidential Series, War Department to AEF, roll 18.

TAG, War Department, to Pershing.

Cable A-1297-R. Confidential.
The following from the Secretary of War:
"The President asked me to say to you that he has been much impressed and disturbed by representation officially made to him here by French and British Ambassadors showing the steady drain upon French and British replacements and the small number of replacement troops now available. He feels that you on the ground have full opportunity to know the situation and fully trusts your judgment as to how far we ought to give additional priority to infantry and machine gun units, in view of the fact that such troops seem to be the most immediately serviceable and urgently needed. The Abbeville agreement, of course, provides less priority for infantry machine gun units than was recommended by the Supreme War Council, but with shipping at present in prospect will result in practically 120,000 infantry and machine gun units, Signal Corps, and Engineer Corps per month during May and June. It has been suggested to the President that General Foch may reopen the subject with you and the President hopes you will approach any such interview as systematically as possible, particularly if the suggestion as to replacements which have been presented to him is as critical as it seems."

In this connection, for your confidential information, there is now left in the United States, excluding 3 divisions at ports of embarkation, 263,852 infantrymen of sufficient training for overseas service, so that unless the acceptance untrained infantrymen is desired, there is a practical limit to the extent to which the infantry and machine gun program can be carried. The number quoted above troops augmented during this month by some 200,000 men but of course these men should not be sent abroad without at least 3 months training. March. [Reply—May 15, P-1124-S; Vol. 5, May 23, P-1170-S]

NARA, RG 120, M930, Confidential Series, War Department to AEF, roll 18.

May 12

Pershing's Personal Diary

With 2nd Division. Left Bar-le-Duc at about 9 a. m. and inspected the 1st Battalion, 9th Infantry, Major Travers commanding, at Savonnieres; thence went with General Lewis to Fains where I inspected the 3rd Battalion of the 9th Infantry. Men of both battalions presented very good appearance; generally in need of clothing. Thence went to Robert-Espagne. Had lunch with General Bundy. Received General Blandelat, commanding 2nd Corps, with which 2nd Division had been serving. He spoke in very high terms of the Colonial Division; particularly of General Bundy and Colonels Malone and [Albert J.] Bowley [2nd Artillery Brigade]. He stated that he thought that the Americans could very soon, to advantage, begin training their own troops in quiet sectors. He thought the difference in language and temperament between Americans and French was a handicap to the present system of having Americans train with French. He stated, however, that his relations with the Americans had been most pleasant and that he personally would be glad to have them serve either with him or beside him. Went from Robert-Espagne to Blesmes, railhead of the 2nd Division. Saw there Lieutenant Colonel Carson, Q. M. Corps, and had talk with him about conditions generally. He seemed to think that the supply of troops is very well accomplished but that there was some delay in transmitting requisitions to Is-sur-Tille due to their having to pass through G-1 of the Division instead of going directly from the Division quartermaster to the Regulating Officer at Is-sur-Tille. He also stated that the Division quartermaster is not supposed, according to present interpretation of orders, to be able answer directly an inquiry from the Chief Quartermaster as to whether or not supplies are being received. He stated that the reply to such telegrams is now obliged to pass through Division Headquarters for the Division Commander's approval. He did not see why the Division Quartermaster should not answer this telegram directly.

A few broken bags of oats and potatoes were to be seen in the uncovered stacks by the railroad, but on the whole the situation was not bad. Returned to Bar-le-Duc for dinner. Worked until about 1 a. m. on promotion list.

LC, Pershing Papers, Diary, May 7, 1917–September 1, 1918, box 4.

Haig to Pershing, reply to Pershing to Haig, May 7 (not located).

[*Ed.*—This letter from Haig to Pershing was undated, so I have selected May 12 arbitrarily because it fell midway between Pershing's original letter of May 7 and his response of May 16 to Haig's undated letter. Although Pershing's letter of May 7 is mentioned in Scott's *Robert Bacon*, which reproduced both this Haig letter and Pershing's reply of May 16, the letter of May 7 was not published or quoted (pp. 334–37).]

I beg to thank you for your letter of May 7th, and I note that it is your intention to combine the office of the American Mission and the Commanding General of American Units serving with the British Expeditionary Forces. I consider that this arrangement should work very well until American divisions are grouped into an Army Corps. When that takes place I presume that the Commanding General will have to be relieved of the work of the Mission. This, however, is not likely to take place for some months, and the arrangement you propose will, in the meantime, be quite satisfactory. I shall be glad to receive General William W. Harts as the Chief of the American Mission.

As regards Colonel Bacon, I am very glad to learn of your decision to leave him on duty at my Headquarters. In view of the large number of American troops which will shortly be operating with the British forces, I suggest that it will be advantageous to attach him to my Personal Staff as my Personal Liaison Officer with American

Units in the British Area. In my dealings with the French and Belgian Units operating in close touch with my troops, I have found the presence of a French or Belgian Liaison Officer attached to my Personal Staff of very great value. I therefore hope that you will agree to Colonel Bacon being attached to my Personal Staff in the same way.

LC, Pershing Papers, folder: Field Marshal Sir Douglas Haig (1917–1918), box 86.

Edward M. House, New York City, to President Wilson.

Here is a cable which has just come from Sir William [Wiseman]. While interesting it is in some ways disturbing.

When I was in Paris I saw that Pershing needed someone to help him do the things that were not strictly military but were more or less diplomatic. I talked with him frankly about it and he seemed to realize the need and asked my advice as to what was best to do. He has too much on his shoulders.

Pershing knows as well as we do that the Roosevelt-Wood crowd are trying to push him out, and he is also conscious of your desire and that of the entire Administration that he should succeed.

I hope Sir William is mistaken in believing that he and Bliss are at outs for while Bliss has not great initiative, he has the saving quality of good sense and Pershing would not go far wrong if he advised with Bliss and they acted in unison. Bliss also has the quality of getting along with others. . . . [*Ed.*—Hereafter followed a lengthy cable of May 11 from Wiseman in London in which he outlined his strong opposition to the Abbeville Agreement and attacked Pershing's views. The text of this cable can be found in the source cited below.]

Link (ed.), *The Papers of Woodrow Wilson*, vol. 47: *March 13–May 12, 1918*, pp. 616–20.

Editor's Note—Sir William Wiseman, a British military attaché and spy as well as a confidante of House, provided a direct back channel from Prime Minister David Lloyd George and his Foreign Secretary, Arthur J. Balfour, to President Wilson via House. Lloyd George and Balfour used Wiseman's closeness to House to influence him with frequent criticism of Pershing and his policies against amalgamation, troop shipments, and other British positions. The British and French both increased their pressure on Washington concerning Pershing and his policies following the Abbeville Conference in early May, often to no avail. Later that month Lloyd George sent a cable to Lord Reading for Wilson, which he first took to House. The British wanted Wilson to send House to the next Supreme War Council meeting in early June in hopes that he would override Pershing in the ongoing dispute on amalgamation and troop shipments (see House's recommendation to Wilson in Vol. 5, May 20). Having played the role of facilitator at Abbeville, Fowler explained how Wiseman now turned into a fierce critic of Pershing, trying to undermine his position and policies with House and Wilson:

Having played a part in the Abbeville agreement did not make Wiseman a defender of it. On the contrary, he soon decided that the Allies had erred by giving in to Pershing. They should have, he thought, admitted inability to agree with Pershing, placed Foch's arguments for amalgamation before Wilson, and let him make a decision. Acting on his second thoughts, Wiseman set about undermining Pershing's position before the next discussion of the use of American soldiers came up in June. As soon as the Abbeville meeting broke up he visited Clemenceau and urged him to dispatch Foch's statement criticizing Pershing to Washington. Clemenceau replied that the statement had already gone to Washington as an expression of the sentiments of both the French and British governments. Wiseman cabled the Allies' unhappiness with Abbeville to House and induced Frazier to report similarly to the State Department. To House he characterized Pershing as suspicious of the Allies, obsessed with the idea of an autonomous army, and unable to get along with Bliss. Pershing acted, Wiseman said, as if he were a head of government rather than a field commander. Plainly, Wiseman hoped to impress on House and Wilson, who received a copy of the cable, that the Allies signed the Abbeville agreement only because of Pershing's unrestrained power.

Nonetheless, the British by signing the agreement weakened the force of these tardy objections to it. House, although he agreed with Wiseman's preference for Foch's plan and forwarded Wiseman's reports to Wilson, realized that there was little chance of undoing Abbeville. (Fowler, *British-American Relations*, pp. 147–48.)

Pershing to TAG, War Department, in reply to TAG, War Department, to Pershing, cables A-1217-R, May 1, A-1247-R, May 5, and A-1251-R, May 6 (not reproduced), in addition to Pershing to TAG, War Department, cables P-891-S, April 11, P-961-S, April 24, P-1042-S, May 3, and P-1064-S, May 6.

Cable P-1099-S. Confidential.
For the Chief of Staff.

1. Reference all previous cables on priority of troop shipments and especially your 1217 and my 1042. Abbeville agreement given in my 1042 and especially that set forth in my 1064 require a change in program outlined in your 1217. The latter agreement is much more favorable to ultimate formation of a distinctly American Force. Therefore recommend following priority for May and June, schedule for July subject to future consideration.

2. Recommend for May, assuming that available shipping will be British, 130,000 and American 70,000, priority to conform as far as practicable to the following British shipping to bring A units (see my 961) of 6 divisions for training with British, total about 118,000, the balance of available space to be utilized for replacements Item 650 R; American shipping to bring, in order stated, units to complete 3d and

5th Divisions about 9,600, 19,000 service of supply, B and attached units for 3 divisions about 27,400, 6 balloon companies and 3 photograph sections about 1,200, and remaining available space to be utilized for replacements Item 650 R.

3. For June, assuming available shipping will be British 150,000 and American 70,000, recommend priority as follows: British shipping to bring, in order stated, A units of 6 divisions about 118,000, B and attached units of 3 divisions about 27,400, and remaining available space to be utilized for replacements Item 666 R, grand total about 150,000; American shipping to bring, in order given, B and attached units of 6 divisions about 54,700 and remaining available space to be utilized for replacements Items 666 R.

4. B units referred to above are remainder of each division after deducting A units outlined in my 961. Attached units comprise for each division 2 sanitary squads, 1 mobile laboratory, 1 bakery company, 1 butchery company, dentists Corps, 2 base hospitals (reduced from 4) and 3 laundries.

5. It will be noted that foregoing requires further suspension priority of shipment of units referred to in 1B and 1H my 891 and your 1217. Reference paragraph 1H my 891 request substitution of depot battalion Item S-302, page 4, Priority Schedule, in place of 1 construction battalion, Item S-404, page 13.

6. Your 1247 concerning replacements understood. Essential that divisions be completed by bring over all units contemplated in foregoing, only a few replacements will be delayed to meet this necessity. Considering number of A units already shipped it will be noted that upon completion of program herein outlined there will be several divisions in France without their B units. Please cable action taken on these recommendations as soon as practicable.

7. Reference paragraph 12, your number 1251. Agreement with British precludes sending sanitary train companies with A units. However no objection to attaching camp infirmaries to infantry regiments. Will endeavor to have some ambulance and field hospital companies join their A units after former arrive in France. [*Ed.*—In cable A-1251-R, May 6, March asked for Pershing's decision on the Surgeon General's recommendation that two ambulance companies and two field hospitals accompany the infantry units of divisions shipped to France ahead of the rest of the divisions.] [Reply—May 14, A-1316-R-1]

NARA, RG 120, M930, Confidential Series, AEF to War Department, roll 7, and Main Series, War Department to AEF, roll 12.

Pershing to TAG, War Department, in addition to TAG, War Department, to Pershing, cable P-1052-S, May 4.

Cable P-1102-S.

2. For Chief Signal Officer. 2C. With reference to paragraph 2A, our cablegram 1052 disapproving production of SE 5 airplanes in United States. This question is still open pending final report of Board of Air Service Officers now in England investi-

gating types of airplanes and engines for 1918 and 1919 production. Final recommendations will be cabled upon completion of Board investigation, about 10 days. [Reply—Vol. 5, May 31, A-1432-R-4; in addition—Vol. 5, May 26, P-1192-S-5]

NARA, RG 120, M930, Main Series, AEF to War Department, roll 3.

May 13

Pershing's Personal Diary

With the 2nd Division. Went to Ancemont where some troops of Division were embarking. Saw on the road elements of the 2nd Engineer Train, which were badly strung out over road. Saw Machine Gun Companies of 5th and 6th Marines on the road. These were marching in good order. Saw also some sanitary columns and ammunition columns. Stopped at Souilly and talked to Lieutenant Colonel Bridges and Salvage Officer there, who had a stack of salvage material which, he stated, would make 40 carloads. Talked to Colonel Bridges about advisability of having requisition system for obtaining clothing for troops and having Quartermaster detailed to visit companies and ascertain their wants and to be responsible that the companies receive what they need. Returned to Bar-le-Duc for luncheon. After luncheon went to Vanault-les-Dames, headquarters of General Harbord's Brigade of Marines. Not finding him there, went through Changy where 6th Marines were billeted, or were to be billeted.

Inspected the 2nd Battalion, 6th Marines, Major [Thomas] Holcomb, commanding [Commandant of the Marine Corps, 1936-43]. These men had arrived in their billets after midnight and presented an excellent appearance. They were shaved and clean, and their arms were in good condition. Also inspected the 1st Battalion of the 6th Marines, Major [Maurice E.] Shearer commanding, at Buisemont. This Battalion presented a very good appearance. However, in view of the fact that they had been in billets for 2 or 3 days, I told the Battalion Commander to transmit my instructions to the Regimental Commander that he inspect this Battalion within the next few days. Returned to General Harbord's headquarters, found him there and had long talk with him. Saw also Majors Leigh and Smith of the Marine Corps. Had dinner at Bar-le-Duc. Talked to Colonel Mitchell of the Air Service, who outlined to me the work he is doing with his squadrons near Toul.

LC, Pershing Papers, Diary, May 7, 1917–September 1, 1918, box 4.

Lord Milner, Secretary of State for War, London, to Pershing, reply to Pershing to Milner and Haig, May 7 (see note with Pershing to Haig, May 5).

Your letter of May 7th about the employment of coloured Divisions with our British forces in France. I am rather hoping that this difficult question may not after all be going to trouble us, for I see, from a telegram received from General Wagstaff [British Liaison Officer at GHQ AEF], that the Divisions so far arrived for training with the British do not include the 92nd.

I hope this is so, for, as a matter of fact, a good deal of administrative trouble would, I think, necessarily arise if the British Army had to undertake the training of a coloured Division.

LC, Pershing Papers, folder: Hon. Lord Milner, box 137; Pershing, *My Experiences in the World War*, vol. 2, p. 46.

Brig. Gen. Alfred E. Bradley, Chief Surgeon, SOS, AEF, to Pershing, reply to Pershing to Bradley, April 30.

I find on my return from my trip to Southern France your very kind letter of April 30th which I greatly appreciate. It is a gratification to me to feel that my services have been satisfactory to you, and I think you have known from the very first that I have given everything in me to make the organization of the Medical Department a successful one. Time will tell whether or not these efforts will be successful, but I believe with General Ireland to carry on the work of the department that there can be no question of the results.

If you have not already done so, I would greatly appreciate, if it meets with your approval, a letter to the War Department as to my work while associated with you. [*Ed.*—Pershing swiftly complied with Bradley's request and sent a strong letter of commendation to The Adjutant General at the War Department on May 15.]

I expect to be in headquarters in a day or two prior to my going to hospital for an operation on my tonsils and I trust I may have the pleasure of finding you there. As soon as I have recovered from this operation I shall proceed at once to the United States.

LC, Pershing Papers, folder: Bradley, box 33.

Secretary of War Newton D. Baker to Pershing.

I am taking advantage of the fact that General Babbitt [Edwin B. Babbitt commanded the 4th Field Artillery Brigade, 4th Division, AEF] is about to sail to send you this personal letter with regard to two or three questions which have been under discussion between us by cable. It seems to me difficult to get into a cablegram a full statement of one's views, and I am particularly anxious that none of the condensed and abbreviated language of our papers should ever be misconstrued by you. Your views are of the greatest value to us and we study them very carefully.

A particular instance of my anxiety on this subject is caused by cablegram 1159 [April 23], paragraph 2, of which you sent me a copy with your letter of April 23, which I had not previously seen and which expresses the policy which the necessity of the case dictated, but does it so abruptly that it might be open to misconstruction. Clearly, we must rely upon your judgment for promotions of men who are with the American Expeditionary Force, and in the nominations which were sent to the Senate our thought was to do so, but at the same time there is a very large number of officers here in the United States, many of whom are doing excellent work under the great handicap of being denied, for the present at least, the opportunity to go to Europe where of course all officers of spirit want to be. If we were to limit promotions to the men who are in France, and exclude those who are in this country, it would have a most damaging effect upon the spirit and hopes of the men here. I think there will be no difference of opinion among us in working out this policy, although of course it does have this apparently insuperable difficulty, mainly, that we will appoint some men to the rank of general officers here who will shortly thereafter be sent to you in France, and when there will have rank greater than some of your own men, although if the two men had been before you for choice at the same time you would have preferred to have the man in France given the increased rank rather than the one in the United States. I do not see how this can be avoided, but I hope its difficulties may be minimized.

Some time ago we sent you a cablegram with reference to a "permanent intelligence department for the Signal Corps." It is cable 1143, paragraph 3, dated April 20. You replied by your cable 1050 [sic, 1016], dated April 28. I do not think the cable we sent gave you any sort of data upon which to judge of the thing we had in mind. We have been having very great difficulty with the aircraft situation here, largely due to the fact that the cables afford so meagre and unsatisfactory a mode of working out engineering problems. Your aircraft section is undoubtedly working as hard as it can and accomplishing excellent results, but on this side our engineers frequently find themselves unable to understand and apply studies made Over There, and it was thought that sending two or three men from this side who had lately been in contact with our engineering and manufacturing difficulties and knowing intimately of our resources would enable them to work with your aircraft section to get this information into a more usable and intelligible form. I think some of my associates here, particularly my civilian associates, have an idea that this group of men would be independent and responsible only to the aircraft section on this side, but of course as soon as the matter came to my attention, which was after this exchange of telegrams between you and General March, I pointed out the impossibility of having any such independent group in France, and that no matter who the persons are or what their purposes, they must still operate under your general direction and in cooperation with agencies which you have established there. It would not do to have your section make one set of reports and this independent body make another set. As the new men whom we have put into aircraft production are very earnest in their insistence upon having a closer appreciation of the difficulties on the American side as the basis for the studies made on the French side, I am going to send to you several men from the Signal Corps and hope you will be able to associate them with your aircraft section. They will be men familiar up to the last minute with the manufacturing and engineering difficulties on this side, manufacturing resources here, and they will therefore be able to help General Foulois and his associates to make their studies and report their results in more usable form over here. Of course when these men have come they will report directly to you, and if you find them an element of discord in any way they, like all other officers sent to France, are subject to your orders and can be directed to return to the United States whenever you think that the wise course.

Your cablegram 1051 [*sic*, 1043] of May 3 deals generally with the aircraft situation as presented by the assignment of certain engines and aircraft to the Navy. As you perhaps recall, the development of aircraft in this country has been largely under the advice of a joint board upon which Army and Navy representatives have sat, and the manufacturing facilities of the country have been lumped so as to avoid complications between the Army and Navy in their use. The net result of this has been that practically all the aircraft made in America have been made under Army direction, but with the understanding that a certain portion would be allocated to the Navy and the major portion to the Army. It is therefore a part of the general working plan over here to have the Navy get a certain number of Liberty engines and planes, and the number assigned to them is so much smaller than that assigned to the Army that there is really no preference for the Navy in the distribution. We have taken care, too, that the Navy draws its share currently, rather than by any priority, so that out of every lot of engines made the major part goes to the Army and a minor part to the Navy until their program is completed, after which the Army will go on absorbing the full production of all the factories.

The whole Department is now busy with the estimates for 1918-1919, and the Committees of Congress are pressing forward with the consideration of both bills, so that for a little while we will be absorbed in this subject. In the meantime, I am deeply grateful to you for your cablegram 1086 [see May 10, P-1086-S] giving a concise account of the present distribution of our forces in France. This is an excellent showing and enables us for the first time to have an exact and comprehensive view of the extent of our assistance to the Allies. I have sent a copy to the President and am sure he will he both deeply interested and greatly gratified at the showing.

We are still troubled on this side about the distribution of news. The arrangement which you and I worked out in France and which seemed so simple and logical apparently fails entirely to work, for the reason that all kinds of questions are raised by the newspapermen over here which you do not know about and therefore the information which you release through European sources is not responsive to the questions in which our people are specially concerned. I think it will be necessary for us to give out a daily statement, now that the number of our troops engaged is growing so large, and upon some subjects which arouse public interest over here we will have to make statements based upon the information which you send for the Department's use. We will of course exercise all the discretion we can to prevent any statement we make being indiscreet. In the meantime, the newspapers on this side insist that we are losing a great advantage in the stimulation of our country's morale by not giving out the accounts of individual actions in Europe. The Stars and Stripes when it comes contains very inspiring news which our newspapers would be very glad indeed to have had and would have been able to make great use of, and of course it is true that the various sections of the country are interested in their own soldiers and whenever a man from a particular place is given a War Cross or commended for the performance of a particular exploit, an account of it would stir the emotions of the community from which he came profoundly. I confess I hardly know what we could do to remedy this, but it has occurred to me that somebody connected with the Stars and Stripes might be directed to make a daily cablegram for us, giving the more important incidents of this character for release on this side, since their publication in the Stars and Stripes shows that they are not withheld for any military reasons. It is a little hard to realize in France how eager and insistent the newspapers are in the United States, and yet of course their eagerness does represent the eagerness of the people of the country, and if we could manage to supply them daily with an account of the operations and exploits which come through the War Department, in addition to those things which are sent by European correspondents, it would relieve a very great deal of pressure and prevent the War Department from being regarded as suppressing and withholding news to which they soon discover to have been distributed in Europe through the Stars and Stripes, and therefore plainly to have been regarded as proper publicity.

We have all been a good deal puzzled as to just what ought to be done in the matter of preferential shipment of infantry and machine gun units. Our program in this country of course was not adapted to the production of those arms, but rather to the production of complete divisions, and as a consequence at the present rate of shipment it looks as though we would soon exhaust our men in these arms and be unable to continue the accelerated program unless we tendered new men who had less than the minimum of training which you regard as necessary in this country, and in which minimum we concur. No doubt by the time you have received this letter, however, that question will be quite definitely set at rest. I understand that General March has sent you figures as to the number of men in the training camps, therefore in subsequent conferences you will be able to discuss the question with these figures in mind.

The phase of this question which has most disturbed me, however, is not the one we have been discussing, but rather the questions of supply. Our program for cargo ships has been based on the theory that we were going to send you about 91,000 troops every month from now until the first of January, with the necessary supplies, and the cargo tonnage has been carefully estimated so that under favorable conditions we will be able to do that. Accelerating the movement of troops, however, places in Europe a large body of American soldiers who will have to depend upon British and French supplies, as there is no way in sight of increasing the cargo tonnage available as rapidly as we have been able to increase the troop transport capacity with the aid of the British. The whole question is exceedingly intricate, and now that we have a Supreme Commander who moves American divisions from one part of the line to another, as he has already moved the First and Second Divisions, it looks as though an arrangement will ultimately have to be made either for a common supply system or else an arrangement whereby the British will undertake to supply all the troops from the Channel to a given point, the French from that point to another point, and the American the sector farthest east. As I remember the transportation facilities in France, the British from the Channel ports would be able to supply troops as far east as Montdidier, the French system centering north of Paris could then take it up and carry it until it reached a place where our distribution system from the

Is-sur-Tille station could perform the work. I confess I do not see how we can expect to follow our divisions from one end of the line to another with a distributing system which will cut into and disarrange the French and British systems, but no doubt all of this has been under consideration and arrangements are in progress. The only point of it all is that so far as we on this side are concerned the accelerated troop movement without accelerated cargo movement is causing us some concern and we would like to be sure that the supply arrangements have been perfected on the other side, and also whether the accelerated program of troop shipment ought to continue beyond July in the absence of such an arrangement for supplies.

I hope by this time that Sergeant Lanckton has reached you safely, and I cannot forebear again thanking you for letting me have his attentions. He is certainly a most comforting and comfortable person to have about, and whatever his previous history may have been I confess he appeals to me as a most worthy and competent boy. We are all very happy in the things you are doing and, as you know, our confidence in you is unlimited.

LC, Pershing Papers, folder: Newton D. Baker, January–June 1918, box 20.

TAG, War Department, to Pershing.

Cable A-1302-R.

1L. Ordnance Department has under manufacture 4 16-inch, 50 caliber guns, forgings for which have been completed and machine work underway. It is estimated that the first gun will be completed during 1918. Due to length of gun and limitations of railway clearance it is probable that considerable preparation of firing platform will be necessary to secure maximum elevation of 45 degrees. This will prevent use of the sliding type carriage. The gun car would be about 125 feet overall in length and would be 84 feet between truck centers. The total number of axles would be about 24 limiting weight per axle to 17 tons. Considering amount of track preparation which will be necessary do you desire these guns on railway carriages? Williams [Chief of Ordnance]. [Reply—Vol. 5, May 30, P-1214-S-1H]

NARA, RG 120, M930, Main Series, War Department to AEF, roll 12.

TAG, War Department, to Pershing, in part in reply to Pershing to TAG, War Department, cables P-747-S, March 18, and P-1052-S, May 4, in addition to TAG, War Department, to Pershing, cables A-1151-R, April 21, and A-1246-R, May 5 (not reproduced).

Cable: A-1306-R.

1. For General Atterbury. 1D. Your 1052, paragraph 4, understood. Are negotiating for metal parts for 6000 cars to be built at Bordeaux. Will place orders promptly

and advise probable dates of deliveries as soon as possible. Please answer all questions in our 1151, paragraph 3A, and 1246, paragraph 1A. We are not sure that we should go ahead and order equipment for Belgian shops? We should have this information immediately. . . . Do you want any more American locomotives and cars? [Reply—Vol. 5, May 22, P-1163-S-11; June 6, P-1259-S-1]

1E. We have 33 locomotives completely set up aboard steamers and can probably get 2 additional boats of the same capacity. We feel assured this will be successful. We can load about 65 refrigerators completely set up in a boat of this kind. Which do you need shipped this way, locomotives or cars? Felton [Director General of Military Railroads]. [Reply—Vol. 5, May 24, P-1179-S-2A; June 22, P-1352-S-9]

2. The President has acted upon the Court-Martial cases of Privates Cook, Sebastian, Fishback and Ledoyan, 16th Infantry. In the cases of Privates Cook and Sebastian, while confirming the sentence, he granted them a full and unconditional pardon and directed that they report to the company for further military duty. In the case of Privates Ledoyan and Fishback, he confirmed the sentences but commuted them to 3 years penal servitude at the Disciplinary Barracks, Fort Leavenworth, Kansas. March

3. With reference to your 747. The provisions of Section 7 of Act April 26th, 1898, paragraph 639, Military Laws of the United States and the delegation to you of power to assign officers under the provisions of 119th Article of War provide sufficient means for the accomplishment of object desired and Secretary of War has decided that it is inexpedient and inadvisable for the War Department to recommend at this time as a war measure legislation relating to the subject of promotion. March.

NARA, RG 120, M930, Main Series, War Department to AEF, roll 12.

Editor's Note—For more on the issue of these court martial cases, see Vol. 3, March 2, Editor's Note following cable A-857-R.

May 14

Pershing's Personal Diary

With 2nd Division. Went to Ancemont to see 1st Battalion, 5th Marines, entrain, Major [Julius S.] Turrill, commanding. Saw also there Colonel [Wendell C.] Neville, commanding the Regiment, Lieutenant Colonel [Logan] Feland and Captain [Keller] Rockey, officer in charge of entraining. Battalion had been relieved from the trenches at 4 that morning and had marched 10 miles to the train. The men presented a very good appearance and entraining was done in an orderly manner.

On the road to and from Ancemont I saw a number of units of the 2nd Division on the march. Part of the 2nd Trench Mortar Battery—no officer was in charge of the detachment which consisted of 4 or 5 wagons and about 25 men. The horses were poor and ungroomed. Detachment marching without any appearance of order. Saw horse section of ammunition column, Captain Hoover commanding Wagon Company. His animals were not in good condition. He stated that most of the poorest ones he had only received a short time ago. He however stated that they are receiving 8 pounds of oats for mules and 10 pounds for horses and 10 pounds of hay for both horses and mules and that this is not sufficient. He stated that about 25 percent of the hay is not good and that the oats often of inferior quality. This train needs road discipline. Men sat on horses at halt and have no proper idea of keeping well to the right-hand side of the road.

Saw the 1st Battalion of the 15th Field Artillery. Colonel [William M.] Cruikshank accompanied the column [newly appointed Commander, 2nd Artillery Brigade], which marched in very good order. The horses were in fair condition. Gave better evidence of grooming than animals of wagon train. Colonel Cruikshank stated that his Regiment is very efficient in sector artillery work; that most of them are young and inexperienced in open warfare firing.

Saw also number of trains of 5th and 6th Marines and Machine Gun Companies of each of these Regiments on the road. None of these elements had proper idea about road discipline. There was a tendency to string out on the road. Men sat on horses during halt. Wagons were traveling in middle of road instead of keeping well over to the right. Returned to Bar-le-Duc. Left for Chaumont at about 5 p. m.

LC, Pershing Papers, Diary, May 7, 1917–September 1, 1918, box 4.

Dawes, GPA, SOS, AEF, Paris, to McAndrew, CS, GHQ, AEF, for CINC, AEF.

Telegram. GPA 35.

Please call attention Commander in Chief to this telegram. Am mailing today minutes interallied conference of May 6th called to discuss your proposition. Next meeting of Conference is held this afternoon [with the French only]. If as a result of it we approach nearer definite agreement consider it advisable if possible for you to come to Paris for consideration of certain important elements of same. Will wire you later as to progress made at Conference [see May 15, Dawes to McAndrew for CINC, AEF, telegram GPA 37].

LC, Pershing Papers, folder: Gen. Charles G. Dawes (1918), box 59.

Pershing to TAG, War Department, in reply to TAG, War Department, to Pershing, cable A-1284-R, May 10.

Cable P-1115-S. Confidential.
For the Chief of Staff and Secretary of War.

1. With reference to paragraph 2, your cablegram 1284. Not understood, as no arrangements have been made regarding sending troops to Italy and there has been

no intention of making such arrangements without approval of War Department. No communication received from Italy or elsewhere except one from M. Orlando with whom question was discussed at Abbeville resulting in his proposition already cabled you [see May 6, P-1064-S-2].

2. Further reference recommendation approving his second plan, purpose of transporting troops direct to Italy is in order that they may be sent by rail through Italy to show people visually that American troops are actually there. It is believed result will be tremendous reception similar to that given our troops in London which was authorized after consultation with British authorities and at their request.

3. Troops sent to Italy should be practically all Americans and not naturalized Italians, as M. Orlando thinks his people might otherwise be in doubt regarding their nationality. Am strongly of opinion that if we send troops we should plan to send eventually 1 division in order to maintain Italian morale by successive arrivals, and demonstrate to Italian government our desire to be of material aid. Unless there should be some reason of which I am unaware hearing on general situation, believe plan outlined is best and that any smaller number of troops would in the end be likely to react against us. Sending 1 division by detachments as proposed would not materially reduce the number to be sent to France within the next 3 or 4 months and hence would meet with no opposition from other Allies, especially if partially trained troops could be selected for the purpose. [Reply—May 19, A-1350-R-3]

NARA, RG 120, M930, Confidential Series, AEF to War Department, roll 7.

TAG, War Department, to Pershing, in reply to Pershing to TAG, War Department, cable P-1099-S, May 12.

Cable A-1316-R. Confidential.

1. With reference to your 1099. It is impossible now to change shipping schedule for May. Bulk of troops to be shipped in May are at port or about to move. We expect to ship 200,000 in May and 225,000 in June. With this increase our schedule is not materially different from yours. It is as follows: Already shipped in April "A" units, 5 divisions, 2nd and 3rd Corps, 95,000. May, "A" units, 7 divisions, 2nd and 3rd Corps, 104,000. "B" units, 6 divisions, 2nd and 3rd Corps, 48,000. Service of rear, replacements, et cetera, 19,000. Total 200,000. June, "A" units, 6 divisions, 4th Corps 100,000, 4th Corps 114,000. "B" units, 6 divisions, 2nd and 3rd Corps, 48,000. Service of rear, replacements, et cetera 63,000. Total 225,000. This will leave "B" units of 4th Corps for July. 6 balloon companies, 3 photographic sections and depot battalion, S-302, will be shipped this month. [Reply—Vol. 5, June 3, P-1237-S-4]
March.

NARA, RG 120, M930, Confidential Series, War Department to AEF, roll 18.

May 15

Pershing's Personal Diary

Worked in office all day. Saw General Foulois and Colonels Ireland, Winter and Nolan...

LC, Pershing Papers, Diary, May 7, 1917–September 1, 1918, box 4.

Editor's Note—As was often the case in his personal diary, Pershing did not go into any details about the substance of his meetings with the individuals who visited him on any given day. However, in 1923, as he gathered information for his wartime memoirs, he did reach out to many of his former colleagues for details that he could add to his story. One of those was the then Surgeon General of the Army, Maj. Gen. Merritte W. Ireland, who had known Pershing since their service in the Philippines and who served as the Deputy Surgeon and then Surgeon of the AEF in 1917–18. On May 25, 1923, Ireland sent Pershing notes of their meetings during the war drawn from his personal diary. Ireland's comments for their meeting of May 15 are as follows:

> In the morning I had a long interview with you, I had just returned from England, where I had been sent by you to meet Mr. Henry P. Davison [Chairman, American Red Cross] and to make arrangements for the proper hospitalization of our soldiers in England.
> While there I was also detailed to attend a conference with the British authorities on the question of venereal diseases in the Allied armies. In this talk with you I took up.
> First, hospitalization in England. For some reason we had not been able to make satisfactory arrangements for the hospitalization of our soldiers. It was most difficult to secure from the British building material, and we had not, up to that time, been able to secure suitable buildings for hospital purposes. During the several days I was in England I made arrangements for the American Red Cross to buy Salisbury Court and erect a thousand bed hospital there. I also arranged with the British authorities to give us a sufficient number of buildings so we could send base hospital units to England and establish suitable hospitals to care for our own men. The arrangements I made were entirely satisfactory to you. Colonel Francis Winter, Medical Corps, was sent to England to become the Chief Surgeon of that base section. This assignment assured a satisfactory Medical Department for the future.
> I also reported to you the result of the Venereal Conference in London with the British authorities. This conference was called by the British Home Office at the instigation of the Archbishop of Canterbury. I told you that the conference had not produced results which would be of benefit to us, or to anyone else. It did disclose the fact that the American army had by far the low-

est venereal rate. In fact, it was difficult for the conference to believe an army could be kept in the field in France with as low a rate as we had at that time.

I took up with you the question of hospitalization in France, and explained the difficulty we were having in procuring sites for new construction and securing suitable buildings for hospital purposes. You gave reassurances of your support in this matter and told me you would take the matter up with the French authorities.

I discussed with you on this occasion the importance of the promotion of a good many men of the temporary forces who were prominent in their Profession and who had come to France to assist us. You gave me assurances of your support in this matter and directed me to bring my recommendations to you at another conference we were to have in a short time. I was so much impressed with your attitude in this conversation that I entered in my diary "I wish I could have reduced to paper the entire conversation we had. It was perfectly splendid and he made the most assuring statements of his hearty accord with the efforts the Medical Department was making and of his support in the future." (LC, Pershing Papers, folder: Data for Book *My Experiences in the World War,* folder no. 3: Medical Corps (Notes by Gen. Ireland)—Maj. Gen, Merritte W. Ireland, Surgeon General, U.S. Army, to Pershing, May 2, 1923, box 351.)

Haig to Pershing, reply to Pershing to Haig, May 11.

I must express to you my sincere thanks for your kind offer of the services of a regiment of heavy artillery, conveyed in your letter of May 11th.

I regret very much that no Field Artillery personnel is available as my Heavy Artillery have suffered to the same extent as the Field Artillery.

I quite understand that you would of course prefer that the training of all your heavy batteries should be carried out at the usual centres, and I therefore appreciate all the more your generous readiness to assist me.

Unfortunately, owing to our heavy expenditure of artillery material during the last two months' operations, I have only sufficient complete howitzer equipments to maintain British batteries in action and cannot hope to provide equipments for your six batteries under present conditions.

I am, therefore, very sorry to say that I am unable to accept your kind offer.

LC, Pershing Papers, folder: Field Marshal Sir Douglas Haig, 1917–1918, box 86.

Foulois, Chief, Air Service, SOS, AEF, to CS, GHQ, AEF.

Subject: Study of the aircraft industrial relations in Europe and recommendations reference priority of American Air Services over Allied Air Services.

1. In my opinion, the military emergencies on the Western front will be sufficiently settled by July 1, 1918, to demand that the Air Service, A.E.F., be given priority over the Air Services of the United States Navy and of England, France, and Italy, as regards the allocation of aeroplanes, Liberty engines, and other aircraft materials manufactured in the United States,

2. During the past three or four months, thousands of tons of raw materials for aircraft purposes have been received in France and the greater part of this raw material has been put *into storehouses for future use*. This statement also applies equally as well to England.

3. Therefore, after July 1, regardless of whether this crisis on the Western front is past, and regardless of whether it results favorably or unfavorably for the Allies, I believe, from that date, we should take a firm stand as regards securing priority on the aircraft materials necessary for the rapid and efficient growth of the Army Air Service, A.E.F. In order to effect this, the authorities in the United States must give me their full support in our recommendations reference allocation of raw, semi-finished, and finished aircraft materials to the Allies and to ourselves, as the weapon of "raw materials" is the most powerful weapon, in my opinion, that can be used with the Allies, not only in the effective and rapid building of our American Air Service, but our entire American Army as well.

4. The Chief of Air Service, in his industrial relations, during the past six months, with the Air Ministries of England, France, and Italy has frequently been approached, first by Italy, then by France, and finally by England, with the proposition to establish Aircraft industrial agreements with the United States to the exclusion of the other Allies. More recently, representatives of the Air Ministries of France and England have *endeavored to reach the Commander-in-Chief direct*, with their industrial propositions instead of dealing with the Chief of Air Service. [See April 27, Loucheur and Dumesnil, to Pershing, and following correspondence, and May 10, Editor's Note following Pershing Personal Diary entry.]

5. On account of the fact that neither the Commander-in-Chief, nor the Chief of Air Service, in carrying out the instructions of the Commander-in-Chief, have deviated from the policy of playing fair with all Allies, the Air Ministries of each of our Allies have transferred their efforts to their Embassies in the United States with the hope of more successful results at that end. Their efforts have been more successful on the Washington end, as evidenced by the recent receipt of a cablegram from Tardieu, the French High Commissioner in the United States, urging General Pershing to add his protest to the French protest, against the English Government being allowed to take all the available supply of spruce in the United States to the exclusion of France and Italy—a request which the Commander-in-Chief promptly complied with. Several other instances have recently occurred which tend to show that the French Government is still trying to persuade the United States to favor France in securing industrial control, against England, and the English Government is also attempting to play the same game, with the United States, against France.

6. As a military officer, with no industrial training, I feel that, ordinarily, neither the Commander-in-Chief or myself, should become involved in the industrial rela-

tions between our Allies and the United States, but in view of the fact that the Aircraft industry of the world, in its present stage of development, is so closely bound together by military and civil control, that in order to protect the interests of the United States and fulfil the policies and promises of the United States, as regards the development of an efficient and adequate American Air Service, both for duty in this present war and for future use in the defense of the United States, that it is imperative that the Commander-in-Chief, A.E.F., continue to exercise his influence and impress his views and recommendations on the Washington authorities regarding the course to be followed in our aircraft industrial relations with the Allies.

7. To this end, I recommend the following:

(a) Instruct Major Grayson M. P. Murphy, the selected representative of Mr. John D. Ryan, (in charge of Aircraft Production in the United States) to report for duty at G.H.Q., A.E.F., at once, and proceed to make careful survey of the aircraft industrial situation with the Chief of Air Service. [For additional correspondence pertaining to Murphy, see May 11 and May 15 (following), Foulois to Chief of Staff.]

(b) Instruct Major Murphy to attend the next Inter-Allied Aviation Committee (Production) meeting, with the Chief of Air Service—meeting scheduled for May 18—in order that he may immediately come in contact with the Inter-Allied Aviation Representatives.

(c) Instruct Major Murphy to proceed to England as soon as practicable, with the Chief of Air Service, to make a careful survey of the situation in England.

(d) As soon as Major Murphy is thoroughly conversant with the situation in England and France, he should then proceed to the United States and lay the whole situation before the State, War and Navy Departments, and receive his instructions as to how he shall carry on his work.

8. Major Murphy should then return to France with a clear understanding as to:

(a) Whether our aircraft industrial policy is to favor one nation to the exclusion of another, or to treat them all alike.

(b) Whether our recommendations, regarding allocation to the Allies of raw, semi-finished and finished aircraft materials, will have any weight against political pressure from foreign Embassies in the United States.

(c) Whether our home policy, after July 1, shall be one which will insure priority for the rapid and efficient development of our own American Air Service in Europe.

9. Pending the settlement of the foregoing recommendations, and based on my knowledge and belief of aircraft conditions in England, France, and Italy, as I believe they will exist after July 1, 1918, I recommend that the following aircraft industrial policy be adopted and recommended by cablegram to the War Department:

Inter-Allied Aircraft Industrial Policy.

That beginning July 1, 1918, the United States Government shall allocate its aircraft production of Liberty engines, other types of engines, aeroplanes, and all other aircraft materials manufactured in the United States, in the following order of priority:

(a) U.S. Army Air Service, A.E.F.

(b) U.S. Army Air Service, at home.

(c) U.S. Naval Air Service, in Europe.
(d) U.S. Naval Air Service, at home.

After the monthly needs (to include June 30, 1919) of the United States Army and the United States Naval Air Services have been first insured and provided for, all surplus production of Liberty engines, other engines, aeroplanes, and all other aircraft materials, over and above the monthly needs and requirements of the United States Air Services, shall be available for allocation to England, France, and Italy on a percentage basis and *in proportion to the size of their respective programs of aircraft production.*

10. The present percentage basis of allocation of aircraft materials from the United States to the Allies is as follows: England 53%, France 37%, and Italy 10%. It is recommended that these figures be allowed to stand, until future military emergencies, or future facts, establish the necessity for their change.

11. The establishment of a policy, that after July 1, 1918, the United States Air Services shall receive priority over the Allied Air Services, in aircraft materials manufactured in the United States, will undoubtedly cause us more or less trouble in our future relations with our Allies. Such troubles, however, in my opinion, will be insignificant, as compared to the difficulties and complications which we are bound to encounter if we change our present policy and attempt, in the near future, to establish aircraft industrial agreements with any single one of our Allies to the exclusion of the others.

12. Attached herewith is a proposed cablegram reference the future policy as proposed, which it is recommended be sent to the War Department.

1 Enc.

Proposed Cablegram [Edited]

Paragraph.   For Chief of Staff.

Recommend that beginning July 1, 1918 the United States Government allocate its production of Liberty engines, other engines, aeroplanes, and all other aircraft materials in the following order of priority: first United States Army Air Service A.E.F., second United States Army Air Service at home, third United States Naval Air Service in Europe, fourth United States Naval Air Service at home. After the monthly needs and requirements of the Air Service programs of the United States Amy and the United States Navy to include June 30, 1919 have been insured and provided for it is recommended that allocation of any Liberty engines, other engines, aeroplanes, and all other aircraft material which may be in excess of our own needs be allocated to England, France and Italy on a percentage basis, in accordance with and in proportion to the size of their respective programs of aircraft production. It is further recommended that the present percentage basis of allocation that is England 53 per cent, France 37 per cent and Italy 10 per cent be continued until future military emergencies or future facts demonstrate the necessity for change in these figures in which case you will be promptly advised. Please acknowledge as soon as possible and inform me as to final decision reference our future Air Service policy. Pershing.

LC, Foulois Papers, folder 12: AEF, Air Service, Allied Air Service, box 7.

Dawes, GPA, SOS, AEF, Paris, to McAndrew, CS, GHQ, AEF, Chaumont.

Telegram. GPA 37.

Will you please bring this telegram to the immediate attention of the Commander-in-Chief at whatever point he may be:

While the English were not present at the conference yesterday afternoon, having filed a statement which I transmitted to you yesterday, I am glad to state to you that the French government at the conference which M. Clemenceau presided, definitely announced agreement with your plan, adopting specifically practically all our suggestions and adding other features of value. The French agreed with us that the way to secure the English acquiescence in the plan which they believe is ultimately inevitable was to make the proposition for the military control committee along the lines of your letter read at the conference and our joint letter in which we made the suggestion that to set the military authority of the committee in action the unanimous agreement of its three members was necessary. This leaves veto power in you representing the American army and the Commanders of the other two armies. The French went further and along the line of your general proposition for centralization of civil as well as military authority make most valuable suggestions. I was careful to point out that while you had suggested that the principles of this plan should be beneficially extended over all civil as well as military allied activities, yet in-so-far as the adoption the French suggestions interfered with the status quo of civil authority that you wished it understood it was a matter for your government to deal with. The French fully realized and appreciate this point as well as your insistence upon the immediate adoption of a plan coordinating the military control over the allied supply activities in the immediate rear of the armies they therefore adopted practically in detail your plan of the military executive committee of supply you suggested this adoption is in such terms that the English upon notification can immediately join or defer joining until some later date without interfering with the immediate institution of the plan between your army and the French army. It is very desirable that I make verbal report and receive further instructions as to my course of action. Please wire me whether you are to pass through Paris and if not to what point I shall come for immediate personal conference. The French Government is communicating with the English Government as to results of conferences. [*Ed.*—Pershing replied to Dawes by telegram on May 16: "Most hearty congratulations on successful outcome most recent conference."]

LC, Pershing Papers, folder: Gen. Charles G. Dawes (1918), box 59.

Pershing to TAG, War Department, in reply to TAG, War Department, to Pershing, cable A-1283-R, May 10.

Cable P-1118-S. Confidential.
For the Chief of Staff.

1. Reference your cablegram 1283. Following Brigade Generals recommended for promotion to the grade of Major General: Mason M. Patrick, Peter E. Traub, E. Lewis, William Lassiter, James G. Harbord, Charles P. Summerall, John L. Hines

Following Colonels recommended for the promotion to the grade of Brigadier Generals in the following order: [40, including Upton Birnie, Jr., A. J. Bjornstad, W. B. Burtt, Fox Conner, W. D. Connor, Malin Craig, LeRoy Eltinge, H. E. Ely, H. B. Fiske, P. B. Malone, D. E. Nolan, F. Le J. Parker, and S. D. Rockenbach; entire list not reproduced]

Following Colonels recommended for promotion to the grade of Brigade General in Quartermaster Department, National Army: [4, including J. A. Logan, Jr.; entire list not reproduced]

Following Colonels for promotion to the grade of Brigadier General in Medical Department, National Army: J. R. Kean

2. Have recommended increased number of Colonels to be Brigadier Generals in order to provide for officers of this grade as heads of Staff Sections, GHQ, and 1 as Deputy Chief of Staff, according to approved Tables of Organization, and also to provide 1 officer as head of Staff College and 1 for head of Tank Corps.
[In addition—Vol. 5, June 8, P-1266-S, June 27, P-1380-S-7, July 9, P-1433-S; reply—July 2, A-1644-R-16, July 9, A-1687-R-3]

NARA, RG 120, M930, Confidential Series, AEF to War Department, roll 18.

Pershing to TAG, War Department, in part in reply to TAG, War Department, to Pershing, cable A-1200-R, April 28.

Cable P-1119-S.
8. For Felton. With reference to paragraph 1A, your cablegram 1200. We may be able to obtain further cessions Belgian locomotives. Matter now under negotiation and you will be advised definitely at early date. [In addition—Vol. 5, May 26, P-1192-S-1]

NARA, RG 120, M930, Main Series, AEF to War Department, roll 3.

Pershing to TAG, War Department, in reply to TAG, War Department, to Pershing, cable A-1297-R, May 11.

Cable P-1124-S. Confidential. Rush.
For the Chief of Staff and Secretary of War.
Reference cable 1297. The original recommendation by the military representatives on the Supreme War Council of an exclusively infantry program for troop shipments from America was evidently made without considering the serious effect upon our plans, although it was explained to them that certain classes of troops and service of the rear organizations would be necessary not only to carry out our purpose of building Army and to meet present requirements. However, the Abbeville conference

took little note of the original recommendations as the sole request made was that the London agreement be extended to include June and July. I stated in substance that our program had been already materially reduced and that the extension of infantry program for 3 months would defer the shipment of artillery and other troops and make it impossible with the shipping then in sight to catch up for several months and the organization of American Divisions would be indefinitely postponed and our service of the rear would be unable to function sufficiently to meet our increasing demands for supplies, and urged that we could meet the situation later if the crisis seemed to demand it. After full discussion in committee, Mr. Lloyd George said: "I agree that you should form American divisions and I think we shall be able to bring over all the infantry we want and also bring over the extra troops you want." He then guaranteed the extra shipping mentioned in the agreement, and we agreed to include June in the infantry program leaving July to be reviewed later. This was declared entirely satisfactory by all concerned. Lord Milner came to me afterwards and said: "I wish you to know that I have been no party to this as I was entirely satisfied with the London agreement." General Foch afterwards said in the most friendly manner: "We are in thorough accord as always, I am very satisfied." His Chief of Staff sent word that General Foch was very much pleased. Although the British War Office was quite satisfied with the London agreement, it is understood that Lord Reading took Lord Milner severely to task for accepting the London program.

A. The aid we shall furnish with shipping promised during May and June will be: First, the 240,000 infantry and machine gun units, and, according to British estimates, possibly about 50,000 more in June; Second, practically 5 divisions in line, 2 in Picardy, or on the way, and 3 in Lorraine, including the 32nd, now moving into line; and Third, 3rd and 5th Divisions, which will be hurried as much as possible and will replace French divisions within a short time. This will make about 175,000 men in divisions plus 240,000 men in infantry units with possibly 50,000 additional in the battle or preparing to go in, besides 4 regiments of colored troops and several batteries of heavy artillery already with the French and British, not to mention the divisional artillery that follows the infantry in May and June – approximately half a million men.

B. If we include July in the program, the troops would not be ready to take their places in the line until some time in August. But the British state that in August they will have 400,000 to 500,000 drafts and the French 1919 Class, about 200,000, will also be coming in then. The main reason for our hurried infantry units for service with the Allies is to help out until the Allied drafts are available. Notwithstanding Allied demands for infantry alone, a recent request comes from the British for 10,000 artillery. While appreciating that we should give every early assistance possible to meet an emergency, I am strongly of the opinion that we must form our own divisions and corps as rapidly as possible and use them as such for the additional moral effect such an Army would have. Many French officers of high rank hold this view and want entire divisions. Sir Douglas Haig said he would like to have our divisions placed beside the British divisions as soon as possible. Our own officers and men are constantly asking whether newspaper reports are true that we are to be amalgamated with French and British units, and are unanimous in their desire to fight under our own flag. It is not impossible that we shall find Irishmen refusing to fight under the British. We cannot ignore what our own soldiers and our people will think and should not keep units too long with either Ally. The Germans are now saying that Americans are inefficient and the French and British will not trust them and so are absorbing them in Allied divisions.

C. In conclusion, I think we have fully and fairly met the situation. We have given the Supreme War Council all it asked at Abbeville. The statement in your cable places a limit upon further concessions which have really been about reached in the Abbeville agreement. It is believed that the action at Abbeville should be consider as the deliberate expression of the Supreme War Council's latest view that the matter be regarded as definitely settled as to May and June, otherwise as long as there is the slightest hope of getting further concessions, there will be a continual clamor regardless of how it affects us. I have fully set forth the above to present the matter as it appears to me.

D. Judging from what occurred at Abbeville and from the expressions of approval by General Foch, I think he cannot consistently reopen the subject until the question of July needs arises. But above all, I wish to be understood as having every desire to meet this question in the broadest way possible and do everything to aid in this emergency, and both the President and the Secretary of War may be fully assured that I shall approach any future discussion in the spirit suggested by the Secretary of War.

NARA, RG 120, M930, Confidential Series, AEF to War Department, roll 7.

TAG, War Department, to Pershing, in part in reply to Pershing to TAG, War Department, cable P-952-S, April 19.

Cable A-1317-R.

1. In view of the large number of officers contemplated for the Army during fiscal year 1918-19, amounting to 175,000, Secretary of War is of the opinion that the following with the excess leather necessary to equip these officers with Sam Browne belts is indispensable [indefensible] and the cost to these officers aggregating over $2 million in addition to their having to provide themselves with the standard belts in the United States is unjustifiable from any military point of view, it being understood that this belt is not permitted to be worn in the trenches in France but is largely ornamental. As this belt was adopted on your recommendations for use in France only, he desires you to consider the matter from the standpoint indicated in the foregoing and communicate your views probably. [Reply—Vol. 5, May 23, P-1172-S-6C]

2. . . . With reference to paragraphs 1K and 1L, your 952. A course for higher commanders and staff officers has been prescribed and is to be conducted by selected French and British officers under the supervision of Division Commanders. It is contemplated giving this instruction to divisions in turn in groups of 5 each. With reference to paragraph 1M, your 952, letters of instruction being issued to division commanders on the subject, and three copies mailed you today. With reference to paragraph 1R, your 952. The entire proposition was gone over with Major Requin

before definite action was taken. Further recommendations from Requin based on his understanding your views now being studied by General Staff. [Reply—Vol. 5, August 27, P-1630-S]
March.

NARA, RG 120, M930, Main Series, War Department to AEF, roll 12.

TAG, War Department, to Pershing, in part in reply to Pershing to TAG, War Department, cables P-913-S, April 14, P-916-S, April 14, and P-1052-S, May 4.

Cable A-1318-R.

3. Attention Morrow. Replying London 216 [not reproduced], paragraph 1. Your 916, paragraph 9A, urges us to immediately put in production single-seater fighter. Your 913, paragraph 1F, advises SPAD and SE 5 best of this class on the front. We took immediate action on this recommendation and have given order for 1000 SE 5s. Your 1052, paragraph 2A, exactly reverses these recommendations. In view of this inconsistent information and also due to request for production of SE 5 from Air Division for training purposes, we have long ago changed our production on these machines and request that samples be sent promptly in accordance with our London 216, paragraph 3.

NARA, RG 120, M930, Main Series, War Department to AEF, roll 12.

TAG, War Department, to Pershing, in part in reply to Pershing to TAG, War Department, cables P-1015-S, April 28, and P-1019-S, April 29 (not reproduced).

Cable A-1323-R.

1B. With reference to your 1015, paragraph 1E, and 1019, paragraph 2C [not reproduced]. Based on present conditions it is estimated deliveries of 155-millimeter ammunition in United States at seaboard can be made for Howitzer high explosive shells July 50,000, August 150,000, September 250,000, October 400,000, November 600,000, December 600,000. Gun high explosive shells August 50,000, September 100,000, October 175,000, November 300,000, December 300,000. Howitzer shrapnel August 5,000, September 8,000, October 15,000, November 21,000, December 33,000. Gun shrapnel September 5,000, October 7,000, November 14,000, December 17,000. Howitzer gas shells July 5,000, August 15,000, September 25,000, October 40,000, November 55,000, December 80,000. Gun gas shell August 5,000, September 15,000, October 25,000, November 35,000, December 45,000. Figures are not cumulative. All of these shells are of the medium thick-walled steel type. No shells with thin walls ordered but additional manufacturing capacity for thin-wall shells being developed.

NARA, RG 120, M930, Main Series, War Department to AEF, roll 12.

May 16

Pershing's Personal Diary

Worked in office until 5 p. m. Saw Messrs. Egan and [Dwight] Morrow, Lieutenant Colonel Stimpson, Captain de Marenches and General Bethel. Talked with Colonel Eltinge and Major Shannon about re-organization of headquarters S.O.S. Left for Paris at 5 p. m. with Colonel Boyd.

LC, Pershing Papers, Diary, May 7, 1917–September 1, 1918, box 4.

Pershing to Haig, reply to Haig to Pershing, May 12.

In answer to your letter of recent date, I have directed Brigadier General William W. Harts to present himself to your headquarters as Chief of the American Mission there. As such, I would like to have him, in addition to his other duties, control all detached units, such as Engineer, Hospital and Aviation, serving with the British Expeditionary Forces. It was never intended, however, that General Harts should have control over the American divisions serving with your forces. I am glad that the plan is satisfactory to you.

As regards Major Bacon, I shall be very glad to attach him to your personal staff as your personal liaison officer with American units in the British area, and am issuing instructions that he report to you for such duty.

LC, Pershing Papers, folder: Field Marshal Sir Douglas Haig, 1917–1918, box 86.

Sims, Commander, U.S. Naval Forces Operating in European Waters, London, to Pershing, reply to Pershing to Sims, May 10.

Personal.

With a view to answering your letter of May 10, 1918, in detail, I have instituted a very thorough investigation of the internal organization and operation of our Naval Air Service, the result of which will be communicated to you together with such suggestions as may appear pertinent looking to a closer co-operation than exists at the present time.

It certainly seems most essential that our two Air Services should work in the closest possible manner and with the utmost harmony to ensure ultimate victory which is our common cause and for which we have been mobilized.

It gives me grave concern to hear that you are of the opinion that some of the officers who are handling our respective Air Services are not working together as they should, and I agree with you heartily in that such a state of affairs must be remedied at once. In this connection, however, and for your information I quote the following letter which I wrote on January 24, 1918, and which to date remains unacknowledged:

A-1. 7262.   24 January, 1918.

From: Force Commander.
To: Major General G.T. Bartlett, U.S.A.
           Commanding Officer, Base Section 3,
           Line of Communications,
           American Expeditionary Force.
Subject: Aeronautical Liaison between U.S. Army and Navy.

1. Inasmuch as Naval and Military Aviation are very closely allied and with a view to eliminating duplication of requests to the British Admiralty for information on this subject, it appears highly advisable to establish Aeronautical Liaison between our respective Headquarters.

2. If, therefore, you concur with me in this view of the situation, I will detail an officer from this office who will, in addition to his other aviation duties, act as Aeronautical Liaison Officer to your command.

3. In return, if you think it to our mutual interests to do so, I will be pleased to have you nominate a similar Officer in your office through whom all matters aeronautical may be transmitted.

                                                  s/Wm. S. Sims.

Pending the reception of the reports which I have called for and which will assist me in clearing up this difficulty, please accept my high admiration of the splendid work which your aviation Service is performing and which I feel confident it will continue with credit to all of us.
[In addition—Vol. 5, June 7, Sims to Pershing]

LC, Pershing Papers, folder: Adm. Wm. S. Sims, box 184.

Editor's Note—On May 16, Sims forwarded a copy of this correspondence to Capt. Hutchinson "Hutch" I. Cone, Commander, U.S. Naval Aviation Forces, Foreign Service, Paris, and on May 17 sent him a telegram requesting "a comprehensive statement showing what has been done in order to promote and ensure cooperation between U.S. Naval Aviation Force, the French, British and U.S. Army Air Services also the extent to which such cooperation is and has been practiced." On May 22, Cone replied in detail to Sims. Because of the importance of this subject to Pershing, Cone's letter has been included here, so that a more complete background on this issue might be available:

                                                  May 22, 1918

Capt. Hutchinson I. Cone, Commander, U. S. Naval Aviation Forces, Foreign Service, Paris, to Sims, Commander, U. S. Naval Forces Operating in European Waters, London, in reply to Sims to Cone, May 16 and 17, 1918.

Subject: Report on Co-operation with French, British and U.S. Air Services.

I. I have to submit the following statement showing what has been done in order to promote and insure cooperation between the U.S. Naval Aviation Forces, the French, British and U.S. Air Services. It has been the aim of this organization to cooperate in every way possible with all the different interests with whom we deal. For this reason the very general statement of General Pershing, that we have failed to cooperate with the U.S. Air Service without stating in what particular, is to be deplored. This organization is put on the defensive much to our disadvantage and it is believed solely because General Pershing has been misinformed.

French

1. The following relations exist between these Headquarters and the various French Departments and Ministries with which we come into contact in the prosecution of our work. The chief French authorities with whom we deal are, in the order of their importance to us:

(a) The Ministere de la Marine (especially the Service Aeronautique).
(b) The Service Technique et Industriel d'Aeronautique Maritime.
(c) The Sous-Secretariat d'Etat d'Aeronautique Militaire et Maritime.

2. We have an active and what I deem efficient liaison between these headquarters and the above departments, which is accomplished in the following manner: . . .

3. Our liaison work with the French has concerned itself principally with the following activities:

(a) The construction of Patrol Stations on the French Coast.
(b) The supplying of these stations.
(c) The operation of these stations.
(d) The construction of bases for the Northern Bombing Project
(e) The supplying of these Bases.

4. In all this work we have not only aimed at keeping the Ministere de la Marine fully informed of our movements and plans and of doing nothing without their approval, but we have scrupulously endeavoured to have them act directly as our agent or representative wherever possible. Thus, where question arise which concern French Ministries other than the Ministere de la Marine, we refrain from dealing officially and directly with those Ministries and instead present the matter to the Ministere de la Marine, requesting them to act in our behalf. Our liaison with other Ministries is thus mainly verbal and informal. In order that we may be able competently to handle all these questions the Ministere de la Marine has appointed Commandant Pamard as an officer especially detailed to furthering of our interests in all matters concerning the various French Bureaus connected with Aviation.

5. The policy of dealing as far as possible directly with one Ministry only has been exceedingly successful and has been the means of avoiding many complications in which we might have become involved through an excusable lack of knowledge of the complicated French bureau system and its intricacies. . . .

British

1. Our liaison with the British Air Service is maintained through your office, Lieut. Edwards, in charge, and of course the Force Commander is thoroughly familiar with this matter. As far as my information goes and from conversations with different British Air Officers, I have met on all sides with enthusiastic praise of the cordial relations existing between Lieut. Edwards and all British officials.

2. In Paris the British maintain what amounts to a Supply Division, whose knowledge of the character and performance of the various French firms engaged in the manufacture of aviation material has always been at our service and has been invaluable to us. This section helps us almost daily in the matter of contracts, and is generally giving us the benefit of their extended experience in a business way in securing aviation supplies in France.

3. Three British Officers, Commander Spenser Grey, Major Davis and Captain Ollerenshaw, are working with us as part of our organization and are rendering to us invaluable service. The services of Commander Grey were temporarily loaned to us by our Army with whom he is serving.

4. In addition to this there has been established cordial relations with British Air Authorities who are in control of the air activities in the region of Dunkerque and as far as I know our relations have been everything that could be desired.

U.S. Air Service

1. The Force Commander is referred to my letter of May 7th, number 6978, which covers this subject quite fully [not located]. In November, 1917, we established a liaison officer with the U.S. Air Service. He was given a room at their office building and our relations were cordial and intimate. These relations have been maintained here in Paris with the U.S. Air Service office, but as explained in my letter above mentioned, it has been impracticable to thoroughly cooperate with the controlling authorities.

2. They have always been promptly informed verbally of our plans as they were conceived and have been furnished with definite written statements as soon as such plans were completed. They have been given our organization chart, lists of our Patrol Stations, program for 1919, bombing program and in fact everything is exactly as it has been furnished to the Force Commander. No comment or criticism has ever been received from them on any of these plans nor has the U.S. Air Service furnished us with its own program or organization charts, although requested to do so. Our attempt to cooperate was taken to the extent that all communications to the

Force Commander on the subject of the disbanding of the European Committee of the Aircraft Production Board were previously submitted to the Chief of Air Service for comment, criticism and advice and they were frequently changed at the suggestion of the Chief of the Air Service. On our part we have received only copies of correspondence with the Commander-in-Chief of the American Expeditionary Force after it had been forwarded and without opportunity to comment.

II. There is forwarded herewith the correspondence between the Secretary of the Navy and Secretary of War, which was received from Washington this date. It is not known in what manner General Pershing considers that these Forces have failed to cooperate with the Army authorities, but if by chance it should concern the Northern Bombing Project, the decisions of the Secretary of the Navy and the Secretary of War are clear on this point, and, of course, this office is in no way responsible for such matters.

III. It is hoped that the Force Commander will fully understand that all of our liaison and obligations to other organizations here suffers greatly from a lack of sufficient officer personnel.

IV. In conclusion, it is desired to emphasize the fact that the U.S. Army has helped us in every possible way and up to date the benefit from all our cooperations has been largely in our favor. (For Sims to Cone, no. 2246, May 16, NARA, RG 45, ONRL, T829, Miscellaneous Records of the Navy Department, Miscellaneous Materials, 1–6/1918, 7–12/1918, Miscellaneous Material Printed Files, World War, roll 409; for Sims to Cone, no. 2263, May 17, NARA, RG 45, ONRL, T829, Miscellaneous Records of the Navy Department, Miscellaneous Materials, 1–8/1918, Miscellaneous Material Printed Files, World War, roll 411; for Cone to Sims, May 22, 1918, Naval History and Heritage Command, website: Wars, Conflicts, and Operations, World War I, Documentary Histories, May 1918; original document at NARA, Record Group 45: Naval Records Collection of the Office of Naval Records and Library (ONRL), Entry 517B.)

Pershing to CS, GHQ, AEF, Chaumont.

1. There has been much complaint and criticism of the manner of handling our ration in several of the divisions. This led to the establishment of a cooking school. I am not advised as to just how far this cooking school has progressed nor how well it is functioning, but the necessity for cooks who can handle our ration and make the most out of it is imperative. Please have this matter studied with a view to sending cooks from the various companies to this school—two from each company in France I should think.

2. A report from General Winn was referred by me several days ago, approved, regarding the reorganization of the leave areas, which he reported—after an investigation—were in need of proper supervision. I have heard nothing of this since and desire to have it taken up without delay. Please inform the proper section that it has been delayed entirely too long.

3. It was observed that the water cart in the Second Division is heavy and cumbersome and considerable complaint was made about it. The harness used in some cases had the breast collar which caused sore shoulders on the animals. The Quartermaster's Department should make a new study of this with a view to suspending the construction of further carts of this character until the matter can be fully investigated.

4. There are many supplies arriving for divisions in bad condition, especially forage and vegetables. The sacking seems to be very bad, and these supplies are shipped from regulating stations in rotten sacking so that when the supplies arrive at destination there is great waste. Arrangements should be made to resack and repack all such supplies in new sacking before it is shipped. Please give positive orders that this be done to stop this waste. It is not a question of Is-sur-Tille receiving and shipping out whatever they can get their hands on, but supplies should leave there in proper condition for the long trip to the railheads. It seems to me that this matter should have been attended to without having to call especial attention to it. The Q. M. D. at Is-sur-Tille, under the direction of the regulating officer, should be held responsible for this condition of supplies.

5. There seems to be a great deal of delay in the administration of justice in a great many divisions, and also some confusion, especially in those divisions where civilian judge advocates are in charge. I wish you would direct the Judge Advocate to make a thorough investigation of this, either by himself in person or by assistants from his office.

It is also my belief that our court-martial system is going to break down; that divisions in the line even in quiet sectors, and more especially in active sectors, the question of handling court-martial cases is going to be very difficult, and I wish you would have the Judge Advocate to make study of a plan for a traveling court which could go from division to division as occasion might require and try all cases presented to it, so that the officer of the division would not be taken from their more important combative duties possibly just at a time when they could illy be spared. This method was in vogue in the Confederate army and worked very successfully, so records say.

6. With reference to the criticisms presented by Colonel Fiske and Colonel Drum as to the road discipline of the Second Division, we must insist upon the train commander's responsibility in this connection at all times. The train commander, whether the train is for the moment serving with its various units or not, should take advantage of every opportunity to train these separate units, so to speak, in road discipline. I mean by this that when they are hauling supplies such as wood, etc., from the railheads, road discipline should be insisted upon at all times. I suggest that this be included in the new memorandum you are sending out to the Second Division so that you will have the whole thing in one communication.

7. I am not at all satisfied with the system of supply of our troops which requires a requisition to be submitted for clothing. The system is antiquated and it never has worked, even in peace times and is not working now. I desire a change. There is no more reason why a company officer should be required to make out a requisition for clothing than they should be required to make out a requisition for potatoes. The responsibility for the supply of articles of clothing should rest with the Q. M. D., working, of course, through the regulating station according to a general plan. To carry this out, please have

an order prepared covering the entire subject in detail, abolishing clothing requisitions in this entire command and substituting therefor some system such as is used by the ordinary traveling salesman who goes around to the country stores and finds out what the merchants need and sends in slips—the supplies to be sent out direct. This system should apply to the companies, and the Q. M. D. should furnish the agents who travel about periodically semi-monthly to see just what the companies need, and it should be shipped in this way to the organization, properly marked. All of this preparation must be done by the Q. M. D. at the regulating station.

This memorandum will form a basis of a study of the system and preparation of necessary orders which will be submitted to me for approval.

LC, Pershing Papers, folder: vol. 2: Memoranda, A.E.F., 1918, box 133.

Pershing to TAG, War Department, in part in reply to TAG, War Department, to Pershing, cables A-1203-R, April 30, and A-1233-R, May 3.

Cable P-1123-S.
  1. For Chief of Ordnance. With reference to paragraph 1B, your cablegram 1203. It is not believed advisable to equip less than Corps units with different model machine guns. Would recommend that in view of deliveries promised paragraph 1N, your cablegram 1233. That 25th Division arriving overseas be equipped with Browning guns. [Reply—Vol. 5., May 24, A-1385-R-1]
  1A. Will these divisions be completely equipped with Vickers guns and replacements for their maintenance or will it be necessary to use part of Vickers machine guns now floated for this purpose? This information urgently needed to determine disposition of Vickers guns now arriving since if altered for Air Service they will not be available in emergency. [Reply—Vol. 5, May 22, A-1371-R-2A]

NARA, RG 120, M930, Main Series, AEF to War Department, roll 3.

Pershing to TAG, War Department, in part in reply to TAG, War Department, to Pershing, cables A-1266-R, May 8, and A-1285-R, May 10, in addition to Pershing to TAG, War Department, cable P-1057-S, May 5, and P-1092-S, May 10.

Cable P-1126-S. Confidential.
For Chief of Staff.
  1. With further reference Marseille our cablegram 1057 and your cablegram 1266. We are offered by the French immediately use of at least 6 berths accommodating vessels drawing 29½ feet when breasted 16½ feet from the quays, with estimated

daily discharge capacity of 2,500 tons. This will be expanded to 3,500 tons when 2 additional berths with daily capacity of 1,000 tons accommodating ships of same draft are turned over to us probably next October. Also we are offered use of 3 berths at new piers under construction, which at estimated date of completion next November and accommodating vessels drawing 39½ feet will have daily discharge of at least 2,000 tons. All the foregoing minimum figures and believe that if emergency arises may be very considerably enlarged. All facilities from Marseille north are excellent and require practically no work except possibly a few storage depots. We can secure storehouses which are immediately necessary for our needs at Marseille and Miramas. Orders have been given to establish a base at this port ready to receive cargoes after June 10. Request you commence to divert ships of type, et cetera, indicated in cablegram 1092 so as to commence cargo deliveries at Marseille to maximum capacity of this port after June 10th. For reasons already cabled certain classes of material for the present can only be received at ports already indicated, as for example railway rolling stock, oil and gasoline, explosives, et cetera. Troop ships should of course not be sent to this port. There is unquestionably some additional risk in shipments to Marseille, but as previously reported, Admiral Sims is of opinion that this additional risk is not substantial. However, to be on the safe side judgment must be used at your end to see that as little embarrassment as possible would be occasioned here by possible loss of supplies not readily replaceable. On this account, would recommend not shipping any particular item of supply solely to Marseille or any individual shipments of which a stock is not maintained through other ports. In view aviation situation do not recommend for the present shipment of aeroplanes or aeroplane motors to Marseille. Subject to foregoing have no other recommendations to offer at this time as to cargoes for Marseille. Request that information be cabled covering arrangements finally agreed upon with Navy Department, also date you will commence diverting ships to this port. [Reply—Vol. 5, May 20, A-1352-R-2; in addition—May 23, P-1202-S-2] [Copy to Sims, May 17 (see May 17).]

3. Reference your cablegram 1285. Realize necessity of using Cavalry Division along border and believe active service there will be beneficial but suggest that organization be kept at full strength and receive all training possible with a view to their being ready for service here later on.

NARA, RG 120, M930, Confidential Series, AEF to War Department, roll 7.

Pershing to TAG, War Department, in reply to TAG, War Department, to Pershing, cable A-1255-R, May 6.

Cable P-1132-S. Confidential.
For Chief of Staff.

In compliance with your number 1255 of May 6 rescinding the rule for handling publicity prescribed by the Secretary of War while here. Instructions have this date been given to the troops concerned to submit, not later than 3:45 p. m. daily, by telephone or in case it is impossible to communicate by telephone, then by telegraph a full summary of the activities during the preceding 24 hours. These instructions will enable the cable for the War Department to be coded not later than 9 p. m.

Considering the size of our forces now in France and the increasingly important part being taken by these forces in the operations now in progress on the western front and the necessity on that account of issuing an authoritative official statement from these headquarters regarding these activities, it is deemed advisable to begin issuing an official communique from these headquarters of the Allied Armies in France. This communique will each day constitute the first part, marked A, of the daily cable for the information of the Secretary of War.

The second portion of the cablegram, marked B, will contain the information of general interest which is given daily to or is ordinarily known by the accredited correspondents accompanying the army and will be additional to that given in the communique. It will, among other things, contain the names of officers and men who have been mentioned for heroism with a brief description of the action which occasioned the mention for heroism.

The third portion of the cablegram, marked C, will deal with the Allied operations and changes in the order of battle on the western front, which information is now covered in a separate confidential daily cablegram.

The fourth section, marked D, will contain confidential information regarding movements of troops, actions, etc., which ordinarily would not be made public at the time and elaborating if necessary the information contained in the other three sections of the cablegram.

Owing to the congestion of telegraphic and telephonic communications particularly as regards divisions serving in British and French areas, it may frequently happen that information will arrive too late to be included in the cable of that date, in which case it will of course be included in the cable of the following day.

NARA, RG 120, M930, Confidential Series, AEF to War Department, roll 7.

Pershing to TAG, War Department, in part in reply to TAG, War Department, to Pershing, cables A-1203-R, April 30, A-1233-R, May 3, and A-1254-R, May 7 (not reproduced).

Cable P-1133-S.
    1. For Chief of Ordnance. With reference to paragraph 1N, your cablegram 1233. This cable not understood when read in connection with paragraph 1B, your cablegram 1203 and paragraph 1B, your cablegram 1254 [not reproduced; it was a long list of Ordnance equipment sent to France in April]. Please indicate clearly your plans for arming 13th to 25th Divisions. Are Vickers guns included in paragraph 1B, your cablegram 1254 sent to us to be used for arming part of these troops? If so have tri-

pods and indirect fire control equipment been shipped? Schedule given in paragraph 1N, your cablegram 1233, will apparently meet our plans for replacement of Hotchkiss. Our plans contemplate having sufficient machine guns shipped us to exchange machine guns in 12 divisions during months of October, November and December. Reserves and replacements for these guns should be provided. If your manufacturing schedule permits it is desirable to exchange these guns at an earlier date. [Reply—Vol. 5, May 27, A-1406-R-1C]

NARA, RG 120, M930, Main Series, AEF to War Department, roll 3.

Pershing to TAG, War Department, in part in reply to TAG, War Department, to Pershing, cables A-1148-R, April 20 (not reproduced), A-1155-R, April 22, A-1193-R, April 27, A-1205-R, April 30, A-1233-R, May 3, and A-1291-R. May 11.

Cable P-1134-S.

1. For Chief of Staff. 1A. With reference to paragraph 1, your cablegram 1205. We have had several conferences with French authorities in charge of ports regarding payment of port dues, who advise us to make no payments at any ports until a complete decision has been reached between the two governments. Ports authorities and French War Ministry are collecting certain information for consideration of a lump sum payment and will advise me when they are in position to further discuss same. Will not conclude agreement until after receipt of information you are forwarding by mail but will advise you of details when decision reached.

1H. With reference your 1193. Have delayed answer awaiting final allotment of priority of shipment for June. In our opinion will be necessary to include Ordnance replacement requirements in accordance with French High Commissioner's offer. We however find it almost impossible to allot more than 10,500 short tons to cover these replacements without too seriously encroaching upon 350,000 tons allotted us by Ship Control Committee for June. Hope therefore that remainder of replacement material amounting approximately to 38,000 short tons or 12,000 ship tons can be furnished by Ship Control Committee as an addition to our June allotment. Please confer Ship Control Committee and advise if this is possible. [*Ed.*—Goethals replied on May 22 in A-1370-R-8 that the 38,000 tons additional was allotted for June.]

1L. With reference to paragraph 1, your cablegram 1155. It is recommended that all officers in the line of the Army graduating from observers schools in the United States, be attached to the Aviation Section of the Signal Corps, but not detailed therein. All officers so attached, who are placed on duty requiring regular and frequent flights, are made eligible to 25% increase of pay. This is in accordance with section 6, Act of Congress published on page 3, Bulletin 46, War Department, August 15th, 1917. The policy has been adopted here of attaching observers to the Air Service and of returning them to their organizations at intervals so that touch therewith may not be lost. This rotation of duty between the Air Service and their own organization is considered very necessary.

1P. With reference to paragraph 10, your cablegram 1291. The number of missing reported in Seicheprey fight is 5 officers and 181 enlisted men.

1Q. With reference to paragraph 7B, your cablegram 1148 [not reproduced]. In view of deliveries of caliber 30 Chauchat already made and delivered Browning machine guns and automatic rifles promised in paragraph 1N, your cablegram 1233, believe your provisions for 260,000,000 rounds adequate.

NARA, RG 120, M930, Main Series, AEF to War Department, roll 3.

TAG, War Department, to Pershing, in part in reply to Pershing to TAG, Department, cable P-1084-S, May 10.

Cable A-1331-R.

1. The plan proposed by you for taking over the army postal service in France has been submitted to the Postmaster General, who agrees to it in following sense: "1. I am willing to turn over to the military authorities at port of embarkation mail for the troops in France, worked to companies and unit, et cetera, as it is now worked in New York, or with such modifications as may be necessary from time to time to meet any new conditions in France. 2. I agree to accept the mail from the military authorities at a station to be operated at Bordeaux, or such other port as transportation conditions may make desirable. 3. I agree to permit all postal clerks now in France who desire to enter the military postal service to do so, and will give indefinite leave for that purpose. The military authorities must operate this service with men entirely on its rolls and not with postal clerks on the rolls of the Post Office Department. However, should the necessity arise, postal clerks will be temporarily detailed with the military postal service to insure efficiency. No postal clerk is to be retained in France against his will, except such as I may direct for that temporary service. 4. The military authorities must permit the Post Office Department to operate its money order and stamp service unhampered, or must depend upon the international money order service for transmission of funds by the men. There is no objection on the part of the Post Office Department to the military postal service conducting the Registry Service." This has been accepted by the Secretary of War for the War Department and you will proceed to organize your postal service along the lines indicated. March.

[*Ed.*—Indeed, Pershing had already done this. GHQ, AEF, established the Military Postal Express Service (MPES) in Europe in accordance with its General Orders No. 72 on May 9.]

NARA, RG 120, M930, Main Series, War Department to AEF, roll 12.

May 17

Pershing's Personal Diary

At Paris. Saw General Patrick, Colonel Mott, Colonel Dawes, General Langfitt [Chief, Service of Utilities, SOS] and Mr. Pomeroy Burton. Had lunch with the Ambassador and had long confidential talk with him. Mr. Sharp told me that he had talked with M. Clemenceau, M. Loucheur, M. Cambon and a number of other officials on the general situation and that he heard on all sides the very highest praise for the American soldiers and nowhere had he heard any criticism of the American attitude in the present crisis.

Saw M. Clemenceau at his office. He also seems confident. Had talk with General Foulois and General Patrick together, and orated them on their new roles, with General Patrick as head of the Air Service.

LC, Pershing Papers, Diary, May 7, 1917–September 1, 1918, box 4.

J. L. Dumesnil, Under-Secretary of State, Military and Naval Aeronautics, Ministry of Munitions, Paris, to Foulois, Chief, Air Service, SOS, AEF, reply to Pershing to French Minister of Munitions, May 4.

2nd Bureau
11507 2/12
Re Scheme of collaboration of American and French Aviation Construction Service.

By letter of the 4th, inst., the Commander-in-Chief of the American Expeditionary Forces replied to a dispatch sent to him by the Minister of Armament and Munitions and myself [see April 27], concerning the necessity of coordinating more closely the resources of the United States and France for Aeronautic Construction.

I have the honor to forward you some additional information relative to this matter.

1. <u>Chasse Airplanes</u>. I quite agree with General Pershing as regards the SPAD-Hispano 300 h. p. As soon as the definite tests are terminated, I will let you know and will ask you what number of Hispano Suiza 300 h. p. engines it will be possible to send from America to France. These engines will be used to equip the cellules intended for the American Formations.

2. <u>Army Corps & Day Bombing Planes</u>. As regards this category of airplanes, France would be able at the most to place at the disposal of the American Services, the following material:

During July	150 Breguet	B2 Liberty & 350 A.C. Airplanes
" August	200 Breguet	[B2 Liberty & 400 A.C. Airplanes]
" [September]	200 Breguet	[B2 Liberty & 500 A.C. Airplanes]
" [October]	250 Breguet	[B2 Liberty & 500 A.C. Airplanes]
" [November]	250 Breguet	[B2 Liberty & 500 A.C. Airplanes]
" [December]	250 Breguet	[B2 Liberty & 500 A.C. Airplanes]

The Army Corps airplanes would be of the (Breguet A2 Liberty)(Salmson C.U.Z. 9) or (SPAD 16 Lorraine 275 h.p.) types, in a proportion to be determined hereafter.

These supplies, however, are subject to the conditions:

That the tests of the Liberty engine on the Breguet A2 & B2 shall give every satisfaction, and second, that the Liberty engines necessary for the equipment of the cellules, shall reach the airplane constructors one month before the machines are sent out, that is to say, in this case France would receive:

During June	500 Liberty engines
" July	600 Liberty engines
" August	700 " "
" September	750 Liberty engines
" October	750 " "
" November	750 Liberty engines

I may add that these engines are to be delivered in addition to those ceded by the United States to France in execution of the order A.E.64. They may be either of the Army or Navy type.

3. <u>Night Bombing Airplanes</u>. The French Aeronautic Department may be able to deliver you a certain number of airplanes of this category in exchange for a certain number of Liberty engines. But the construction of airplanes of this type is not yet sufficiently advanced to allow my making any definite engagement in regard to the matter.

I think, however, that I shall soon be able to make a definite proposition.

4. I quite agree with General Pershing as regards the precautions to be taken concerning the building in America of an Airplane invented in France.

5. One of the first C.UZ. 18 engines has been reserved for the American Aviation. I agree with General Pershing in thinking that this model may be sent to America in charge of French engineers, in order that the American engineers may study the possibility of its being constructed. If this construction is decided on, we will then come to an agreement as to the type of cellule to be made in France for its utilisation, and also con-

cerning raw material. By arrangements which have been made, the Federal Government is to supply raw material in exchange for cessions granted by the French Government.

I should be greatly obliged if you would bring these matters before General Pershing, and would let me know as soon as possible how many of the above-mentioned airplanes you wishus to reserve for American formations.

LC, Foulois Papers, folder 12: AEF, Air Service, Allied Air Service, box 7.

Pershing to Sims, Commander, U. S. Naval Forces in European Waters, London, in addition to Pershing to Biddle for Sims, telegram, May 10.

May 17th. Confidential. For Admiral Sims.

Following cablegram sent to War Department May 16th quoted for your information "No. 1126 May 16th Confidential. For the Chief of Staff. 1 Paragraph 1. With further reference to Marseille my cablegram 1057 [May 5] your cablegram 1266 [May 8]. We are offered by the French immediately use of at least 6 berths accommodating vessels drawing 29 1/2 feet when breasted 16 1/2 feet from the quays, with estimated daily discharge capacity of 2,500 tons. This will be expanded to 3,500 tons when 2 additional berths with daily capacity of 1000 tons accommodating ships of same draft are turned over to us probably next October. Also we are offered use of 3 berths at new piers under construction, which at estimated date of completion next November and accommodating vessels drawing 39-1/2 feet will have daily discharge of at least 2000 tons. All the foregoing minimum figures and believe that if emergency arises may be very considerably enlarged. All facilities from Marseille north are excellent and require practically no work except possibly a few storage depots. We can secure storehouses which are immediately necessary for our needs at Marseille and Miramas. Orders have been given to establish a base at this port ready to receive cargoes after June 10th. Request you commence to divert ships of type etcetera indicated my cablegram 1092 [May 10] so as to commence cargoes deliveries at Marseille to maximum capacity of this port after June 10th. For reasons already cabled certain classes of material for the present can only be received at ports already indicated, as for example railroad rolling stock, oil, explosives, etc. Troopships should of course not be sent to this port. There is unquestionably some additional risk in shipment to Marseille, but as previously reported, Admiral Sims is of the opinion that this additional risk is not substantial. However on the safe side judgement must be used at your end to see that as little embarrassment as possible would be occasioned here by possible loss of supplies not readily replaceable. On this account would not recommend shipping any particular items of supply solely to Marseille or any individual shipments of which a stock is not maintained through other ports. In view of aviation situation do not recommend for the present shipment aeroplanes or aeroplane motors to Marseille. Subject to foregoing have no Oscillation recommendations to offer at this time as to cargoes for Marseille. Request that information be cabled covering arrangements finally agreed upon with Navy Department, also date you will commence diverting ships to this port. Pershing."

Naval History and Heritage Command, website: Wars, Conflicts, and Operations, World War I, Documentary Histories, May 1918, Pershing to Sims, May 17, 1918; original document at NARA, Record Group 45: Naval Records Collection of the Office of Naval Records and Library (ONRL), Entry 517B.

Editor's Note—Although Pershing downplayed Sims's concerns about using Marseille and other French Mediterranean ports for transports, Sims indeed had serious questions about such an approach. He expressed those concerns to the Chief of Naval Operations, Adm. William S. Benson, in a confidential cable [8289] sent on May 23:

> 8289. Army authorities hope to handle tonnage program for 1918 in French Atlantic Ports, assisted by French Channel Ports. Any embarrassment in military situation however may require greater coal shipments from England and larger use of French Atlantic Ports. At any time availability of freight cars may seriously delay ships. Only alternative seems to be use of Marseille and other French Mediterranean ports.
>
> I have pointed out to Army authorities the disadvantages of using Mediterranean Ports. The route will be 1400 miles longer all in submarine Waters. Furthermore, the Convoy between Gibraltar and Marseilles [sic] are not strongly escorted. I have impressed on Army Authorities the desirability of using to the maximum first French Atlantic Ports, Second French Channel Ports, and at last resort French Mediterranean Ports. I am assured Mediterranean ports will be used only if other Ports become badly congested.
>
> At present and for some months past, the submarine situation west of Gibraltar is not such as to warrant establishing a convoy between United States and Gibraltar. Small submarines en route to Mediterranean generally stop in area west of Gibraltar to expend torpedoes, and some losses are to be expected there. From Gibraltar to Marseilles and return ships will be in Convoy. The losses in this convoy average 1.5 per cent.—that is 8 ships sunk out of every 500 ships convoyed. The percentage is somewhat greater than losses in convoys to French Atlantic Coasts.
>
> If it becomes necessary to use French Mediterranean Ports vessels should be routed independently to Gibraltar to join Convoys to Marseilles. Present practice is to sail vessels independently in Mediterranean if over 13 knots speed, as they are considered safer than in slow convoys.
>
> Vessels destined for Mediterranean should be of the smaller type, not exceeding about 7500 tons dead weight, and should be well armed to guard against attack by cruiser submarines. Vessels should be of good speed so as to further increase their safety. (Naval History and Heritage Command, website: Wars, Conflicts, and Operations, World War I, Documentary Histories, May 1918, Pershing to Biddle for Sims, May 10, 1918; original document at NARA, Record Group 45: Naval Records Collection of the Office of Naval Records and Library (ONRL), Entry 517B.)

Pershing to Theodore Roosevelt, Oyster Bay, Long Island, N.Y.

Please accept my congratulations upon the enviable record made by your son, Captain Archibald Roosevelt, 26th Infantry, who has been officially cited for splendid courage in battle March 8, 1918, upon the occasion of his receiving wounds at the head of his company during a heavy bombardment.

It is with extreme satisfaction that I report he is now convalescing and will probably return with his regiment within a relative short time to add new luster to his already brilliant record.

LC, Pershing Papers, folder: Col. Theodore Roosevelt and Family, box 177.

Pershing to TAG, War Department.

Cable P-1131-S
1. For Chief Signal Officer. 1F. 6 Liberty engines taken apart here and all but one found defective. Only one of them should have been allowed to pass shop inspection. Only two of these engines have been run here. One engine had bevel gear at base of vertical shaft not properly secured. Engine number 17,479 which had not been run here had crank pin bearings with cracked and broken babbitt. A Navy low compression engine not yet run here has crank pin bearing very badly dented on outside of bronze shell in manner showing gross negligence in erection and inspection. The damage to this bearing was not due to wear. Engine would have been wrecked if run in service with this bearing. Engine number 17,480 had grit in crank case and bearings not cleaned. An engine in England had bearings in condition not fit to run. This entire situation of utmost gravity and if production engines are no better than those we have they should not be used here. Suggest you send Major Hall and Captain James G. Heaslett here at once on flying trip on first available liner for consultation. [Reply—Vol. 5, May 23, A-1382-R-7B]

NARA, RG 120, M930, Main Series, AEF to War Department, roll 3.

Pershing to TAG, War Department, in part in reply to TAG, War Department, to Pershing, cable A-1217-R, May 1.

Cable P-1139-S. Confidential.
For the Chief of Staff.
1B. Reference your cablegram 1217, paragraph 1. It is understood that following Divisions are assigned to 3rd Corps: 3rd, 5th, 27th, 33rd and 78th. Please repeat designation of the other division.
1C. In the 2d, 3d and 4th Corps which divisions are organized as replacement divisions? Which are organized as depot divisions?

1D. Cable name of Commander of 89th Division. [Reply—Vol. 5, May 20, A-1352-R-4; May 29, A-1418-R-4]

NARA, RG 120, M930, Confidential Series, AEF to War Department, roll 7

May 18

Pershing's Personal Diary

At Paris. In morning went to Versailles and had talk with General Foch. He made two propositions; 1st, the establishment of an American sector; 2nd, adoption, in agreement with General Pétain, of a schedule prescribing the American troops which shall serve with the French for certain periods of instruction and the duration of these periods. I also ascertained from him that he seemed to be satisfied with the measures adopted at the Abbeville conference, May 1st and 2nd, and that he appeared pleased with the American effort. He was well pleased to learn that I had given orders for placing with the French all available aviators which they might desire. Also had talk with General Bliss. Returned to Paris and saw Major Perkins, Mr. Ganne, Colonel Dawes, Mr. Martin Egan, Colonel Ireland and Miss Birkhead.

LC, Pershing Papers, Diary, May 7, 1917–September 1, 1918, box 4.

Editor's Note—Col. Ireland, Chief Surgeon, AEF, presented these additional details of his meeting with Pershing in Paris.

> I again reminded you of the difficulty of providing sufficient hospitalization for our sick and wounded. This you assured me you had in mind and would take up with the French authorities.
>
> I again mentioned our great shortage in Medical Department personnel, which you said you understood and assured me that you would do everything you could to have additional personnel sent from the United States.
>
> I explained the difficulties we had encountered when our sick and wounded soldiers were treated in French formations and suggested that the scheme of having the French hospitalize our patients when they were fighting with the French Army would always prove unsatisfactory. You seemed to have a full grasp of this unsatisfactory condition and said you would assist in having our men sent to American hospitals. (LC, Pershing Papers, folder: Data for Book *My Experiences in the World War,* folder no. 3: Medical Corps (Notes by Gen. Ireland)—Maj. Gen. Merritte W. Ireland, Surgeon General, U.S. Army, to Pershing, May 2, 1923, box 351.)

Report on Conversation with General Foch, May 18th, at Trianon Palace, Versailles.

General Foch asked General Pershing to give him a general statement of the American forces now in France, or expected to arrive. After a general statement by General Pershing on the situation as to American troops, General Foch stated that he wished to make two propositions to General Pershing:

1st. That we now contemplate the establishment of an American sector. That when the 1st Division shall have been withdrawn from the battle front which it now occupies and shall have had a period of rest, it be placed in this American sector. And that it be followed by the successive American divisions as they are withdrawn from the battle front, as the 2nd, 26th, etc., and that we contemplate turning over this sector to the First American Corps and successive American Corps and Armies as they are ready to take their place.

2nd. That General Pershing draw up with General Pétain what General Foch called a "calendar". This schedule should show what American troops are to train with the French for the next few months, should designate French divisions to which American regiments are to be assigned for training, and should prescribe the length of time which these regiments are to spend with the French divisions.

General Foch expressed his opinion that when American troops are thus assigned to the French for training they should, during the period prescribed, follow the sort of the French troops to which they are assigned—if they remain in a quiet sector, remain there with them; if they go to the battle front, go there with them; and that there is every reason why the time which they are to remain with the French division be prescribed in advance. After this period with the French is finished these troops should pass into the American Army proper.

General Foch wished to know what General Pershing thought of these two propositions. General Pershing stated that he agreed with the policy which they outlined.

General Pershing mentioned the possibility of placing the 2nd Division by the First on the battle front and uniting the two as an American Corps. He brought out that this would afford for our government an effective answer to those who are disposed to criticize the brigading of American infantry with the French and the British, and stated that this would also afford a good opportunity for giving to our division and corps commanders an opportunity to function in battle and that it would show to our people that as soon as our troops have finished their training in the brigade and so on, they are placed in the American Army, properly speaking.

General Foch stated that since the 2nd Division would, in all probability, not be placed in line before the last of May and the 1st Division will, in all probability, be so worn out by that time as to necessitate its withdrawal from the line, the two would hardly be there together. However, he thought the way to decide this would be to have General Pershing visit the 1st Division, see how they are getting along, and the question would be regulated after General Pershing decides whether or not the 1st Division can remain in line after the Second goes in.

General Pershing stated that as soon as two American Corps take their place in line the American government expects him to take direct command of them.

General Foch suggested that the division and higher commanders and their staffs who are now in the States would do well to precede their commands to France and be assigned to staffs of units that are now engaged in the battle; that this would afford them valuable experience. He stated that he thought that these commanders and staffs could train with either the French, the British or the American staffs that are now functioning.

General Pershing stated that he would give careful consideration to this proposition. He stated that he had been thinking for some time of the advisability of establishing himself in a sort of advance headquarters near to General Foch's headquarters so that he might be in closer touch with General Foch, study the work of General Foch's staff and other staffs at the front, and also might treat more promptly questions arising between General Foch and himself.

General Foch stated that this was an excellent idea and he hoped that General Pershing would do so at the soonest possible moment, and that he himself and his staff would be at General Pershing's entire disposition for any assistance in carrying out this idea. He mentioned having just chosen as Deputy Chief of Staff General Lerond, who commanded the Artillery of the 6th Army. This officer is to be used especially for dealing with the Americans.

General Pershing asked General Foch if he was satisfied with the resolutions adopted by the Supreme War Council at Abbeville May 1st and May 2nd.

General Foch stated that he was obliged to content himself with what the governments decided; that these agreements were very well; that he had been dealing with the war and with Allies for 4 years and that after all one had to decide things according to circumstances. He made some remark which intimated that the decisions taken thus could not always be absolutely adhered to.

General Pershing stated that he wished General Foch to understand that he himself is not disposed to place a strict interpretation upon the resolution adopted in the Versailles conference; that he is disposed to do everything that he possibly can to accomplish results and that, if at any time General Foch sees a means for accomplishing better results, he would be always disposed to listen to any suggestions which General Foch might have to make for the improvement of the situation.

General Pershing stated that according to the Abbeville agreement the British are to bring over 150,000 troops in June—120,000 of which are to be infantry and machine gun units and 30,000 such troops as America might decide to send; that if the British bring 50,000 in addition to these, they were to be infantry and machine gun units.

General Pershing proposed that if it appears that the British will be able to bring 200,000 men, he will let all the infantry and machine gun units come first and the 30,000 other troops afterward.

General Pershing stated to General Foch that the Americans had reported that they hoped to embark 200,000 troops in May and 285,000 in June.

General Foch asked General Pershing the status of the question concerning the American aviators which the French wished assigned to their squadrons.

General Pershing stated that there had been some misunderstanding between his staff and General Pétain's staff on this subject; that he had just discovered this and had given instructions to the Chief of his Air Service to place every available aviator at the disposition of the French for service as they might deem best. General Pershing stated that he wished them to serve in whatever way they would be of the greatest aid.

General Foch summed up the two propositions which he had made in the beginning of the conversation, stating that it was understood that General Pershing agreed to the principle of forming an American sector and that if General Pershing would draw up with General Pétain a schedule prescribing the assignment of American units for instruction with the French, General Pershing could then consider that this would practically finish his direct relations with General Pétain and after that General Pershing could deal directly with him.

LC, Pershing Papers, folder: Conferences and Agreements, Folder No. 1, box 50.

Pershing to TAG, War Department, in part in reply to TAG, War Department, to Pershing, cable A-1067-R, April 8.

Cable P-1142-S.
  8. For Chief Signal Officer. 8C. With reference to paragraph 2A, your cablegram 1067. 17 cases containing 4 DH 4 planes and spares unpacked and all pieces found to be in perfect condition. First machine nearly assembled at Romorantin [Air Service Production Center No. 2] and will be flown in day or 2. Assembly being performed without difficulty no warping or distortions appearing thus far. Notify Cleveland Office.

NARA, RG 120, M930, Main Series, AEF to War Department, roll 3.

TAG, War Department, to Pershing, in part in reply to Pershing to TAG, War Department, cable P-1063-S, May 6; in addition to TAG, War Department, to Pershing, cable A-1233-R, May 3.

Cable A-1341-R.
  1L. With reference to paragraph 3, your 1063. Troops arriving after July 1st will be equipped with Browning machine guns and Browning machine rifles with adequate reserve of both types unless troops movements still further speeded up. Are now starting to complete equipping Fifth Corps. The Second Corps (British) and the Fourth Corps completely equipped with Vickers machine guns. It has been assumed these 2 corps as well as First and Third will be equipped by you with Chauchat. This plan will fulfill your requirements that each corps have complete complement of the same types of rifle. Reference replacement of present 8 m.m. arms in service with Browning machine guns and rifles. See our 1233, paragraph 1N which gives complete

After months of promises from the War Department, the first of the American-manufactured DeHavilland 4 aircraft finally arrived at Brest early in May 1918. Individual aircraft, engine, instruments, and spare parts came crated in boxes for ease of shipment and to prevent damage. Loaded on flatcars, the crated aircraft were then shipped to Air Service Production Center No. 2 at Romorantin, where they were reassembled, test flown, and moved forward to Air Service units for training and operations. Source: NARA, Still Picture Branch, RG 111, 111-SC-13419.

shipping schedule in both arms by months and indicated are this can be lived up to. No more Chauchat rifles desired in the United States therefore your suggestion to hold 6000 as emergency supply Second Corps and cancel remainder of order is approved. Williams [Chief of Ordnance]. [In addition—Vol. 5, May 24, A-1385-R-1]

NARA, RG 120, M930, Main Series, War Department to AEF, roll 12.

TAG, War Department, to Pershing, in part in reply to Pershing to TAG, War Department, cable P-1066-S, May 7.

Cable A-1342-R.
    1A. Your 1066, paragraph 2. 100 refrigerator cars complete loaded on steamship Ticonderoga, invoice 50; 200 on Rondoless; 414 tons miscellaneous parts which,

through causes beyond control of Engineering Department, was floated on Suwanee; 100 refrigerator cars complete floated on Suwanee; 50 refrigerator cares complete being floated on Newton.

NARA, RG 120, M930, Main Series, War Department to AEF, roll 12.

TAG, War Department, to Pershing, in part in reply to Pershing to TAG, War Department, cable P-1083-S, May 9, in addition to TAG, War Department, to Pershing, cable A-1224-R, May 2.

Cable A-1347-R. Confidential.

2. For Air Service. French Military Mission advises French Government can supply minimum 150 Breguet machines per month. We could supply Liberty engines for the same but would interfere with squadrons quoted in our 1224 for which we expect DeHaviland planes will be ample production. Consider carefully and advise if you wish to figure on deliveries of engines for Breguet machines and what number per month for how many months taking into account that such engines will be supplied at expense American made planes. [Reply—Vol. 5, May 23, P-1175-S-1]

2B. With reference to your 1083, paragraph 6C. Await with interest advices results of negotiation. Will prepare to make duplicate jigs, et cetera, for Caproni. [Reply—Vol. 5, June 18, P-1330-S-2D]

NARA, RG 120, M930, Confidential Series, War Department to AEF, roll 18.

May 19

Pershing's Personal Diary

Left Paris at 9:30 a. m. for Chantilly, where I had a talk with General Pétain. He stated that he would soon have to meet what would amount to a reduction of 25 Divisions to half strength; that it would be a great help if he could get sufficient American troops, either by battalions, regiments or brigades, to fill up these divisions until about the 1st of October when the 1919 Class would become available. This makes still another estimate as to the time when the 1919 Class will become available. I thought General Foch said yesterday that it would be ready in August.

Before asking that these troops come by battalions, regiments or brigades, General Pétain remarked that it would be difficult for him to break up any regiments as each regiment had a history and it would be regrettable that the regiment go out of existence, therefore he would like to have American battalions to go into his regiments, having two French and one American battalion per regiment. When he asked for our troops to come into these depleted divisions by battalions, regiments or brigades he did not state how this would obviate his breaking up some regiments.

Went from Chantilly to Headquarters, 1st Division, at Le Mesnil-St.-Firmin, and spent afternoon and night with General Bullard. Slept in dugout which they have arranged for sleeping quarters for staff under house.

LC, Pershing Papers, Diary, May 7, 1917–September 1, 1918, box 4.

Conference, Pershing and Pétain, at Chantilly, May 19, 1918.

Very Secret
Interview of the 19th of May, 1918, at Chantilly between General Pétain and General Pershing.

I. Question of an American Sector.
 The following is agreed upon:
 As soon as circumstances permit, the American Army will take complete charge of the sector of the Woevre.
 The nucleus of this sector is formed by the sector actually occupied at the present by the 26th U. S. Division.
 As other American divisions become available, each of them will be sent to take its place on the right and left of this subsector.
 Until the moment when four American Divisions are in the line and two in reserve, these divisions will continue to be placed under the authority of the French General Commanding the Army in which the sector is located.
 As soon as there are four American Divisions in the line and two in reserve, the sector will be definitely turned over to the American Army and will function with the American Army's resources (supply stations, ammunition depots, etc.) as an Army Sector.
 If the fluctuations of the battle make it necessary for the Supreme Command to take American Divisions from the American sector, after such sector has been definitely established, and to replace these divisions by French divisions, the French divisions would, during their tour in the American Sector, be placed under the American Command.
 Incidentally, *General Pershing* makes it understood that:
 1st—The American Divisions now in the zone of the British Armies will, as soon as their instruction is completed and the present crisis has reached its termination, be brought to the American Sector of the Woevre.
 2nd—The instruction of the 3rd and 5th Divisions is being pushed with great activity and these divisions will be ready to appear on the front with but little delay.

II. American Personnel put at the Disposition of the French High Command.
 The Aviation pilots and the personnel of the Signal Corps which have been recently requested are put at the disposition of the Commander-in-Chief of the French Armies.
 The orders to this effect have been given.

III. Colored Regiments.

For certain internal reasons a certain number of American units have negroes as their officers.

General Pershing is in some doubt as to the aptitude for command of these negro officers. He asks that the French Command report to him all cases in which these negro officers appear to be incapable in order that he may immediately take such measures as may be necessary. A suitable method seems to be to place a French officer alongside of each negro field officer. This method gave good results when applied by the English to the Hindoo officers.

General Pershing sees no objection to the French employing, in case of necessity, the negro troops by battalions instead of by regiments.

IV. French and American Decorations.

The following is agreed upon:

In the future propositions for bestowing French decorations on American officers and soldiers will be, before being put into effect, transmitted to the American General Headquarters in order to obtain the opinion of those Headquarters.

Similarly, *General Pershing* will transmit in the near future to the French General Headquarters lists of French officers and soldiers upon whom he proposes to bestow American decorations.

V. Reinforcing French Divisions.

General Pétain set forth to General Pershing the grave disadvantages which would result if French divisions were broken up on account of a lack of a sufficient number of replacements.

The most critical period from this point of view will exist during the months of July, August and September; that is, this period will extend up to the time when the class of 1919 will be available for the front.

He asked General Pershing to examine what can be done to assist in this matter through temporarily incorporation for short tours, the tour of one unit to be followed by the tour of another unit, American battalions, regiments or brigades in French Divisions. It being well understood that these units would be returned to their own commands as soon as the class of 1919 is available.

During the critical period he (General Pétain) would keep General Pershing thoroughly informed as to the exact situation of our (French) effectives.

General Pershing promises to study the question in all its detail and to do all that he may be able to do. [See Vol. 5, May 29, Conner to CS.]

General Pershing made it clear that in the future American units arriving in France will have had much more instruction than any of the units which may have preceded them and that this fact will have as a result the reduction of the tour which American regiments now have or instruction purposes in French divisions.

VI. Pooling of all of the Resources of the Allies
(Supplies of all Kinds and Means of Transport)

General Pershing and *General Pétain* are both very strongly in favor of this idea and consider that it must be fully developed, whatever reservations may be made by the English.

VII. Manufactures of Aviation Materiel.

General Pershing stated that the manufacture of the Liberty Motors is progressing very favorably.

On the other hand the manufacture of airplanes is not progressing very well in the United States.

On the other hand the manufacture of airplanes is very satisfactory in France.

As a result, General Pershing considers it desirable to find a solution without delay to the question of the adaptation of Liberty Motors brought over from America to airplanes manufactured by the French.

Incidentally, *General Pétain* stated that the American sector, once it is constituted, should be provided with a sufficient number of American Air squadrons.

In case of need, the materiel of French squadrons could at that time be turned over to the American Army.

VIII. Headquarters of General Pershing.

General Pershing made it known that the influx of American troops into the northwestern [northeastern] region of France would oblige him to organize an advance General headquarters from which he could easily visit the northwestern [northeastern] region of France.

The interview of the two Generals terminated at this moment.

[*Ed.*—For the report of Maj. Paul H. Clark, American Military Mission to French GHQ, on additional French comments on Pershing's meeting with Pétain, see Vol. 5, May 22.]

LC, Pershing Papers, folder: Conferences and Agreements, Folder No. 2, box 50.

Editor's Note—Pershing provided these additional details in his memoirs:

> The purpose of my visit was to discuss the possibility of assembling our divisions to form an American army. I recalled to Pétain that the earlier plans for their concentration in the vicinity of Toul had been postponed at my suggestion on account of the emergency that then confronted the Allies. He replied that he did not see how it could be done now, and that the matter of immediate concern to him was the reinforcement of his own divisions in such a way as to preserve both their number and their strength. He was willing to accept our men by battalions, regiments, or brigades, but preferred the assignment of two American battalions to each of twenty-five divisions until October. Foch had asked for assignments of American troops only until August, when, it was said, the French 1919 class would be available for service. As fifty battalions of infantry would have been equiva-

lent to that of at least four of our divisions, it would have compelled us to break up that number of incoming units, with little hope of reorganizing them. Of course, it was out of the question to consider such a possibility.

While his needs were appreciated, this was another request that could not be granted without yielding in my determination to bring about the formation of an American army. After some further discussion, we simply renewed the understanding previously reached that, for the present, American divisions with the French and not yet prepared for offensive action should occupy portions of the front in quiet sectors, relieving French divisions when the exigencies of the situation demanded that they should enter the battle. Thus for each partially trained division we would be able to free two French divisions. A few days later this arrangement received Foch's approval. (*My Experiences in the World War*, vol. 2, pp. 53–54.)

Bliss to Pershing, reply to Pershing to Bliss, May 5.

I received your kind note of May 5th but have neglected to acknowledge it earlier, for which I tender you my apology. Your note inclosed a tabulated statement in regard to the shipments, made and hoped for, of rolling stock from the United States.

I also note what you say about the mechanics that have been turned over to the French to repair French rolling stock. I am greatly obliged to you for the information.

LC, Pershing Papers, folder: General Tasker H. Bliss, 1917–1918, box 26.

Pershing to TAG, War Department, in addition to Pershing to TAG, War Department, cable P-1064-S, May 6.

Cable P-1147-S. Confidential.
For the Chief of Staff.

Reference my cable 1064, paragraph 3. It is gratifying to report that conferences by representatives of Allied Governments have resulted in adoption of working plan for pooling supplies and utilities in accordance with plan outlined in cable above referred to. M. Clemenceau himself presided at one of these conferences. Under the arrangement a General Office of Supplies is to be established near the Commander-in-Chief of the Allied Armies; and an Allied Board consisting of one military representative from each army will bring to the notice of the General Office of Supplies all means of unifying and coordinating the allotment of utilities and the distribution of supplies for their respective army organizations. Allotment of supplies from the common stocks upon the unanimous decision of the respective Allied representatives on the Board and these decisions will have the force of orders to various military supply agencies. The French and ourselves have fully agreed to the foregoing plan and it is expected that the British will also approve. If the question of unification of supplies for civil population should eventually be considered it will follow the same general plan, but so far the arrangement applies only to military supplies. It is believed by all concerned that the plan will result in great economy of resources in general and that construction such as warehouses and barracks and regulating stations will be reduced and that rail transportation will be simplified. The question of munitions and aviation will probably be brought under the plan and a closer understanding reached as to their allotment.

NARA, RG 120, M930, Confidential Series, AEF to War Department, roll 7.

TAG, War Department to Pershing, in part in reply to Pershing to TAG, War Department, cables P-1093-S, May 10, and P-1115-S, May 14.

Cable A-1350-R. Confidential.
 3. With reference to your 1093 and 1115. In view of demands which are being made upon United States by Great Britain and France for increased shipment of troops, Secretary of War believes it impossible at present to make definite engagement with regard to furnishing troops direct to Italy, but is entirely sympathetic with the project and hopes shortly to make definite decision in the matter. In this connection you are informed that the 4 steamboats mentioned in your telegram, namely the Duke D'Abruzzi, Duke Aosta, Taormina and Verona, are included in list of ships which the British authorities have advised us are part of their convoy to take American troops to Great Britain. If we are to carry out our agreement with the British these ships cannot be used for the purpose of taking troops to Italy. It is noted also that the Verona and Taormina which your dispatch lists with a carrying capacity of 6,000 are listed by the British as having joint carrying capacity of 3,947. If you are called upon to say anything about the matter, express sympathetic attitude and pointing out obligations of this Government during May and June express the hope that favorable determination of the question may soon be made for execution to begin later than June. [Reply—Vol. 5, June 5, P-1250-S]
March.

NARA, RG 120, M930, Confidential Series, War Department to AEF, roll 18.3

Bibliography

Official Records

NATIONAL ARCHIVES AND RECORDS ADMINISTRATION, ARCHIVES II, ADELPHI, MARYLAND

RG 45: Miscellaneous Records of the Navy Department, 1803–1859.

Miscellaneous Records of the Office of Naval Records and Library (ONRL), Miscellaneous Material Print Files, World War. Microfilm Publication T829. (See also Internet Sources below: National Archives and Records Administration.)

RG 120: General Headquarters, American Expeditionary Force (GHQ, AEF).

The Adjutant General, GHQ, AEF.

The Adjutant General's Office, Cables Division, Cablegrams Exchanged between General Headquarters, American Expeditionary Forces, and the War Department, 1917–1919, Microfilm Publication M930. (See also Internet Sources below: National Archives and Records Administration.)

Gorrell's History of the U.S. Army Air Service, American Expeditionary Forces, Microfilm Publication M990. (See also Internet Sources below: National Archives and Records Administration.)

Office of the Commander-in-Chief, Office of the Secretary of the General Staff, Entry 22, Reports of the Commander-in-Chief, GHQ War Diary, folder 34: January 24–April 28, 1918; folder 35: April 28–June 12, 1918, box 4.

Records of the American Section of the Supreme War Council, 1917–1919. Microfilm Publication M923. Most of the folders missing from the M923 collection can be found in the Library of Congress, Manuscript Division, Papers of Tasker H. Bliss. (See also Internet Sources below: National Archives and Records Administration.)

The Assistant Chief of Staff, Operations (G-3), GHQ, AEF, file 1003: Employment of Troops, boxes 3110–12.

Manuscript Collections

LIBRARY OF CONGRESS, WASHINGTON, DC

Papers of Henry T. Allen
Papers of Newton D. Baker

Papers of Tasker H. Bliss
Papers of Charles H. Brent
Papers of Robert L. Bullard
Papers of Paul H. Clark
Papers of Benjamin D. Foulois
Papers of Lloyd C. Griscom
Papers of James G. Harbord
Papers of Peyton C. March
Papers of William Mitchell
Papers of George S. Patton Jr.
Papers of John J. Pershing
Papers of Theodore Roosevelt Sr.
Papers of Hugh L. Scott
Papers of William S. Sims

AMERICAN HERITAGE CENTER, UNIVERSITY OF WYOMING, CHEYENNE

Papers of Senator Francis E. Warren

MANUSCRIPTS AND ARCHIVES, YALE UNIVERSITY LIBRARY, NEW HAVEN, CONNECTICUT

Edward Mandell House Papers
Series 1: Correspondence, folder 3072: John J. Pershing, box 89.

MASSACHUSETTS HISTORICAL SOCIETY, BOSTON

Papers of Clarence Ransom Edwards, box 22.

Photographs

NATIONAL ARCHIVES AND RECORDS ADMINISTRATION, ARCHIVES II, ADELPHI, MARYLAND

Special Archives Division, Still Picture Branch

RG 111: U.S. Army Signal Corps
RG 165: War Department General Staff

LIBRARY OF CONGRESS

Prints and Photographs Division

John J. Pershing Collection, Lot 7719
Bain News Service Collection
Harris & Ewing Collection
Chase, Joseph Cummings. *Soldiers All: Portraits and Sketches of the Men of the AEF.* New York: George H. Dorn, 1920.

Books, Articles, etc.

Alexander, Robert. *Memories of the World War, 1917–1918.* New York: Macmillan, 1931.
Andrews, Avery D. *My Friend and Classmate John J. Pershing. With Notes from My War Diary.* Harrisburg, PA: Military Service Publishing, 1937.
Association of Graduates, U.S. Military Academy. Robinson, Col. Wirt (ed.). *Biographical Register of the Officers and Graduates of the U.S. Military Academy at West Point, New York, Since Its Establishment in 1802.* Supplement, Vol. VI-A and VI-B: *1910–1920.* Saginaw, MI: Seemann & Peters, Printers, 1920. (Also available online at http: //digital-library.usma.edu/libmedia/archives/cullum/VOLUME_6A_cullum.pdf and http://digital-library.usma.edu/libmedia/archives/cullum/VOLUME_6B_cullum.pdf.)
Beaver, Daniel R. *Newton D. Baker and the American War Effort, 1917–1919.* Lincoln: University of Nebraska Press, 1966.
Blake, Robert (ed.). *The Private Papers of Douglas Haig, 1914–1919. Being Selections from the private diary and correspondence of Field-Marshal the Earl Haig of Bemersyde, K.T., G.C.B., O.M., etc.* London: Eyre & Spottiswoode, 1952.
Blumenson, Martin (ed.). *The Patton Papers: 1885–1940.* 2 vols. Boston: Houghton Mifflin, 1972.
Bruce, Robert B. *A Fraternity of Arms: America and France on the Great War.* Lawrence: University Press of Kansas, 2003.
Buck, Beaumont B. *Memories of Peace and War.* San Antonio, TX: Naylor, 1935.
Bullard, Robert L. *Personalities and Reminiscences of the War.* Garden City, NY: Doubleday, Page, 1925.
Callwell, Charles E. *Field-Marshal Sir Henry Wilson: His Life and Diaries.* 2 vols. London: Cassell, 1927.
Chase, Joseph Cummings. *Soldiers All: Portraits and Sketches of the Men of the AEF.* New York: George H. Dorn, 1920.
Clark, Edward B. *William L. Sibert: The Army Engineer.* Philadelphia, PA: Dorrance, 1930.
Coffman, Edward M. *The Hilt of the Sword: The Career of Peyton C. March.* Madison: University Press of Wisconsin, 1966.
———. *The War to End All Wars: The American Military Experience in World War I.* New York: Oxford University Press, 1968.
Cooke, James J. *Pershing and His Generals: Command and Staff in the AEF.* Westport, CT: Praeger, 1997.
Cooper, Duff. *Haig.* 2 vols. London: Faber and Faber, 1935 and 1936.
Crowell, Benedict, and Robert F. Wilson. *The Road to France.* Vol. 2: *The Transportation of Troops and Military Supplies, 1917–1918.* New Haven, CT: Yale University Press, 1921.
Davis, Henry Blaine, Jr. *Generals in Khaki.* Raleigh, NC: Pentland Press, 1998.
Davison, Henry P. *The American Red Cross in the Great War.* New York: Macmillan, 1920.
Dawes, Charles G. *A Journal of the Great War.* 2 vols. Boston: Houghton Mifflin, 1921.
Doughty, Robert A. *Pyrrhic Victory: French Strategy and Operations in the Great War.* Cambridge, MA: Harvard University Press, 2005.
Du Cane, Lt. Gen. Sir John. *With Marshal Foch: A British General at Allied Supreme Headquarters, April–November 1918.* Edited by Elizabeth Greenhalgh. Warwick, UK: Helion, 2018.
Finney, J. M. T. *A Surgeon's Life: The Autobiography of J. M. T. Finney.* New York: G. P. Putnam's Sons, 1940.
Foch, Ferdinand. *The Memoirs of Marshal Foch.* Translated by Col. T. Bentley Mott. Garden City, NY: Doubleday, Doran, 1931.

556 Bibliography

Foulois, Benjamin D., with Col. C. V. Glines. *From the Wright Brothers to the Astronauts: The Memoirs of Major General Benjamin D. Foulois.* New York: McGraw-Hill, 1968.
Fowler, W. B. *British-American Relations, 1917–1918: The Role of Sir William Wiseman.* Princeton, NJ: Princeton University Press, 1969.
Frothingham, Thomas G. *The American Reinforcement in the World War.* Garden City, NY: Doubleday, Page, 1927.
Ganoe, William A. *The History of the United States Army.* New York: D. Appleton-Century, 1942.
Gleaves, Albert. *A History of the Transport Service: Adventures and Experiences of United States Transports and Cruisers in the World War.* New York: George H. Doran, 1921.
Goldhurst, Richard. *Pipe Clay and Drill: John J. Pershing, the Classic American Soldier.* New York: Reader's Digest Press, 1977.
Grasty, Charles H. *Flashes from the Front.* New York: Century, 1918.
Greenhalgh, Elizabeth. *Foch in Command. The Forging of a First World War General.* New York: Cambridge University Press, 2011.
———. *Victory through Coalition: Britain and France during the First World War.* New York: Cambridge University Press, 2005.
Griscom, Lloyd C. *Diplomatically Speaking.* Boston: Little, Brown, 1940.
Hagood, Johnson. *The Services of Supply. A Memoir of the Great War.* Boston: Houghton Mifflin, 1927.
Hankey, Lord (Maurice Hankey). *The Supreme Command, 1914–1918.* 2 vols. London: George Allen and Unwin, 1961.
Harbord, James G. *The American Army in France, 1917–1919.* Boston: Little, Brown, 1936.
———. *The American Expeditionary Forces: Its Organization and Accomplishments.* Evanston, IL: Evanston Publishing, 1929.
———. *Leaves from a War Diary.* New York: Dodd, Mead, 1931.
Harris, Frederick, Frederic H. Kent, and William J. Newlin (eds.) *Service with Fighting Men: An Account of the Work of the American Young Men's Christian Associations in the World War.* 2 vols. New York: Association Press, 1922.
Herwig, Holger H., and Neil M. Heyman. *Biographical Dictionary of World War I.* Westport, CT: Greenwood Press, 1982.
Hewes, James E., Jr. *From Root to McNamara: Army Organization and its Administration, 1900–1963.* Washington: U.S. Army Center of Military History, 1975.
History of the U.S.S. Leviathan, Cruiser and Transport Forces, United States Atlantic Fleet. Brooklyn, NY: Brooklyn Eagle Job Department, 1919.
Holley, Irving B. *Ideas and Weapons. Exploitation of the Aerial Weapon by the United States during World War I: A Study in the Relationship of Technological Advance, Military Doctrine, and the Development of Weapons.* Washington: Office of Air Force History, 1983.
Holmes, Richard (ed.). *The Oxford Companion to Military History.* London: Oxford University Press, 2001.
Lacey, Jim. *Pershing: A Biography.* New York: Palgrave Macmillan, 2008.
Levine, Isaac Don. *Mitchell: Pioneer of Air Power.* New York: Duell, Sloan and Pearce, 1943.
Liggett, Hunter. *A.E.F. Ten Years Ago in France.* New York: Dodd, Mead, 1928.
———. *Commanding an American Army: Recollections of the World War.* Boston: Houghton Mifflin, 1925.
Link, Arthur S. *Woodrow Wilson and the Progressive Era, 1910–1917.* New York: Harper and Brothers, 1954.
———, et. al. (eds.). *The Papers of Woodrow Wilson.* Vol. 47: *March 13–May 12, 1918.* Princeton, NJ: Princeton University Press, 1984.

Lloyd George, David. *War Memoirs of David Lloyd George*. 2 vols. London: Odhams Press, 1938.

Lonergan, Thomas Clement. *It Might Have Been Lost! A Chronicle from Alien Sources of the Struggle to Preserve the National Identity of the A.E.F.* New York: G. P. Putnam's Sons, 1929.

March, Peyton C. *The Nation at War*. Garden City, NY: Doubleday, Doran, 1932.

Marshall, George C. *Memoirs of My Services in the World War, 1917–1918*. Boston: Houghton Mifflin, 1976.

Millett, Allen R. *The General: Robert L. Bullard and Officership in the United States Army, 1881–1925*. Westport, CT: Greenwood Press, 1975.

Mitchell, William. *Memoirs of World War I: From Start to Finish of Our Greatest War*. New York: Random House, 1960.

Morison, Elting E. *Admiral Sims and the Modern American Navy*. Boston: Houghton Mifflin, 1942.

Mott, T. Bentley. *Twenty Years as Military Attaché*. New York: Oxford University Press, 1937.

O'Connor, Richard. *Black Jack Pershing*. Garden City, NY: Doubleday, 1961.

Palmer, Frederick. *Bliss, Peacemaker: The Life and Letters of General Tasker H. Bliss*. New York: Dodd, Mead, 1934.

———. *John J. Pershing, General of the Armies: A Biography*. Harrisburg, PA: Military Service Publishing, 1948.

———. *Newton D. Baker: America at War*. 2 vols. New York: Dodd, Mead, 1931.

———. *With My Own Eyes: A Personal Story of Battle Years*. Indianapolis: Bobbs-Merrill, 1933.

Pershing, John J. *My Experiences in the World War*. 2 vols. New York: Frederick A. Stokes, 1931.

Pogue, Forrest C. *George C. Marshall: Education of a General, 1881–1939*. New York: Viking Press, 1963.

Rabalais, Steven. *General Fox Conner: Pershing's Chief of Operations and Eisenhower's Mentor*. Philadelphia, PA: Casemate, 2016.

Réquin, E. *America's Road to Victory*. New York: Frederick A. Stokes, 1919.

Robertson, William R. *From Private to Field-Marshal*. Boston: Houghton Mifflin, 1921.

———. *Soldiers and Statemen, 1914–1918*. 2 vols. New York: Charles Scribner's Sons, 1926.

Ryan, Stephen. *Pétain the Soldier*. South Brunswick, NJ: A. S. Barnes, 1969.

Scott, Hugh L. *Some Memories of a Soldier*. New York: Century, 1928.

Scott, James Brown. *Robert Bacon: His Life and Letters*. Garden City, NY: Doubleday, Page, 1923.

Service Historique, État-major de l'armée, Ministère de la Guerre [Historical Service, French Army General Staff, Ministry of War]. *Les armées françaises dans la grande guerre* [The French Army in the Great War].

———. *L'hiver 1917–1918. L'offensive allemande (1 novembre 1917–18 julliet 1918)* [Winter, 1917–1918: The German Offensive (1 November 1917–18 July 1918)]. Vol. 6.

———. *Le préparation de la campagne 1918: L'offensive allemande de 1'Oise à la mer du nord (1 novembre 1917–30 avril 1918)* [Preparations for the Campaign of 1918: The German Offensive from the Oise toward the North Sea (1 November 1917–30 April 1918)]. Vol. 1. Paris: Ministry of War, 1931.

———. *Annexes* (Appendices). Vols. 2, 3. Paris: Ministry of War, 1932.

———. *L'offensive allemande contre les armée françaises (1 Mai–18 Julliet 1918)* [The German Offensive against the French Army (1 May–18 July 1918)]. Vol. 2. Paris: Ministry of War, 1934.

———. *Annexes* (Appendices). Vol. 1. Paris: Ministry of War, 1935.

Shay, Michael E. *Hunter Liggett: A Soldier's General*. College Station: Texas A&M University Press, 2019.

———. *Revered Commander, Maligned General: The Life of Clarence Ransom Edwards, 1859–1931*. Columbia: University of Missouri Press, 2011.

———. *The Yankee Division in the First World War: In the Highest Tradition*. College Station: Texas A&M University Press, 2008.

Sheffield, Gary, and John Bourne. *Douglas Haig: War Diaries and Letters, 1914–1918*. London: Weidenfeld & Nicholson, 2005.

Shiner, Col. John F. *Foulois and the U.S. Army Air Corps, 1931–1935*. Washington: Office of Air Force History, 1983.

Simmons, Edwin H., and Joseph H. Alexander. *Through the Wheat: The U.S. Marines in World War I*. Annapolis, MD: Naval Institute Press, 2008.

Sims, William S. *The Victory at Sea*. Garden City, NY: Doubleday, Page, 1920.

Smith, Gene. *Until the Last Trumpet Sounds: The Life of General of the Armies John J. Pershing* New York: John Wiley & Sons, 1998.

Smith, Richard Norton. *The Colonel: The Life and Legend of Robert R. McCormick, 1880–1955*. Boston: Houghton Mifflin, 1997.

Smythe, Donald. *Guerrilla Warrior: The Early Life of John J. Pershing*. New York: Charles Scribner's Sons, 1973.

———. *Pershing: General of the Armies*. Bloomington: Indiana University Press, 2007.

———. "Pershing and General J. Franklin Bell, 1917–1918," *Mid-America* 54 (January 1972): 34–51.

———. "'Your Authority in France Will Be Supreme': The Baker-Pershing Relationship in World War I," *Parameters* 9, no. 2 (June 1979): 38–45.

Spencer, John. *Wilson's War: Sir Henry Wilson's Influence on British Military Policy in the Great War and Its Aftermath*. Warwick, UK: Helion, 2020.

Stackpole, Pierpont L. *In the Company of Generals: The World War I Diary of Pierpont L. Stackpole*. Edited by Robert H. Ferrell. Columbia: University of Missouri Press, 2009.

Stallings, Lawrence. *The Doughboys: The Story of the AEF, 1917–1918*. New York: Harper & Row, 1963.

Still, William N., Jr. *Crisis at Sea: The United States Navy in European Waters in World War I*. Gainesville: University Press of Florida, 2006.

Sweetser, Arthur. *The American Air Service: A Record of Its Problems, Its Difficulties, Its Failures, and Its Final Achievements*. New York: D. Appleton, 1919.

Tardieu, André. *France and America: Some Experiences in Cooperation*. Boston: Houghton Mifflin, 1927.

Toulmin, H. A., Jr. *Air Service, American Expeditionary Force, 1918*. New York: D. Van Nostrand, 1927.

Trask, David F. *The AEF and Coalition Warmaking, 1917–1918*. Lawrence: University Press of Kansas, 1993.

———. *Captains and Cabinets: Anglo-American Naval Relations, 1917–1918*. Columbia: University of Missouri Press, 1972.

———. *The United States in the Supreme War Council: American War Aims and Inter-Allied Strategy, 1917–1918*. Middletown, CT: Wesleyan University Press, 1961.

Twitchell, Heath, Jr. *Allen: The Biography of an Army Officer, 1859–1930*. New Brunswick, NJ: Rutgers University Press, 1974.

U.S. Air Force. Office of Air Force History. *The U.S. Air Service in World War I*. Edited by Maurer Maurer. 4 vols. Washington: Office of Air Force History, 1978. (This is an edited compilation of Col. Edgar S. Gorrell's History of the U.S. Army Air Service, American Expeditionary Forces, NARA, RG 120, Microfilm Publication M990, 1974.)

U.S. American Battle Monuments Commission. *American Armies and Battlefields in Europe.* Washington: U.S. Army Center of Military History, 1992. (A reprint of the ABMC's 1938 edition.)

———. *A Guide to the American Battle Fields in Europe.* Washington: GPO, 1927.

U.S. Army. Center of Military History. *Order of Battle of the United States Land Forces in the World War.* 3 vols. Washington: U.S. Army Center of Military History, 1988.

———. *United States Army in the World War, 1917–1919.* 17 vols. Washington: U.S. Army, 1948. Reprinted by U.S. Army Center of Military History, 1991.

U.S. Army. Office of the Chief of Chaplains.

———. Earl F. Stover, *Up from Handymen: The United States Army Chaplaincy, 1865–1920.* Washington: Department of the Army, Office of the Chief of Chaplains, 1977.

———. Roy J. Honeywell, *Chaplains of the United States Army.* Washington: Department of the Army, Office of the Chief of Chaplains, 1958.

U.S. Department of the Navy. *Annual Reports of the Navy Department for the Fiscal Year 1919.* Washington: GPO, 1920.

U.S. Department of the Navy. Naval History Division.

———. Lewis P. Clephane. *History of the Naval Overseas Transportation Service in World War I.* Washington: GPO, 1969.

U.S. Department of the Navy. Office of Naval Records and Library, Historical Section. *The United States Naval Railway Batteries in France.* Washington: GPO, 1922.

U.S. Department of State. *Papers Relating to the Foreign Relations of the United States, 1918. Supplement 1: The World War,* Vol. 1. Washington: GPO, 1933.

U.S. War Department. The Adjutant General's Office (TAGO). *American Decorations: A List of Awards of the Congressional Medal of Honor, the Distinguished Service Cross, and the Distinguished Service Medal Awarded under Authority of the Congress of the United States, 1862–1926.* Washington: GPO, 1927.

———. *America's Munitions, 1917–1918: Report of Benedict Crowell.* Washington: GPO, 1919.

———. *Final Report of Gen. John J. Pershing, Commander-in-Chief, American Expeditionary Forces.* Washington: GPO, 1920.

———. *Historical Report of the Chief Engineer, Including All Operations of the Engineer Department: American Expeditionary Forces, 1917–1919.* Washington: GPO, 1919.

———. *Official Army Register.* (Published annually.) Washington: GPO, 1897–1956.

Vandiver, Frank E. *Black Jack: The Life and Times of John J. Pershing.* 2 vols. College Station: Texas A&M University Press, 1977.

Venzon, Anne Cipriano (ed.). *The United States in the First World War: An Encyclopedia.* New York: Garland Publishing, 1995.

Webster's American Military Biographies. Springfield, MA: G. & C. Merriam, 1978.

Webster's Biographical Dictionary. Springfield, MA: G. & C. Merriam, 1972.

Webster's Encyclopedic Unabridged Dictionary of the English Language. New York: Gramercy Books, 1989.

Weigley, Russell. *History of the United States Army.* New York: Macmillan, 1967.

Who Was Who in American History—The Military. Chicago, IL: Marquis Who's Who, 1975.

Wilgus, William J. *Transporting the A.E.F. in Western Europe: 1917–1919.* New York: Columbia University Press, 1931.

Wilson, John B. *Maneuver and Firepower: The Evolution of Divisions and Separate Brigades.* Washington: U.S. Army Center of Military History, 1998.

Woodward, David R. *The American Army in the First World War*. New York: Cambridge University Press, 2014.

———. *Lloyd George and the Generals*. Newark: University of Delaware Press, 1983.

———. *Trial by Friendship: Anglo-American Relations, 1917–1918*. Lexington: University Press of Kentucky, 1993.

Wright, Peter E. *At the Supreme War Council*. New York: G. P. Putnam's Sons, 1921.

Yockelson, Mitchell A. *Borrowed Soldiers: Americans under British Command, 1918*. Norman: University of Oklahoma Press, 2008.

Young, Hugh. *Hugh Young: A Surgeon's Autobiography*. New York: Harcourt, Brace, 1940.

Zabriskie, Alexander C. *Bishop Brent, Crusader for Christian Unity*. Philadelphia, PA: Westminster Press, 1948.

Internet Sources

American Battle Monuments Commission, at http://www.abmc.gov/commission/history.php.

Biographical Directory of the United States Congress, at http: //bioguide.congress.gov/.

"Biographies in Naval History," Naval Historical Center, at http: //www.history.navy.mil/bios/.

Biography United States Air Force, at http://www.af.mil/information/bios.

National Archives and Records Administration. Available online at www.fold3.com.

———. RG 45. Miscellaneous Records of the Navy Department, 1803–1859. Miscellaneous Records of the Office of Naval Records and Library (ONRL), Miscellaneous Material Print Files, World War. Microfilm Publication T829, at https://www.fold3.com/publication/1004/miscellaneous-records-of-the-navy-department.

———. RG 120. General Headquarters, American Expeditionary Force (GHQ, AEF). The Adjutant General's Office, Cables Division, Cablegrams Exchanged between General Headquarters, American Expeditionary Forces, and the War Department, 1917–1919, Microfilm Publication M930, at https://www.fold3.com/title/487/wwi-military-cablegrams-aef-and-war dept.

———. Records of the American Section of the Supreme War Council, 1917–1919. Microfilm Publication M923, at https://www/fold3.com/title/488/wwi-supreme-war-council-american-records.

———. Gorrell's History of the U.S. Army Air Service, American Expeditionary Forces, Microfilm Publication M990, at https://www.fold3.com/title/80/gorrells-history-aef-air-service.

[William S. Sims]. "Sims," in *Dictionary of American Naval Fighting Ships*, Naval Historical Center, at http://www.history.navy.mil/danfs/s13/sims-iii.htm.

U.S. Army, Command and General Staff College, Combined Arms Research Library, Digital Library, World War Records, 1st Division, American Expeditionary Forces: Operations Reports, at cgsc.contentdm.oclc.org/cdm/singleitem/collection/p4013c0117/id/1030/type/singleitem/pftype/pdf.

U.S. Navy, Naval History and Heritage Command, website: Wars, Conflicts, and Operations, World War I, at https: //www.history.navy.mil/browse-by-topics/wars-conflicts-and-operations/world-war-i.html, Documentary Histories.

Wikipedia. At www.en.wiki.org/wiki/.

Index

Abbeville Conference and Agreement (Supreme War Council), xxii–xxiv, 233, 268, 334, 345, 370–71, 380, 386–96, 404–14, 415, 418–19, 423, 450–51, 455, 457–58, 488, 497, 504–5, 515, 522, 542, 544

Abbeville meeting (British-French only), 225–26, 278, 333–34

African American division (92nd). *See* Black division

aircraft engines/motors: development and production, xi, 6, 175–76, 200, 223, 229, 290, 317, 328, 337, 352, 375–77, 385, 418, 427, 429, 433, 483, 500, 533, 546; Liberty engines/motors, 17, 72, 154, 176, 206, 212–13, 224, 229, 279, 328, 335–36, 353, 375–78, 417, 428–29, 452, 475–76, 500, 510, 519, 519–20, 538, 541, 547, 550

aircraft, bombing, 278, 376; Caproni night bombers, 107, 151, 277–78, 376–77; day bombing, 335–36, 376, 428, 537; development and production, 6–7, 72, 151, 154, 212–13, 223, 230, 278–79, 289–90, 317, 328, 417–18, 443, 452, 500, 508–9, 509–10, 517–20, 525; discussions on contracts for aircraft and engines and proposals for future cooperation with the French, 335–37, 344, 352–53, 375–77, 385, 427–30, 547; Handley Page night bombers, 107, 123, 150–51, 181, 199, 247, 278–79, 303, 341, 343, 417, 428, 460, 474; machine guns, 46, 223, 383; observation (reconnaissance), 335, 376, 383, 428; pursuit (fighter), 7, 153, 229, 317, 335, 383, 427–28, 476; training, 7, 88, 93, 153, 525; production agreements for Handley Page bombers and discussions for pursuit aircraft and future cooperation with Great Britain, 151, 175, 177, 181, 279, 190, 303, 315, 317, 324, 341, 343, 433, 460, 474, 477–78, 506–7, 528

Aircraft Production Board, Council of National Defense (CND), 530

Air Service, 120, 150–51; aircraft, engine, and training programs with Italy, 7–8, 72, 154, 177, 208–9, 212, 242, 279, 299, 377–78, 430, 518–20; Air Service Program, 6–9, 120, 176, 324, 382–83, 480–84, 520; aircraft acceptance parks, 460, 482–83; Air Service Production Center No. 2, 107, 181, 279, 343, 545–46; balloon schools, companies, and squadrons, 7–8, 185, 188, 205, 482–83, 506, 515; cooperation with the Trenchard and Royal Air Force, 150–51, 199–200, 278–79, 367–68; criticism of U.S. Navy over allocation of Liberty engines and on naval air operations in Europe, 154, 176–77, 212, 224, 377–79, 423–25, 475–77, 479–80, 484–85, 510, 517–20, 526–30; Handley Page night bomber program with British (*see* aircraft); liaison with the French Air Force, 8, 483; mechanics for the French Army, 185, 205, 401, 491; mechanics training program with the British, 7, 91, 162, 229, 324; personnel, 6–8, 107, 120, 185, 188–89, 324, 341, 350, 352, 431, 460, 479, 482–83; photographic sections, 188, 483, 515; squadrons, 6–8, 91–92, 120, 154, 188–89, 208, 229, 238–39, 242, 302–3, 382–83, 417–18, 428, 460–61, 480–84, 491, 507, 550; training, 6–9, 208, 242, 352, 546; training schools and centers, 6–8, 460; training and service with the French Air Service, 8, 401, 431,

561

Air Service *(continued)*
461–62, 470, 479, 482, 544–45, 548; training and service with the Royal Air Force, 154–55, 193–97, 450–51, 517–19

Alden, Herbert W., 327

Allaire, William H., Jr., 420, 499; correspondence with Pershing *(see* Pershing)

Allen, Henry T., xii, 468; correspondence with Pershing *(see* Pershing)

Allied anti-submarine warfare. *See* Germany (German)

Allied Maritime Transport Council. *See* Inter-Allied Councils

Allied services of supply (later Military Board of Allied Supply): Clemenceau and French accept pooling proposal, 339–41, 514, 521; Dawes's proposals to Pershing for creation of unified Allied supply services, 217–21, 232–34, 438–39; Pershing proposes pooling Allied supplies to Clemenceau and Milner, 256–57, 263–64; Pershing informs War Department of his concept for pooling Allied supplies, 274, 551–52; Pershing discusses unified supply concept with American members of Allied Maritime Transport Council, 325–26

Alvord, Benjamin, 371, 381; meetings with Pershing *(see* Pershing)

amalgamation of American troops with British and French units, xvii, xxii, 19–20, 23, 48, 57, 60, 147, 149, 249, 263, 296–99, 331–32, 357, 361, 389–90, 419, 504–5; discussions on American cooperation at Supreme War Council meeting at Beauvais, 133–34, 138–39; Pershing's disagreement with Bliss at Permanent Military Representatives' discussion of Joint Note No. 18, 55–60, 62; Pershing's opposition to, 55–60, 62, 249–50, 263, 297–98, 360–61, 504. *See also* Six-Division Plan, Joint Note No. 18

American Expeditionary Forces (AEF): Air Service, AEF *(see* Air Service); ambulance companies, 493, 506; Ambulance Service, 325, 452, 491; American liaison officers, xii–xiii, 150, 199, 215–16, 239–40, 280, 323, 332–33, 403–4, 503–4, 526 *(see also* Bacon, Robert, Clark, Paul H., Fowler, Harold, Griscom, Lloyd C., and Mott, T. Bentley); army artists, 247, 302; army corps, xxii, xxiv, 10–11, 18, 35–36, 60, 65–66, 73, 104, 133, 144, 148, 68–69, 179, 185, 188, 221, 231, 245, 297, 308, 312, 331, 335, 356, 398, 400, 404, 410–11, 415, 421–22, 440, 445, 450, 483–84, 523, 532, 537–38, 543–45; barracks, xi, 139–40, 274, 552; billeting, xi, 39, 43, 65, 68, 201; Chief Ordnance Officer, 112, 311 *(see also* Williams, Clarence C., Jordan, Harry B.); Chief Quartermaster Officer, 311, 504 *(see also* Rogers, H. L.); commanders of brigades, divisions, and corps, 36, 44, 57, 158, 201, 216, 227, 249, 272, 275, 280–81, 313, 360, 372, 375, 411, 423, 435–36, 449, 454, 496; Director General of Transportation (DGT), 50, 71, 140, 175, 312, 342, 371 *(see also* Atterbury, William W. and Transportation Department, AEF); engineers (military), 22, 40–41, 47, 63, 91, 98, 165, 169, 287, 302, 307, 339, 442, 446, 491; foresters and forestry units, 251, 491; formation of an American sector of the front, xxiv–xxv, 38, 70, 403, 453–54, 542–43, 545, 548; Gas Service, AEF *(see* Gas Service); General Headquarters, AEF (GHQ, AEF), viii, xviii, 42, 74, 246, 418, 444, 453, 483–84, 536, 549–50; General Organization Project (Plan), 302, 480–81, 484; General Purchasing Agent (Agency, Board)*(see also* Charles G. Dawes), 219–20, 250, 257; General Staff, xiv–xvi, 9, 11, 72–73, 120, 196 198, 256, 284, 288, 368, 498; General Staff officers (staff officers), xvi, xviii, 11, 24, 33, 73, 196, 315, 440, 442; General Staff: Assistant Chief of Staff, Administration (G-1), 65, 83, 120, 196, 431, 503 *(see also* Logan, James A., Jr.); Assistant Chief of Staff, G-2 (Intelligence), xv, 78, 198 *(see also* Nolan, Dennis E.); Assistant Chief of Staff, G-3 (Operations), viii, xiv–xvi, 24, 52, 186, 207, 368 *(see also* Conner,

Fox); Assistant Chief of Staff (G-4), 440 (*see also* Connor, William D., Moseley, George Van Horn); Assistant Chief of State, G-5 (Training), 83, 368, 463(*see also* Fiske, Harold B.); historical section, 302, 325; Line of Communication (LOC), AEF (*see* Services of Supply (SOS)); Priority Schedule, 10-11, 166, 178-80, 185-89, 204-5, 271, 310, 495, 506; promotions in, 33, 112, 146, 262, 274-75, 299-301, 509; replacement division(s), 21, 128, 157, 244, 305, 541; replacements (troops), 17, 60, 86-87, 93, 128, 145, 148, 165-66, 168-69, 170, 172, 178-80, 186-88, 204, 227, 242, 248, 256, 259, 267, 275-77, 282-83, 292-93, 295, 315-16, 329, 395, 404, 441-43, 446, 459, 491, 502-5, 515; replacement raw materials for purchases from Allies, 15-16, 151, 154, 200, 212, 326, 336-37, 353, 378, 424, 427-30, 500, 518-19, 539; replacement (spares) for weapons and equipment, 112, 181, 230, 260-61, 279, 343, 385, 450, 474, 545-46; schools (army, corps, staff, training, etc.), xvi, 7, 98, 100, 161, 194, 273, 295-96, 384, 396-98, 401, 436, 482, 489, 499, 530; staff college (Langres), 198, 273, 404, 432, 436, 475, 522; strategic plan for 1918 and 1919 (September 25, 1917), viii-ix; suitability of general officers for command, 43, 101-2, 444; training areas (camps, centers), xi, xxiv, 7, 29, 43, 257, 374, 461, 492; training cablegram, no. 11, 489-90; training with the British (*see also* Six-Division Plan), xxi-xxii, 12-13, 31-32, 68, 245, 266, 297, 327, 458, 471, 491, 508; training with the French Army, 21, 35-40, 44, 51-53, 57-58, 62-63, 144-45, 163, 204-5, 206-8, 227-28, 259, 297, 304-5, 320-21, 356-58, 396-400, 411, 422-23, 453-56, 478-79, 492, 502-3, 523, 542-45, 547-51; Transportation Department, 270-71 (*see also* Atterbury, William W., and Director General of Transportation)

—BRIGADES: Coast Artillery, 44; NUMBERED: 2nd Artillery, 502, 514; 4th Artillery, 508; 31st Artillery, 491; 32nd Artillery, 491; 1st Infantry, 22, 216; 3rd Infantry, 495; 4th Marine, xii, 146, 372, 435-36, 440, 507

—CORPS, NUMBERED: I Corps, 21, 38, 52, 63-64, 189, 207, 211, 246, 287, 304-5, 454, 481-83, 491, 542-43, 545; II Corps, 11, 39, 167, 178, 186-87, 231, 244-46, 276, 287, 404, 450, 515, 541, 545-46; III Corps, 186-87, 231, 244-46, 287, 404, 515, 541, 545; IV Corps, 246, 468, 515, 541, 545; V Corps, 246, 545; VI Corps, 496;

—DIVISIONS: 1st Division, 22, 36, 38, 44, 52, 76, 89, 106, 157, 163, 189, 193, 201, 216, 232-23, 239-41, 257, 259, 301, 405, 416, 444-46, 461, 491, 543, 548; 2nd Division, xii, 22, 36, 39, 44, 62, 162, 187, 207, 372, 403, 436, 491, 496, 502-3, 507, 513, 543; 3rd Division, 10, 36, 104, 204, 207, 210, 231, 306, 372, 403-4, 461, 470, 479, 491, 523, 541, 548; 4th Division, 198, 231, 244-45, 404; 5th Division, 10, 104, 122, 198, 210, 231, 244-45, 287, 306, 404, 454, 461, 478-79, 491, 506, 523, 541, 548; 6th Division, 198, 231, 244-45, 474; 7th Division, 316, 459; 26th Division, 20-22, 36, 38-39, 44, 52-53, 62, 66, 88-89, 158, 162-63, 207, 209, 259, 301, 304-5, 319, 374-75, 402-3, 444, 446, 454, 461, 478-79, 491, 541, 548; 27th Division, 231, 244-45, 263, 404, 479, 541; 28th Division, 18, 231, 244-45, 404, 491; 29th Division, 474-75; 30th Division, 18, 231, 244-45, 263, 404; 32nd Division, 21, 184, 204, 207, 209-10, 226-27, 239, 259, 287, 305-6, 319, 349-50, 454, 461, 478-79, 491, 523; 33rd Division, 231, 244-45, 404, 541; 35th Division, 231, 244-45, 342, 404, 479, 491; 37th Division, 474-75; 41st (Depot) Division, 64, 491; 42nd Division, 20-22, 36, 38-39, 52-53, 62, 66, 207, 209, 239, 259, 301, 305-6, 319, 402-3, 454, 461, 478-79, 491; 77th Division, 18, 104, 216, 231, 244-45, 279-80, 287, 301, 309, 404, 479, 491; 78th Division, 18, 231, 244-45, 404, 541; 80th Division, 18, 244-45, 404; 82nd Division, 244-45, 491; 83rd Division, 18, 474; 89th Division (*see also* Wood,

American Expeditionary Forces *(continued)*
Leonard), 474–75, 542; 90th Division *(see also* Allen, Henry T.), 474–75; 92nd Division, 324, 372, 468, 474–75, 508; 93rd Division, 94, 491
—REGIMENTS, NUMBERED: 54th Artillery (Heavy), 491; 53rd Coast Artillery, 53; 6th Engineer, 125, 164; 35th Engineer, 72, 222, 271; 36th Engineer, 271; 30th Engineer (Gas and Flame), 491; 15th Field Artillery, 514; 9th Infantry, 502; 16th Infantry, 216, 513; 18th Infantry, 436; 23rd Infantry, 495; 26th Infantry, 541; 61st Infantry, 122; 102nd Infantry, 447; 369th Infantry, 306, 479; 370th Infantry, 306; 371st Infantry, 306; 372nd Infantry, 306; 5th Marine, 372, 507, 513–14; 6th Marine, 507, 514
American Red Cross, 462, 516. *See also* Davison, Henry P.
Amiens, 2, 49–50, 66, 78, 80, 82, 87, 115–16, 204–5, 236, 82, 408, 413
ammunition, xi, 44, 46, 93, 153, 194, 261, 289, 295, 326, 354, 474, 477, 501, 525, 548
Andrews, Avery D., 126; meetings with Pershing *(see* Pershing*)*
animals, 16–18, 271, 514
Ardery, Edward D.: meetings with Pershing *(see* Pershing*)*
army group, 400; French, Group of Armies East (GAE), 39, 402; Group of Armies Reserve (GAR), 455
artillery, xi, xxi, xxiv, 16, 37, 39, 41, 44, 48, 53, 56–57, 60, 76, 79, 81, 99, 104, 115, 144–45, 147, 157, 164, 169, 171, 178–79, 185–87, 204, 207, 210–11, 216, 222, 231, 259–60, 262, 273, 276, 281, 286–89, 292–93, 297, 301, 308, 310, 312–14, 319–21, 325, 334, 354, 356–58, 360, 374, 394, 400, 410–11, 422, 434, 439, 442, 446, 448, 455, 458, 482, 487, 489, 491, 494, 497, 501, 514, 517, 523
Atterbury, William W., 51, 71, 84, 126, 177, 196, 285, 290, 355, 512; correspondence and meetings with Pershing *(see* Pershing*)*
Austria, 95, 98–99, 115, 339
automatic rifles, 104, 296, 450, 536; Browning Automatic Rifles, 262, 426, 450, 536, 545; French Chauchat, 262, 450, 536, 545–46

Bacon, Robert, 78, 235, 503–4, 526; correspondence and meetings with Pershing *(see* Pershing*)*
Baker, Newton D., vii–viii, x, xii, xvii–xix, xxi–xxiv, 6, 30–31, 48, 59–60, 65–66, 94–97, 117, 119, 157–58, 233, 235, 292, 297–98, 303–4, 309, 320, 363, 366, 370; Baker Memorandum, 264–69; cables exchanged with Wilson while in Europe, 66–67, 85–87, 89–90, 104–6, 157–58, 160–61, 165; correspondence with Bliss, 29–30, 83–85, 110–11, 164–65, 183–85, 281–82, 311, 338, 361–64, 366–67, 421–22, 458; correspondence with Woodrow Wilson, 264–69, 312–14, 338–39, 364, 366–67, 422–23, 450–51, 481, 490–92; correspondence (including cables) and meetings with Pershing *(see* Pershing*)*; meeting with Pershing and Bliss, 74
Balfour, Arthur J., 41–42, 48, 174, 217, 504
Bartlett, George T., 527
Beauvais Conference (Supreme War Council), xxii–xxiv, 48, 96–97, 116–17, 126–39, 143–44, 155, 225, 298, 407, 421
Belgium, 108, 124, 350, 405, 485, 490, 492, 504; locomotives for AEF, 250, 294, 355, 438, 522; repair of railway cars, 175, 494, 513
Bell, J. Franklin, 32, 71, 101–4
Belleau Wood, 435, 496
Benson, William S.: cables exchanged with Sims, 67–68, 120–21, 196, 540
Bethel, Walter A., 51; meetings with Pershing *(see* Pershing*)*
Biddle, John, 328; correspondence (including cables) with Pershing *(see* Pershing*)*
Black, William M., 363; correspondence and meetings with Pershing *(see* Pershing*)*
Black division (92nd) (aka "Negro division"; "colored division"), 324, 372, 468, 474–75, 508; officers, 549; regiments, 11, 105, 187, 204, 231, 306, 324, 396, 490, 549; soldiers, 51, 427, 437, 459, 468, 549

Bliss, Tasker H., xii, xviii, xxi, xxiii, 19–20, 26, 41, 78, 95, 119, 167–68, 215, 226, 270, 289, 332, 358, 504–5; at Supreme War Council's Abbeville Conference with Pershing, 386–96, 404–14; at Supreme War Council's Beauvais Conference with Pershing, 128–39; at Permanent Military Representatives meeting with Pershing and drafting of Joint Note No. 18, 55–60, 61; correspondence with Baker (*see* Baker); correspondence and meetings with Pershing (*see* Pershing); correspondence with the War Department and March, 24, 143–44, 282–84, 380, 421–22, 432; meeting with Pershing, Foch, Harbord, and Weygand at Sarcus, 318–24

Bolling, Raynal C., 205–6, 252, 282

Boyd, Carl, 257; meetings with Pershing (*see* Pershing)

Bradley, Alfred E., 371, 381; meetings with Pershing (*see* Pershing)

Brent, Bishop Charles H., xii, 382; meetings with Pershing (*see* Pershing)

Brewster, André W.: meeting with Pershing (*see* Pershing)

British ports, 68; cross-Channel traffic to France, 145, 180, 278, 341–42, 460, 475; Folkestone, 286, 318, 323; Liverpool, 57, 68, 121, 154; problems with transporting American troops through England and across the Channel to France, 68, 124; Southampton, 68, threat 293, 461, 520

Bullard, Robert L., xii, 201–2, 216–17, 237, 241; meetings with Pershing (*see* Pershing)

Bundy, Omar, 435, 496; meetings with Pershing (*see* Pershing)

Bureau of Aircraft Production, 426, 519. *See also* Ryan, John D.

Burton, Pomeroy: meetings with Pershing (*see* Pershing)

Burtt, W. B., 202, 522; meetings with Pershing (*see* Pershing)

cablegrams, War Department, xii–xii

Cadorna, Luigi, 99, 332

Cambon, Jules, 354, 537

Carter, E. C., 248; meetings with Pershing (*see* Pershing)

censorship, 284–85, 302

Central Powers, 16. *See also* Austria and Germany

chaplains, 106, 255–56, 382

Chaumont, x, xxiii, 19, 24, 30, 66–67, 73–74, 84–85, 89, 92, 106, 128, 155, 157, 162, 167, 178, 181, 210, 220, 226, 232–33, 243, 249, 268, 298, 306, 330, 344, 351, 374, 427, 436, 445, 479, 495, 514

Chief of Ordnance, 92, 145, 153, 194, 222–23, 230, 290, 295, 315, 344, 382, 449, 474, 499, 534. *See also* Crozier, William, Wheeler, Charles B., Williams, Clarence C., and Ordnance Department

Chief Signal Officer, 72, 188–89, 229–30, 247, 250, 289, 302, 315, 324, 341, 355, 382, 417, 433, 442, 474, 506, 541, 545

Churchill, Winston S.: meeting with Pershing (*see* Pershing)

Clark, Paul H.: GHQ, AEF, Liaison with Pétain and French GHQ, xii; correspondence and meetings with Pershing (*see* Pershing)

Claveille, Albert, 16, 84, 363

Clemenceau, Georges, x, xvii, xxi, 67, 108, 116–17, 126–27, 225–26, 232–34, 269, 274, 333–35, 345–48, 350, 386, 421–22, 451, 470–71, 505, 521, 551–52; at Abbeville Conference (Supreme War Council), 386–96, 404–14; at Beauvais Conference (Supreme War Council), 128–39; at British-French Doullens Conference, 49–50; correspondence and meetings with Pershing (*see* Pershing)

coal, 145, 197, 250, 269–70, 318, 321, 325, 340, 341–42, 346, 441, 460, 475; for refueling American ships, 67–68, 120, 154–55, 195; shipment to Italy, 3, 15, 125–26, 441; supplies for AEF, 88, 274, 285–86, 384, 540

Collins, James L., 1; for correspondence and meetings with Pershing (*see* Pershing)

Compiègne (French GHQ), xxi, 31, 35, 47

Conner, Fox, viii, xv, 275, 522; AEF divisions training with the British, 82–83, 147–48; AEF divisions training with the French, 44, 51–52, 402–3; comments on the

Conner, Fox *(continued)*
   Abbeville Agreement, 457; shipment and use of American troops, 147–48, 178–80, 184–88; correspondence and meetings with Pershing (*see* Pershing)
Connor, William D., 140, 275, 300, 440, 522; meetings with Pershing (*see* Pershing)
convoys, 14, 69, 214, 396, 464, 486, 492, 501, 540
correspondents, xiv, 302, 511, 534
Craig, Malin, 522
Crowder, Enoch H., 364; correspondence with Pershing (*see* Pershing)
Crozier, William: meetings with Pershing (*see* Pershing). *See also* Chief of Ordnance and Ordnance Department
Currie, A. W., 222; meeting with Pershing (*see* Pershing)

Dawes, Charles G., xix, 34–35, 216–17, 264, 326, 346–47, 469, 514; correspondence and meetings with Pershing (*see* Pershing)
Davison, Henry P., 516; correspondence with Pershing (*see* Pershing)
de Chambrun, Aldebert Pineton: meeting with Pershing (*see* Pershing)
de Maud'huy, Louis: correspondence with Pershing (*see* Pershing)
Debeney, Marie-Eugene, 217, 455
Derby, Lord, 13–14, 84, 259, 369; meeting with Pershing (*see* Pershing)
di Robilant, 387, 406
Doyen, Charles A., 161, 371–72, 435, 500; correspondence with Pershing (*see* Pershing)
drafts. *See* amalgamation of American troops with British and French units
Drum, Hugh A., viii, 178–79, 215, 302, 531; meetings with Pershing (*see* Pershing)
DuCane, J. P., 406
Duncan, George B., 123, 201–2, 216

Edwards, Clarence R., 237, 371, 446; Harbord's criticism of Edwards's behavior, 53–54, 109; meeting with Pershing (*see* Pershing)
Egan, Martin, 70, 444; meetings with Pershing (*see* Pershing)

Eltinge, LeRoy R., viii, 215, 275, 300, 395, 495, 522; meetings with Pershing (*see* Pershing)
Executive War Board. *See* Inter-Allied General Reserve

Felton, Samuel M., 71–72, 175, 194, 255, 459, 474, 499, 513, 522
Fiske, Harold B., 178, 217, 522, 531; meetings with Pershing (*see* Pershing)
Foch, Ferdinand, ix–x, xiv–xv, xvii, xxii–xxv, 48, 67, 82, 87, 92–93, 105–6, 110–11, 143–44, 158, 200–201, 208, 215–16, 218–19, 225–26, 232–34, 237–38, 246, 248–50, 258, 268–69, 291, 293, 301, 304–6, 332–33, 338, 346–49, 350–51, 367, 370–71, 381, 415, 421–23, 432, 439, 471, 477, 488, 502, 523, 547; at Abbeville Conference (Supreme War Council), 386–96, 404–14; at Beauvais Conference (Supreme War Council), 128–39; at British-French Doullens Conference, 49–50; at Sarcus meeting with Pershing and Bliss, 318–24; Foch agrees to American sector at Chantilly meeting with Pershing, 542–45; Pershing offers Foch and Clemenceau full support of the AEF, 74–78; weaknesses of and corrections to Doullens Agreement making Foch Allied CINC, 107–8, 114–17, 155, 225; correspondence and meetings with Pershing (*see* Pershing)
Foulois, Benjamin D., xii, 73–74, 341; correspondence with Trenchard (RAF) on air operations, 150–51, 199–200; correspondence with French air minister on production of aircraft and engines for AEF Air Service, 335–37, 375–77, 401–2, 477–78, 537–39; replaced as Chief, Air Service, 537; correspondence and meetings with Pershing (*see* Pershing)
France: Ministry of War, ix, xvii, xxi, 108, 129, 354, 387, 406; Minister of Munitions (*see* Loucheur, Louis)
Frazier, Arthur H., xviii, 235, 237, 387, 419, 423, 505; at Abbeville SWC session, 386–96, 404–14; correspondence and meetings with Pershing (*see* Pershing)

French air service, 8, 335, 483
French aircraft production for Air Service, 352–53, 430, 478
French army, 58, 62, 134, 221, 264, 276, 288, 333, 336–37, 350, 388, 431, 452, 521, 542; 1st, 36, 61; 2nd, 162; 3rd, 75, 111; 5th, 202, 228, 232, 455; 6th, 544; 7th, 53, 203; 8th, 402; 10th, 414; corps, I Corps, 52; VII Corps, 52; X Corps, 204; XXI Corps, 203; XXXII, 454; 69th (Infantry) Division, 44, 52, 62; General Headquarters (GQG), xvi, xxi, 203, 549
French ports, 46, 164, 166, 191–92, 367; Atlantic ports, 68, 253, 540; Bassens, 252, 254; Bordeaux, 65, 197, 252, 254, 462; Boulogne, 286, 318, 323, 412; Brest, 65, 67–68, 120–21, 139, 154, 167, 195, 197, 252, 494, 546; Channel ports, 105, 293, 308–10, 408, 511, 540; Cherbourg, 13, 68, 83, 140; congestion at, 66, 68, 139, 191–92, 294, 300; docks and wharves at, xi, 139, 191–92, 465; facilities at, xi, 31, 67–69, 96–97, 112, 139–40, 191–93, 195–96, 209, 217–18, 254, 264, 300–301, 363, 441, 533, 539; Gironde River, 254; La Pallice, 252, 473; La Rochelle, 252; Le Havre, 83; Mediterranean ports, 126, 198, 540; Marseille, 3, 193, 196–98, 213, 300–301, 441, 469, 486–87, 500, 532–33, 539–40; Miramas, 197, 533, 539; Montoir, 139–42, 252; Nantes, 140–41; St. Nazaire, 65, 139–42, 218, 252–53, 371, 462; St. Sulpice, 252
French railways, 3, 15, 30, 178, 271, 474; locomotive and rolling stock problems and shortages, 3, 11, 28, 65, 71, 84–85, 112, 123, 177, 222, 246–47, 255, 271, 303, 355, 437–38, 466, 513, 522; railway (transportation) facilities, 67, 84, 421–22, 511
Fries, Amos: meetings with Pershing (see Pershing)

gas warfare, 2, 80, 106, 119, 262, 280, 312, 525
General Organization Project (GOP). See American Expeditionary Forces
General Purchasing Agent. See American Expeditionary Forces

General Staff and General Staff officers. See American Expeditionary Forces
Germany: x, xv, 2, 95, 156, 221, 309, 316, 337, 339, 349, 354, 381, 416; March and April offensives, xxi–xxii, xxiv, 1–5, 19, 21, 25, 27, 41, 57, 66, 68, 73, 76, 78–81, 92, 95, 108, 110, 115–16, 130, 156, 159, 163, 181–83, 188, 196, 204, 225, 227, 236, 258, 265, 268, 278, 296, 308, 310, 315–16, 349, 381, 408–9, 412–13, 472; German submarine threat and Allied anti-submarine warfare, 40, 68–69, 161, 176, 196–97, 212, 214, 291, 340, 348, 376–77, 424, 476, 484–86, 492, 540
Giardino, Gaetano, 19, 26, 46–47, 55–59, 99, 208, 364
Gièvres, 140, 152, 382, 462
Glenn, Edwin F., 198
Goethals, George W., xii, 112, 128, 221, 231, 384, 424, 460, 465, 475, 494, 533
Gondrecourt, 436
Great Britain: Admiralty, 67, 527; Air Board, 175, 385; Air Ministry, 367; British General Staff, xii, xvi; Chief, Imperial General Staff (CIGS), xii, xv, 47, 129, 170, 173, 292, 387, 406 (see also Hutchison, Robert; Robertson, William R.; Whigham, Robert Dundas; and Wilson, Henry H.); Ministry (Minister) of Munitions, 296 (see also Churchill, Winston S.); Ministry (Minister) of Shipping (Shipping Controller), 17, 67, 146, 270, 292, (see also Maclay, Joseph); Secretary of State for War (Minister of War), xii, xxiv, 13, 258–59, 268, 291–92, 307, 345, 387, 406, 468 (see also Derby, Lord; Milner, Lord); War Cabinet, 47–48, 84, 94, 135, 146, 173–74, 258–59, 267, 292, 298, 345 (see also Hankey, Lord); War Office, xii, xv, 14, 42, 47, 124, 167, 171–74, 180, 186, 203, 268, 276–77, 292–93, 298, 310, 406, 427, 437, 449, 456, 468, 497, 523 (see also Wilson, Henry H.)
Griscom, Lloyd C., xii–xiii, 70, 235, 280

Hagood, Johnson, 123, 139, 196
Haig, Douglas, xiv, 3, 39, 63, 66, 69, 76, 89, 105, 115, 143–44, 172, 225–26, 233, 240, 248–50, 257, 259, 268, 292–93, 301,

568   Index

Haig, Douglas *(continued)*
312–14, 320–21, 333, 350–51, 366–67, 374, 404, 423, 443, 453, 468, 523; at Abbeville Conference, 386–96, 404–14; at Beauvais Conference, 129–39; at Doullens Conference (British-French), 49–50; Pershing-Haig meeting on British training of AEF divisions (Six-Division Plan), 262–63, 280–81; correspondence and meetings with Pershing (*see* Pershing)
Hankey, Lord, 129, 135, 292, 345, 388, 406
Harbord, James G., xii, xiv–xv, xviii, 97, 100–101, 128, 199, 220–21, 307, 331–32, 365, 371–72, 374–75, 435–36, 440, 487, 507, 522; Harbord's criticism of Edwards's behavior, 53–54, 109; correspondence and meetings with Pershing (*see* Pershing)
Harjes, Henry Herman: meetings with Pershing (*see* Pershing)
Heights of the Meuse, 21–22, 39, 305
Hines, John T., 123, 216–17, 522
Holcomb, Thomas, 507
hospitals, 79, 90–91, 97–98, 122, 139–40, 162, 338, 371, 403, 491, 493, 506, 516–17, 526, 542
House, Edward M., xii–xiii, xviii, 41–43, 60, 104, 235, 334, 414, 504–5; correspondence with Woodrow Wilson, 504–5; correspondence with Pershing (*see* Pershing)
Hutchison, Robert, xvii, 167–68, 266–67, 292, 330, 334; meeting with Baker in Washington, 358–60; meetings with Baker and Pershing in Paris (*see* Pershing)

Inter-Allied Councils: Allied Maritime Transport Council, 125–26, 325–26, 340–42, 345, 418–19, 429; Aviation, 151, 200, 279, 350, 377, 425, 428–30, 500, 519; Transportation, 3, 177–78, 209–10, 242, 281, 294
Inter-Allied General Reserve, 3, 85, 110, 136, 283–84; Executive War Board of, 4, 30–31, 85, 110, 421
Ireland, Merritte W., 516–17, 542. *See also* Surgeon General
Is-sur-Tille, 24, 140, 287, 498, 503, 511–12, 531–32

Issoudun, 7
Italy, 29–30, 34, 111, 115, 161, 196, 218, 232, 301, 369–71, 380, 404–5, 407, 421, 465; AEF Air Service programs with Italy, 7–8, 72, 107, 151, 154, 177, 208–9, 212, 242, 279, 377–78, 424–25, 430, 517–20; British and French forces in Italy, 3, 98–99, 414–16; coal supplies for Italy, 3, 15, 125–26, 441; Italian army, 98–99, 348, 370, 425, 432, 452; Italian front, 46–47, 66–67, 108, 116, 208–9, 242, 278, 311, 337, 362–63, 366, 407, 421, 443; Mott's report on Italian situation, 98–99; Secretary Baker's visit to, xxiii, 30, 94, 117, 119, 127, 150, 157–58, 236, 311, 362–63; the question of sending U.S. troops to Italy, 46–47, 57, 311, 337, 362–64, 366–67, 443, 451, 472–73, 485, 493–99, 514–15, 552

Joffre, Joseph, x
Joint Army and Navy Aircraft Committee (Paris), 73–74, 279
Joint Note Nos. 12, No. 18 (SWC). *See* Permanent Military Representatives (SWC)
Johnson, Evan M.: meeting with Pershing. *See* Pershing
Jordan, Harry B.: meetings with Pershing. *See* Pershing

Kean, J. R., 140, 522
Kernan, Francis J., 152, 291; correspondence and meetings with Pershing (*see* Pershing)

laborers, 34–35, 67, 187, 191, 205, 227, 332. *See also* workmen
large passenger liners and cargo ships used as troop transports, 13–14, 68, 146, 160, 205, 286; *Aquitania, Mauretania,* and *Olympic,* 12–14, 17, 31–33, 67, 127; *Great Northern,* 68; *Northern Pacific,* 68; U.S.S. *Leviathan,* 67–68, 120–22, 154, 195, 231
Langfitt, William C., 139
Lassiter, William, 123, 522
Lawrence, H. A., 49, 262, 280, 292, 333, 387; memorandum of Haig-Pershing

conversation, 280–81; meeting with Pershing (*see* Pershing)
Liffol-le-Grand, 498
Liggett, Hunter, 62, 64, 109; meeting with Pershing (*see* Pershing)
Line of Communication (LOC). *See* Services of Supply
Lloyd George, David, xvii, xxii, 41–42, 54, 56, 94–97, 105–6, 120, 126–27, 142–44, 156, 160, 174, 225, 232–34, 237–38, 258–59, 265–69, 274, 297, 320–21, 348, 351, 359, 361–62, 419, 421, 423, 450–51, 464, 471–72, 523; at Abbeville Conference, 386–96, 404–14; at Beauvais Conference, 129–39; dislike of and attempts to undermine Pershing, xxi–xxiii, 41–43, 174, 297–99, 504–5; correspondence and meetings with Pershing (*see* Pershing)
Lochridge, P. D., 114, 387, 406
Logan, James A., Jr., 6, 194, 196–97, 213, 522; correspondence with Foulois on Air Service program, 6–9, 120; meetings with Adm. Sims on use of French Mediterranean ports, 194, 196–99, 213; meetings with Pershing (*see* Pershing)
London (Milner-Pershing) Agreement, xxiv, 268–69, 281, 296–99, 307–14, 409–10, 450–51, 457, 470–72, 523; French disagreement with, 318–24, 333–35, 413–14
Lorraine, 88, 163, 259, 301, 453, 523
Loucheur, Louis, 75, 77–78, 232, 375, 478; correspondence and meeting with Pershing (*see* Pershing)
lumber, 250–51, 255, 264, 274, 345. *See also* American Expeditionary Forces: foresters and forestry units

machine guns, xi, 57, 70, 78–81, 104, 148–49, 167, 172–73, 204, 206, 277, 280, 307, 332–33, 347, 369, 388, 391, 395–96, 398–99, 408, 450, 484, 532, 535; Browning, 315, 383, 426, 450, 536, 545; Hotchkiss, 223, 315, 426, 535; Lewis, 70, 261, 280; Marlin, 223, 296, 425–26; Vickers, 46, 223, 383, 450, 532, 545
Maclay, Joseph, 292, 307, 321, 346

Malone, Paul B., 123, 522; meeting with Pershing (*see* Pershing)
manpower, Allies, xxi, 94; American, x, xxi, 60, 119, 167–68, 282, 419; British, 23, 148, 159, 259, 282–84, 309, 390, 409, 472, 523; French, 309, 472, 487, 523
March, Peyton C., xii, xviii–xix, 33, 97, 160, 233, 235, 300, 364, 369, 509, 511; correspondence with Pershing (*see* Pershing)
mechanics, 6–7, 489; Air Service mechanics for training in Great Britain, 7; motor mechanics for French, 185, 205, 401, 437–38, 491, 551
Meuse River, 44, 52–53, 372
Military Board of Allied Supply, 326
Milner, Lord, xii, xxiv, 48, 76, 84, 136, 223, 239, 268–69, 281, 291, 307, 320–21, 323–24, 327, 332–35, 346, 350, 380, 386–96, 404–14, 421, 450, 458, 470–72, 488, 523; at Doullens Conference (British-French), 49–50; London (Milner-Pershing) Agreement (*see* London [Milner-Pershing] Agreement); correspondence and meetings with Pershing (*see* Pershing)
Mitchell, William: meeting with Pershing. *See* Pershing
Montreuil, 1, 233
morale: Allies, 28, 34, 272, 394; American, 28, 34, 43, 410, 431 445–46, 472, 510; British, 81, 203; French, 27; Italian, 99, 311, 362, 366, 393, 451, 515
mortars, 477; heavy, 63, 112, 260, 477; Stokes and Newton Stokes, 477; trench, 477, 513–14
Moseley, George Van Horn, 215, 369, 440
motor transport, 13, 32, 211, 264, 34; automobiles and cars, xi, 253, 255, 364; tractors, 211, 255, 342; trucks, xi, 44, 211, 253, 494
Mott, T. Bentley, 327, 333, 381; interprets during Foch, Bliss, Pershing, Harbord meeting on London Agreement, 318–24; Pershing designates as his liaison with Foch, 239–40; remains with Baker in Paris, 155, 157; report on Italian situation, 98–99; report on mission

570   Index

Mott, T. Bentley *(continued)*
  to Foch, 344–49; correspondence and meetings with Pershing *(see* Pershing)
Murphy, Grayson M. P., 426, 519
Murray, Peter, 371

Nancy, 36, 150–51, 199–200
Nash, P. A. M., 3, 16, 84–85, 348, 363
National Army, 70; divisions, 33, 279, 309 *(see also* American Expeditionary Forces, divisions); 77th, 78th, 82nd, 83rd, 89th, 90th, 92nd, and 93rd; officers, 45, 123, 162, 325, 369, 371, 381, 436, 440, 480, 487, 522
National Guard: divisions, 305, 309 *(see also* American Expeditionary Forces, divisions); 26th, 27th, 28th, 30th, 32nd, 33rd, 35th, 37th, and 42nd Divisions; officers, 54, 494
Neville, Wendell C., 513
newspapers, 1, 69, 95, 102, 203, 236, 285, 354, 510–11. *See also* press
Nolan, Dennis E., xv, 198, 217, 275, 286, 426, 440, 522; meetings with Pershing *(see* Pershing)

open warfare, 2, 32, 201–2, 211, 215, 316, 399–400, 445, 514; Pershing criticizes trench warfare training and emphasizes open warfare training to War Department, 2, 272–74. *See also* trench warfare
Orlando, Vittorio Emanuele, 233, 345, 387, 394, 406–7, 421, 423, 451, 473, 493, 515
ordnance: material, 104, 145, 211, 230, 247, 339, 417, 534–35; personnel, 123, 165, 339, 368, 442
Ordnance Department, 69–70, 153–54, 211–12, 224, 260, 327, 475, 512. *See also* Chief of Ordnance; Crozier, William; Wheeler, Charles B., and Williams, Clarence C.

Palmer, Frederick, xvii, 267–68, 304; notes of observations on 1st and 26th Divisions, 444–48; correspondence and meetings with Pershing *(see* Pershing)
Palmer, John McAuley, viii
Patrick, Mason M., 74, 418, 522; Pershing transfers Foulois to Air Service, Zone of Advance, and Patrick to be Chief, Air Service, 537; meetings with Pershing *(see* Pershing)
Patton, George S., Jr.: correspondence with Pershing. *See* Pershing
Parker, Frank Le J., 522
Permanent Military Representatives, SWC, xii, xxi, 19–20, 41–42, 59–60, 85–87, 89–90, 129, 131, 177, 248, 265–67, 289, 329–32, 345, 358–64, 423; Joint Note No. 12, 58; Joint Note No. 18, 41–43, 58–60, 62, 118–19, 170–74, 275–77, 289, 297, 330, 388
Pershing, Francis Warren, vi, 150, 157, 236–37
Pershing, John J.: Abbeville Agreement *(see* Abbeville Conference and Agreement); attends Supreme War Council sessions at Abbeville, 386–96, 404–14; attends conference at Beauvais, 128–39; court martial cases, 442, 513, 531; Dawes proposes creation of unified Allied services of supply to Pershing, 217–21, 232–34, 438–39 *(see also* Allied services of supply); disagreement with Bliss at Permanent Military Representatives' discussion of Joint Note No. 18, 55–60, 62 *(see also* Permanent Military Representatives, SWC, Joint Note No. 18); discussions with French on aircraft and engine production contracts, 352–53; doctrinal and training emphasis on open warfare and maneuver, 2, 272–74; Lloyd George's dislike of and attempts to undermine Pershing, xxi–xxiii, 41–43, 174, 297–99, 504–5; London (Milner-Pershing) Agreement *(see* London (Milner-Pershing) Agreement); meeting with Haig on British training of AEF divisions (Six-Division Plan), 262–63, 280–81 *(see also* Six-Division Plan); opposition to amalgamation of American troops, 55–60, 62, 249–50, 263, 297–98, 360–61, 504; proposes pooling Allied supplies to Clemenceau and Milner, 256–57, 263–64; pushes for an American sector of the front, xxiv–xv, 38, 403, 453–54, 542–43, 545, 547–51; stresses creation of

an independent, autonomous American Army in France, xxii, 62, 86, 168, 218, 265, 282, 366–67, 405, 410, 443, 455–56, 472, 505

—CORRESPONDENCE WITH, Allaire, William H., 420; Allen, Henry T., 468; Atterbury, William W., 125–26, 210; Bacon, Robert, 125, 403–4; Baker, Newton D., 40–43, 92–93, 99–101, 156–57, 174–75, 256, 259–60, 275–77, 299–300, 302–4, 312–14, 317, 329–32, 339–41, 358–61, 369–71, 422–23, 431, 443, 450–51, 470–72, 494–95, 502, 508–13, 522–24, 533–34, 552; Biddle, John, 31, 127, 203, 353, 380, 486; Black, William M., 327–28; Bliss, Tasker H., 30–31, 54–55, 90, 111, 117–19, 126–27, 146–47, 200–201, 208–9, 234, 237–38, 242, 437–38, 473, 497; Blatchford, Richard M., 444; Bradley, Alfred E., 90–91, 97–98, 242–43, 379–81, 508; Cambon, Jules, 474; Clark Paul H., 203–4, 209–10, 226–28, 349–51; Clemenceau, Georges, 62, 234, 237–38, 263–64, 419–20; Collins, James L., 30, 403; Conner, Fox, 44, 51–52, 63–65, 82–83, 147–49, 184, 201, 402–3, 457; Crowder, Enoch H., 33–34, 51; Davison, Henry P., 353, 380; Dawes, Charles G., 24, 151–52, 191–92, 217–21, 438–39, 542; de Maud'huy, Louis, 158; Doyen, Charles A., 379; Foch, Ferdinand, 76–78, 327, 460–62, 478–80; Foulois, Benjamin D., 6–9, 120, 352–53, 367–68, 377–79, 429–30, 480–84 (on Air Service organization), 484–85 (Army vs Navy Air Operations), 517–20 (aircraft industrial relations in Europe); Frazier, Arthur H., 9, 337; Haig, Douglas, 22, 117, 163–64, 434, 437, 497, 503–4, 517, 526; Harbord, James G., 51–52, 63, 193, 201–2, 215–17, 308–11, 368–69; House, Edward M., 9, 143, 339; Kernan, Francis J., 50–51, 125–26, 139–40, 158–59, 188, 193, 234–35, 311–12, 480; Lloyd George, David, 344–46; Liggett, Hunter, 242; Loucheur, Louis, 335–37, 427–30 (French and AEF Air Service Production cooperation); March, Peyton C., 31–32, 164, 300–302, 486–88; Milner, Lord, 437, 456–57, 507–8; Mott, T. Bentley, 98–99, 344–49, 414–16; Palmer, Frederick, 221, 444–48; Patton, George S., Jr., 109, 229, 243–44; Pétain, Henri Philippe, 21–22, 189–90; Ragueneau, Camille M., 15–16, 21–22, 62–63, 189–90, 402–3; Rawlinson, Henry, 48; Roberts, Elmer, 354; Roosevelt, Theodore, 369, 541; Simonds, George S., 78–83, 159; Sims, William S., 31, 40, 55, 127, 152–53, 193–94, 299, 463–64, 479–80, 486; 196–98, 213–15, 539–40 (views on the use of French Mediterranean ports and Marseille), 73–74, 526–30 (Naval Air-Air Service relations); Thornton, Henry W., 3–4, 28; Wagstaff, Cyril M., 22–23, 124–25; Warren, Francis E., 69–71, 101–4, 235–37

—MEETINGS WITH, Alvord, Benjamin, 162; Andrews, Avery D., 15; Ardery, Edward D., 107, 311; Atterbury, William W., 15, 224, 342; Bacon, Robert, 279, 286; Baker, Newton D., 1, 46, 55, 67–68, 74, 89, 150, 167, 170–74; Bethel, Walter A., 189, 373, 443, 453, 526; Biddle, John, 286, 291; Black, William M., 1; Bliss, Tasker H., 14, 55–61, 62, 74, 128–39, 150, 318–24, 386–96, 404–14; Boyd, Carl, 1, 35 75, 77, 89, 155, 162, 199, 232, 239, 262, 279, 318–24, 325, 332, 344, 373, 386–96, 404–14, 495, 526; Bradley, Alfred E., 224; Brent, Charles H., 373, 444, 453, 456; Brewster, André W., 199; Bullard, Robert L., 162, 232, 239–40, 405, 548; Bundy, Omar, 162, 495, 502; Burton, Pomeroy, 1, 453, 537; Burtt, W. B., 332, 344; Carter, E. C., 444; Churchill, Winston S., 296; Clark, Paul H., 1, 332–33, 453; Clemenceau, Georges, 74–78, 129–39, 256–57, 386–96, 404–14, 537; Collins, James L., 74; Conner, Fox, 124, 155, 162, 178–80, 184–89, 477; Connor, William D., 189; Crozier, William, 344, 418; Currie, A. W., 280; Dawes, Charles G., 232–33, 239, 249–50, 256–57, 332, 344, 427, 542; Duncan, George B., 338; Edwards, Clarence R., 162; Egan, Martin,

Pershing, John J. *(continued)*
453, 536, 542; Eltinge, LeRoy R., 386–96, 404–14, 526; Fiske, Harold B., 162, 189, 460, 495; Foch, Ferdinand, 74–76, 128–38 (Beauvais Conference), 239–40, 318–24 (Sarcus), 386–96 and 404–14 (Abbeville Conference), 542–45 (Chantilly); Foulois, Benjamin D., 176–77, 332, 344, 418, 460, 477, 516, 537; Frazier, Arthur H., 248, 386–96 and 404–14 (Abbeville Conference), 418; Fries, Amos, 248, 373; Gibbons, Floyd, 124; Haig, Douglas, 129–39 (Beauvais), 262–63 (Montreuil), 386–96, 404–14 (Abbeville); Harbord, James G., 114, 155, 232, 249, 262, 279–80, 291–92, 297–99, 304, 318–24 (Foch, Bliss, Pershing, and Harbord at Sarcus), 325, 434, 507; Harjes, Henry Herman, 124, 176; Hines, John T., 525–26; Hutchison, Robert, 170–74; Jordan, Harry B., 332, 344, 418; Johnson, Evan M., 279; Kernan, Francis J., 176; Lawrence, H. A., 286; Liggett, Hunter, 525–26; Lloyd George, David, 129–39 (Beauvais), 296, 386–96, 404–14 (Abbeville); Logan, James A., Jr., 189, 199, 325, 342, 344, 477; Loucheur, Louis, 537; Malone, Paul B., 495, 502; Milner, Lord, 259, 292–93, 296–99, 304; Mitchell, William, 507; Mott, T. Bentley, 94, 155, 318–24, 332, 537; Nolan, Dennis E., 189, 86, 373, 460, 469, 516; Palmer, Frederick, 1, 74, 199, 256, 460; Patrick, Mason M., 477, 537; Pétain, Henri Philippe, 1, 35–40 (at Compiègne), 74–78 (at Clermont, Foch's GHQ), 129–39 (Beauvais), 386–96 and 404–14 (Abbeville), 547–51 (at Chantilly); Quekemeyer, John G., 286, 453; Ragueneau, Camille M., 35–40 (at Compiègne), 89, 124, 224, 453; Rawlinson, Henry, 46; Rethers, Harry, 286; Roberts, Elmer, 150; Rockenbach, Samuel D., 373; Rogers, H. L., 176; Russel, Edgar, 460; Sackville-West, C. J., 248; Simonds, George S., 17, 279; Sims, William S., 291; Wagstaff, Cyril M., 291–92; Weygand, Maxime, 318–24 (Sarcus with Foch, Pershing, Bliss, and Harbord), 386–96 and 404–14 (Abbeville); Whigham, Robert Dundas, 170–74; Williams, Clarence C., 176; Wilson, Henry H., 128–39, 296, 304, 386–96, 404–14; Winter, Francis, 516; Wiseman, William, 418; Wood, Robert E., 114

Pétain, Henri Philippe, ix–x, xii, xiv–xv, xvii, xxi, xxiv–xxv, 1, 20, 31, 57–58, 66, 87, 89, 105, 143–44, 163, 207–8, 346–47, 350–51, 366–67, 471, 478, 542, 545; attends British-French conference at Doullens, 49–50; attends meeting with Clemenceau, Foch, and Pershing, 74–78; attends Supreme War Council sessions at Abbeville, 386–96, 404–14; at Beuavais, 129–39; discussion with Pershing on establishing an American corps, 35–40; informs Foch on status of American forces, 304–6; memorandum on training American infantry, 396–400; discussions on establishing an American sector, xxiv–xxv, 38, 453–54, 547–51; correspondence and meetings with Pershing (*see* Pershing)

Poincaré, Raymond, 49, 225

press, 7, 93, 104, 131, 277, 284–85, 370. *See also* newspapers

Priority Schedule. *See* American Expeditionary Forces

Quartermaster, 161, 165, 442, 452, 503, 507; Quartermaster Department (Corps), 17, 191–92, 343; Quartermaster General, 114, 473 (*see also* Wood, Robert E.)

Quekemeyer, John G., 76, 82; meeting with Pershing (*see* Pershing)

Ragueneau, Camille M., 51–52, 184–85, 226–27, 306, 333; correspondence to/from Pétain and French GHQ, 206–8, 453–56, 469–70; correspondence and meetings with Pershing (*see* Pershing)

railways: xi, 2–3, 28, 84, 96, 113, 116, 178, 222, 294, 433, 474; construction, 84; engineers and troops, 72, 222, 271 (*see also* regiments, AEF); equipment, 177–78, 195, 294; locomotives, 3, 28, 84, 112, 123, 177, 222, 246–47, 255, 303, 355, 438, 466, 513, 522; material (tracks, ties, etc.), 84, 140, 142, 194–95, 251, 254–55; repair and car building, 11, 16, 67, 71–72, 112–13, 178, 222, 255, 271, 437, 551; rolling stock (cars, gondolas), 28, 84, 112–13, 222, 255, 438, 466, 437–74, 513, 533. *See also* French railways

raw materials, 6, 16, 151, 154, 212, 326, 335–37, 353, 378, 424, 427, 429, 500, 518–19, 539

Rawlinson, Henry, 19–20, 26, 47, 82, 125; at Permanent Military Representatives meeting with Pershing and Bliss, 55–60, 62; correspondence and meeting with Pershing (*see* Pershing)

Resco, Micheline, vi

reserve officers, 446

reserves: forces, 1–3, 22, 36, 46, 66, 92, 94–95, 110, 115, 124, 149, 157, 161, 171, 227, 248, 265, 276, 283, 333, 384, 389, 409; supplies (stocks), 113, 145, 198, 451, 535, 551. *See also* Inter-Allied General Reserve

Rethers, Harry: meeting with Pershing. *See* Pershing

Roberts, Elmer: correspondence and meeting with Pershing. *See* Pershing

Robertson, William R., xv, 13, 56, 69, 156, 297, 304, 334

Rockenbach, Samuel D., 123, 522; meeting with Pershing (*see* Pershing)

Rogers, H. L.: meeting with Pershing. *See* Pershing

Roosevelt, Archibald, 541

Roosevelt, Kermit, 369

Roosevelt, Theodore, 104, 504; correspondence with Pershing (*see* Pershing)

Roumania, 2, 349

Royal Air Force (Royal Flying Corps), 150, 176

Russel, Edgar: meeting with Pershing. *See* Pershing

Russia, xxi, 2, 14, 27, 285, 316, 407, 416, 422

Ryan, John D., 426, 519. *See also* Bureau of Aircraft Production

Sackville-West, C. J., 177, 387, 406; meeting with Pershing (*see* Pershing)

Scott, Hugh L., xii

Services of Supply (SOS), AEF, xi, xvi, xxii, xxiv, 29, 34, 66, 91, 140–42, 149, 179, 185, 220, 233, 235–36, 298, 309, 347, 394, 440, 458, 491–92, 506; base sections, 253–54, 286, 371, 433, 516, 527; Commanding General, xii, 51 (*see also* Kernan, Francis J.); depots, xvi, 44, 140, 145, 192, 253, 255, 264, 274, 345, 356, 454, 466, 474, 533, 539, 548; Line of Communication construction, 7–8, 65, 84, 90–91, 123, 139, 142, 174, 192, 220, 236, 251, 254, 267, 274, 300, 361, 464, 466, 498, 517, 552; port construction, 192, 264, 345, 533, 539; ports of embarkation, 105, 244, 255, 458, 502; ports of debarkation, xi, 65–66, 84, 281, 363, 490, 492; reorganization of LOC, 50–51; Service of the Rear, 60, 169, 178–79, 220–21, 232, 308, 522–23; Service of the Rear (Line of Communication) Project, 302; warehouses (storehouses), xi, 140, 192, 217–19, 236, 254, 264, 274, 300, 345, 462, 465, 518, 533, 539, 552

Service of the Rear. *See* Services of Supply

shipping, xxii, 6, 40, 56, 87, 96, 151, 171, 189, 222, 253, 325–26, 341–42, 363, 367, 424, 429, 439, 488, 502, 506, 515, 523, 531; American shipping program, 105, 134, 168, 171, 186, 204–7, 264–66, 276, 286, 288, 292, 307–11, 313, 325–26, 344–45, 361, 385, 409–10, 413, 505–6; British shipping assistance, 13–14, 17, 31, 54, 57, 67–68, 94, 97, 134, 138–39, 146–47, 168, 186, 204–7, 244, 265, 268, 288, 292, 297–98, 307–11, 313, 321, 324, 361, 409–10, 413, 450, 472, 505–6; U.S. Shipping Board and Ship Control Committee, 17, 88, 128, 139, 161, 164, 167, 191–92, 207, 269–70, 278, 286, 325–26, 328–29, 332, 341–42, 418–19, 460, 487. *See also* Abbeville Conference and Agreement; convoys; Inter-Allied Councils, Allied Maritime Transport Council; London (Milner-Pershing) Agreement.

Sibert, William L., 43

Signal Corps, xix–xx, 123, 165, 250, 273, 296, 307, 325, 347, 442, 457, 470, 475, 491, 493, 502, 509, 535, 548. *See also* Chief Signal Officer

Simonds, George S., 178; reports on British operations against German March offensive, 78–83, 159; correspondence and meetings with Pershing (*see* Pershing)

Sims, William S., xii, 33, 60, 67–68 (Brest), 94, 126, 146, 154, 196–97, 199, 269–70, 302, 341–42, 391, 440–41, 452, 492–93, 533; position on Navy Air-Air Service relations, 73–74, 526–30; suitability of Brest as a harbor for large passenger liners such as U.S.S. *Leviathan*, 67–68, 120–21; views on the use of French Mediterranean ports and Marseille, 196–98, 213–15, 539–40; correspondence and meetings with Pershing (*see* Pershing)

Six-division plan (six AEF divisions to be transported to France and trained by the British), xxii, xxiv, 11–14, 20, 54, 58, 82–83, 95, 124, 159, 173, 180, 244–46, 266–69, 292–93, 296–99, 307–8, 332–35, 350, 386, 457–58

small arms, pistols, and rifles, xi, 70, 124, 245, 261, 450, 501

Smith, Holland M., 372

Spalding, Philip L., 367–68, 426

St. Mihiel, 21, 39, 163, 372

statistical bureau, 45, 112–13

submarines and U-boats, 40, 61, 68–69, 196, 291, 340, 348, 377, 424, 484–85, 540

Summerall, Charles P., 522

Supreme War Council (SWC), x, xii, xxiv, 19, 59–61, 85–87, 89–90, 108, 118–19, 126, 144–45, 157, 160–61, 165, 168, 170, 177–78, 210, 233, 257, 264, 266, 274–75, 294, 320, 330, 334, 344, 350–51, 358, 361, 370–71, 380, 419, 421–22, 425, 439, 450, 470, 488, 497, 502, 504, 522, 524, 544; Beauvais Conference, 129–39; Fifth Session (Abbeville), 386–96, 404–14. *See also* Permanent Military Representatives, SWC

Surgeon General, 516–17, 542. *See also* Ireland, Merritte W.

Tables of Organization, 18, 377, 482–83, 522

tanks, 80, 109, 377; Anglo-American production agreement, 373, 425, 498; armament, 223, 296; Chief of, 373, 522 (*see also* Rockenbach. Samuel D.); corps, 18; Liberty engines for, 154, 176, 212, 417, 475; personnel, 185, 205; table of organization, 18

Tardieu, André, 424–25, 475, 518

Thornton, Henry W., 177–78; correspondence with Pershing (*see* Pershing)

tonnage, 10–11, 16, 29, 32, 34, 45–46, 88, 112–13, 125–26, 146–47, 160–61, 177–78, 185, 189–93, 195, 197, 207, 211, 218–20, 231, 250–51, 255, 257, 263, 166–67, 270, 27, 292–93, 297, 300, 309–10, 314, 319, 326–27, 329, 334, 337, 340–41, 344–48, 360–62, 391, 404, 408, 411–13, 419, 421–22, 424, 429, 433, 441, 450, 452, 458, 465–66, 471, 475, 481, 511, 540; British tonnage, 12–14, 32, 180, 293, 310, 346, 413, 450; requisitioned Dutch tonnage, 146, 161, 166

Tours, xvi, 8, 21, 51, 191, 477

transportation, xi, xiv, 6, 29, 51, 68, 84, 86, 125, 144, 160, 178–79, 190, 218, 232–33, 357, 265–66, 270–71, 291, 318, 340, 464–65, 469, 489, 536; facilities, 84, 96, 411, 421–22, 439, 511; land (ground), 8, 12–13, 147, 172–73, 219–20, 255, 263, 277; rail, 15, 65, 170, 281, 552; sea, 56, 218, 264, 326, 341, 344; troops, 12–13, 24, 31–32, 54, 83–84, 104–5, 165, 168, 185, 298, 309, 327, 329, 338, 359–60, 371, 380, 386, 411, 413, 421–22, 451, 458, 471–73. *See also* Abbeville Conference and Agreement, London (Milner-Pershing) Agreement

Traub, Peter E., 275, 522

trench warfare, 2, 79, 81, 211, 215, 272–74, 394, 399–400. *See also* open warfare

Trenchard, Hugh M.: correspondence with Foulois on air operations, 150–51, 199–200

U.S. Marine Corps: 4th Marine Brigade, xii; 435–36; 5th Marines, 372, 507, 513–14;

6th Marines, 507, 514; personnel, 123–24, 146, 256, 379, 500. *See also* Charles A. Doyen

U.S. Navy Department, 14-inch railway gun program, 230, 261, 449, 469, 494. *See also* Sims, William S.

U.S. War Department: General Staff, 45, 371

venereal diseases, 420, 453, 456, 516–17

Verdun, 2, 36, 491

Wagstaff, Cyril M., 124, 508; correspondence and meetings with Pershing (*see* Pershing)

Walsh, Robert D., 371

Warren, Senator Francis E., vi–viii, xix, 488; problems of Pershing-Warren correspondence, vii, 71; correspondence with Pershing (*see* Pershing)

Weygand, Maxime, 19, 26, 49, 333, 346; meetings with Pershing (*see* Pershing)

Wheeler, Charles B., 46, 123, 477

Whigham, Robert, xvii, 167–68, 266–67, 292, 334; meetings with Baker and Pershing in Paris (*see* Pershing)

Williams, Clarence C., 426, 512, 546; meeting with Pershing (*see* Pershing)

Wilson, Henry H., 47, 49–50, 84, 128–39, 143–44, 167, 225, 233, 268, 291–93, 296–99, 304, 320, 332–33, 359; at Abbeville Conference, 386–96, 404–14; at Beauvais Conference, 128–39; meetings with Pershing (*see* Pershing)

Wilson, Woodrow, x, xii, xxii, 23, 42, 47, 90, 93, 96, 165, 317. *See also* Baker, Newton D., and House, Edward M.

Winter, Francis, 516; meeting with Pershing (*see* Pershing)

Wiseman, William, 387, 406, 414, 418–19, 504–5; meeting with Pershing (*see* Pershing)

Woevre, 453–54, 548

Wood, Leonard, 60, 69–71, 102–4, 236

Wood, Robert E.: meeting with Pershing. *See* Pershing

workmen, 341, 347, 401. *See also* laborers

Ypres, 349, 408, 413